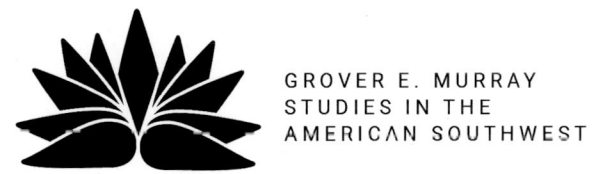
GROVER E. MURRAY
STUDIES IN THE
AMERICAN SOUTHWEST

AUTO TOURING AMERICA'S NATIONAL PARKS

THE PHOTOGRAPHY OF H. A. SPALLHOLZ

JULIAN E. SPALLHOLZ, LANCE O. SPALLHOLZ, AND ARTHUR S. VAUGHAN

TEXAS TECH UNIVERSITY PRESS

This book is typeset in Adobe Caslon Pro. The paper used in this book meets the minimum requirements of ANSI/NISO Z39.48-1992 (R1997). ⊗

Designed by Hannah Gaskamp
Cover design by Hannah Gaskamp

Library of Congress Cataloging-in-Publication Data

Names: Spallholz, Julian E., author. | Spallholz, Lance O., 1947– author. | Vaughan, Arthur S., 1948– author. | Spallholz, H. A. (Henry Albert), 1881–1957, photographer. Title: Auto Touring America's National Parks: The Photography of H. A. Spallholz / Julian E. Spallholz, Lance O. Spallholz, and Arthur S. Vaughan. Description: Lubbock, Texas: Texas Tech University Press, [2024] | Series: Grover E. Murray Studies in the American Southwest |
Summary: "A turn-of-the century photography collection of one family's automobile travels through the early American West"—Provided by publisher.
Identifiers: LCCN 2023048131 | ISBN 978-1-68283-210-3 (cloth)
Subjects: LCSH: West (U.S.)—Description and travel. | West (U.S.)—History—1890–1945. | National parks and reserves—West (U.S.) | Spallholz, H. A. (Henry Albert), 1881–1957—Travel—West (U.S.) | Automobile travel—United States—History—20th century.
Classification: LCC F595.S745 2024 | DDC 917.804—dc23/eng/20240520
LC record available at https://lccn.loc.gov/2

24 25 26 27 28 29 30 31 32 / 9 8 7 6 5 4 3 2 1
Printed in China

Texas Tech University Press
Box 41037
Lubbock, Texas 79409-1037 USA
800.832.4042
ttup@ttu.edu
www.ttupress.org

CONTENTS

PREFACE

In June 1966, after graduating from high school in North Andover, Massachusetts, Art Vaughan fulfilled his military obligation by following family tradition and enlisting in the US Coast Guard. Upon completing basic training, he filled out a form known to new recruits as a "dream sheet," on which he specified his choice of future duty station, location, or Coast Guard district. He entered his preferences: any ice breaker, any of the four ocean station vessels in the North Atlantic Ocean, any lighthouse or light vessel, anywhere in Alaska, and—on advice from his older brother Allan—anywhere, but not on a buoy tender. His first assignment turned out to be the Coast Guard cutter *Cowslip*: an aids to navigation vessel, a Cactus-class buoy tender, stationed at the Coast Guard base in South Portland, Maine. Art always felt that the last phrase on the dream sheet might have had some bearing on his placement. However, the order that sent Arthur to the *Cowslip* was instrumental in his discovery of a photographic treasure trove that decades later would be known as the Spallholz Collection.

After several months on board the *Cowslip*, Art rented a room in Portland where he could get away from the confines of the vessel when he was not on duty. Having a room in town meant he could wear civilian clothes, so in May 1967 he stopped in at the Salvation Army thrift store. While browsing through racks of clothing, he noticed three other shoppers examining some small items very closely. After the trio lost interest and left the store, Art moved over to see what they had been examining with such interest: several boxes filled with three-inch by four-inch glass image slides and a 1,000-watt projection bulb. The slides turned out to be images of old cars and national parks. Art purchased all four boxes of slides, the projection bulb, and the antique Bausch & Lomb home slide projector that accompanied the slides. He carried the whole lot back to his rented room to examine the slides more closely using the surprisingly still functional antique slide projector.

Art began showing the slides during dinner parties given by crew members who had homes in town. After finishing his four-year tour of duty on the *Cowslip*, Art continued to exhibit his slide show at his friends' homes. A common question raised during these presentations was about the kind of vehicle Henry Spallholz—the road-trip photographer—drove west in the summer of 1919. Using a grain magnifier to enlarge a small area of the slide, Art could examine some of the images more closely. The front radiator badge of the car and the hubcaps on two of the slides showed that the automobile manufacturer was the Haynes Motor Company, an early car company located in Kokomo, Indiana. The radiator badge bears the company logo "America's First Car," along with a depiction of their early horseless carriage, the Pioneer.

In 2001, Art presented the Spallholz slide collection at the Photographic Historical Society of New England near Boston, Massachusetts. His program received such a high level of interest that he decided to feature the 1919 cross-country trip program at other camera clubs across New England. As Art became involved with digital photography, he sought out a platform where he could share some of the images, provide information on the subjects, and include technical details on how the images were photographed. He decided to upload the vintage photographs onto Flickr, an image hosting service. The photographs, twenty-three in all, now appeared on Flickr's worldwide archival network in an album he titled the Spallholz Collection. Viewers could leave comments on the photos or ask questions about them. One particular comment that he received referenced an image of a vehicle packed and ready for travel, asking how Art had come into possession of the slides. This inquiry came from the grandsons of Henry Spallholz, triggering a fruitful collaboration among Art, Lance and Julian Spallholz, and their families, culminating in the preparation of this book. In retrospect, Art thanks his brother Allan for his advice about buoy tender duty that led indirectly to the discovery of the Spallholz Collection and the publication of this book, *Auto Touring America's National Parks*.

COINCIDENCE AND SERENDIPITY

Most of the vintage photographs in this book were taken in 1919 by our grandfather, Henry Albert Spallholz, an avid outdoorsman who excelled in fishing, hunting, and golf. He was also a successful businessman and photographer. Above all, he and our grandmother Lizzie Ferguson Spallholz were masters at planning and organizing details for their automobile cross-country round trip.

The eight-year-old Ernest Henry Spallholz in this photographic essay was our father. Over the years he recounted to us his family's 1919 motor trip to Yellowstone National Park, Crater Lake National Park, Mount Rainier National Park, and Grand Canyon National Park. Dad so loved traveling and visiting national parks as a boy that he and our mother, Janice Orton Spallholz, continued his parents' tradition, taking us to visit Yellowstone National Park in 1950 when we were just four (Lance) and seven (Julian) years old. At the entrance to the park, we were greeted by bears on their hind legs leaning against automobiles and being fed by tourists. Dad

took us as far west as Salt Lake City in his 1949 Buick, retracing much of the same Lincoln Highway route his father had followed in 1919. By then most dirt and brick roads were macadam, a form of pavement composed of crushed stone and covered by a light crushed-stone dust surface topped with a cement-like binder. Years later, we used much of our grandparents' 1919 travel gear for our own travel experiences.

In April 1957, Henry Spallholz died suddenly of a heart attack. Grandmother Lizzie Spallholz, known affectionately to us as "Bey," passed away eight years later. They had resided for many years in a small upstairs apartment in Portland, Maine, where they had stored many of their personal items in a basement locker. Small family items and personal effects were saved from the locker upon our grandmother's passing, but all the original glass lantern slides of the 1919 road trip, and additional trips the family took in 1920 and 1922, somehow made their way to the Salvation Army thrift store in South Portland, along with the original lantern slide projector. From there, the photographs came into the hands of Art Vaughan in 1967. The slide collection was all but forgotten until fifty years later when Art posted twenty-three of the images from the Spallholz family road trip onto Flickr.

The following pages feature more than 200 of the Spallholz motor trip images from our grandfather's original collection of glass lantern slides and album prints. The images are presented in the order they were taken during his family's 1919 journey, accompanied by his captions as well as historical research into the locations featured in the images. Some annotated period photographs and postcards are included within the travel sequence when illustrative of places, events, and trip continuity. Also included are images from a number of souvenir lantern slides that were purchased during the expedition. The way in which we—Lance, Julian, and Art—were brought together by a collection of slides and prints is a story of coincidence, luck, and serendipity. We sincerely hope our readers will delight in the 1919 photographs of American cities, landscapes, national parks, and other historic places and the photographic account of our grandfather's and his family's 10,400-mile road trip. We have enjoyed restoring some of this early travel history about the American West and its earliest roads and US national parks, now preserved in time.

HENRY A. SPALLHOLZ: A BIOGRAPHICAL SKETCH

Henry A. Spallholz was born in 1882 in Stuttgart, Germany. He celebrated his third birthday in 1885 as he and his mother crossed the Atlantic by steamship to join his father, who had emigrated to the United States. His father had settled in Salem, New York, and was starting what would become a successful business career. The family lived on a rural road, and when it came time to attend school, Henry walked about two miles every day to a one-room schoolhouse. When he was a teenager, he was stricken with a severe illness that left him almost completely deaf.

Henry's father established various business ventures. Henry's own personal drive helped him overcome his hearing loss, and he soon was on his way to a series of successful positions. He met a young woman, Lizzie Mae Ferguson, who lived on a nearby farm with her grandparents. Henry's diary from the time records two daily entries, one a weather report and the other a notice that he had gone to the Ferguson farm to "court" Lizzie. Lizzie's grandparents wished for her to be educated, so she enrolled at Cornell University and graduated in 1905 as a classics major in Latin and Greek. Soon after her return to Salem, she and Henry were married.

The couple honeymooned in Europe in 1906. The album of the trip featured photographs taken by Henry, first aboard ship, then in London, Switzerland, and eventually Stuttgart, where the Spallholzes visited the house where Henry had been born. Photography for individuals was not common at the time, but this album demonstrates that Henry was interested in preserving his memories in this way.

When the couple returned to Salem, Henry's business success began to expand, as did his family. Son Walter was born in 1909, and Ernest followed in 1911. A series of managerial positions opened up. In nearby Rexleigh, New York, Henry became the manager of a machete factory. A dam on the Battenkill River, now famous for trout fishing, supplied the mill's energy. The machetes were produced in sets of four different blades which were sent to Cuba for use in the sugarcane harvest. Soon after, for a short period of time, Henry became the owner and managing editor of the local newspaper, the *Salem Press*. His father was manager of a Manhattan Shirt factory in Poultney, Vermont, and Henry became manager of the Manhattan Shirt factory in Salem right across the street from his home. His greatest financial success arrived when he became president of the People's National Bank of Salem. All of this was accomplished before his family's 1919 automobile trip.

The 1919 journey recorded about 350 photographs as Henry and his family made a round-trip 10,400-mile, ninety-six-day drive out west. But that was not the end of his traveling. In July 1920, the family went by train to vacation in Glacier National Park for five weeks, producing an album of 128 photographs. In 1922 the family once again took the train to make a six-week-long trip to Yellowstone, with side tours to Wyoming and Utah. The album of that trip has about 120 pictures. In October 1923, Henry traveled alone to Yellowstone to hunt and fish, this time taking fifty-five pictures. At home, his car took him to most of the covered bridges in Eastern New York and nearby New England, producing an album of fifty-five photographs. He had pictures of family trips to Maine, to the Adirondacks, south to Delaware, hiking the hills near Salem, and hunting with his beloved Springer Spaniels.

The bank presidency had provided Henry and his family financial comfort. He invested in property and bought land in Florida, speculating on the growth of the state. But ten years after the Spallholzes' first trip to the west, the banking collapse of 1929 started the decline that would bring an end to Henry's success story and his personal wealth. The People's National Bank remained open because Henry and Lizzie sacrificed to help the Salem depositors, many of whom were their friends and neighbors. Walter and Ernest were withdrawn from prep school; Henry's properties, including the Florida holdings, were sold; and the money they personally had was all put back into the bank. In the mid-1930s the federal government came and closed the bank, as it had done with so many others at the time. While many small banks were returning 19 cents on the dollar to depositors, Henry's personal financial sacrifice allowed his bank to return about 90 cents on the dollar. The family sold their house and most of its contents and moved to Boston. Henry with his sons opened the Good Housekeepers Laundry there, which kept the family afloat. After a few years, Walter bought a commercial laundry, Universal Laundry and Dry Cleaners, in Portland, Maine, and moved there. Henry and Lizzie soon followed their son and retired in Portland.

Henry passed away in 1957 and Lizzie in 1965. The photo albums were kept by Ernest. Ernest and his family, along with the photo albums, returned to Salem, New York.

LANCE AND JULIAN SPALLHOLZ
MARCH 2024

INTRODUCTION

Barely eight months after the armistice of November 11, 1918, had brought to a conclusion the war intended to end all wars, Lizzie and Henry Spallholz set out on June 11, 1919, from Salem, New York with their sons Ernest and Walter on a transcontinental motor tour. Covering over 10,000 miles in just under 100 days, the Spallholz family immersed themselves in three months of recreational delights that ranged from roadside camping to glacier tobogganing in states from New York to California and back again. In doing so, they joined a great horde of travelers, numbering in the hundreds of thousands, who had set out aboard their horseless carriages in a like-minded pursuit of vacation happiness.

Although adventurous individuals had been setting out on such excursions since 1900, Americans as a whole had not done so in substantial numbers until well into the century's second decade. With the accelerating pace of automotive production and increasingly widespread efforts to improve and extend networks of roads, aspiring vacationers by the hundreds and eventually the thousands took off across American landscapes, frequently in pursuit of opportunities to escape the nation's urbanizing and industrializing locales. Developments such as the 1908 introduction of the Model T by pioneering manufacturer Henry Ford, the admission of motor cars to more of the country's national parks, and the proliferation in the years immediately after 1910 of private highway organizations such as the Lincoln Highway, the Dixie Highway, and the Yellowstone Trail reflected the automobile's escalating entrance into ever more phases of American life.

By the time the Spallholz family launched into its grand continental excursion in the summer of 1919, then, the golden age of American auto touring had begun in earnest. With more than 7.5 million registered automobiles in the nation that year (a fifteen-fold increase since 1910),[1] this newest advance in mechanical transportation could be encountered all over the landscape. After a brief hiatus in the production of automobiles for civilian use, supplanted by trucks and other commodities for military purposes, the rapid reconversion by manufacturers resuscitated the supply of motor cars. Similarly, the efforts of the wartime United States Fuel Administration in 1918 to encourage voluntary suspension of recreational driving to preserve stocks of gasoline for the military could now be terminated as peace descended upon the European battle fronts.[2]

Such occurrences by themselves could have made 1919 a pivotal moment for American automobility. Still other events, portentous in their implications for the future of the motor car, enhanced the year's consequence. In the Far West, Oregon, Colorado, and New Mexico became the first states to apply taxes to the purchase of gasoline, while on July 7, 1919, the United States Army dispatched the First Transcontinental Motor Train (37 officers, 258 enlisted men, and

---

1 Eric Burns, *1920: The Year That Made the Decade Roar* (New York: Pegasus Books, 2015), 5.
2 James J. Flink, *The Automobile Age* (Cambridge, MA: The MIT Press, 1988; paperback edition 1990), 80, and "Gasolineless Sundays," *Motor Travel: A Magazine for Automobile Owners* 10, no. 4, September 1918, 19.

81 vehicles) from Washington, DC, as a cross-country expedition to promote the national necessity of good roads.[3]

Within the context of such greater events, the occurrences that unfolded during the travels of the Spallholz family that summer might have been completely lost were it not for the survival of its photographic collection, consisting of more than 330 glass slides and album prints from which the images featured in this book were selected. Amidst the tens of thousands who set out to crisscross the American West in 1919, nothing would have shone posterity's spotlight upon these four individuals were it not for this opportunity to peruse this remarkable documentation of their adventures.

Although unaccompanied by narration from any of the original travelers, the great majority of the photographs speak clearly for themselves. Moreover, the detailed captions written by the present volume's authors generally establish the pertinent details needed to advance the tale. Beginning with the family's departure from their home in Upstate New York, the reader travels with the Spallholz party across space and time. Indeed, given the enormous range of images included, we gain insight into nearly every phase of their outing, from planning and preparation through all the highs and lows of life on the road.

In nearly all aspects of their journey, the Spallholz family exemplified the experiences that would characterize auto touring in the decade after World War I. Like so many of their motoring peers, our adventurers undertook meticulous preparations for their trip, including extensive modifications of their 1917 Haynes Roadster to enhance its cargo capacity. They assembled gear of all kinds for a life in the outdoors, from hunting rifles and fishing poles to nesting cookware and a gasoline-fired camp stove. While loaded down with tent, dining table, and sleeping bags, the family also incorporated

plans for occasional hotel stays and visits with friends located across the country. Interwoven with the original photographs, the collection includes commercial postcards and glass slides of hostelries from Chicago's Blackstone Hotel to Riverside, California's Mission Inn, depicting various settings in which the family took temporary refuge from camp life by the side of the road.

Once the family had set forth, their passion for photography propelled them to capture nearly every imaginable aspect of motoring across every type of terrain. Again and again, their cameras were deployed to depict all of the thousand and one shocks that automobiles were heir to in 1919, from boggy mudflats masquerading as roads to vehicles marooned in culverts or ditches. Henry's series of photographs taken after flash flooding outside of Cody, Wyoming, in particular encapsulated the assorted vulnerabilities of road, car, and motorist when confronted by high water. The engaging views of tourists with pants and skirts rolled up to their knees inspecting a near-sunken Buick roadster highlight both the humorous and the alarming dimension of early twentieth-century motor touring.

Above all, however, the visual archive of the Spallholz family voyage reflected an obvious obsession with recording their encounters with scenic America. From the unbounded expanses of the Great Plains and the boulder-choked canyons of the Rocky Mountains to the Pacific Northwest's towering evergreen forests and the scorching Arizona deserts, the family put its arsenal of cameras to constant use, emphasizing the rugged, empty landscapes so reminiscent of the descriptions in word and picture created by explorers, artists, scientists, immigrants, journalists, and photographers during the previous century. Indeed, with the exception of a few shots of Isleta Pueblo and its inhabitants gathered while crossing New Mexico, the Spallholz photos, like those taken by so many other tourists,

---

3 Flink, *Automobile Age*, 171, and Pete Davies, *American Road: The Story of an Epic Transcontinental Journey at the Dawn of the Motor Age* (New York: Henry Holt and Company, 2002), 6.

would only reinforce the imaginative vision of the Far West held by so many Americans as a vast, empty realm reserved by a beneficent Providence for their exclusive dominion.

All that being acknowledged, however, one subject above all others took pride of place in front of the Spallholz cameras—America's national parks. Having made such all-encompassing preparations for plunging themselves in nature, Henry, Lizzie, and their sons spent many days in the precincts of various national parks, taking the fullest opportunity possible of the increasingly accommodating attitude with which various park administrators came to view the automobile. While initially quite apprehensive in the early years of the twentieth century about the potential impact of the automobile upon park landscapes and services, park superintendents succumbed in time to mounting public pressure. One after the other, various parks opened their gates, including Mt. Rainier in 1908, General Grant in 1910, Crater Lake in 1911, Glacier in 1912, Yosemite and Sequoia in 1913, Mesa Verde in 1914, and Yellowstone in 1915 (the latter a mere four years before the Spallholz visit).[4] By 1919, enthusiastic tourists such as the Spallholz family could plan an excursion that would include motoring ventures in Yellowstone, Mt. Rainier, Crater Lake, Sequoia, and the South Rim of the Grand Canyon, as well as local, state, and private attractions such as Hell's Half Acre and Shoshone Canyon in Wyoming, the Columbia River Highway and Multnomah Falls in Oregon, and Pikes Peak and the Garden of the Gods in Colorado. With their cameras always poised at the ready, the Spallholz family documented an enormous regional infrastructure of scenic wonders that was already achieving national and international renown.

The Spallholz archive thus furnishes us with a marvelously detailed visual account of the burgeoning national park system at a pivotal moment in its history. These vivid images contribute to our understanding of how Americans envisioned the parks and made use of them, just as the automobile made access to them far greater than ever before. Similarly, many other Spallholz photographs illustrated grand swathes of Western landscapes, both rural and industrial, either undergoing or perched on the brink of irrevocable change, often propelled by the influx of the automobile. This wonderfully illustrated account of the Spallholz family's travels is in itself not only a splendid touring narrative but an enduring source document for the history of the trans-Mississippi West in the early twentieth century.

DR. PETER J. BLODGETT
FORMER CURATOR OF WESTERN AMERICAN HISTORY
HUNTINGTON LIBRARY, ART MUSEUM,
AND BOTANICAL GARDENS

---

4 The enumeration of dates at which different parks allowed the entrance of automobiles may be found in Flink, *Automobile Age*, 173. Additional discussion about the evolving relationship of automobiles and the national parks in the early twentieth century may be found in Alfred Runte, *National Parks: The American Experience* (Lanham, MD: Lyons Press, 2022), 140–43.

AUTO TOURING AMERICA'S NATIONAL PARKS

CHAPTER 1

THE AUTOMOBILE IN AMERICA & AMERICA'S FIRST ROAD TRIPS

THE AUTOMOBILE IN AMERICA

The late nineteenth and early twentieth centuries ushered in many technological advances, such as electricity for the home, industrial use, and street lighting. However, the automobile proved the most innovative technology of the day at a time when steam locomotives and the railroads dominated mass transportation of both goods and people. Within twenty years of the transcontinental railroad's completion, the time of the horseless carriage had come; inventors of all kinds produced small steam and internal combustion engines. In 1879, German engineer Carl Benz invented the internal combustion engine, a single cylinder, two-stroke engine with less than one horsepower.

By 1885, Benz had adapted his internal combustion engine to Europe's first car: an open-air, two-seated carriage with a three-horsepower internal combustion gas engine. The following year, Benz received a patent for the world's first automobile under the brand name Mercedes-Benz.[5] The automobile revolution Carl Benz started in Germany continued with the Duryea brothers, who built and sold the very first motorized wagons in the United States. In September 1893, the brothers completed a road test using a horse-drawn wagon retrofitted with an internal combustion engine, dubbed the Duryea Motor Wagon. What followed was the establishment of the Duryea Motor Wagon Company in Springfield, Massachusetts. The Duryea Motor Wagon Company came to an end seven years later when the brothers squabbled over finances.

In the early 1900s, New York State alone was home to more than one hundred small automobile manufacturers. However, the Haynes-Apperson automobile from Kokomo, Indiana, was recognized as, and remains to this day, "America's First Car."

Thirty-four-year-old Elwood Haynes was a teacher, inventor, and automobile and metallurgical entrepreneur when he developed a gasoline-driven horseless carriage. He had originally planned to power his horseless carriage with steam, a method popularized by the Stanley Brothers with their Stanley Steamer. Haynes was aware of the hazards associated with steam technology and feared an explosion. He had also considered an electric-powered horseless carriage, but he could find no practical way to store electric power. He purchased a single-horsepower marine engine from the Stintz Gas Engine Company in Grand Rapids, Michigan, and adapted the engine for use in his horseless carriage. On July 4, 1894, his horseless carriage, which he named the Pioneer, made its first test drive down Broadway in Kokomo, Indiana.

Following the successful drive of the Pioneer and continued engineering improvements to his horseless carriage over the next two years, Elwood Haynes partnered with Elmer and Edgar Apperson to form the Haynes-Apperson Company in 1896. The three men collaborated to improve upon the Pioneer's original design until it could be manufactured for public sale. It was a decidedly beneficial association between Haynes and the Apperson brothers in those years. The Haynes-Apperson collaboration held up during a public dispute with the Duryea brothers about who invented the first car in America.

Haynes-Apperson automobiles were the first built in Indiana and the very first automobiles commercially built and sold in the United States. In 1896, the business sold its first car to P. C. Lewis of Catskill, New York, and delivered it to him by railroad in the summer of 1897. The Haynes-Apperson Company continued to successfully manufacture automobiles in Kokomo after completing a publicity tour in its newest automobile, which they named the

---

5 Christian Huygens, a physicist living in Holland circa 1680, initially experimented with combustion engines using gunpowder. The continuous running internal spark gasoline combustion engines were developed by J. J. Étienne Lenoir in 1858.

Trap. The Trap drew much attention to Haynes-Apperson by winning several early automobile races. During this time, the argument over who built America's first car continued, but the dispute ended abruptly in 1900 with the collapse of the Duryea Motor Wagon Company. Nonetheless, the Haynes-Apperson Company's successes eventually led to the break-up of their own partnership in 1904. Elwood Haynes and the Apperson brothers then formed their own separate automobile companies in Kokomo.

The Haynes portion of the Haynes-Apperson enterprise reverted to Elwood Haynes, who established the Haynes Automobile Company in Kokomo, Indiana, in 1905. With the Duryea Motor Wagon Company now defunct and public discourse concerning who invented the first car in America having evaporated, Elwood Hayes introduced the Haynes Motor Company corporate logo shield, which bore the words "America's First Car," along with a rendering of their original Pioneer. This enameled logo henceforth appeared on the radiator badge of all Haynes automobiles. Unfortunately, a manufacturing plant fire led to the construction of a new and very costly manufacturing plant expansion, followed by the postwar downturn in the US economy and a decline in sales. Until its bankruptcy and cessation of manufacturing operations in 1924, the Haynes Automobile Company built some of the most highly prized motor cars of its day.

AMERICA'S FIRST ROAD TRIPS, 1903–1919

1903: HORATIO JACKSON, SEWALL CROCKER, AND "BUD"

Horatio Nelson Jackson, a thirty-one-year-old physician from Vermont, accomplished the first recorded automobile trip across America in 1903. He was accompanied by his mechanic Sewall K. Crocker and a bulldog they picked up along the way that they named Bud. Jackson was prompted by a $50 bet that an automobile could not be driven across the North American continent. To make the trip, Jackson purchased a used two-cylinder, twenty-horsepower open-air automobile from the Winton Motor Carriage Company. The two men began their trip in Oakland, California, and traveled north through the Rocky Mountains and north of the Donner Summit, as routes through the desert sands of the southwest had brought about the failure of two earlier attempts to cross the country by automobile.[6] Jackson, Crocker, and Bud arrived in New York City on July 26, 1903, after a period just short of sixty-four days, becoming the first to successfully traverse the continent in an automobile. Jackson spent $8,000 on the trip, but he never collected on his $50 San Francisco wager. Others soon followed in their dusty, rocky, sandy, and sometimes very muddy tracks.

1905: PERCY F. MEGARGEL AND DAVID FASSETT

In the summer of 1905, Percy F. Megargel planned America's first round-trip automobile transcontinental journey. He represented the American Motor League and was sponsored by the REO Motor Car Company. For this journey, Ransom E. Olds provided a standard sixteen-horsepower REO touring car that Megargel named the Mountaineer. The Mountaineer was outfitted with certain modifications considered essential for this particular trip: removable seats for in-vehicle sleeping, special protective undercarriage steel plates, and a frame-mounted hand-cranked windlass that would

---

6 This first transcontinental trip was the subject of a Ken Burns documentary film made in 2003 for PBS television, *Horatio's Drive: America's First Road Trip*, based on the book of the same title by Dayton Duncan.

assist the vehicle through deep mud, sand, and up or down severe grades. The intent of this venture was to promote the REO as a reliable vehicle as well as stimulate development and sales within the automobile industry.

On August 19, 1905, Megargel and REO mechanic David Fassett departed New York City's Herald Square for what was expected to be no more than a sixteen-week expedition. Unanticipated difficulties encountered on the return to New York, however, extended the trip to ten months. The pair traveled westward via a northern route, then down the Pacific Coast to Southern California and back towards the east along a southern route. The outbound journey presented a variety of challenges: flooding, nonexistent roads, sandstorms, and snowstorms. The drive down the Pacific Coast to San Francisco and eventually Los Angeles was almost a delight, but as they crossed the Great American Desert on their way back east, they encountered deep sand and near-zero visibility due to a severe sandstorm. They ran into winter upon arriving in Arizona's Padre Canyon, where the area's freezing cold was nearly their undoing. Later on, New Mexico's Rio Puerco quicksand forced the travelers to abandon the bogged Mountaineer in the river for three weeks until a major snowmelt created enough water flow to wash away the quicksand and allow a group of Apache and Navajo natives and their ponies to haul the waterlogged vehicle out onto firm ground.

On June 5, 1906, the somewhat battered Mountaineer and its weary occupants motored back into Herald Square amid much celebration and fanfare. The information Megargel and Fassett obtained on the journey was instrumental in generating interest among government channels for new road development in rural and western areas and road improvement in the east. The record of their experiences proved most useful for other travelers who would follow in their wake.

1908: JACOB MURDOCK AND FAMILY

The next successful transcontinental journey was accomplished by Jacob Murdock, his wife, and their three children from Johnstown, Pennsylvania. For the trip east from Pasadena, Jacob Murdock purchased a used 1908 Packard Touring 30 automobile in California for $4,500. He loaded it up with camping provisions, food, water, tools, ropes, spare tires, gasoline, and a rifle for his son Milton to keep the coyotes at bay. Mechanic Mark Phillip DeMay accompanied the family. The group exited California via San Bernadino, Cajon Pass, and turned north towards Victorville, and crossed Death Valley. They followed much of what eventually became Nevada Route 50, named the "Loneliest Road in America" by *Life* magazine in 1986. Throughout their trip, the family was met with muddy roads, a flat tire, bitter cold, wind, and a blinding Wyoming snowstorm. Upon leaving Laramie, Wyoming, on the trip home, they encountered snow a foot deep, more mud, and deep wet sand, which problem they solved by driving through bad areas at high speed. They arrived home in Johnstown, Pennsylvania, greeted by friends and the press, having unintentionally set a record for cross-country travel.

1909: ALICE RAMSEY AND FRIENDS

In June 1909, twenty-two-year-old Alice Ramsey and three other women—Nettie Powell, Margaret Atwood, and Hermine Jahns—set out for San Francisco from New York City. Theirs was an all-expenses-paid trip by the Maxwell-Briscoe Motor Company of Tarrytown, New York. Alice and her three companions drove a new four-cylinder, thirty-horsepower Maxwell Touring Automobile. The Ramsey drive was fraught with mechanical troubles and very muddy roads, but they arrived in San Francisco on August 7, 1909. Alice Ramsey became the first woman to drive across America, completing the trip in less time than Jackson had, but the group did not even come close to breaking the record set by the Murdocks. Alice Ramsey returned east by train. Over the years she made more than thirty additional transcontinental automobile trips and was named the First Lady of Automotive Travel in 1960.

1915: EMILY POST AND SON

Six years after Alice Ramsey's drive to San Francisco, Emily Price Post—who was later widely known for her books on etiquette—engaged her son Bruce Price Post to drive her across America to San Francisco. The pair made the trip in a highly modified six-cylinder Mercedes with a 144-inch wheelbase and an externally exposed exhaust system that had been customized in England. Setting out in their powerful sixty-horsepower modified Mercedes, they drove north along the new Lincoln Highway, one of the first transcontinental roads in the United States. The Posts' car was plagued by a variety of mechanical failures, among them burnt-out motor bearings and leaks in the oil and exhaust lines. Getting lost was not uncommon due to the lack of updated maps, and the roads were often muddy.

After driving south from Omaha to Denver and becoming discouraged by the time they reached Arizona, Emily placed the modified Mercedes on an automobile freight car of the Atchison, Topeka and Santa Fe Railway (AT&SF) at Winslow, Arizona. From Winslow, she and her son visited the Grand Canyon some sixty miles away and completed their trip to Los Angeles via the AT&SF Railroad. They were reunited with their Mercedes in Los Angeles and traveled north to San Francisco on California's much improved roads. Emily Post's primary commentary on her trip experience included advice for any travelers who wished to attempt the continental crossing in the future: buy new and buy American. American automobiles had a much higher clearance for travel on poor roads, parts required for repairs were more readily available, and tires were not metric.

1915: EFFIE PRICE GLADDING

In April 1915, Effie Price Gladding and her husband "T" borrowed a friend's Studebaker in San Francisco to explore California's wine country, University of California, Berkeley, and other sights. In Winton, California, they left the vehicle at a garage for repairs and boarded a horse-drawn stagecoach into the Yosemite Valley, where they hiked and camped. Upon their return to Winton, the couple picked up their "machine," as Effie referred to the Studebaker, and followed an indirect route east, touring much of Southern California for forty-three days before heading back east via the Lincoln Highway to their home in New York. After their Studebaker developed mechanical trouble outside of Boulder, Colorado, Effie and T replaced the worn-out vehicle with a new Franklin automobile. In 1915, the Lincoln Highway was 3,389 miles in length from coast to coast. The travelers deviated from the direct Lincoln Highway route four times, adding nearly 5,000 miles to go exploring. They returned to New York in September. In the Studebaker and Franklin automobiles, the couple had traveled a total of 8,600 miles in a period of approximately five months.

1916: TWO WOMEN, A CAR, AND A CAT

In 1916 two suffragettes, Alice Snitzer Burke and Nell Richardson, believed that a widely publicized transcontinental tour across America would provide an opportunity for them to collect a multitude of signatures in support of the suffrage movement and bring large-scale recognition to women's right to vote. Their trip was sponsored by the National American Women's Suffrage Association. The pair drove more than 10,000 miles over five months. They began in New York, traveled south to New Orleans, motored west to cities on the California coast, and worked their way north to Seattle. They stopped in cities and small towns to collect an impressive 500,000 signatures. The trials and tribulations Alice Burke and Nell Richardson experienced during their 10,000-mile tour in support of the Nineteenth Amendment mirrored those experienced by other early travelers: mechanical difficulties, flat tires, and, of course, Midwest mud.

1919: US ARMY MILITARY CONVOY

On July 7, 1919, a US Army convoy comprised of more than eighty military vehicles and approximately three hundred enlisted men and officers, including Lt. Dwight D. Eisenhower, drove across America from Lafayette Square in Washington, DC, to San Francisco, California. This was the first transcontinental military convoy to cross the continental United States, mostly along the Lincoln Highway. The convoy included military automobiles, armored cars, and supply trucks that had been used in Europe during the war. The trip was intended both as a celebration of the war's end and as an opportunity to assess the ability of the Army and its vehicles to operate on United States highways.

As they exited Lafayette Square, in Washington, DC, the convoy was immediately wrought with mechanical troubles, limiting the convoy's progress to a mere forty miles the first day. Later, vehicle breakdowns and off-road wrecks, problems with inadequate bridges, and support vehicles in mud or desert sand up to their axles were frequent occurrences. The convoy averaged six miles an hour down the Lincoln Highway and still managed to arrive in San Francisco six days ahead of its traveling schedule. It was called "America's worst cross-country trip." Its success (or the lack thereof) likely contributed to the eventual construction of the modern efficient Federal Interstate Highway System we have today. Credit must also be given to D. D. Eisenhower for his observation of Germany's autobahn during WWII, its design and efficiency leading to construction of our Federal Interstate Highway System.

1919: BEATRICE MASSEY AND HUSBAND

In 1919, Beatrice Learned Massey and her husband, known to their friends as "the Doctor" and his wife "Toodles," were inspired to take a transcontinental voyage by Emily Post's book about her own trip, *By Motor to the Golden Gate*. The couple and their friends departed from the Seymour Hotel in New York City in their twin-six Packard Touring automobile. This journey was different from the transcontinental excursions of the past, which had been undertaken to achieve some goal. This was purely a leisurely tour to experience "motor fever" and enjoy the wide-open country. The Masseys and friends passed through Cleveland, Ohio to Detroit, crossed Lake Michigan by ferry, and motored on into Wisconsin, Minnesota, down to South Dakota, and into Montana. They continued across Nevada and on into California, finally ending in San Francisco. This sightseeing venture lasted forty-nine days, thirty-three of which were spent driving. The group covered 4,154 miles without any gear attached to the outside of their Packard, as opposed to the norm for long trips of the day. The group did not plan to camp out, nor did they bring a camera along. Mrs. Massey did keep a detailed account of hotels and hotel descriptions, listing them as either very comfortable, comfortable, good, or bad. They had made it a rule upon leaving New York City to stay overnight in the best of hotels that money could buy. At the end of the journey, the group concluded that travel for two people could be had for about $13 per day.

The roads the group encountered were like the roads travelers before them had experienced: good, bad, and awful. At one point they rode out of the mud while hanging onto the automobile's running boards. Their traveling companions returned to New York City from Yellowstone National Park by train, arriving before the Masseys reached Utah. The Doctor and Toodles continued on, encountering deep sand, hot sun, and desert monotony. They met a total of two other cars along the seemingly endless and monotonous Western landscape, plus a sandstorm, chuckholes, a rock bridge, and coyotes. Tired and covered with sand from a storm in Utah, the Masseys shelled out $196.69 to ship their car by train to Reno, Nevada. One week later, they were reunited with their Packard in Reno, drove into California, and took the Oakland Ferry across San Francisco Bay. En route they passed the US Naval Pacific Fleet at anchor, signaling that World War I was really over. Fifty US naval vessels lay at anchor, all ablaze with lights and aflutter with flags, as was the entire city, celebrating the Pacific Fleet's arrival in San Francisco. Early that next morning, the Masseys awoke to the sight of the US Army transcontinental eighty-vehicle motor convoy making its way up San Francisco's Market Street. They had traveled coast to coast with no accidents, no sickness and only two punctured tires. It could have been much worse.

1919: THE SPALLHOLZ FAMILY ROAD TRIP

In 1919, Henry Albert Spallholz, his wife Lizzie, and their sons Ernest and Walter hit the road in their 1917 Haynes Light Six Roadster. Henry's travel plans were to explore and photograph the Great Plains, the Rocky Mountains, and most of the designated national parks of the time. Unlike the previously well-publicized transcontinental trip departures, this expedition began somewhat quietly and received only local village attention and rural newspaper coverage. Early during their journey, the Spallholz family stopped at the Haynes automobile factory in Kokomo, Indiana, where Henry gave the company two photographs for inclusion in the August–September 1919 issue of the *Haynes Pioneer* magazine.

Henry planned for a round-trip family excursion, circumnavigating much of the western United States. He had been planning this family vacation in his Haynes Roadster for more than two years. The purpose of this outing was to experience firsthand the great outdoors of the West while preserving a record in notes and photographs of the Western landscapes, rivers, mountains, and America's scenic national parks. The automobile journey took the Spallholz family across much of the Lincoln Highway as well as other national highways, across the muddy Midwest, the Great Plains, into view of the Rocky Mountains in Colorado, and the Cascade Mountains and Pacific Rim. They stopped at Mount Rainier in Washington State, where Henry Spallholz, colleague William Worner, and guide Hans Fuhrer ascended to the summit.

In Oregon they drove the Columbia River Highway and visited Crater Lake. In California they visited San Francisco, drove along the old Camino Real to Los Angeles and San Bernadino, stopping at Catholic missions along the route. Turning east they passed through Arizona, visiting the Grand Canyon and Petrified Forest. After stopping in Albuquerque and Santa Fe, New Mexico, they entered Colorado via Ratón Pass, visited the Garden of the Gods in Colorado Springs, and motored to the summit of Pikes Peak. Driving east, the family passed into Kansas for the final leg, arriving home on September 15, 1919, after motoring more than 10,400 miles in ninety-six days. They photographically recorded and catalogued the entire trip along the way, as documented here, in *Auto Touring America's National Parks*.

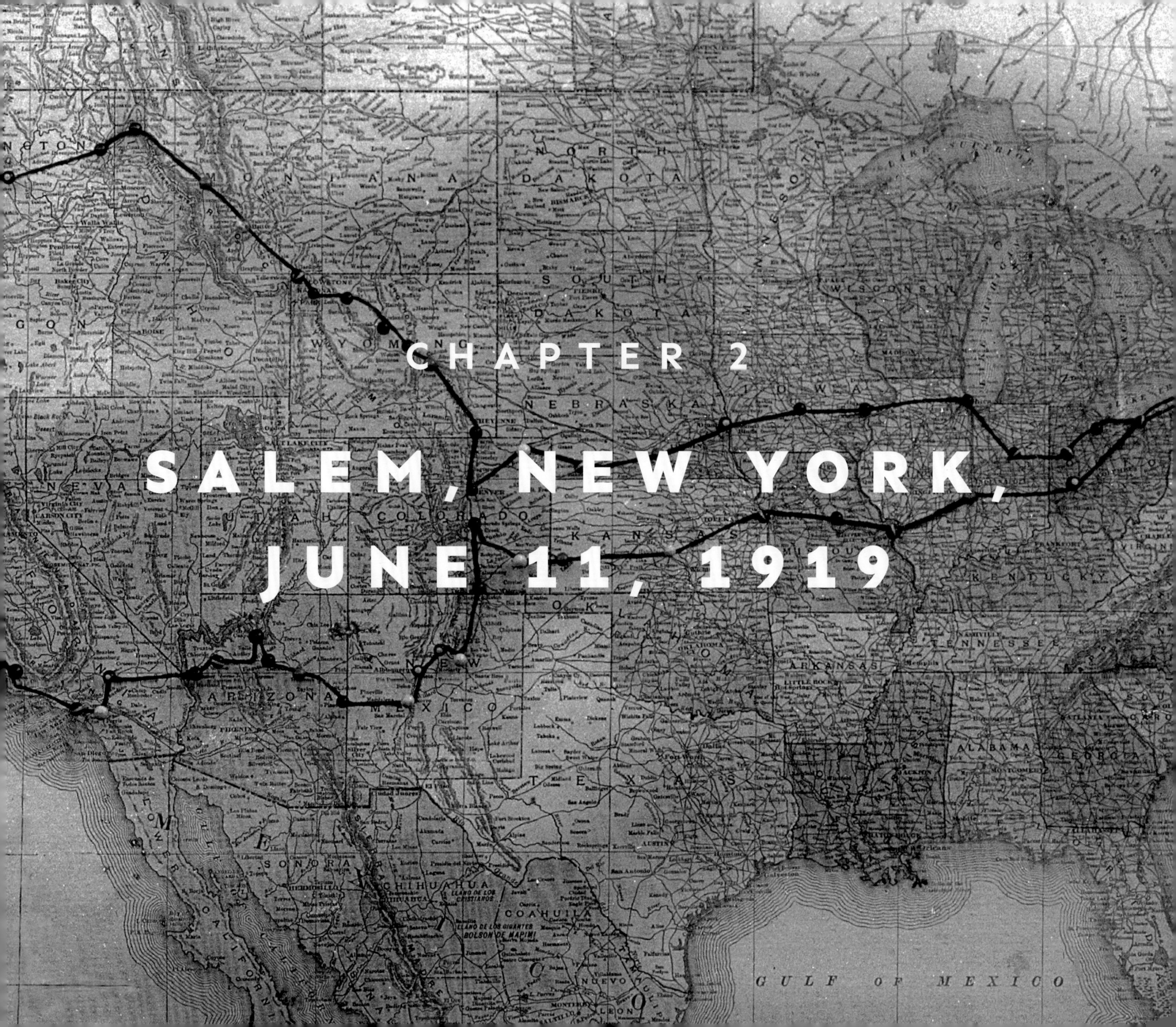

CHAPTER 2

SALEM, NEW YORK, JUNE 11, 1919

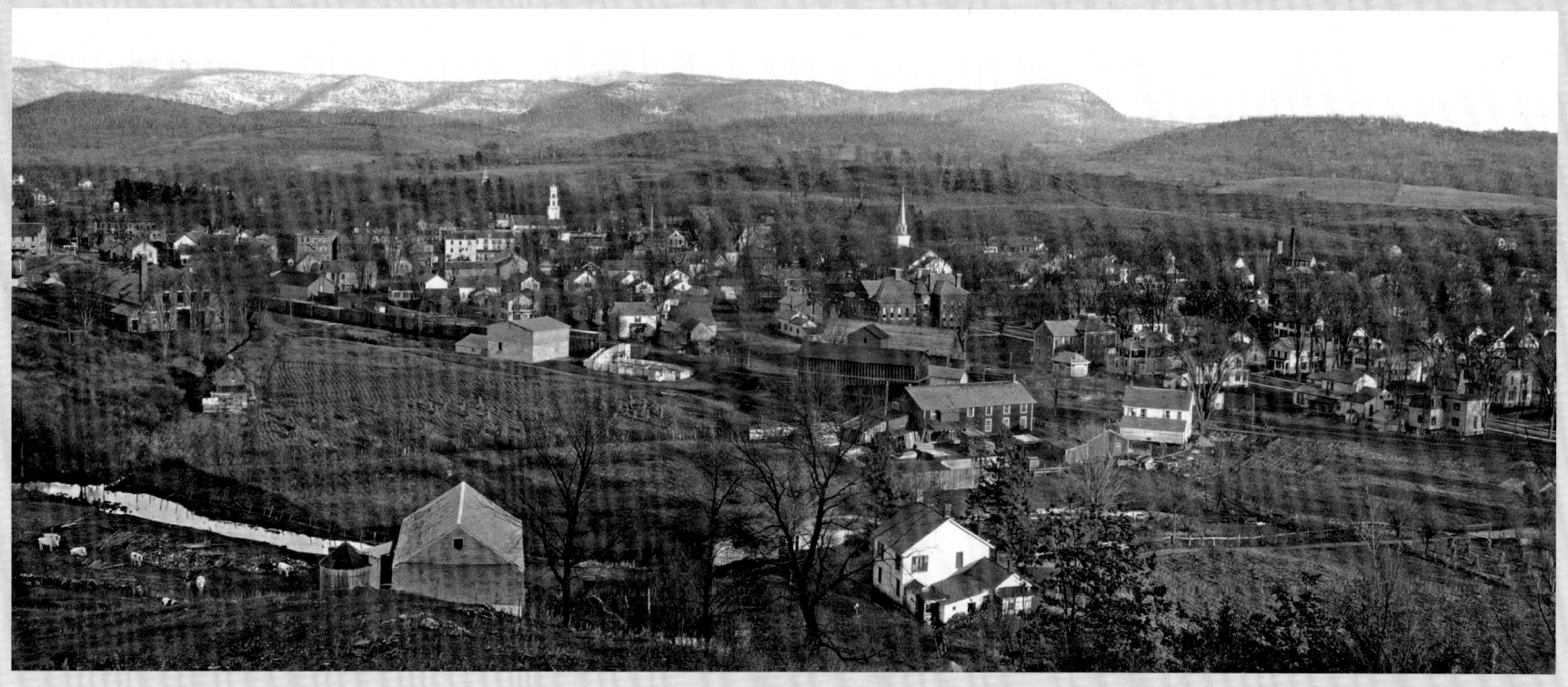

Panoramic photograph of Salem, New York. Two glass slides were fused together to make one panoramic image from photographs taken from Cary Hill in Salem. Visible in the photograph are the courthouse cupola, the Salem Central School Academy, and the Presbyterian and Old White Congregational Church steeples. The Manhattan Shirt Shop and Steam Plant chimney are visible on the right. Mt. Equinox in Vermont is the far distant mountain peak on the left.

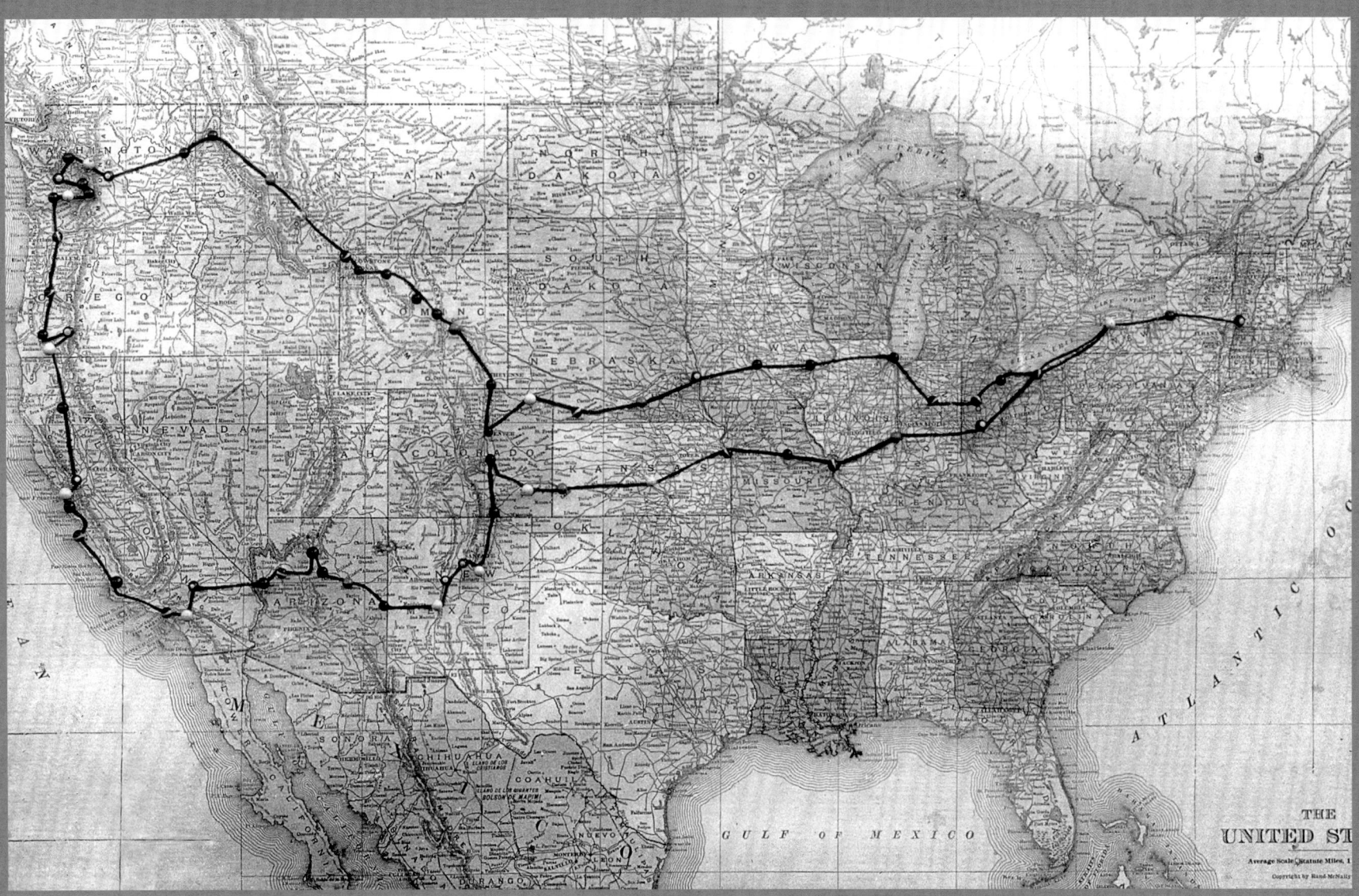

Photograph of the trip progress map with pushpins. This map hung on the wall in the People's National Bank of Salem, New York, on Main Street. Henry, then president of the bank, routinely provided running updates of their traveling location via Western Union Telegraph. Bank employees inserted red pins to indicate the Spallholzes' location during their travel. Other pin colors indicated predetermined mail stops.

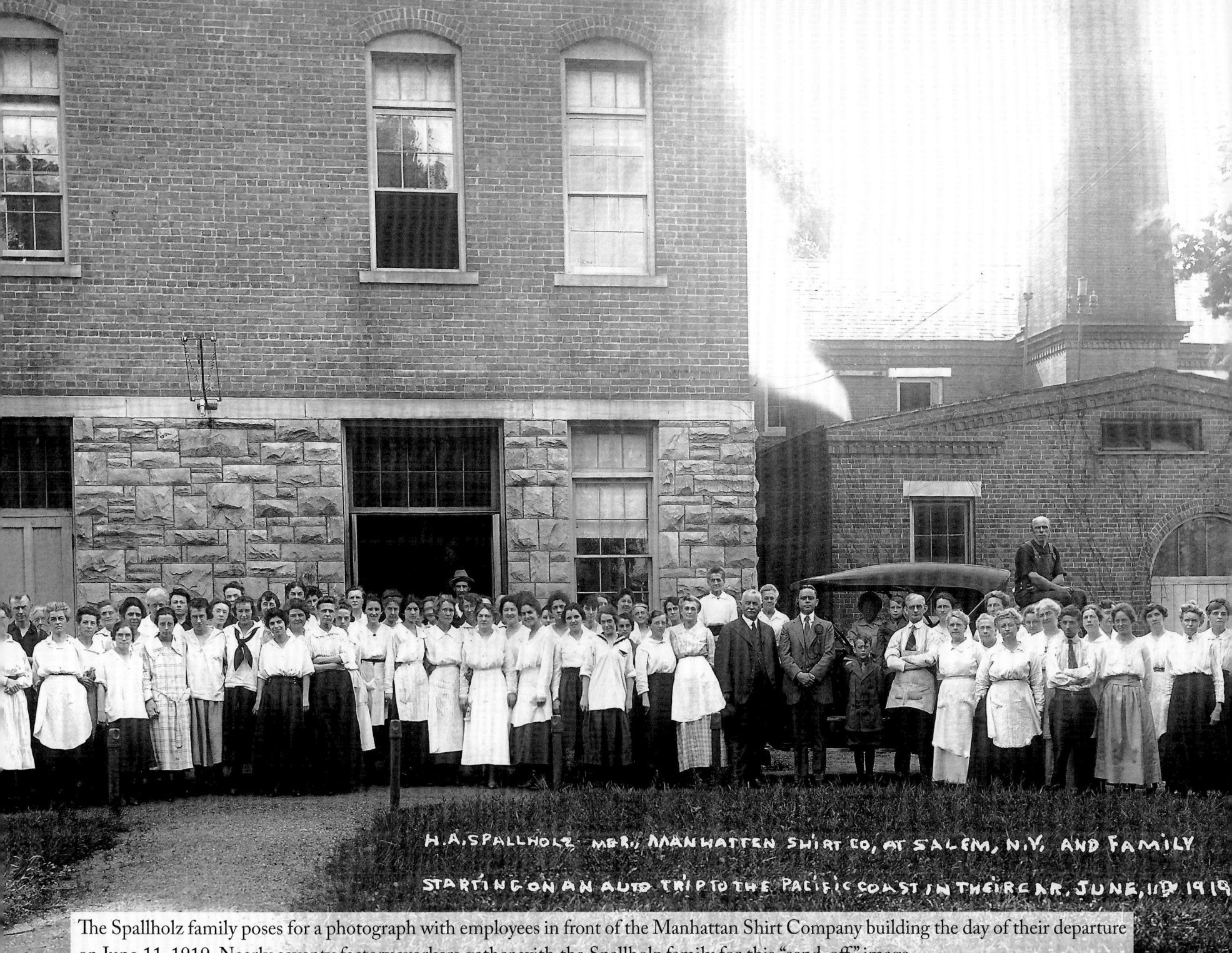

H.A. SPALLHOLZ, MGR., MANHATTAN SHIRT CO. AT SALEM, N.Y. AND FAMILY
STARTING ON AN AUTO TRIP TO THE PACIFIC COAST IN THEIR CAR, JUNE, 11D 1919

The Spallholz family poses for a photograph with employees in front of the Manhattan Shirt Company building the day of their departure on June 11, 1919. Nearly seventy factory workers gather with the Spallholz family for this "send-off" image.

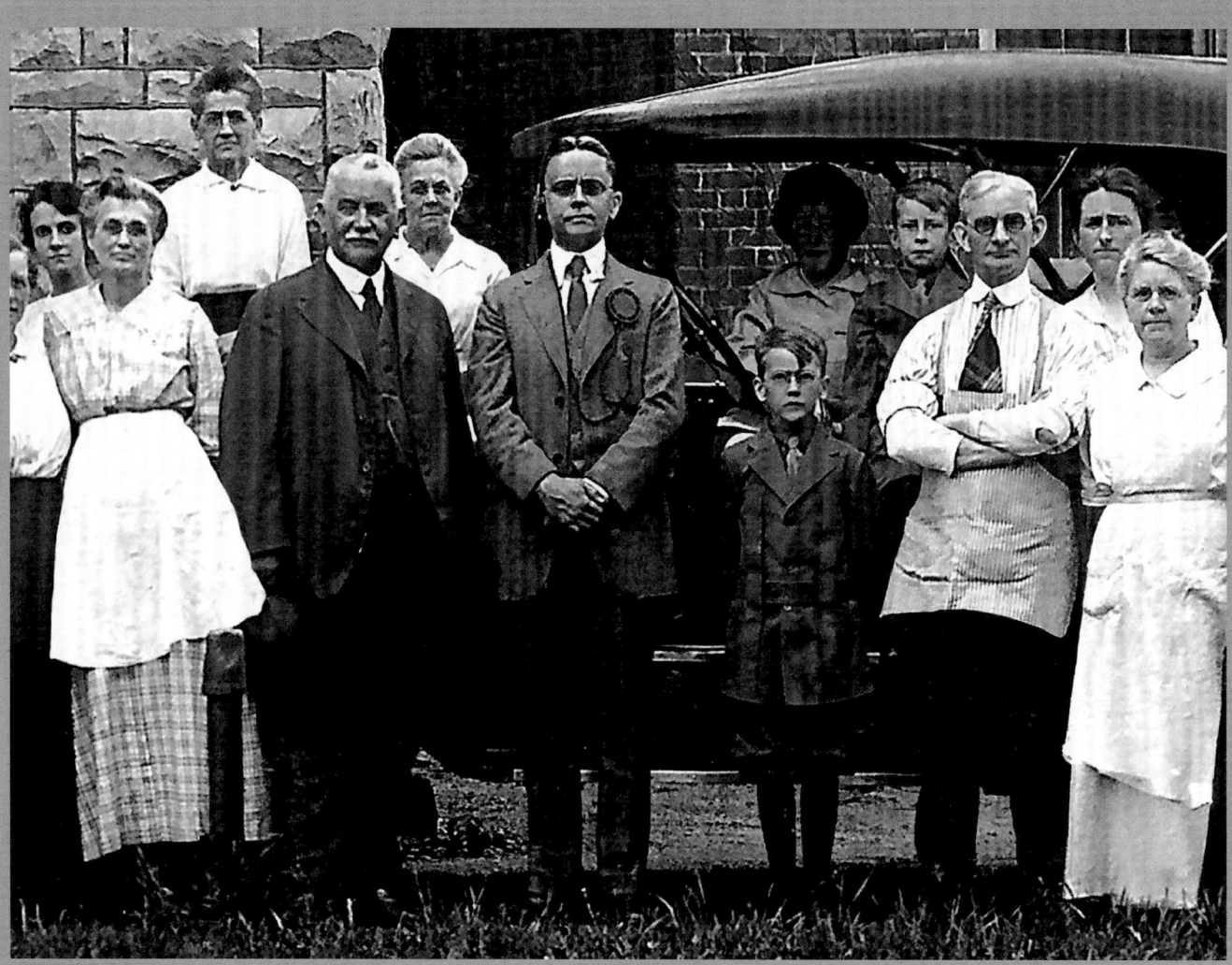

A close-up of a section of the previous photo showing the travelers: Henry Albert Spallholz, with the cable from his hearing aid wound into his front pocket, wired through his coat and looped around his right ear, Walter Lind Spallholz (standing at Henry's left), Lizzie Ferguson Spallholz seated in the Haynes Automobile, and Ernest Henry Spallholz standing on the running board to Walter's left surrounded by employees.

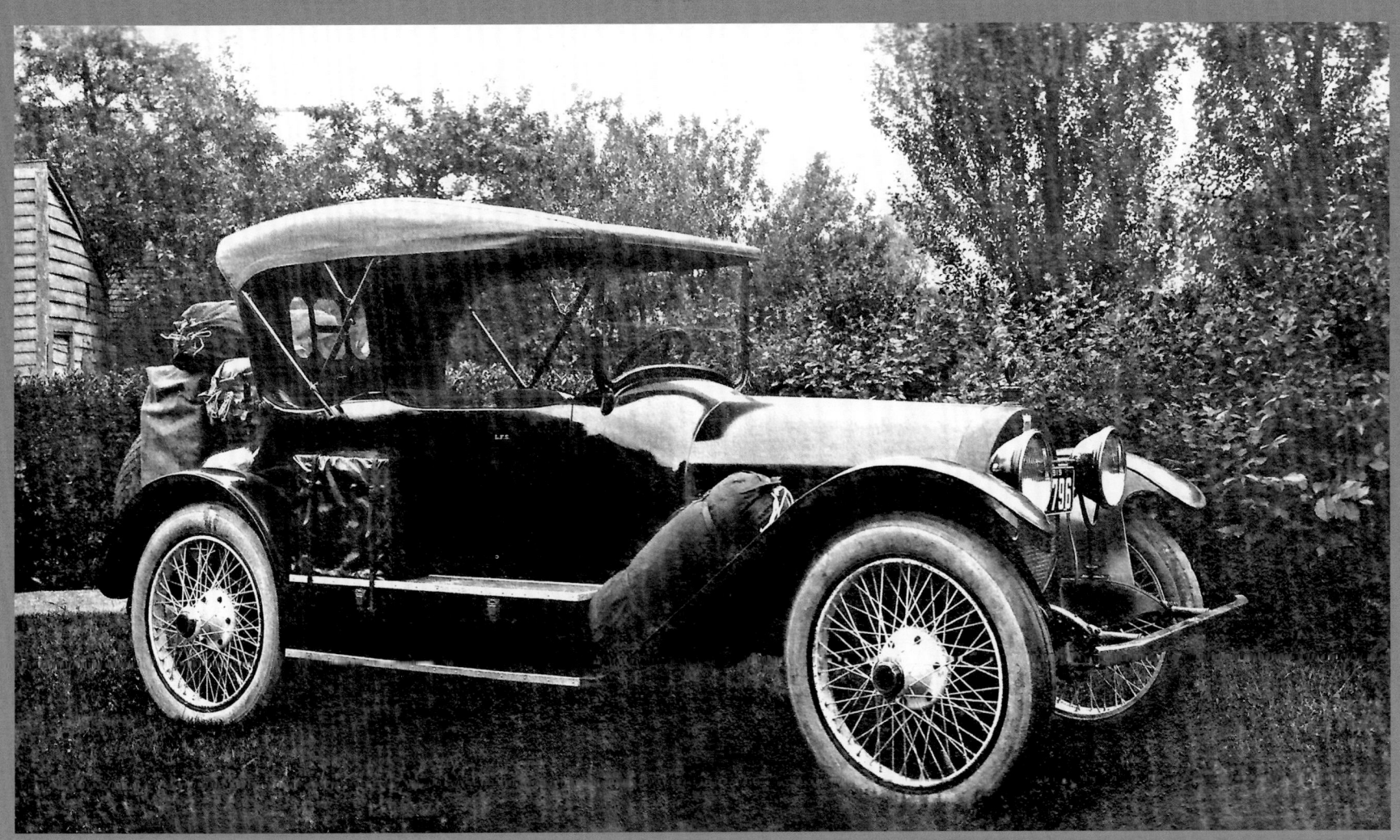

Henry added a front bumper, extended the rear bumper, and attached specially made running board boxes on either side of the automobile. One of the boxes contained a folding gasoline camp stove and a complete set of nested cooking utensils and food containers; the box on the other side held automobile replacement parts and tools, guns, ammunition, fishing reels, rods, and tackle.

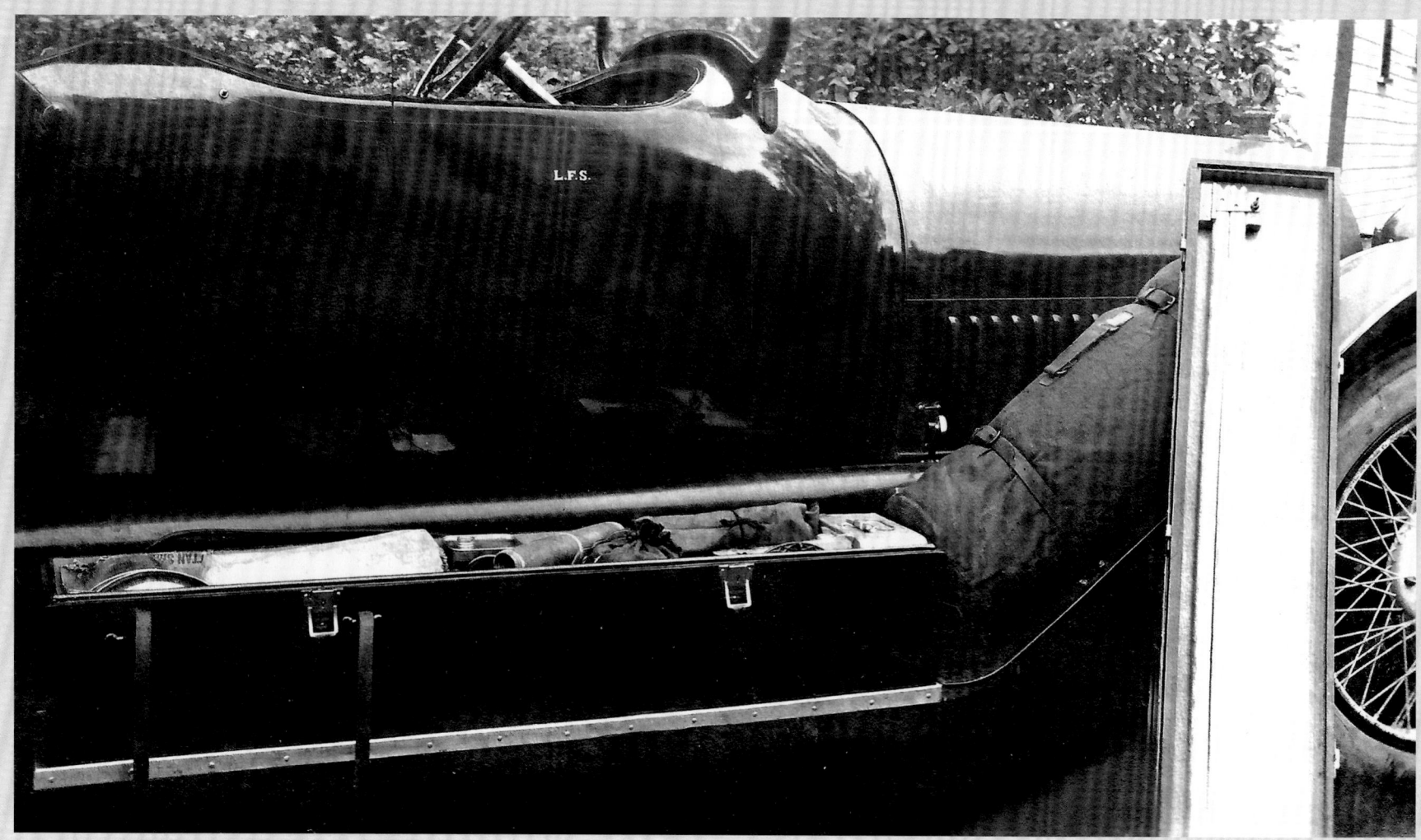

The running board boxes contained provisions and equipment for the trip, the tops of which could be assembled into a dining table. The tent poles—shown attached inside the box cover, which is leaning against the front tire—telescoped together to support a large balloon silk tent.

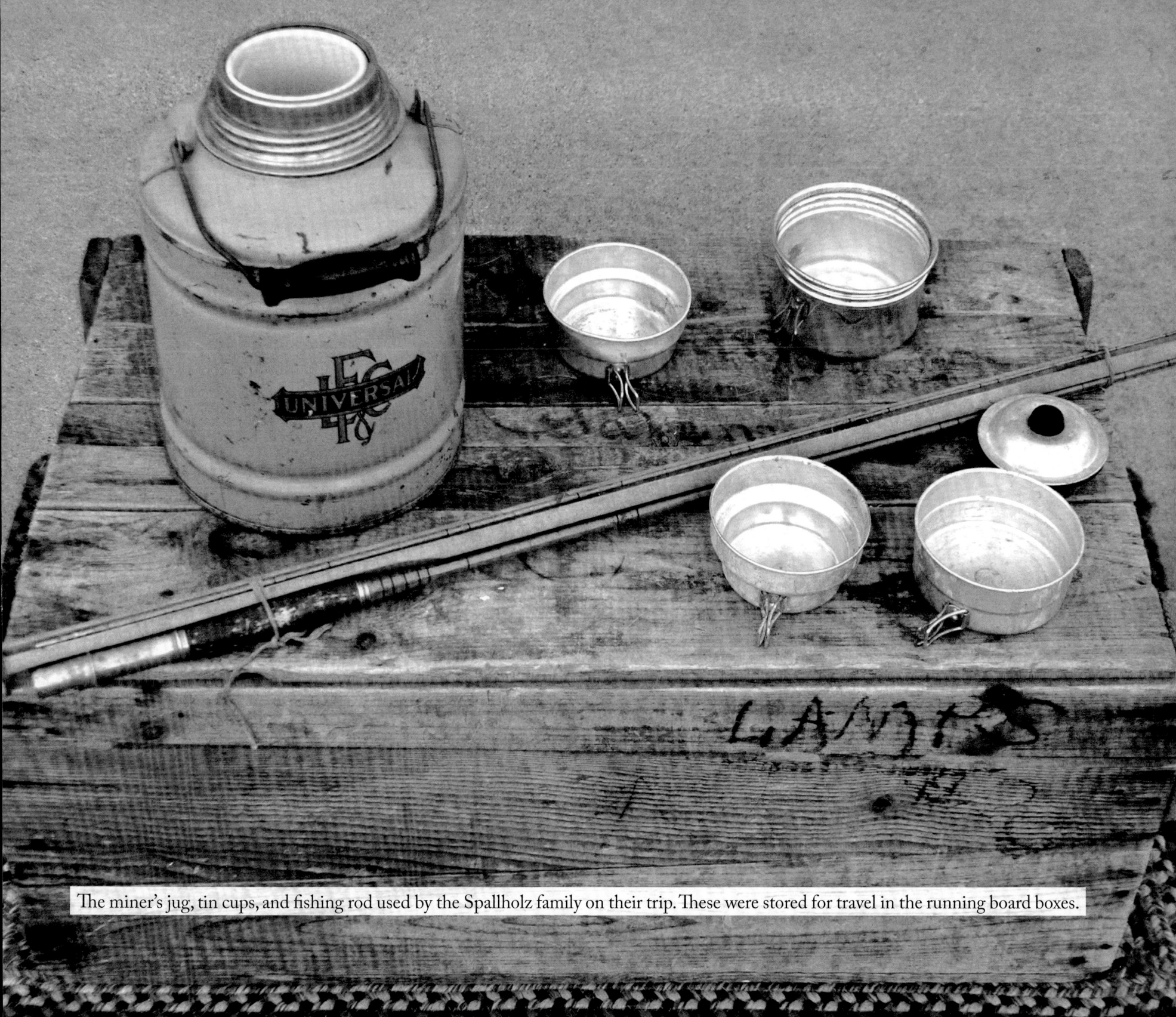

The miner's jug, tin cups, and fishing rod used by the Spallholz family on their trip. These were stored for travel in the running board boxes.

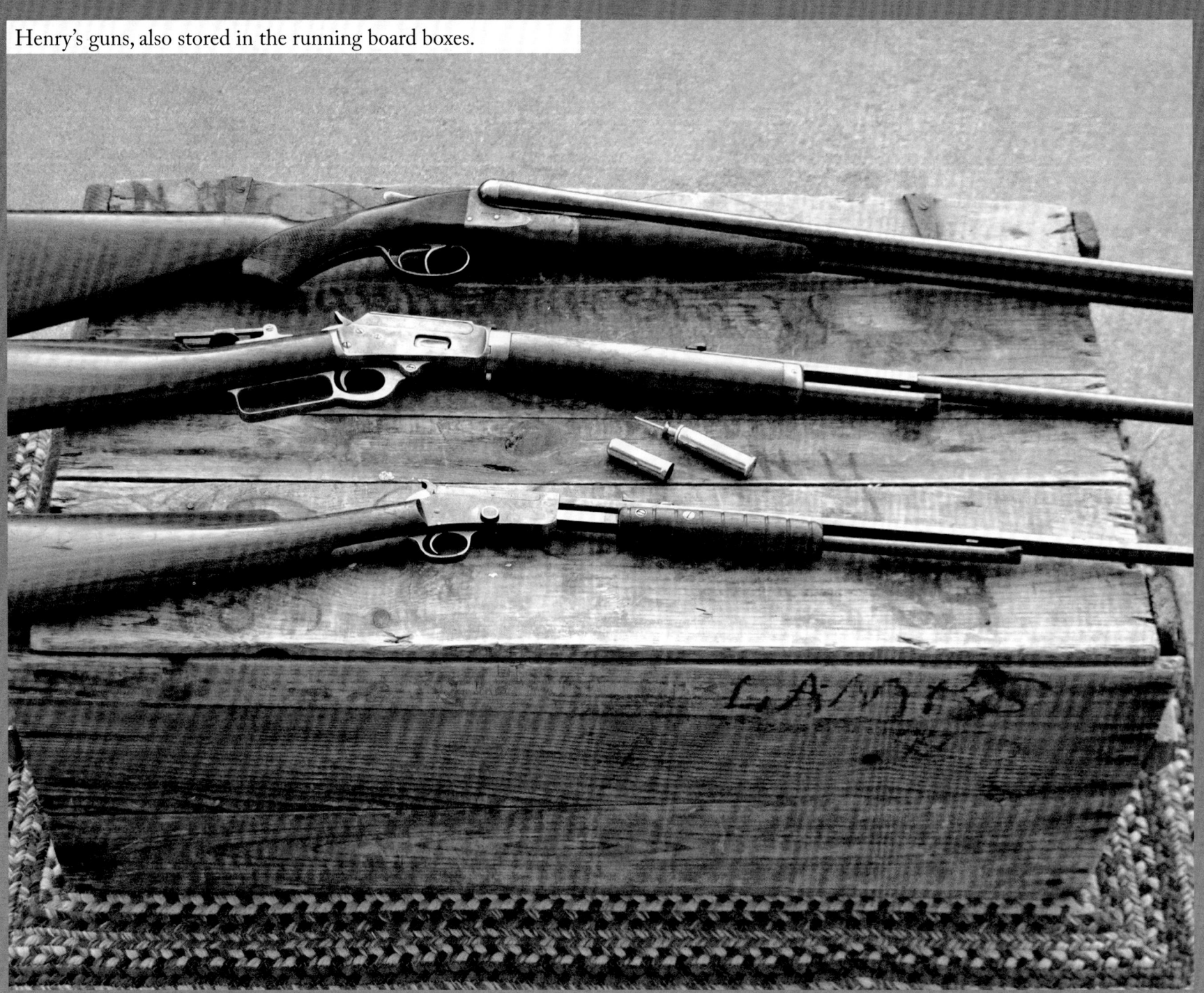

Henry's guns, also stored in the running board boxes.

Henry sits at the wheel of the Haynes Roadster with Walter and Ernest in the back seat. This view shows the rear spare tire rack Henry extended to support the balloon silk tent, duffel bag (with handle), clothes, and sleeping bags. Another sleeping bag is strapped to the front fender. The smaller black satchels behind the driver's door contained maps, notebooks, automobile survival books, and camera equipment.

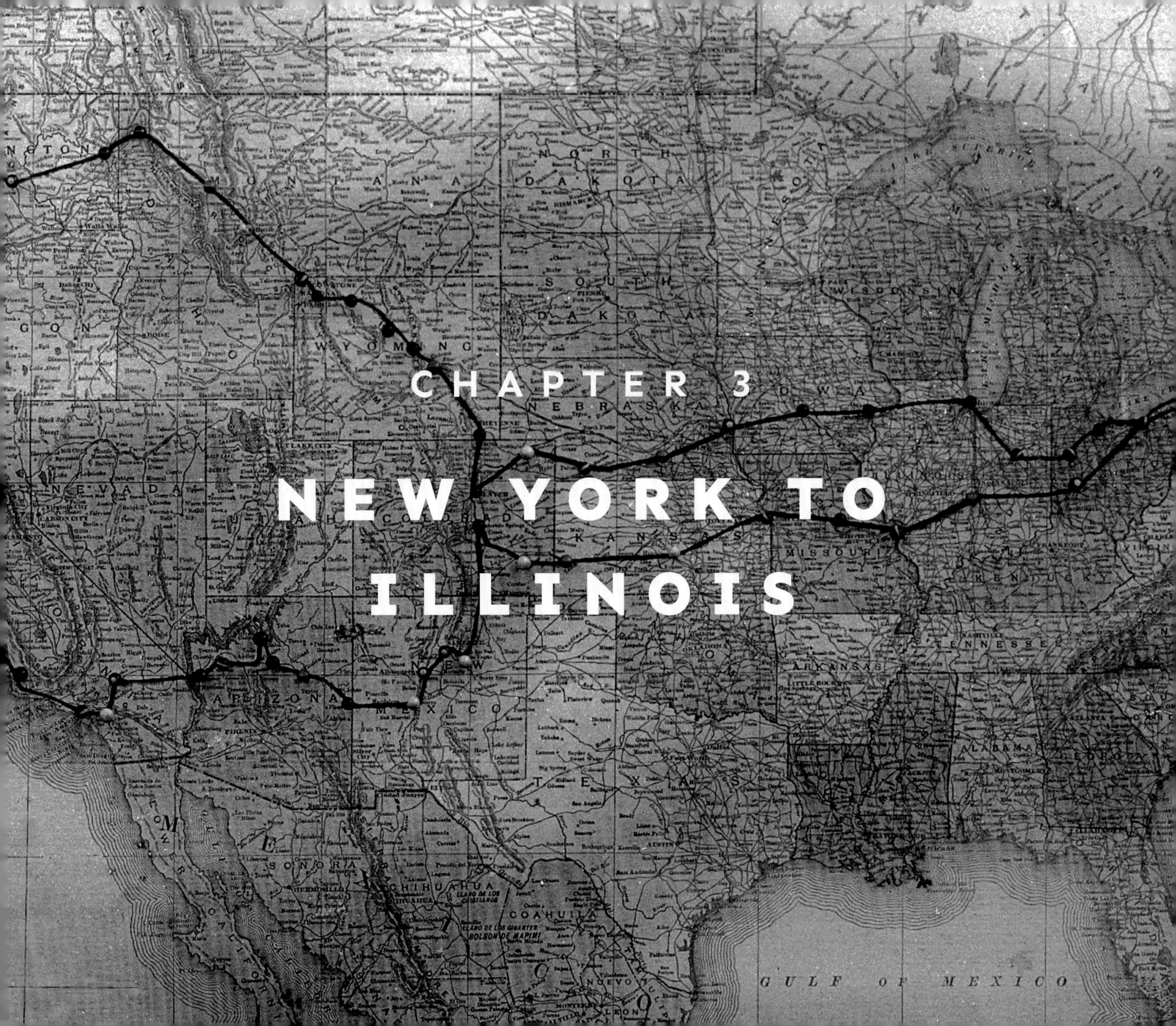

CHAPTER 3
NEW YORK TO ILLINOIS

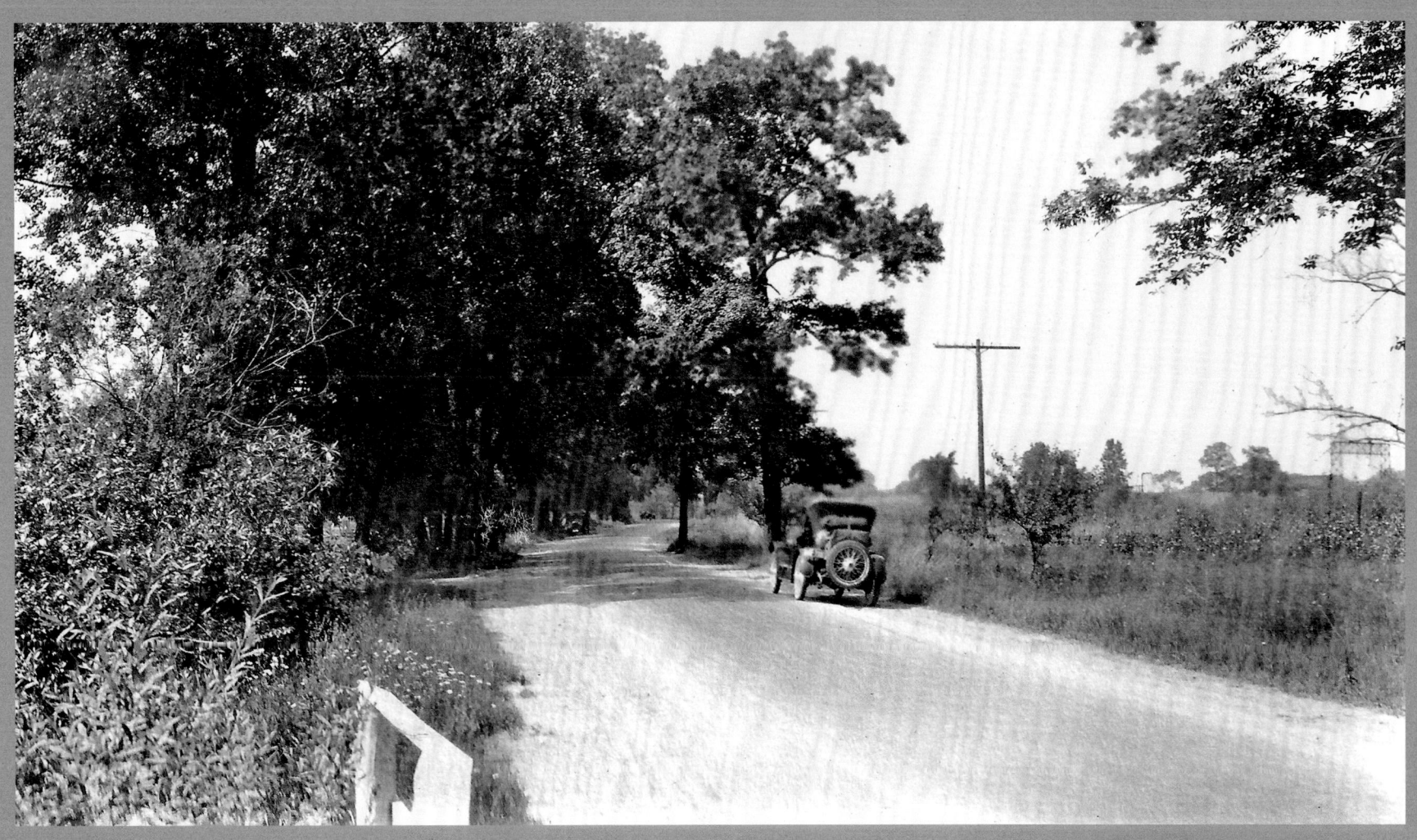

Upon leaving Salem, road conditions were good through the Finger Lakes district of New York State, north of Lakes Seneca and Geneva and the town of Geneva. The road in this picture is now New York State Route 20. Some of New York's best wineries can be found off US Route 20 on the way to the Finger Lakes.

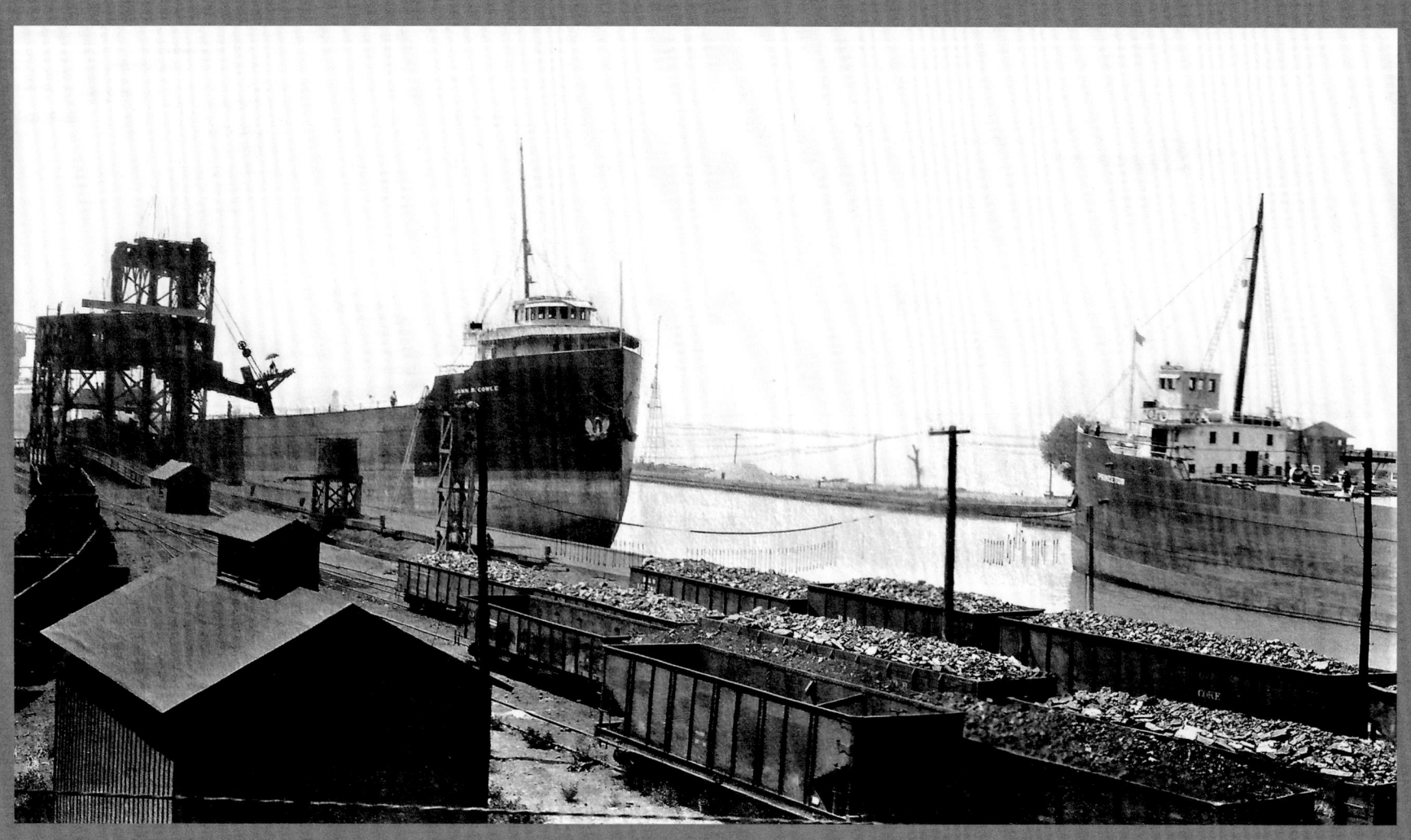

After passing through the northwest section of Pennsylvania, the Spallholzes arrived in Lorain, Ohio. Coal and iron ore were shipped on boats following the opening of the Soo Locks, which operate at the border between Sault Saint Marie, Michigan, and Sault Saint Marie, Ontario, Canada. Around 1864, Johnstown Steel relocated to Lorain, Ohio, on the Black River.

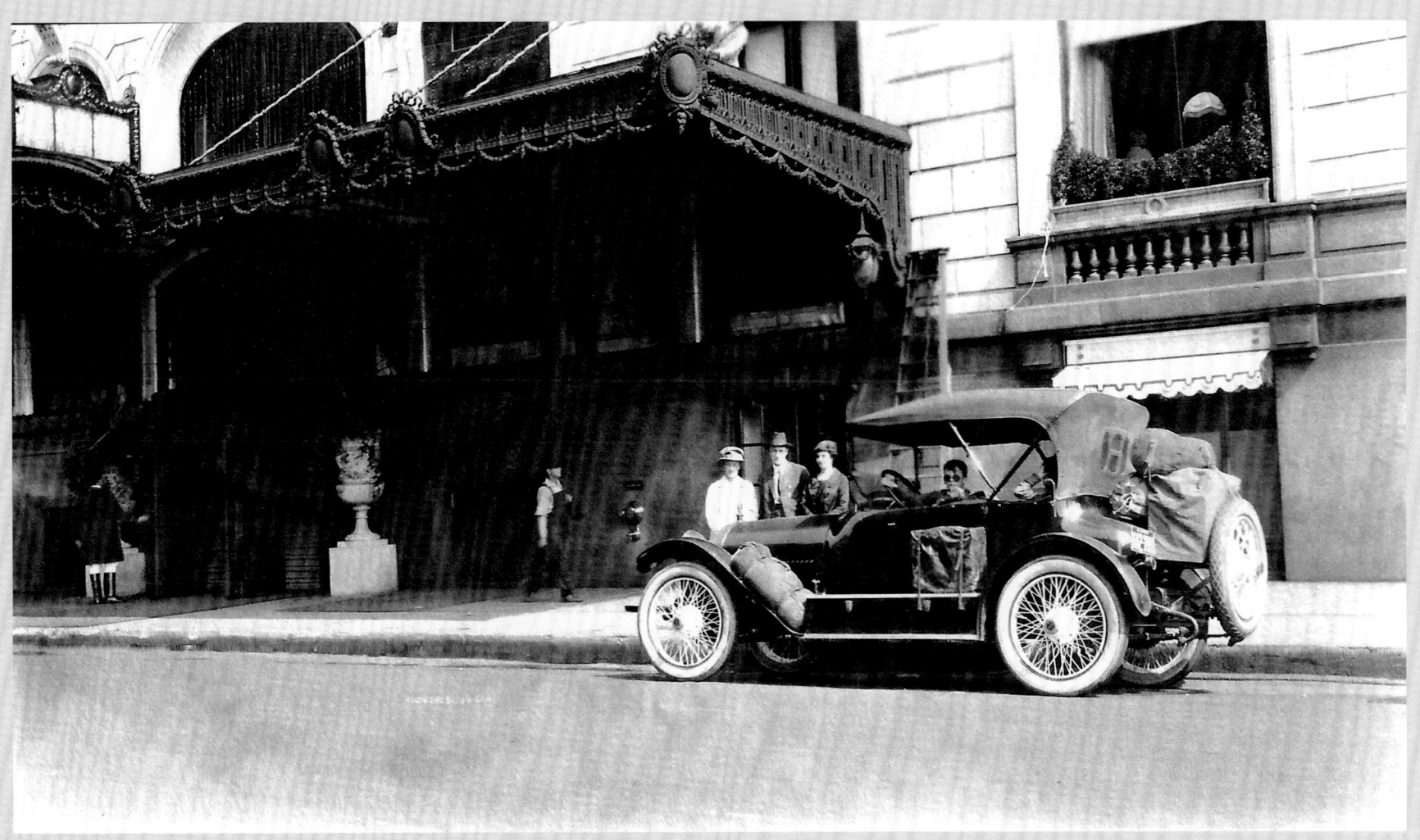

In Chicago, the Spallholz family stayed overnight at the Blackstone Hotel and visited with acquaintances from Salem upon their departure. Lizzie stands next to the Haynes with friends from Salem, John McWorther and his daughter. Walter is at the wheel and Ernest in the back seat of the Haynes.

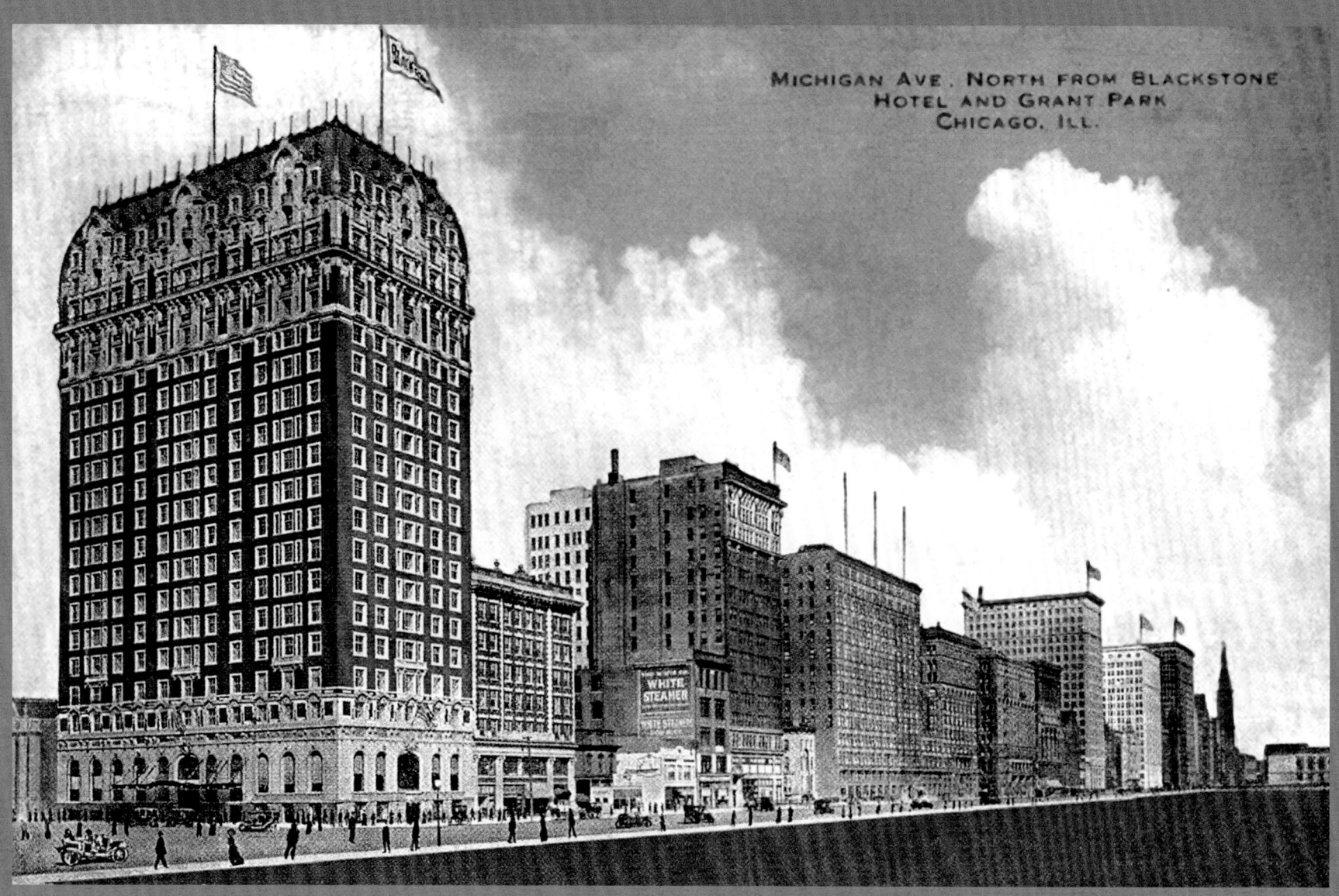

MICHIGAN AVE. NORTH FROM BLACKSTONE
HOTEL AND GRANT PARK
CHICAGO, ILL.

The Blackstone Hotel on Michigan Avenue, completed in 1910, takes its name from Timothy Blackstone, founding president of the Chicago Union Stockyards. It is also known as the Hotel of Presidents, as many twentieth-century presidents resided here in the presidential suite over the years. The hotel was added to the National Register of Historic Places in 1986 and was named a Chicago landmark in 1998.

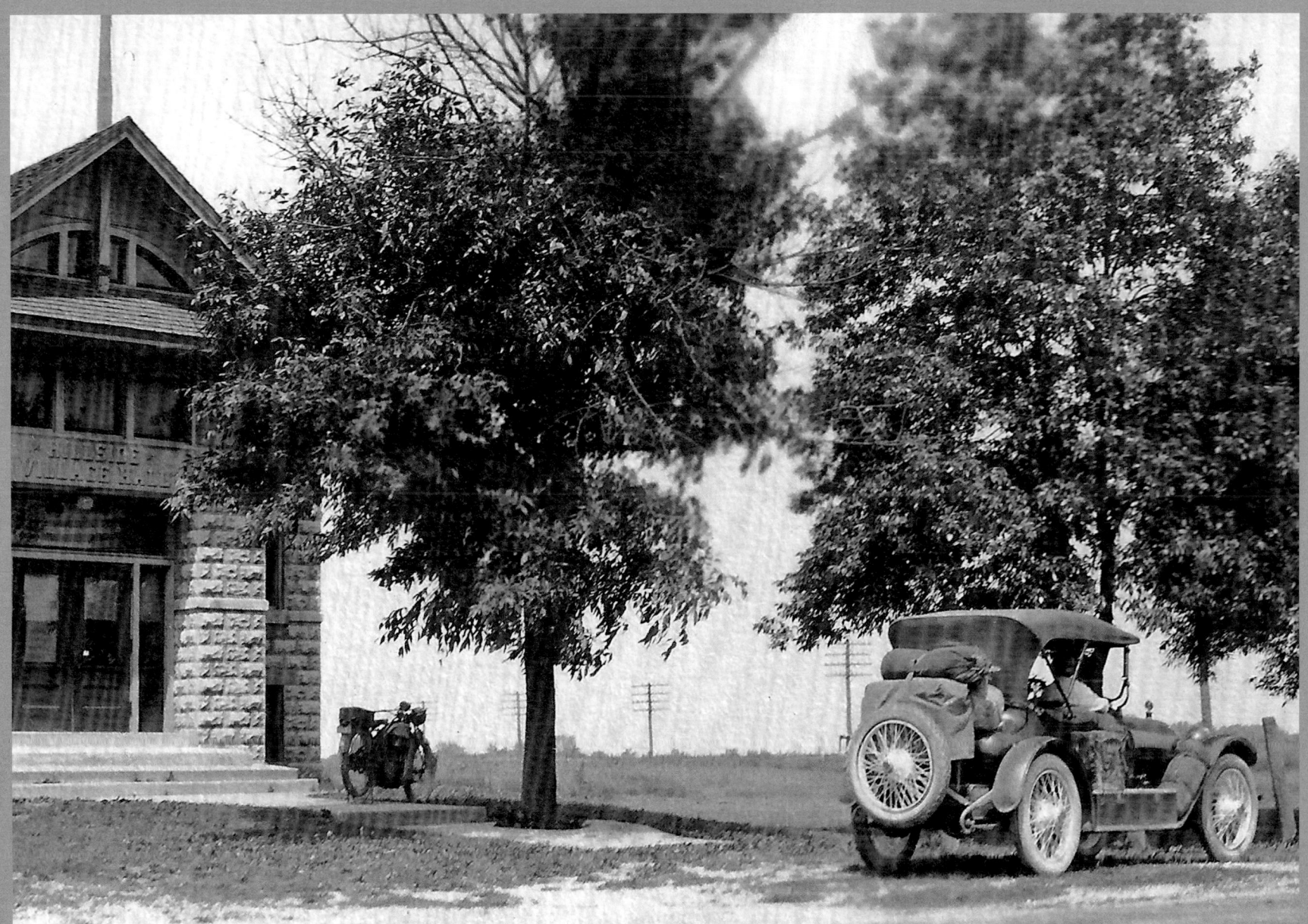

Traveling through Hillside, Illinois, going thirty-two miles per hour, the Spallholz family was stopped for speeding. Henry was directed to immediately appear before the local justice of the peace, which was common at that time for traffic infractions. The police officer's motorcycle is parked to the right of the small courthouse. Lizzie and family sit patiently in the automobile. The justice's building in Hillside was torn down in the 1960s.

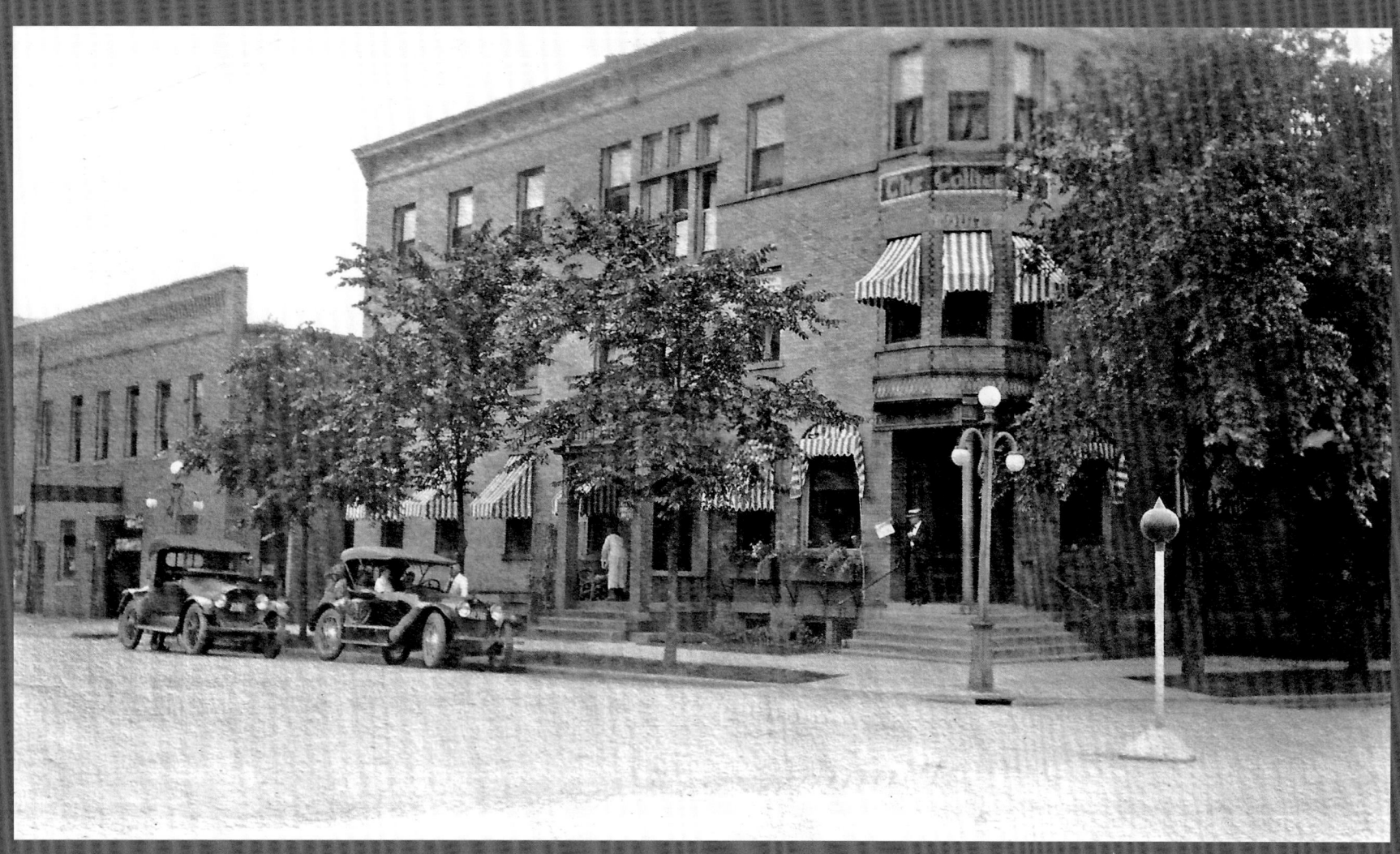

The Spallholzes' encounter with road mud forced them to stay overnight at the Collier Inn in Illinois. They seem to be following in Emily Post's tire tracks: Ms. Post devotes two chapters to mud in the Midwest in her book, *By Motor to the Golden Gate*. The 1922 *Midwest Bluebook* lists the Collier Inn fees: "American Plan $3.50 and up; European Plan $1.50 and up. Hot and cold running water in every room. Rooms with bath. Dining room service unexcelled."

Ernest Spallholz stands on the running board box in this photograph of an unusual bricked section of the Lincoln Highway, with little traffic, probably US Route 30 west from Sterling. From Rochelle, Illinois, through Franklin Grove and Dixon, Illinois, the Lincoln Highway is Route 38. West of Sterling, Illinois, it becomes US Route 30 through Morrison. The billboard beyond the left fender pictures a carload of happy travelers and offers an invitation for folks to stop at The Highway Hotel.

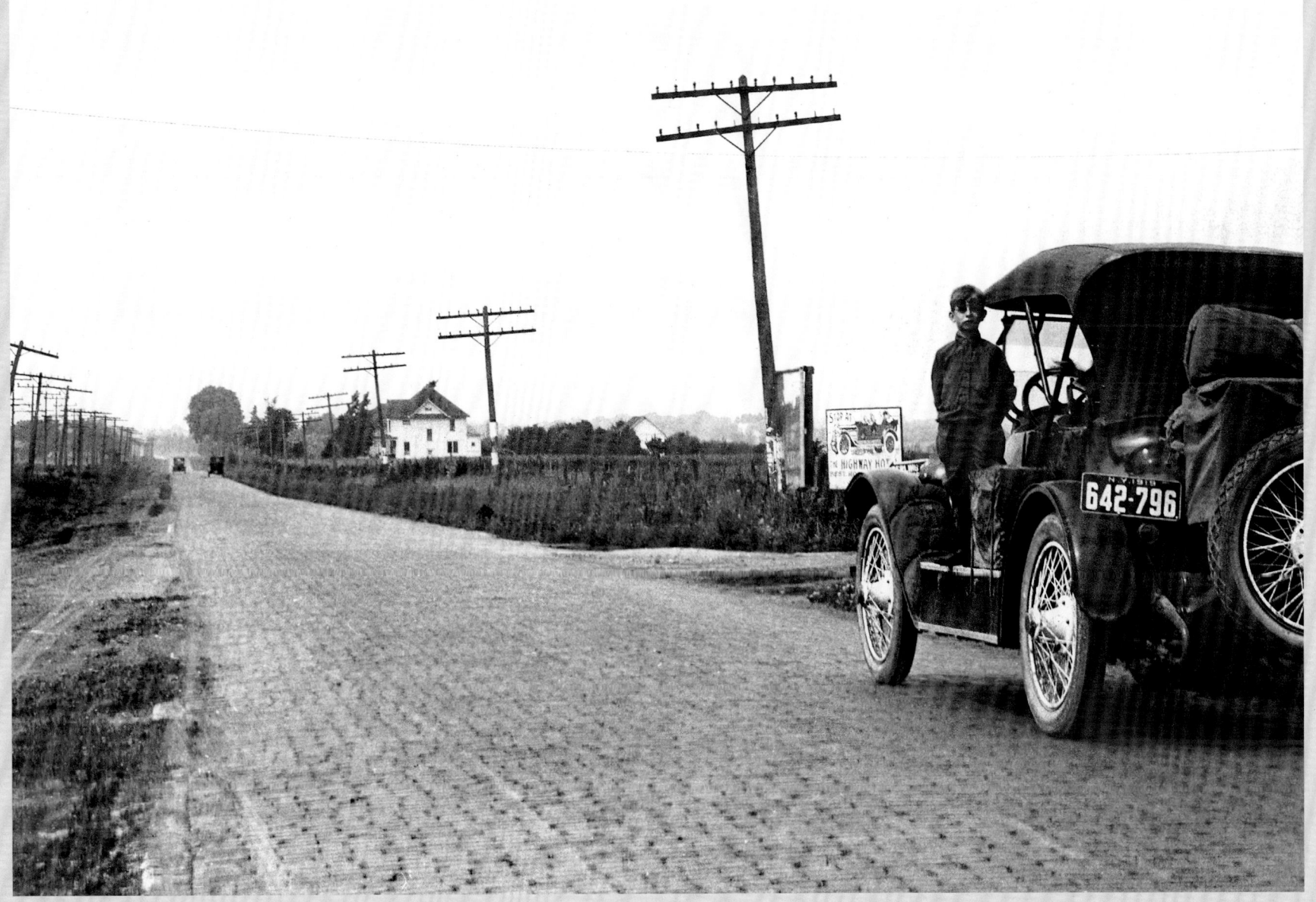

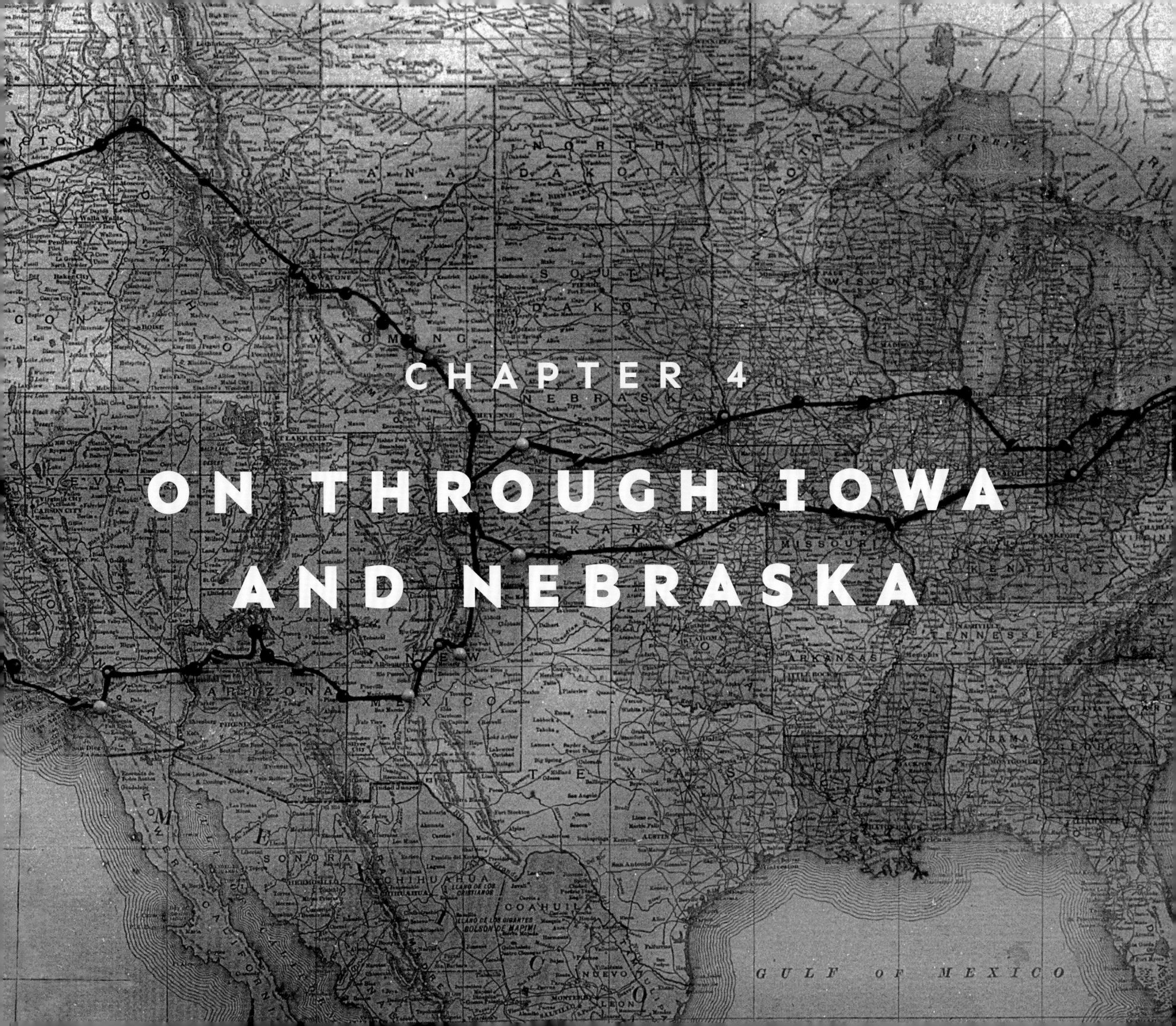

CHAPTER 4

ON THROUGH IOWA AND NEBRASKA

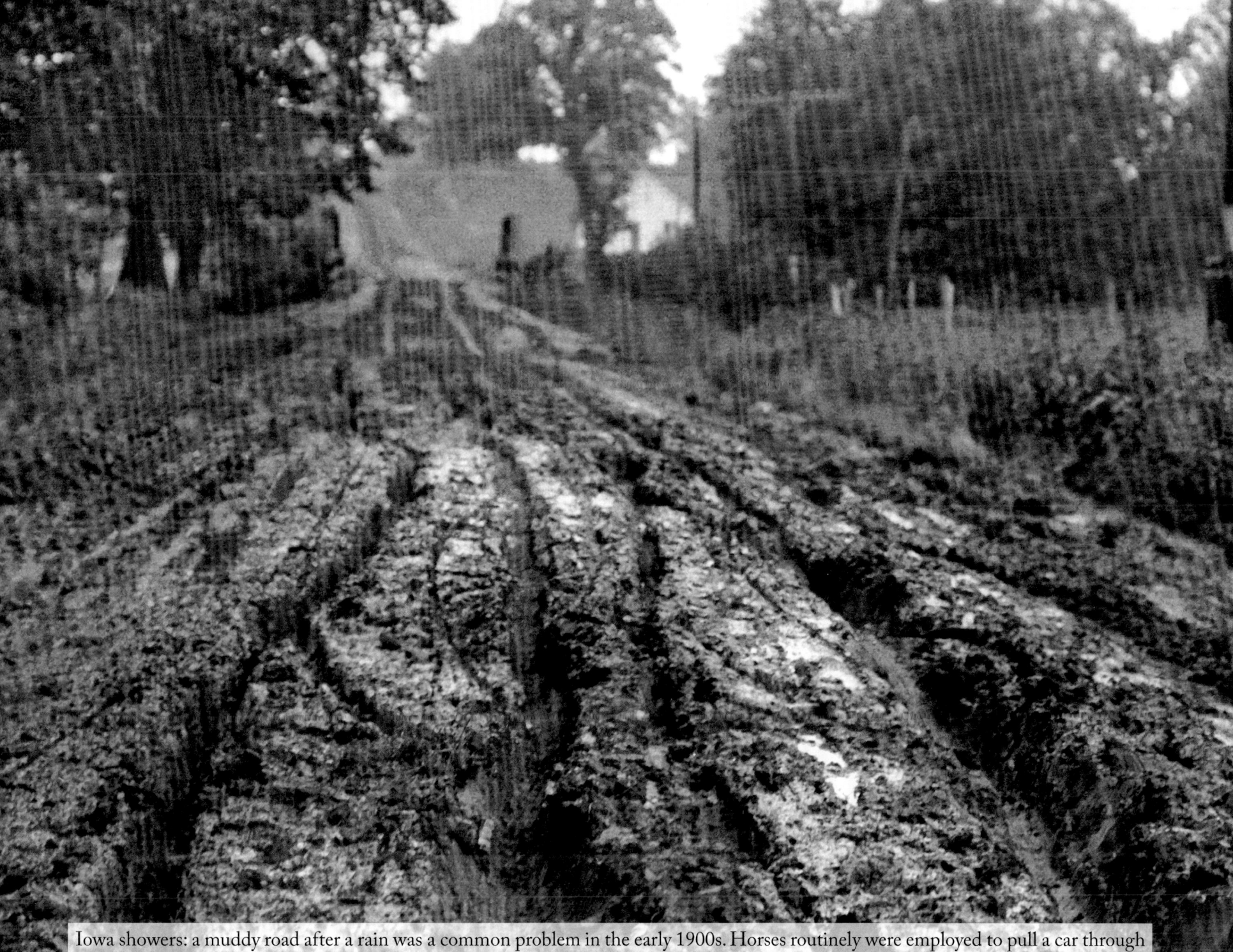

Iowa showers: a muddy road after a rain was a common problem in the early 1900s. Horses routinely were employed to pull a car through particularly impenetrable areas.

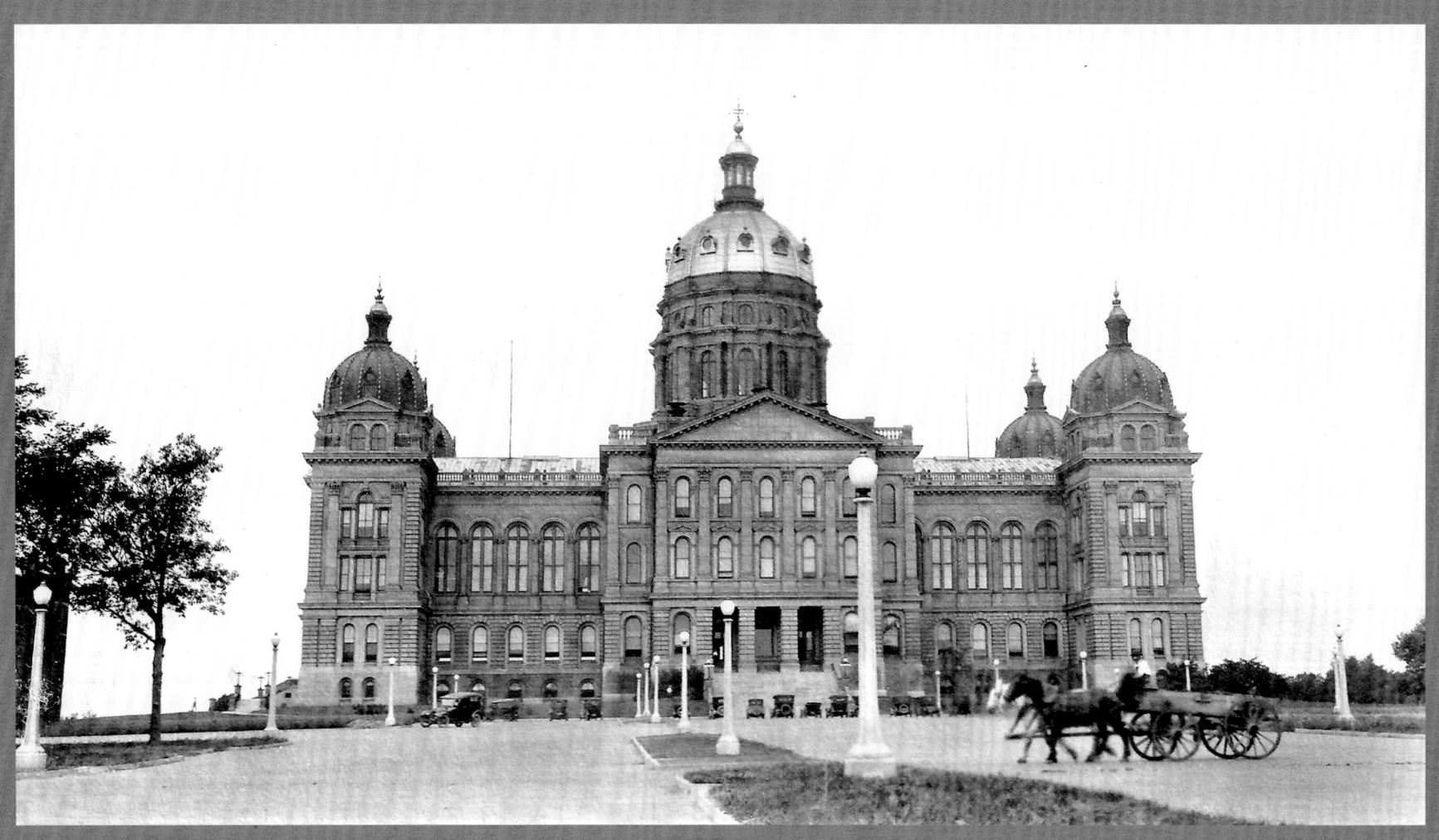

The Iowa Capitol Building was constructed on donated land at the highest point in Des Moines. It was completed, with five domes, in 1886. The central dome is 275 feet tall and covered in gold leaf. In addition to housing legislative functions, the Capitol is also a living museum and a state and international cultural facility.

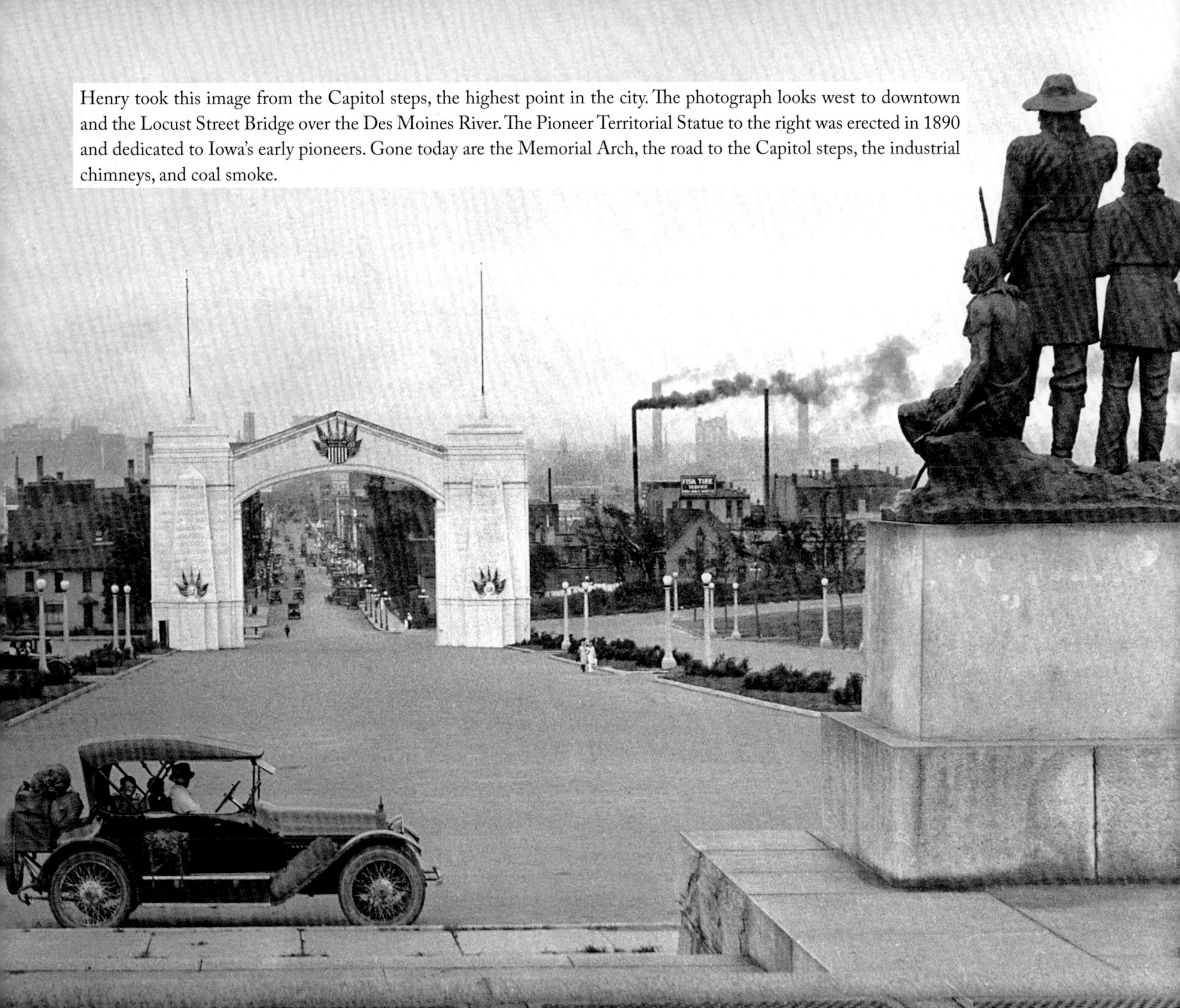

Henry took this image from the Capitol steps, the highest point in the city. The photograph looks west to downtown and the Locust Street Bridge over the Des Moines River. The Pioneer Territorial Statue to the right was erected in 1890 and dedicated to Iowa's early pioneers. Gone today are the Memorial Arch, the road to the Capitol steps, the industrial chimneys, and coal smoke.

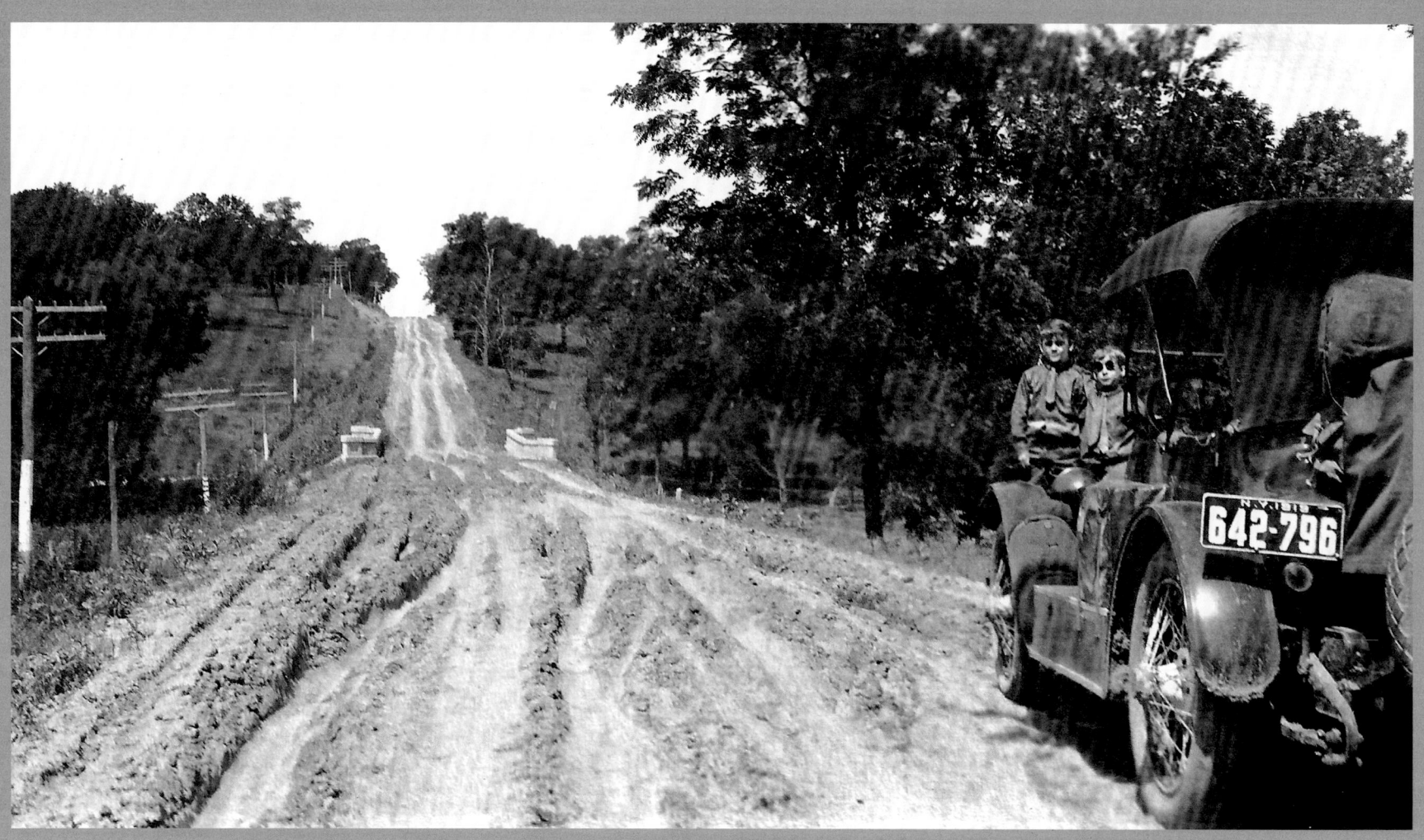

Walter and Ernest stand on the front bumper of the Haynes, which faces west looking toward Atalissa, Iowa. It is parked on a section of a rudimentary highway system that is part of what is now US Route 6. A passing farmer remarked that the muddy road was in better shape than it had been.

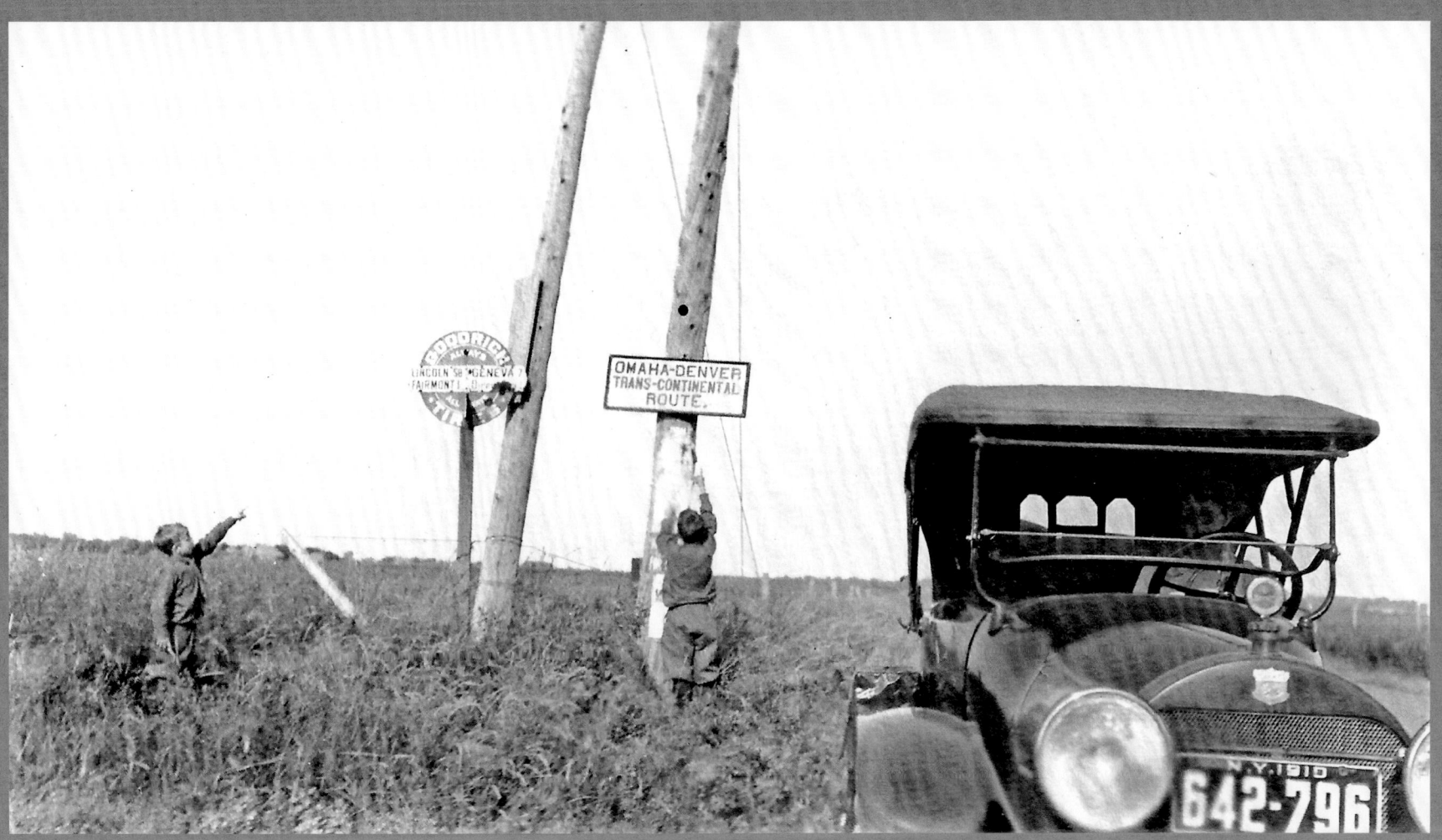

Walter and Ernest point to the sign marking the Omaha–Denver transcontinental highway on the way to Hastings, Nebraska, directly south of Grand Island. The round sign to the left is an advertisement for Goodrich Tires. Lizzie Spallholz sits in the driver's seat of the Haynes, which boasts the distinctive H (Haynes) pattern in the rear window panel.

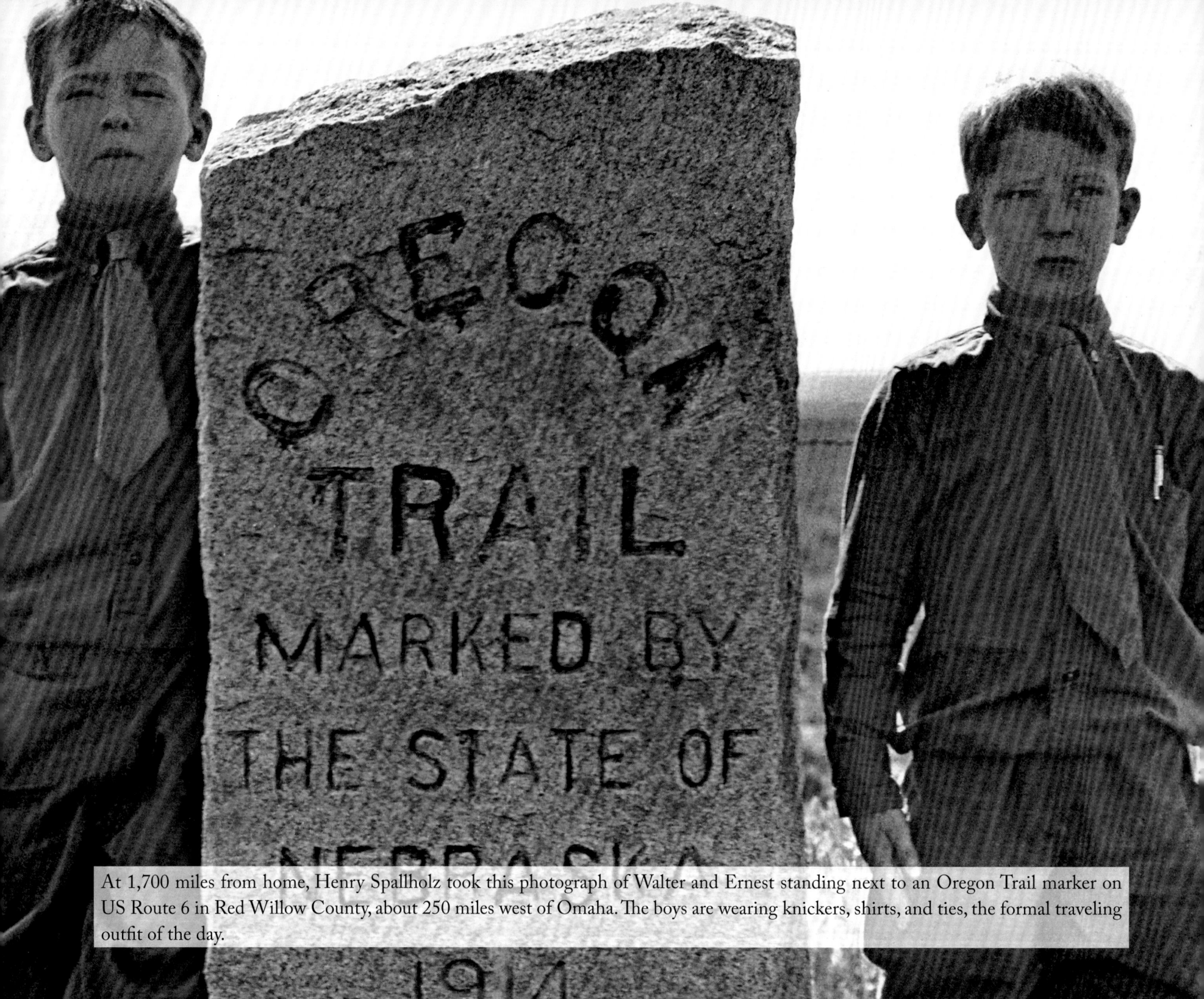

At 1,700 miles from home, Henry Spallholz took this photograph of Walter and Ernest standing next to an Oregon Trail marker on US Route 6 in Red Willow County, about 250 miles west of Omaha. The boys are wearing knickers, shirts, and ties, the formal traveling outfit of the day.

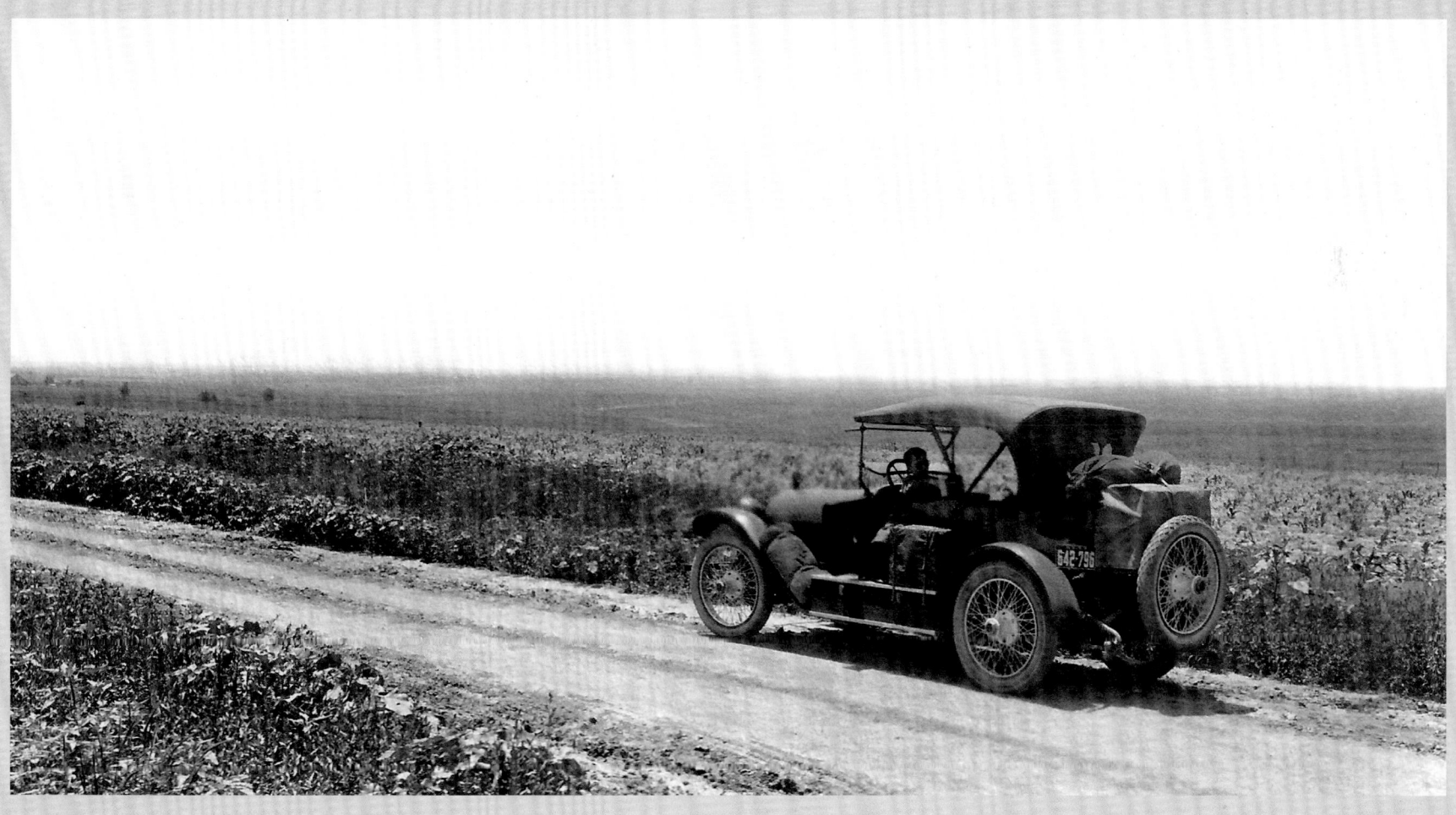

East of Beverly, Nebraska, the family pauses to take this photograph of typical flat prairie. The farm buildings on the far left give a sense of scale for the wide-open spaces of the region. Walter is at the wheel, wearing his sunglasses.

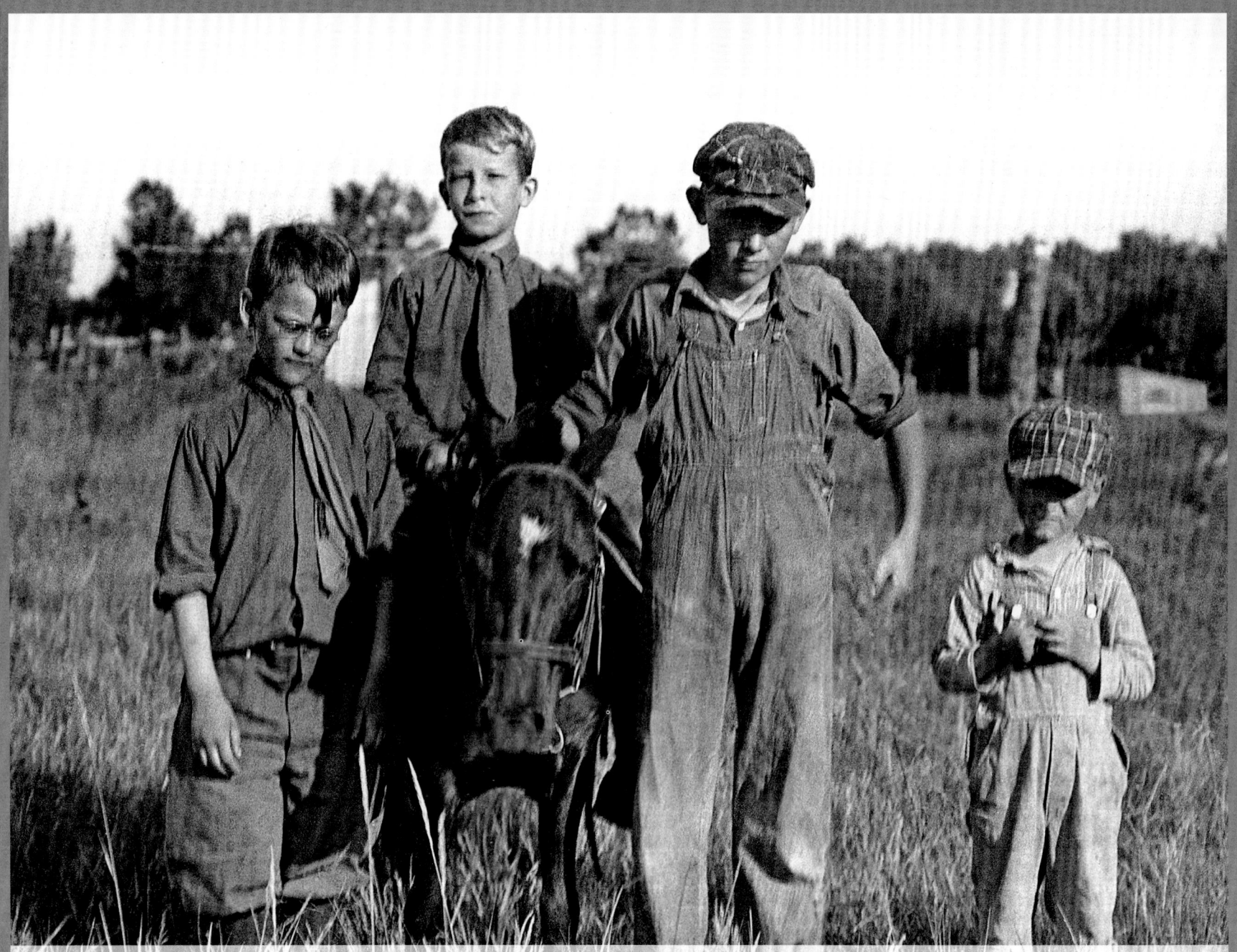

The Spallholzes' first campsite of the trip was at Beverly, Nebraska. Here the boys made acquaintance with children on a nearby farm. Significant differences between the children's Eastern and Western clothing are apparent.

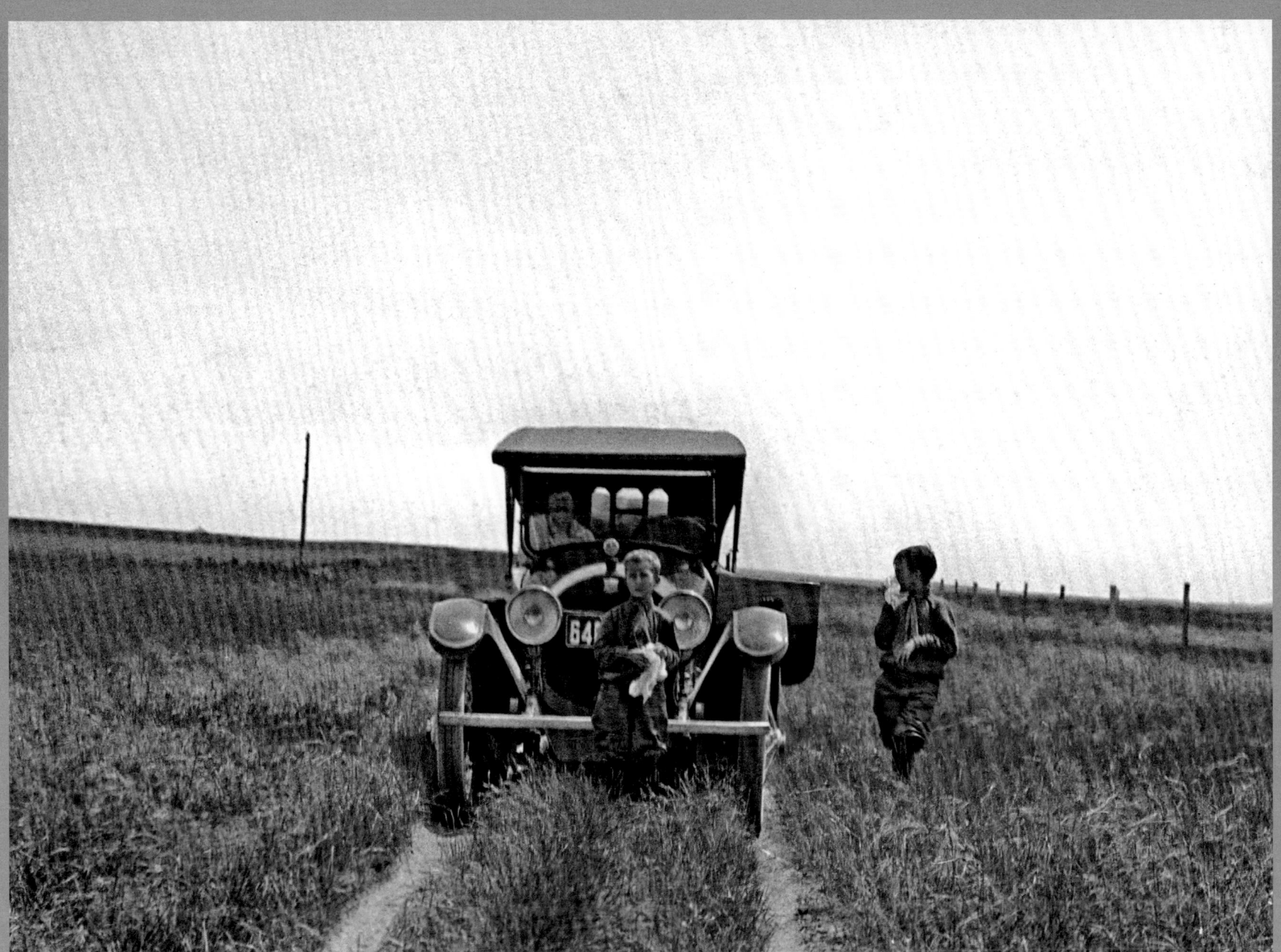

West of Imperial, Nebraska, the family had to make a prairie detour. They might have deviated from their original route to avoid a washout from flooding or to take a shortcut recommended by local residents. Ernest and Walter walk around while their father snaps this photo. The boys are holding rags and are probably wiping away sweat due to the early summer heat.

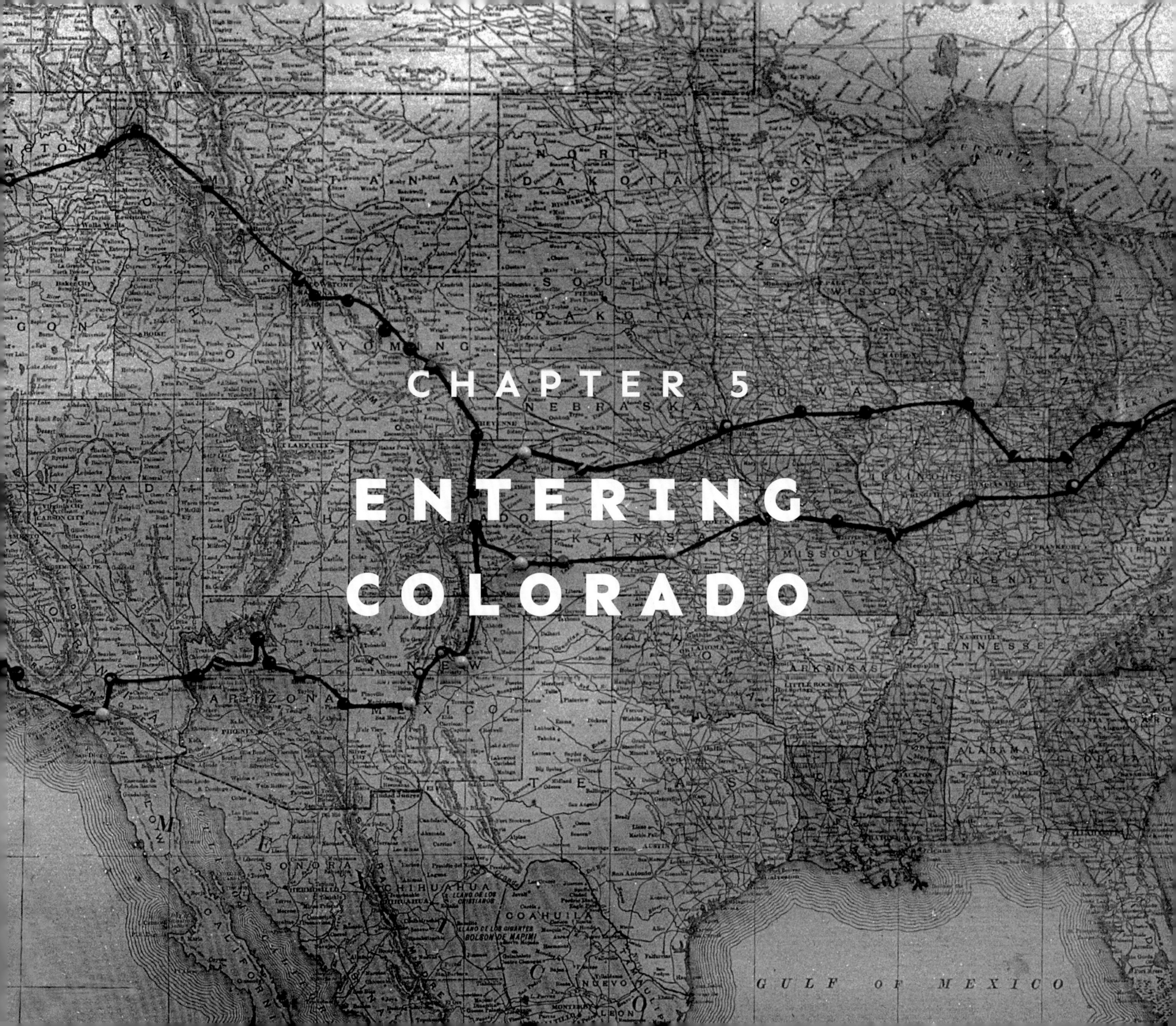

CHAPTER 5

ENTERING COLORADO

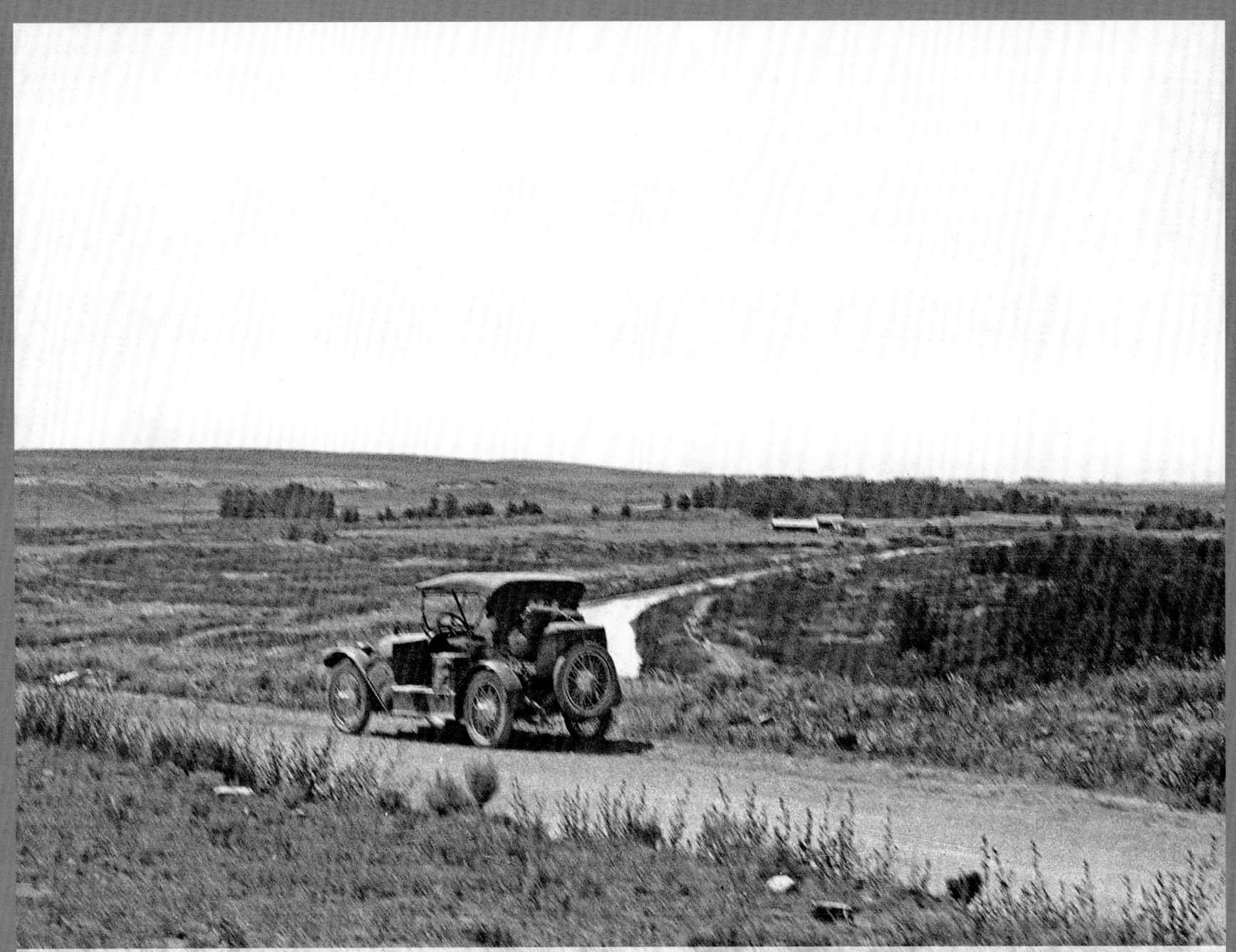

The Spallholz family entered Sterling, Colorado, and found good roads by following an irrigation canal eighty-five miles south towards Fort Morgan. The canal on the right of the road could be part of the North Sterling Irrigation District, which was formed in 1907.

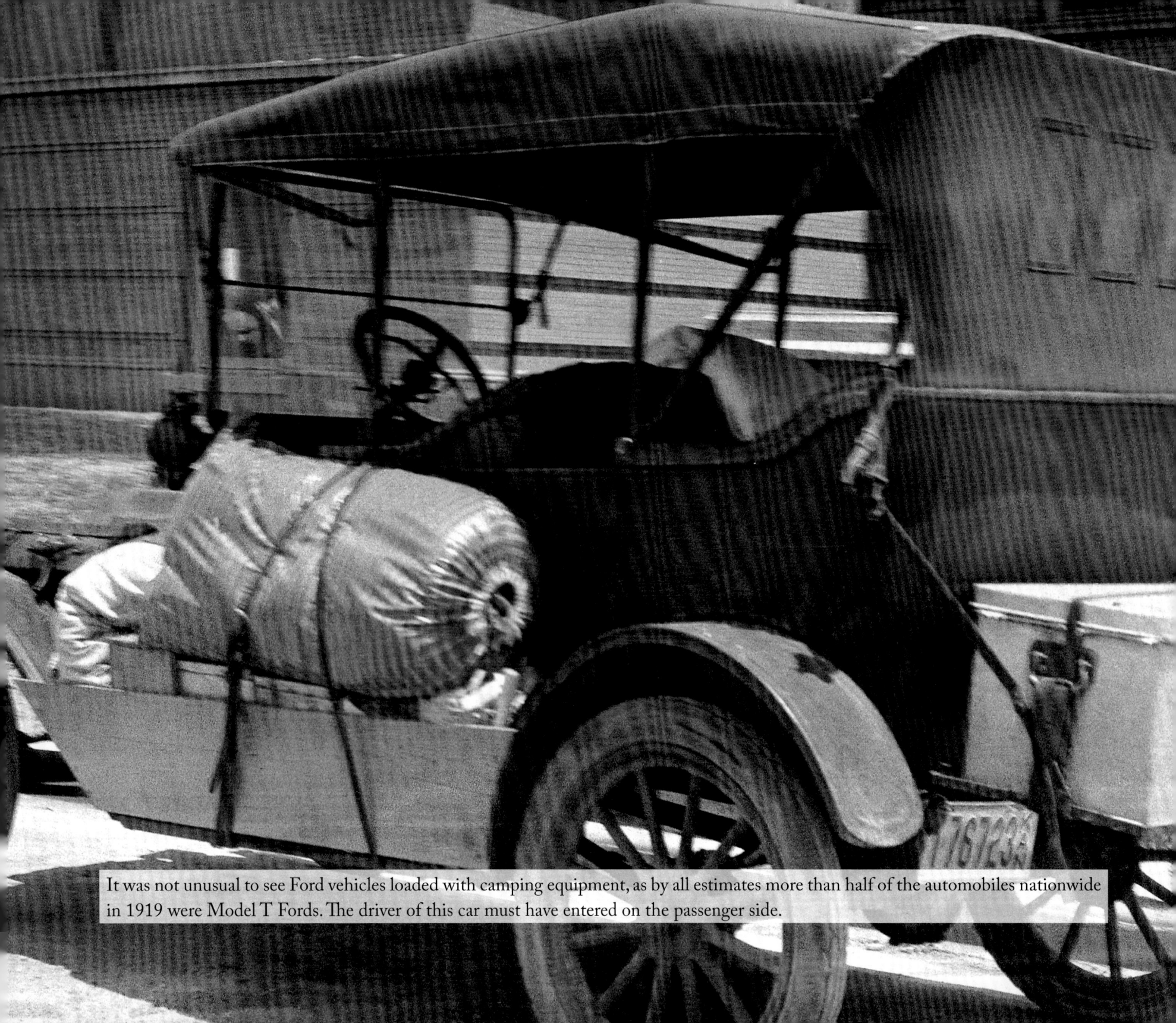

It was not unusual to see Ford vehicles loaded with camping equipment, as by all estimates more than half of the automobiles nationwide in 1919 were Model T Fords. The driver of this car must have entered on the passenger side.

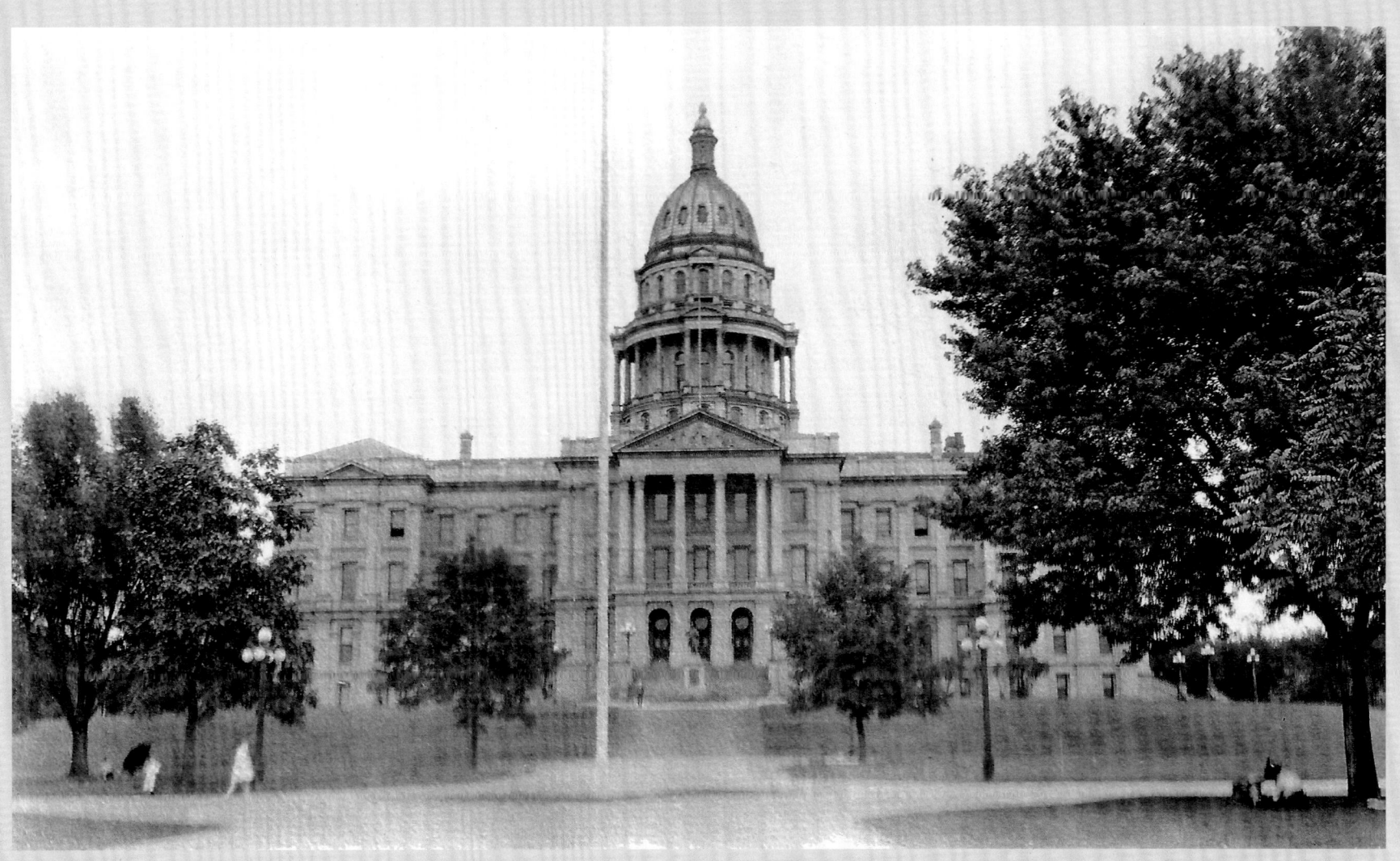

The Colorado State Capitol Building was constructed in the early 1890s in the Neoclassical architectural style using Colorado white granite. The 180-foot dome is covered in gold leaf. The Denver mile-high city survey mark at 5,280 feet elevation can be found on three of the Capitol's steps, each engraved with increasing accuracy as technology improved over the years. When the Spallholzes visited the Capitol Building in 1919, they would have seen the mile-high engraving on step 15.

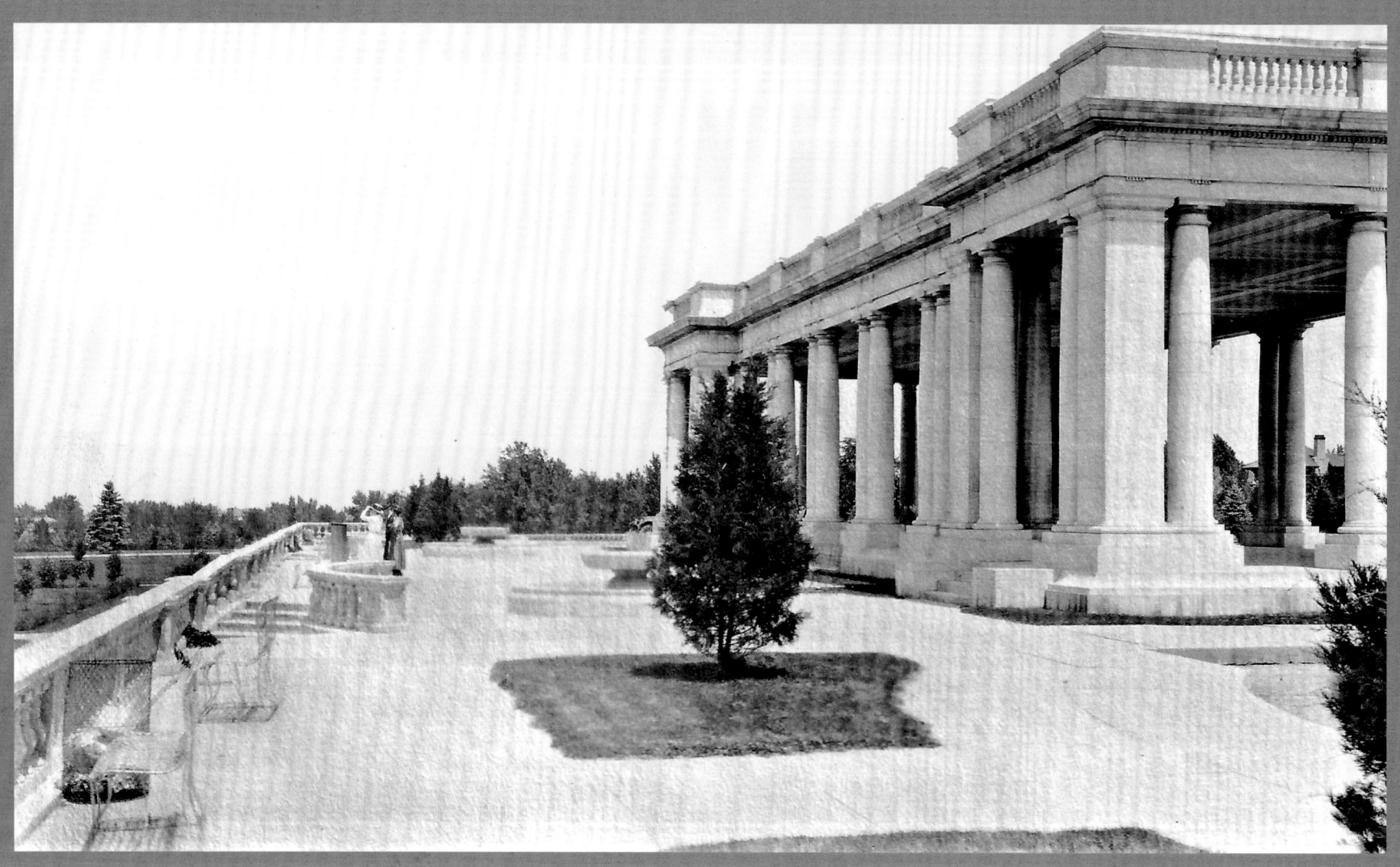

Cheesman Park features a Neoclassical memorial named in honor of Denver pioneer Walter Scott Cheesman. The park is framed on three sides by private residences and sits upon land originally used as a cemetery.

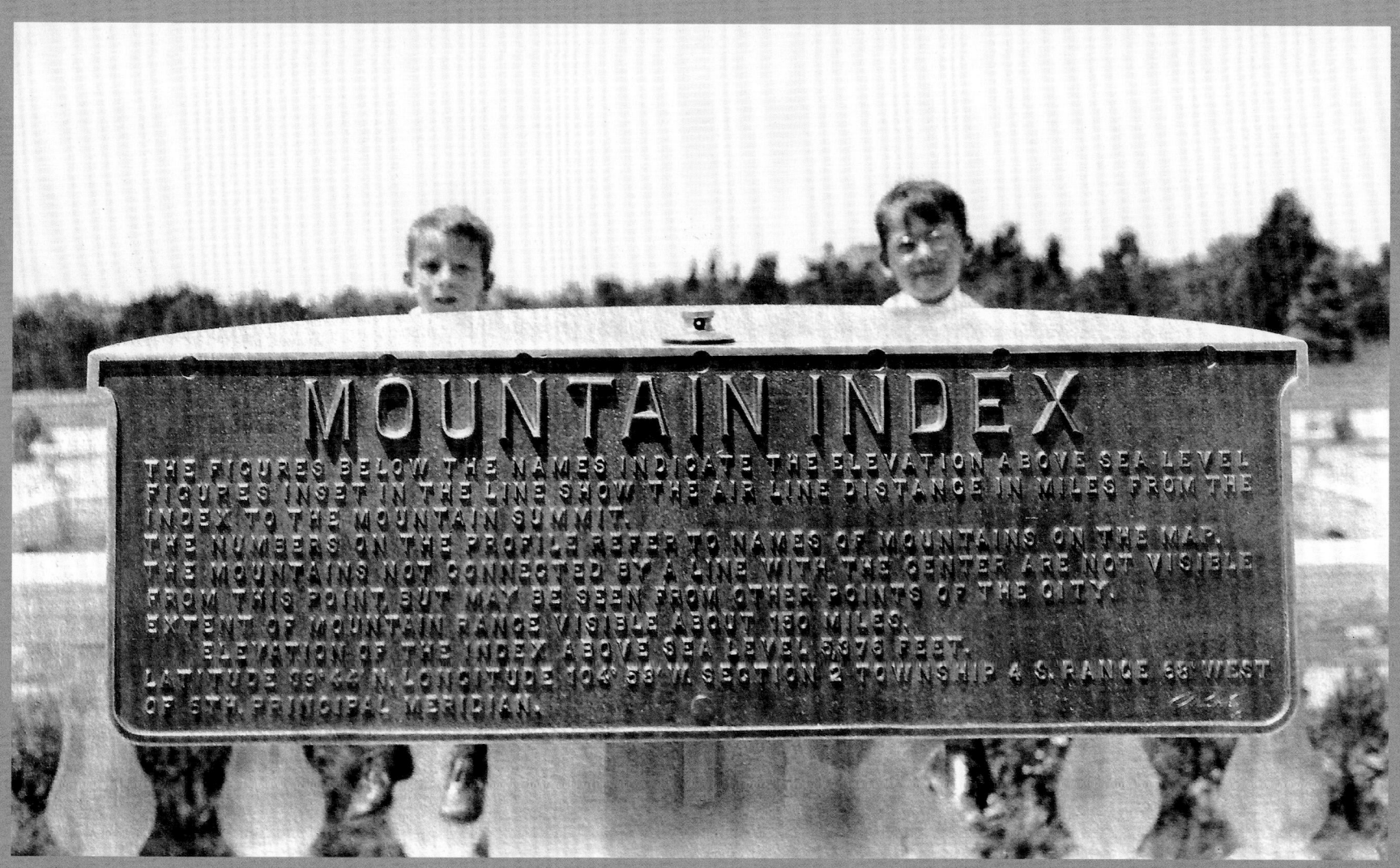

Ernest and Walter look west towards the Rocky Mountains from the Cheesman Mountain Index. From this height, the scope of mountain range visible from the Cheesman pavilion is 150 miles from Pikes Peak (south) to Longs Peak (north). On the opposite side of the index is a list of other high Colorado peaks within view from Cheesman Park.

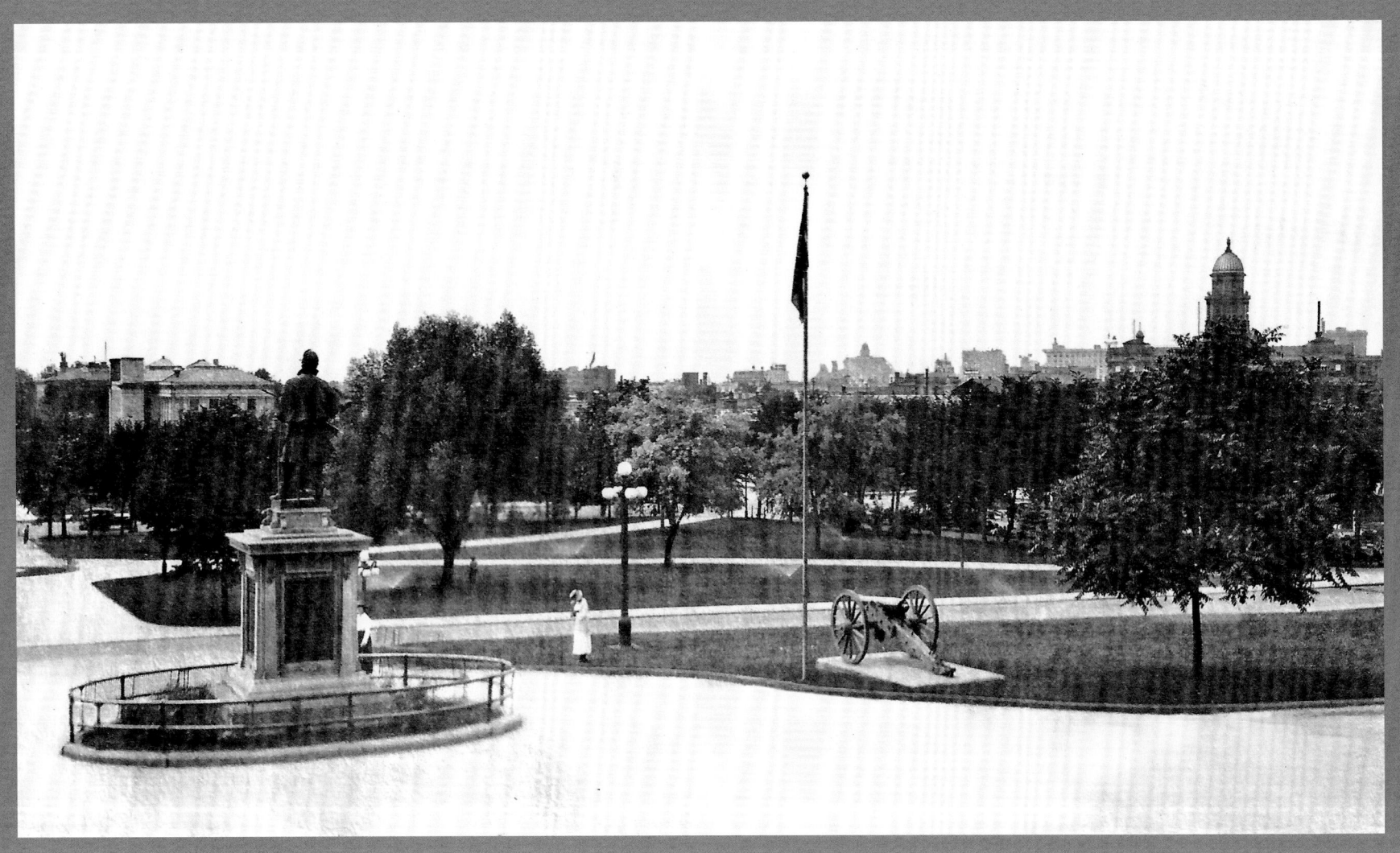

Henry snapped this view of downtown Denver from the Colorado State Capitol Building, looking towards the northwest. The cannon and statue memorialize Colorado soldiers' contributions during the Civil War. The elevated domed building to the right is the Arapahoe County Courthouse.

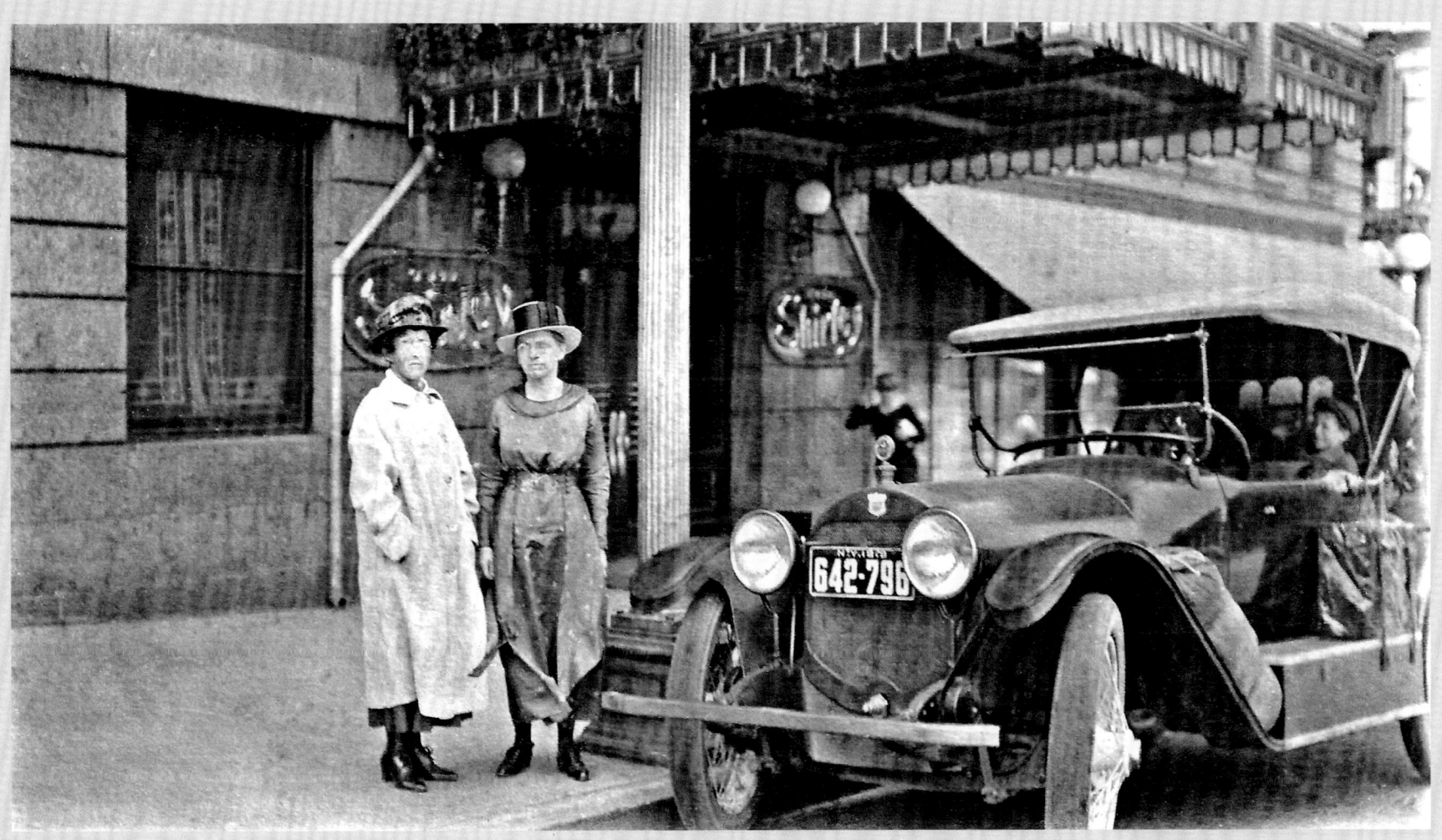

After touring Denver and staying overnight at the very fashionable Shirley-Savoy Hotel, the family says goodbye to some friends. Lizzie Spallholz is on the left, standing in front of the hotel next to a friend from Cornell University. Walter and Ernest are sitting in the Haynes.

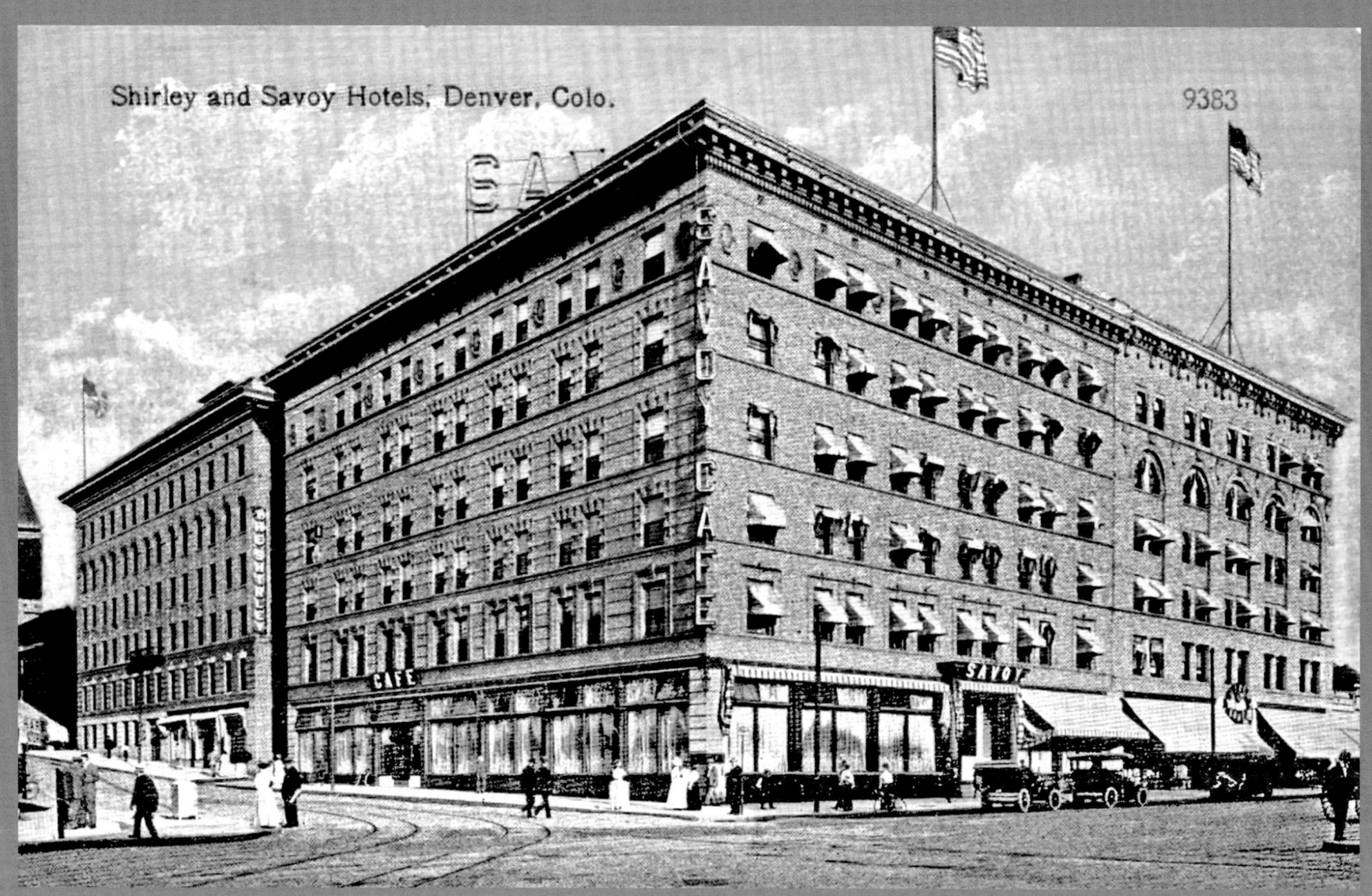

Period postcard of Shirley-Savoy Hotel, Denver, Colorado.

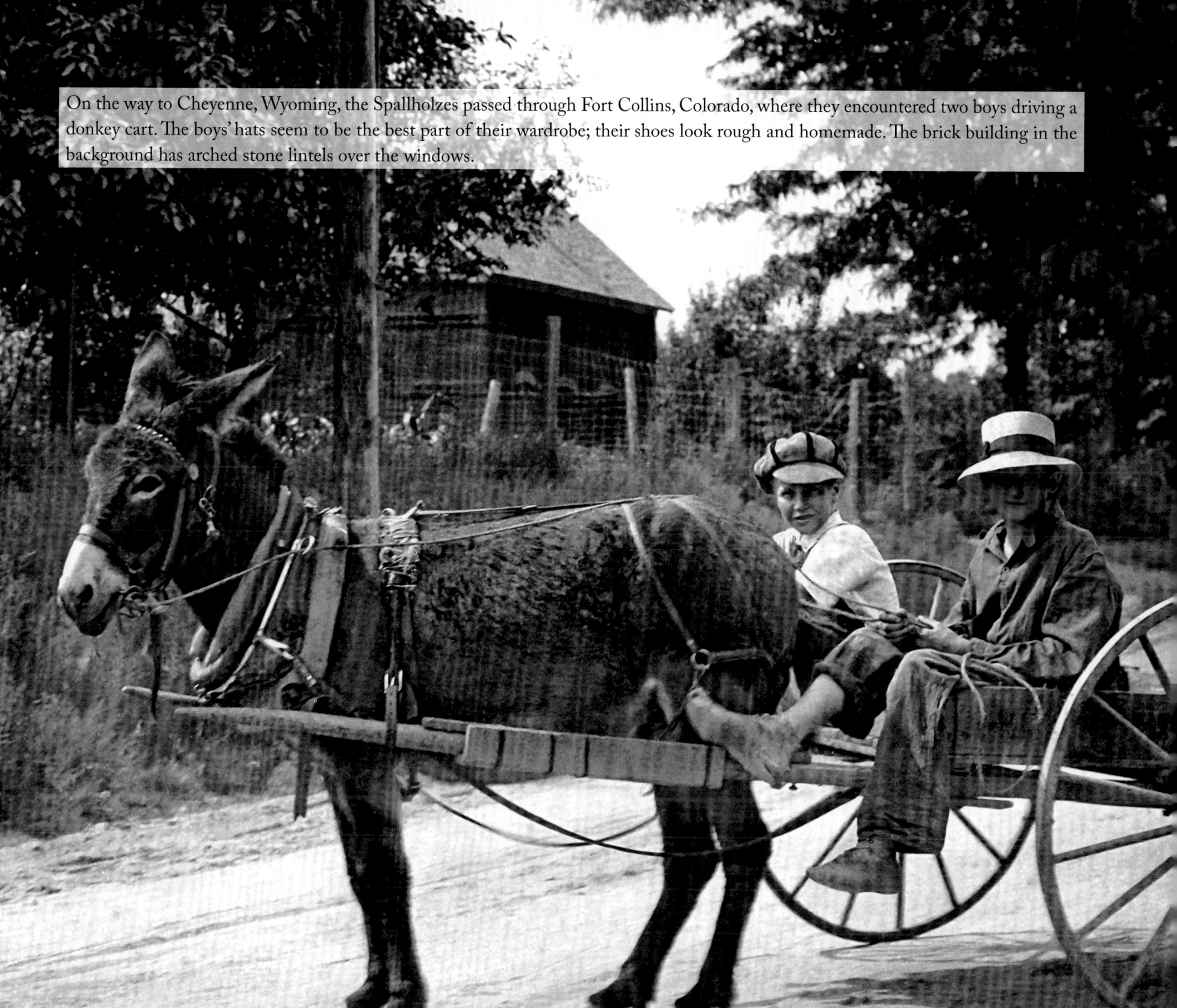

On the way to Cheyenne, Wyoming, the Spallholzes passed through Fort Collins, Colorado, where they encountered two boys driving a donkey cart. The boys' hats seem to be the best part of their wardrobe; their shoes look rough and homemade. The brick building in the background has arched stone lintels over the windows.

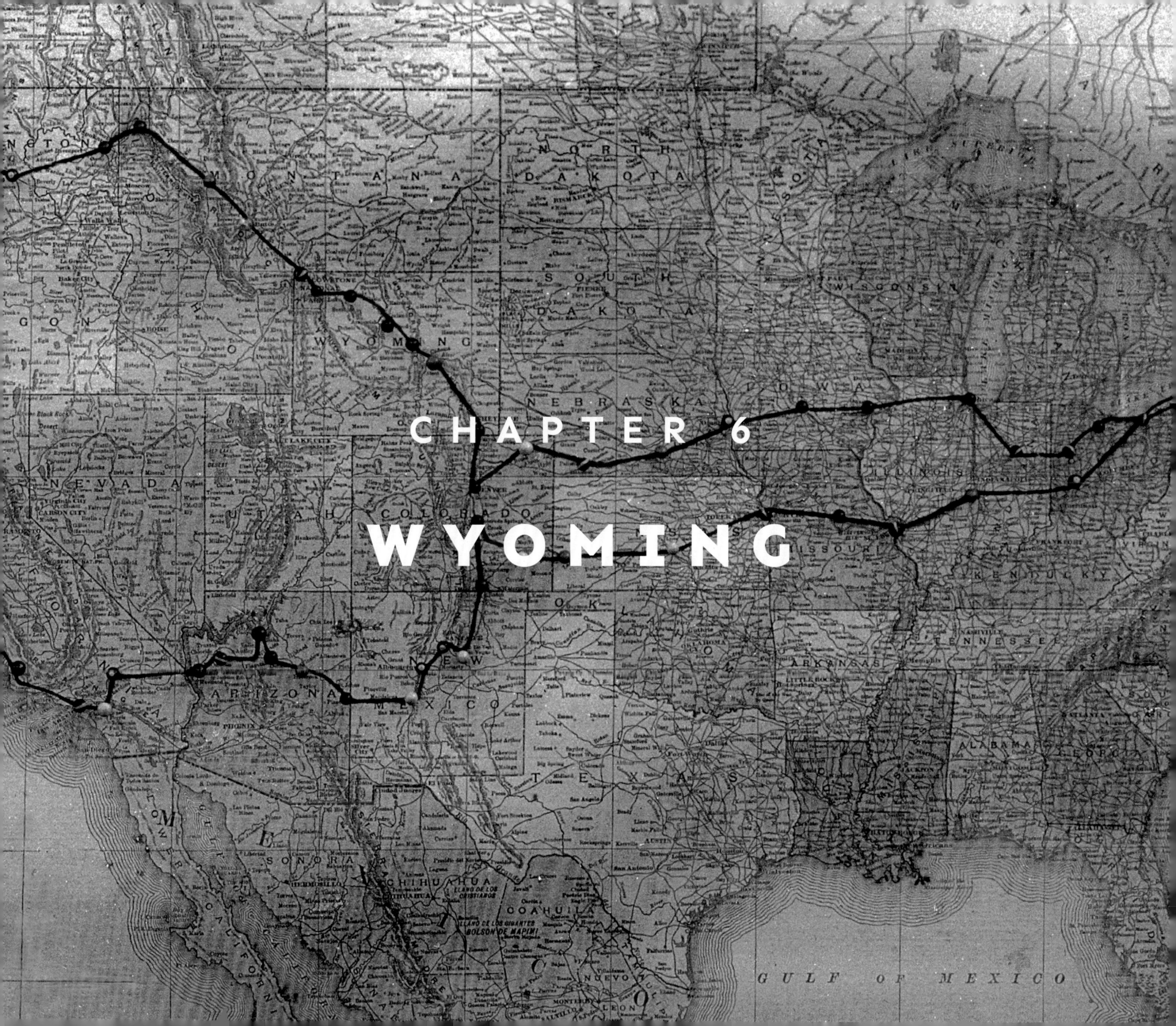

CHAPTER 6

WYOMING

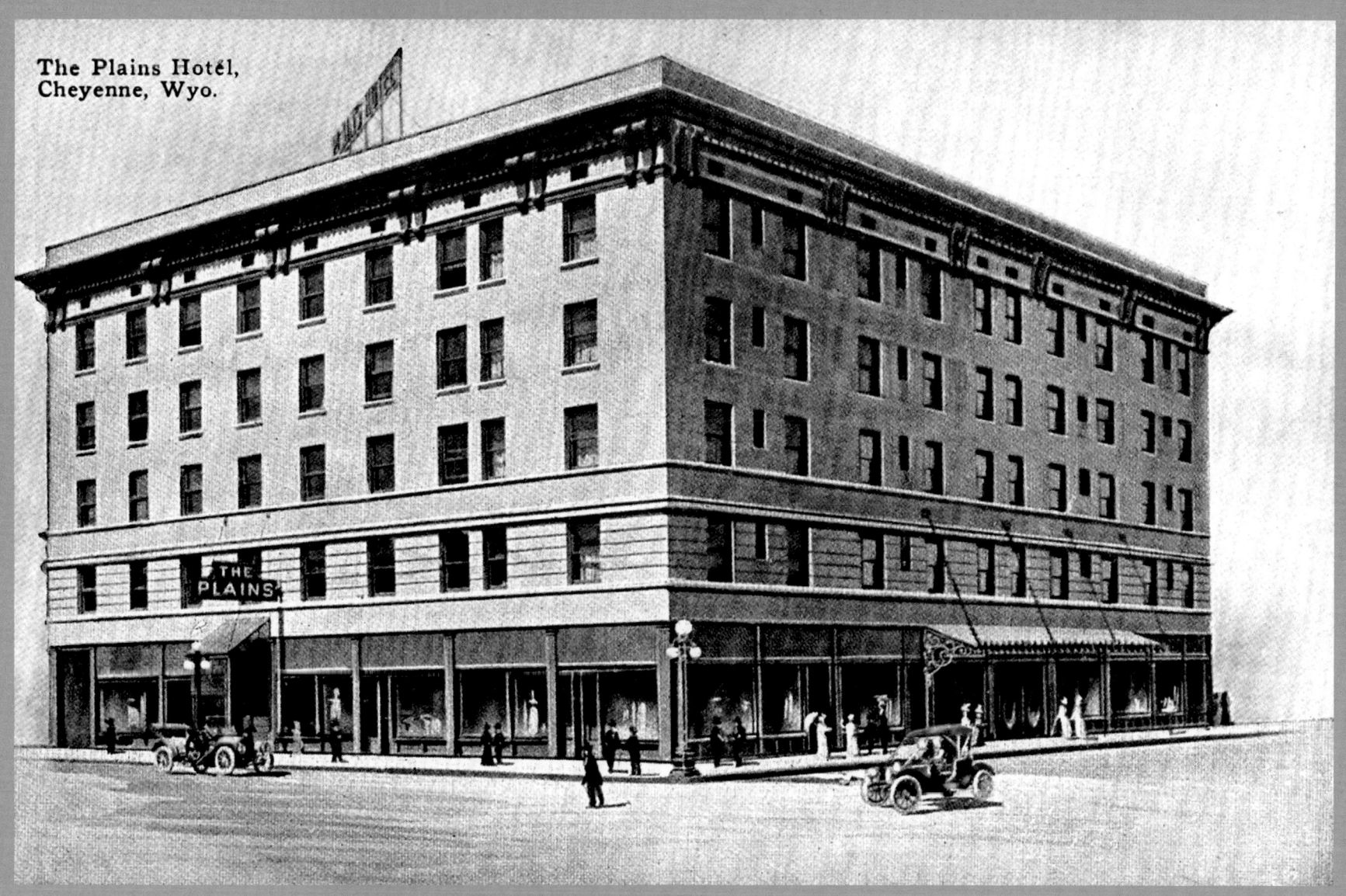

The Plains Hotel,
Cheyenne, Wyo.

When they arrived in Cheyenne, Wyoming, the Spallholzes likely stayed overnight at the Plains Hotel. A 1911 historic landmark, the Plains Hotel was the first luxury hotel in Wyoming. Designed with high-style Western décor, the building is located at the center of Downtown Cheyenne.

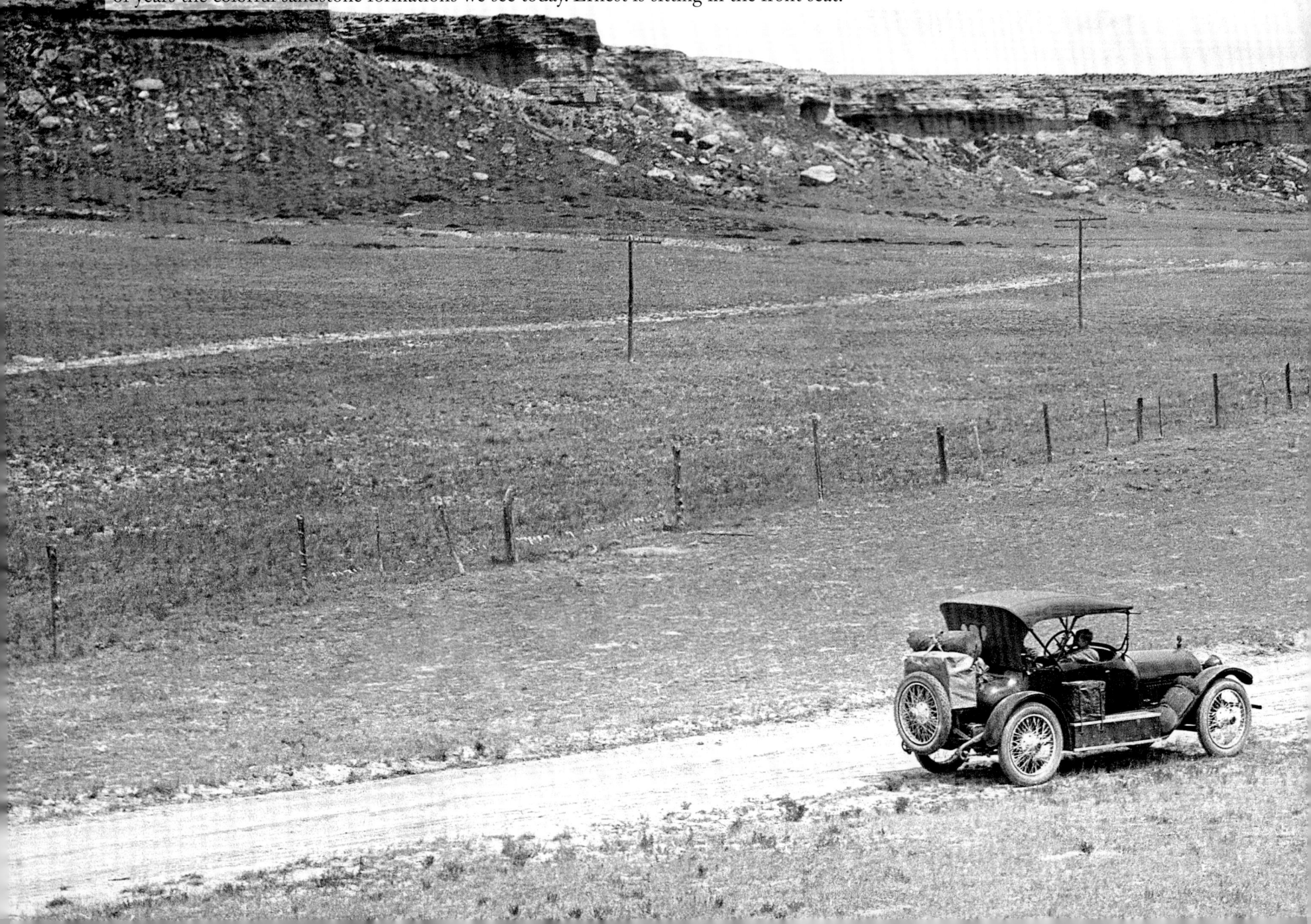

The landscape from Cheyenne to Yellowstone National Park was very rugged. The Spallholz family passed large outcroppings of brick-red cliffs that are part of the Chugwater Formation, found throughout Wyoming, Colorado, and Montana. The formation gets its deep red color from the abundance of iron oxide in the silt that was deposited during the Permian and Triassic periods, becoming after millions of years the colorful sandstone formations we see today. Ernest is sitting in the front seat.

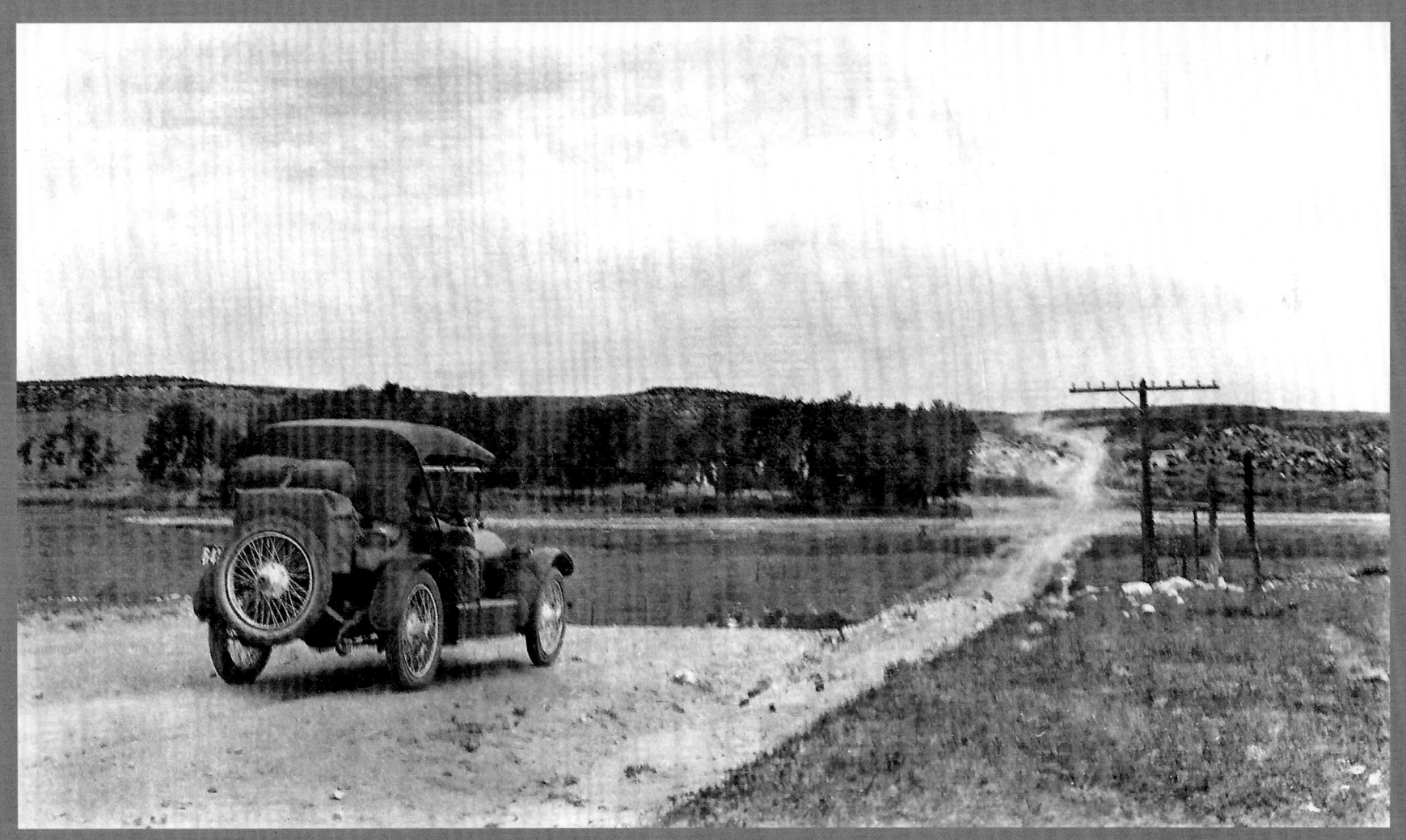

While traveling north through ranching country near Wheatland, north of Chugwater, the Spallholz family passed the Rocky Mountains on their left. Just ahead is a ranch house, surrounded by cottonwood trees.

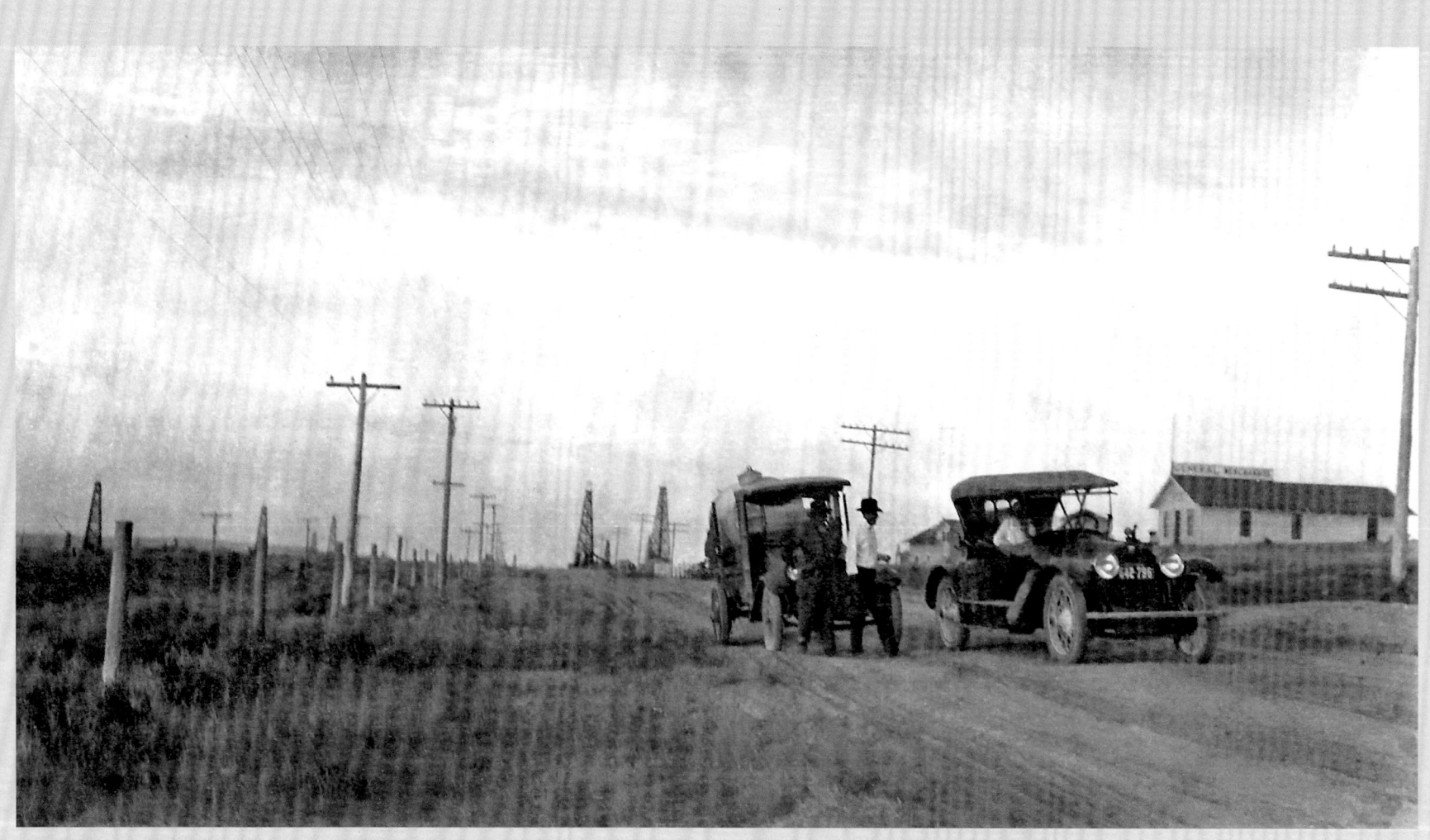

The Spallholzes' route took them through the Big Muddy oil field, about ninety miles past Wheatland, Wyoming. The town of Parkerton, Wyoming, grew up around the oil fields. The Shannon Sandstone stratum in the Big Muddy produced 3.6 million barrels of oil in 1919, the year the Spallholzes drove through.

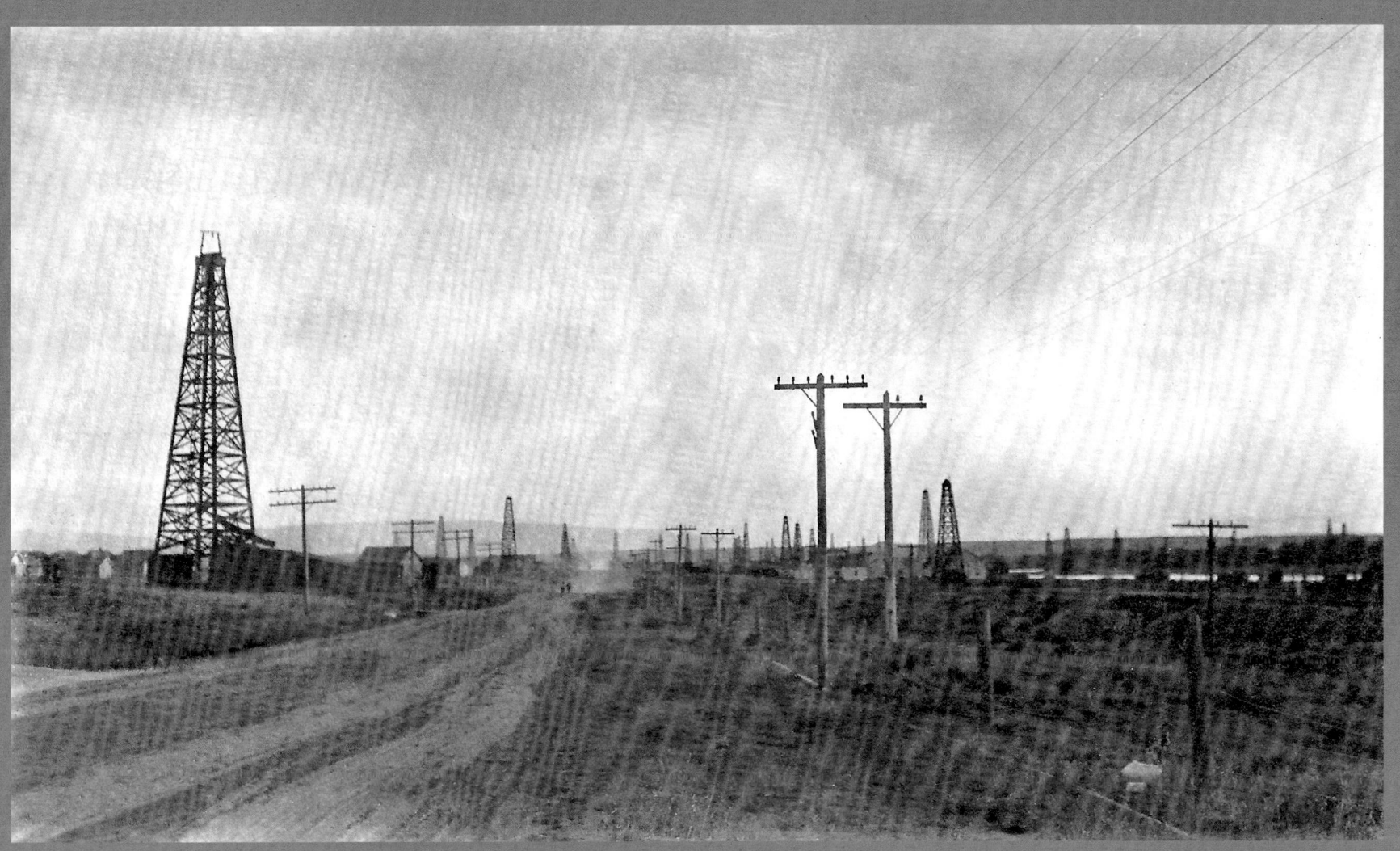

This view of the Big Muddy oil field provides some perspective for its name. En route to Cody, the Spallholz family encountered the remnants of a desert downburst, which created a flash flood and a situation that could have resulted in a drowning fatality.

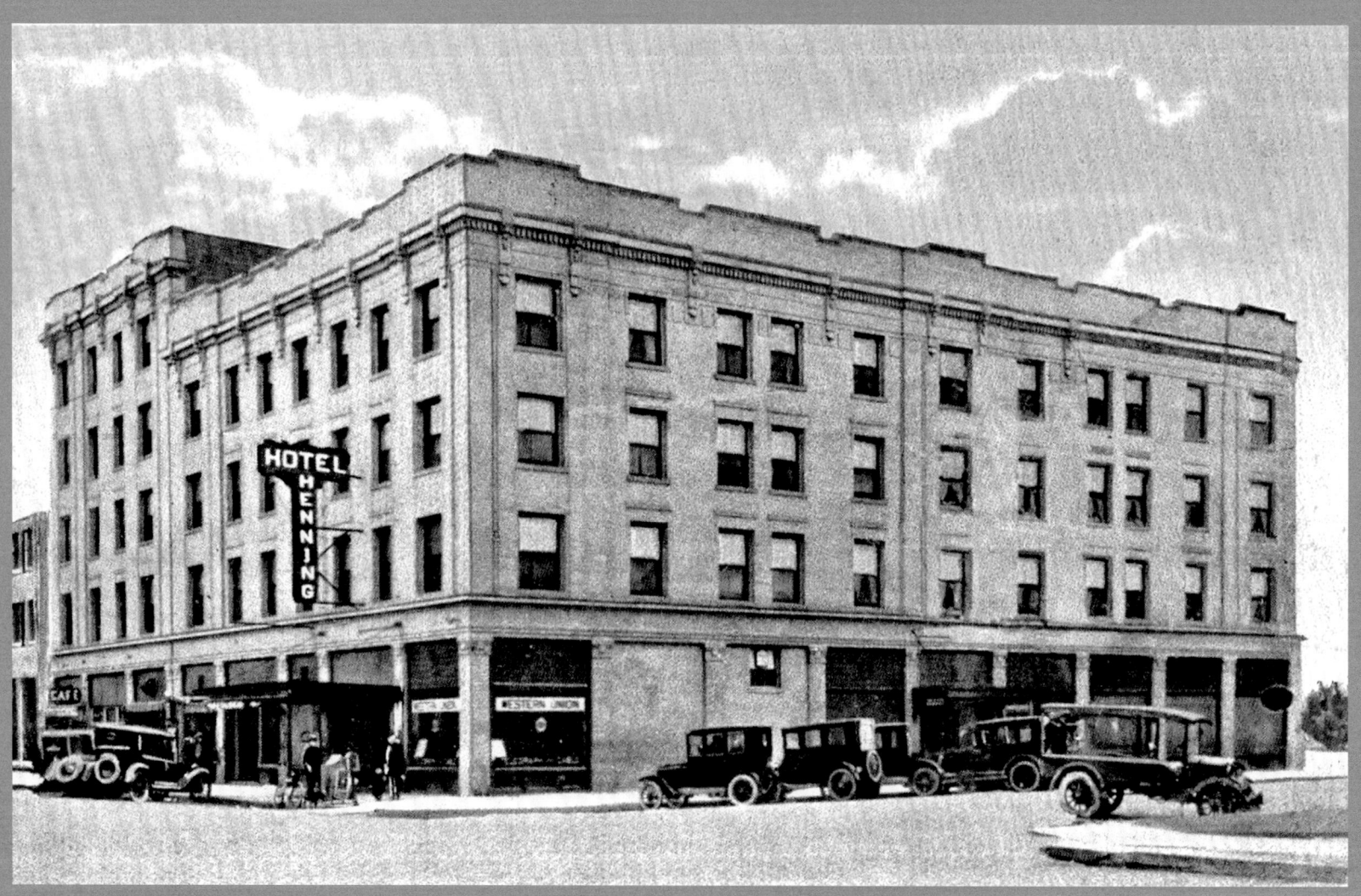

Period postcard of another hotel the family may have stayed at, the Henning Hotel in Casper, Wyoming. Built in 1914 of brick and mortar on the corner of Center Street and 1st Street, the hotel must have stood out conspicuously in a Western town that still had many wooden buildings similar to those seen in old Western movies.

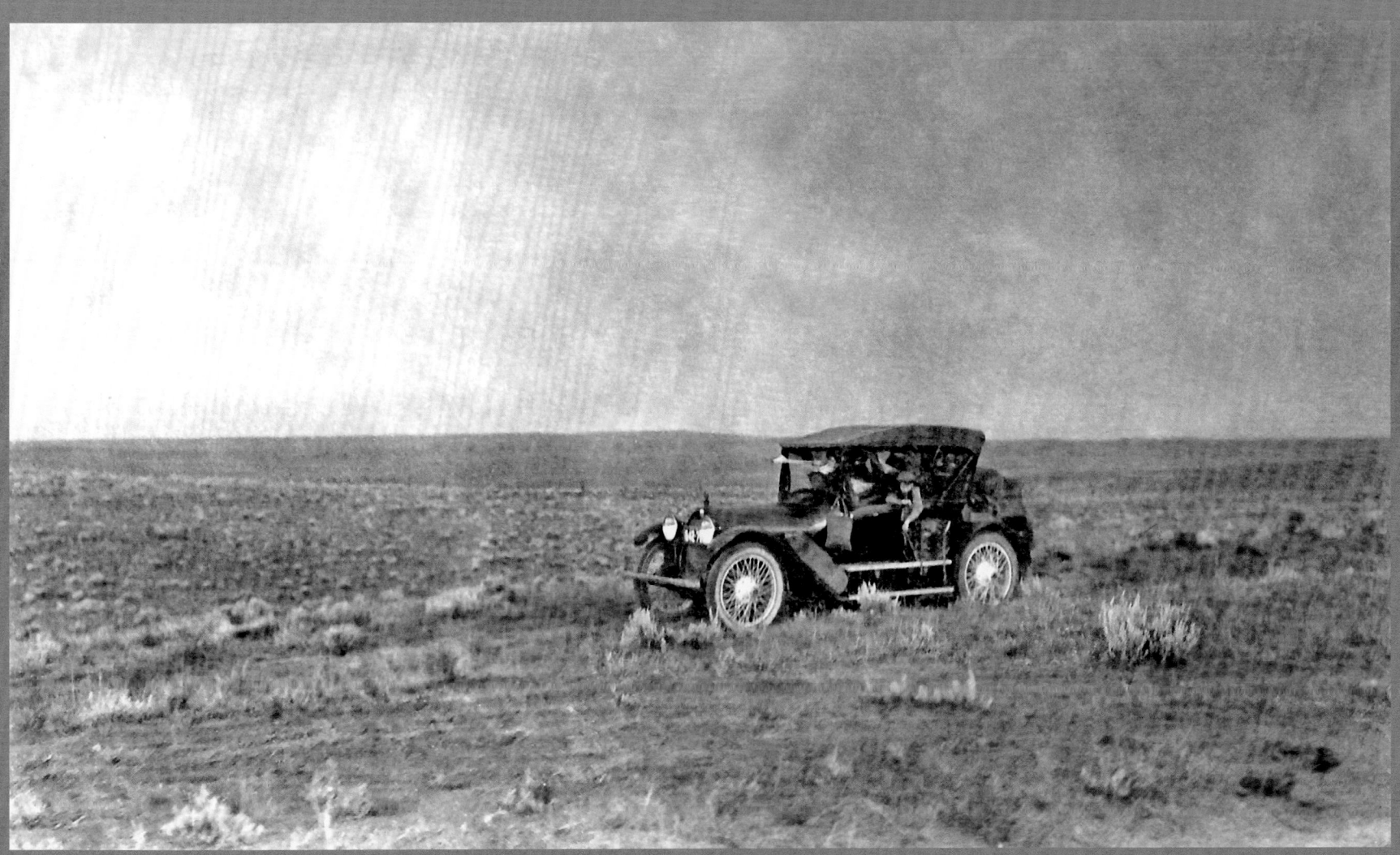

A large storm and heavy rain passed to the northeast of the Spallholzes as they traveled along a prairie road near the small settlement of Powder River, west of Casper, Wyoming. Crossing the prairie was still a hazardous adventure in 1919, with the possibility of encountering automobile trouble, inclement weather, and snow in high elevations. Prairie roads crossing washes and streams were often flooded or turned to mud by heavy rainfall.

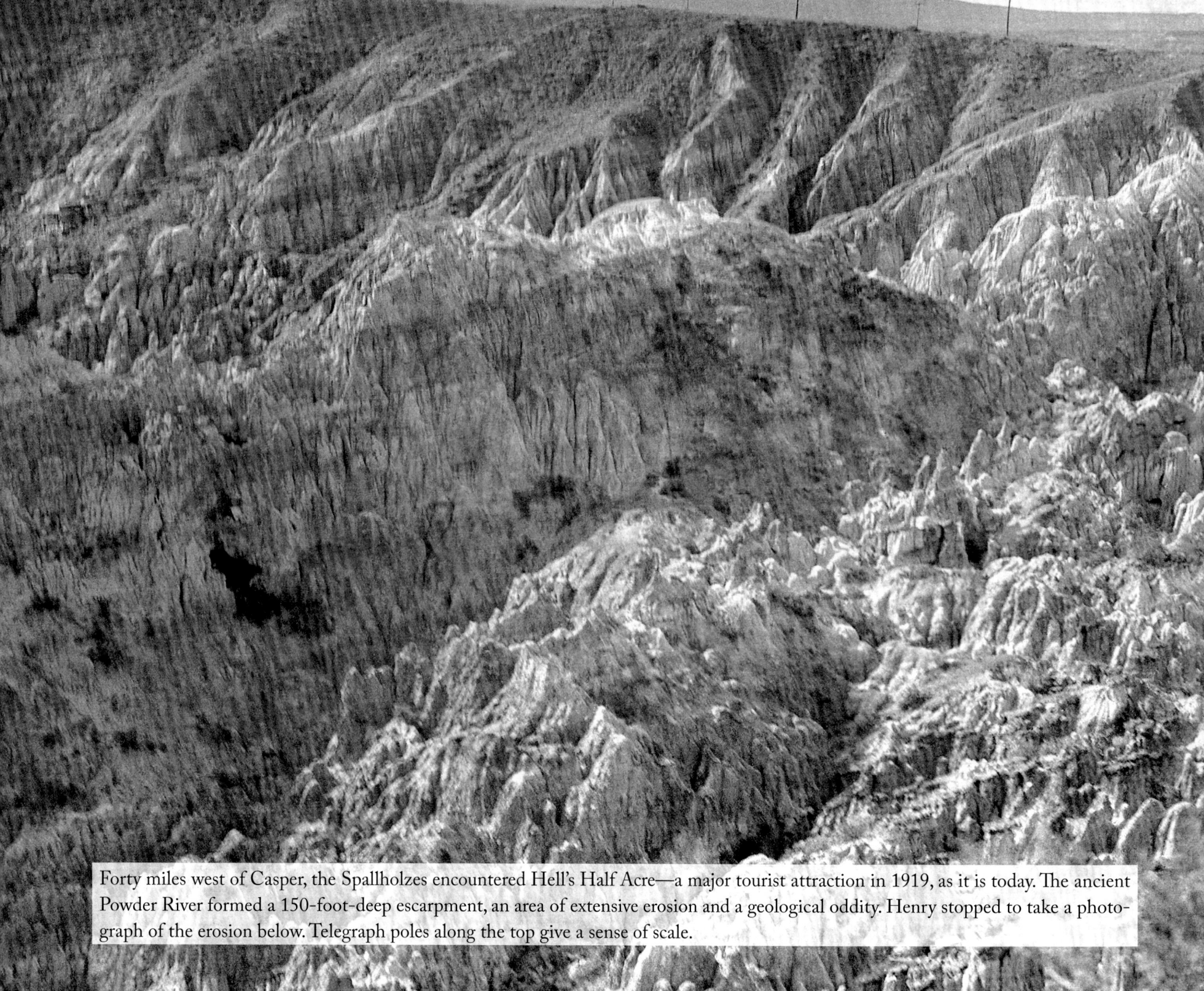

Forty miles west of Casper, the Spallholzes encountered Hell's Half Acre—a major tourist attraction in 1919, as it is today. The ancient Powder River formed a 150-foot-deep escarpment, an area of extensive erosion and a geological oddity. Henry stopped to take a photograph of the erosion below. Telegraph poles along the top give a sense of scale.

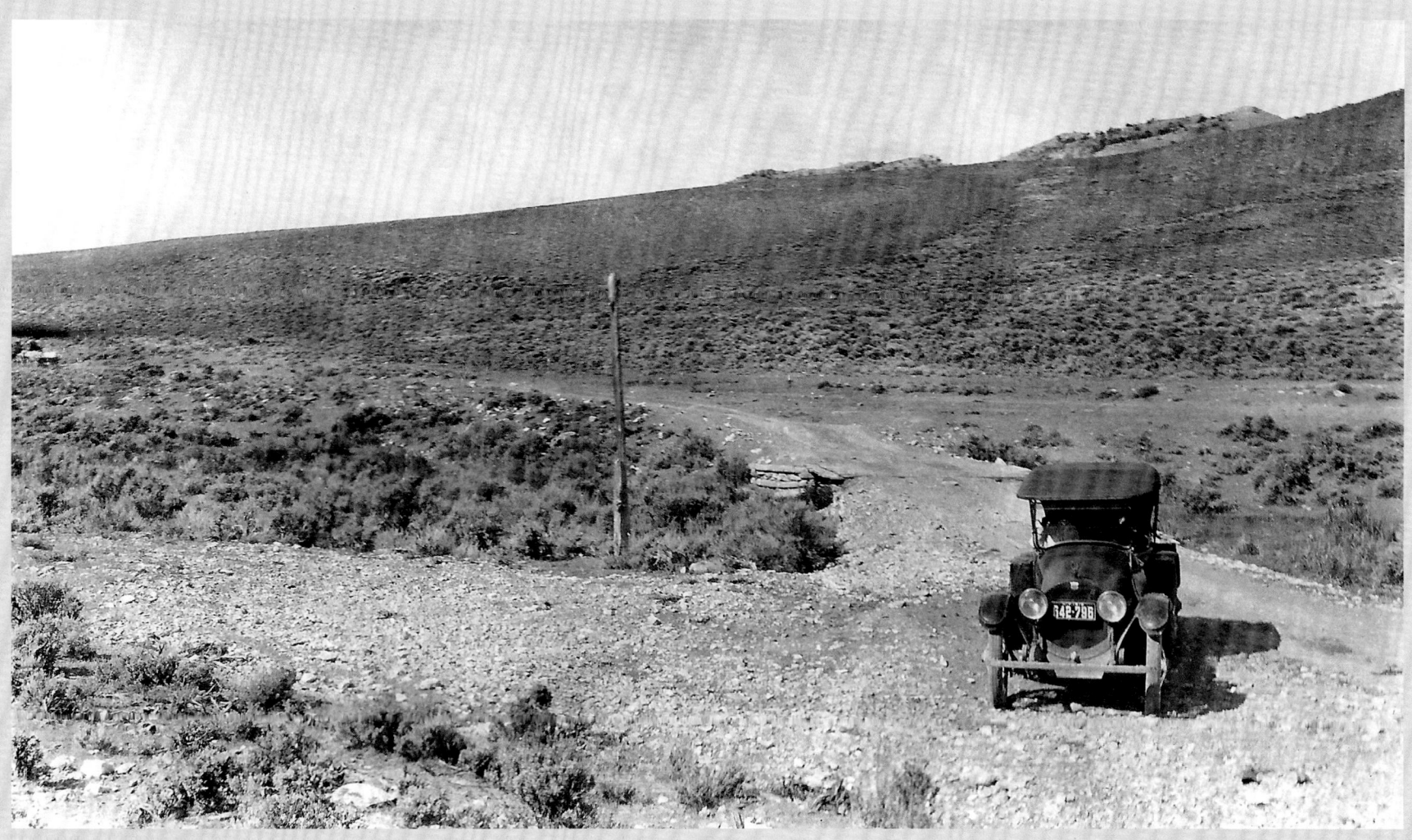

This photograph of a prairie pass was taken after leaving Lost Cabin. Legend has it that early prospectors in the area found a rich vein of gold but were driven from their cabins by Indians living near the site. They returned to find their cabins destroyed, thus "lost." After traveling four miles north on Badwater Road, the Spallholzes turned onto Nowood Road and motored through Nowood Canyon. Although Henry listed the canyon as "No Wood" on his slides and prints, it is shown on all modern maps as *Nowood*. Local lore suggests that the name was coined by a group of men passing through the area who could find no wood to build a fire. The Nowood River is roughly ninety-five miles in length and flows north through Fremont and Washakie Counties into Ten Sleep.

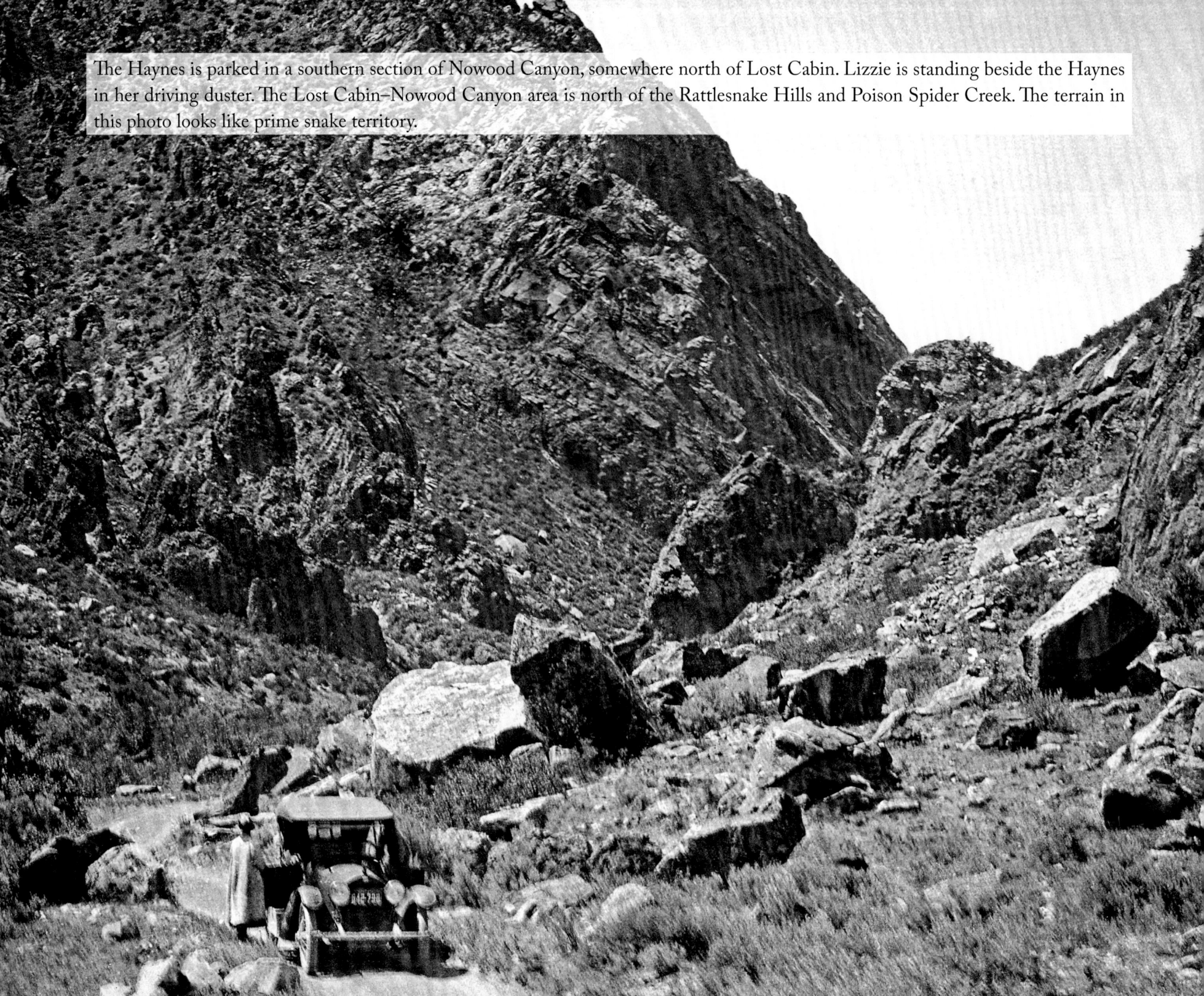

The Haynes is parked in a southern section of Nowood Canyon, somewhere north of Lost Cabin. Lizzie is standing beside the Haynes in her driving duster. The Lost Cabin–Nowood Canyon area is north of the Rattlesnake Hills and Poison Spider Creek. The terrain in this photo looks like prime snake territory.

The narrow road exiting Nowood Canyon opens up into the countryside. The Chugwater Formation and Western Union telegraph poles reappear in the distance.

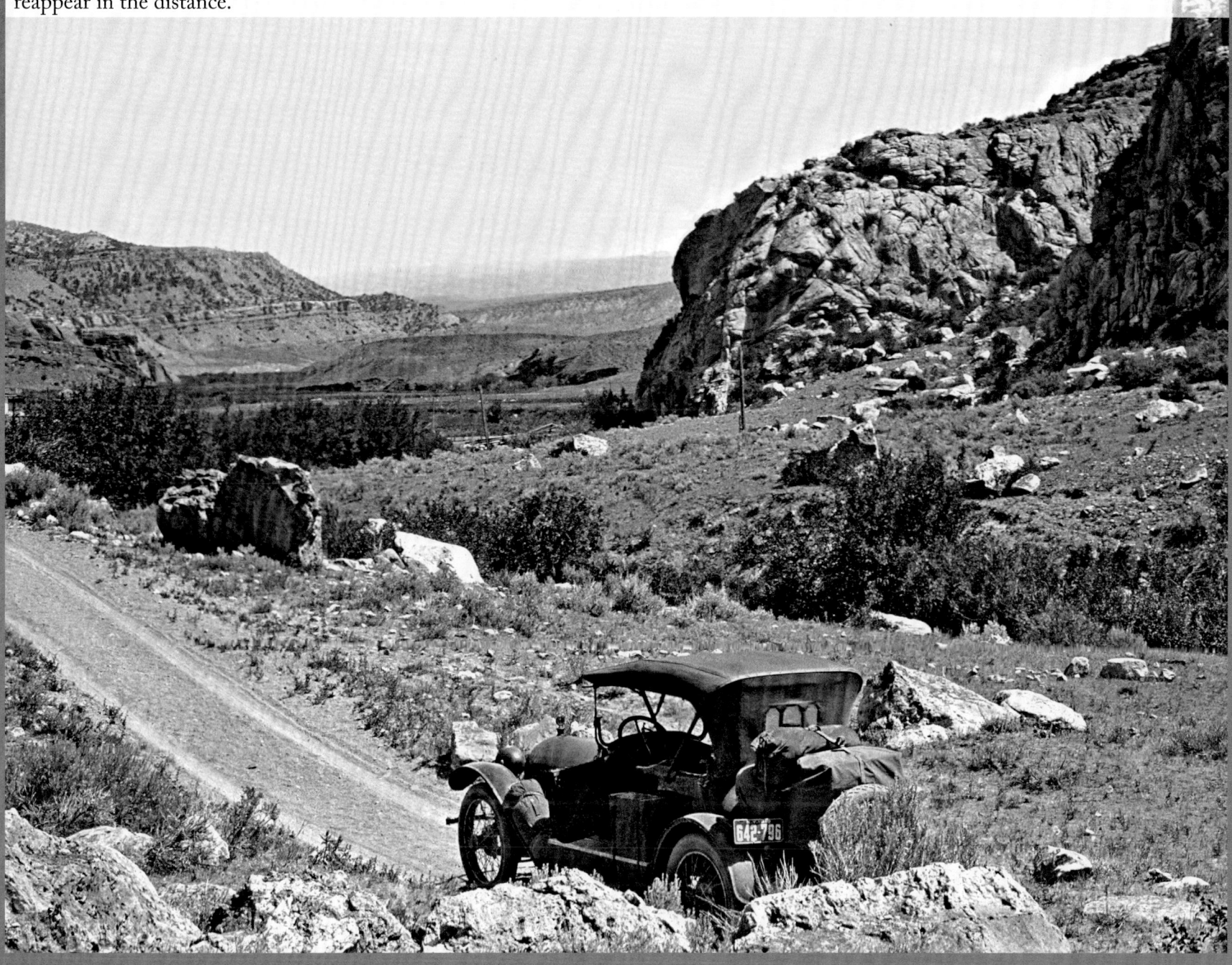

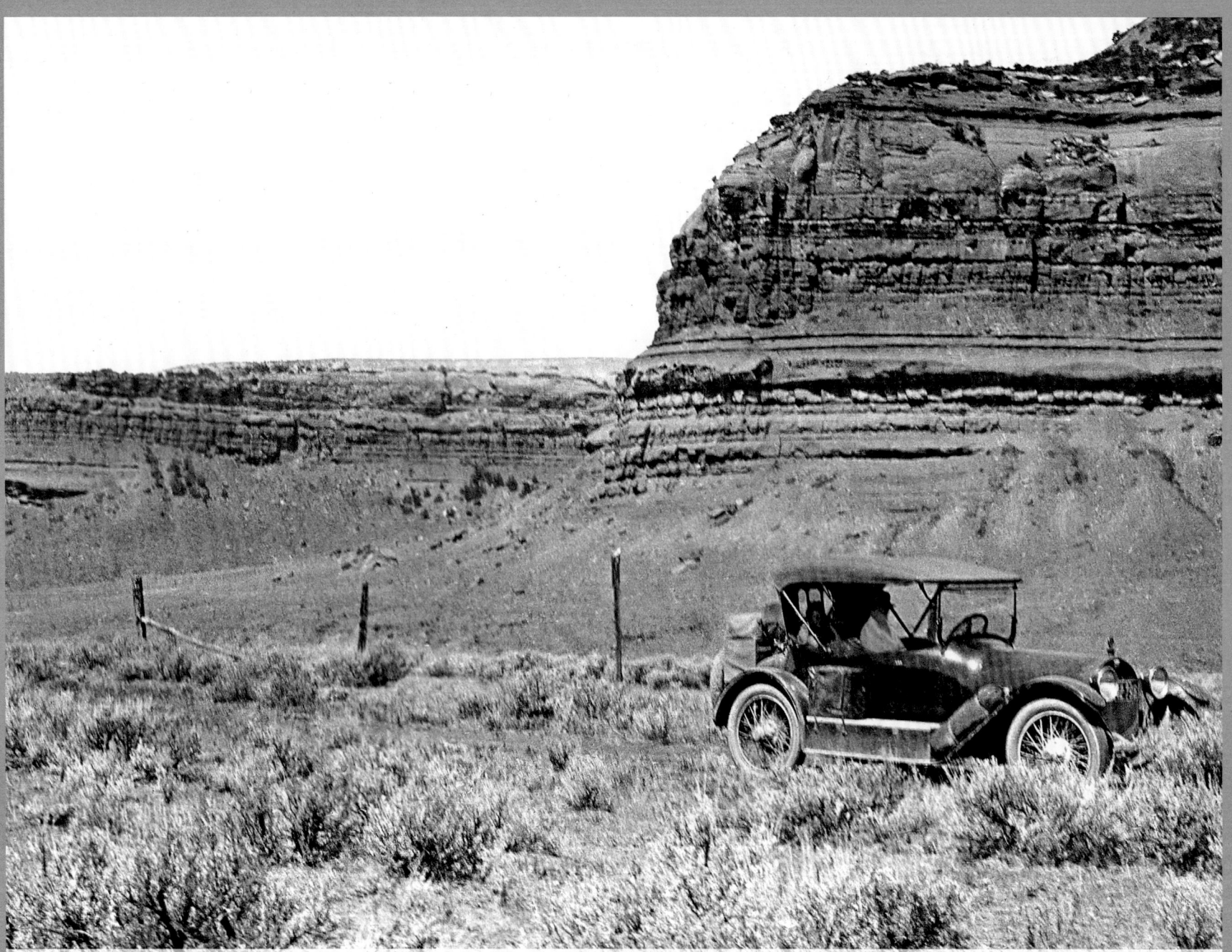

Red sandstone buttes appear at the exit of Nowood Canyon. The light and dark horizontal layering indicate they are a continuation of the Chugwater Formation. Lizzie is seen in the front seat wearing her duster.

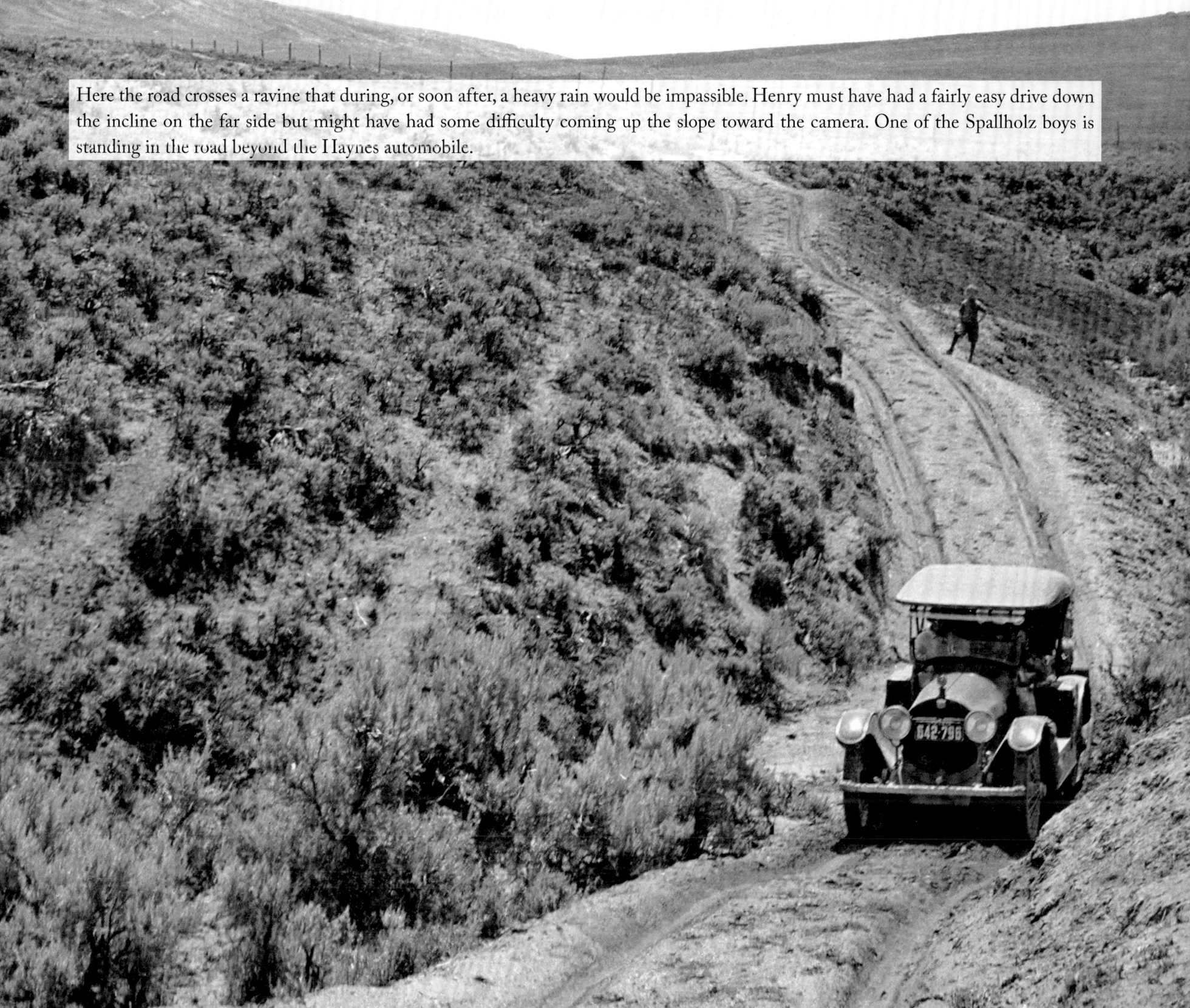

Here the road crosses a ravine that during, or soon after, a heavy rain would be impassible. Henry must have had a fairly easy drive down the incline on the far side but might have had some difficulty coming up the slope toward the camera. One of the Spallholz boys is standing in the road beyond the Haynes automobile.

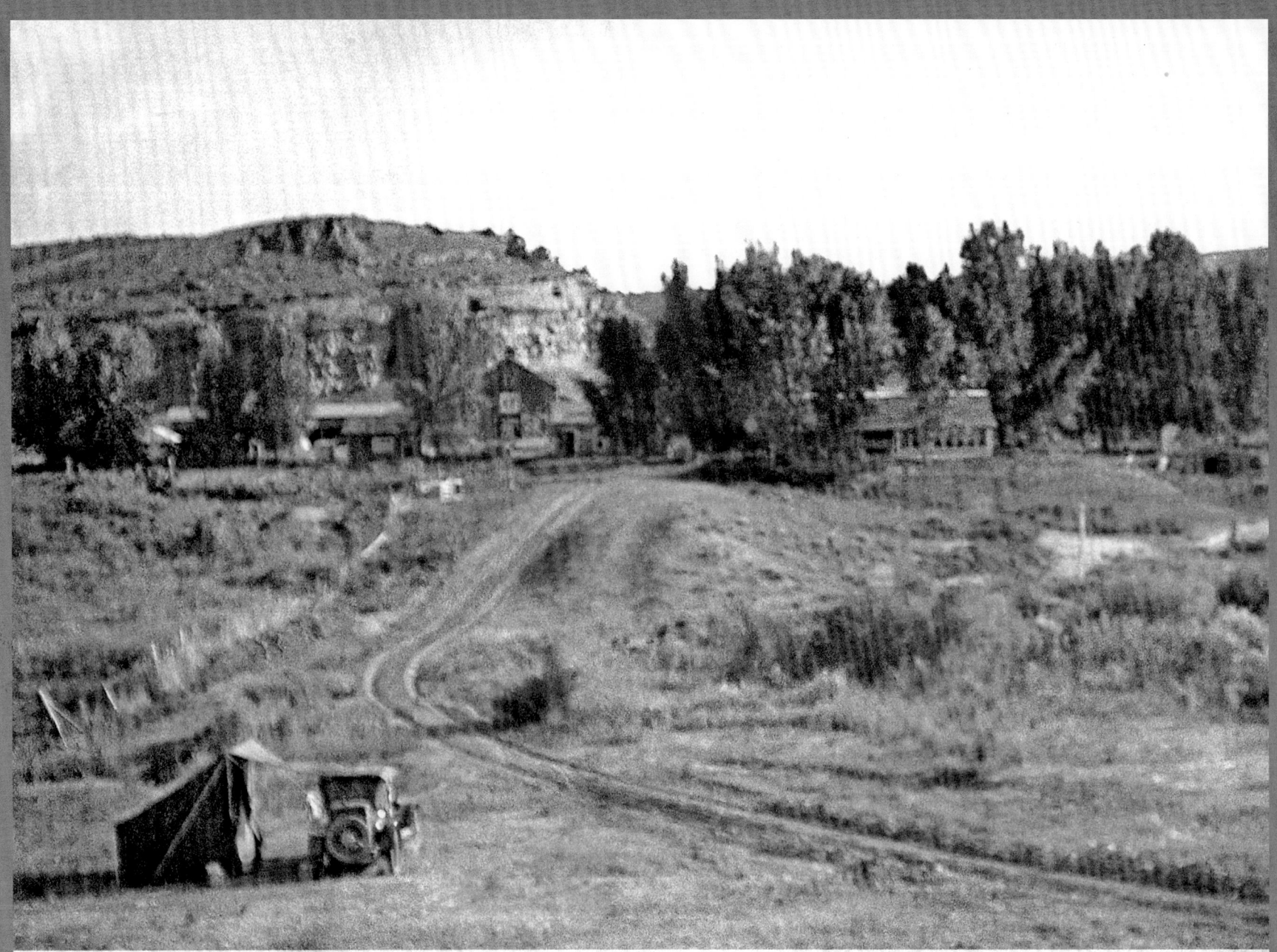

The Haynes' drive shaft suddenly broke during the trip through Wyoming, forcing the Spallholzes to camp twelve miles south of Ten Sleep at the Taylor Ranch. They had to wait for seven days until a new drive shaft that was shipped by rail from the Haynes factory in Kokomo, Indiana, finally arrived at Ten Sleep. This is the only photograph showing their balloon silk tent in use.

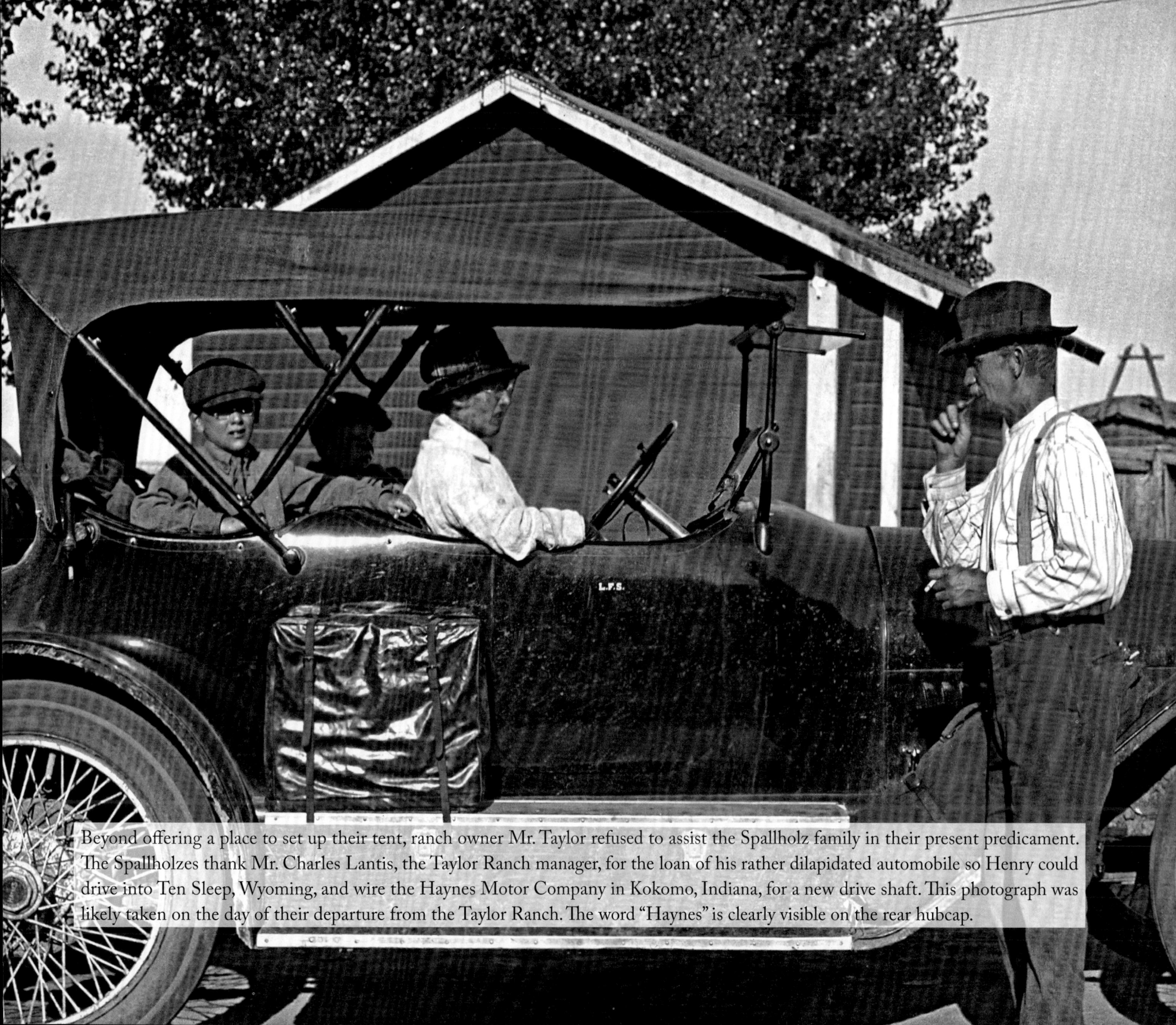

Beyond offering a place to set up their tent, ranch owner Mr. Taylor refused to assist the Spallholz family in their present predicament. The Spallholzes thank Mr. Charles Lantis, the Taylor Ranch manager, for the loan of his rather dilapidated automobile so Henry could drive into Ten Sleep, Wyoming, and wire the Haynes Motor Company in Kokomo, Indiana, for a new drive shaft. This photograph was likely taken on the day of their departure from the Taylor Ranch. The word "Haynes" is clearly visible on the rear hubcap.

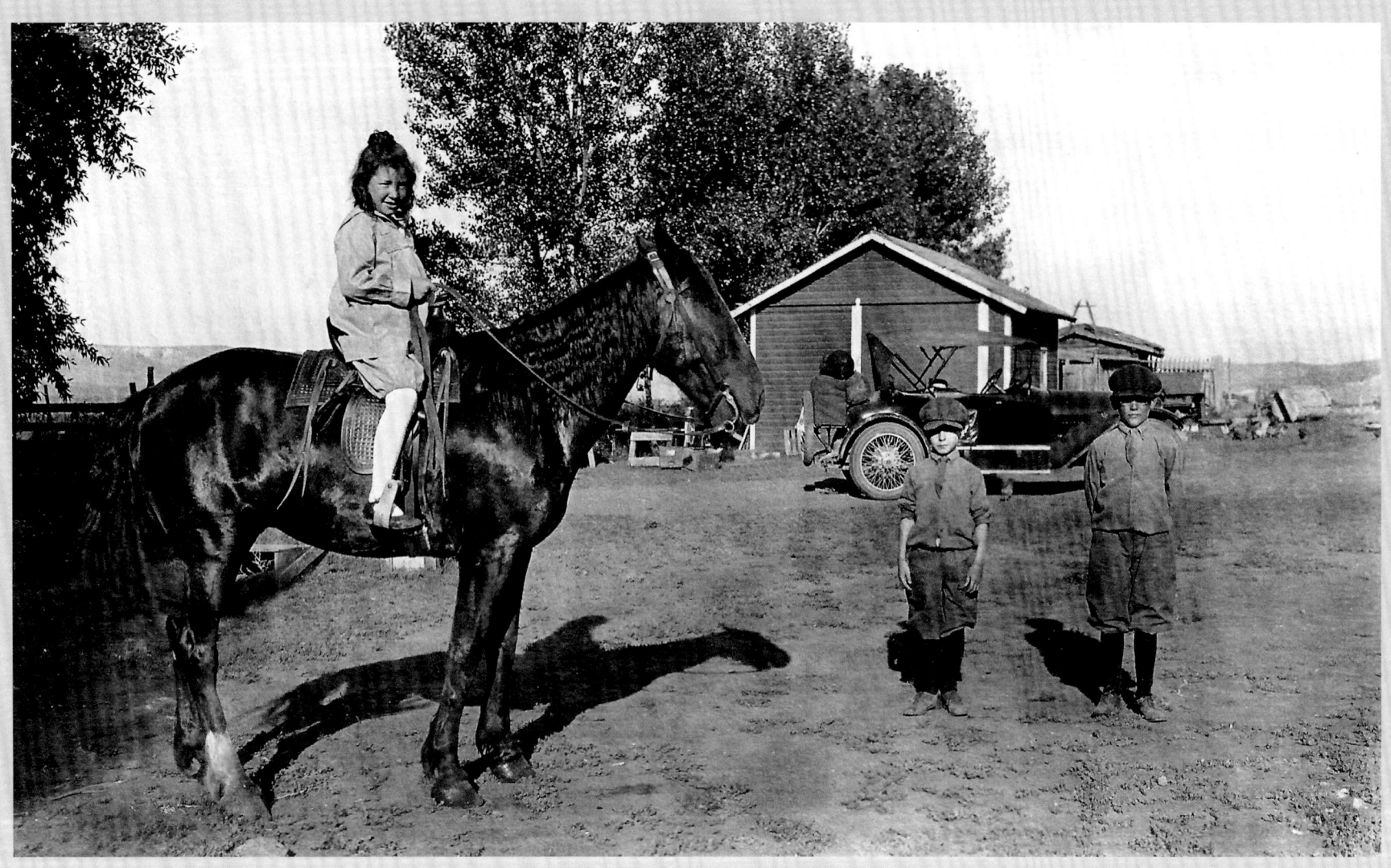

Margaret Taylor, daughter of the ranch owner, is on horseback while Ernest and Walter stand nearby. With the Haynes loaded in the background, the boys say good-bye to the girl and her horse.

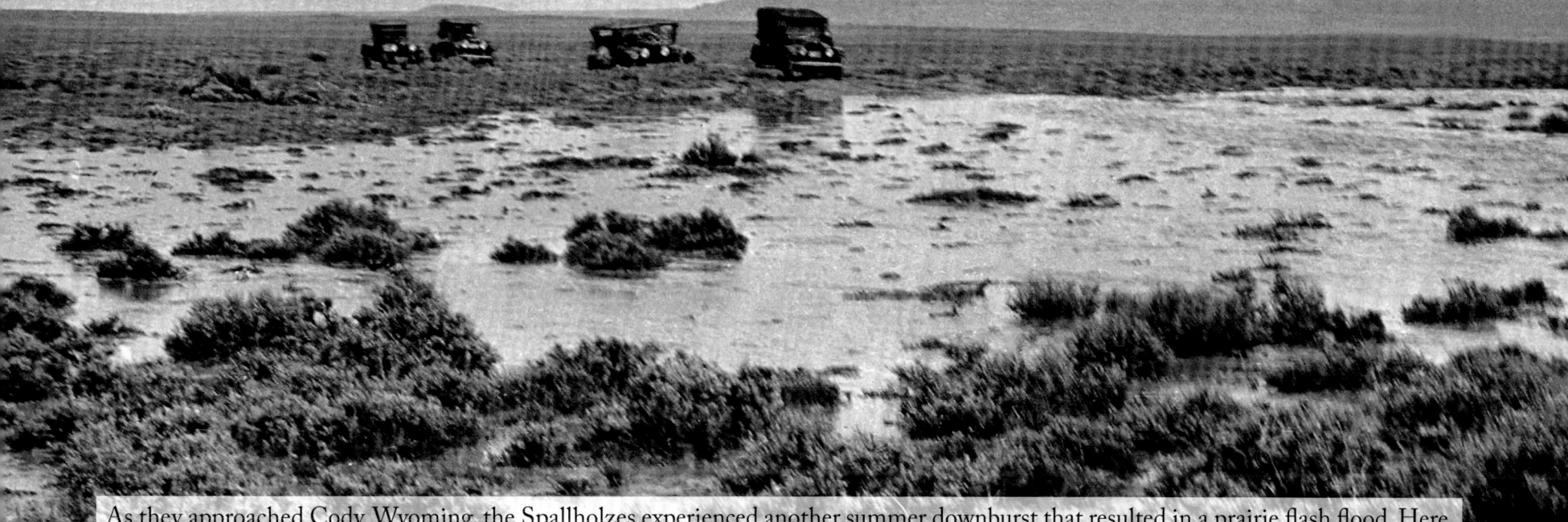

As they approached Cody, Wyoming, the Spallholzes experienced another summer downburst that resulted in a prairie flash flood. Here, the road is under water and cars have backed up; Lizzie wrote in her letters home that there were eleven cars in all. The image shows signs of a slight bit of camera motion. Henry probably took this photograph from the Haynes while it was sitting in shallow water. The unwise drivers of the distant vehicles are probably about to drive into trouble.

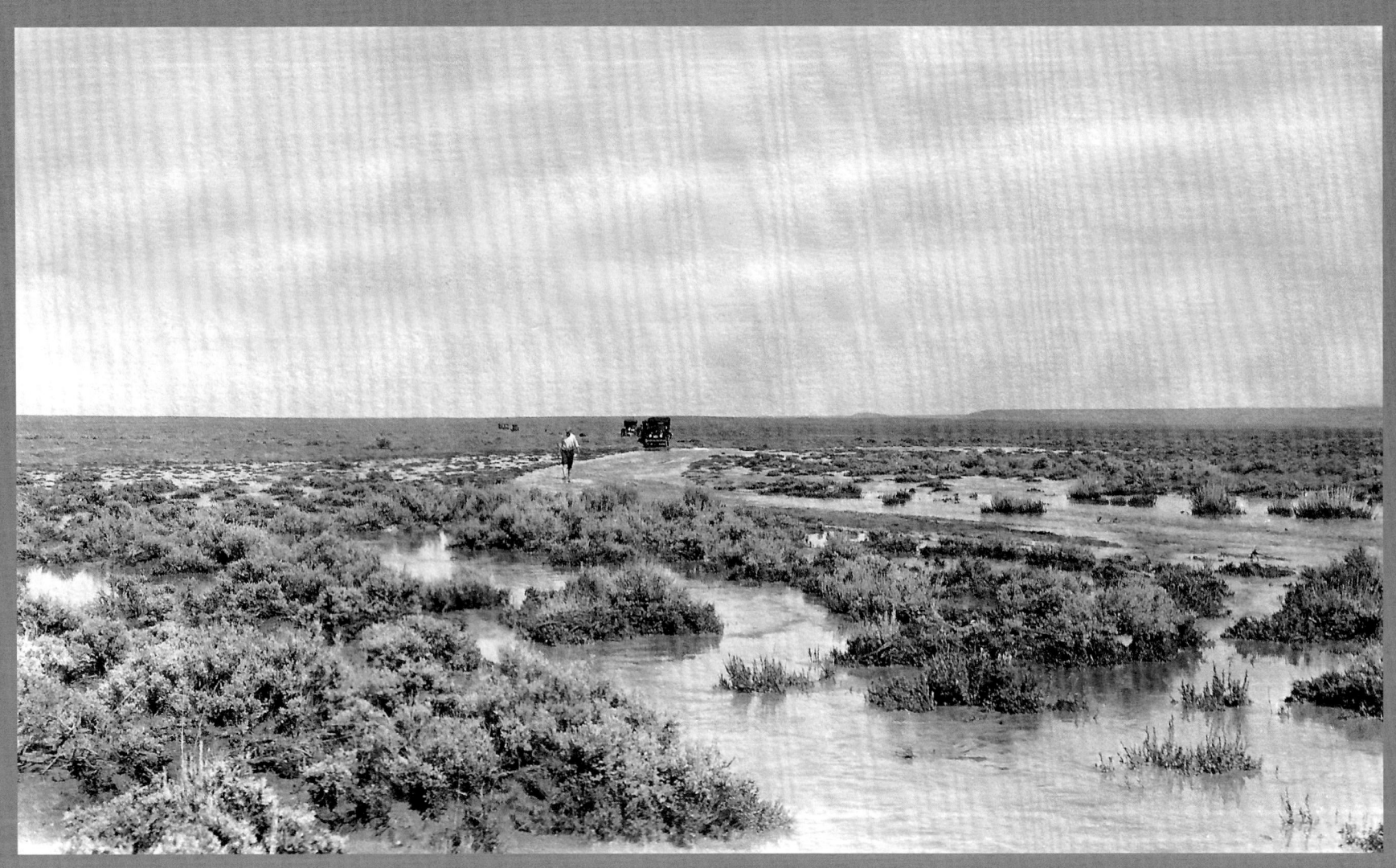

The volume of rainfall overflowed the road, creating a driving hazard for other travelers en route to or from Cody. Some of the men have taken off their shoes, rolled up their trousers, and waded around to scout out the flooded road.

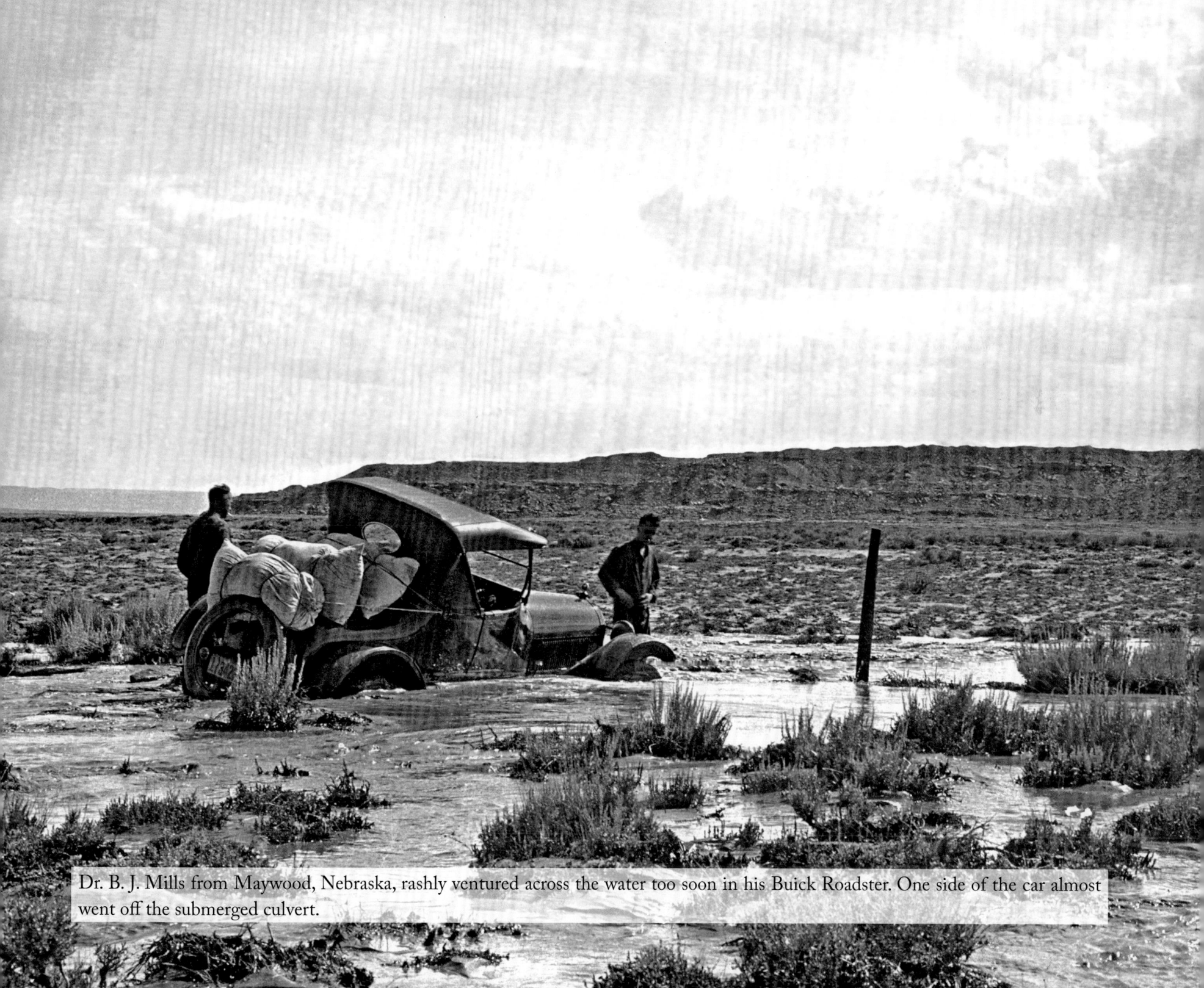

Dr. B. J. Mills from Maywood, Nebraska, rashly ventured across the water too soon in his Buick Roadster. One side of the car almost went off the submerged culvert.

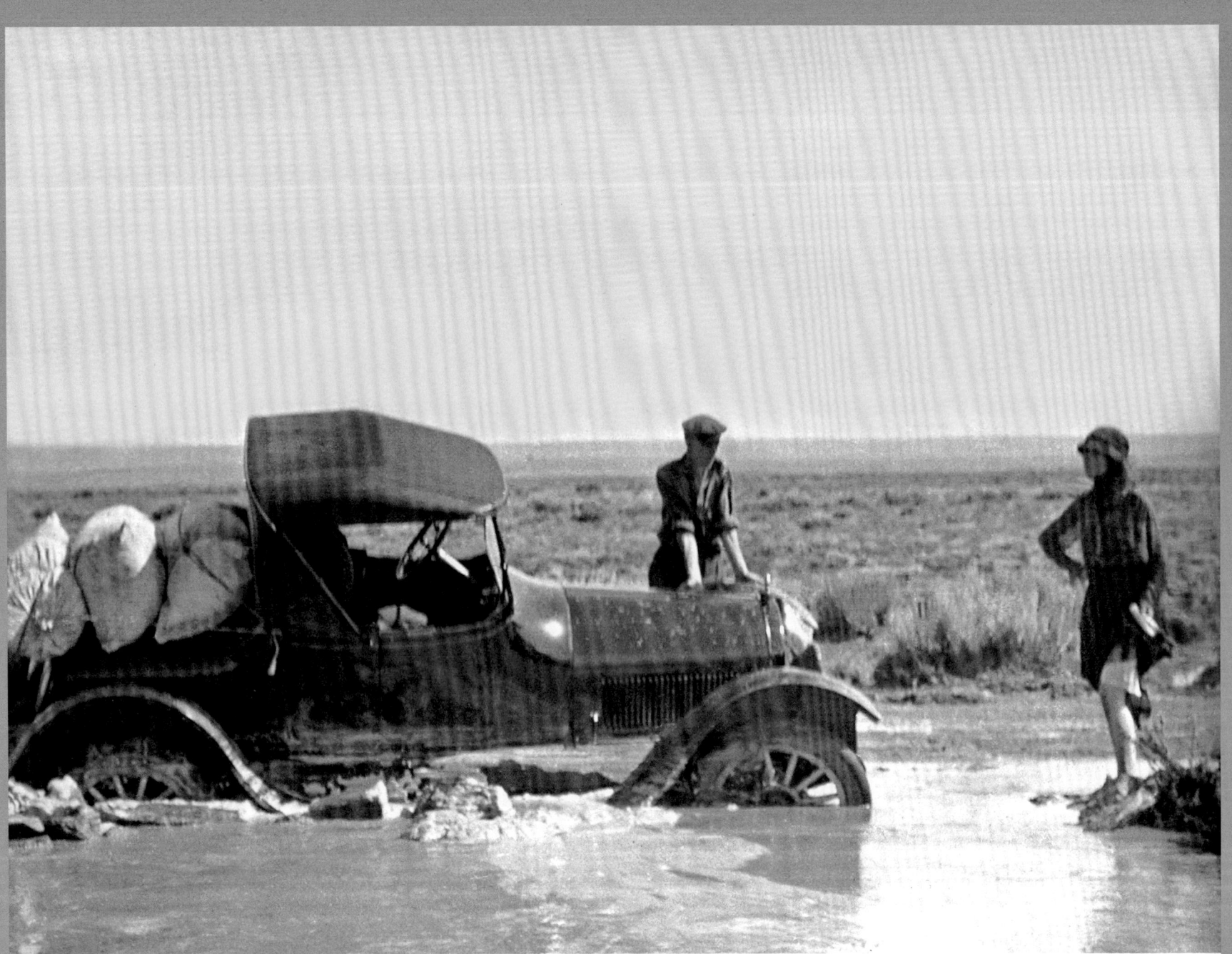

Dr. Mills' wife had to take off her shoes and stockings to wade out from the car. In this image, the water has dropped about a foot from its highest level, as indicated by the mud line near the top of the wheels.

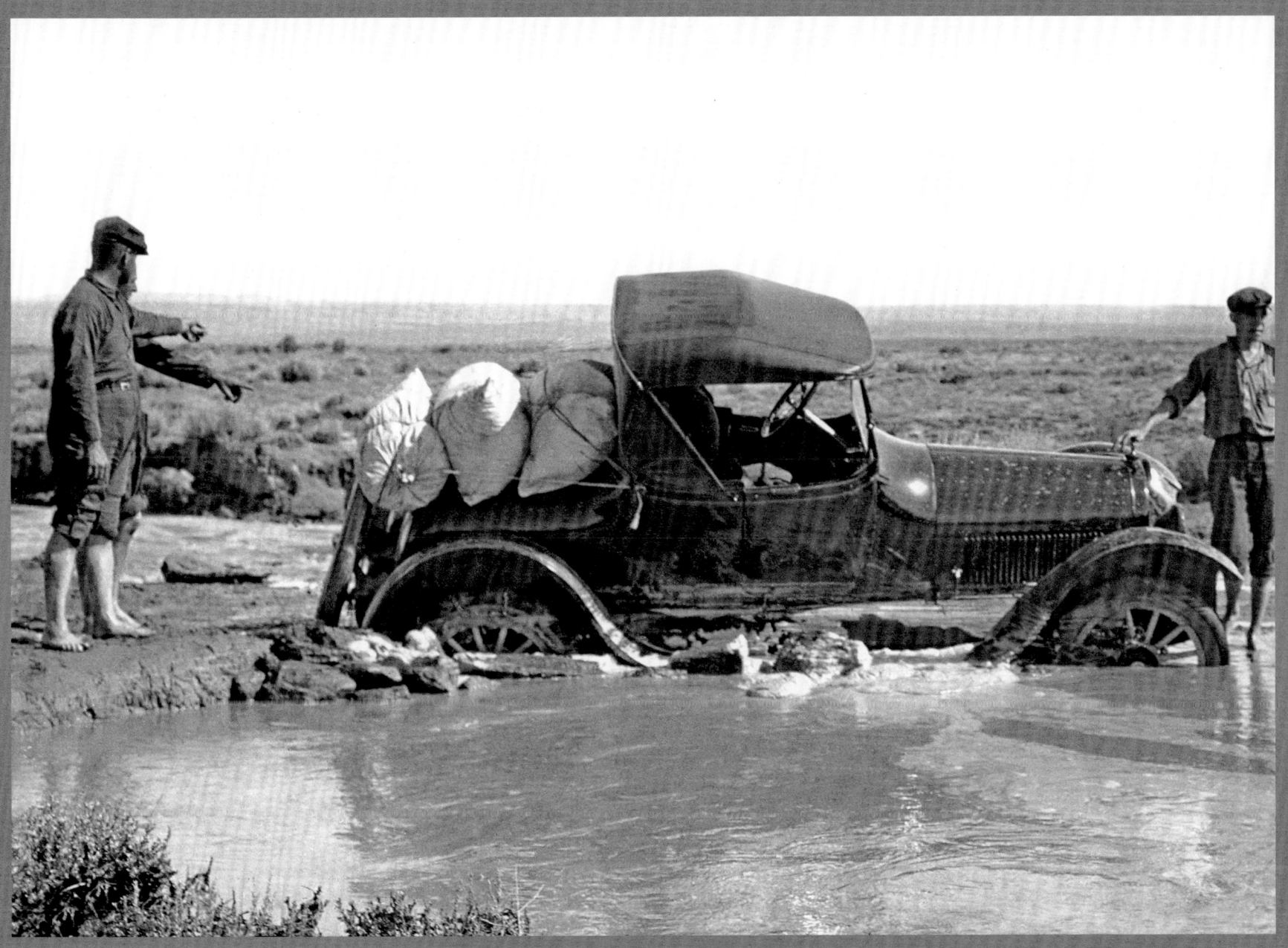

Close-up of other motorists stopping to help the Mills couple out of their predicament; they succeeded in pulling the car out with a rope. The vehicle was not significantly damaged.

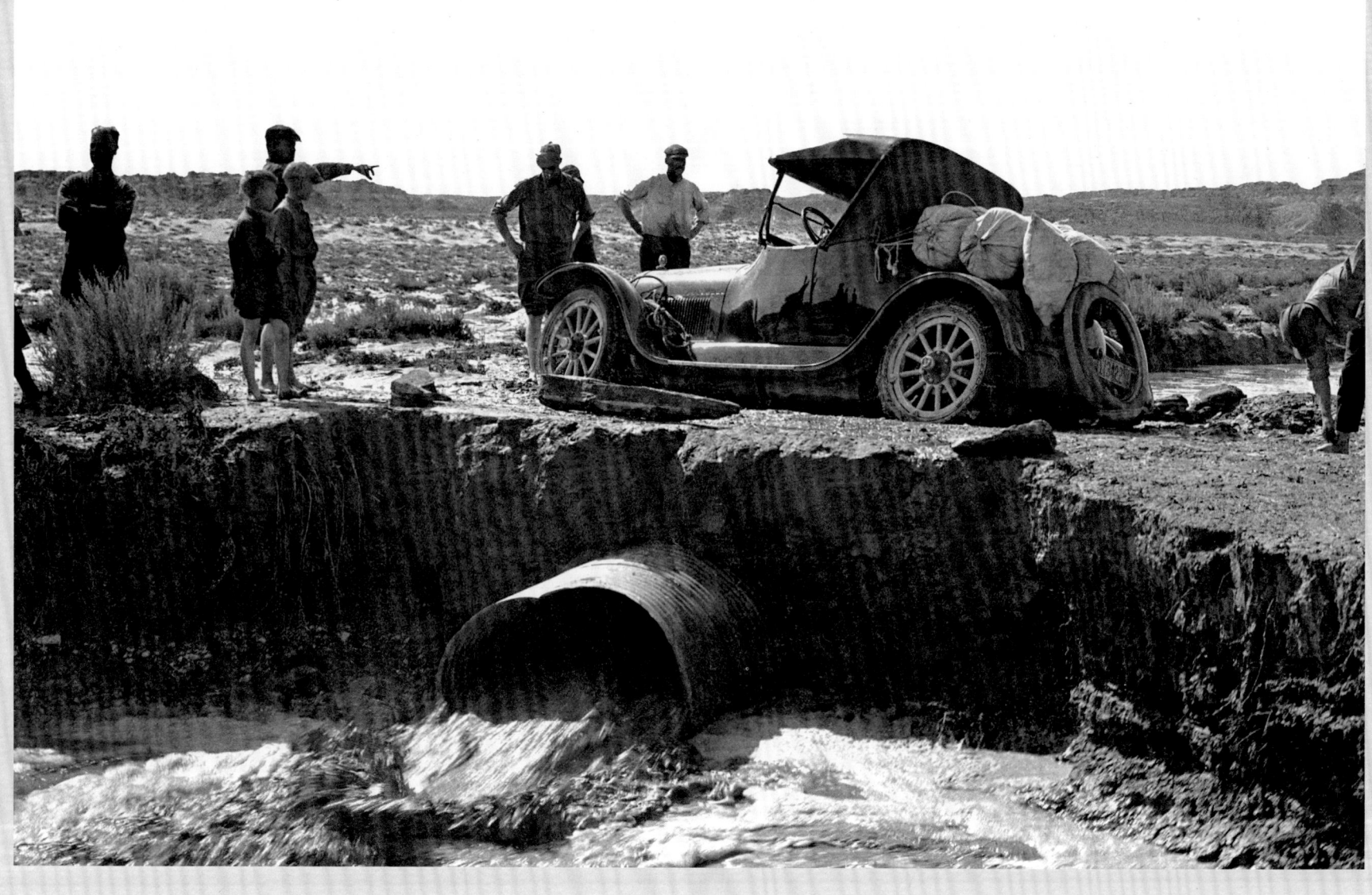

The water level continues to drop, and the Mills' Buick can be worked out of its precarious position. The previous three images give no hint as to how dangerous this situation really was. Here a tow rope rests on the front fender, ready for use. Henry is pointing to something as Walter and Ernest look on beside him. The rear wheels were fitted with desert mud chains, but they were not effective in this situation.

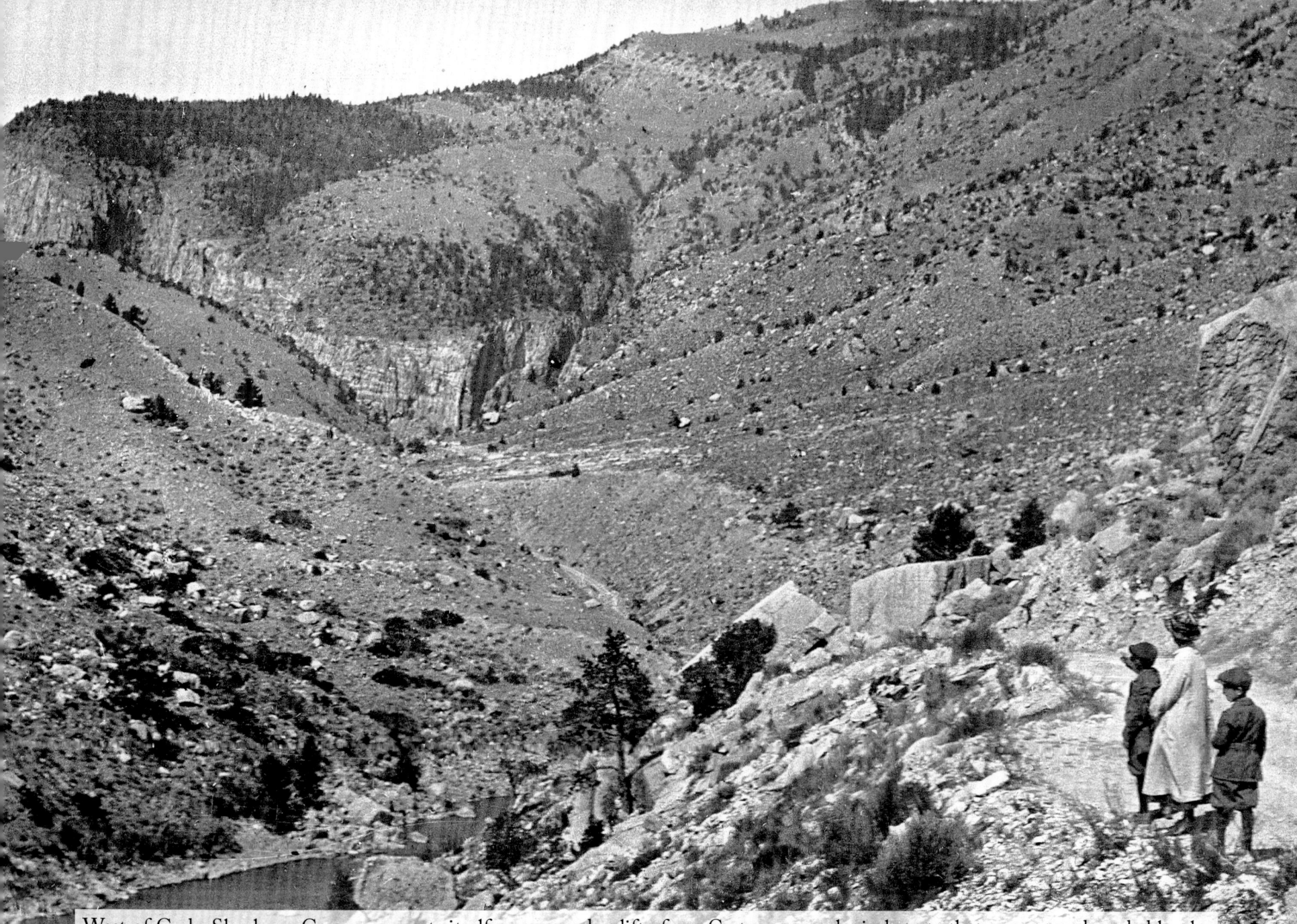

West of Cody, Shoshone Canyon presents itself as a rugged uplift of pre-Cretaceous geological strata that was cut and eroded by the Shoshone River. The headwaters begin in the Shoshone National Forest. The road into the canyon winds high above the river and reaches the Buffalo Bill Dam. In 1919, Lizzie reported in her letters home that it was the highest dam in the world at 328 feet. Walter, Lizzie, and Ernest look over the Shoshone River somewhere east of the dam, between the reservoir and Cody.

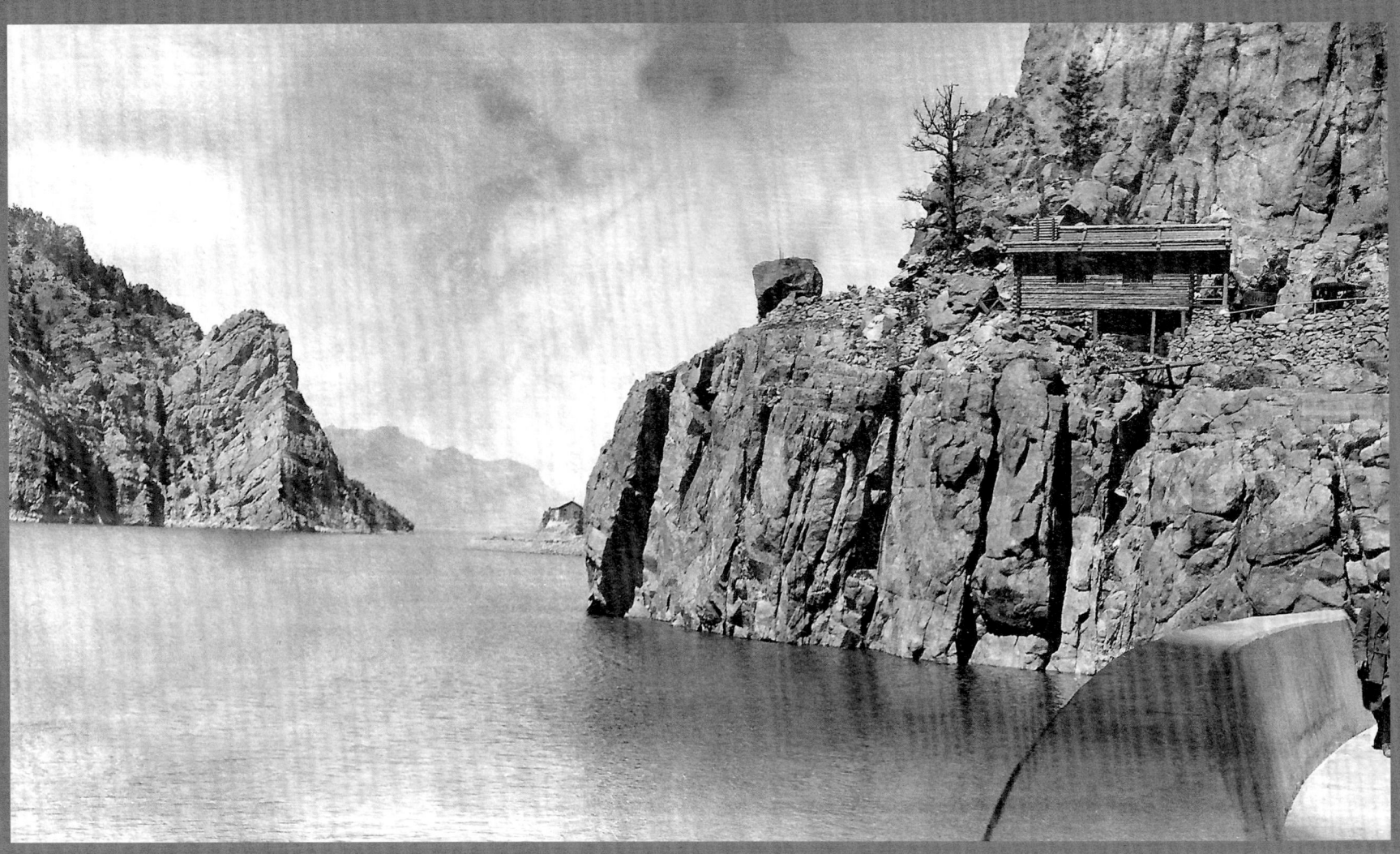

Henry took this picture of the Buffalo Bill Reservoir following the family drive uphill through Shoshone Canyon. As they reached the Buffalo Bill Dam (lower right), the Reservoir came into view. Cliffside are two parked vehicles and a possible visitor center and overlook. The water in the reservoir is used for hydroelectric power generation and recreational and agricultural purposes.

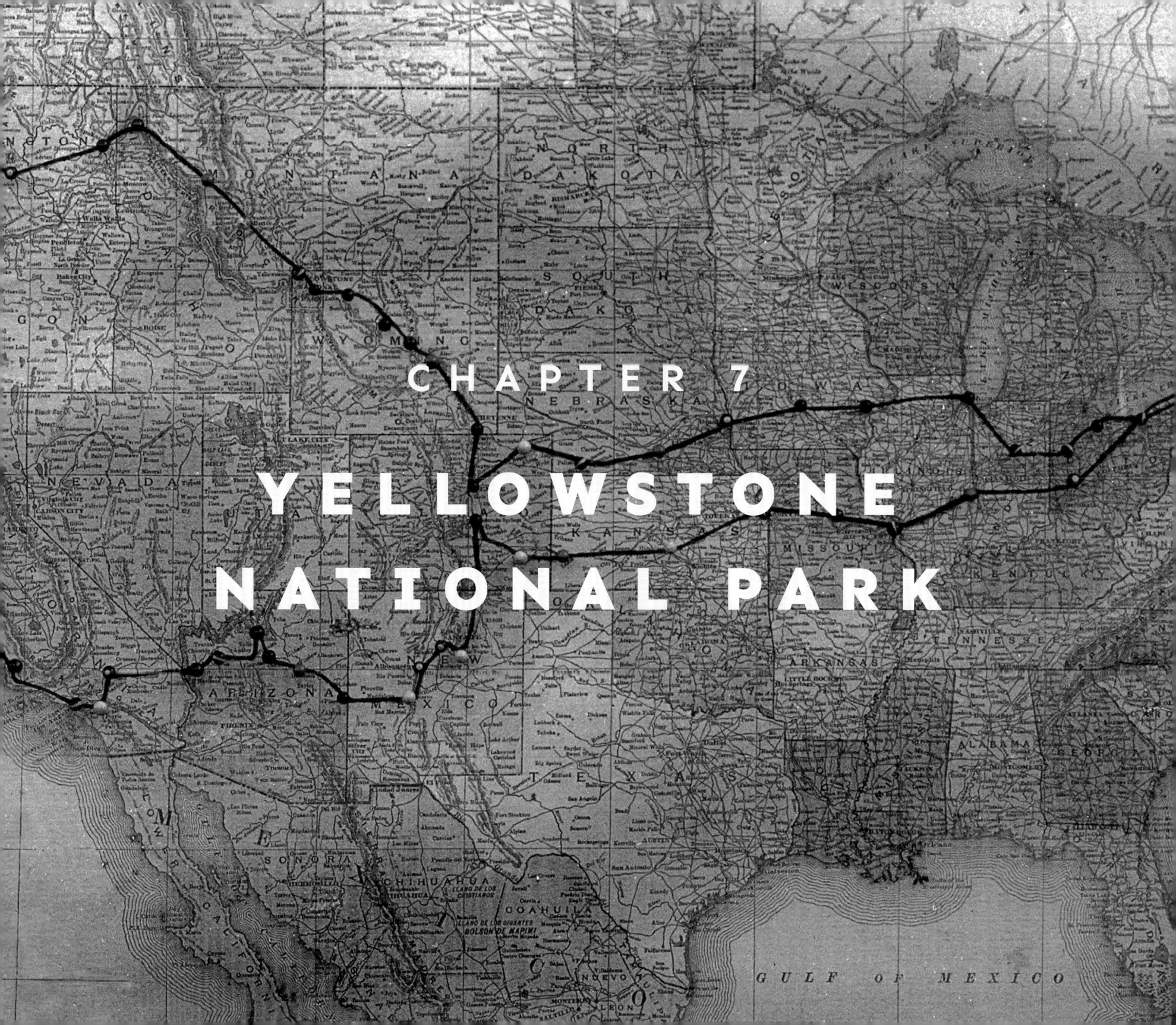

CHAPTER 7

YELLOWSTONE
NATIONAL PARK

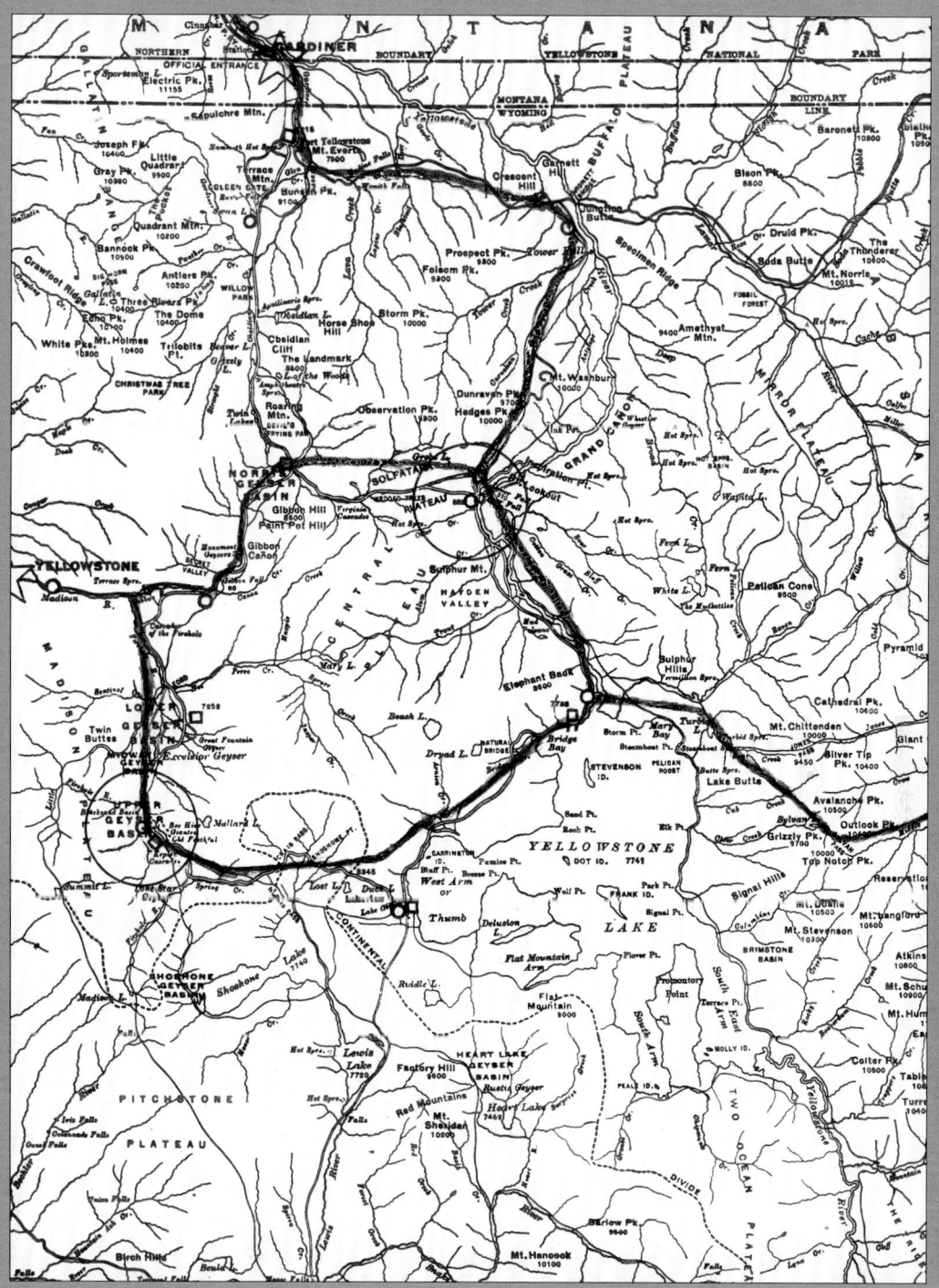

Henry marked this map with the route the family traveled around Yellowstone National Park. They entered through the eastern park entry gate after traversing Shoshone Canyon over Sylvan Pass. They spent about a week within the park viewing most of the major tourist sites and exited the park through the arched Roosevelt Gate into Gardiner, Montana. (Underwood & Underwood monochrome lantern slide.)

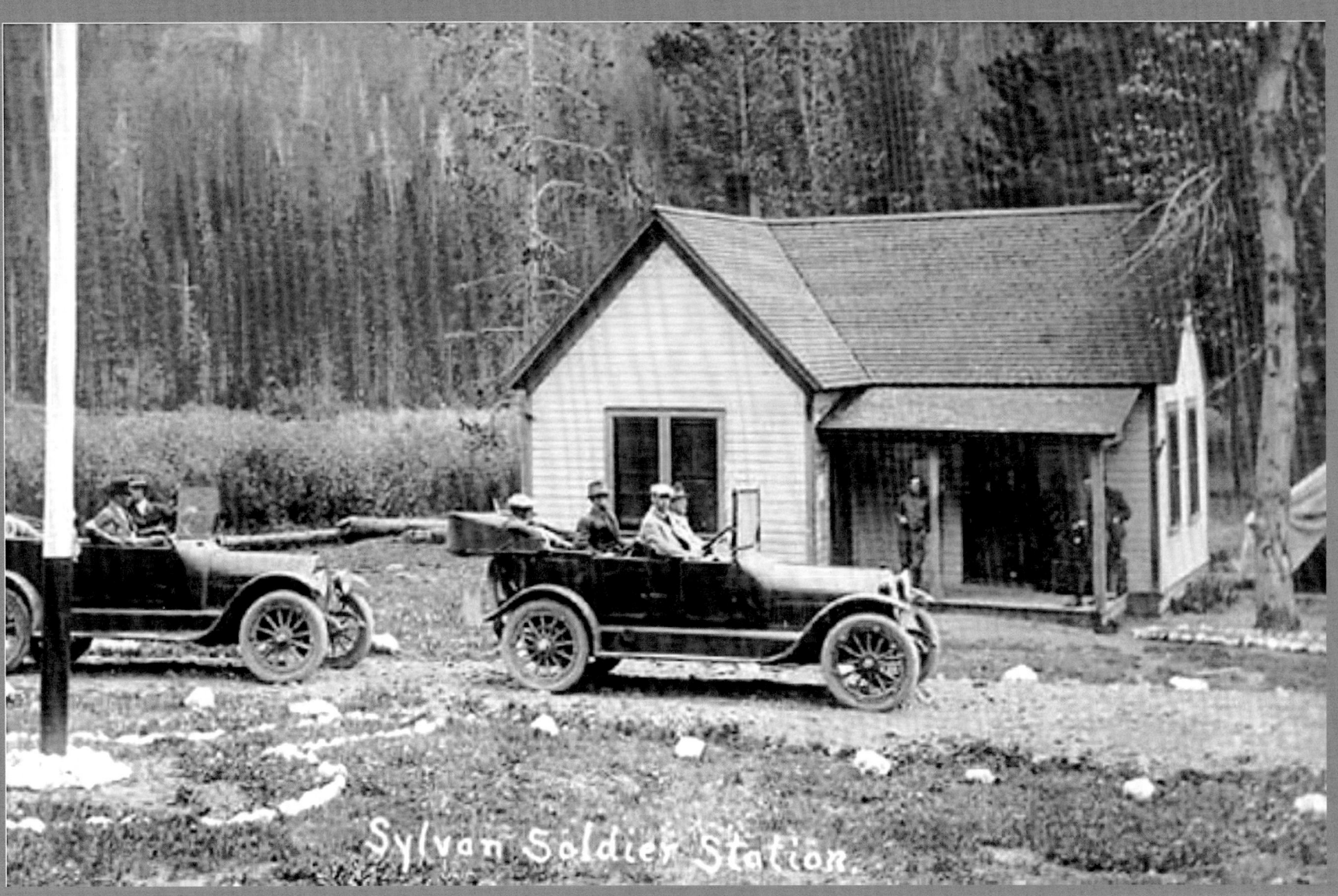

Sylvan Soldier Station.

Sylvan Soldier Station, Soldiers Entrance, Yellowstone National Park. This is how the eastern entrance gate into Yellowstone National Park would have looked at the time the Spallholz family, driving from Cody, Wyoming, arrived in 1919. The terms "Soldier Station" and "Soldiers Entrance" refer to the fact that the US Army controlled Yellowstone National Park from 1886 to 1918. (Photograph provided courtesy of wyomingtrailsandtales.com.)

After entering Yellowstone National Park, Henry stopped to photograph the Loop, a 360-degree up-and-around turn on the road over Sylvan Pass in the Absaroka mountain range east of Yellowstone Lake. The Loop was constructed in 1914 to reduce the steep uphill section at that point on the original pass. Lizzie wrote that the family had to go over Sylvan Pass, the last section of which was a steep eight-mile uphill climb.

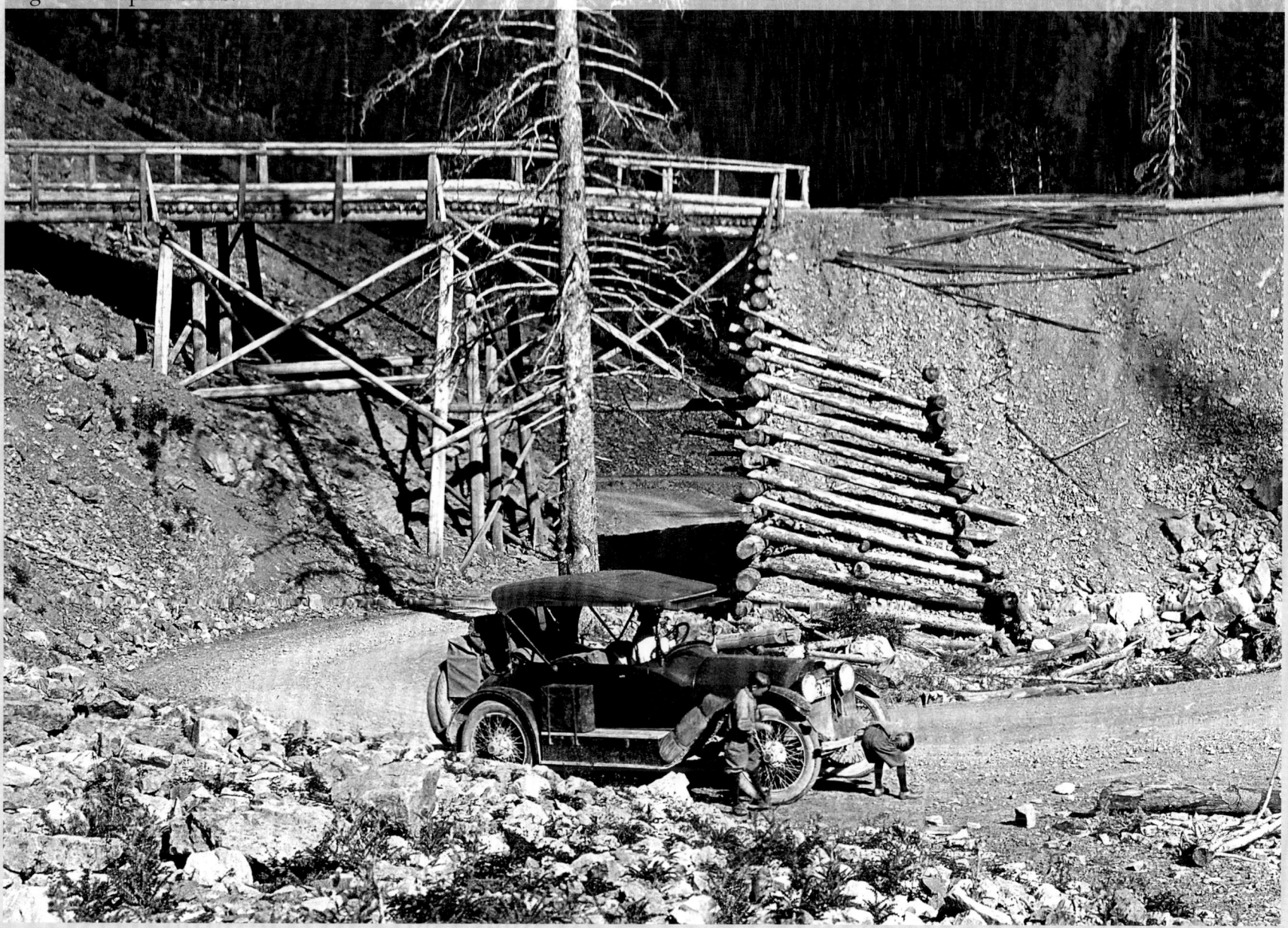

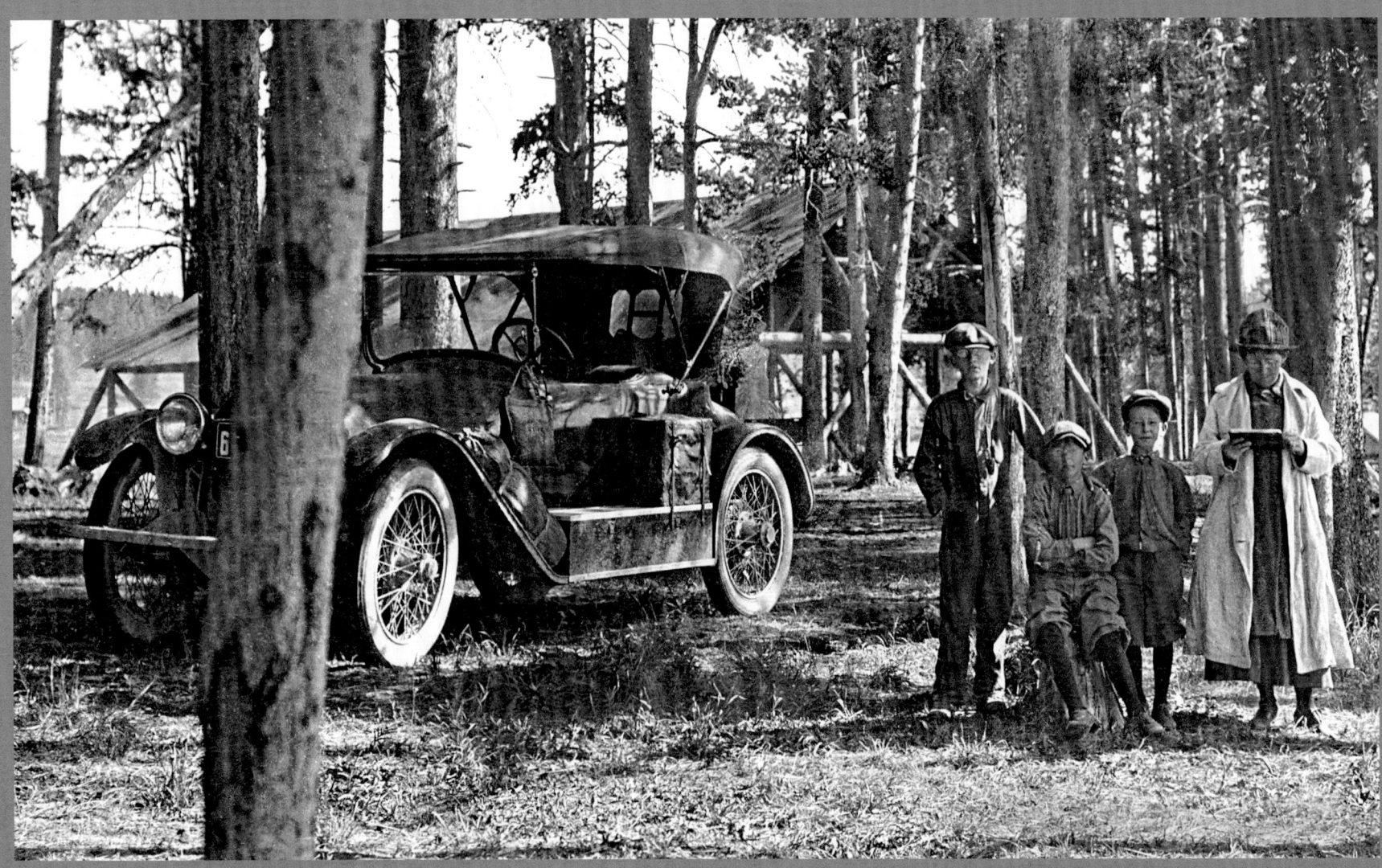

The Spallholz family camped the first night of their Yellowstone National Park trek on the shore of Yellowstone Lake, where they could see the mountain peaks of the Grand Tetons in the distance. They kept their drinking water cool through evaporation in a canvas water bag hanging from the wind screen support or on the bumper in front of the radiator. Bears came around the campsites looking for food at night. Prior to driving around Yellowstone National Park, Walter, Ernest, and Lizzie Spallholz visited with a friend from a nearby campsite. In this photograph, Lizzie is holding what may be a small guidebook. Computer processing has eliminated strong light banding in the right part of the image, possibly caused by lens flare or by loading and removing film in the sun.

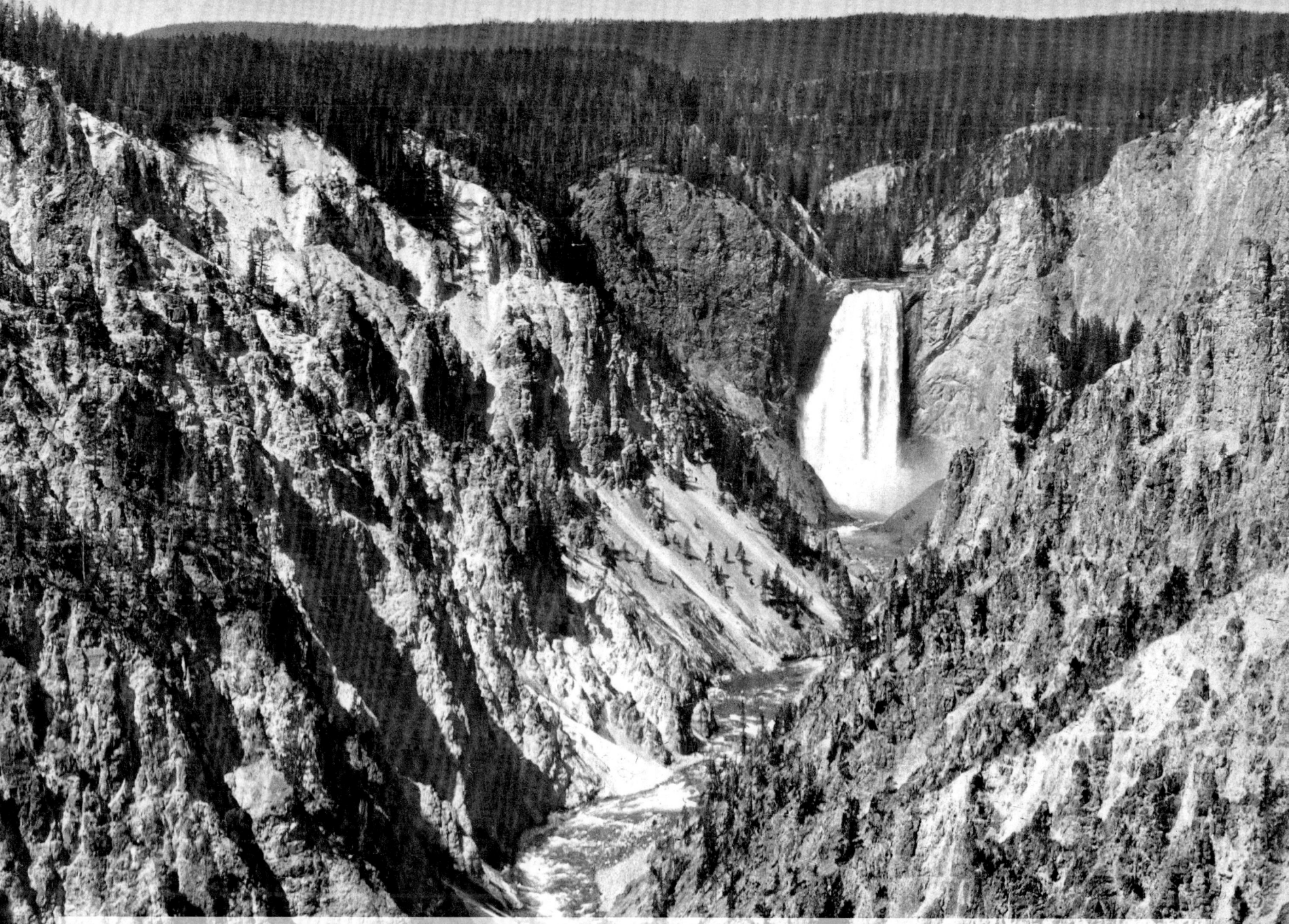

Henry took this photo from Artist Point, looking nearly a mile straight up Yellowstone Canyon towards the Great Falls. Where the river curves, just below the center of the image, stronger, more turbulent current has eroded the base of the slope at that point, resulting in the canyon wall above falling away over time. This steep terrain provides no foothold to support the growth of trees, as seen elsewhere on both sides of the canyon.

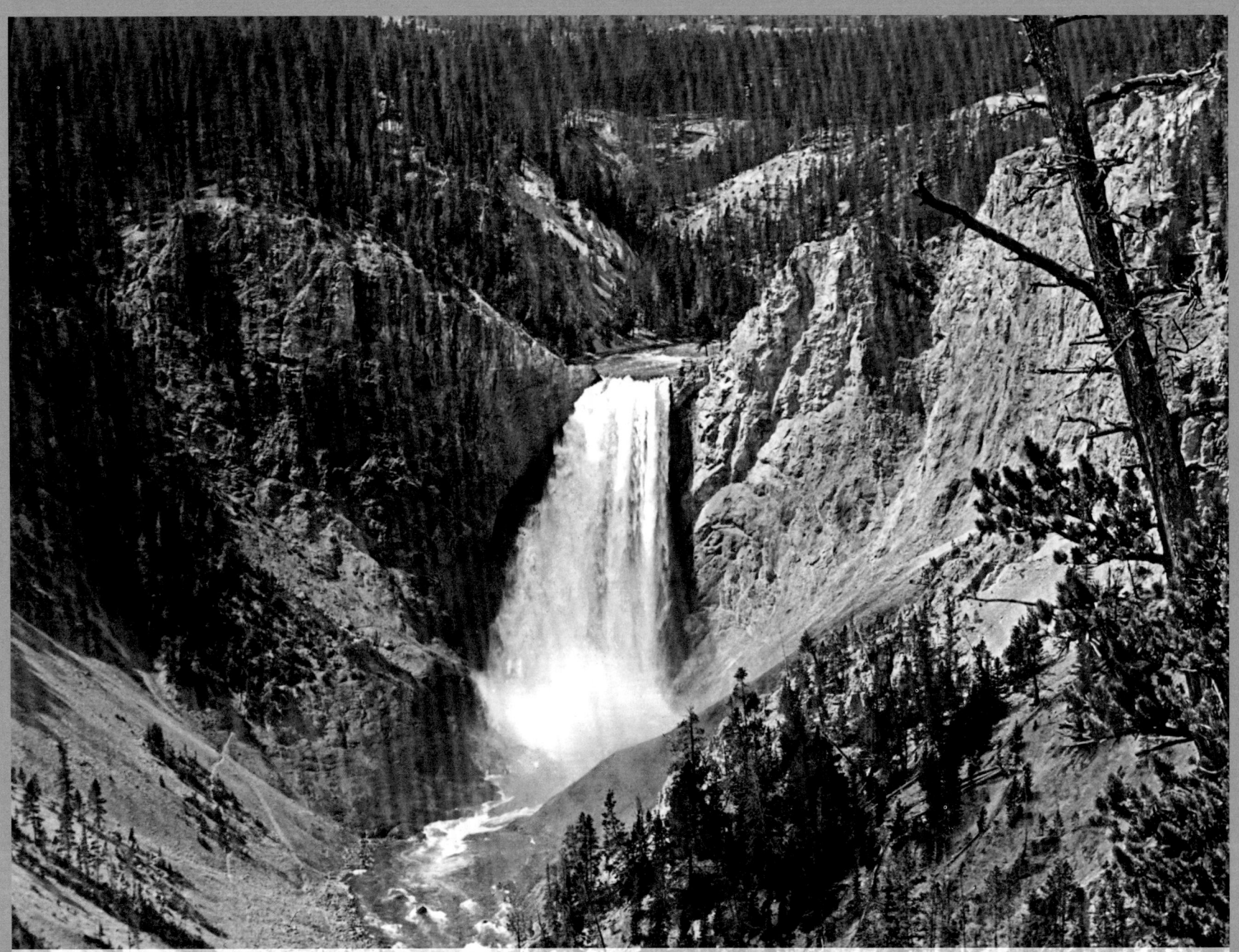

A view from Point Lookout 1,200 feet above the river, looking up Yellowstone Canyon to the lower falls. (Underwood & Underwood hand-colored lantern slide rendered in black and white.)

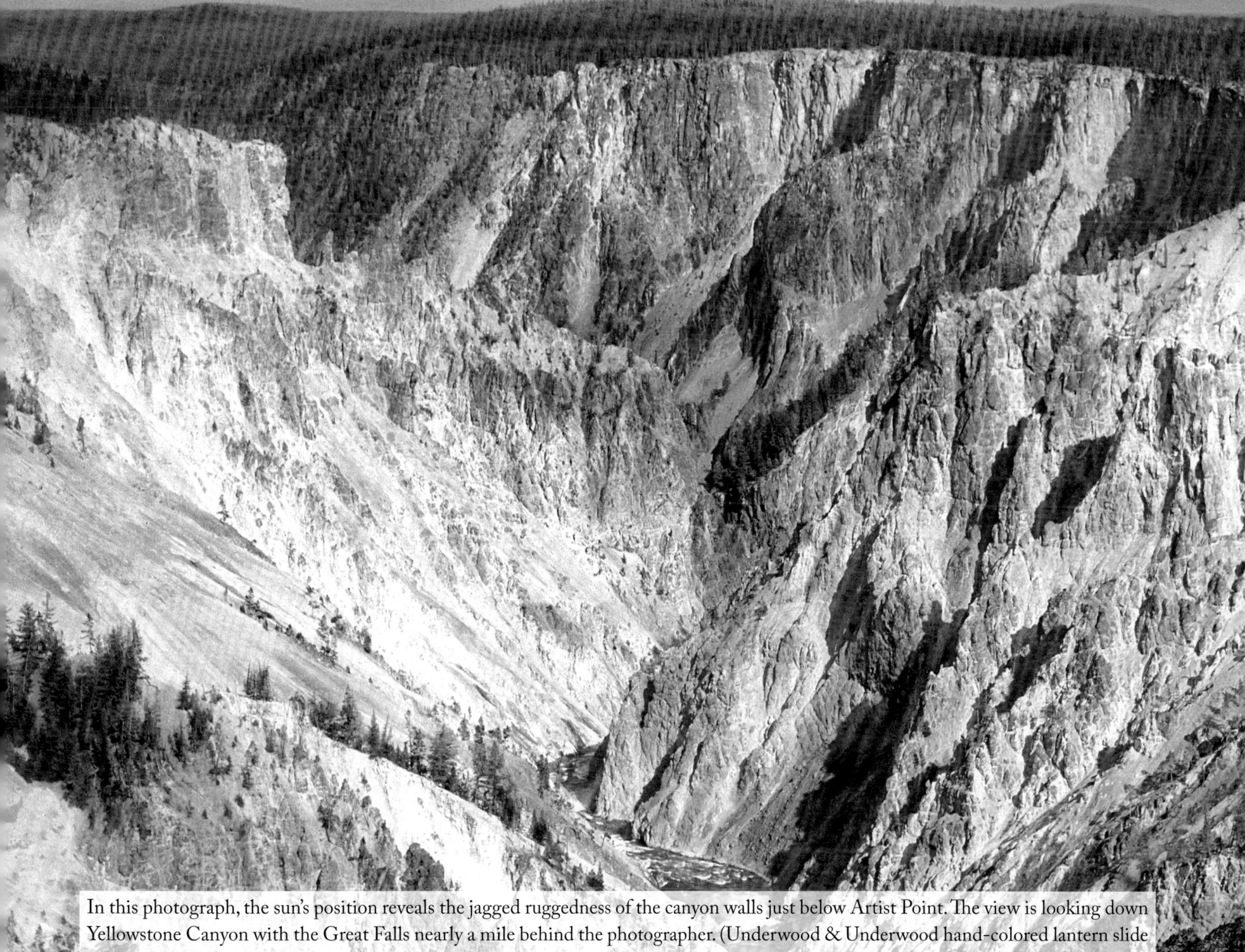

In this photograph, the sun's position reveals the jagged ruggedness of the canyon walls just below Artist Point. The view is looking down Yellowstone Canyon with the Great Falls nearly a mile behind the photographer. (Underwood & Underwood hand-colored lantern slide rendered in black and white.)

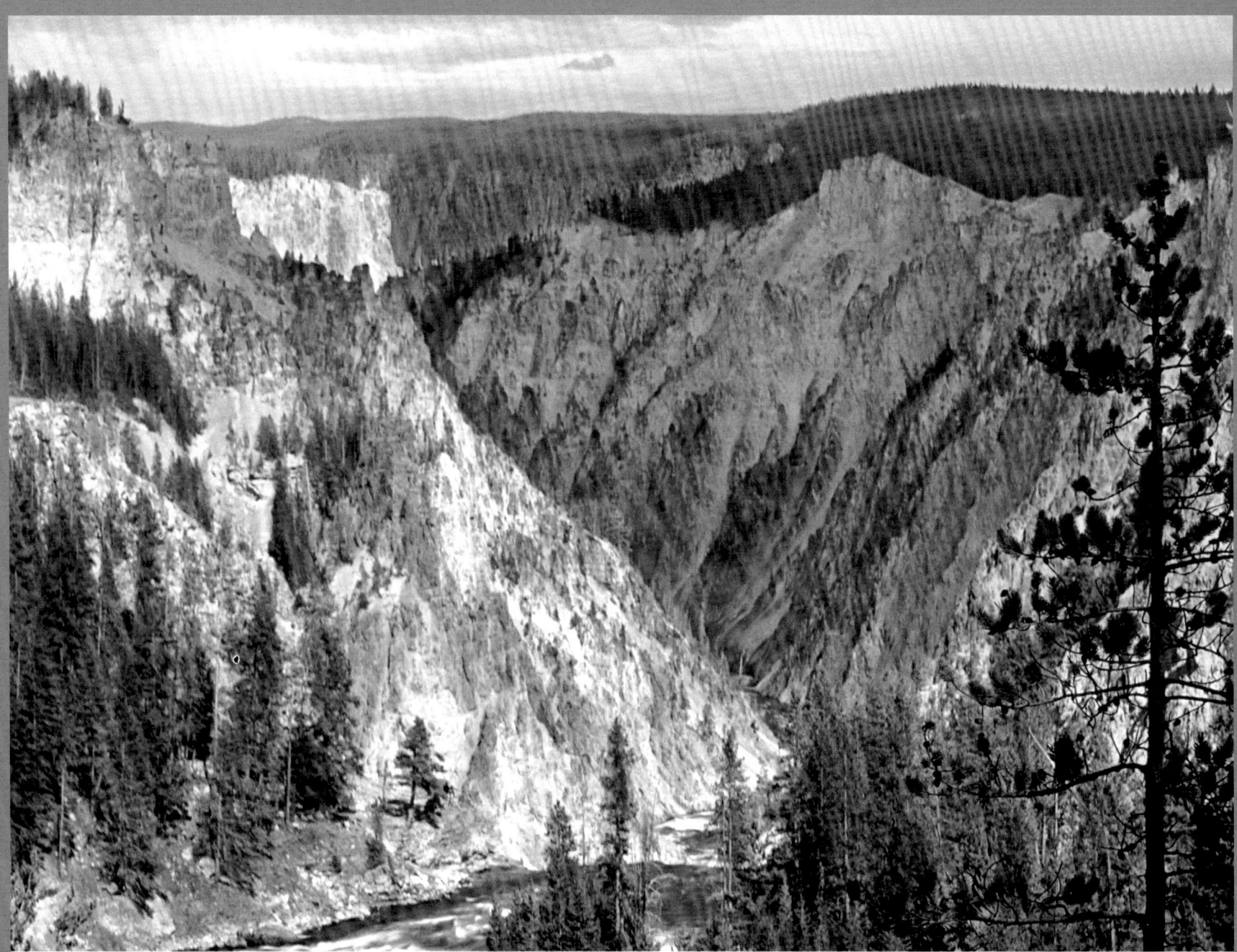

This image offers a closer view of the Yellowstone River and its rugged canyon walls, showing the incredible heights and depths of the canyon. (Underwood & Underwood hand-colored lantern slide rendered in black and white.)

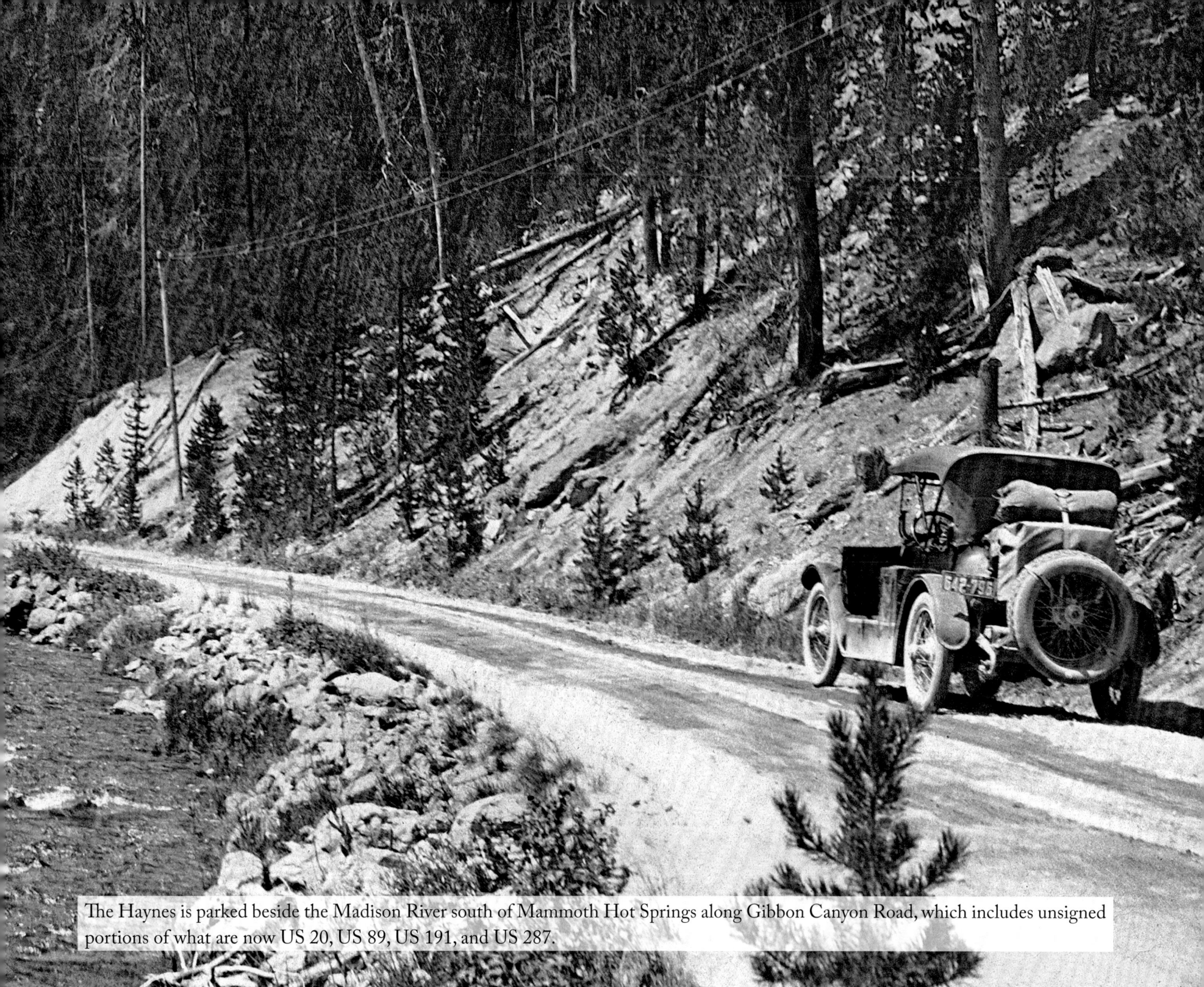

The Haynes is parked beside the Madison River south of Mammoth Hot Springs along Gibbon Canyon Road, which includes unsigned portions of what are now US 20, US 89, US 191, and US 287.

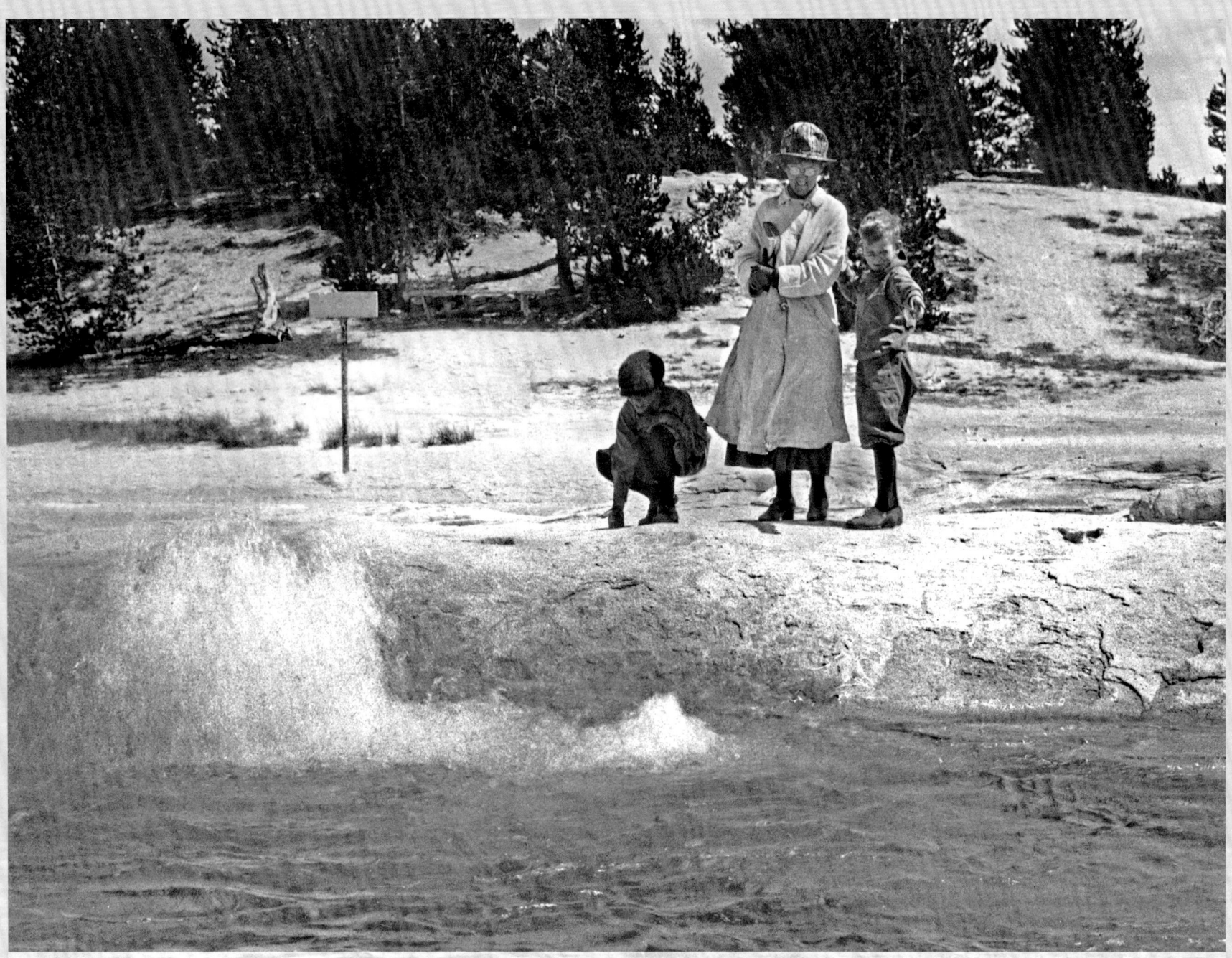

The boys and Lizzie watch the relatively mild bubbling action of the Fountain Geyser. The ground was stable enough in 1919 for visitors to walk right next to the scalding water.

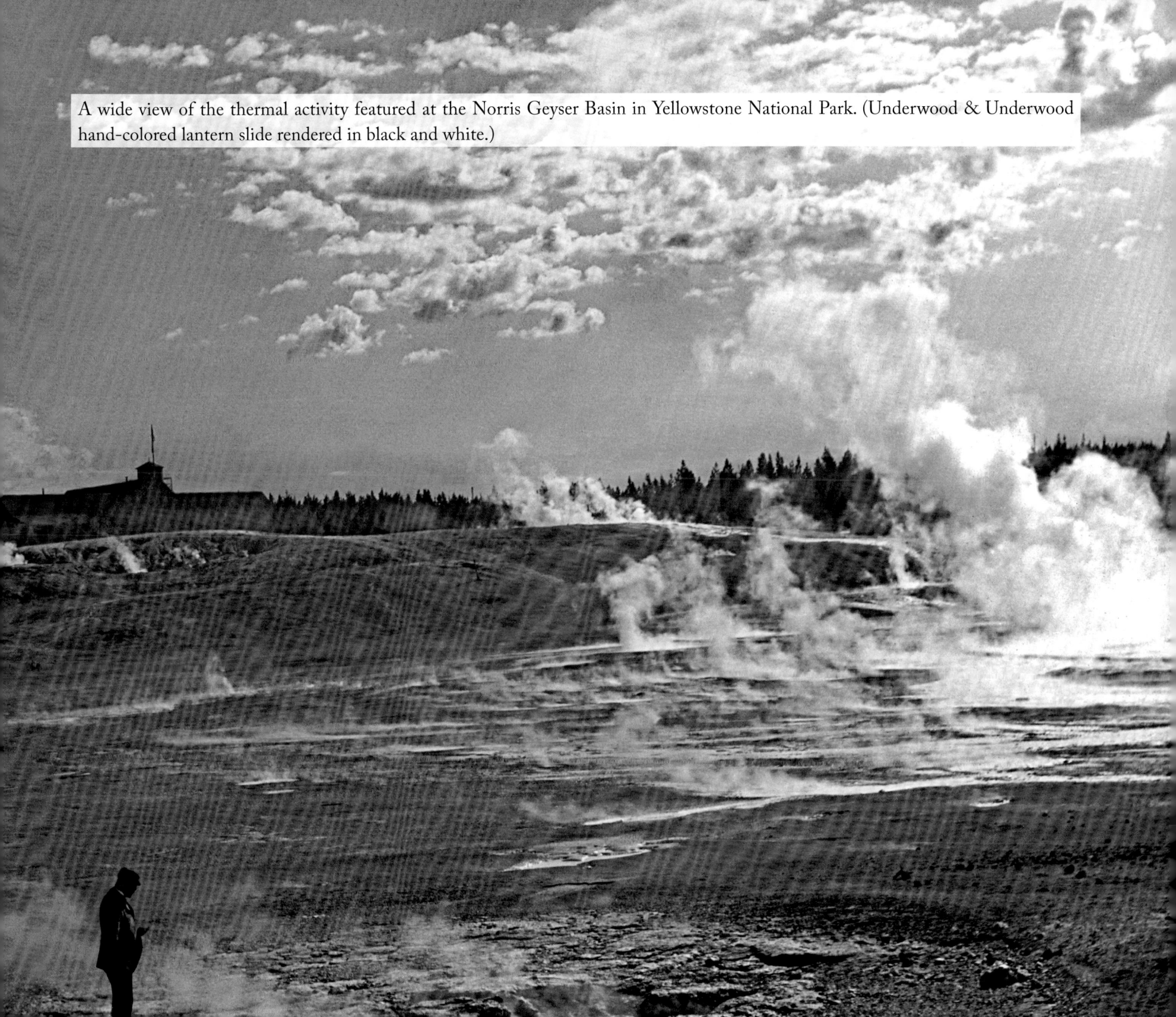

A wide view of the thermal activity featured at the Norris Geyser Basin in Yellowstone National Park. (Underwood & Underwood hand-colored lantern slide rendered in black and white.)

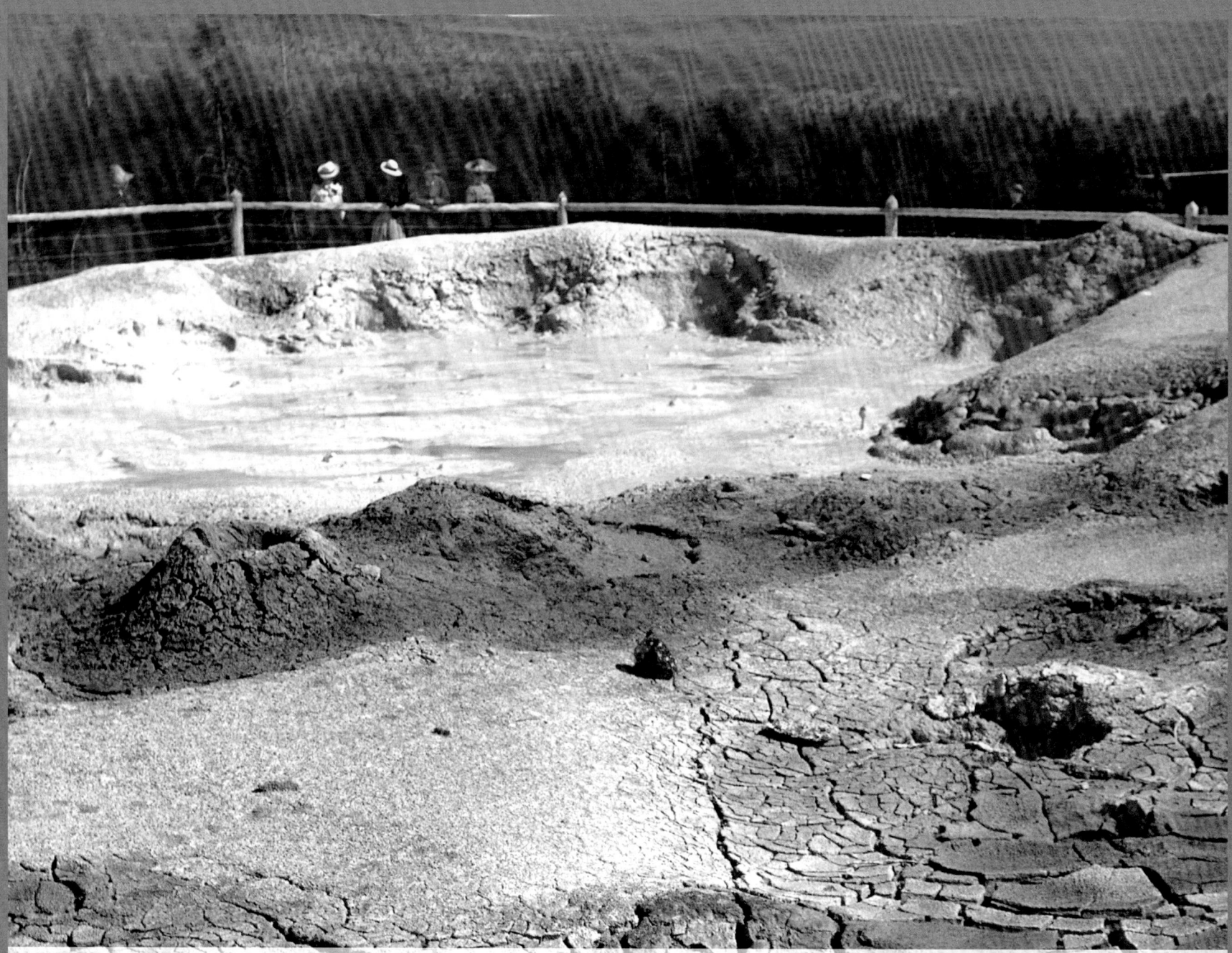

This photograph showing visitors at the Mammoth Hot Springs Paint Pots was taken in 1903. (Underwood & Underwood hand-colored lantern slide rendered in black and white.)

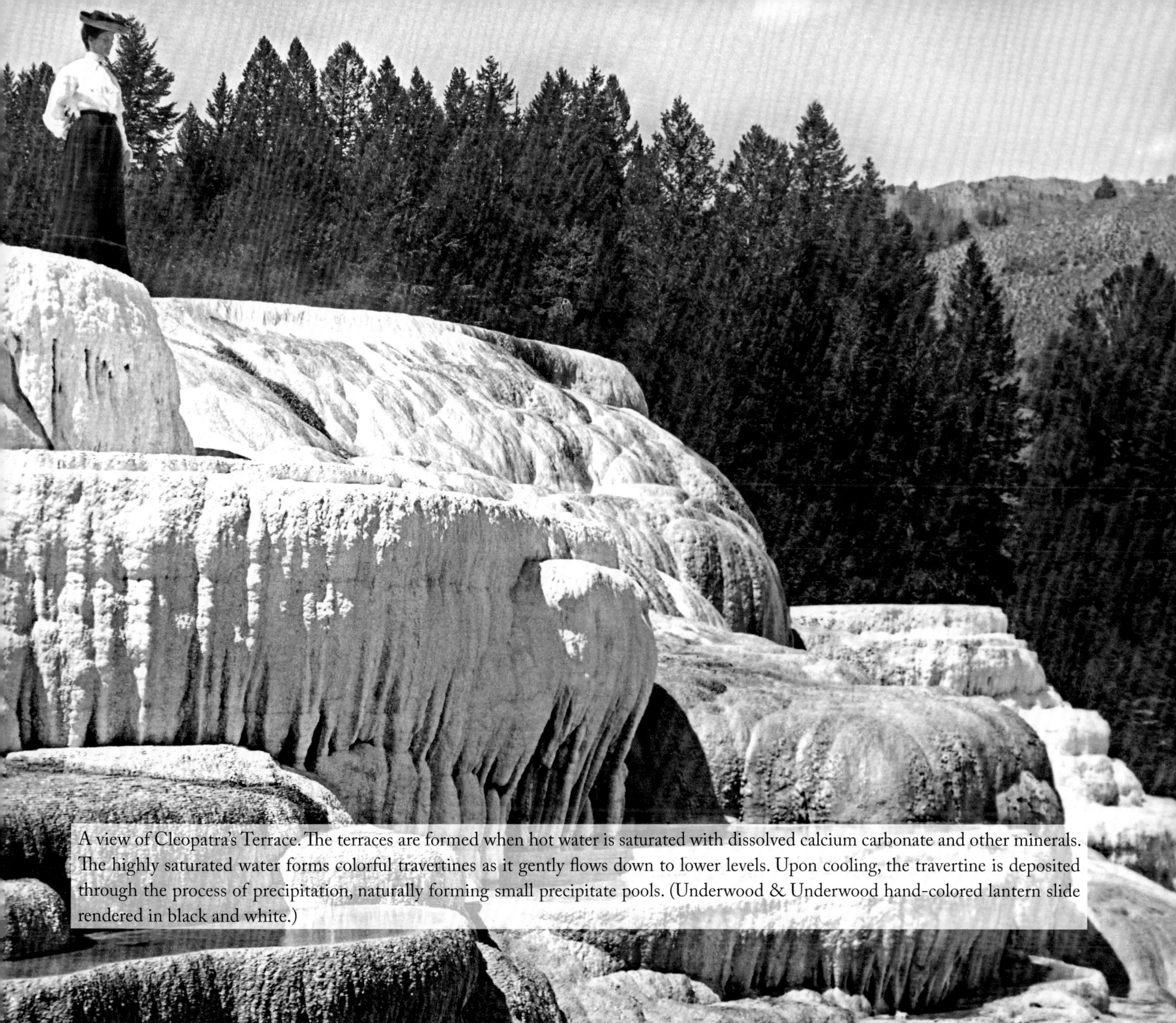

A view of Cleopatra's Terrace. The terraces are formed when hot water is saturated with dissolved calcium carbonate and other minerals. The highly saturated water forms colorful travertines as it gently flows down to lower levels. Upon cooling, the travertine is deposited through the process of precipitation, naturally forming small precipitate pools. (Underwood & Underwood hand-colored lantern slide rendered in black and white.)

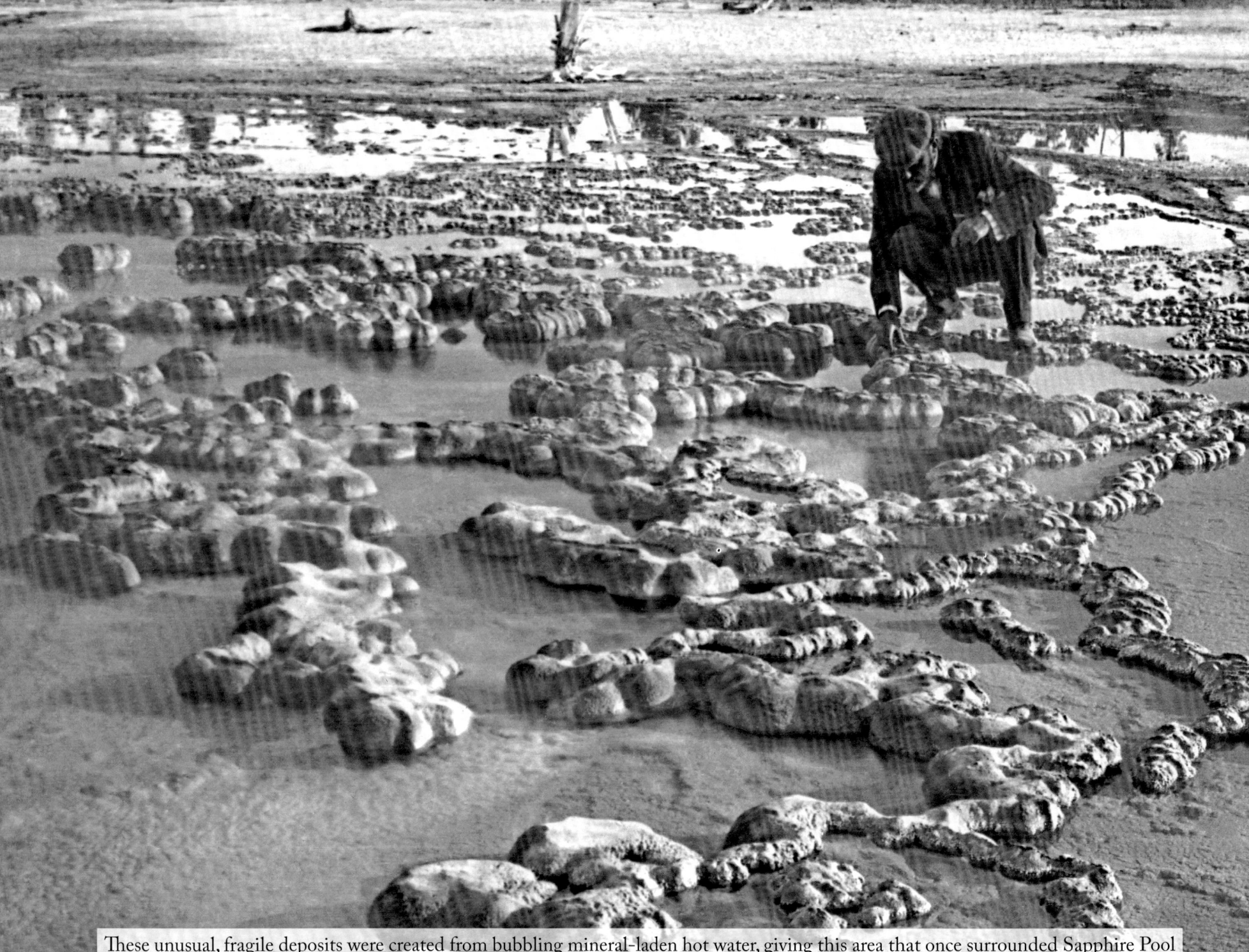

These unusual, fragile deposits were created from bubbling mineral-laden hot water, giving this area that once surrounded Sapphire Pool the name of Biscuit Basin. (Underwood & Underwood hand-colored lantern slide rendered in black and white.)

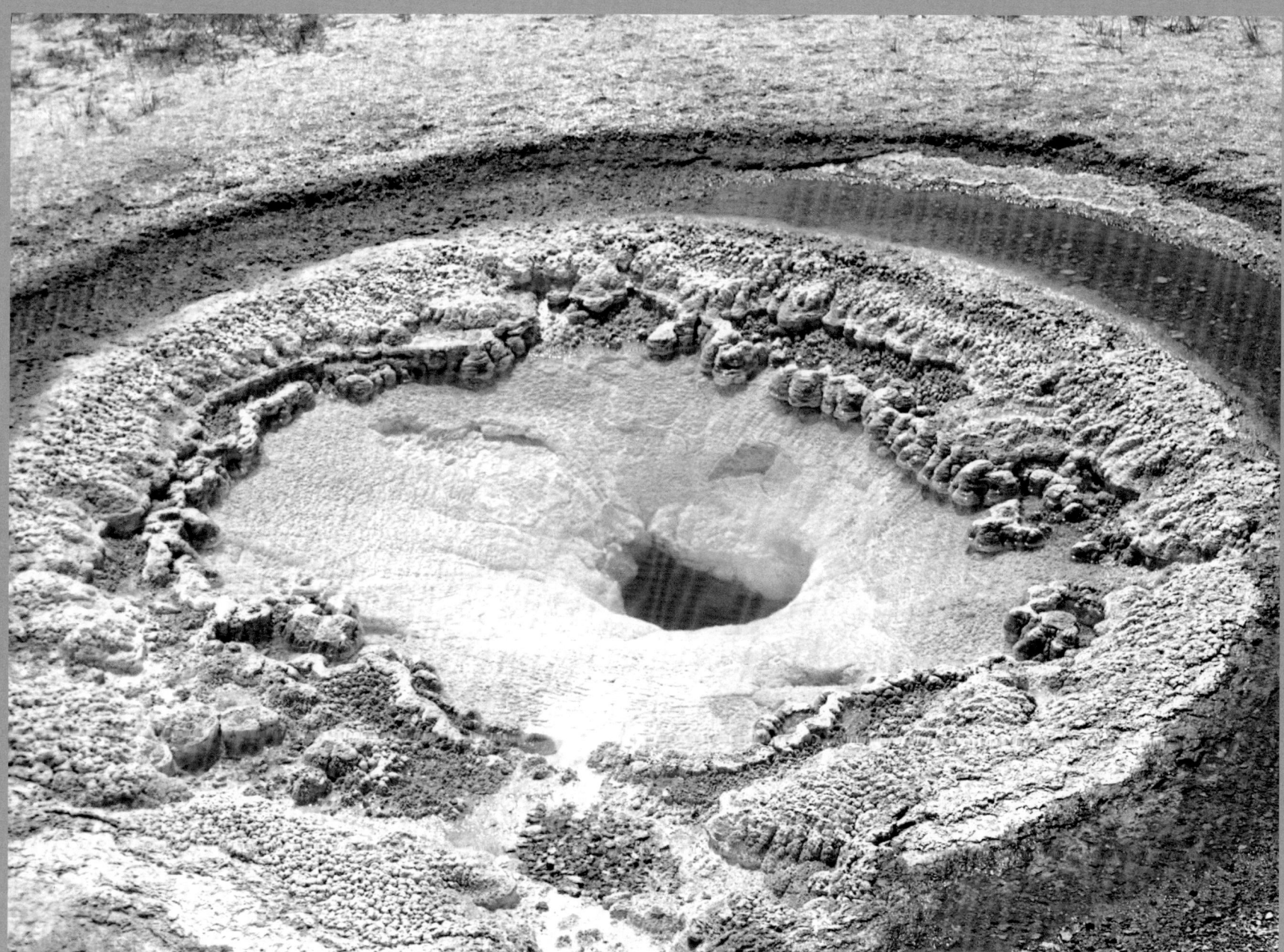

Morning Glory Pool's name derives from its circular arrangement of mineral deposits, which cause it to have the shape of a morning glory flower. Here the pool looks dry but is actually full of scalding water up to the darker algal border. (Underwood & Underwood hand-colored lantern slide rendered in black and white.)

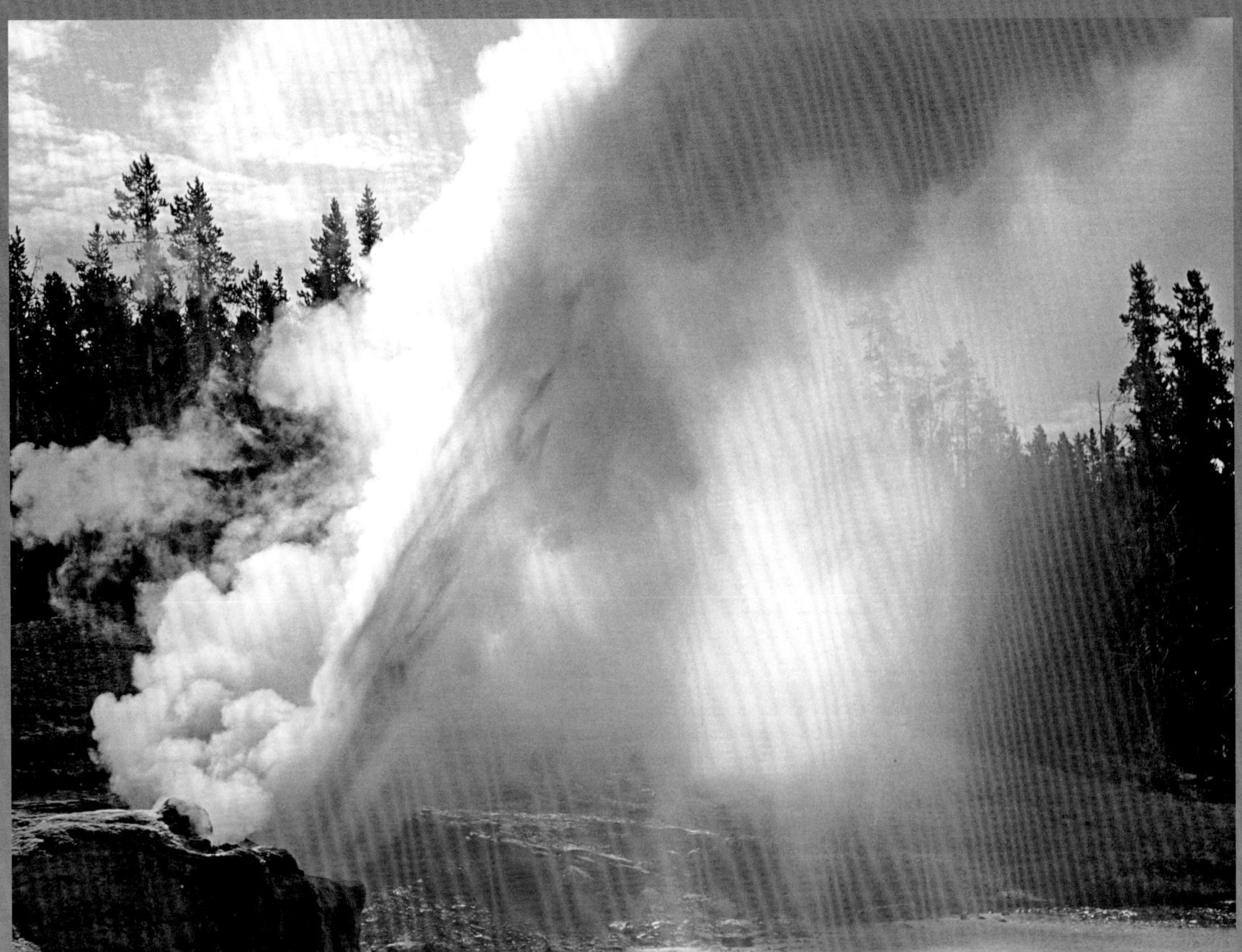

The Riverside Geyser in eruption. The geyser projects a plume of scalding water and steam at an angle over the Firehole River approximately every seven hours. (Underwood & Underwood monochrome lantern slide.)

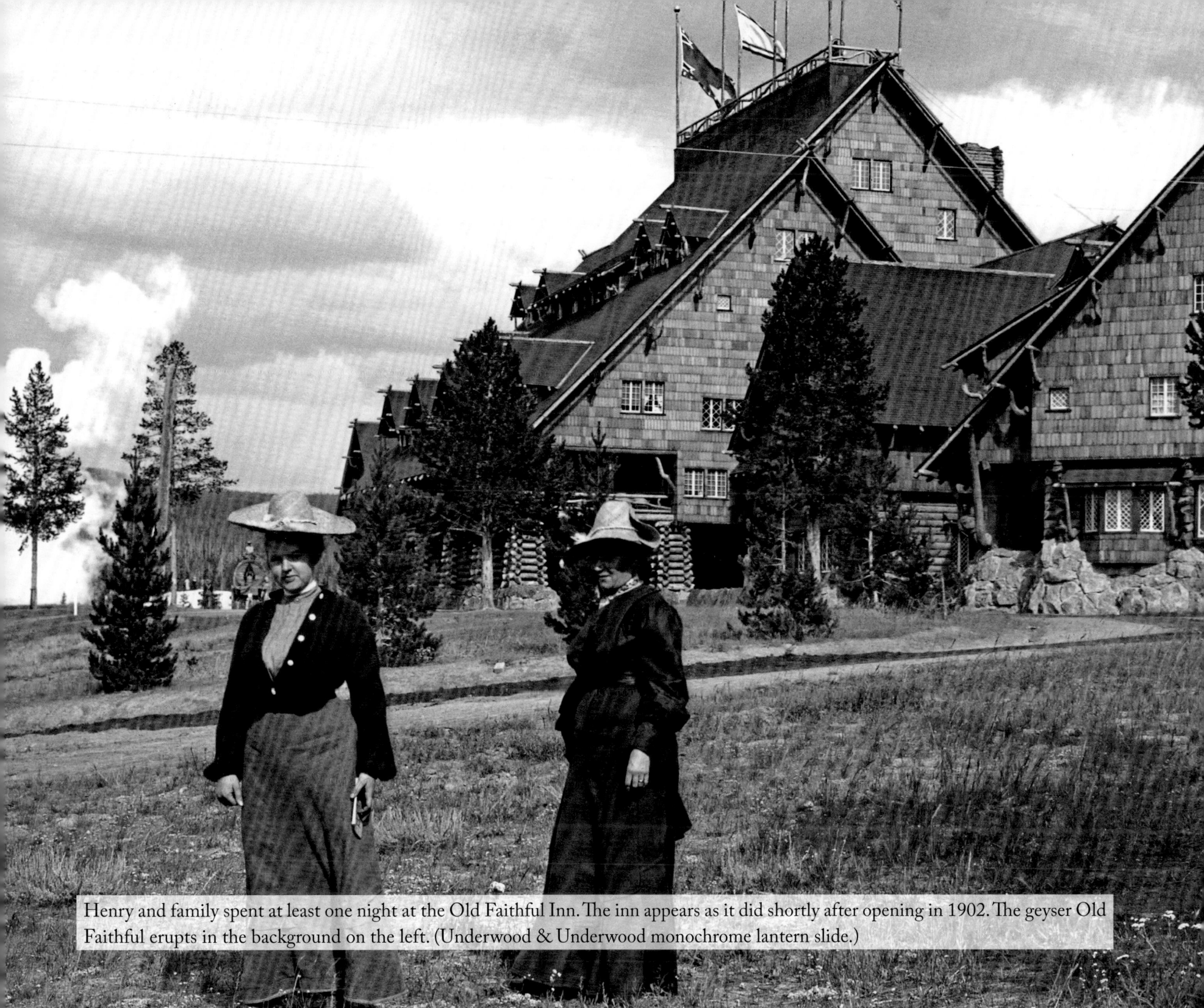

Henry and family spent at least one night at the Old Faithful Inn. The inn appears as it did shortly after opening in 1902. The geyser Old Faithful erupts in the background on the left. (Underwood & Underwood monochrome lantern slide.)

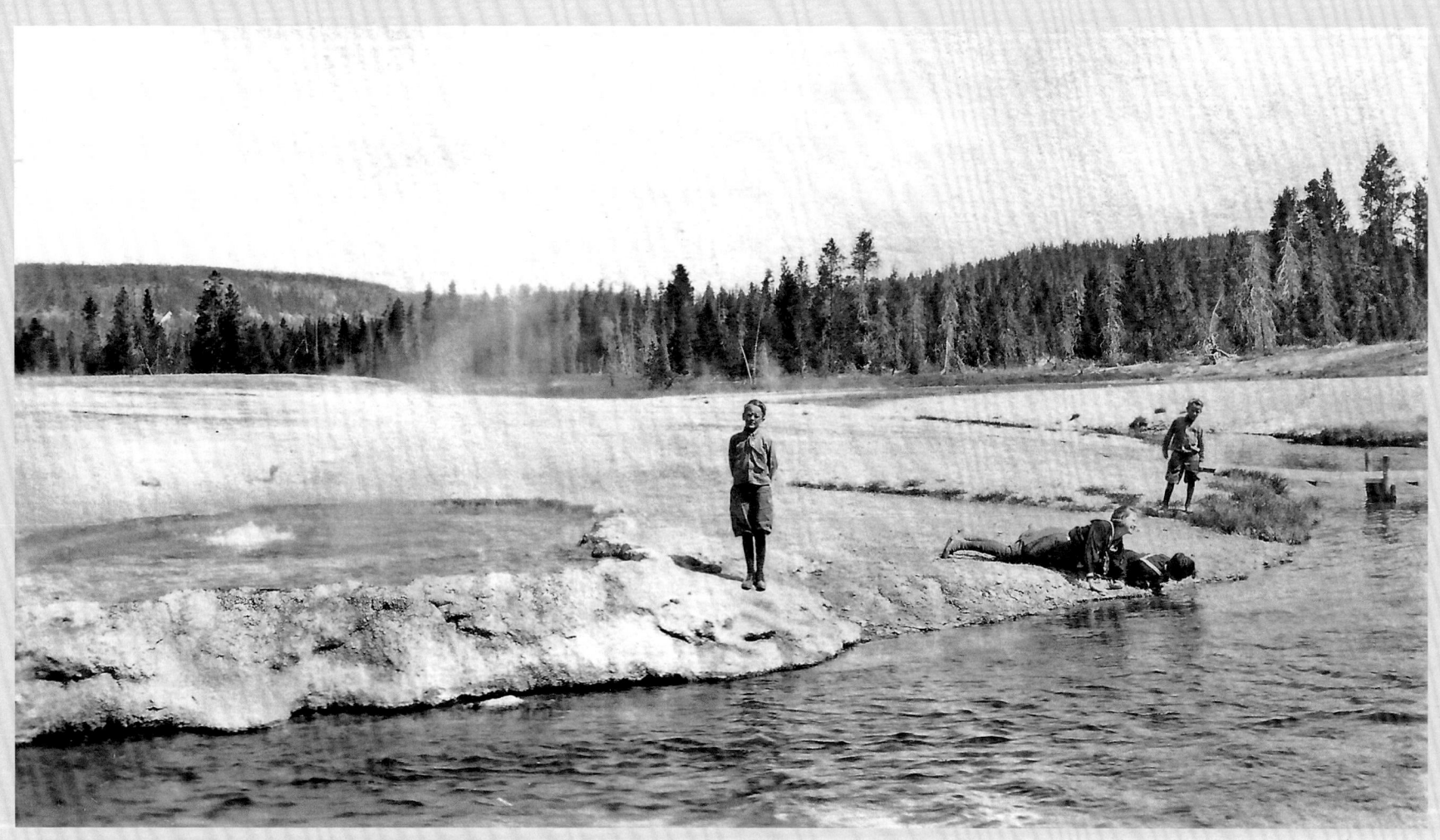

At Iron Spring, the water in the geyser is scalding hot and the creek next to it is swift. Walter stands in the center next to the geyser, and Ernest in the background looks on as two unknown children play beside the running river.

The view of Shoshone Lake in this photograph is to the south of the Continental Divide. Lizzie sits in the passenger seat of the Haynes in her duster. Walter and Ernest must be out exploring while Henry takes the photo. The Grand Tetons are fifty miles away, barely visible as an extremely faint smudge on the horizon to the left.

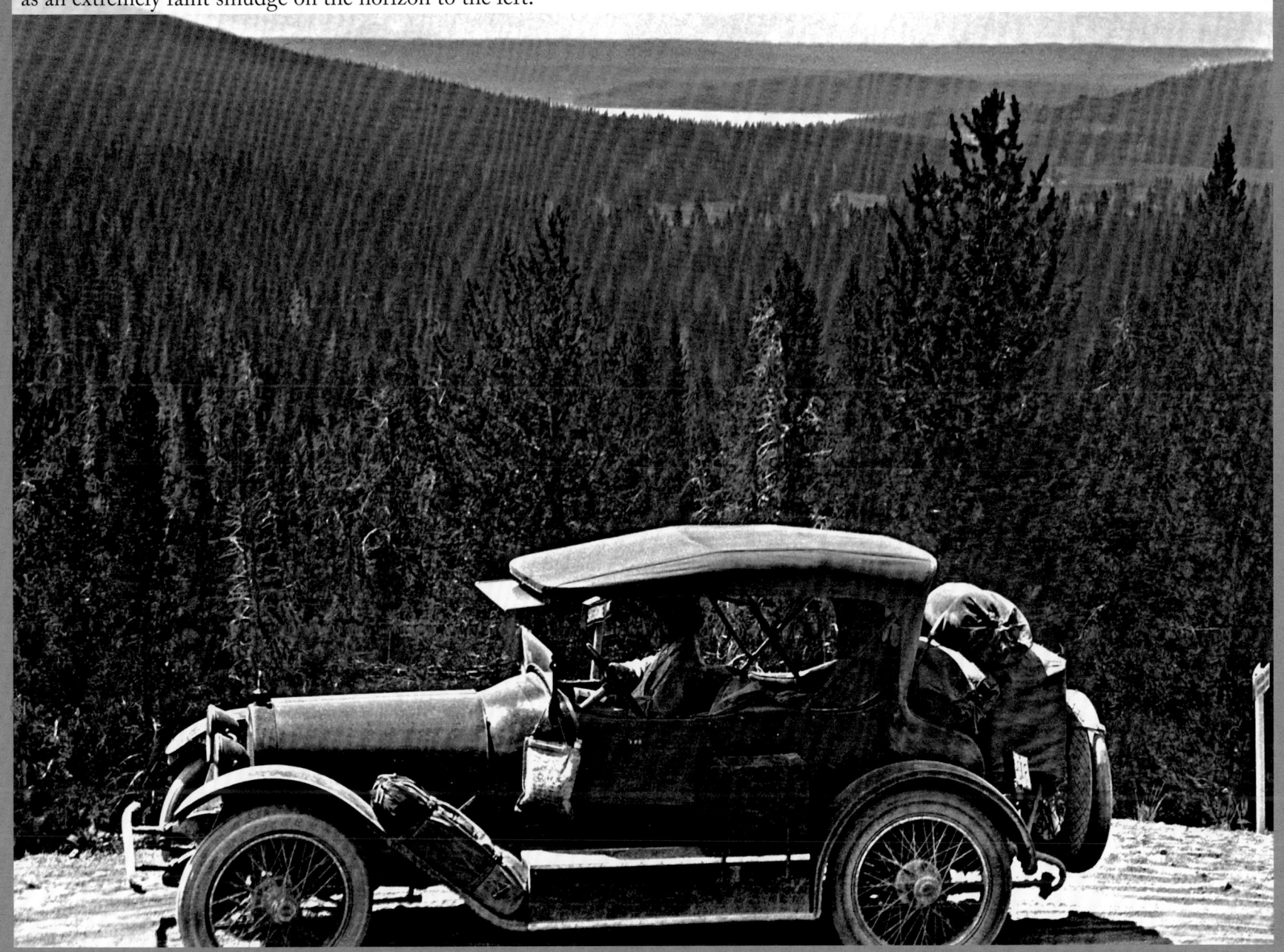

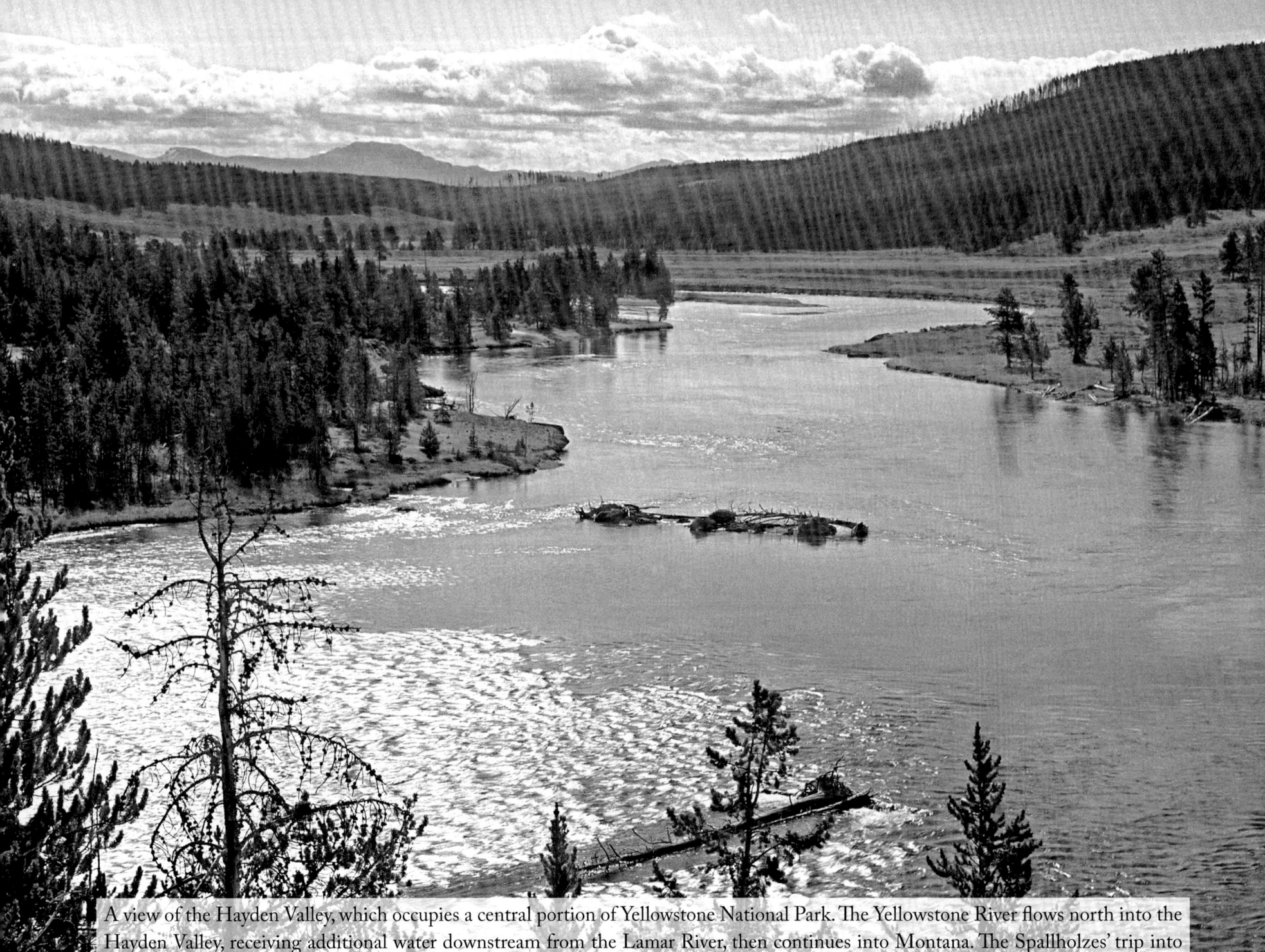

A view of the Hayden Valley, which occupies a central portion of Yellowstone National Park. The Yellowstone River flows north into the Hayden Valley, receiving additional water downstream from the Lamar River, then continues into Montana. The Spallholzes' trip into the valley included stops at the mud volcanoes. (Underwood & Underwood hand-colored lantern slide rendered in black and white.)

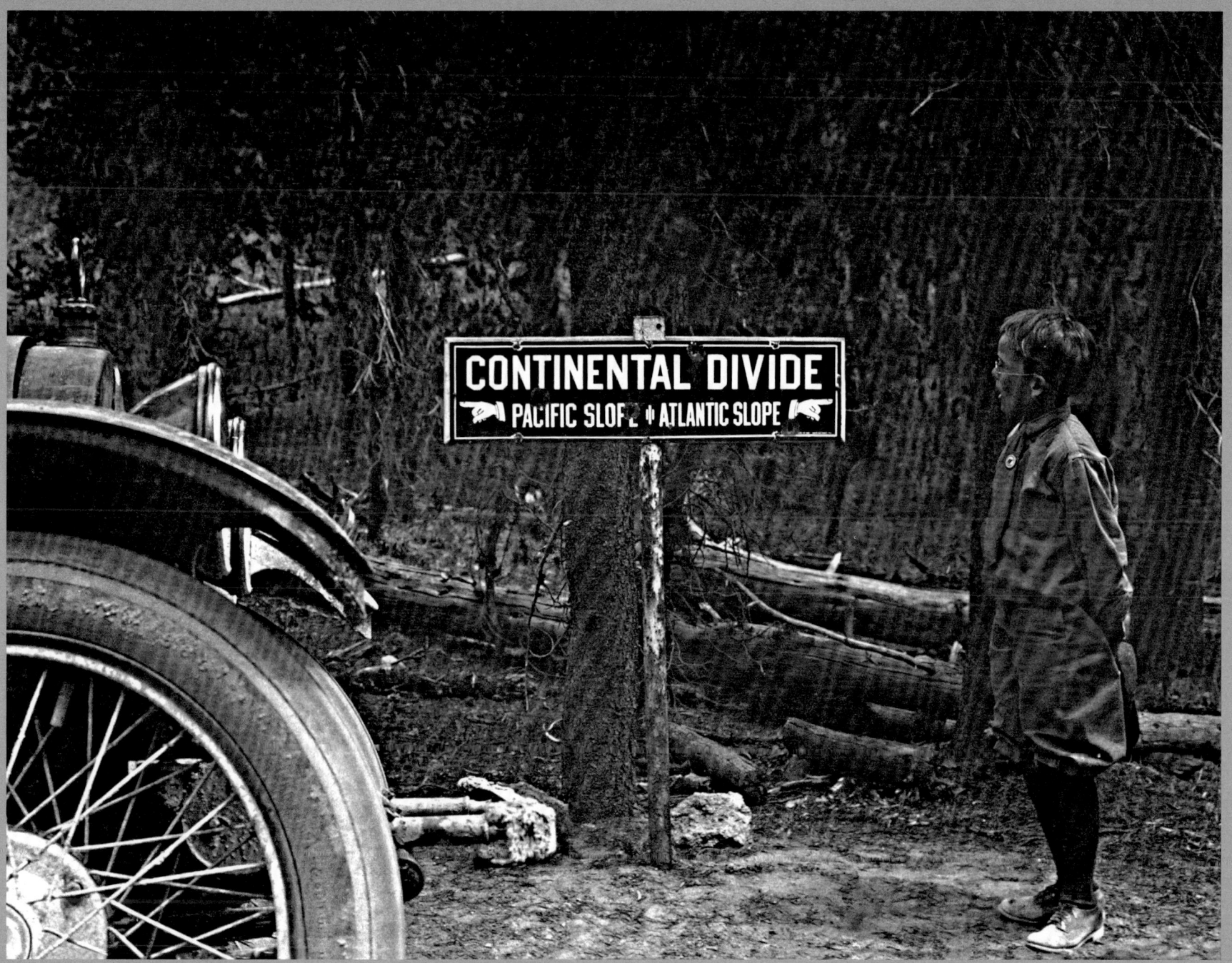

Walter Spallholz stands beside a Yellowstone National Park sign marking the Continental Divide in Wyoming. From this point, water and snowmelt to the left of the sign flow towards the Pacific Ocean and to the right of the sign towards the Mississippi River and the Gulf of Mexico. The sign is peppered with bullet holes.

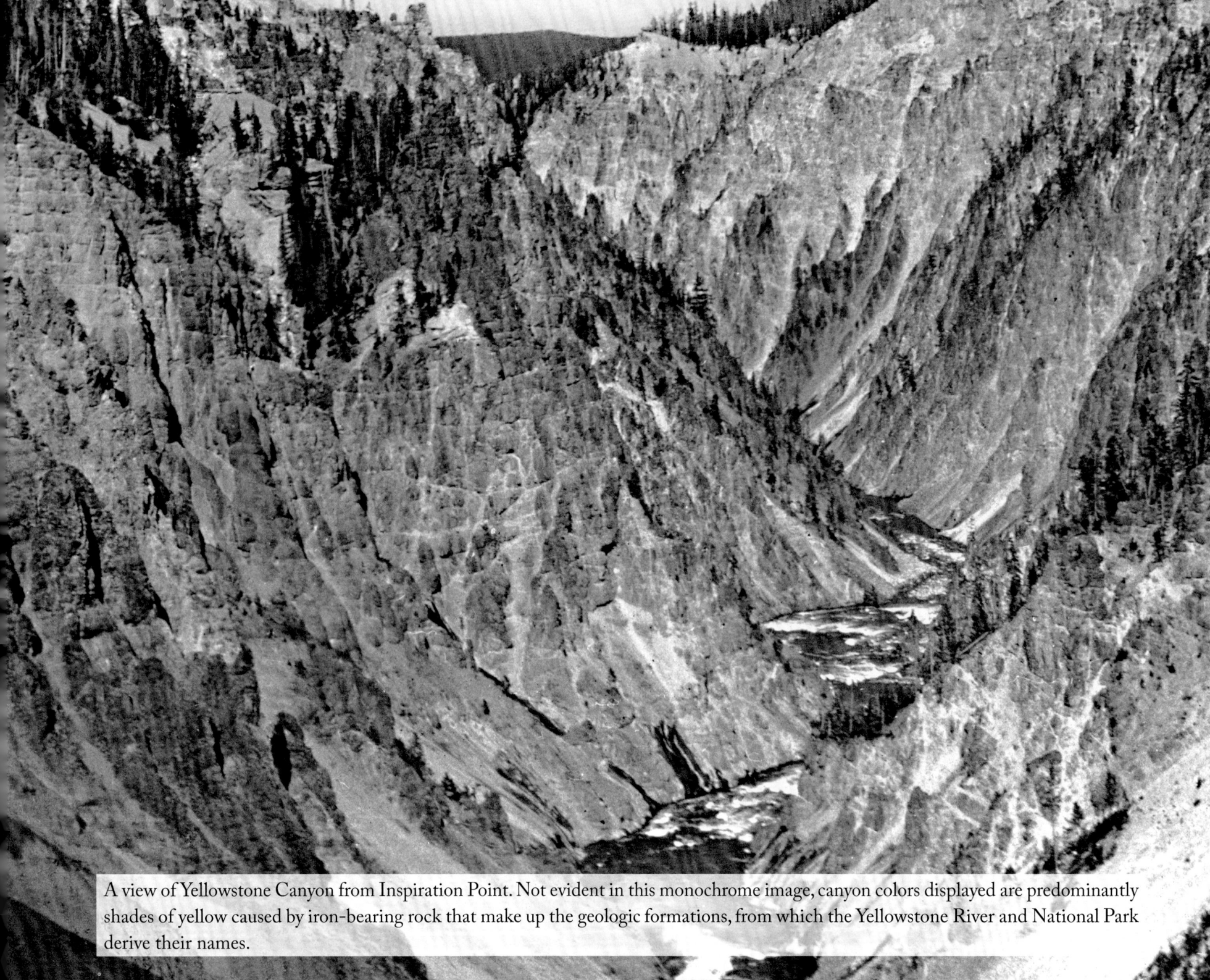

A view of Yellowstone Canyon from Inspiration Point. Not evident in this monochrome image, canyon colors displayed are predominantly shades of yellow caused by iron-bearing rock that make up the geologic formations, from which the Yellowstone River and National Park derive their names.

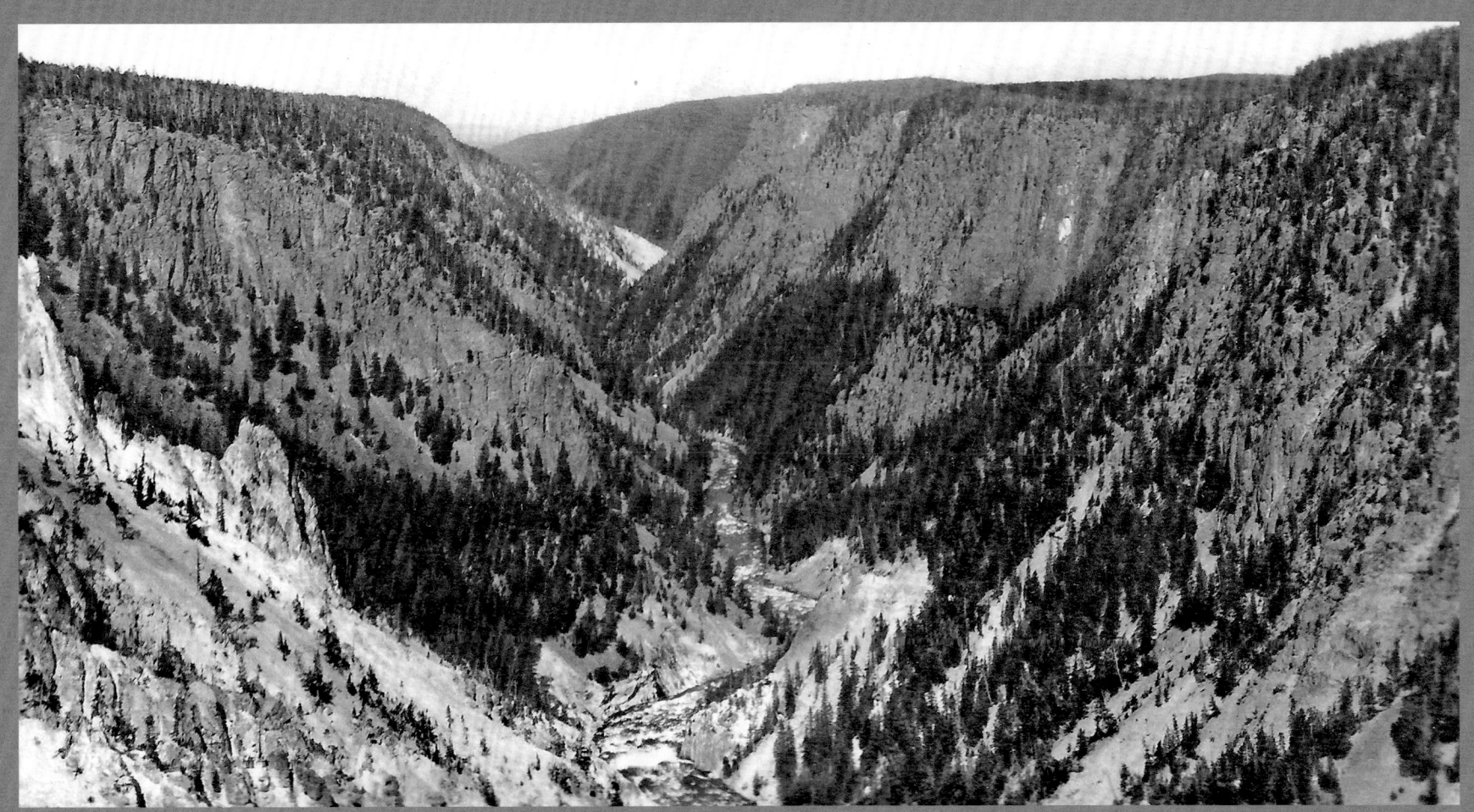

Grand Canyon of Yellowstone from Grand View Point.

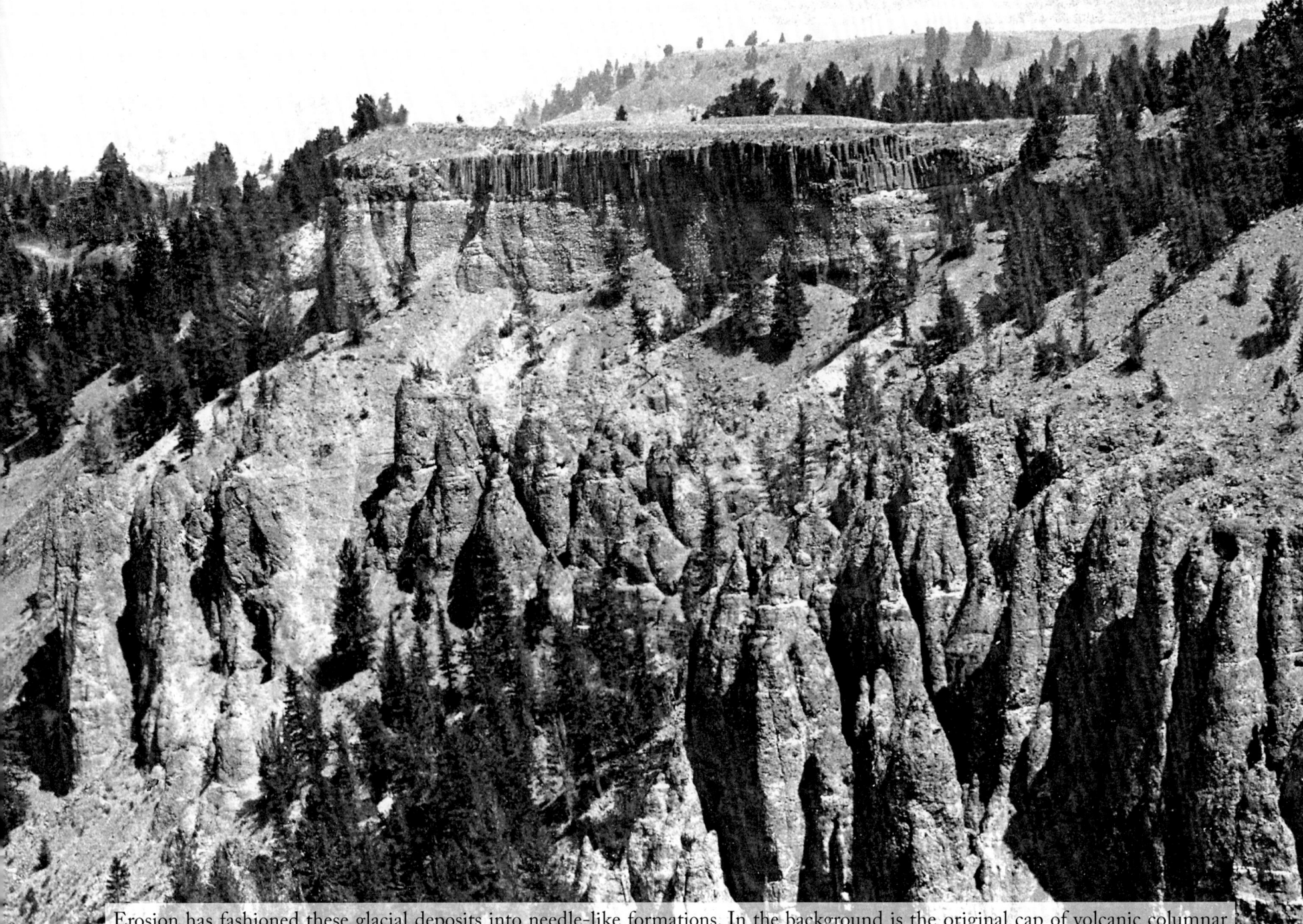

Erosion has fashioned these glacial deposits into needle-like formations. In the background is the original cap of volcanic columnar basalt about twenty-five feet thick. Yellowstone National Park sits atop a super volcano whose hot magma below provides heat for the thermal activity at the surface.

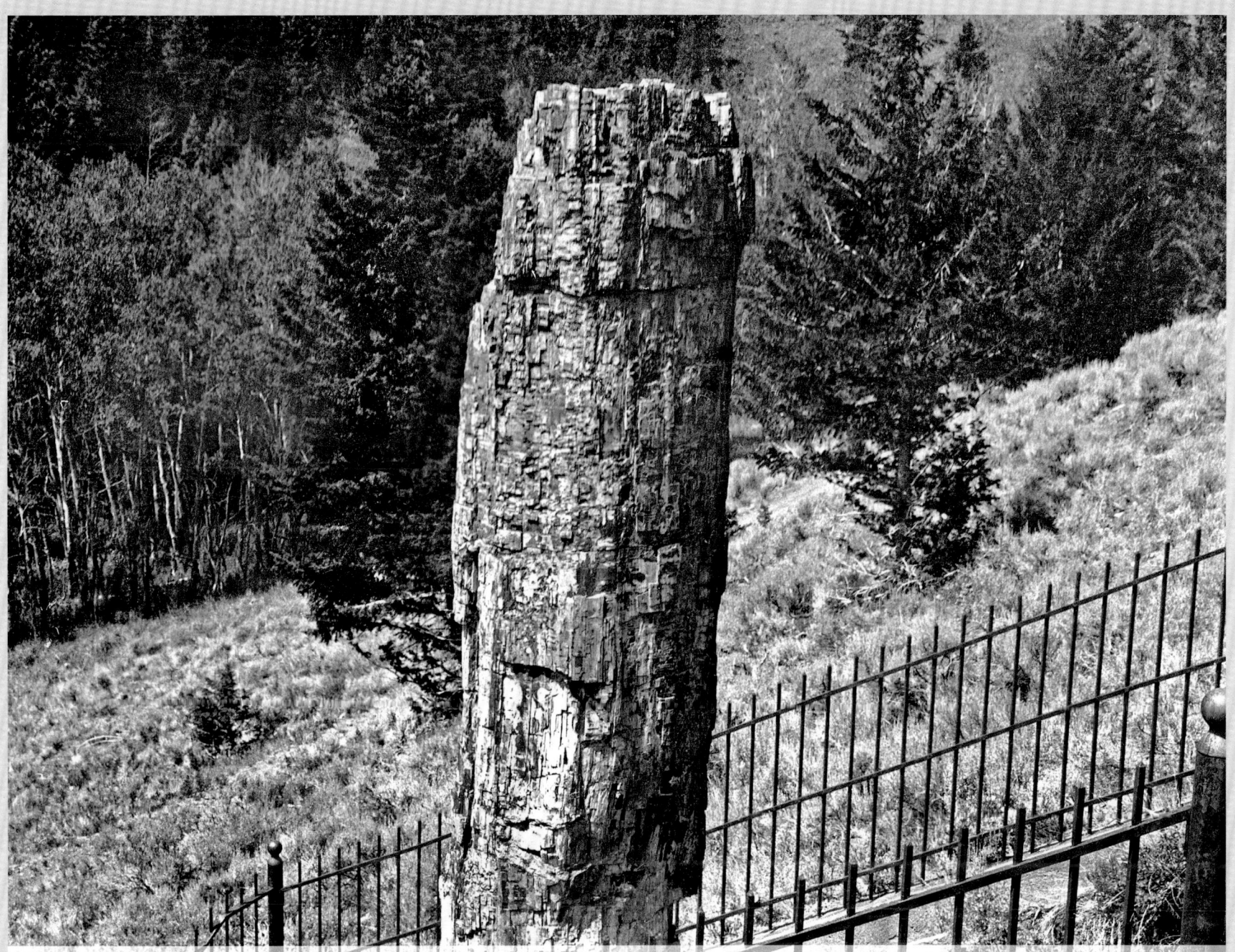

The remains of a fossilized redwood tree in the Petrified Forest section of Yellowstone National Park. Many of the trees here remained upright, standing straight as the day they were buried. This specimen still stands where it is seen here, surrounded by the iron fence.

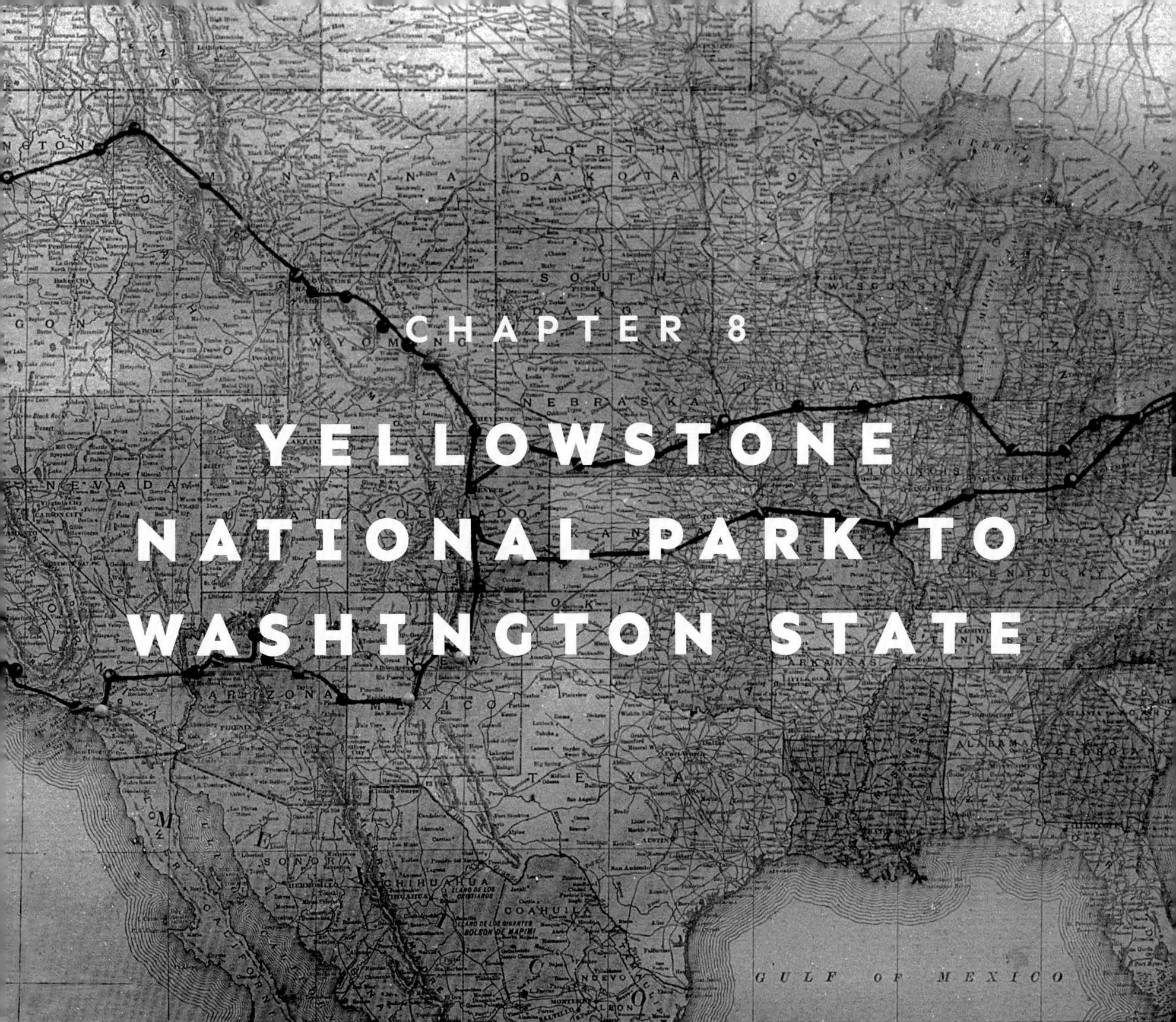

CHAPTER 8

YELLOWSTONE NATIONAL PARK TO WASHINGTON STATE

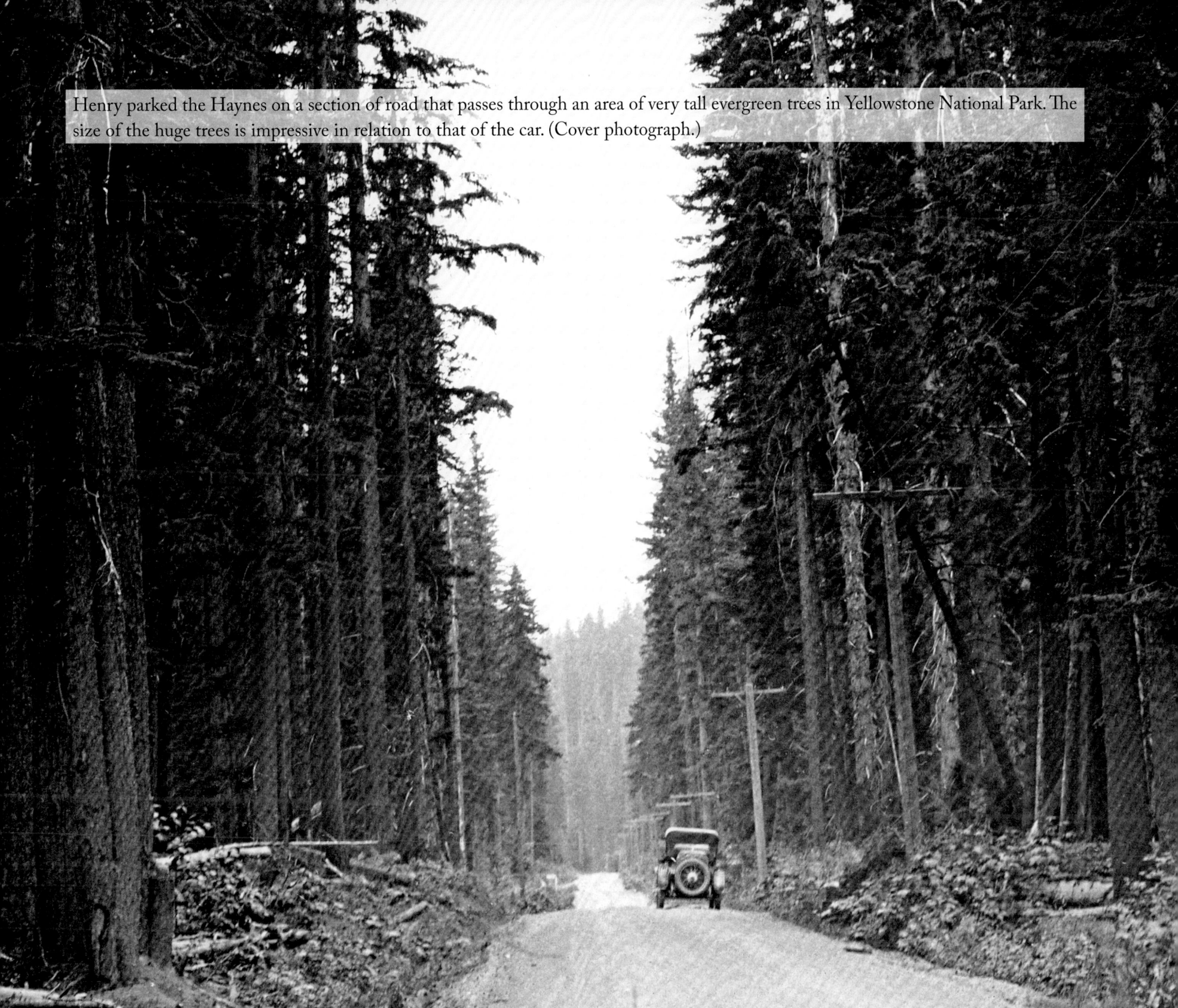

Henry parked the Haynes on a section of road that passes through an area of very tall evergreen trees in Yellowstone National Park. The size of the huge trees is impressive in relation to that of the car. (Cover photograph.)

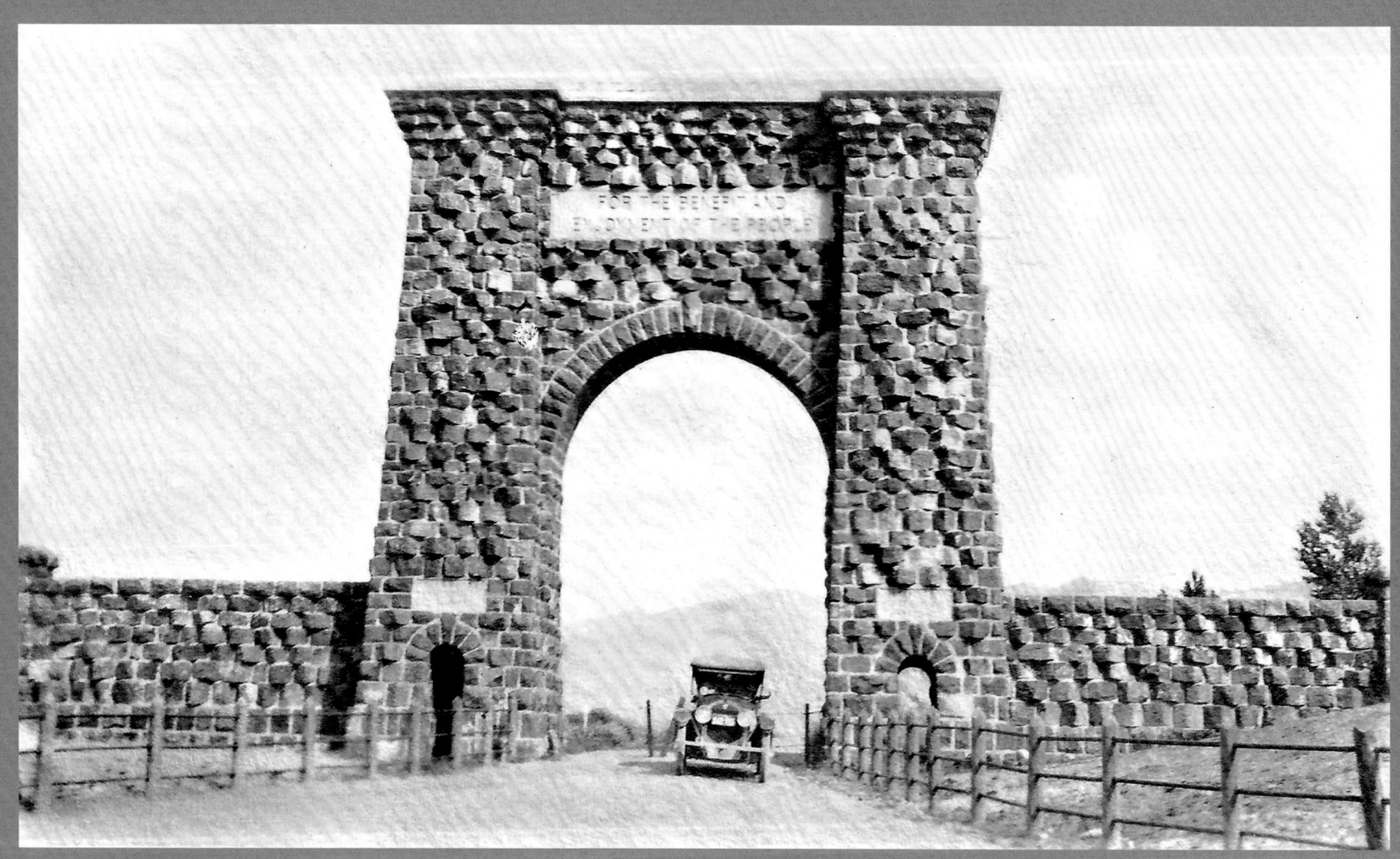

The Roosevelt Arch at Yellowstone's north entrance in Gardiner, Montana, is a rustic triumphal arch gate completed in 1903 in honor of President Theodore Roosevelt. The 52-foot-tall structure bears the inscription "FOR THE BENEFIT AND ENJOYMENT OF THE PEOPLE." At this point the Spallholz family is roughly 2,200 miles from home.

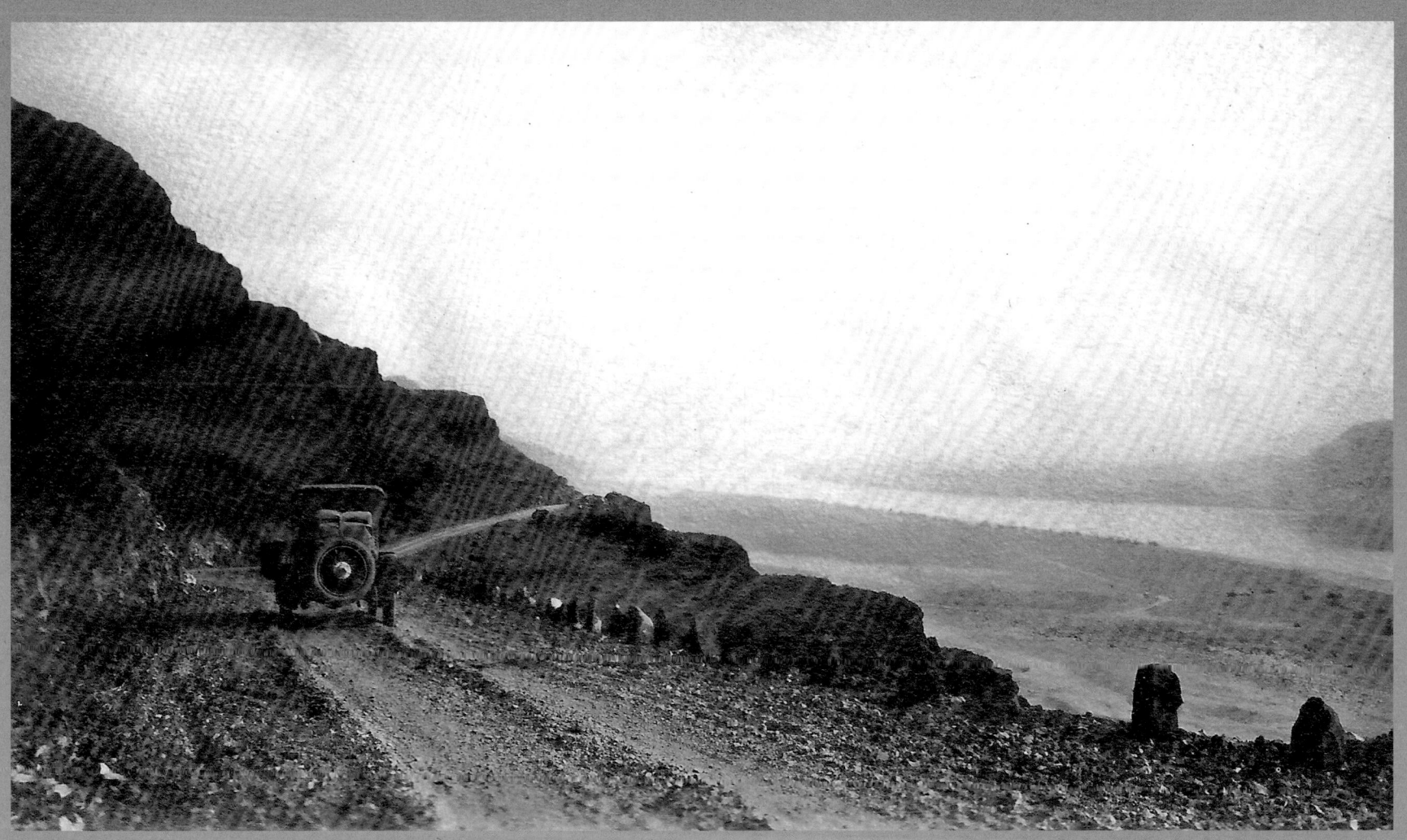

The Haynes sits on the road that winds along the east side of the Columbia River. The view is facing south toward Vantage, Washington, two miles away where the Spallholz family crossed the river by ferry. The first highway bridge at Vantage was constructed in 1927.

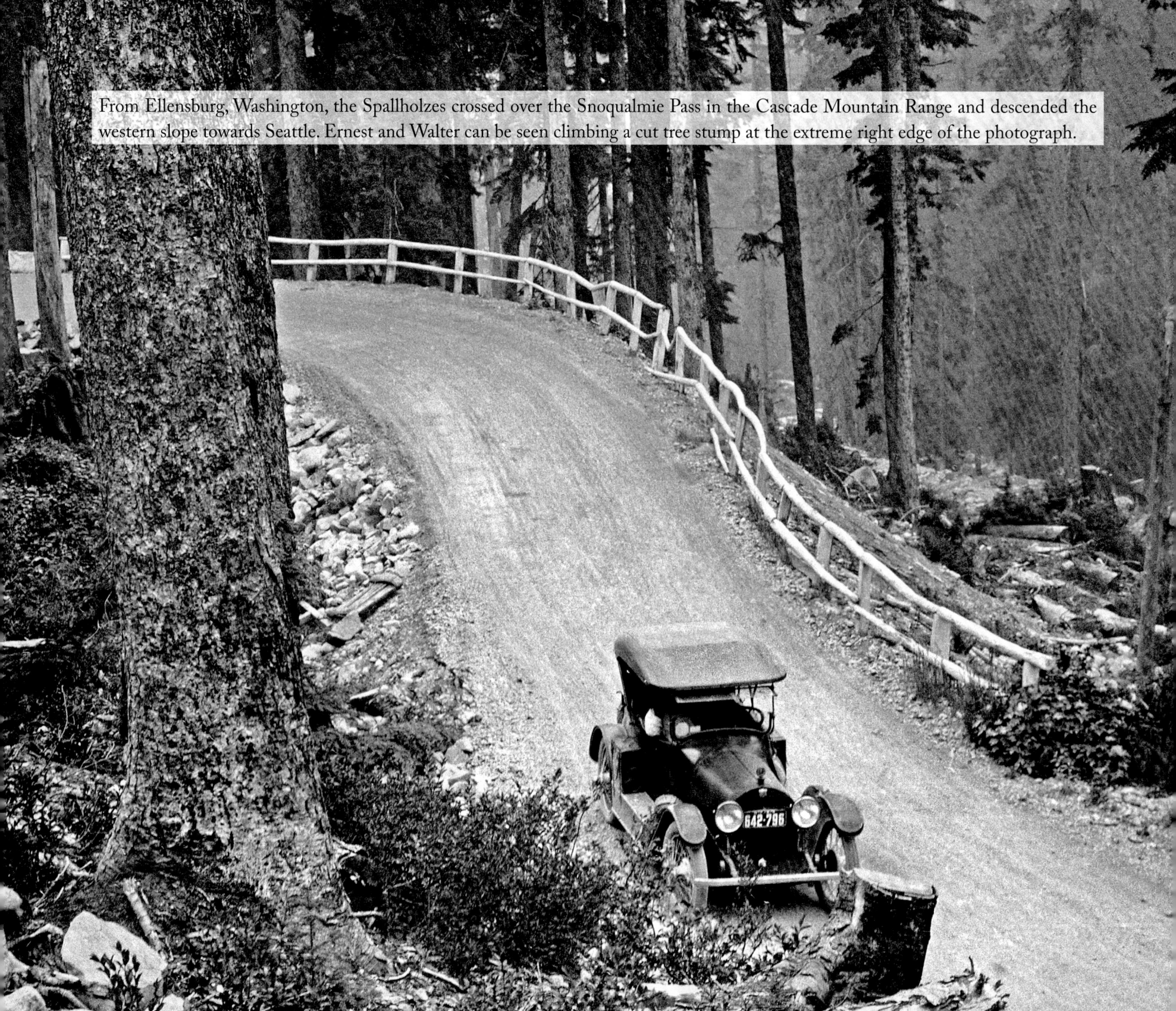

From Ellensburg, Washington, the Spallholzes crossed over the Snoqualmie Pass in the Cascade Mountain Range and descended the western slope towards Seattle. Ernest and Walter can be seen climbing a cut tree stump at the extreme right edge of the photograph.

CHAPTER 9

WASHINGTON STATE: MOUNT RAINIER NATIONAL PARK

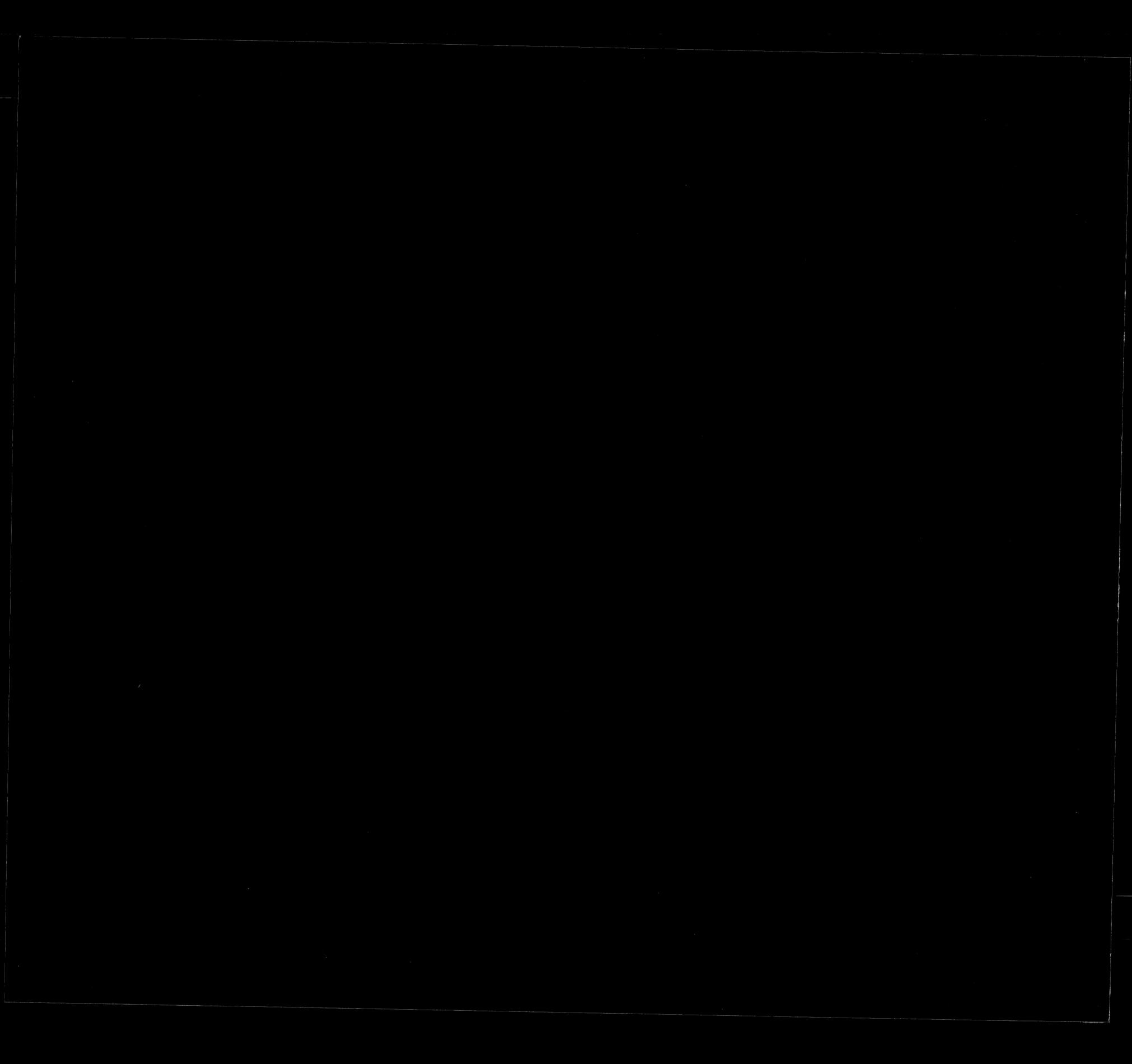

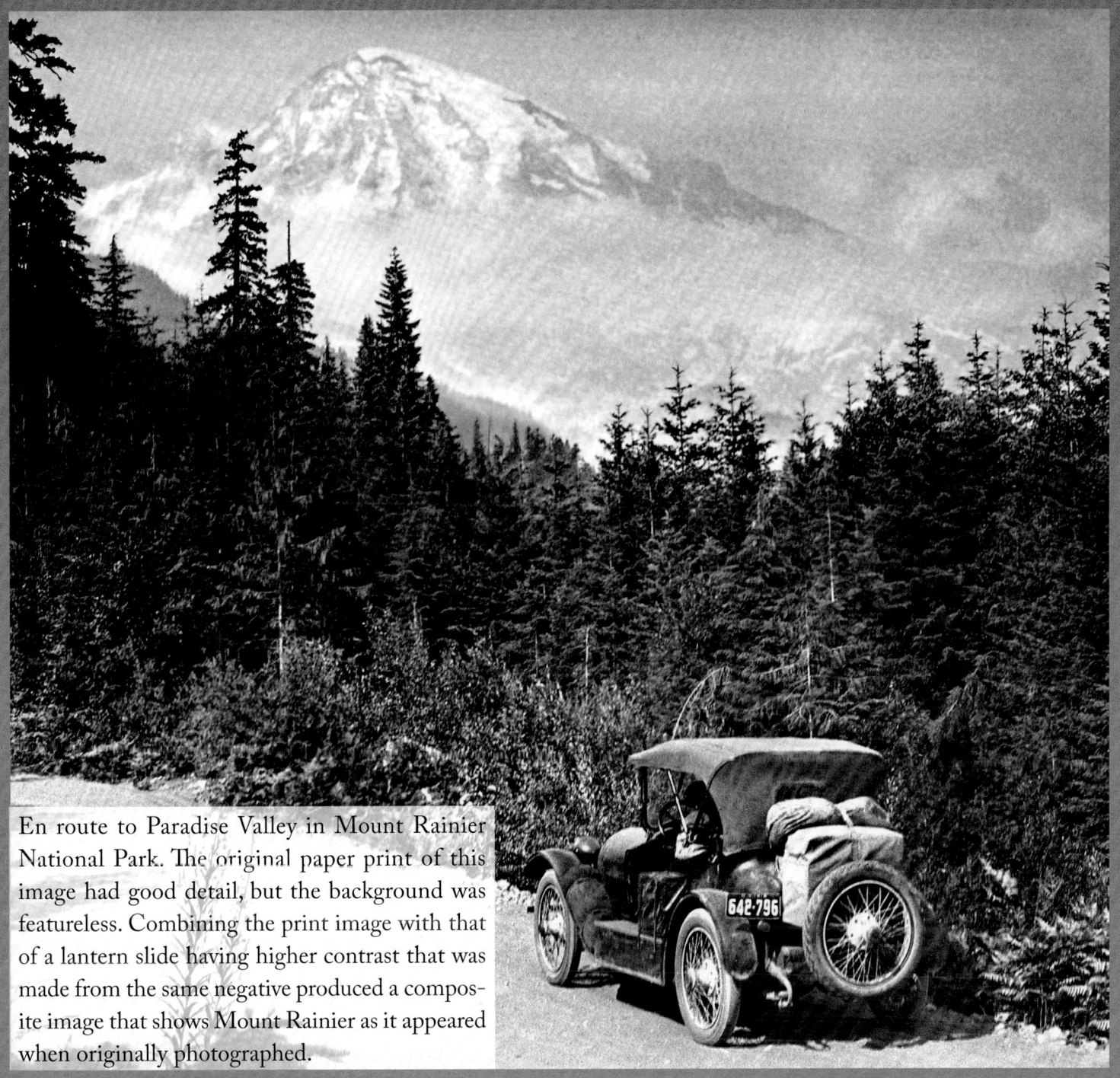

En route to Paradise Valley in Mount Rainier National Park. The original paper print of this image had good detail, but the background was featureless. Combining the print image with that of a lantern slide having higher contrast that was made from the same negative produced a composite image that shows Mount Rainier as it appeared when originally photographed.

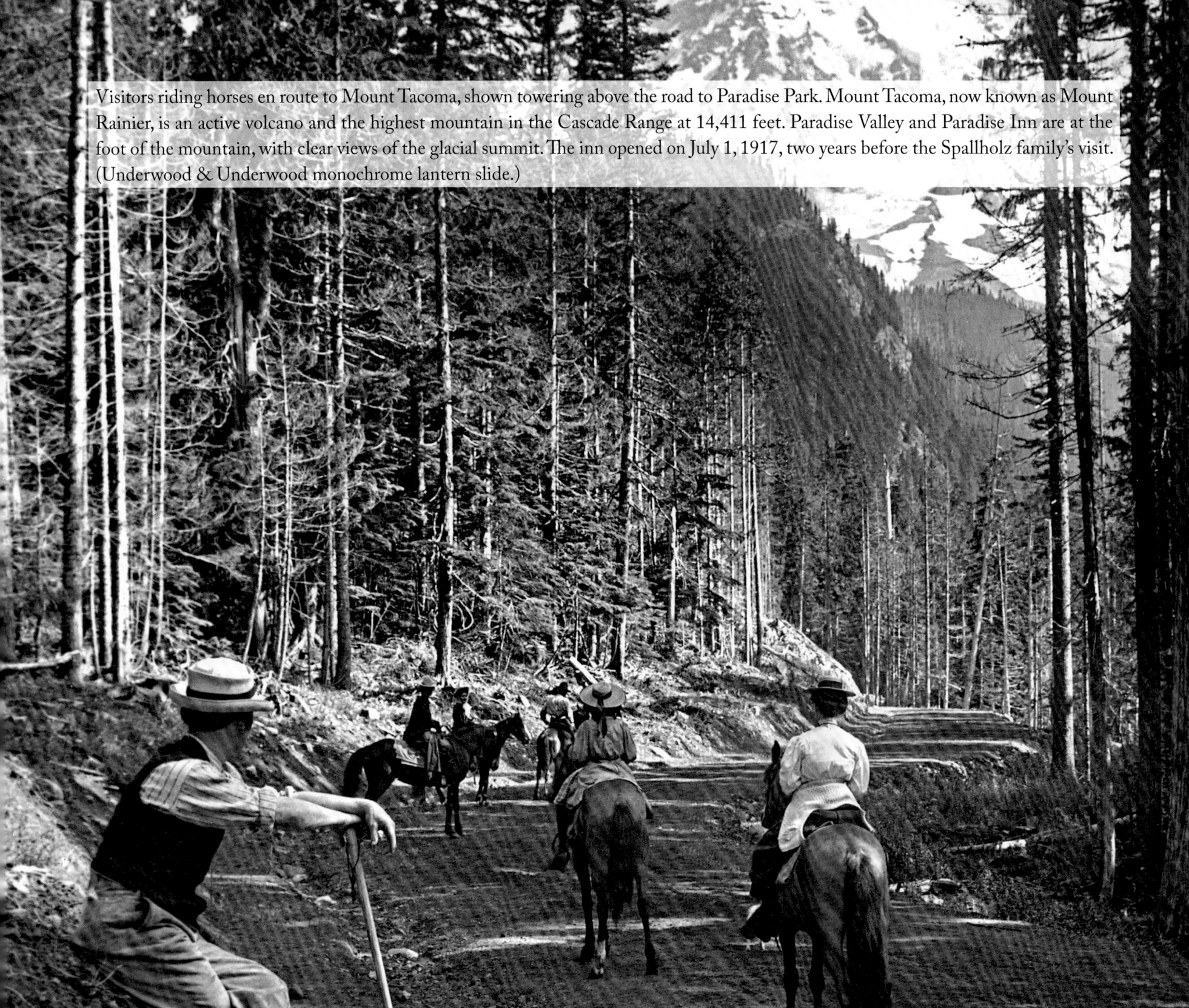

Visitors riding horses en route to Mount Tacoma, shown towering above the road to Paradise Park. Mount Tacoma, now known as Mount Rainier, is an active volcano and the highest mountain in the Cascade Range at 14,411 feet. Paradise Valley and Paradise Inn are at the foot of the mountain, with clear views of the glacial summit. The inn opened on July 1, 1917, two years before the Spallholz family's visit. (Underwood & Underwood monochrome lantern slide.)

Two automobiles motor through a grove of Douglas fir trees on the road to Mount Rainier. On the drive to Paradise Valley, the Spallholz family passed through similar forests of fir, hemlock, and red cedar, many of which exceeded a height of 200 feet. (Asahel Curtis hand colored lantern slide rendered in black and white.)

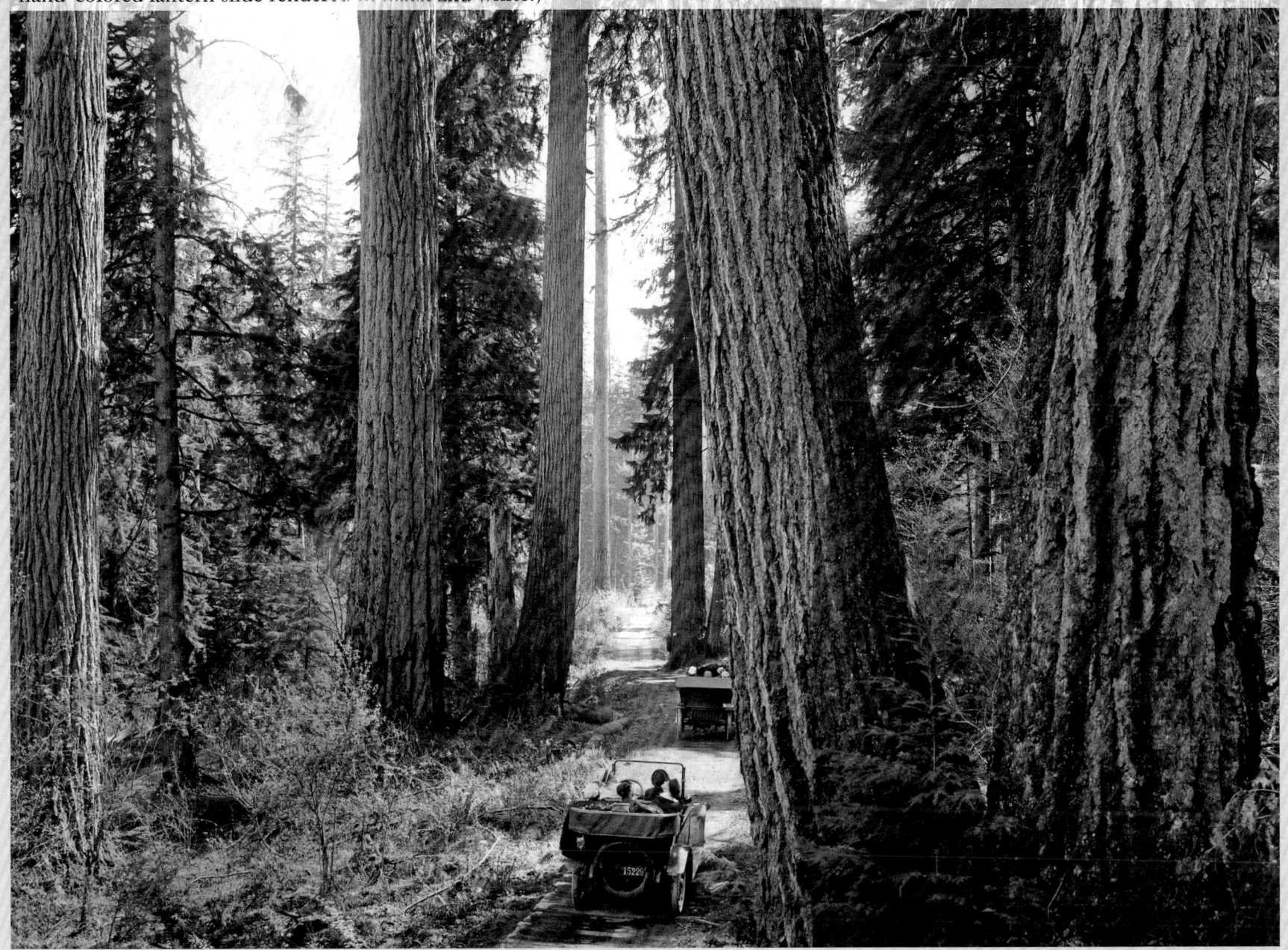

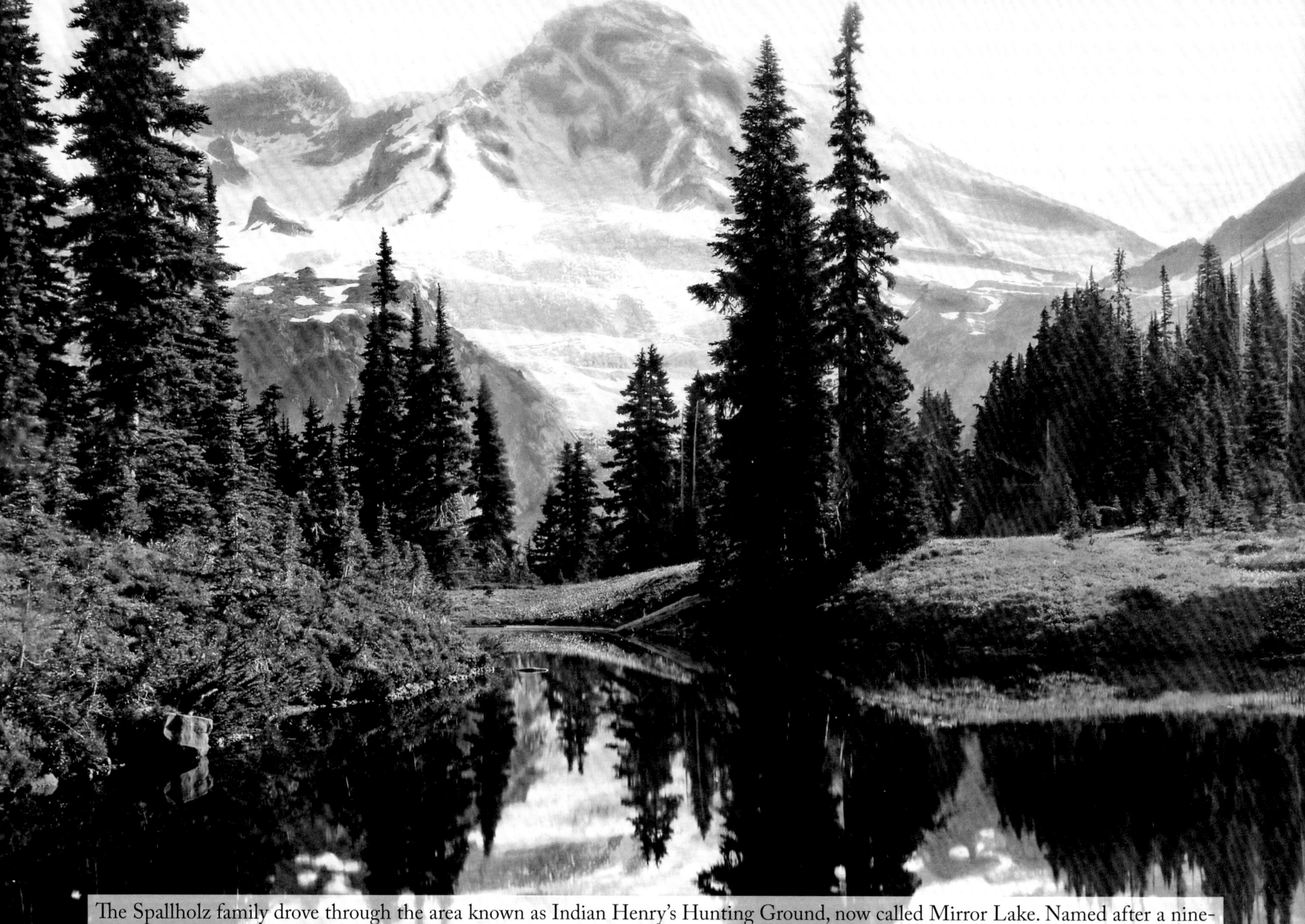

The Spallholz family drove through the area known as Indian Henry's Hunting Ground, now called Mirror Lake. Named after a nineteenth century guide in the Mount Rainier area, Indian Henry's Hunting Ground is one of the most popular hiking destinations in the park. Here the placid lake reflects Mount Rainier and its immediate surroundings. (Asahel Curtis hand-colored lantern slide rendered in black and white.)

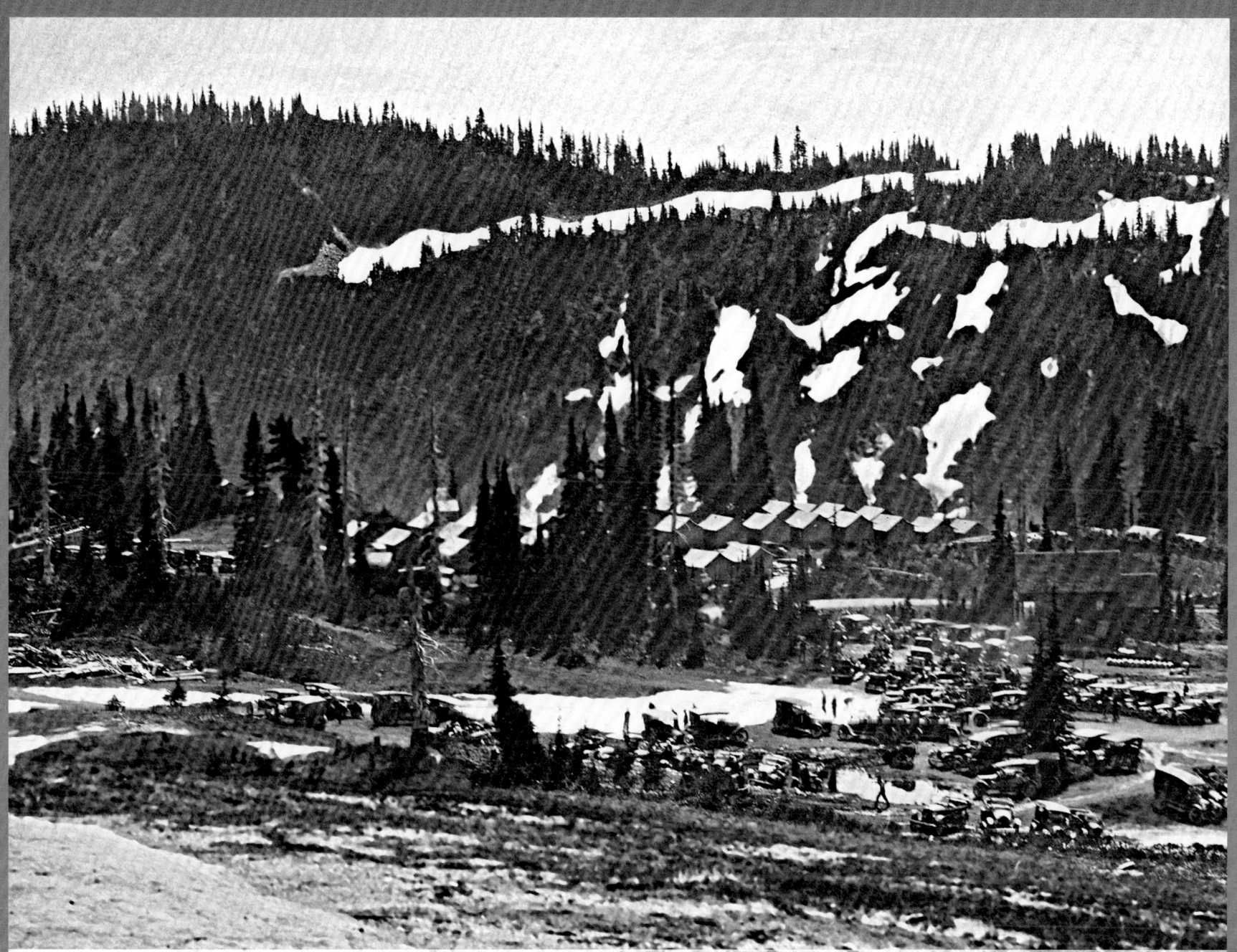

A partial view of Paradise Valley at sunrise. Paradise Inn is on the far left, cottages are in the center, and a full parking lot appears on the right.

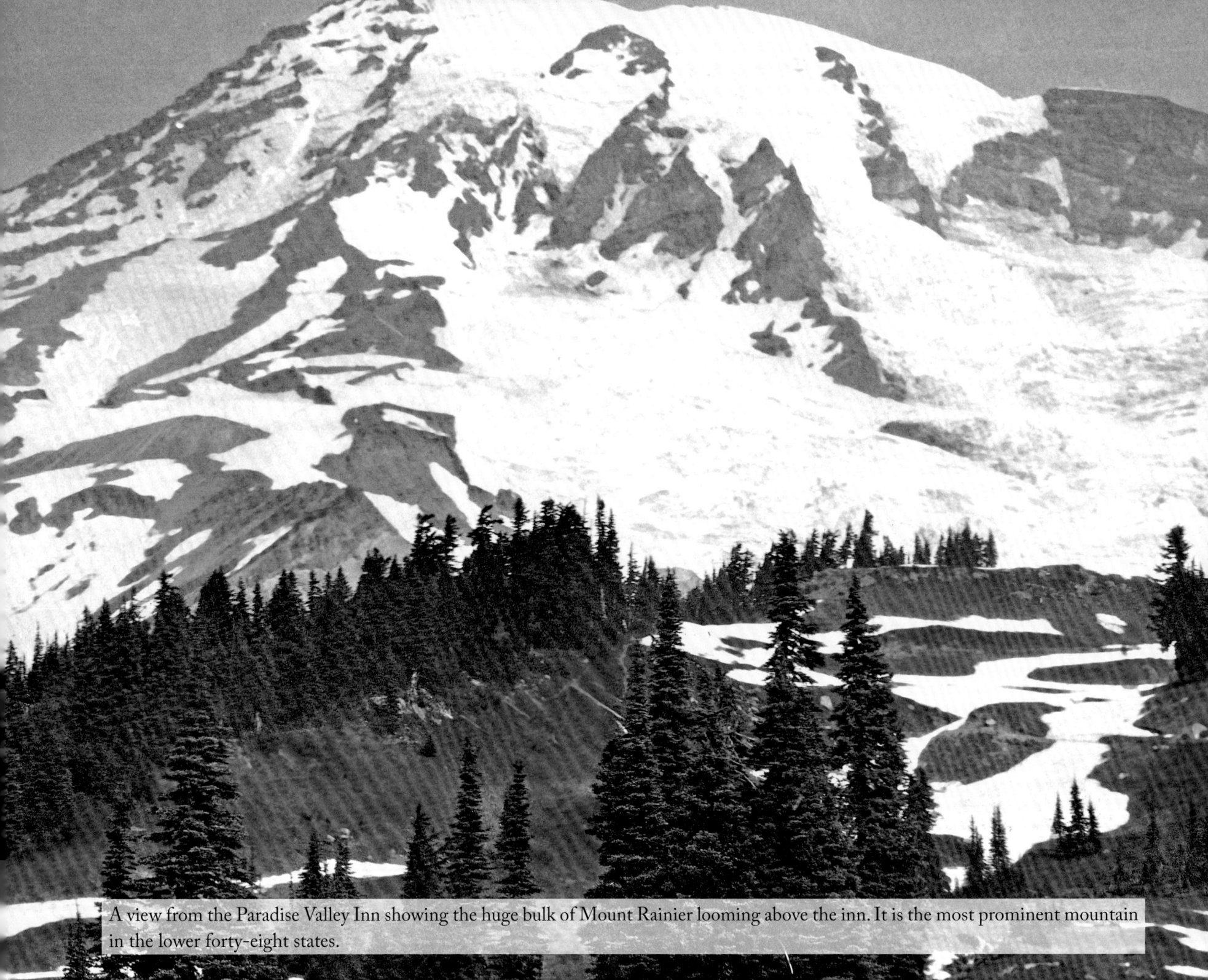

A view from the Paradise Valley Inn showing the huge bulk of Mount Rainier looming above the inn. It is the most prominent mountain in the lower forty-eight states.

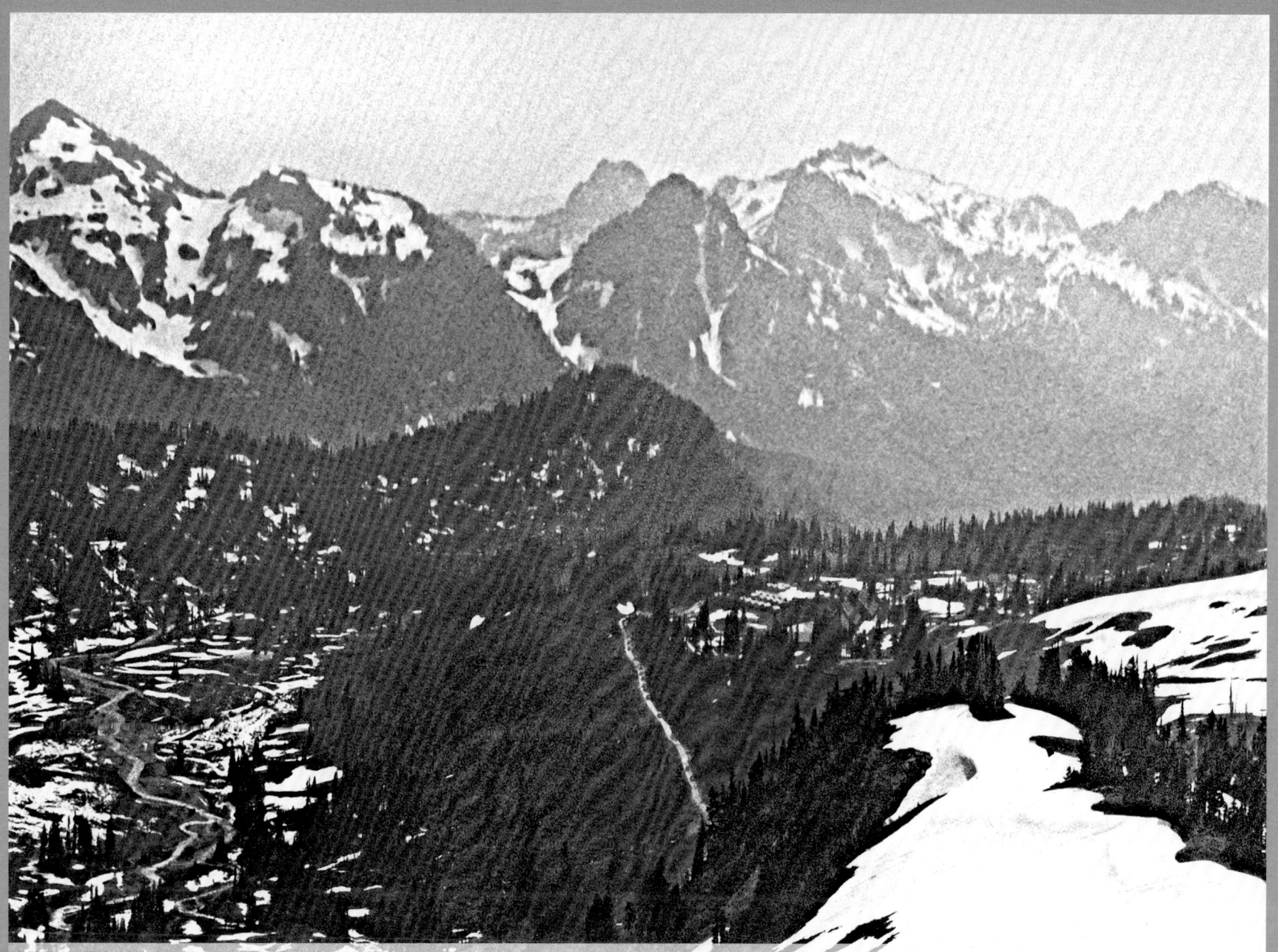

View of the Tatoosh Mountain Range, with Paradise Valley and the Paradise Inn directly below right center. The road into Paradise Valley is seen in the center as a narrow strip leading up to the inn. Travel on the road was seasonal: by horseback in winter, by automobile in the warmer snow-free seasons of the year. The narrow road allowed only single-file automobile travel in one direction at any given time.

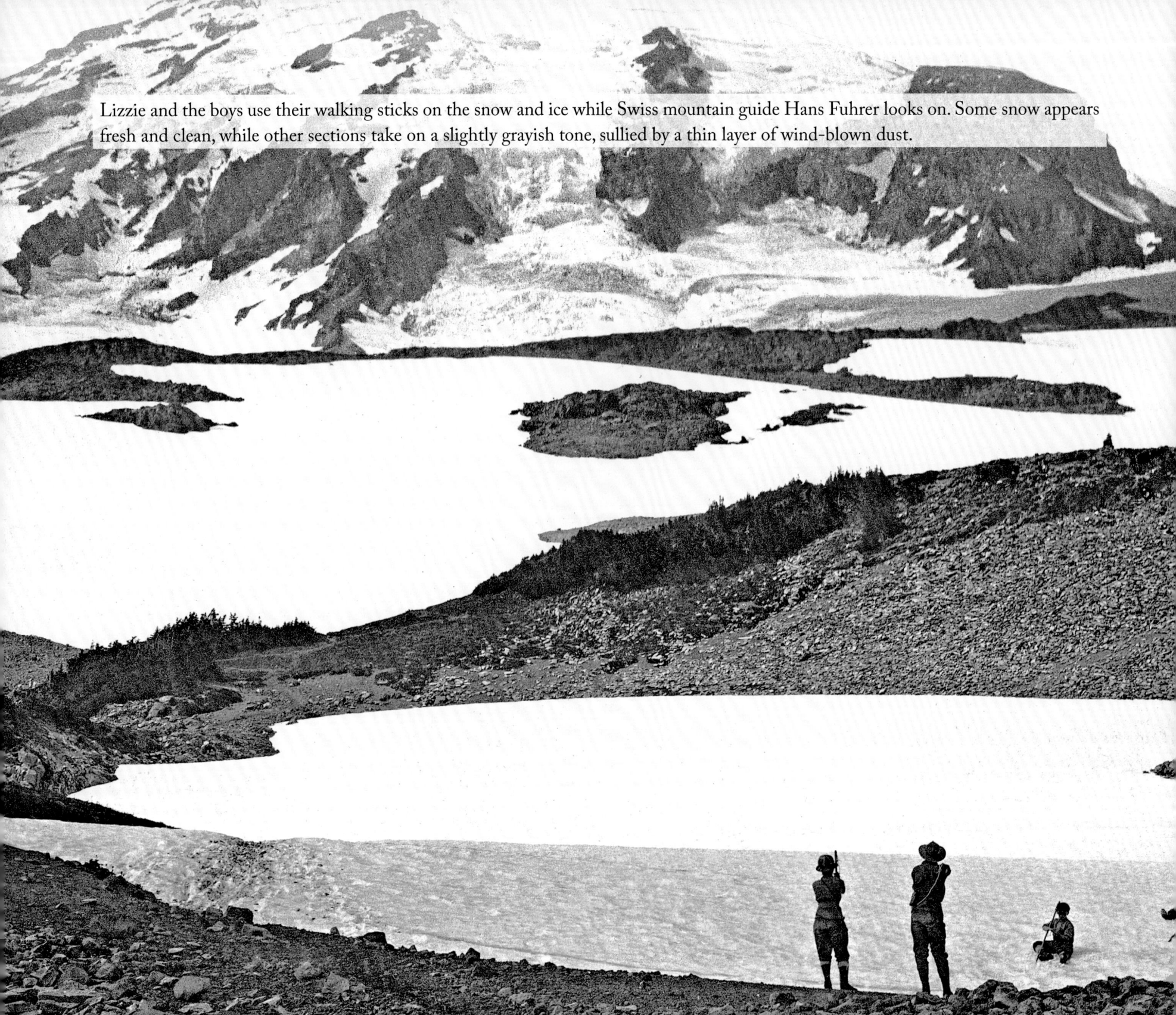

Lizzie and the boys use their walking sticks on the snow and ice while Swiss mountain guide Hans Fuhrer looks on. Some snow appears fresh and clean, while other sections take on a slightly grayish tone, sullied by a thin layer of wind-blown dust.

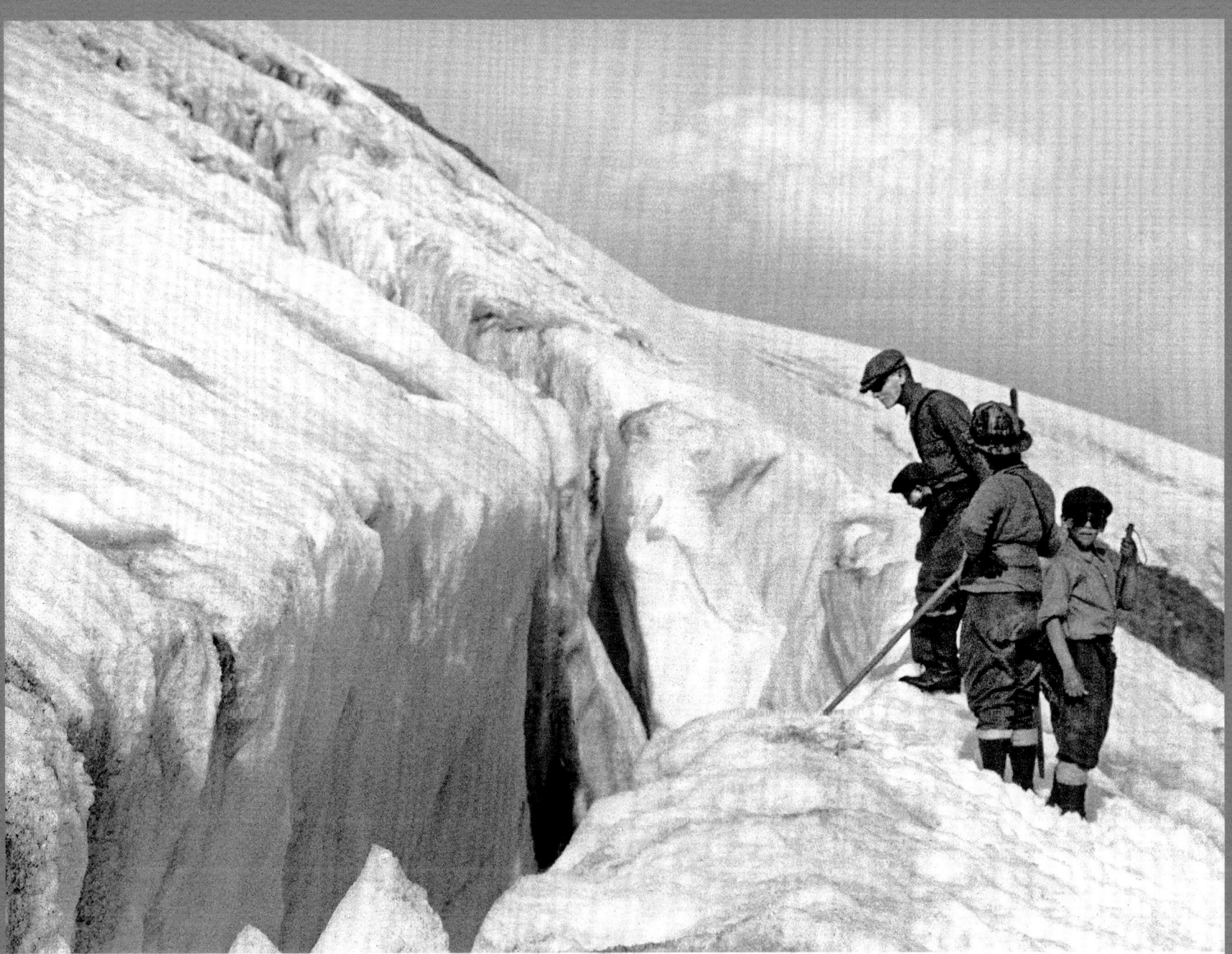

Henry, Lizzie, and the boys stand at the edge of a crevasse on Paradise Glacier, located on the southeast flank of Mount Rainier. The photographer is most likely Hans Fuhrer, their Swiss mountain guide.

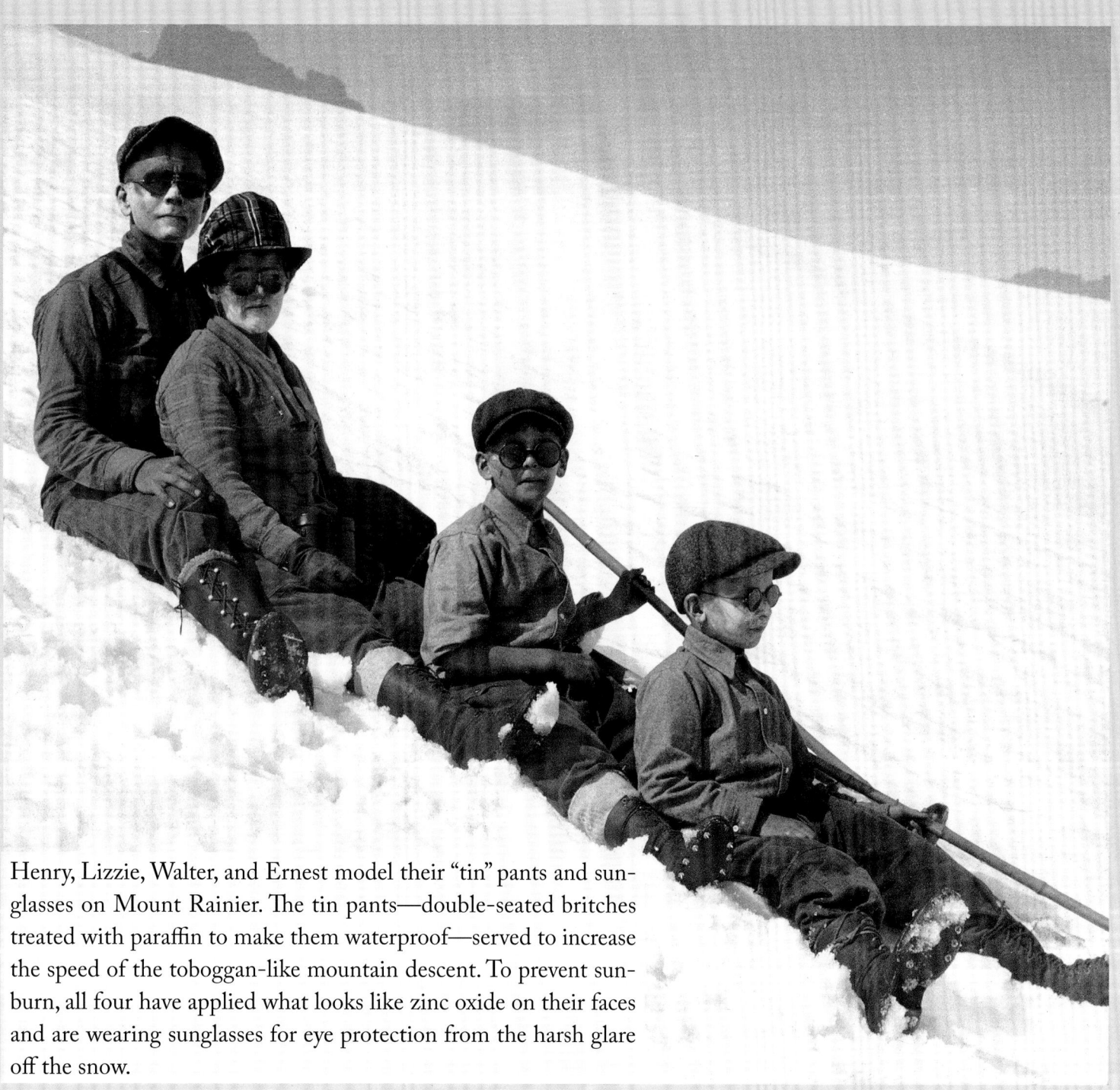

Henry, Lizzie, Walter, and Ernest model their "tin" pants and sunglasses on Mount Rainier. The tin pants—double-seated britches treated with paraffin to make them waterproof—served to increase the speed of the toboggan-like mountain descent. To prevent sunburn, all four have applied what looks like zinc oxide on their faces and are wearing sunglasses for eye protection from the harsh glare off the snow.

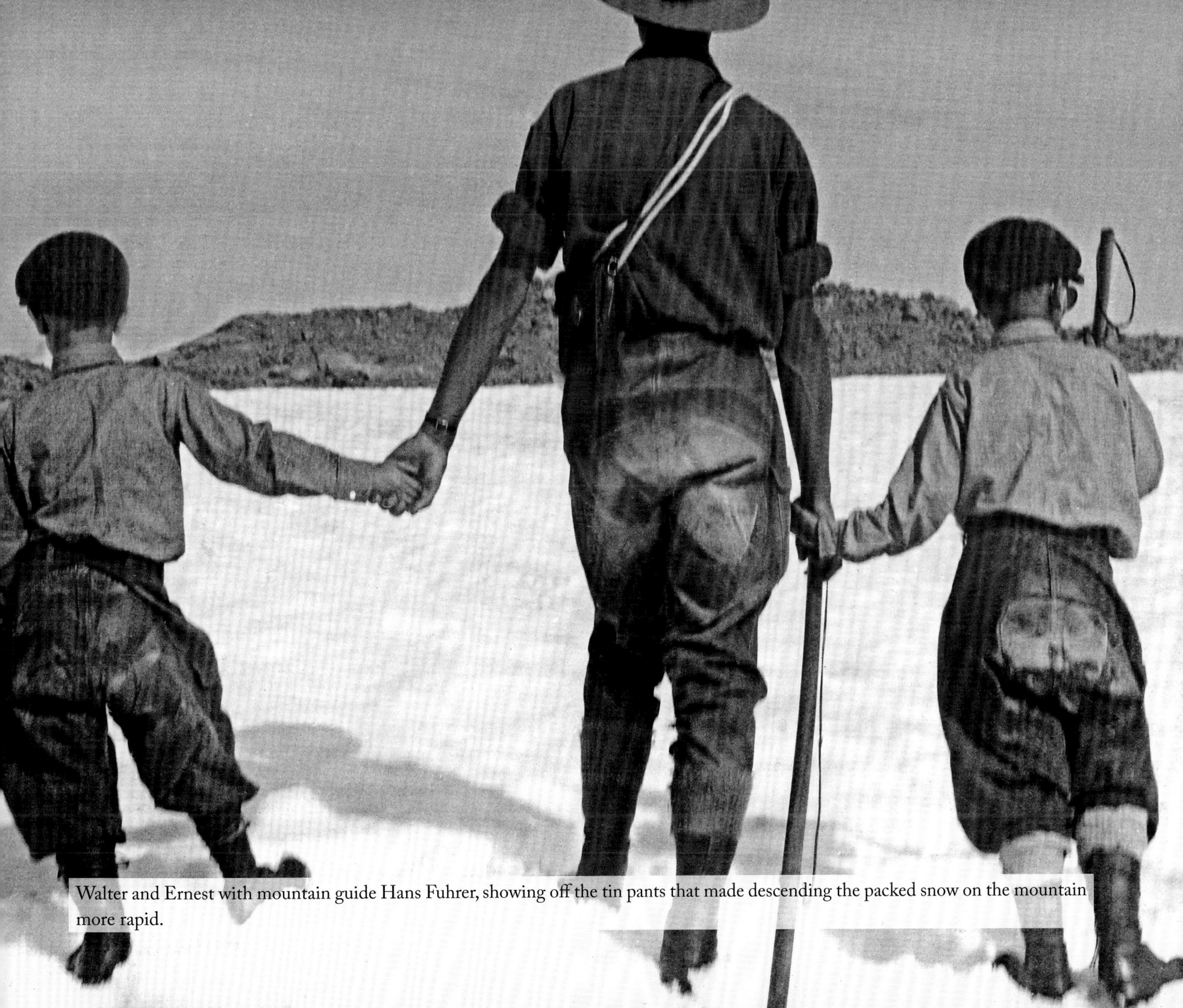

Walter and Ernest with mountain guide Hans Fuhrer, showing off the tin pants that made descending the packed snow on the mountain more rapid.

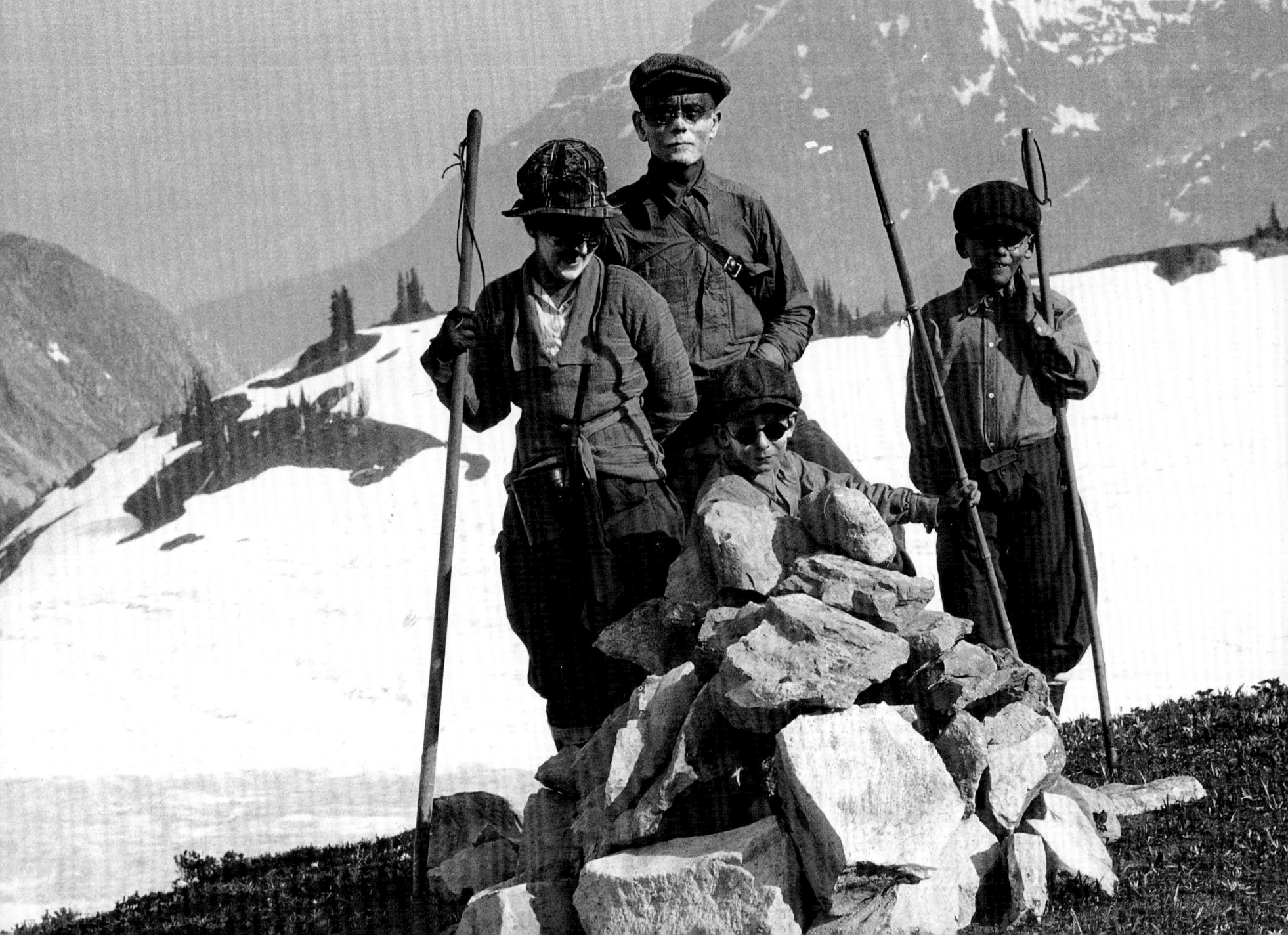

The family stands behind a pile of stones marking the camp from which Hazard Stevens and his climbing companion P. B. Van Trump ascended Mount Rainier in 1870. Sluiskin, their superstitious Indigenous guide, fearful of proceeding farther, waited at this location for the climbers to reappear. Hazard Stevens returned in 1915 to mark this spot.

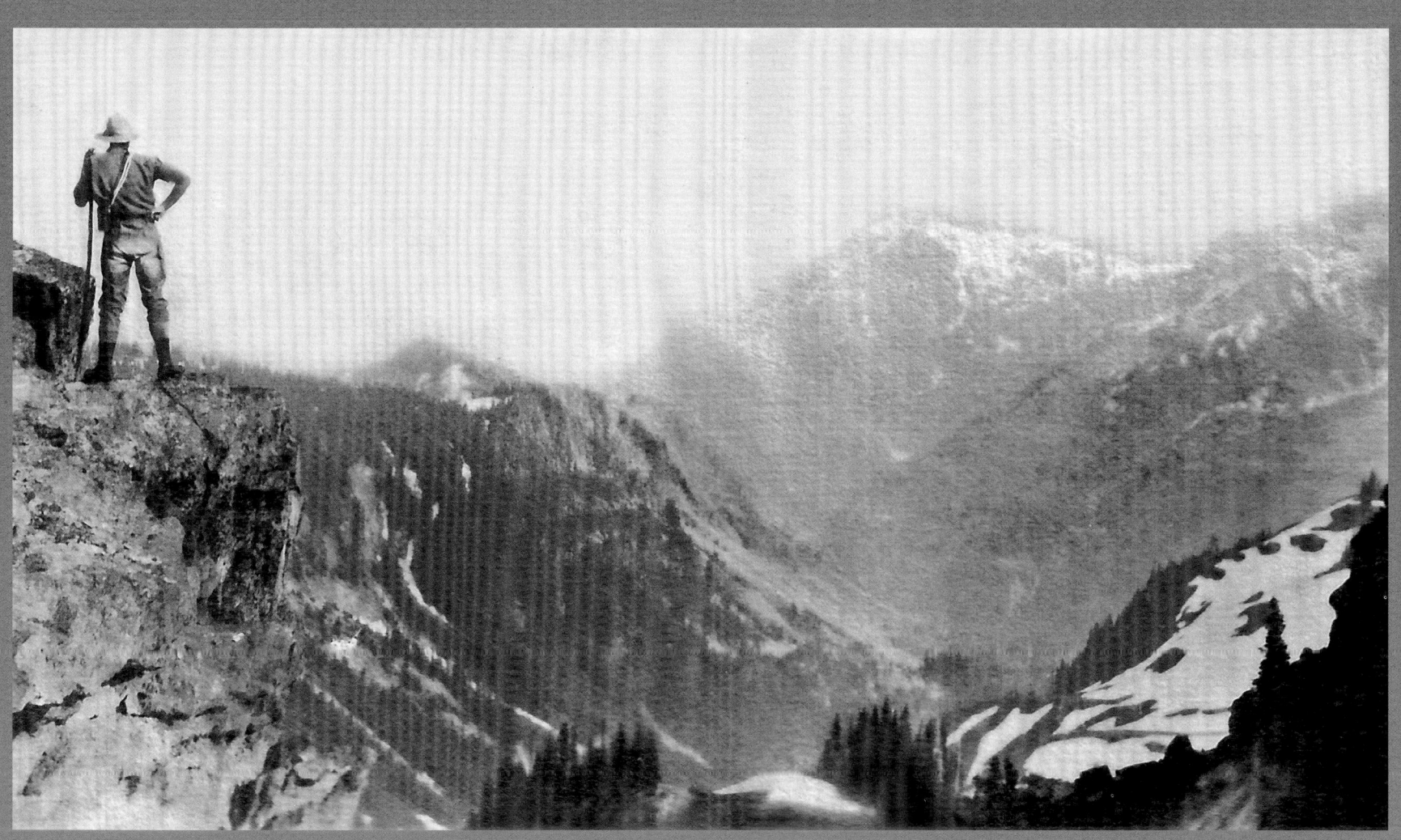

Hans Fuhrer, trail guide for Henry Spallholz, and his climbing companion William Worner of Pennsylvania gaze at the Tatoosh Mountain Range. Located within the bounds of Mount Rainier National Park, the range has twenty-five mountain peaks, each averaging approximately 6,500 feet in elevation. The range can be viewed from many places within Paradise Valley and is a popular wilderness area for hikers.

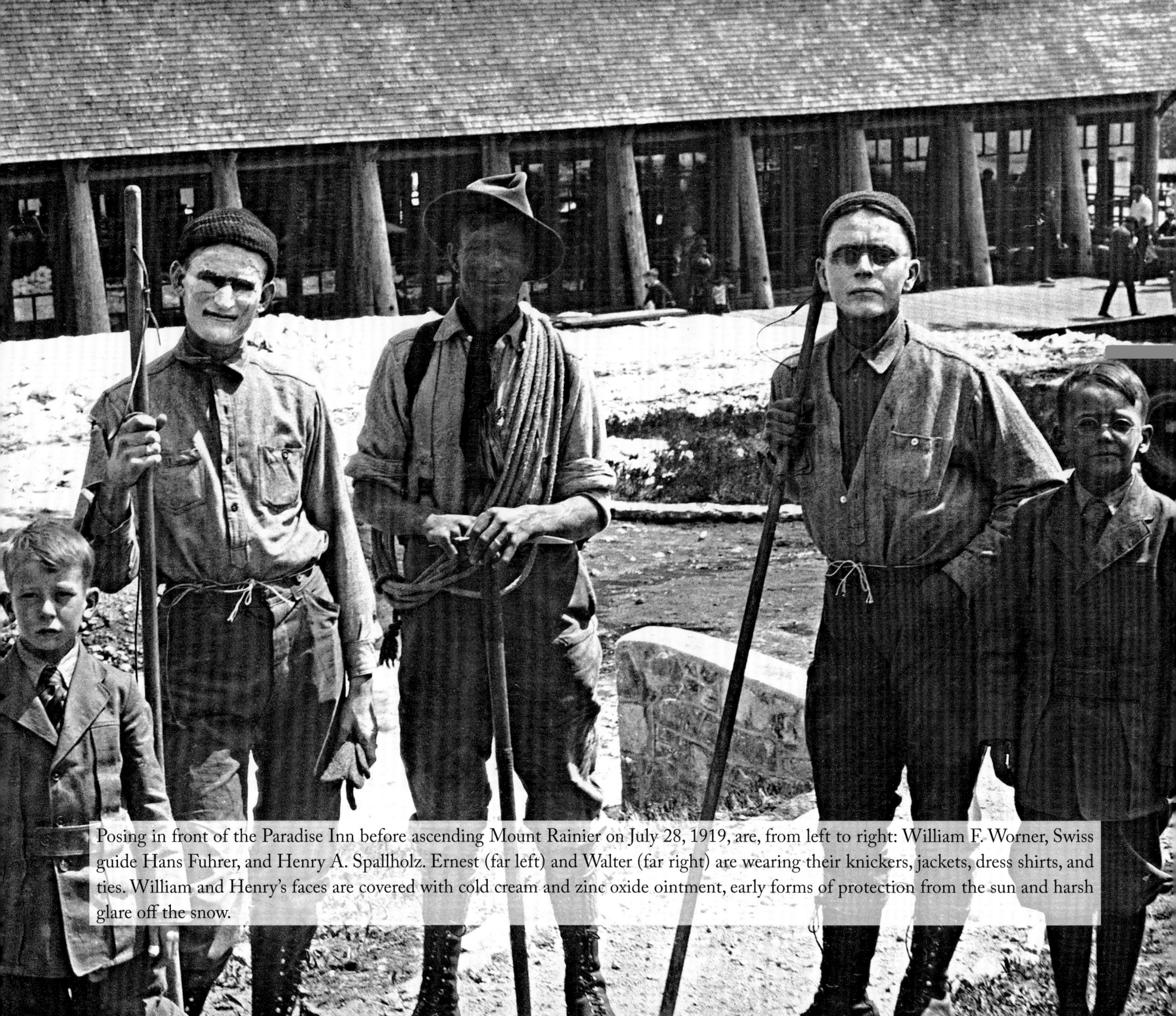

Posing in front of the Paradise Inn before ascending Mount Rainier on July 28, 1919, are, from left to right: William F. Worner, Swiss guide Hans Fuhrer, and Henry A. Spallholz. Ernest (far left) and Walter (far right) are wearing their knickers, jackets, dress shirts, and ties. William and Henry's faces are covered with cold cream and zinc oxide ointment, early forms of protection from the sun and harsh glare off the snow.

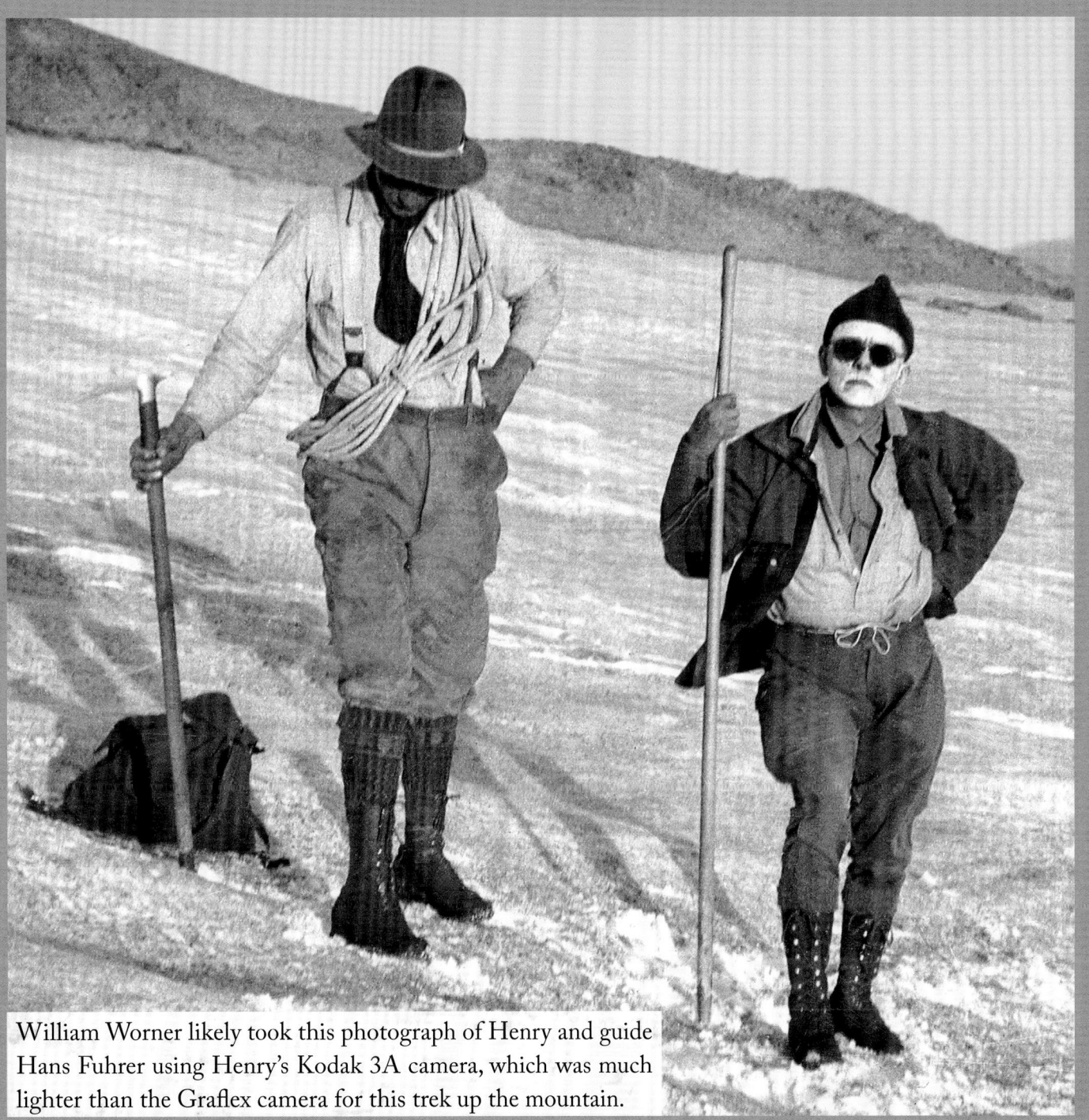

William Worner likely took this photograph of Henry and guide Hans Fuhrer using Henry's Kodak 3A camera, which was much lighter than the Graflex camera for this trek up the mountain.

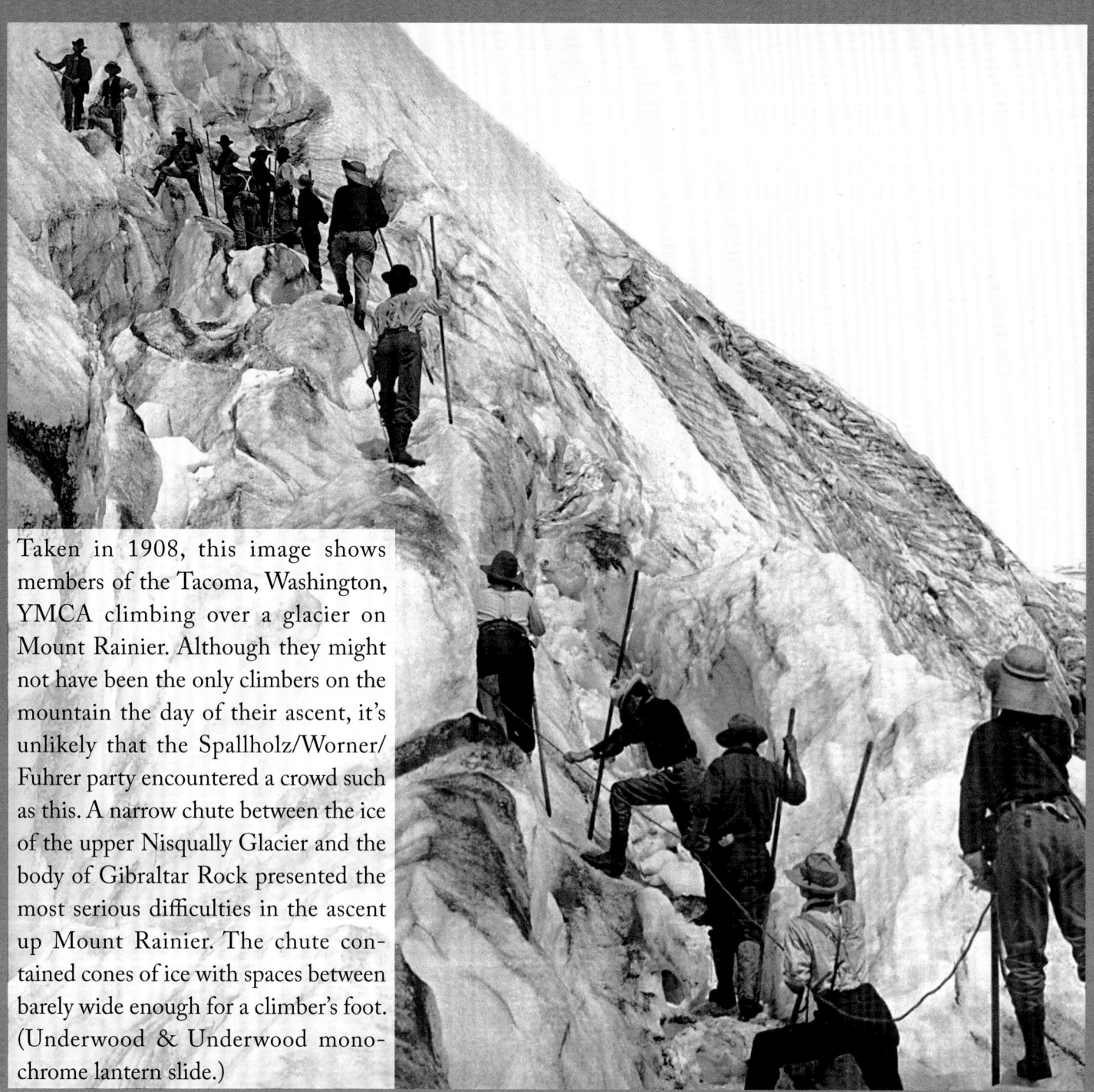

Taken in 1908, this image shows members of the Tacoma, Washington, YMCA climbing over a glacier on Mount Rainier. Although they might not have been the only climbers on the mountain the day of their ascent, it's unlikely that the Spallholz/Worner/Fuhrer party encountered a crowd such as this. A narrow chute between the ice of the upper Nisqually Glacier and the body of Gibraltar Rock presented the most serious difficulties in the ascent up Mount Rainier. The chute contained cones of ice with spaces between barely wide enough for a climber's foot. (Underwood & Underwood monochrome lantern slide.)

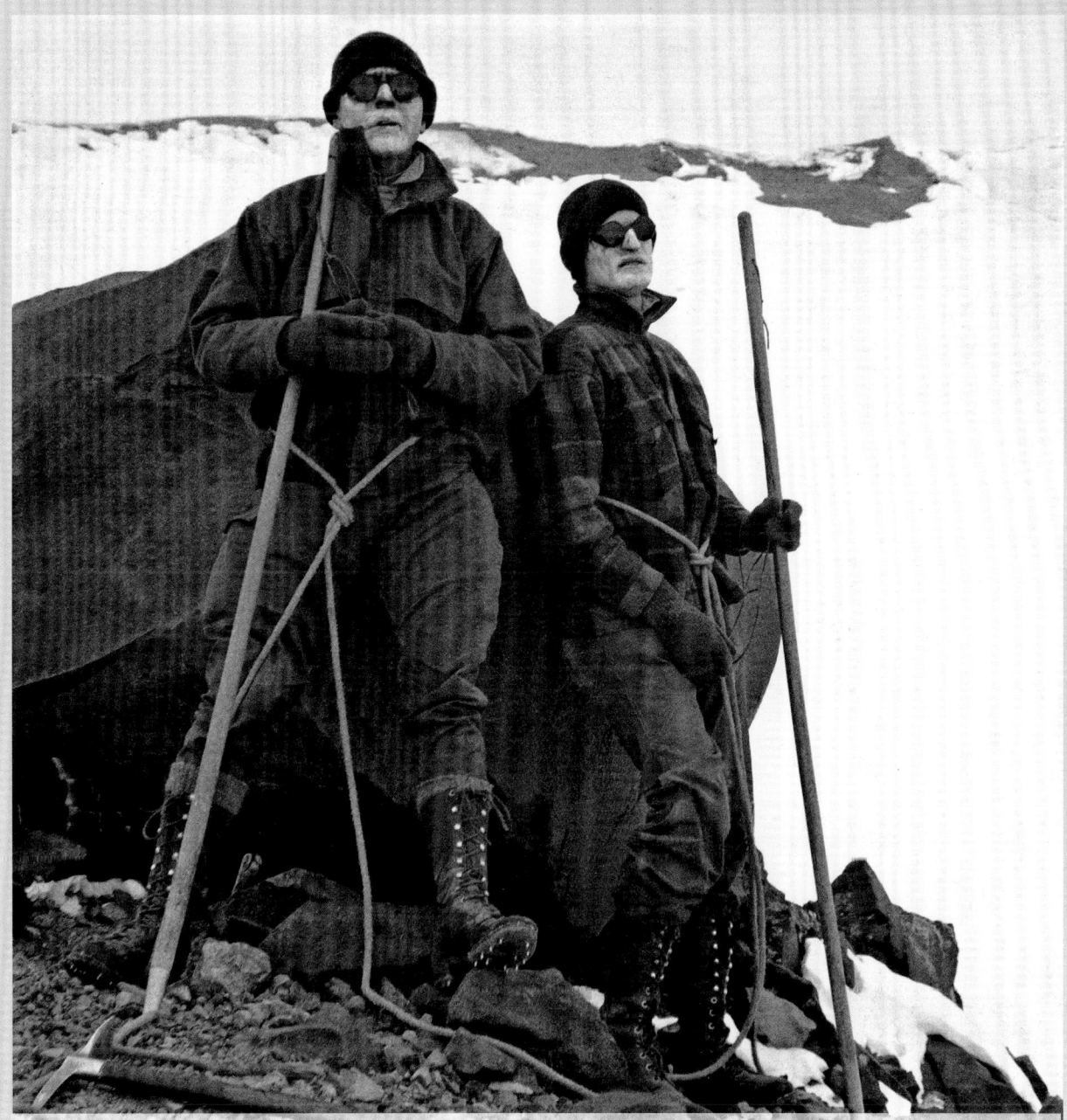

Guide Hans Fuhrer photographed this image of Henry and his climbing companion William Worner leaning on rocks at the Columbia Crest. Note the laced boots with ice grips and the ice axe lying in the foreground.

Henry, his climbing companion William Worner, and their guide Hans Fuhrer spent the night at an elevation of 10,500 feet in a stone hut now known as Camp Muir. Getting a restful sleep was difficult on the cold stone floor, especially with nocturnal rats running about. The following morning, the group ascended to the crater rim at an elevation of 14,411 feet and signed the climber registry. The time taken to complete the ascent of the mountain (ten and a half hours) was record-breaking for the 1919 climbing season. (For a detailed account of their experience see Appendix A: Ascent of Mount Rainier.)

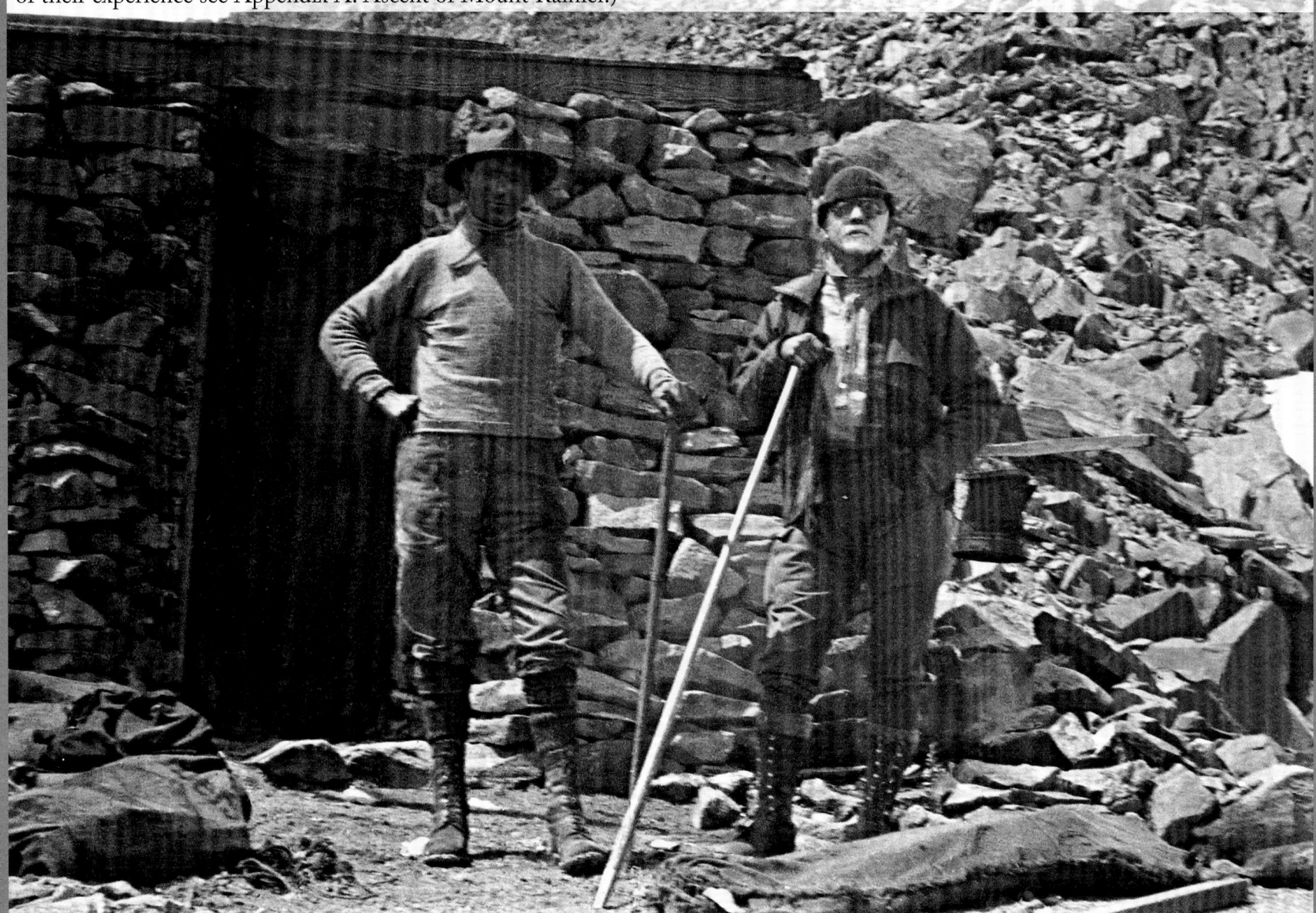

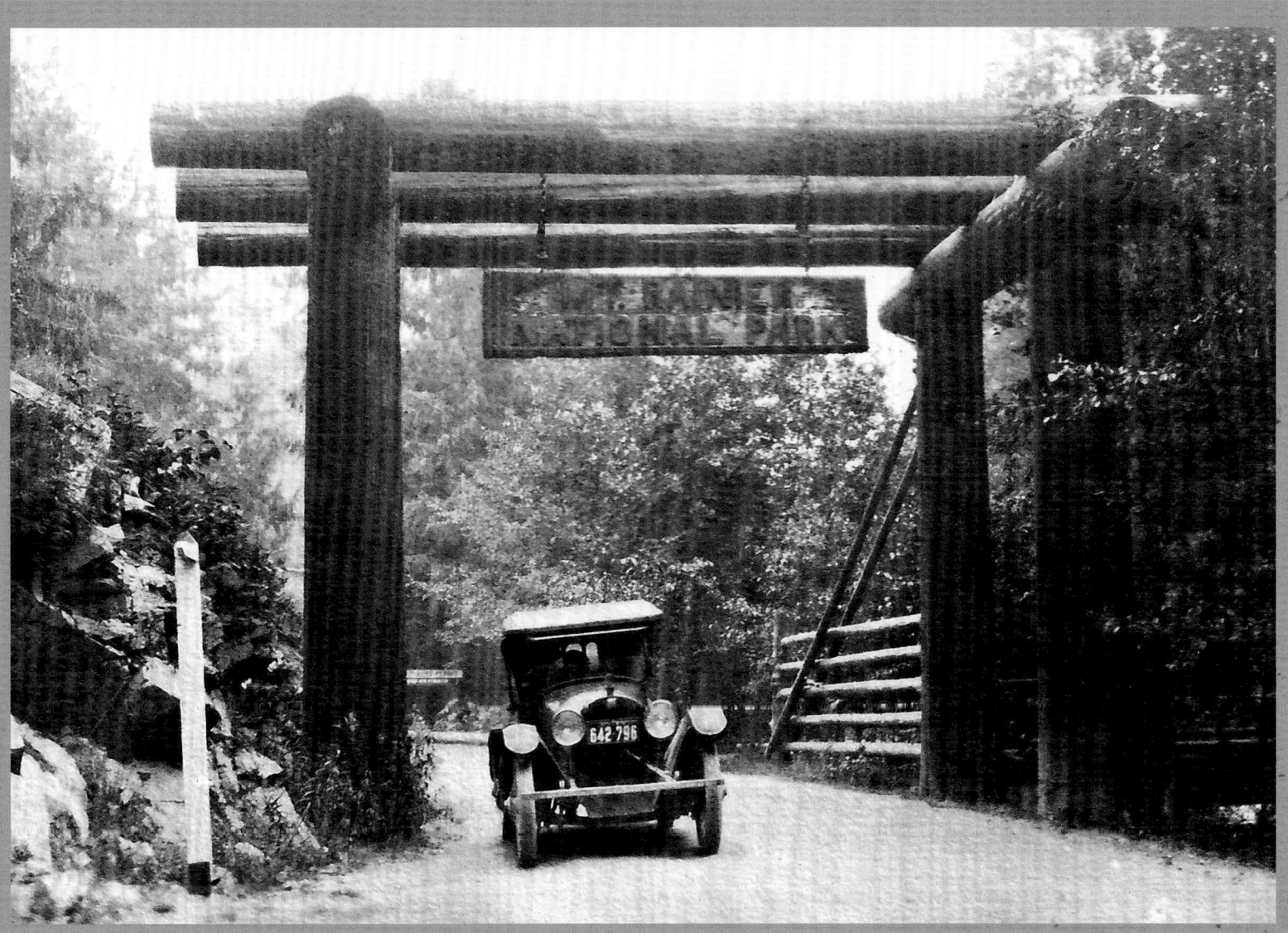

The Spallholz family exited Mount Rainier National Park through the Nisqually Gate and headed south towards Oregon. Upon returning home to Salem, New York, Henry said the climb to the summit of Mount Rainier was for him the most exciting and memorable part of the entire trip.

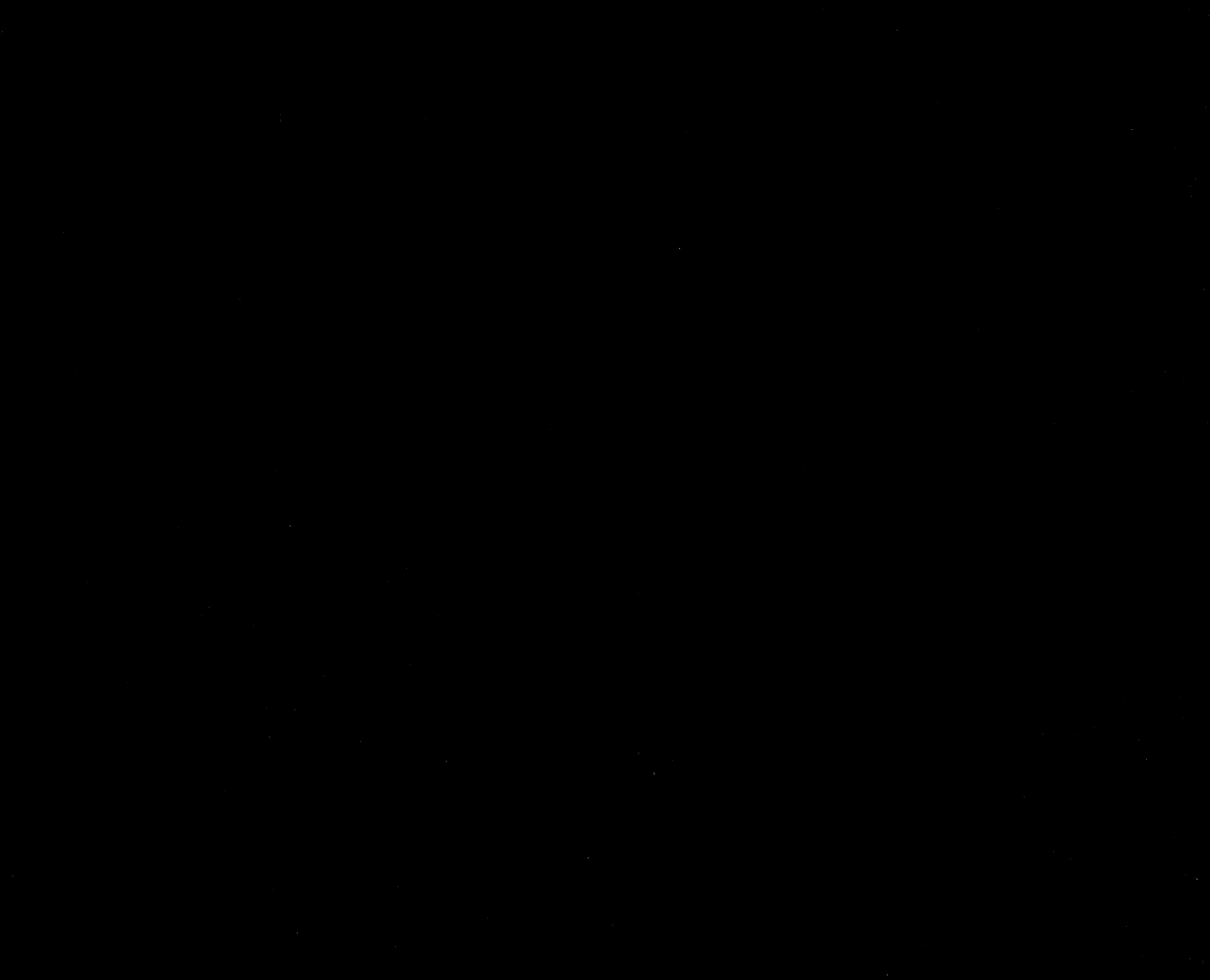

CHAPTER 10

OREGON: CRATER LAKE NATIONAL PARK & COLUMBIA RIVER

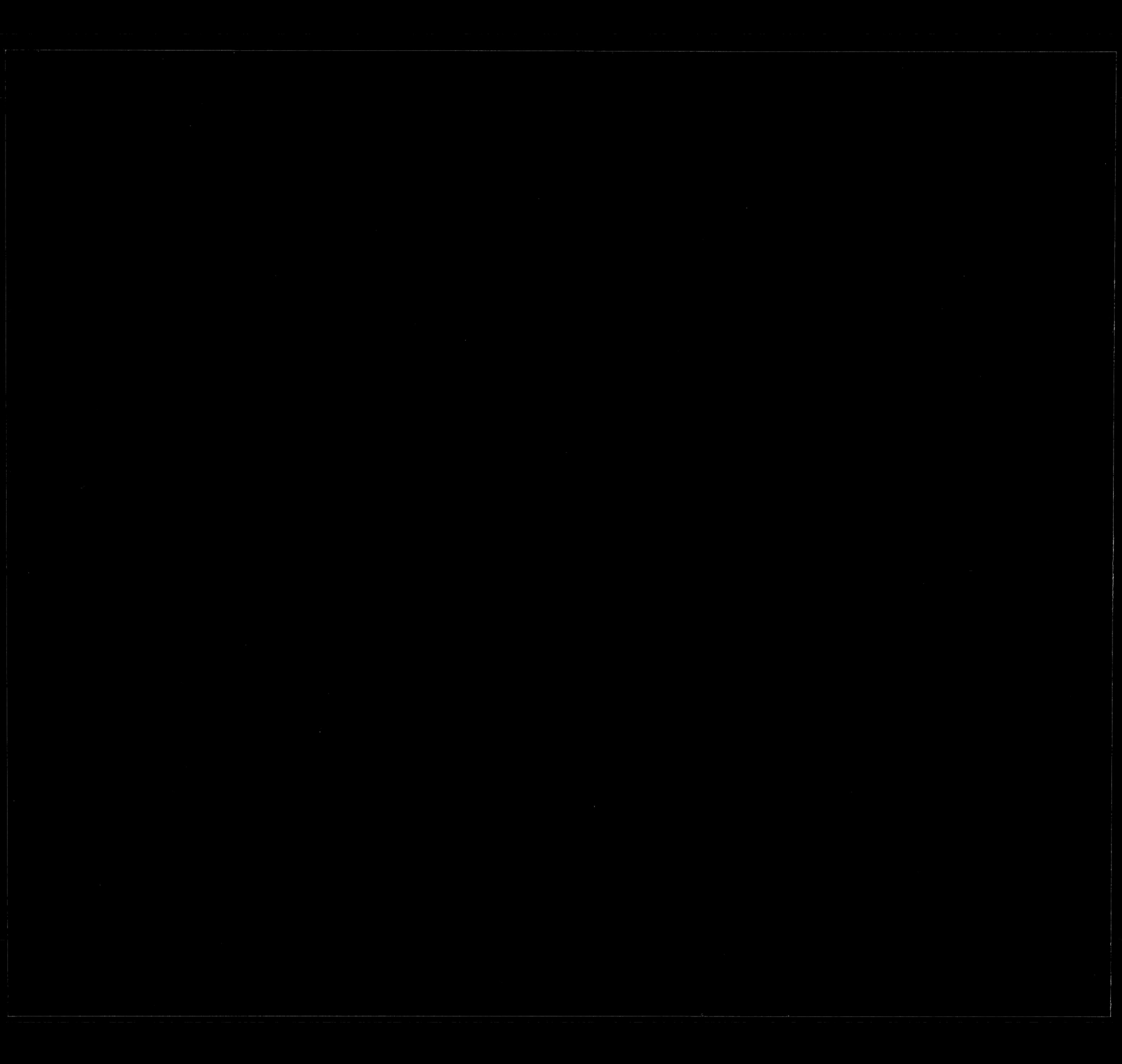

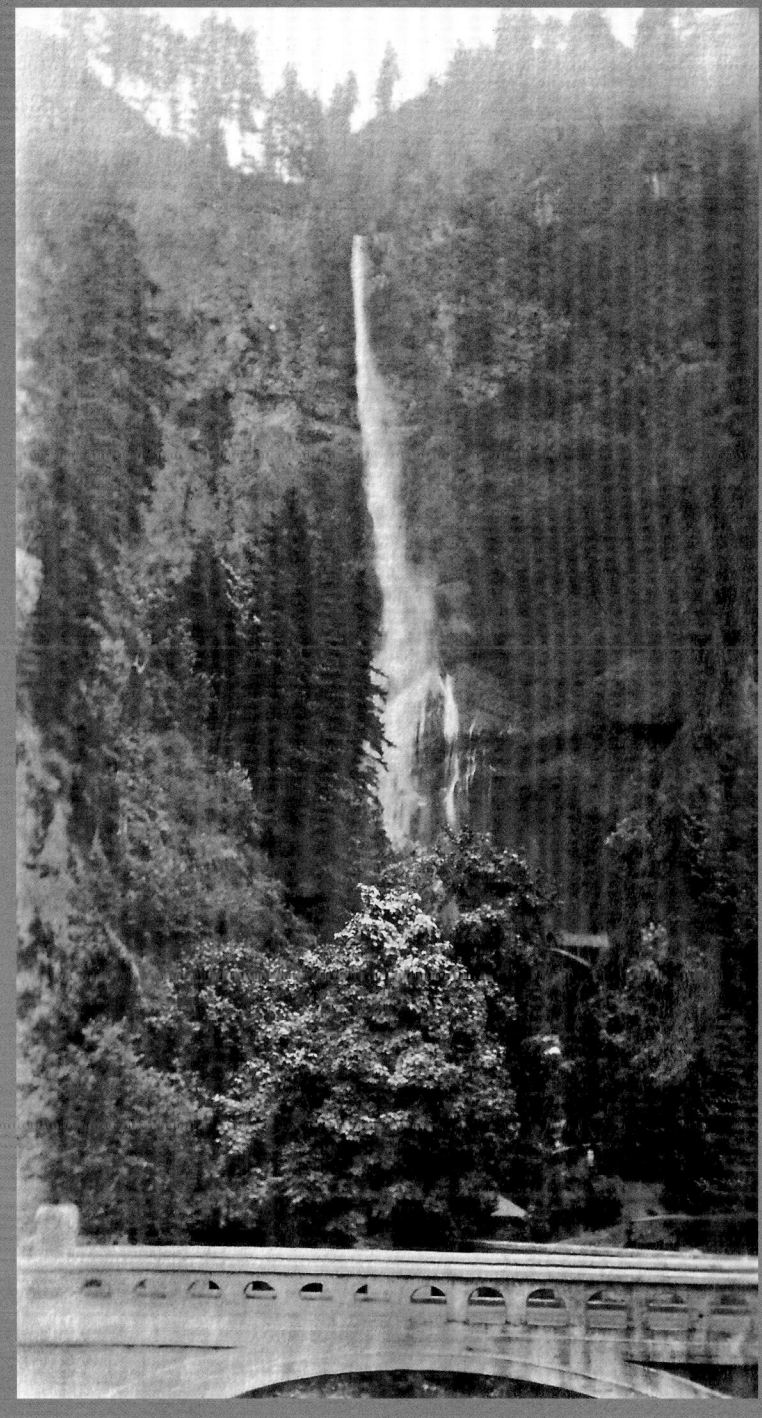

Henry took this photograph of Multnomah Falls from the footbridge crossing Multnomah Creek, beside the Columbia River Highway. The upper waterfall forms a deep pool, with the river then passing under the arch of Benson Bridge before plunging another sixty-nine feet to a lower pool. Multnomah Falls and its bridge remain one of the most photographed locations along the scenic Columbia River Highway.

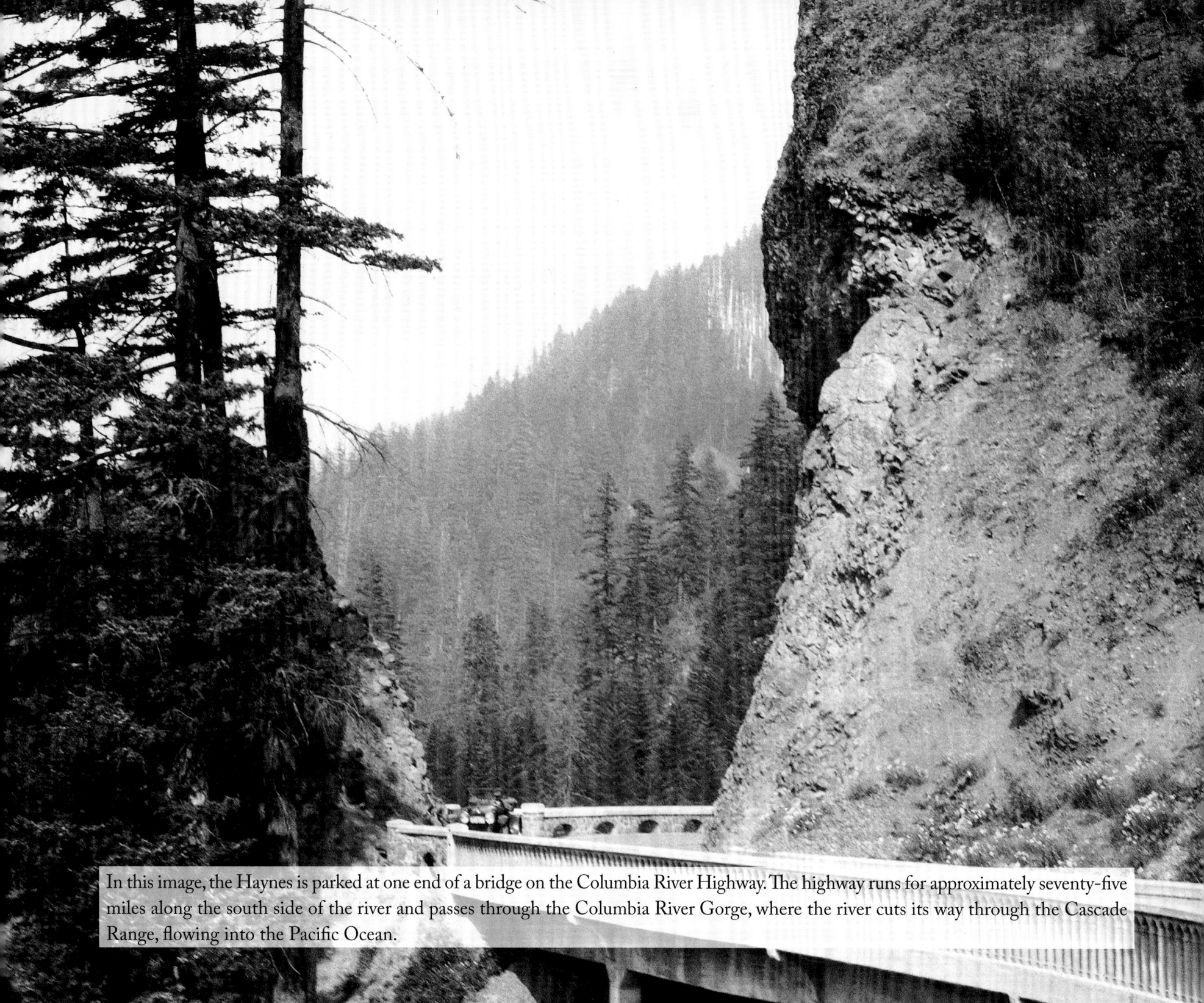

In this image, the Haynes is parked at one end of a bridge on the Columbia River Highway. The highway runs for approximately seventy-five miles along the south side of the river and passes through the Columbia River Gorge, where the river cuts its way through the Cascade Range, flowing into the Pacific Ocean.

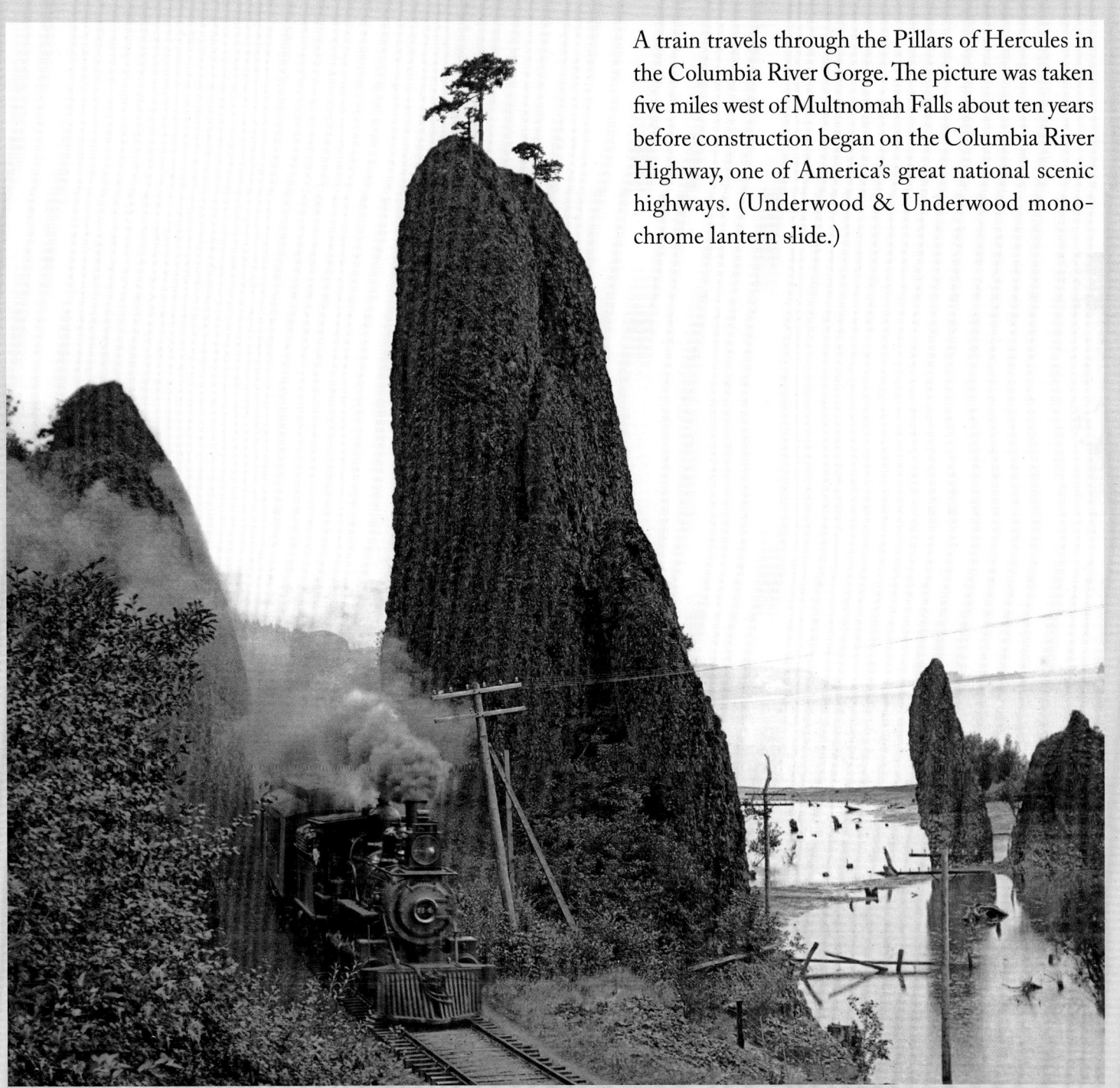

A train travels through the Pillars of Hercules in the Columbia River Gorge. The picture was taken five miles west of Multnomah Falls about ten years before construction began on the Columbia River Highway, one of America's great national scenic highways. (Underwood & Underwood monochrome lantern slide.)

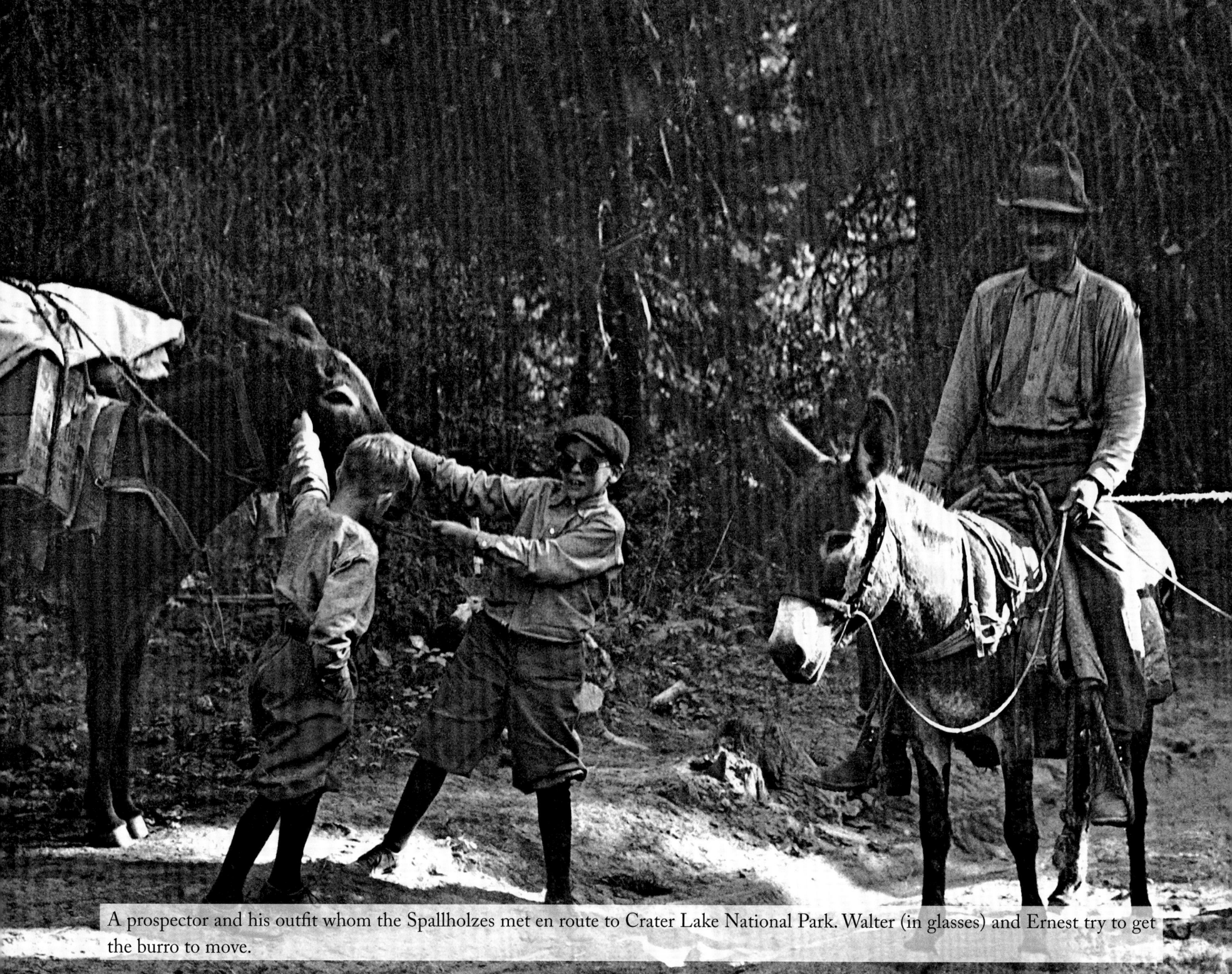

A prospector and his outfit whom the Spallholzes met en route to Crater Lake National Park. Walter (in glasses) and Ernest try to get the burro to move.

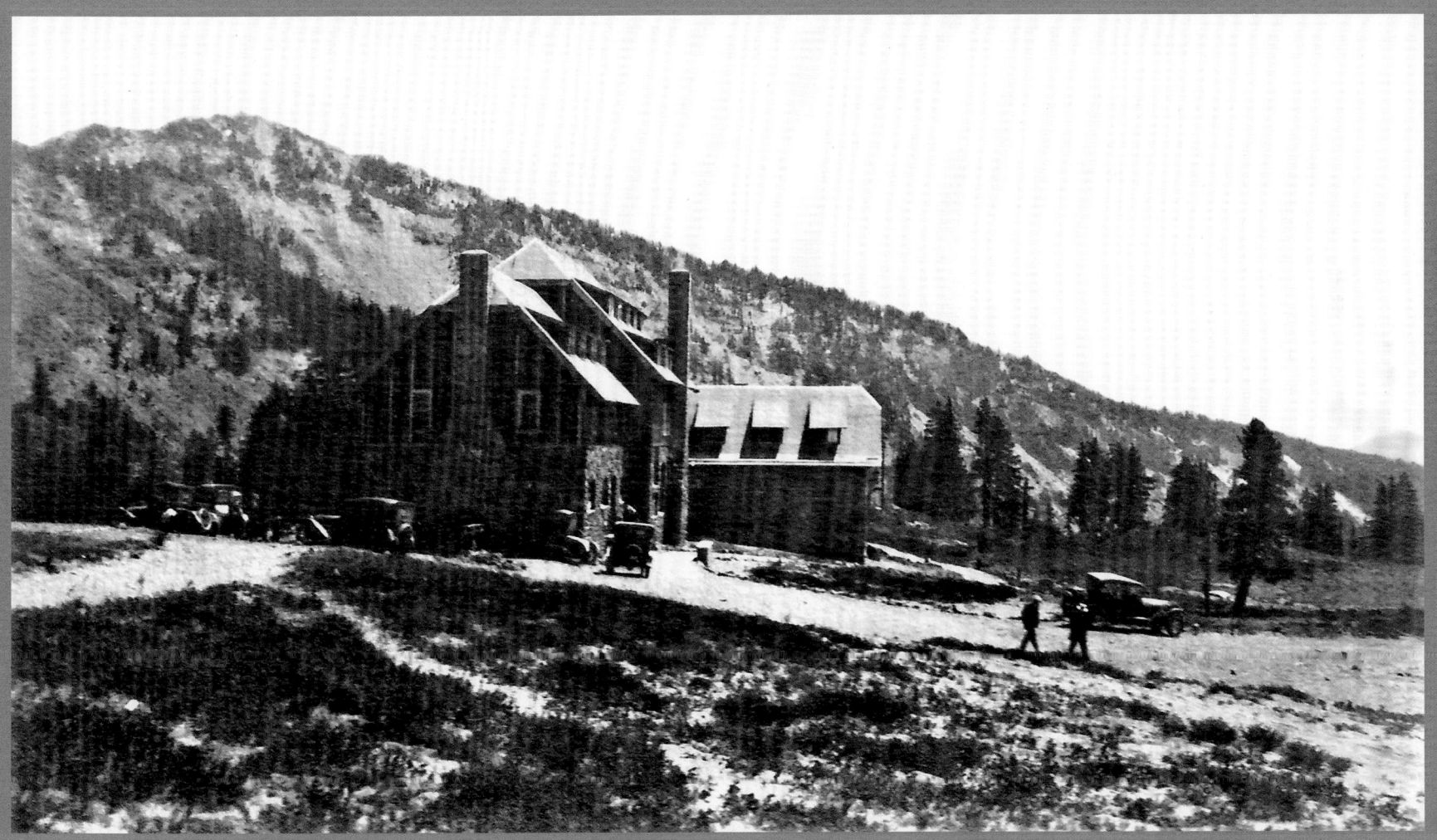

When they arrived in Oregon, the Spallholzes stayed at the Crater Lake Lodge, a hotel on the rim of the crater, with a view overlooking the caldera.

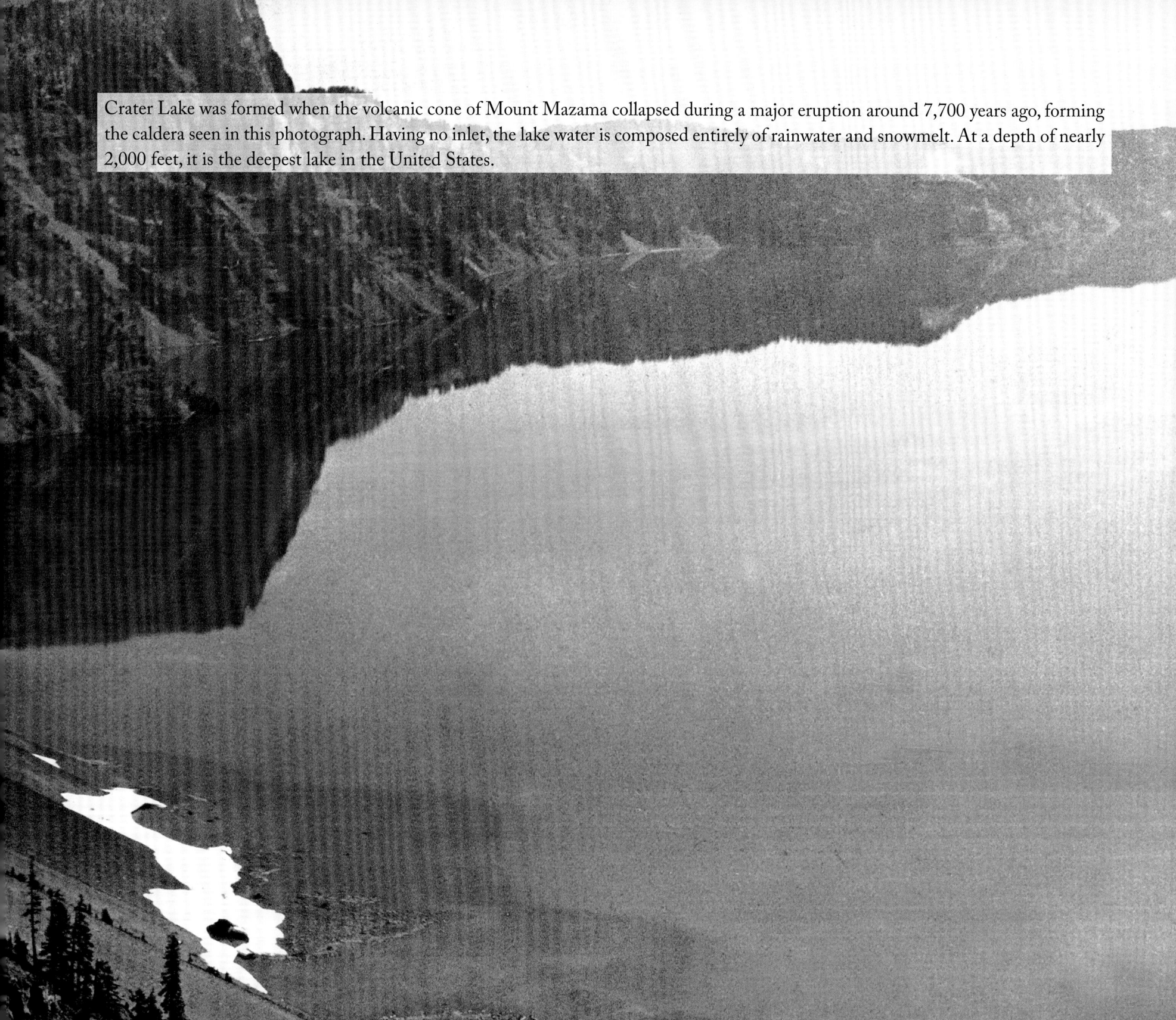

Crater Lake was formed when the volcanic cone of Mount Mazama collapsed during a major eruption around 7,700 years ago, forming the caldera seen in this photograph. Having no inlet, the lake water is composed entirely of rainwater and snowmelt. At a depth of nearly 2,000 feet, it is the deepest lake in the United States.

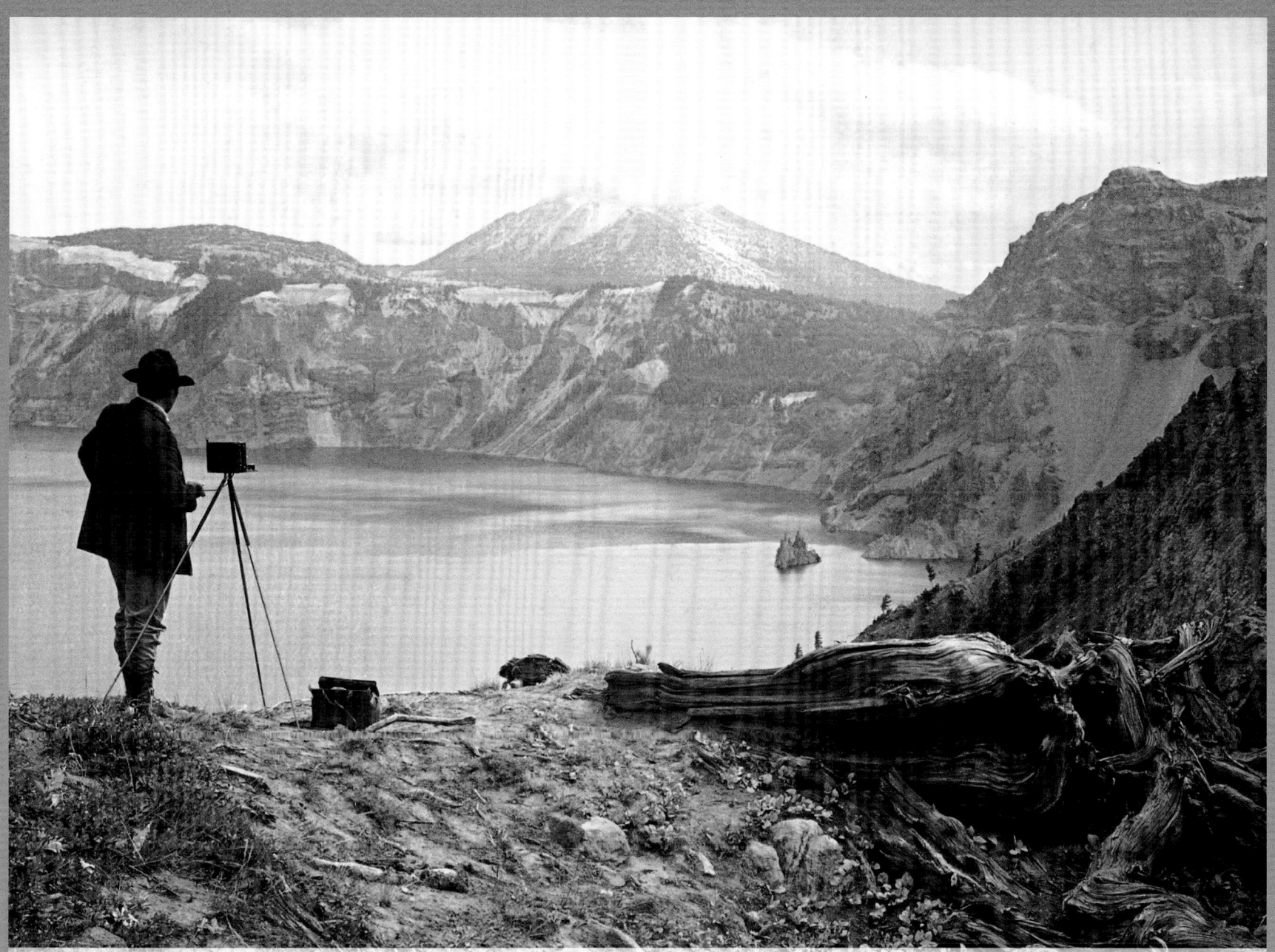

A photographer "in his element" at Crater Lake. The photographer is facing east from a viewpoint not far from Crater Lake Lodge, taking a picture of the Phantom Ship, a small, rugged island formed from an exposed volcanic dike. (Underwood & Underwood monochrome lantern slide.)

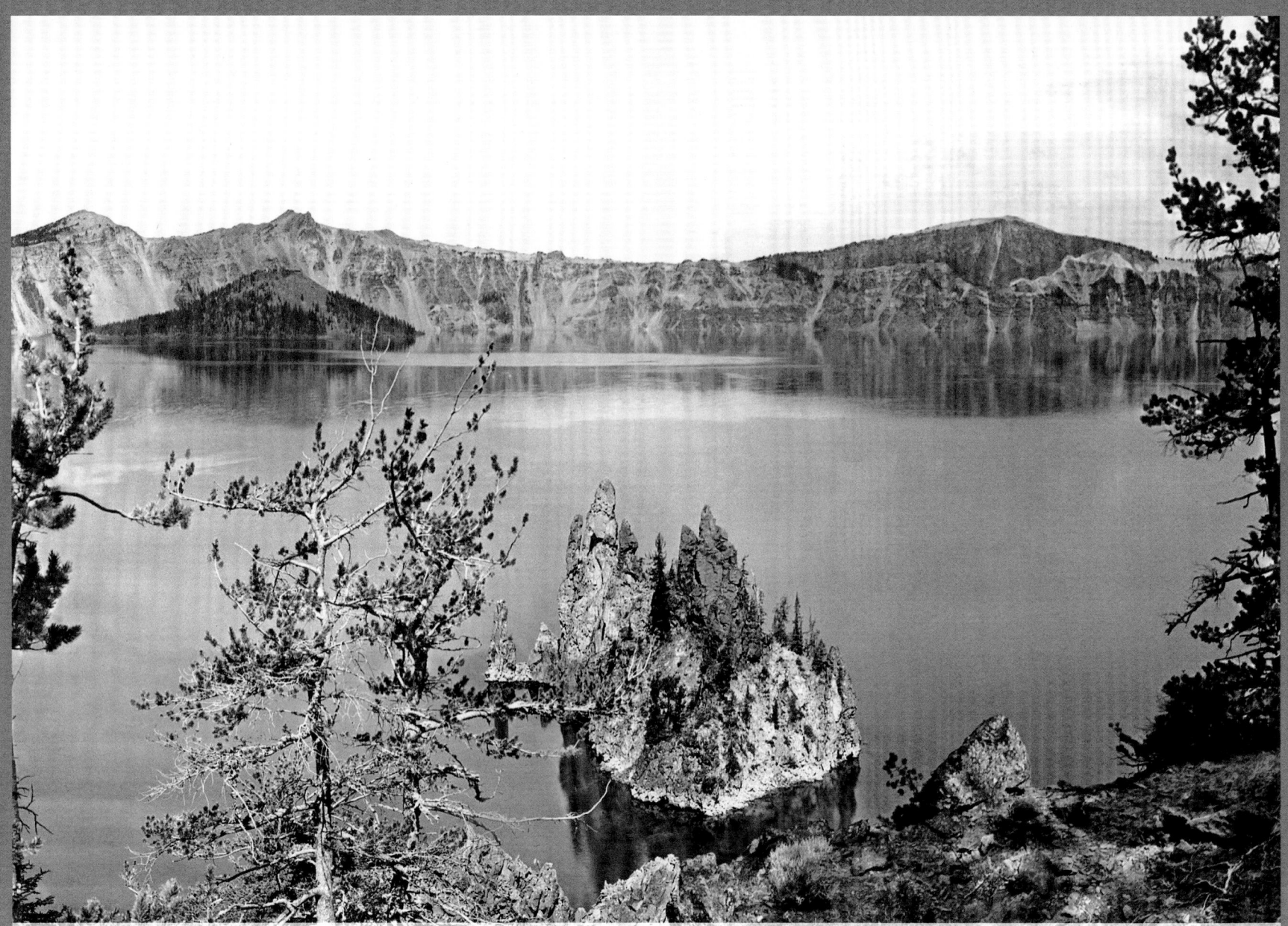

A view of Phantom Ship and Wizard Island. Phantom Ship in the foreground has a jagged appearance and is all that remains of an ancient volcanic cone that shared the same magma reservoir that created Mount Mazama. Wizard Island's graceful cone was created over several thousands of years by a series of smaller eruptions following the cataclysmic caldera-forming event. (Fred H. Kiser monochrome lantern slide.)

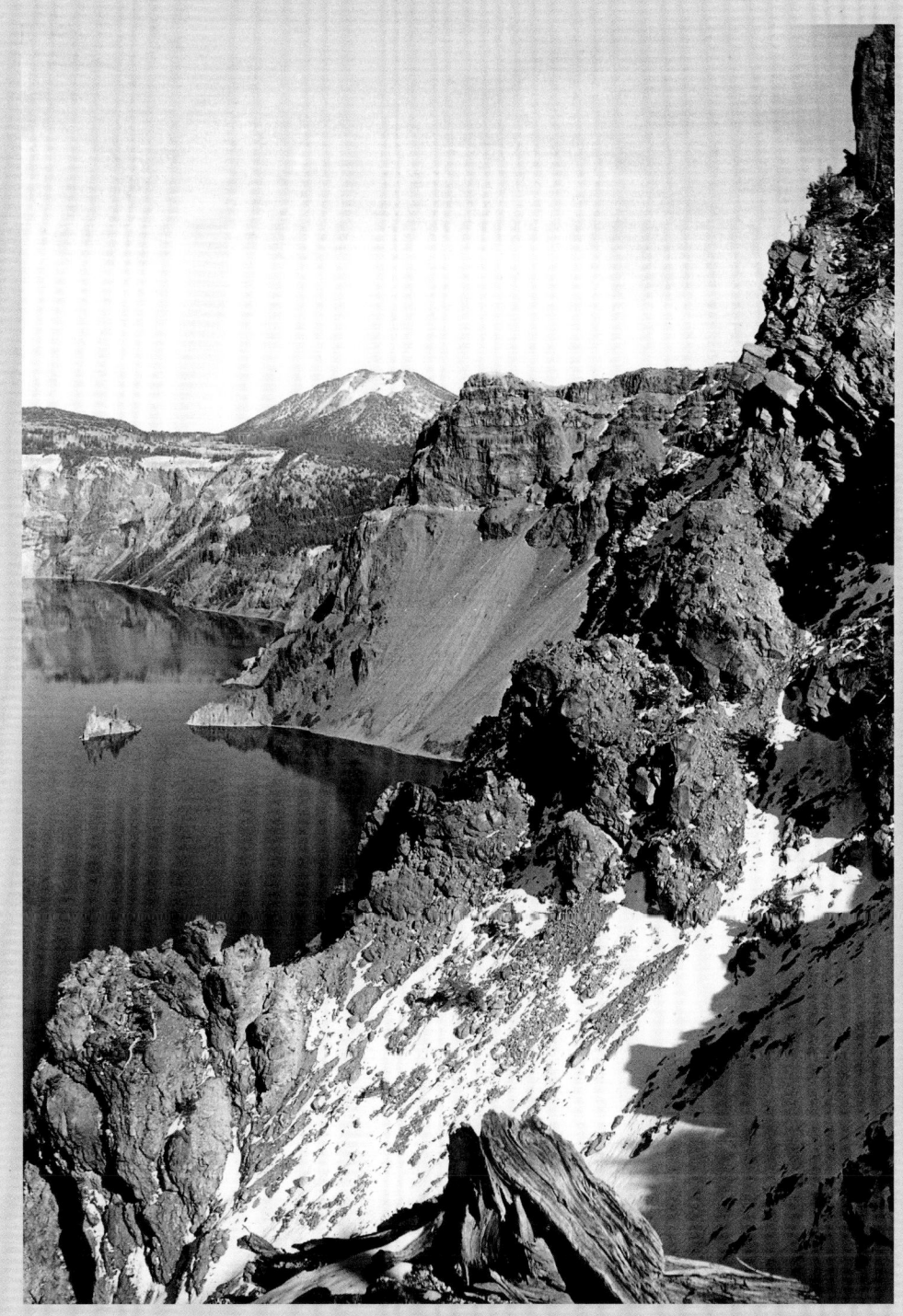

In this view facing to the north from Garfield Peak, snow is still clinging to the steep slopes below the crater rim. No snow remains on the south-facing slopes around the north side of the caldera. (Fred H. Kiser monochrome lantern slide.)

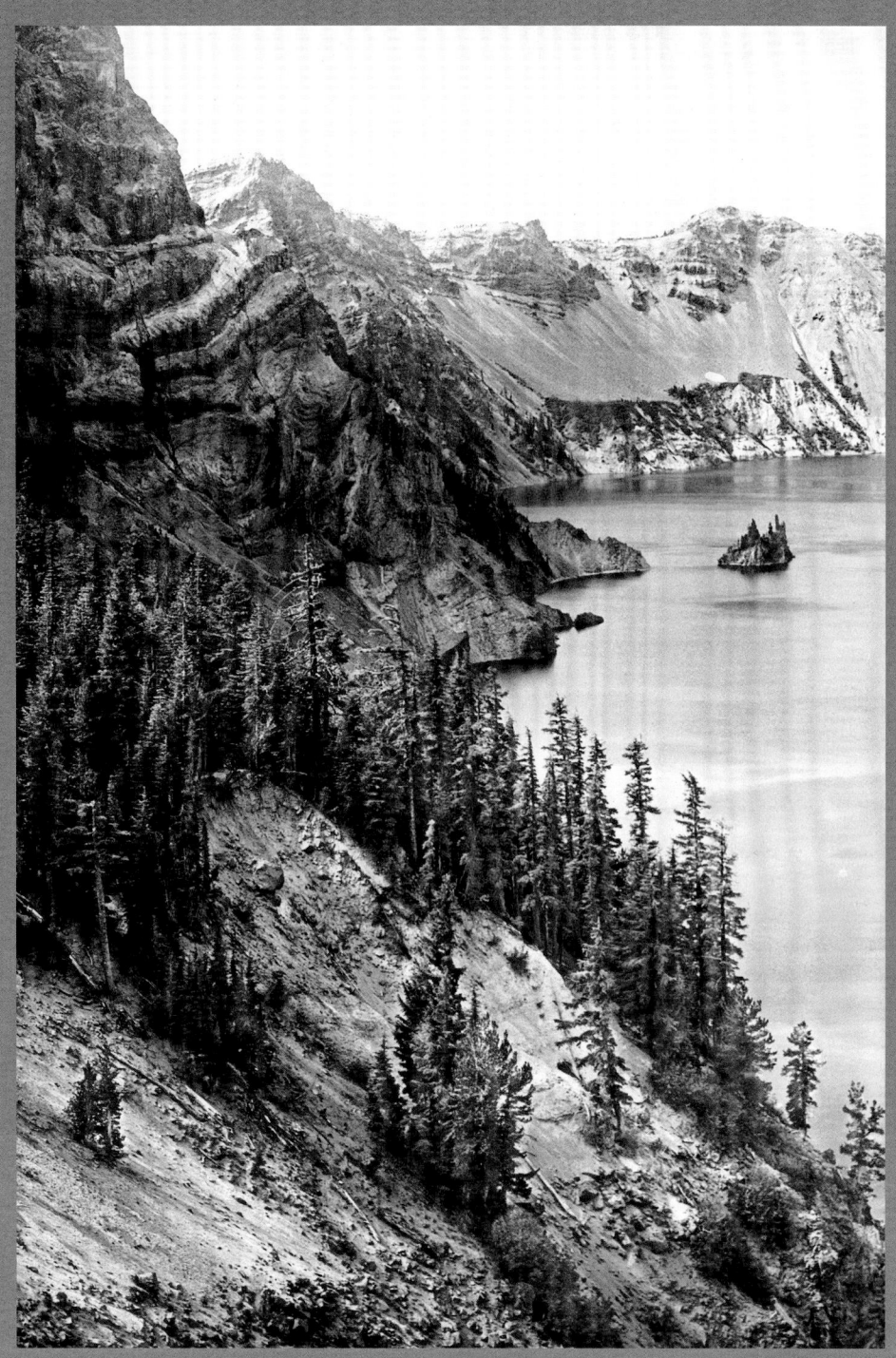

Dutton Cliff and Phantom Ship at Crater Lake. A view facing south, showing snow still clinging to sections of the crater wall that get very little sun during the day in midsummer. Phantom Ship is in the background. (Fred H. Kiser monochrome lantern slide.)

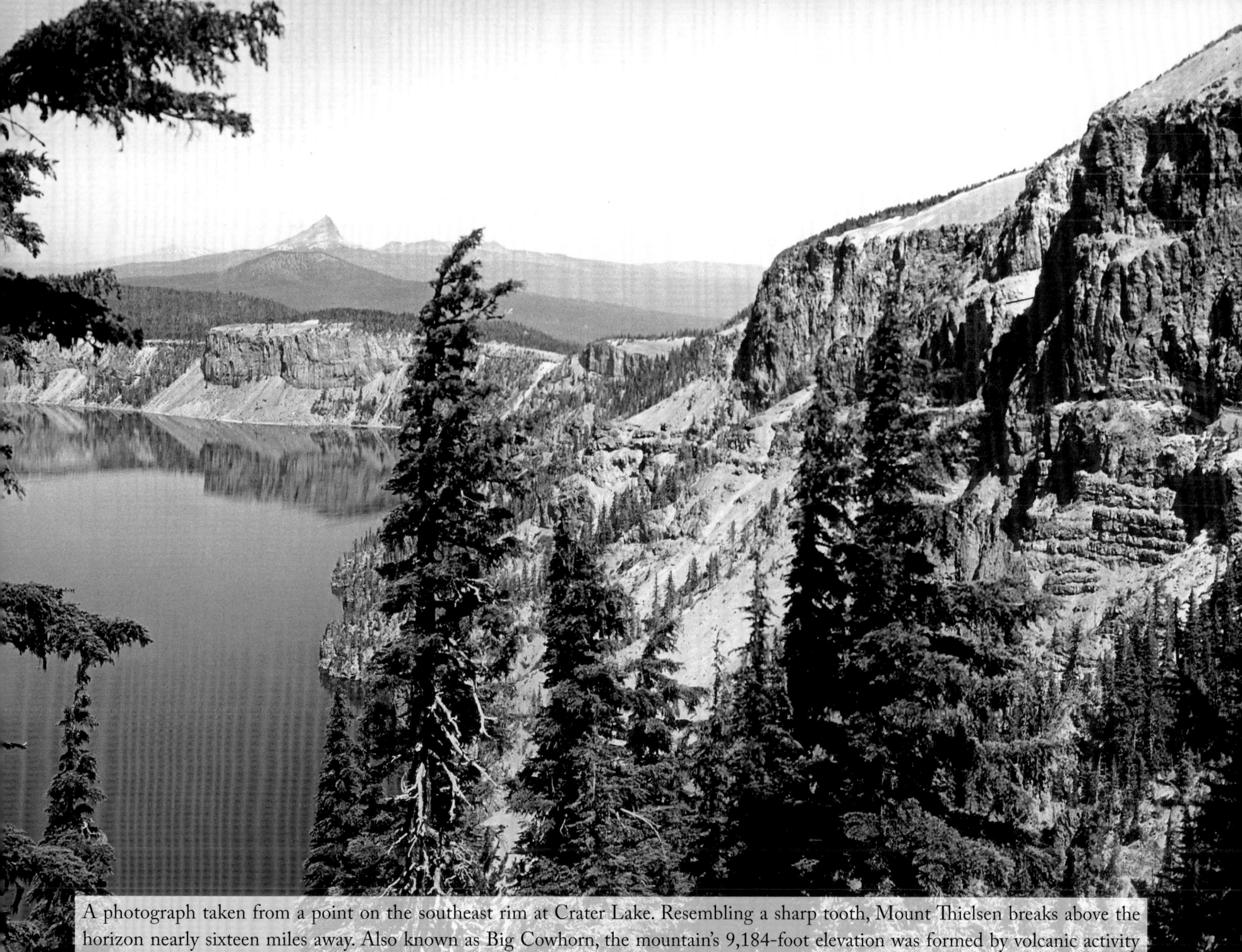

A photograph taken from a point on the southeast rim at Crater Lake. Resembling a sharp tooth, Mount Thielsen breaks above the horizon nearly sixteen miles away. Also known as Big Cowhorn, the mountain's 9,184-foot elevation was formed by volcanic activity approximately 250,000 years ago. (Fred H. Kiser monochrome lantern slide.)

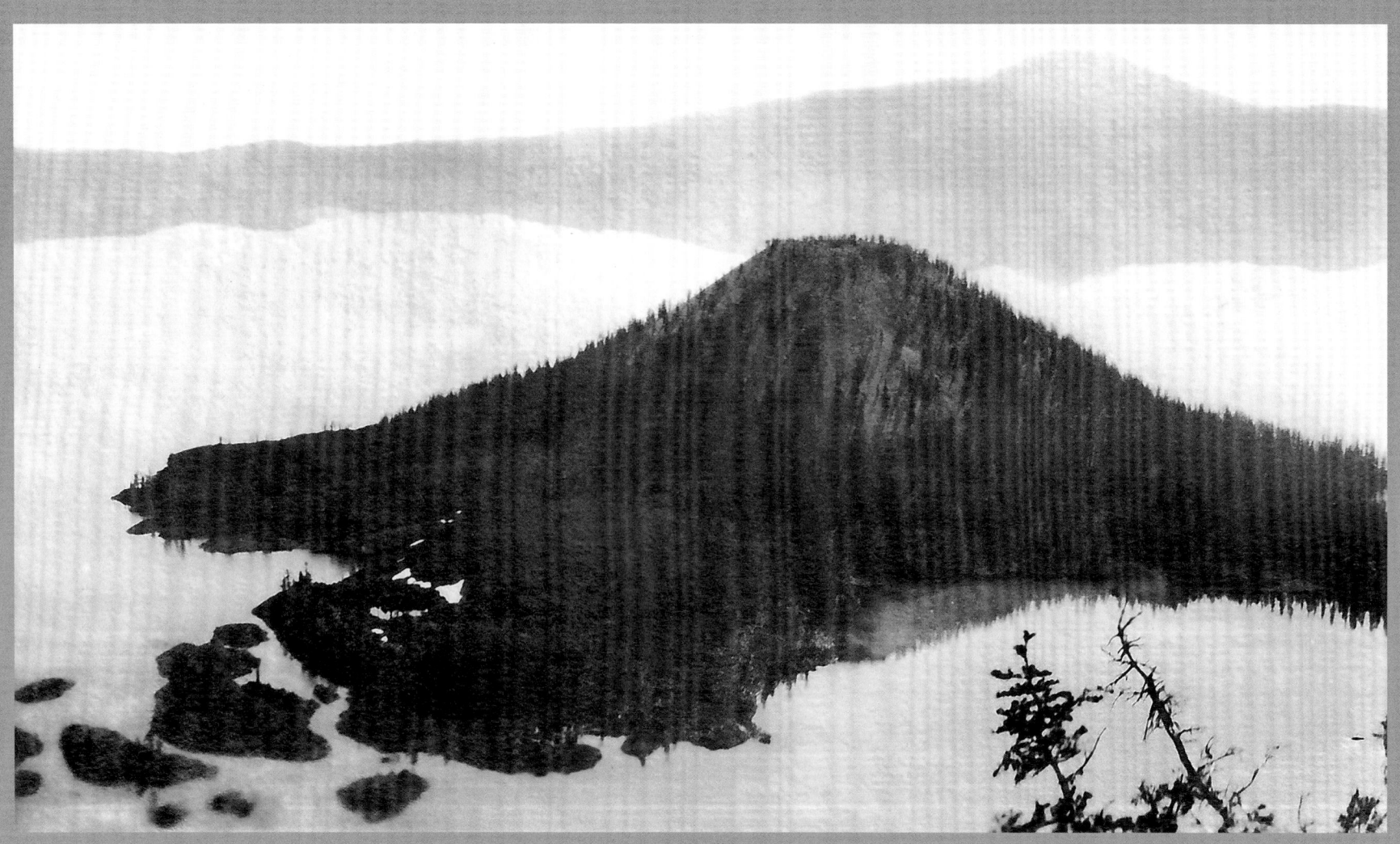

A hazy view from the Watchman Trail looking east over Wizard Island. The haze in the sky and distant detail of the crater rim are the result of using orthochromatic film, an early film especially sensitive to blue light where skies could appear as a featureless white, especially at higher altitudes.

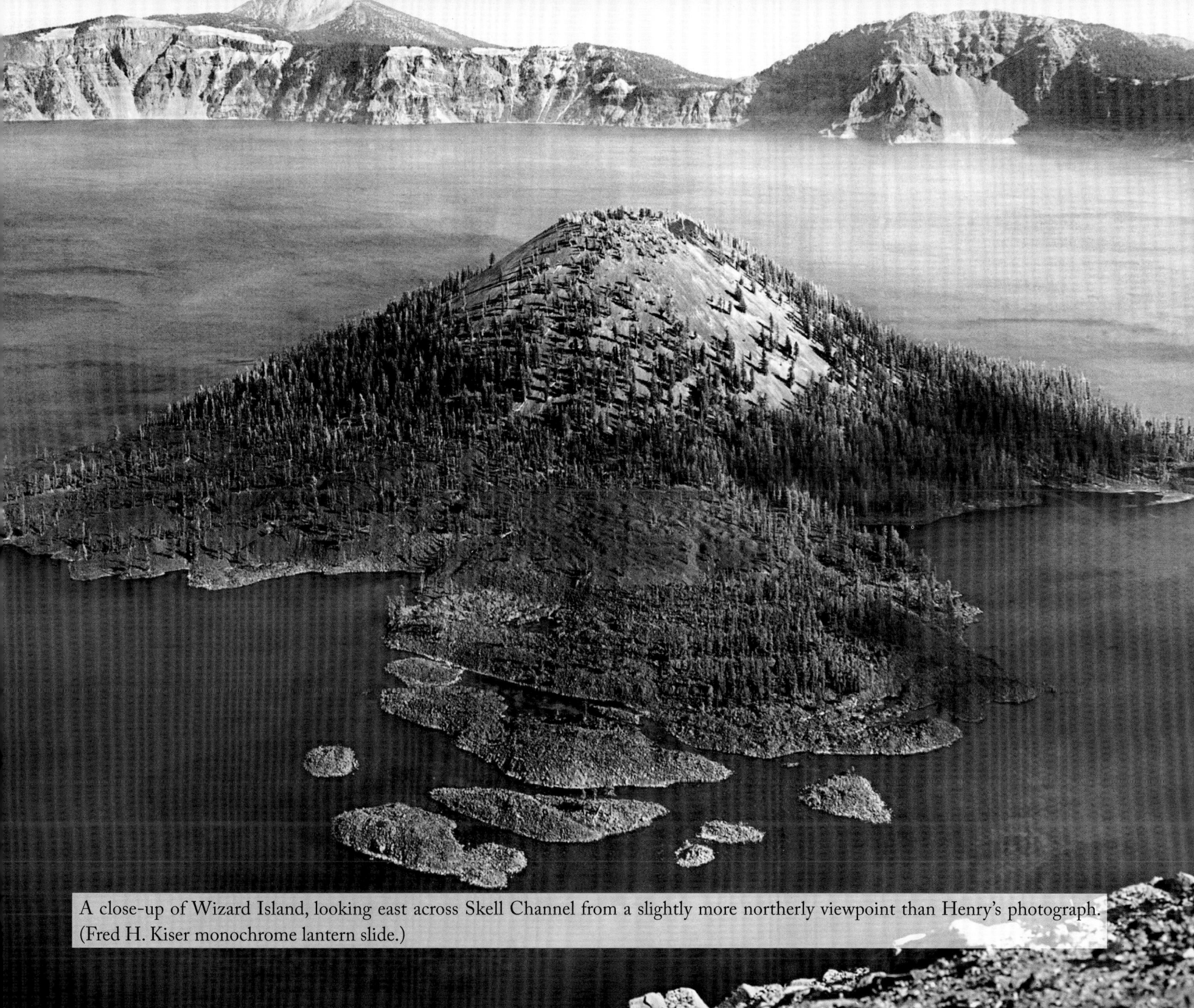

A close-up of Wizard Island, looking east across Skell Channel from a slightly more northerly viewpoint than Henry's photograph. (Fred H. Kiser monochrome lantern slide.)

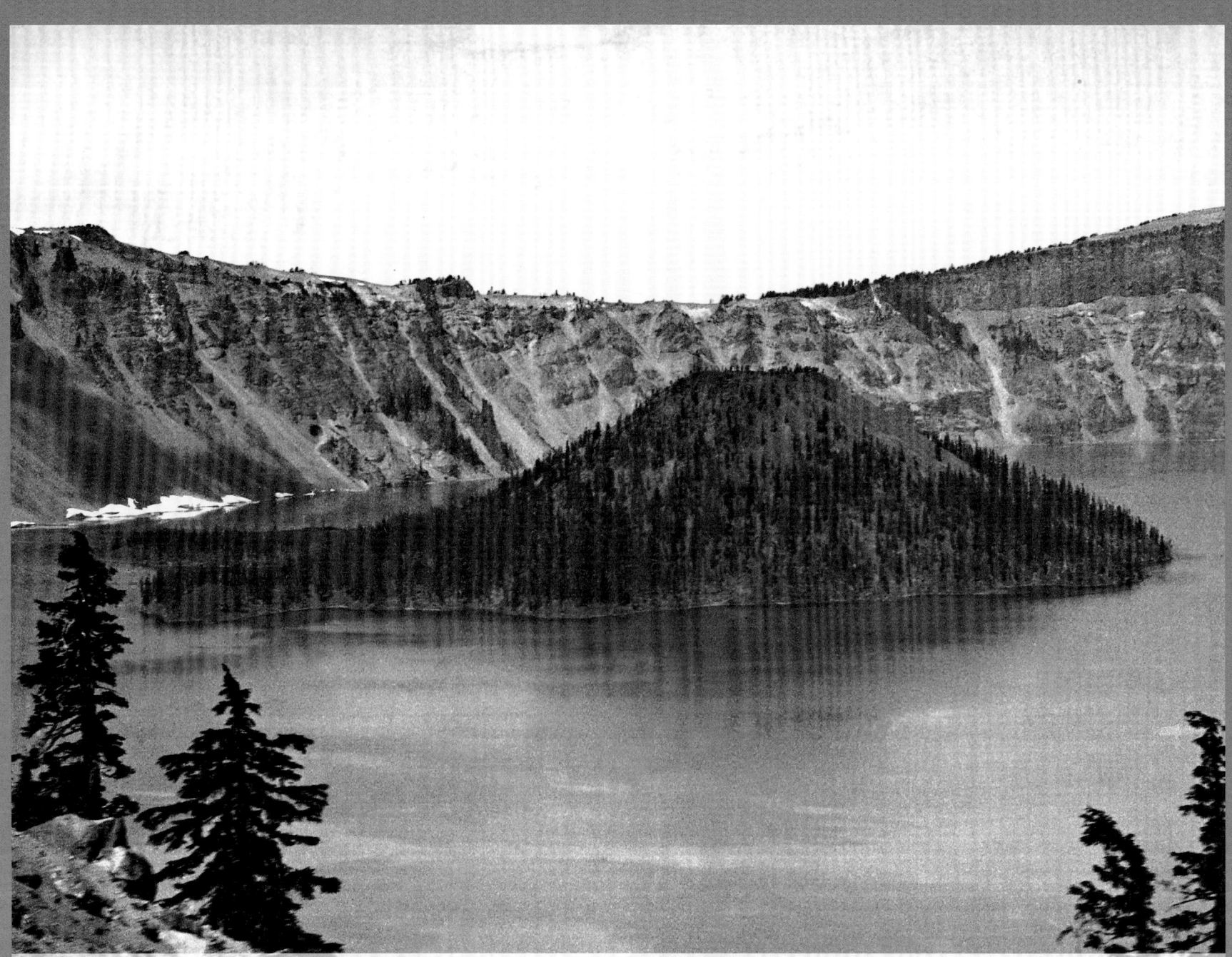

A close view of Wizard Island in Crater Lake taken from near the location of the present-day Rim Village Visitors Center. (Underwood & Underwood monochrome lantern slide.)

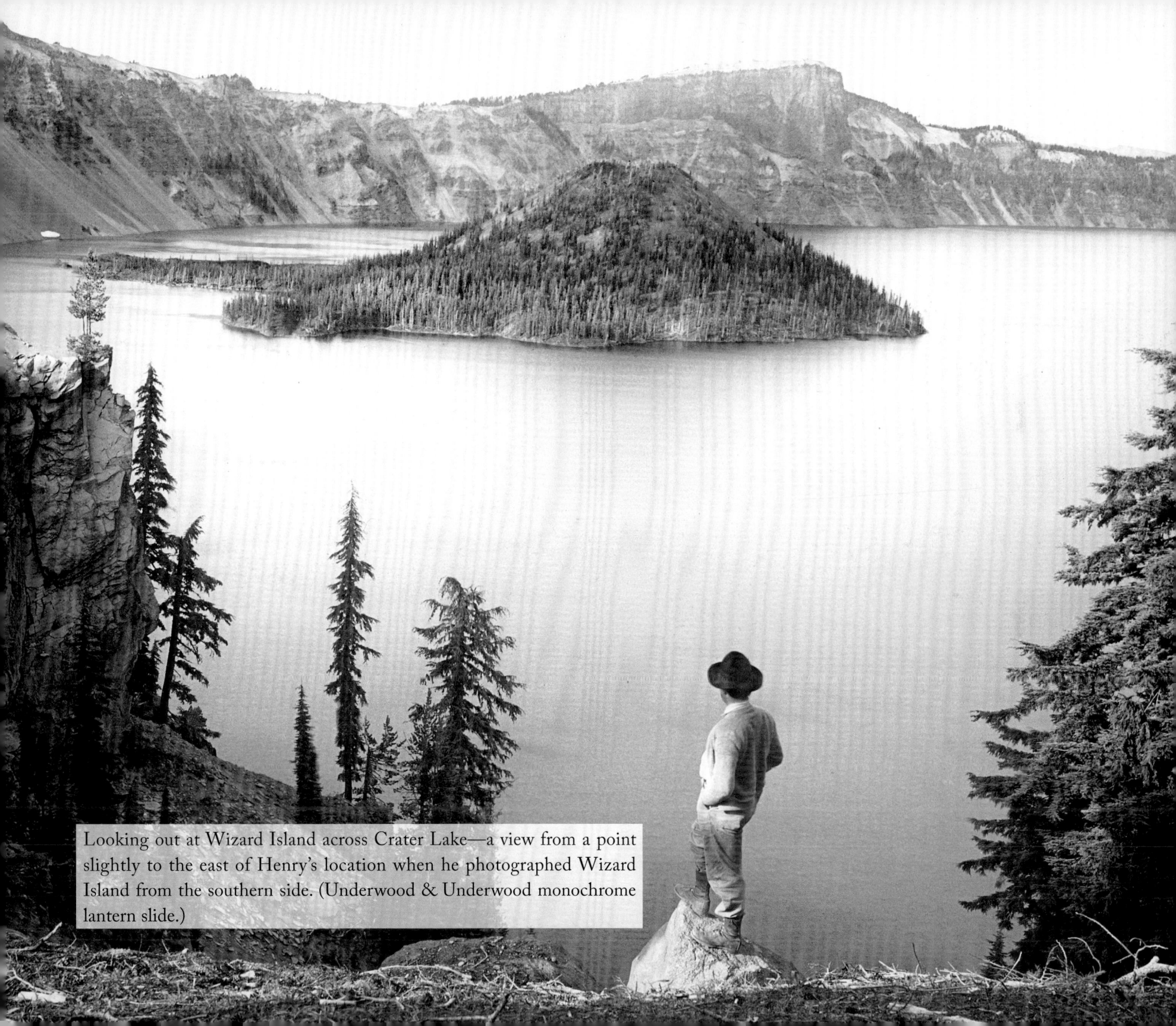

Looking out at Wizard Island across Crater Lake—a view from a point slightly to the east of Henry's location when he photographed Wizard Island from the southern side. (Underwood & Underwood monochrome lantern slide.)

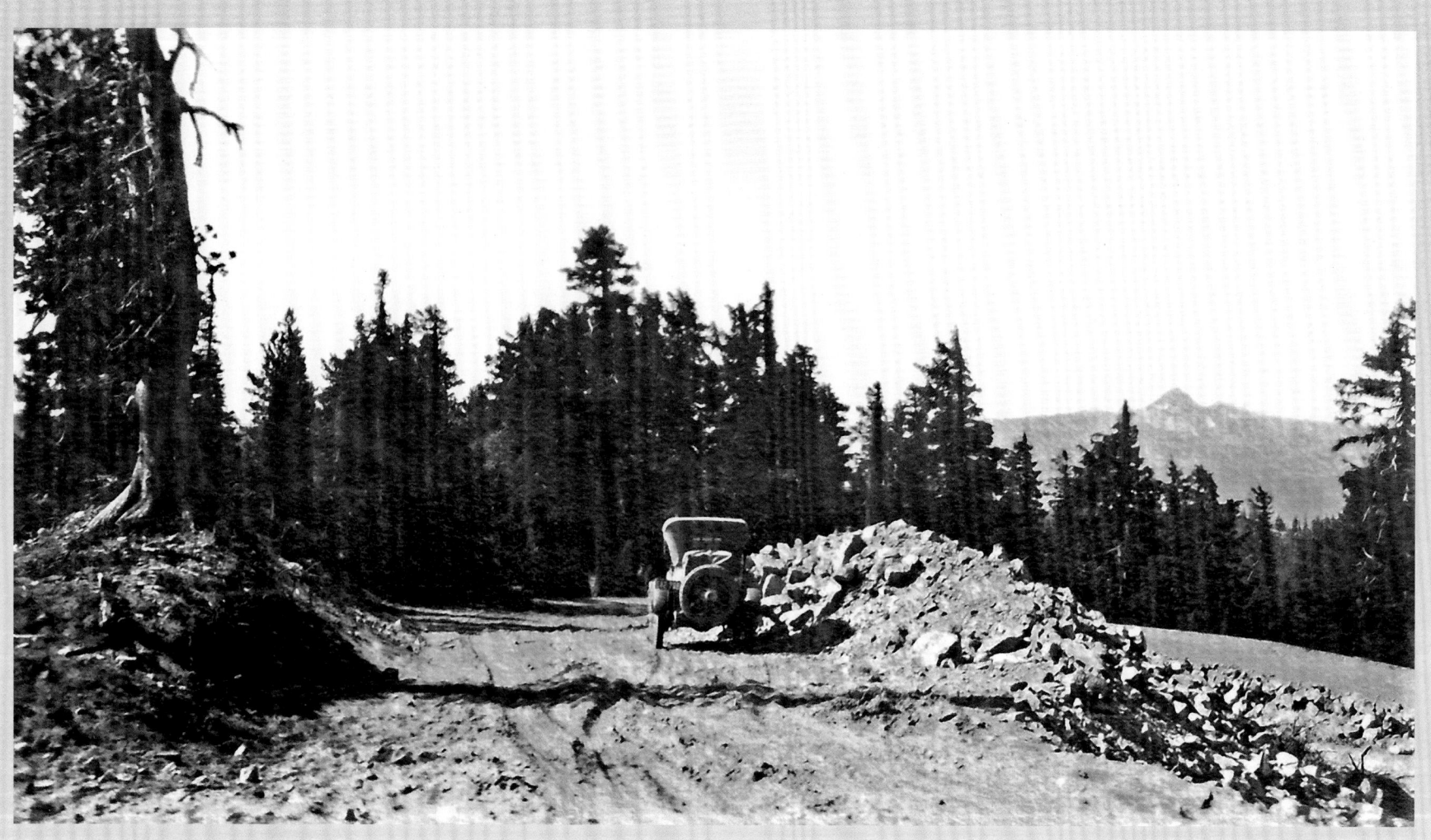

The Spallholzes drove on the rim road while leaving Crater Lake National Park, on the way into California's Mount Shasta volcanic area. Mount Shasta was designated a National Natural Landmark in March 1976.

CHAPTER 11

SOUTH INTO CALIFORNIA AND THE PACIFIC COAST

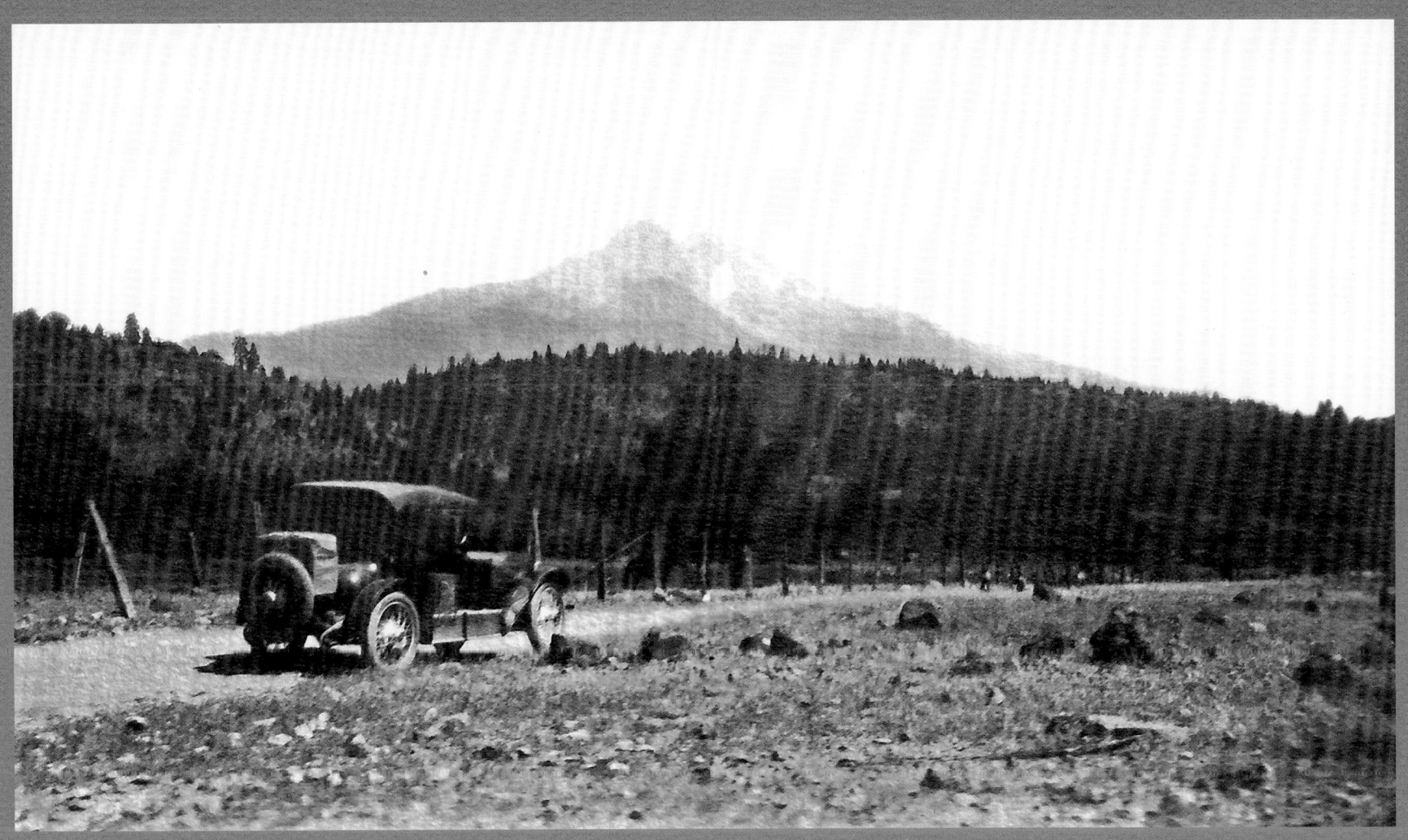

Driving south along a fenced ranch in Northern California, Henry photographed Mount Shasta, the second highest peak in the Cascade Range at 14,180 feet. Mount Shasta is an active volcano and the largest of three confluent volcanic cones.

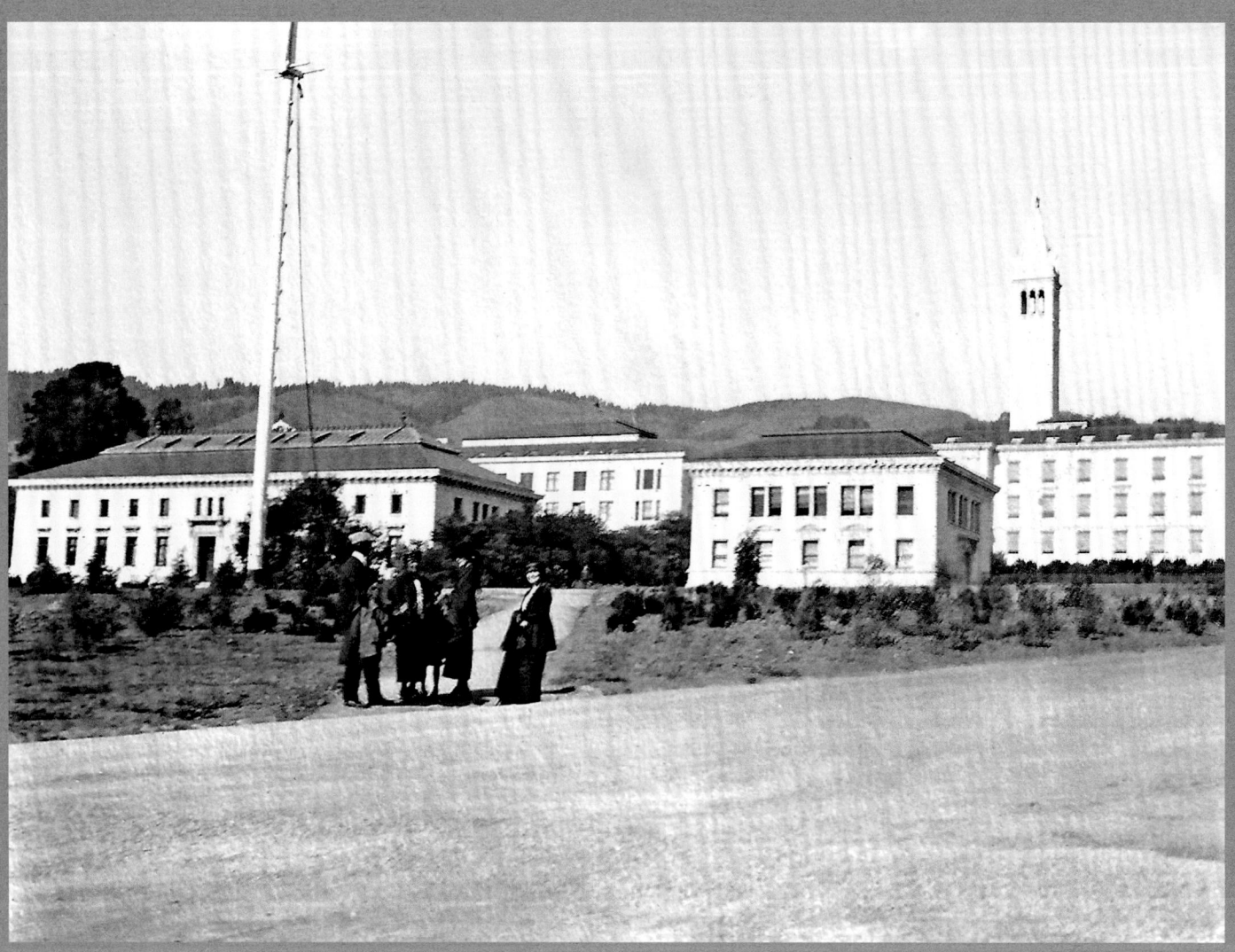

The Spallholz family drove on to Berkeley, California, to visit friends at the University of California, Berkeley. Here the group is on Campanile Way standing in front of California Hall at the left and Durant Hall on the right. The Campanile Bell Tower rises in the background behind Wheeler Hall.

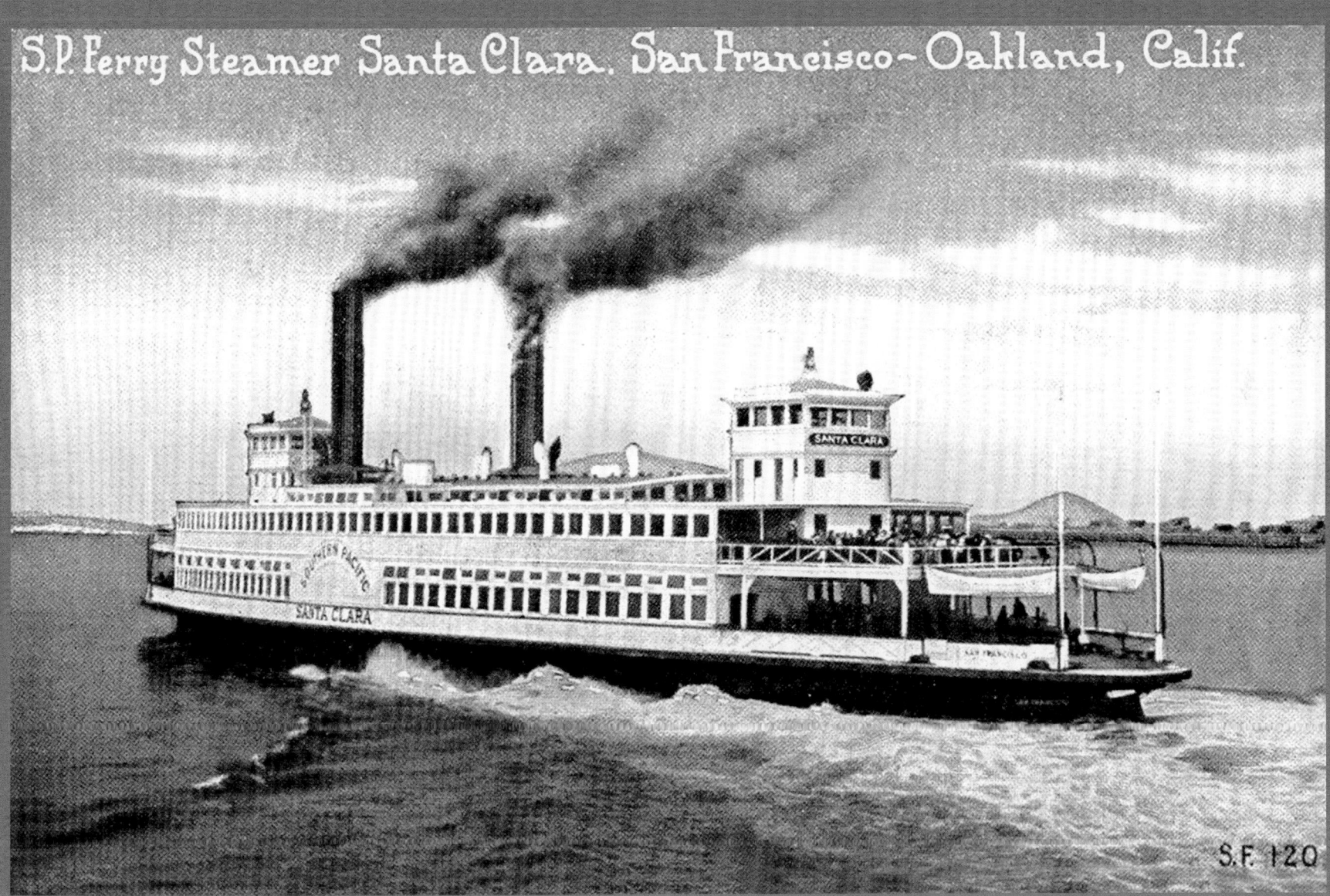

S.P. Ferry Steamer Santa Clara. San Francisco~Oakland, Calif.

S.F. 120

To avoid a lengthy drive south around San Francisco Bay, at the dock in Oakland, the Spallholz family boarded a ferry like the one in this postcard, the *Santa Clara*. The vessel carried automobiles below on a car deck and had an upper deck accommodating about four hundred passengers. Arriving in San Francisco, the ferry unloaded passengers and automobiles at the Embarcadero, at the foot of Market Street.

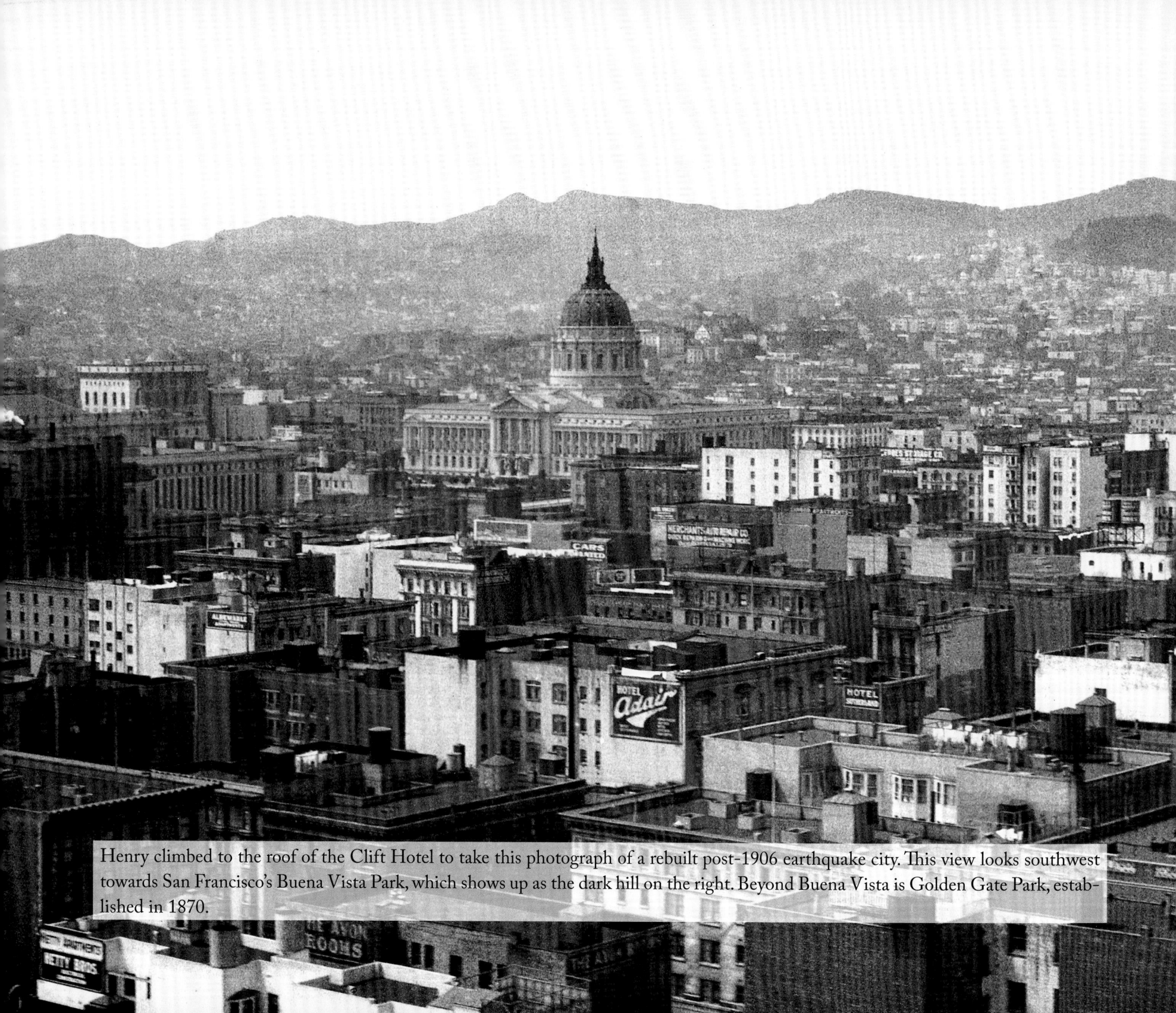

Henry climbed to the roof of the Clift Hotel to take this photograph of a rebuilt post-1906 earthquake city. This view looks southwest towards San Francisco's Buena Vista Park, which shows up as the dark hill on the right. Beyond Buena Vista is Golden Gate Park, established in 1870.

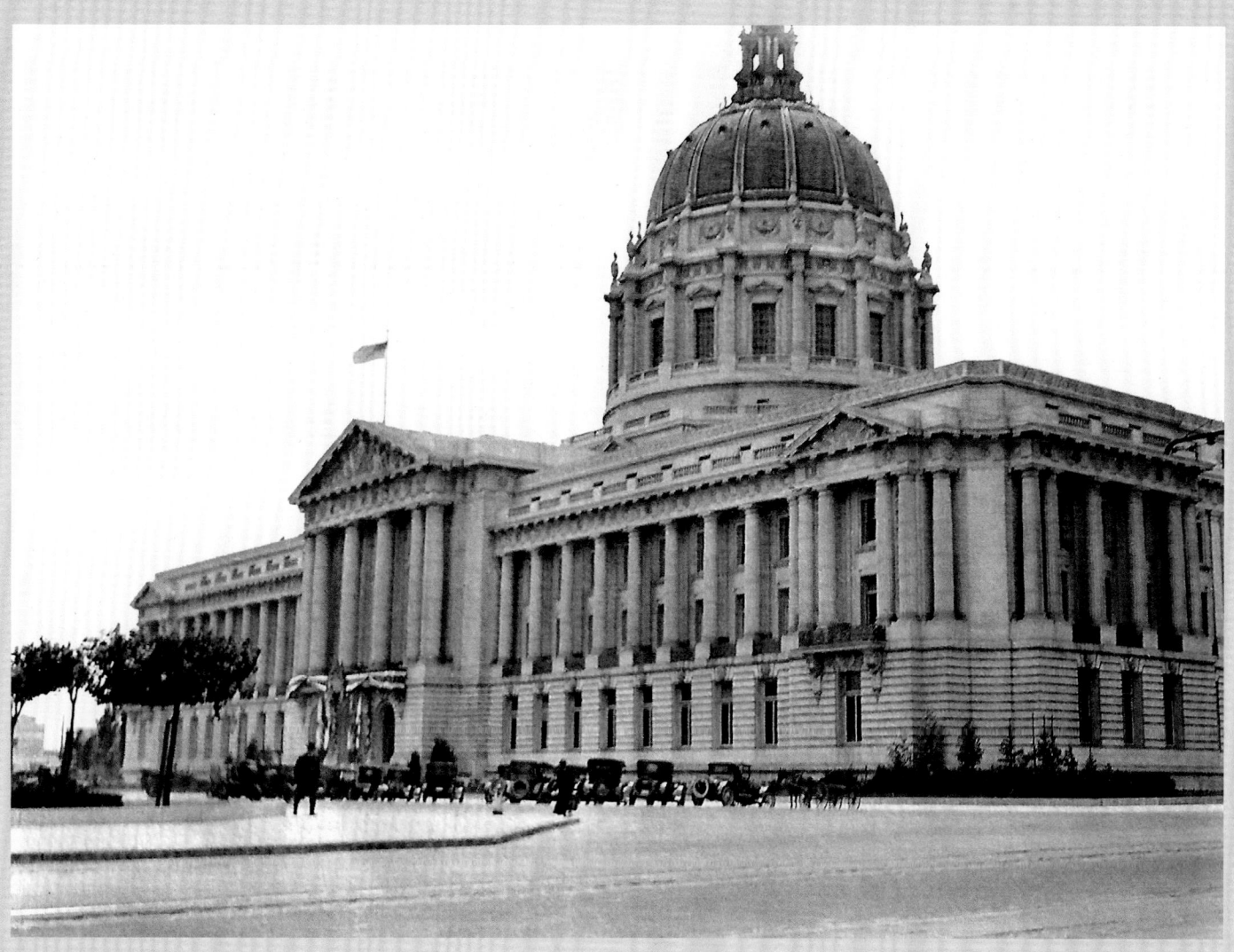

Located just a few blocks from the Clift Hotel was San Francisco's city hall. Having a dome forty-two feet taller than that of the US Capitol, the building dominated the cityscape in 1919.

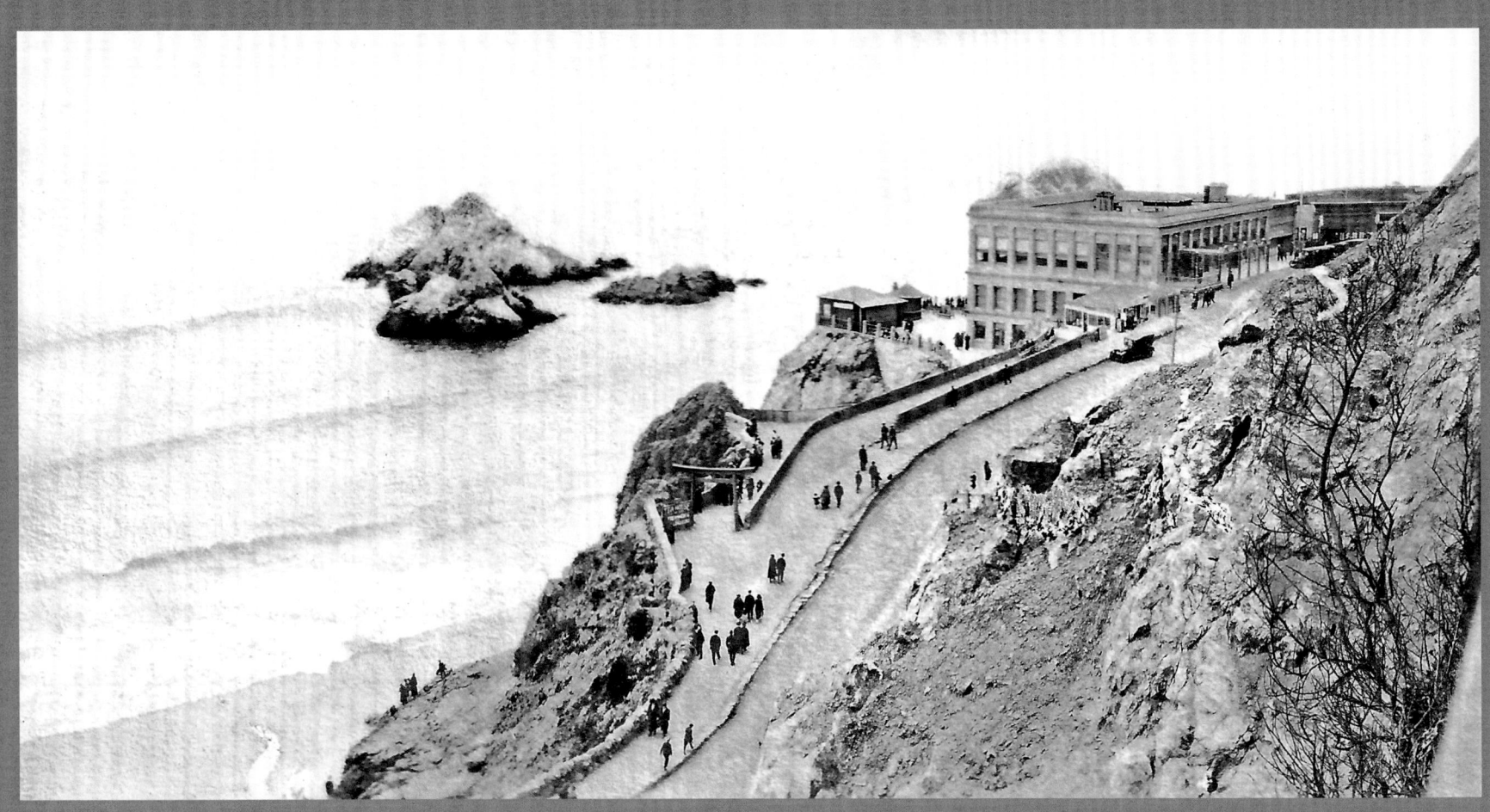

Henry photographed the Cliff House Hotel, designed in a neoclassical architectural style, from the shore south of the Golden Gate. The Cliff House is now part of the Golden Gate National Recreation Area.

From the Cliff House, Henry took a close-up of a small rock formation where Steller and California sea lions lounge in the sunshine. These animals and other resident wildlife are protected in the Golden Gate National Recreation Area.

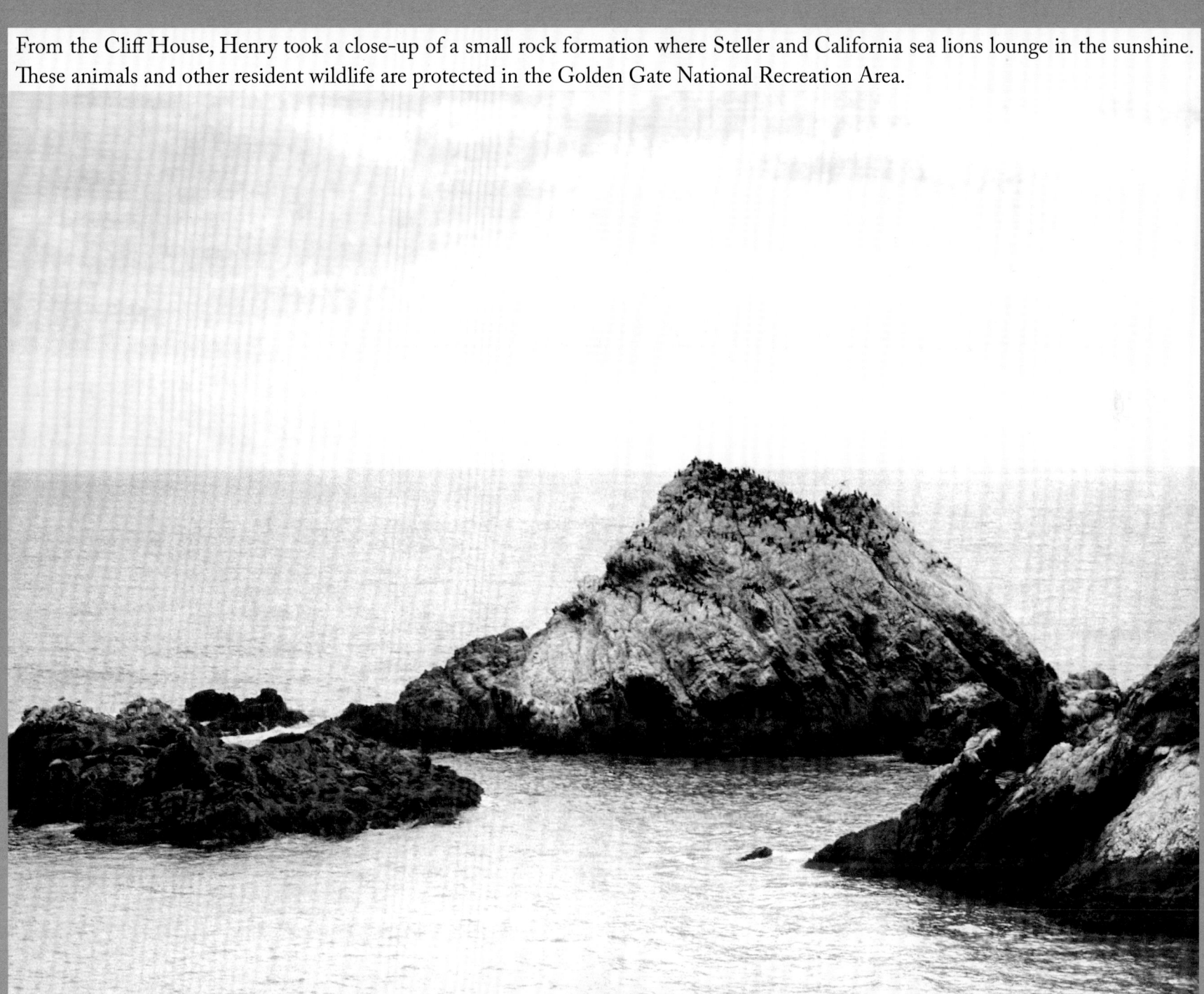

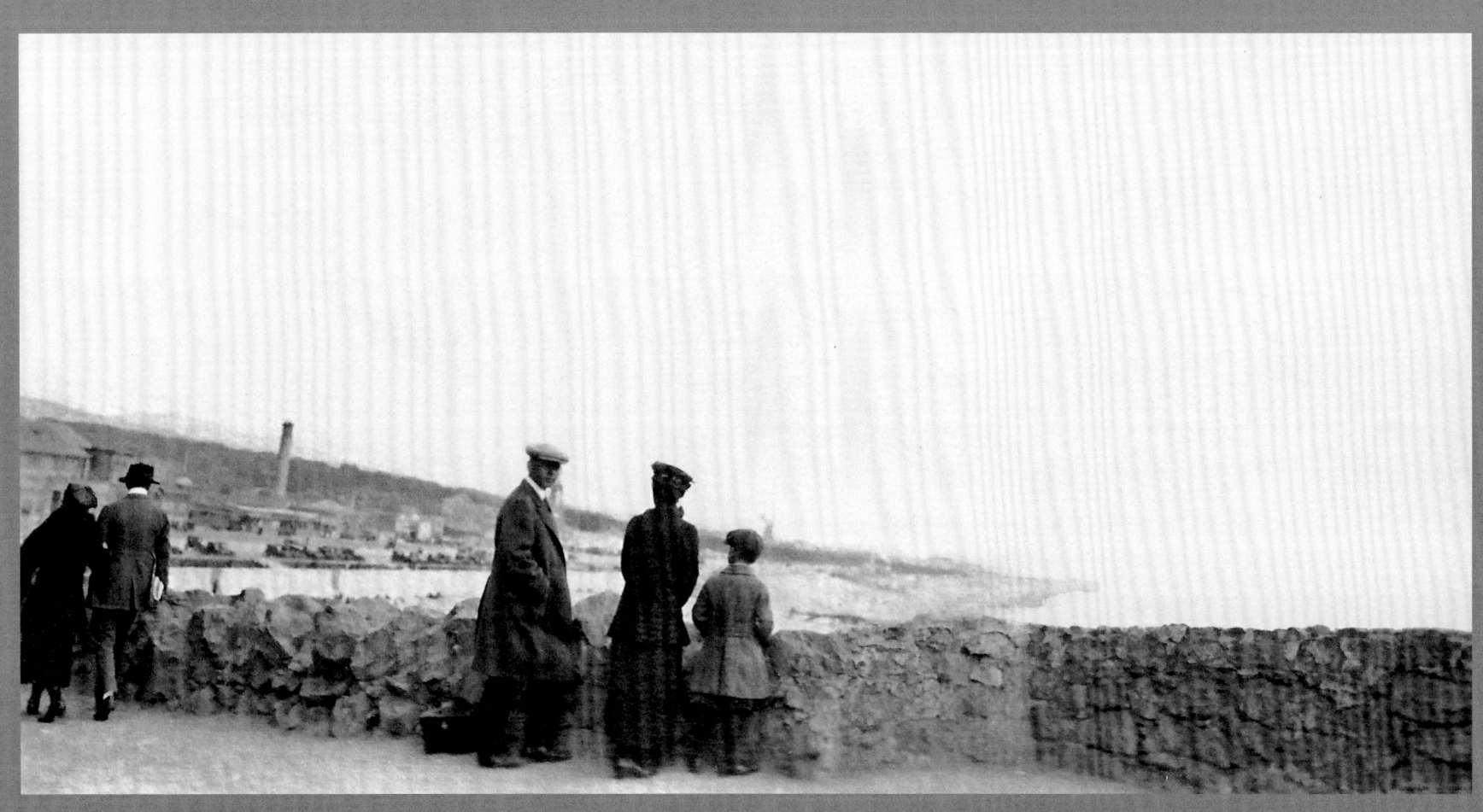

Henry, Lizzie, and Ernest are shown here, on the Cliff Walk at Lands End Lookout. The Graflex camera case is to Henry's left. Judging by their clothing, a cold wind is blowing in from the Pacific. In the far distance the Dutch Windmill appears just to the right of Ernest's cap.

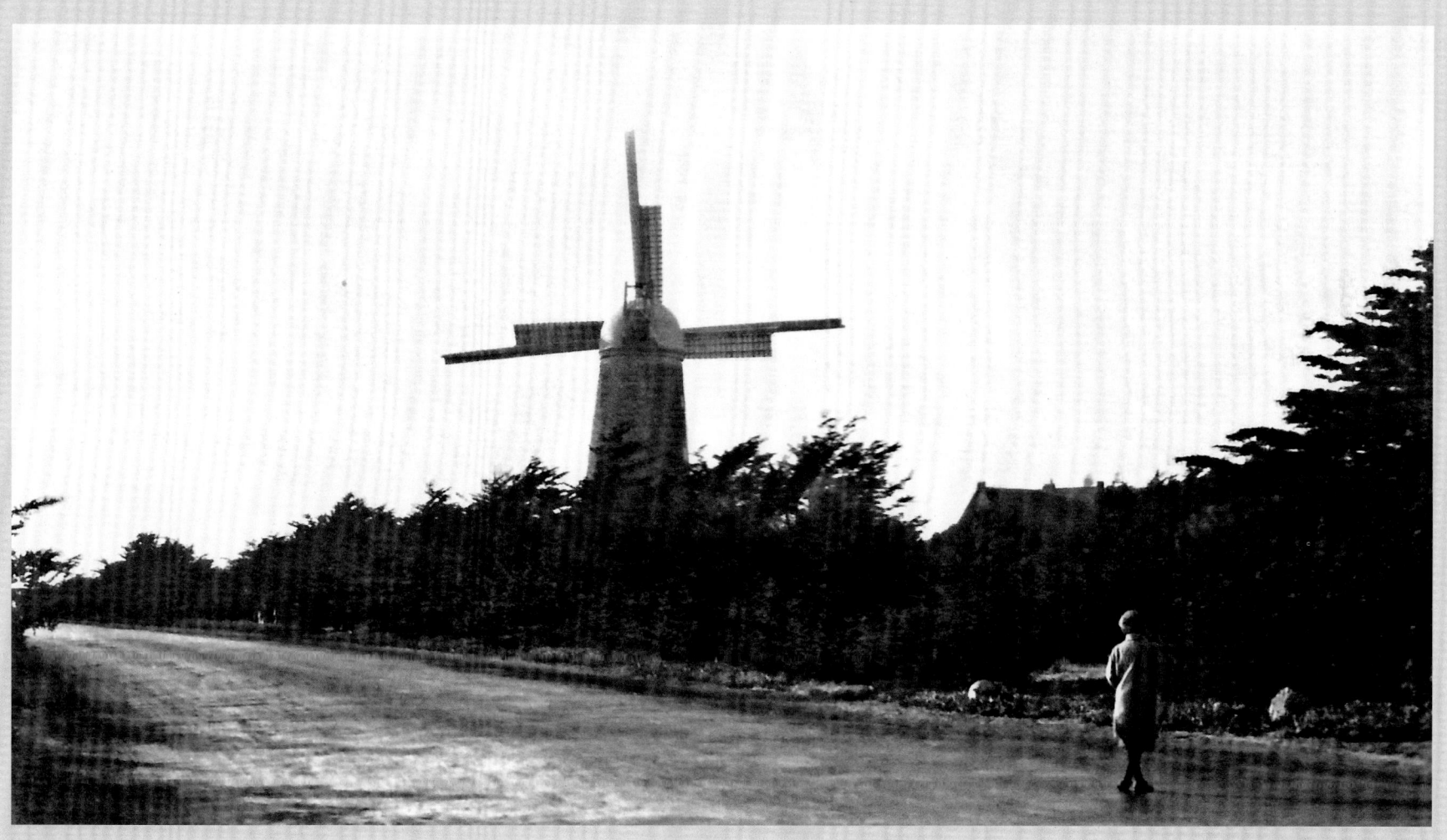

The Dutch Windmill in Golden Gate Park was built in 1903. One of two windmills constructed at about the same time, the Dutch Windmill has a blade span of 102 feet and a height of 75 feet. It was made for pumping groundwater to irrigate Golden Gate Park and the Queen Wilhelmina Tulip Garden. The Dutch Windmill became a San Francisco designated landmark in 1981.

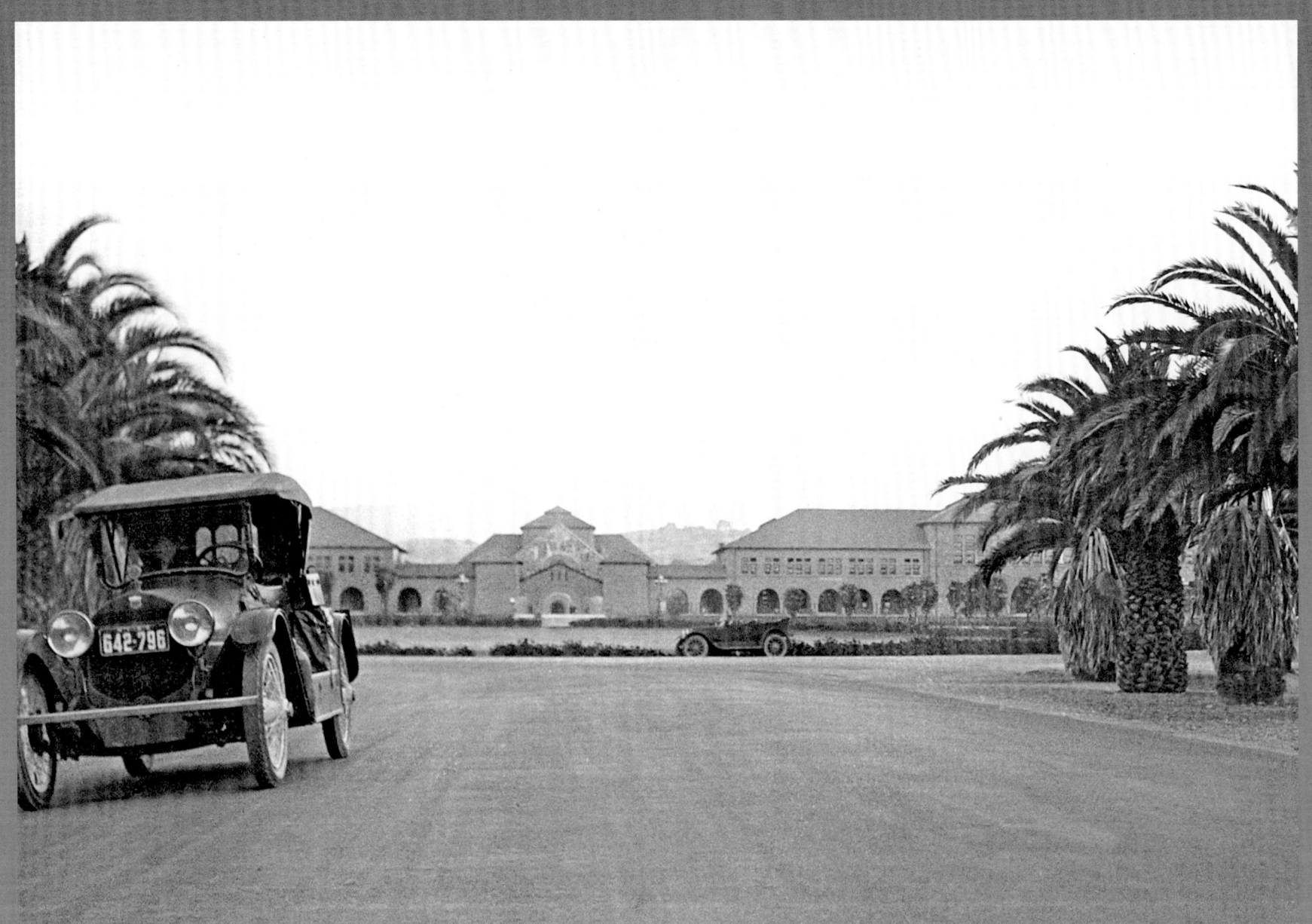

Leaving San Francisco, the Spallholzes stopped at Stanford University in Palo Alto. Lizzie would visit with a classmate from her college days at Cornell University, Dr. Edith Johnson. Here the Haynes is parked on Palmer Drive with the Stanford University entrance in the background. More than half a century later, Palo Alto would become part of the region known as Silicon Valley.

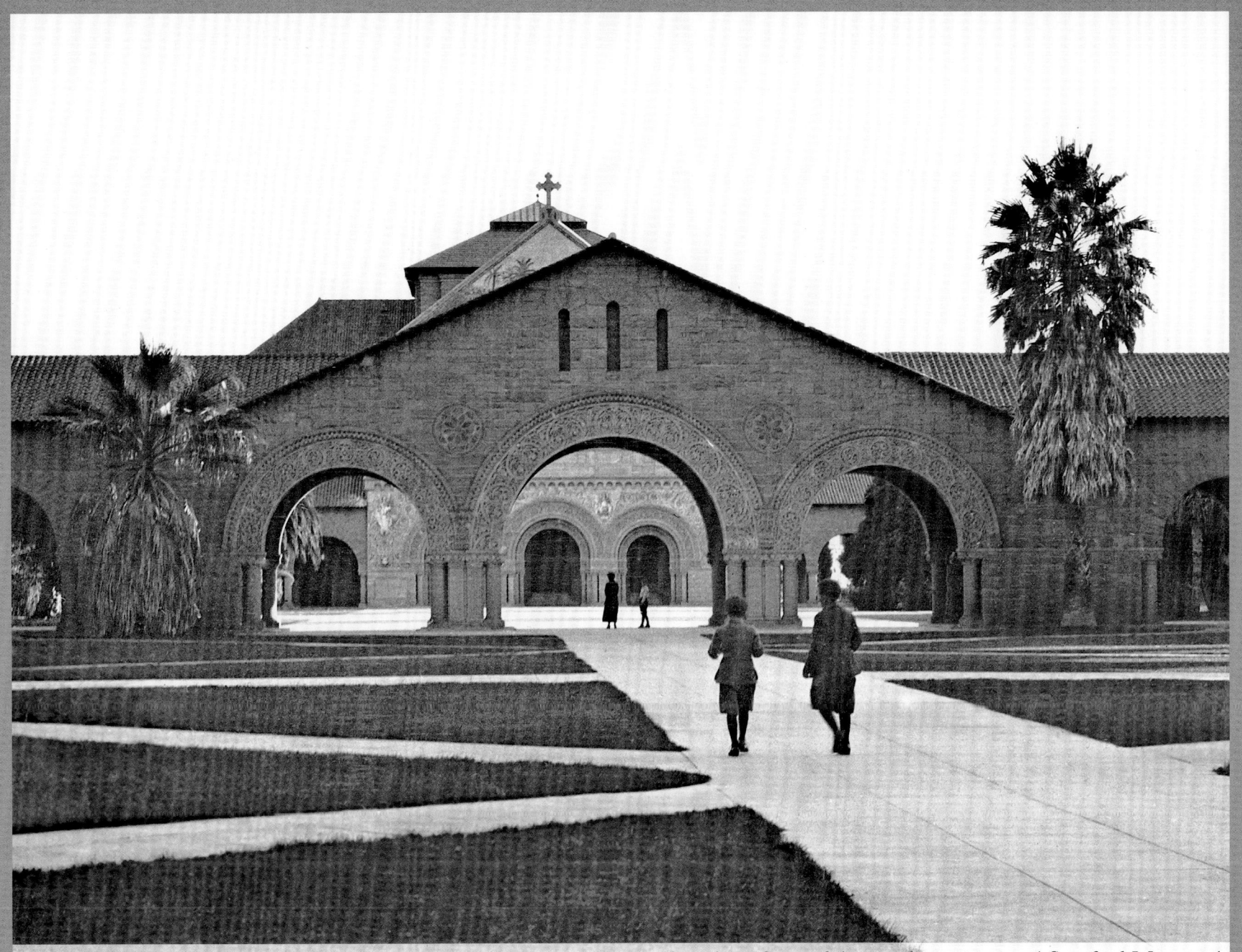

Lizzie and Walter stand under the main entrance arch of the major quadrangle in front of the nondenominational Stanford Memorial Church in Palo Alto, California.

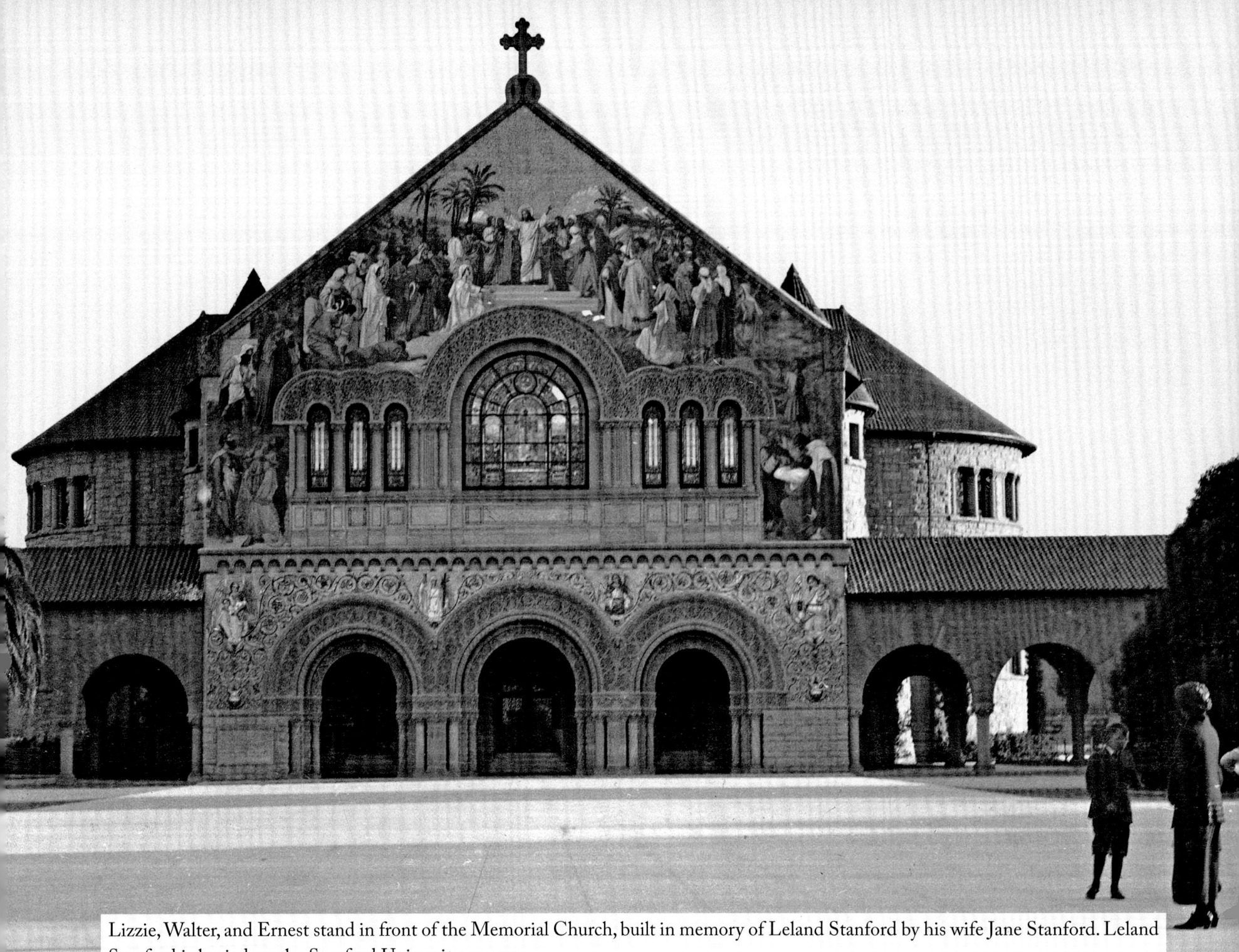

Lizzie, Walter, and Ernest stand in front of the Memorial Church, built in memory of Leland Stanford by his wife Jane Stanford. Leland Stanford is buried on the Stanford University campus.

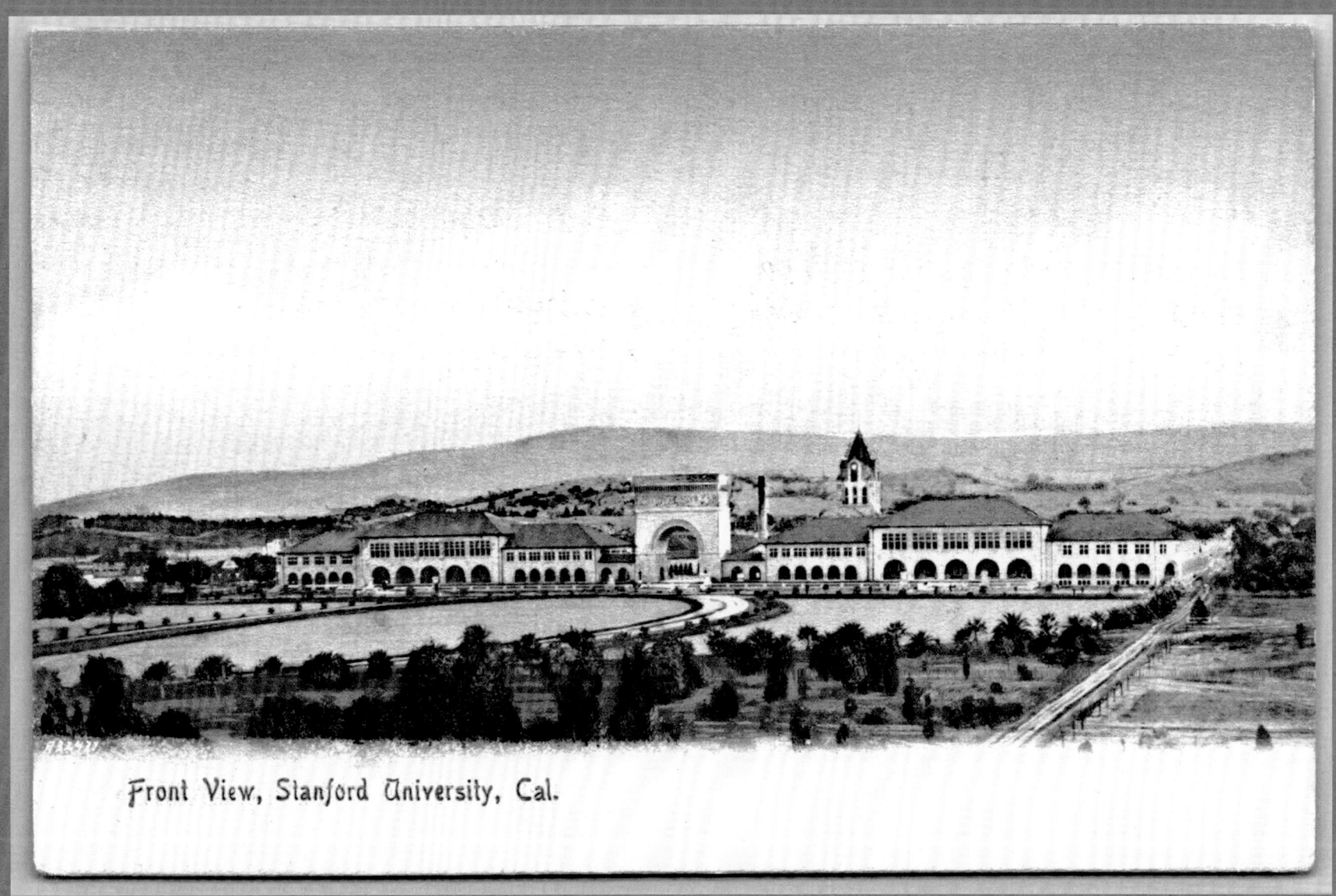

Front View, Stanford University, Cal.

Period postcard showing a front view of Stanford University.

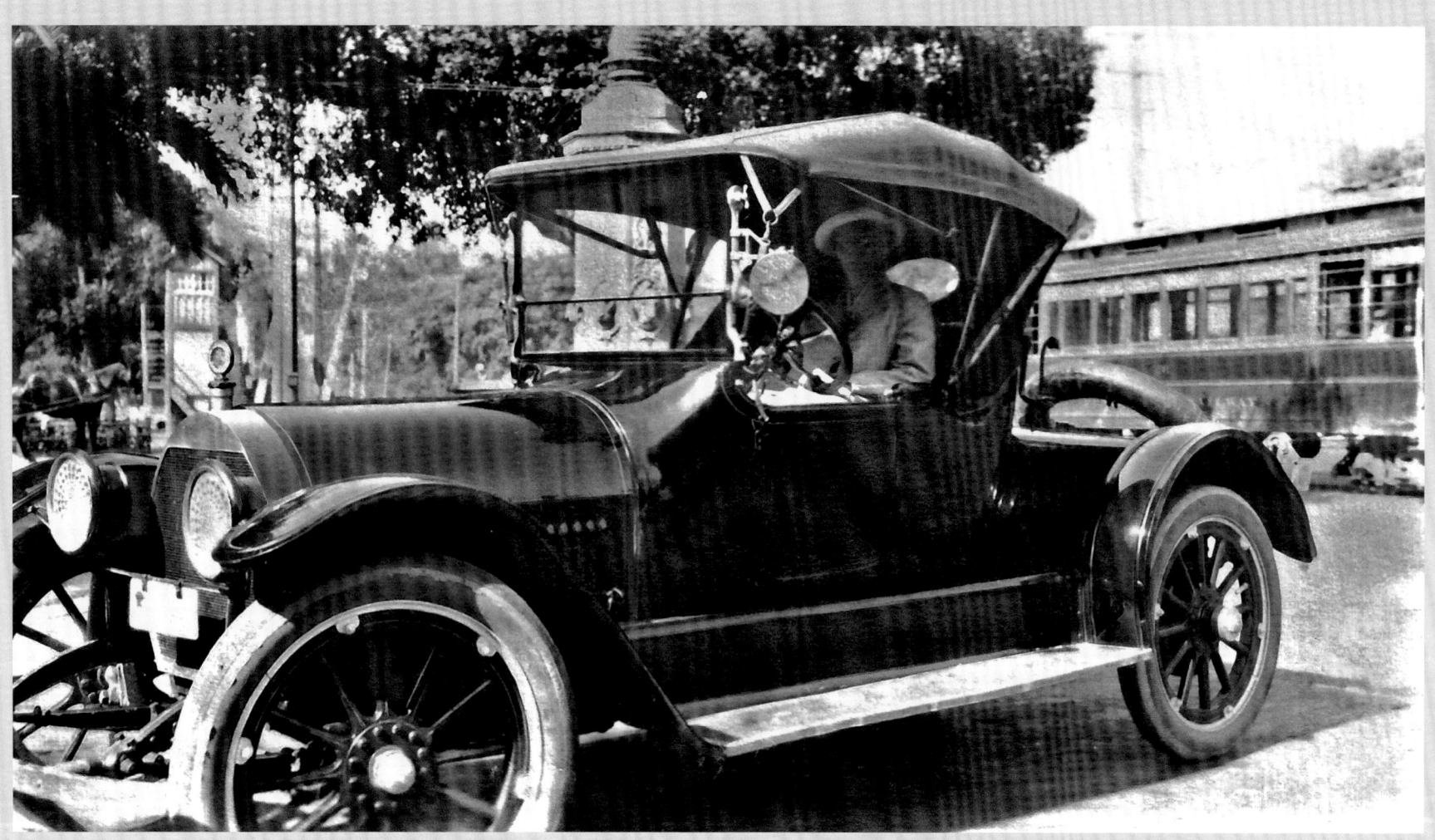

In Palo Alto, California, Lizzie Spallholz visited with Dr. Edith Johnson, a classmate of hers from Cornell University. Dr. Johnson is sitting in her automobile. Note the trolley in the background.

Lizzie, Walter, and Ernest sit in the Haynes on the stagecoach and covered-wagon route south of San Luis Obispo, California, along the Camino Real south of San Francisco. At 1,522 feet, Cuesta Pass connects the eastern Salinas River Valley with the coastal cities north of the Santa Lucia Mountains. The road appears to be in very good condition here, with a sturdy white guard rail.

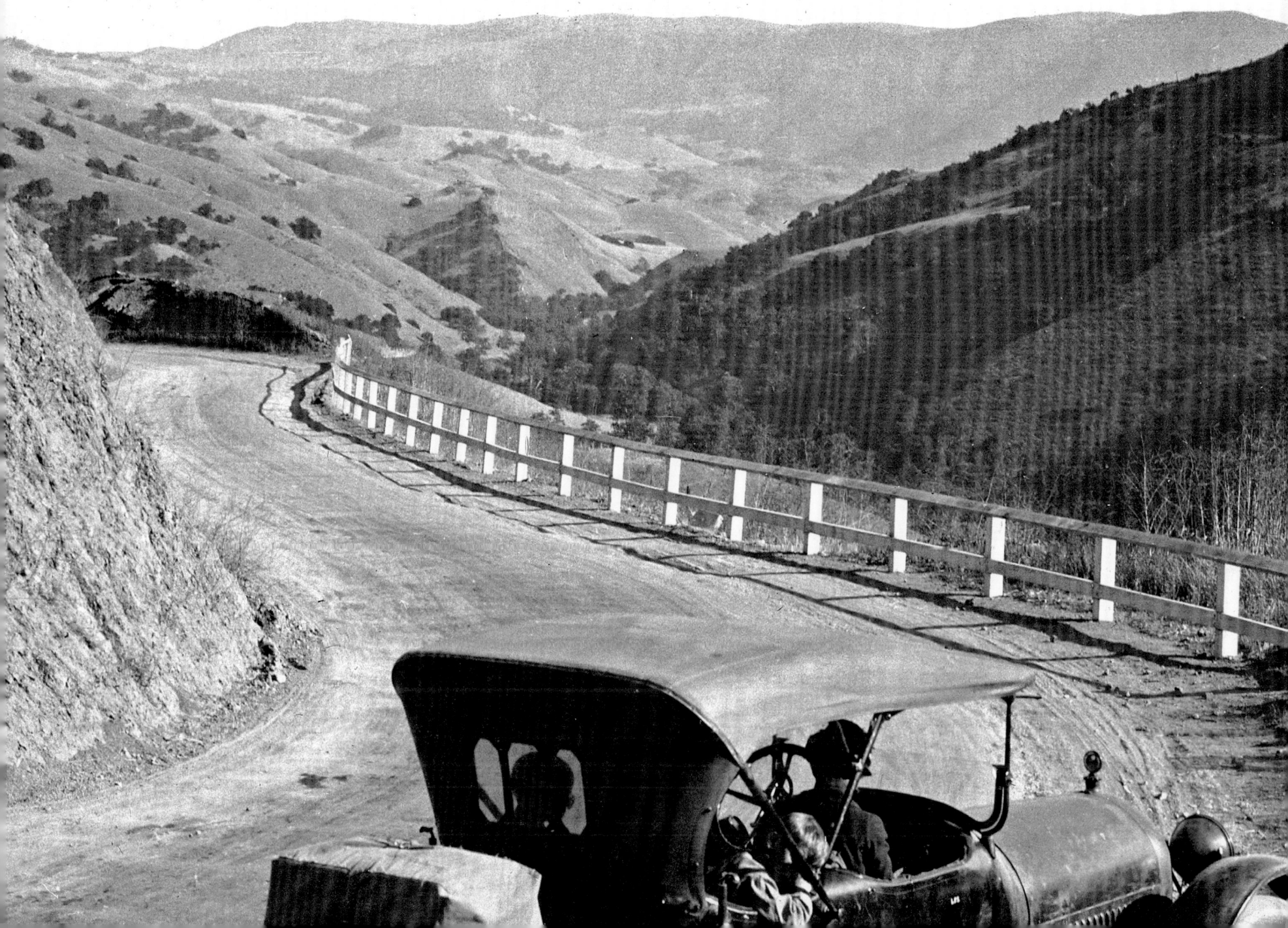

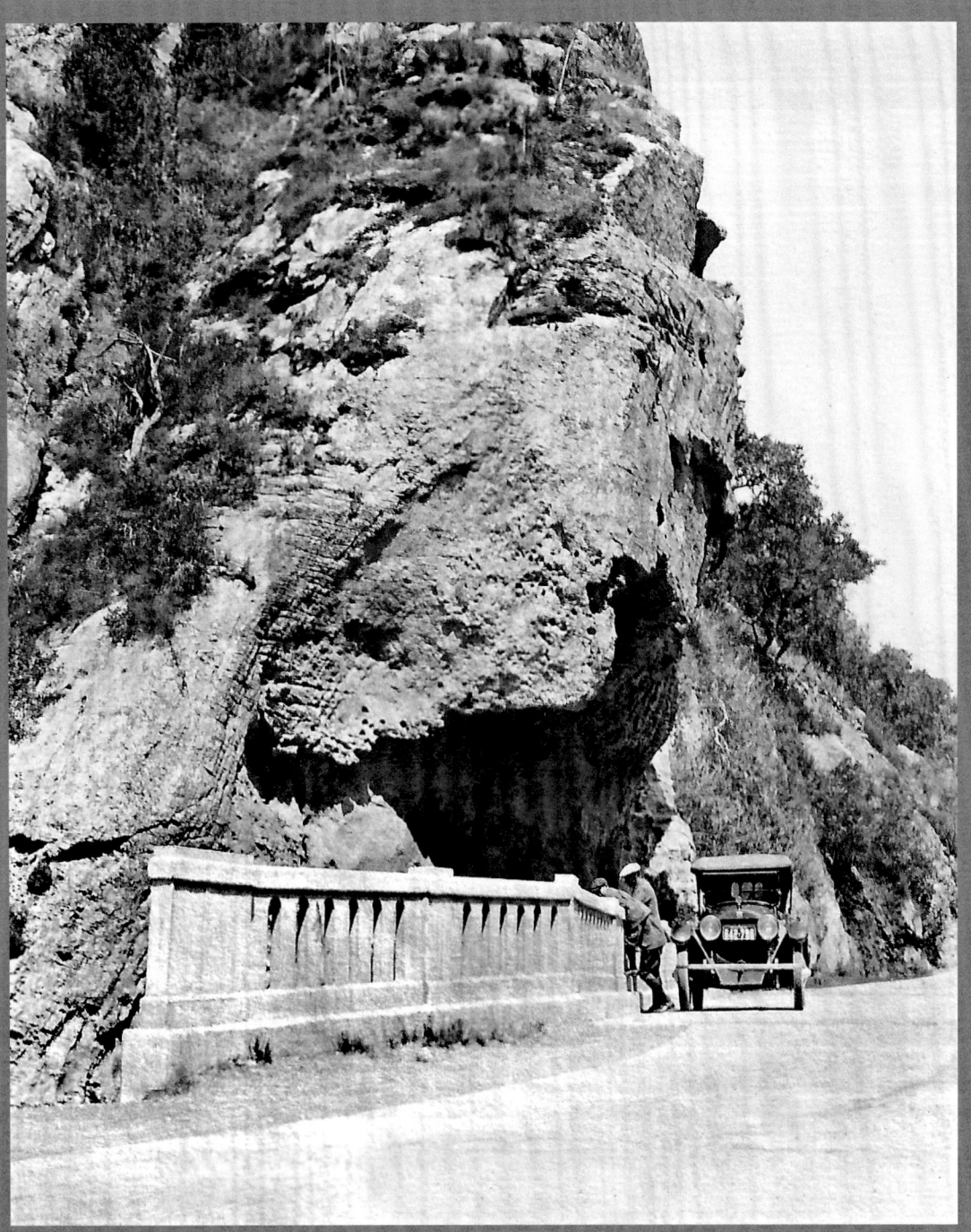

On the downhill side of the Cuesta Pass summit, the Spallholzes stopped on a bridge to inspect a riverbed below. Walter looks over the bridge wall, and above them hangs the exposed face of what appears to be an ancient volcanic basalt flow.

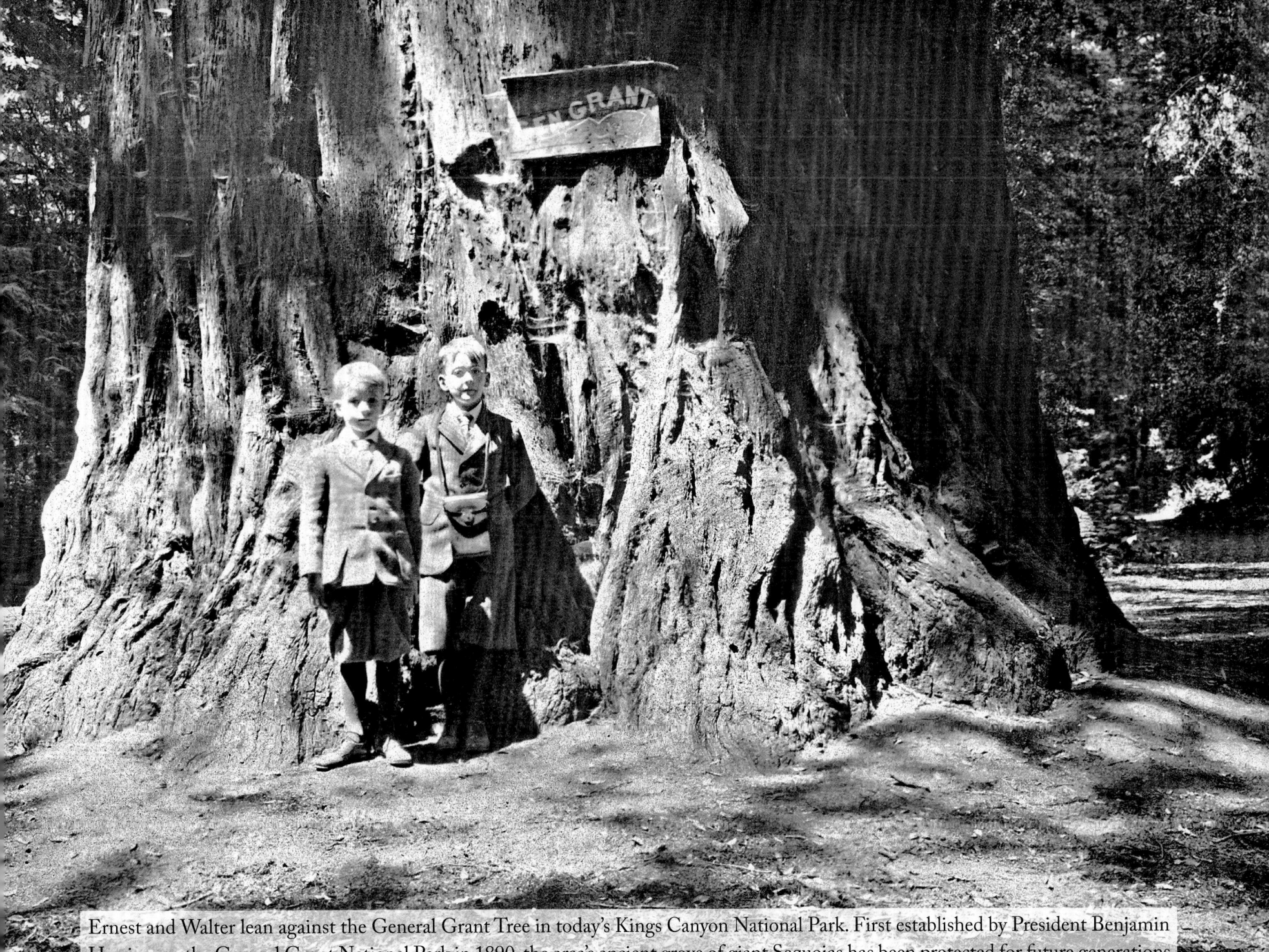

Ernest and Walter lean against the General Grant Tree in today's Kings Canyon National Park. First established by President Benjamin Harrison as the General Grant National Park in 1890, the area's ancient grove of giant Sequoias has been protected for future generations of visitors to enjoy. The tree is the centerpiece of Grant's Grove, the largest of a group of giant sequoias within the park.

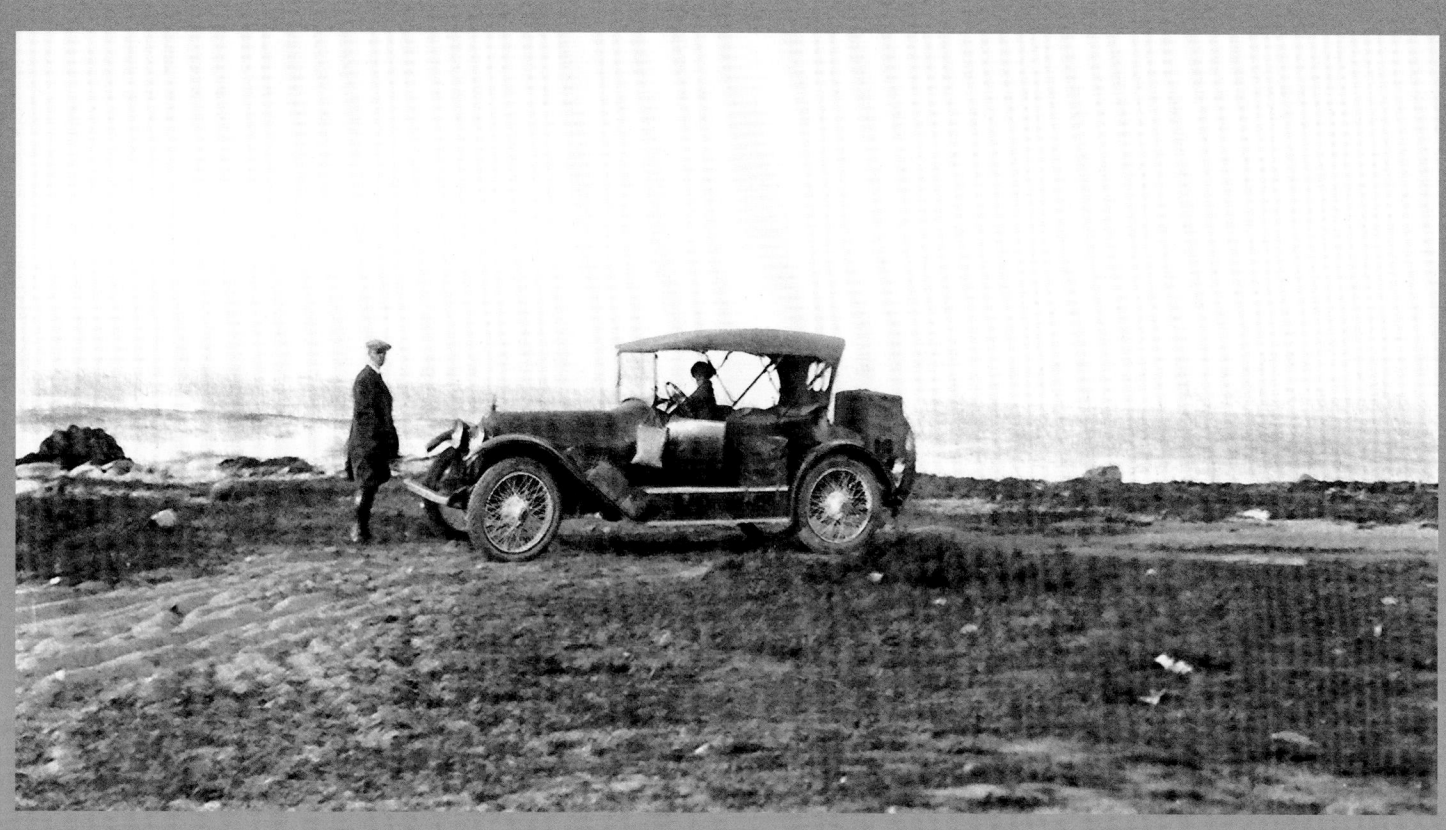

On the beach at Monterey Bay, Henry stands in front of the Haynes and Lizzie sits in the driver's seat. Monterey is on the peninsula to the south of the bay. Discovered and settled by the Spanish in the mid to late 1500s, the locale is home to the Monterey Bay Aquarium and is a designated marine conservation area.

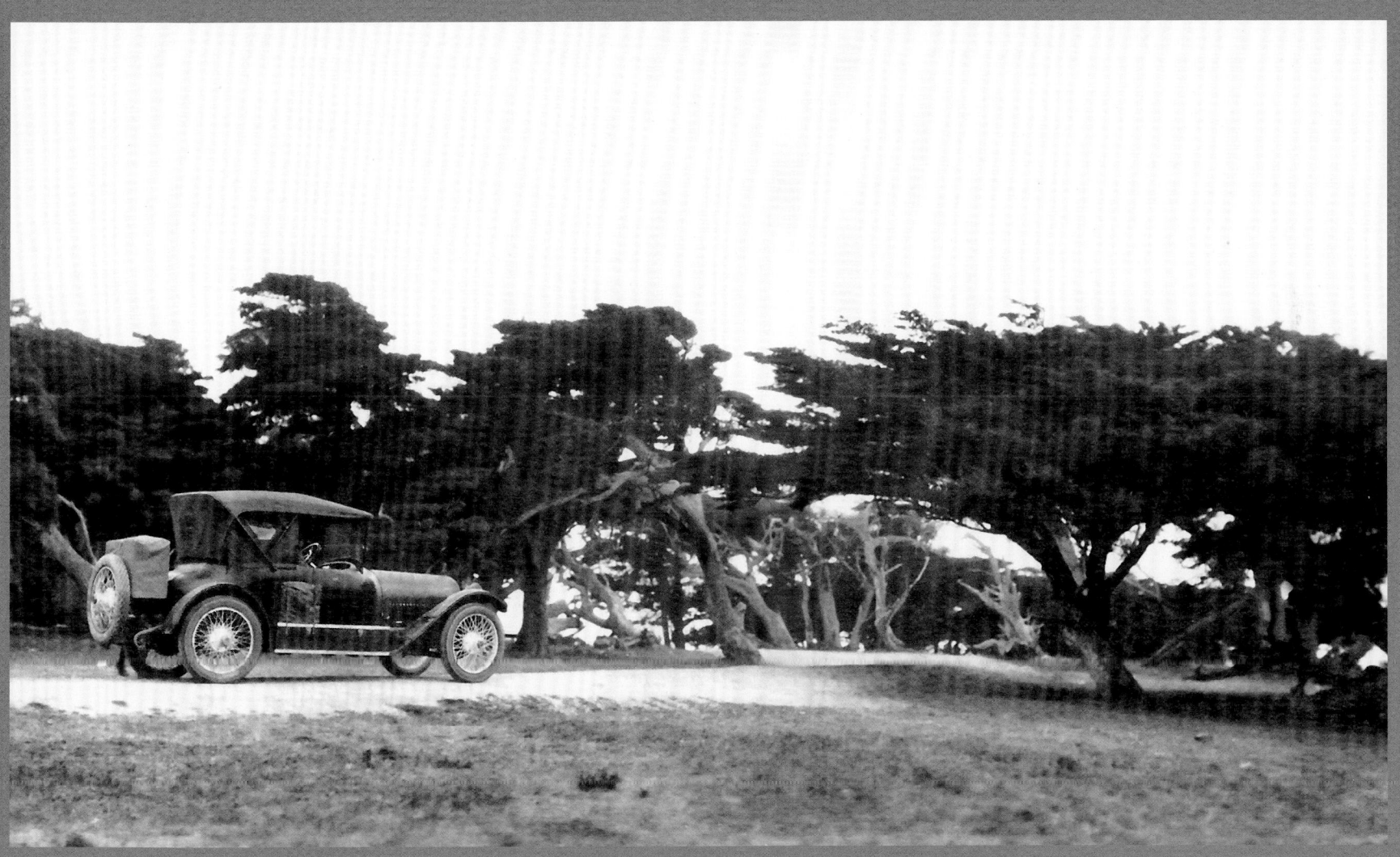

The Haynes sits at Cypress Grove, a popular stop on California's coast near Carmel River State Beach. The slight leaning of the trees indicates the prevailing wind at this location is from the west. Ten miles north of Cypress Grove along the well-known seventeen-mile drive is the Lone Cypress, believed to have been seeded in 1750 when the area was the colony known as New Spain.

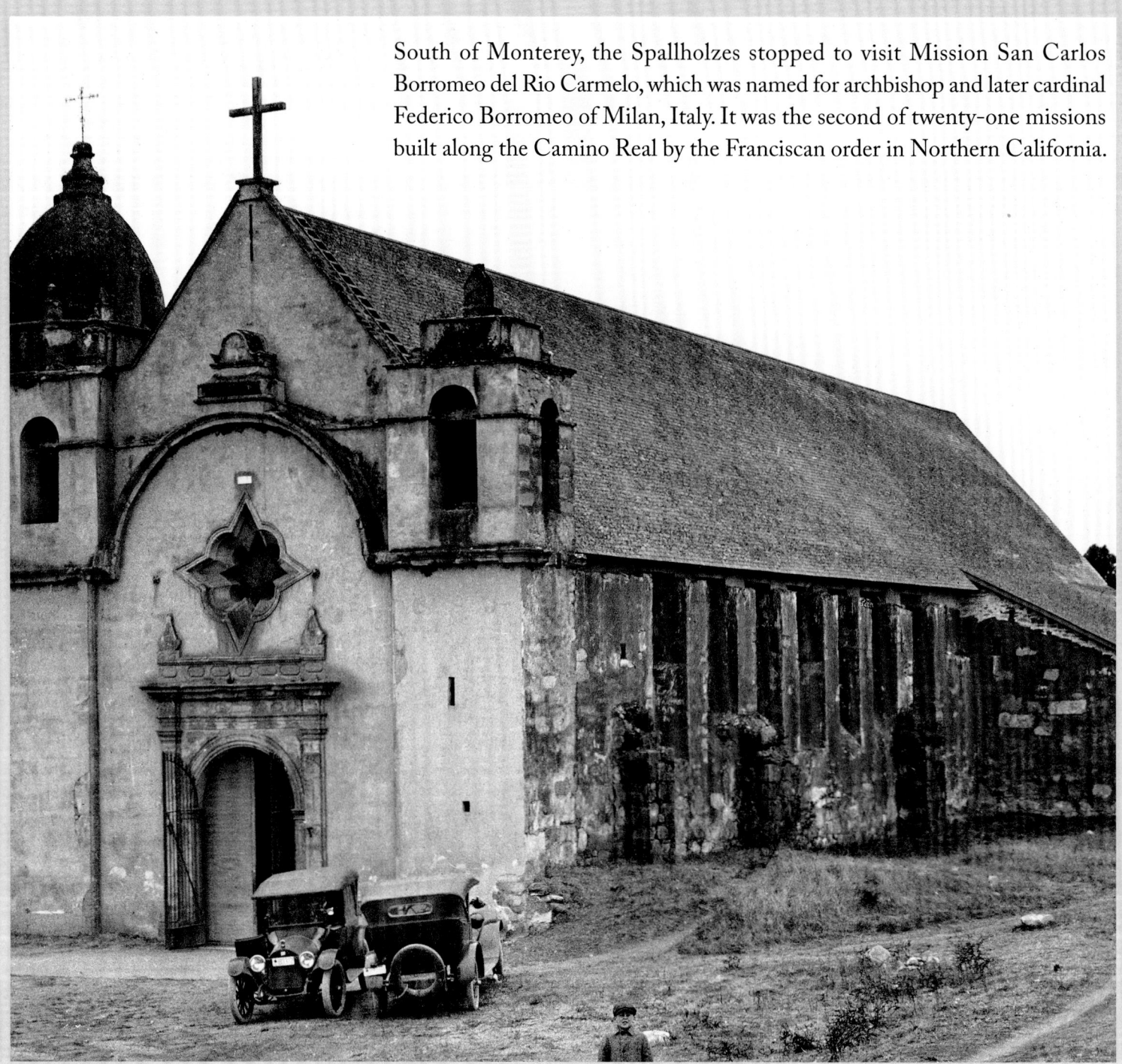

South of Monterey, the Spallholzes stopped to visit Mission San Carlos Borromeo del Rio Carmelo, which was named for archbishop and later cardinal Federico Borromeo of Milan, Italy. It was the second of twenty-one missions built along the Camino Real by the Franciscan order in Northern California.

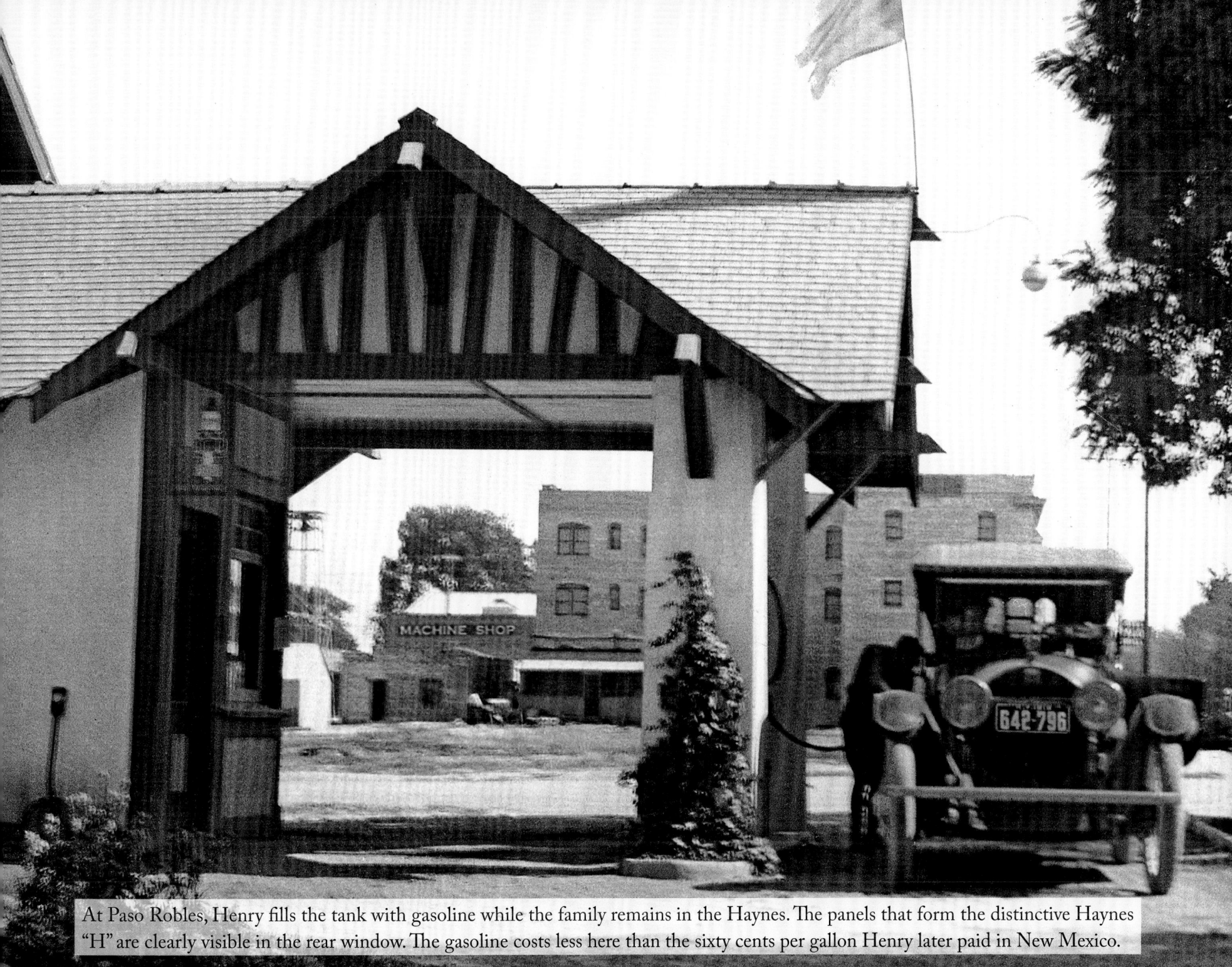

At Paso Robles, Henry fills the tank with gasoline while the family remains in the Haynes. The panels that form the distinctive Haynes "H" are clearly visible in the rear window. The gasoline costs less here than the sixty cents per gallon Henry later paid in New Mexico.

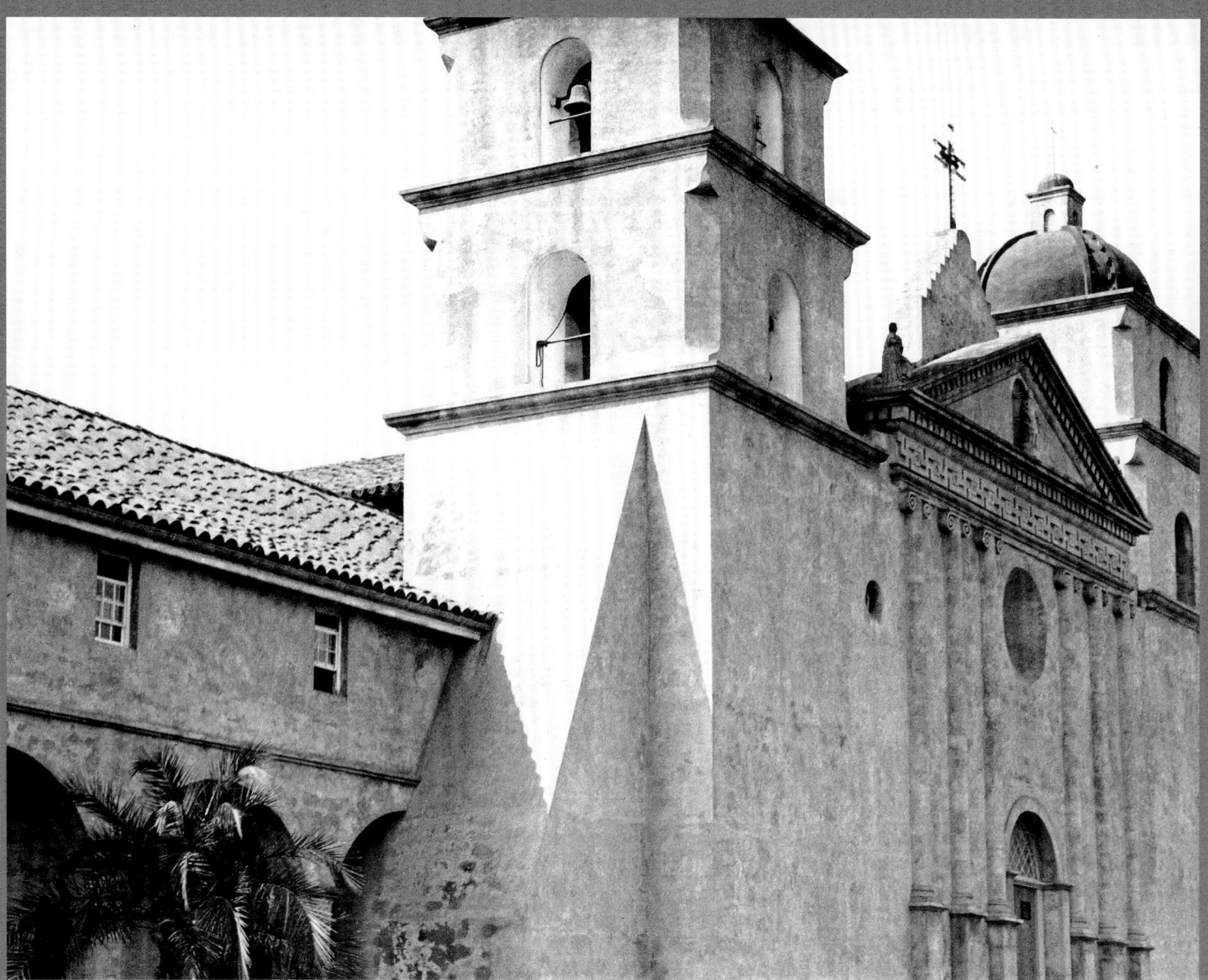

Santa Barbara Mission is one of the twenty-one Franciscan missions on the Camino Real. Named after Santa Barbara, who was beheaded by her pagan father for not recanting her Christian faith, the mission occupies land that faces the Pacific Ocean at the front and the Santa Ynez Mountains to the rear. This Spallholz photograph is of a portion of the long-arched room corridor and the chapel's twin bell towers. The presence of two towers indicates the mission church was once a cathedral.

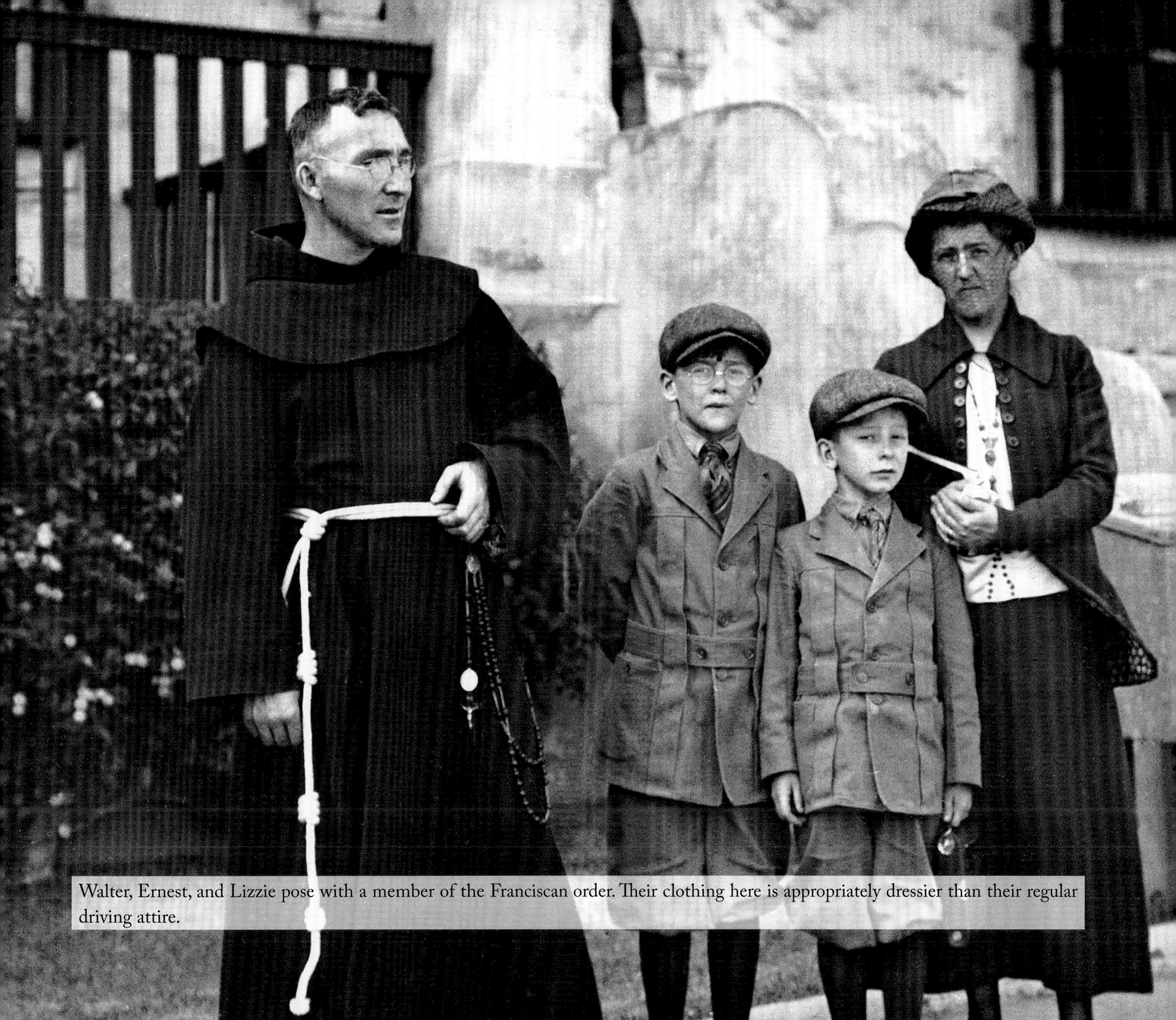

Walter, Ernest, and Lizzie pose with a member of the Franciscan order. Their clothing here is appropriately dressier than their regular driving attire.

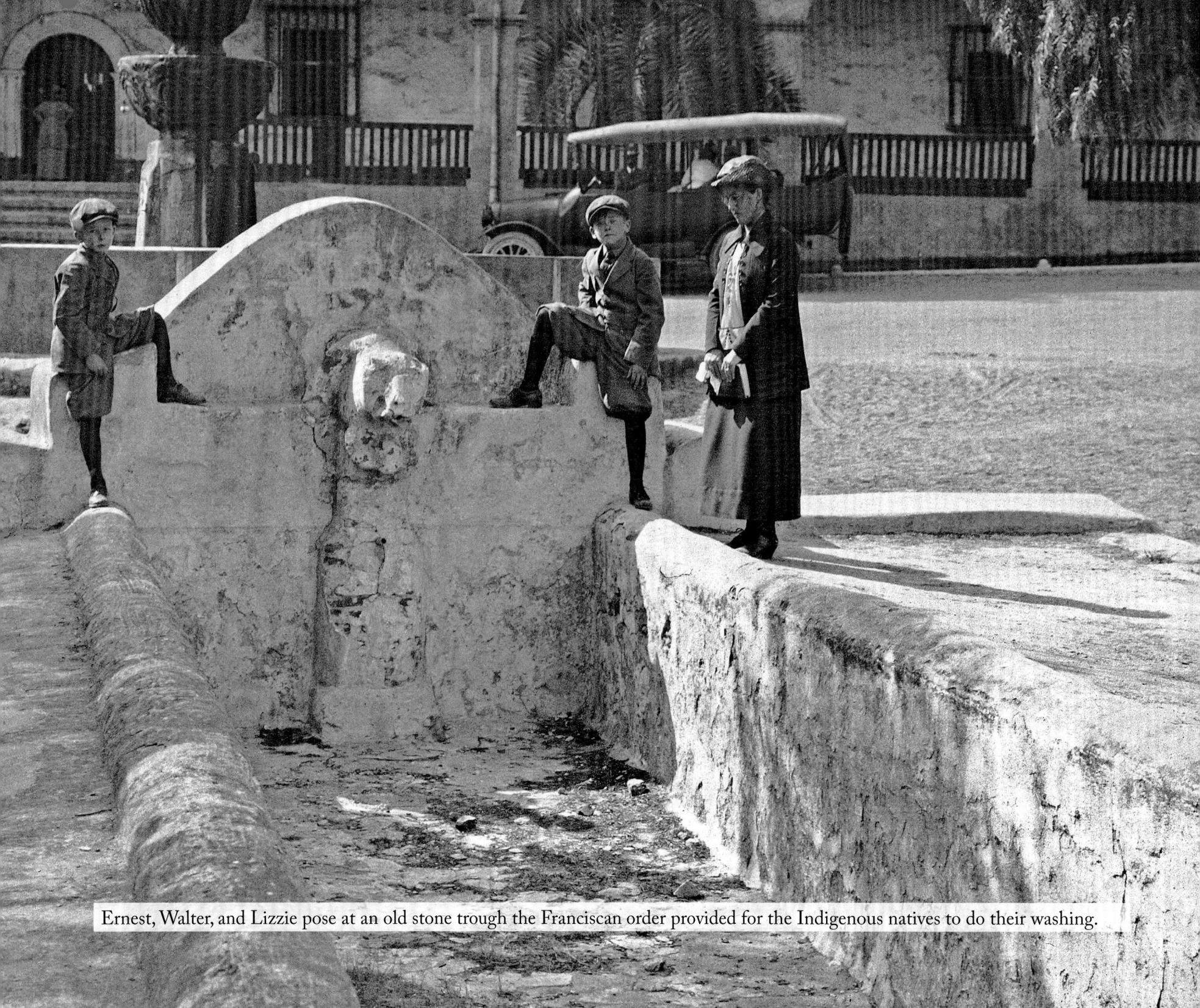

Ernest, Walter, and Lizzie pose at an old stone trough the Franciscan order provided for the Indigenous natives to do their washing.

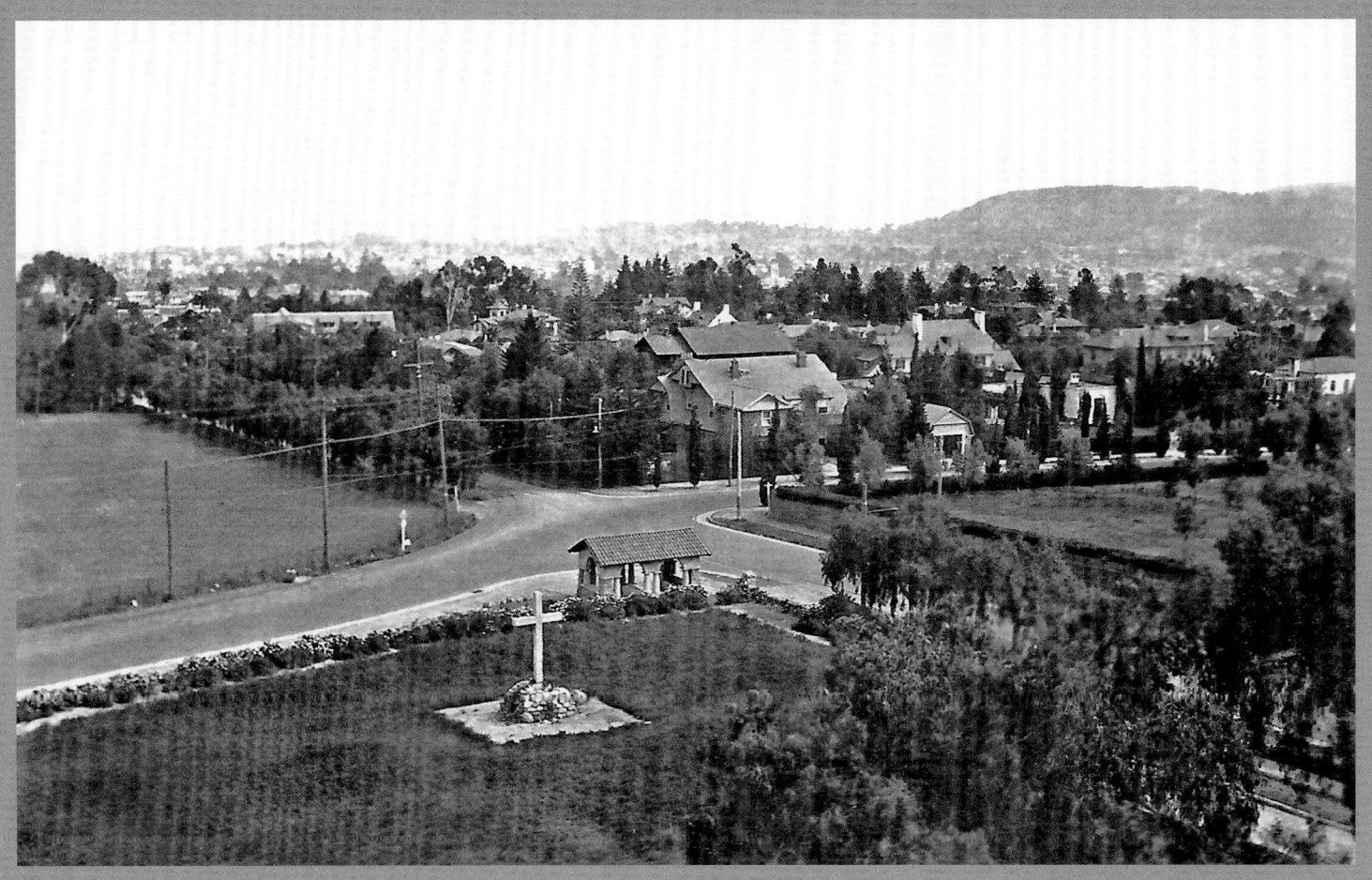

Henry took this photograph from the Santa Barbara Mission tower. The Santa Ynez Mountains are in the background.

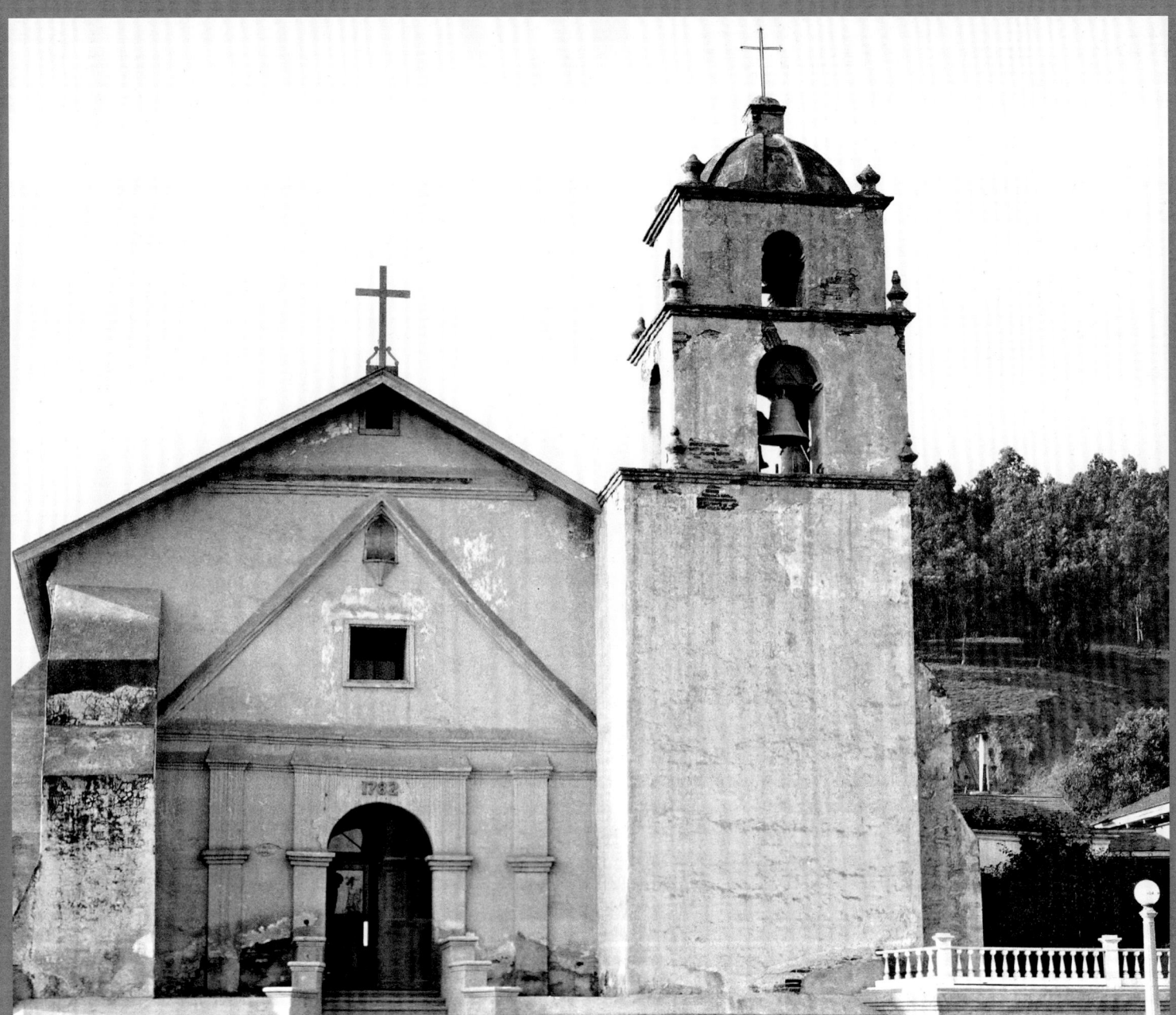

Mission San Buenaventura is named for Saint Bonaventure, patron saint and philosopher in the Catholic Church. It is the ninth and last of the Catholic missions to be established (1782), by Father Junípero Serra, then head of the Franciscan Order.

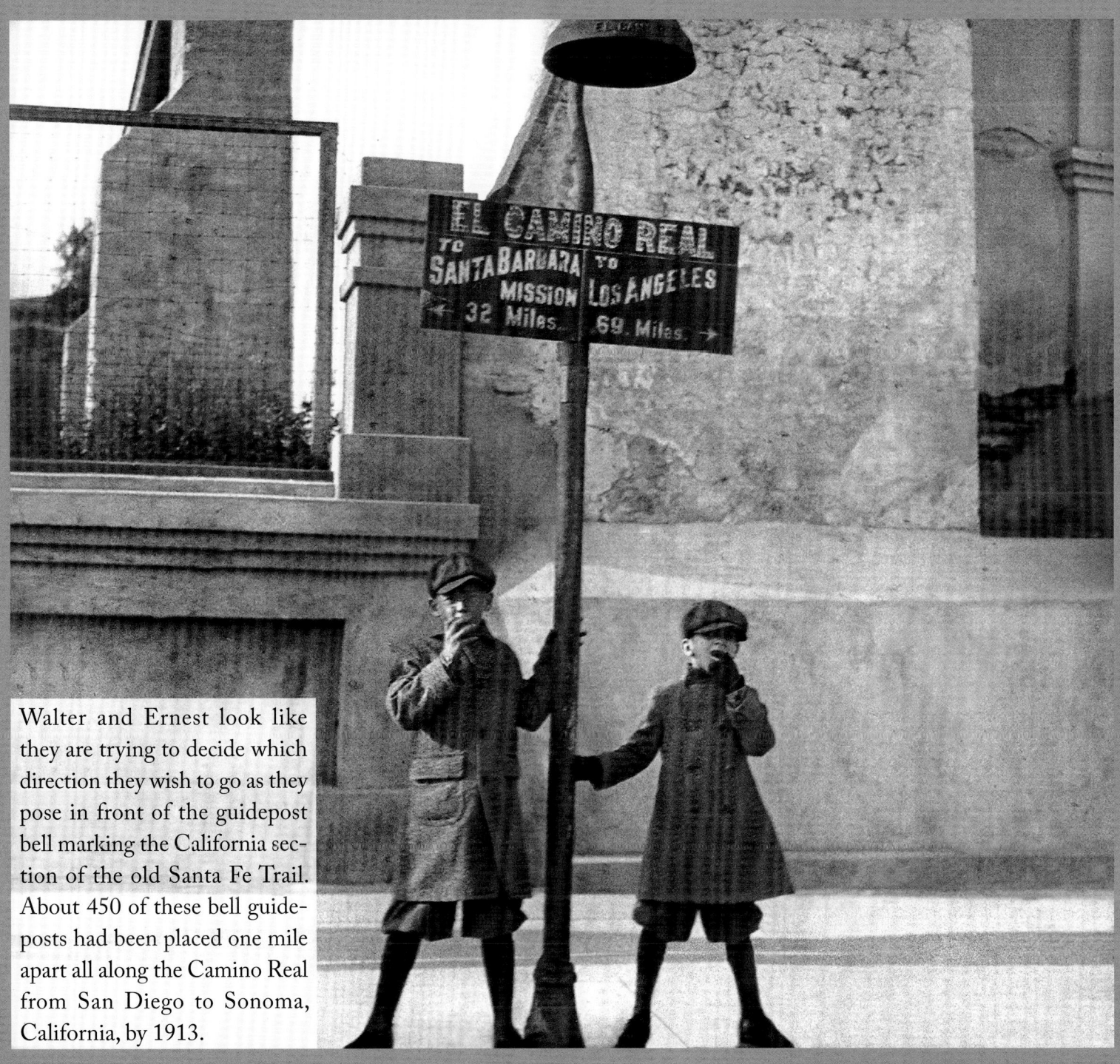

EL CAMINO REAL
TO SANTA BARBARA MISSION ← 32 Miles.
TO LOS ANGELES 69 Miles. →

Walter and Ernest look like they are trying to decide which direction they wish to go as they pose in front of the guidepost bell marking the California section of the old Santa Fe Trail. About 450 of these bell guideposts had been placed one mile apart all along the Camino Real from San Diego to Sonoma, California, by 1913.

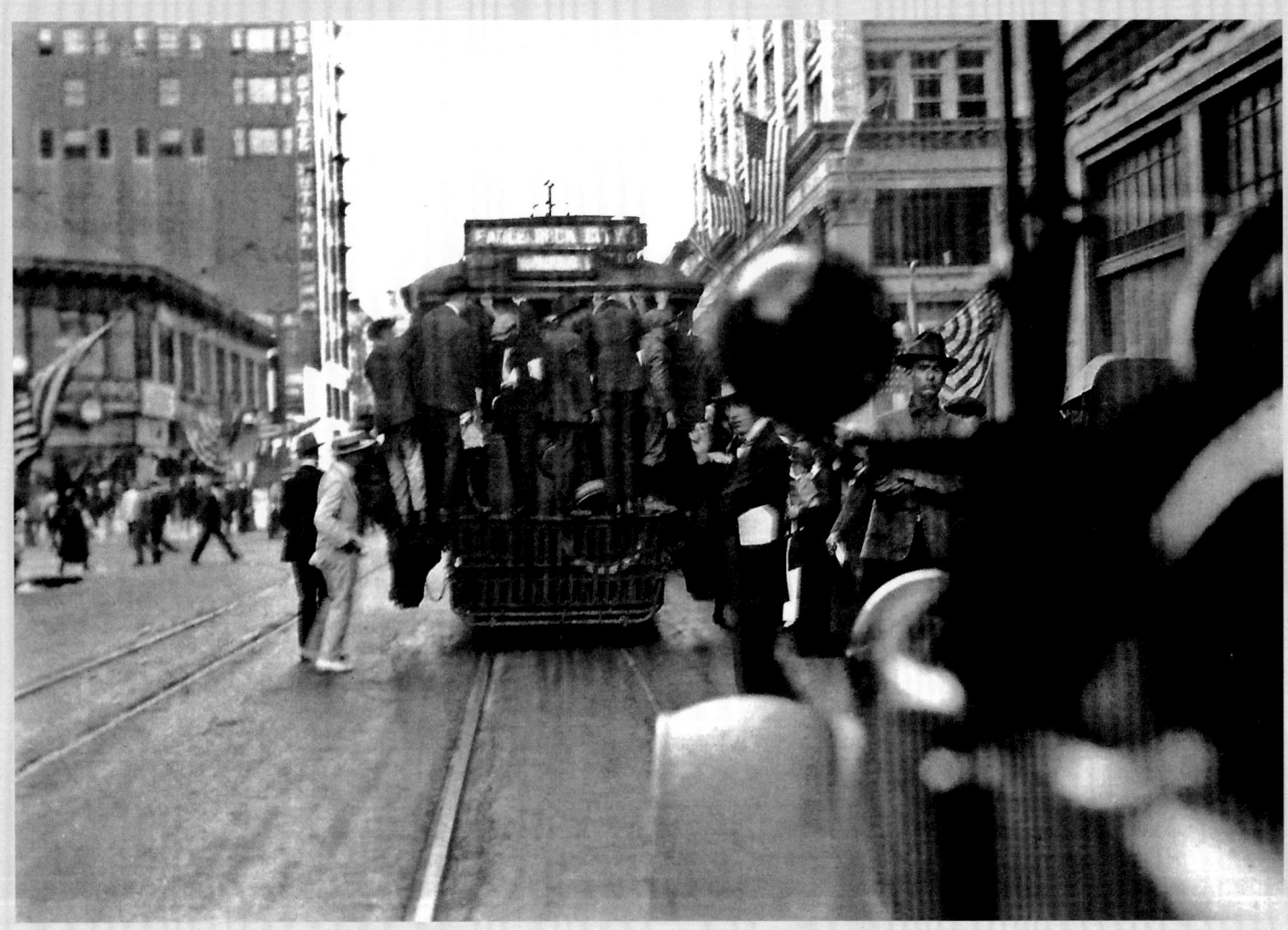

The Spallholzes arrived in Los Angeles at the height of the streetcar strike of 1919. Streetcar men were on strike for additional pay and the right to union organize. Management of the Los Angeles Railway system had just rejected an hourly wage increase. Walter probably took this photograph with the Kodak camera from the rear seat of the Haynes while Henry was driving the car.

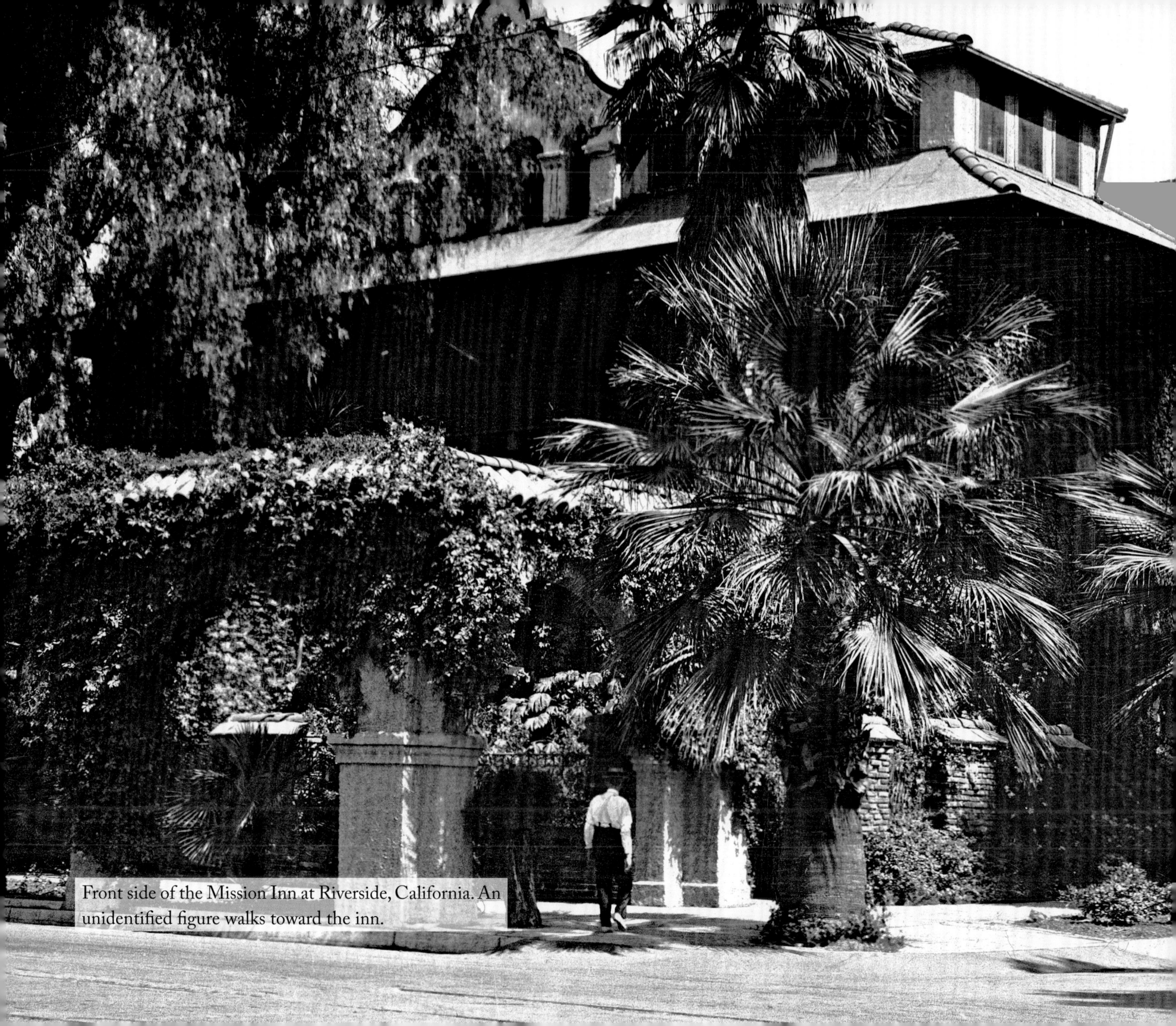

Front side of the Mission Inn at Riverside, California. An unidentified figure walks toward the inn.

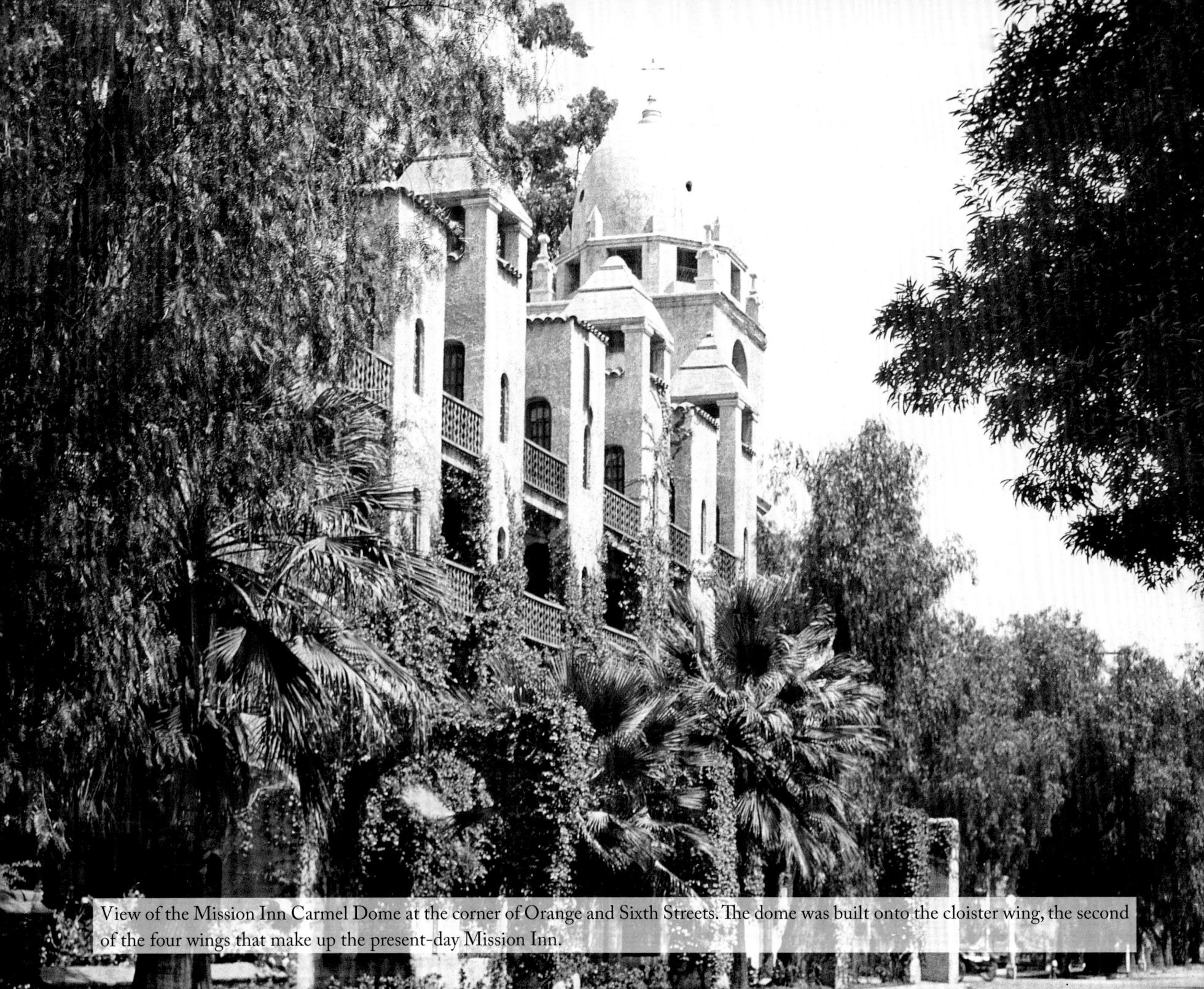

View of the Mission Inn Carmel Dome at the corner of Orange and Sixth Streets. The dome was built onto the cloister wing, the second of the four wings that make up the present-day Mission Inn.

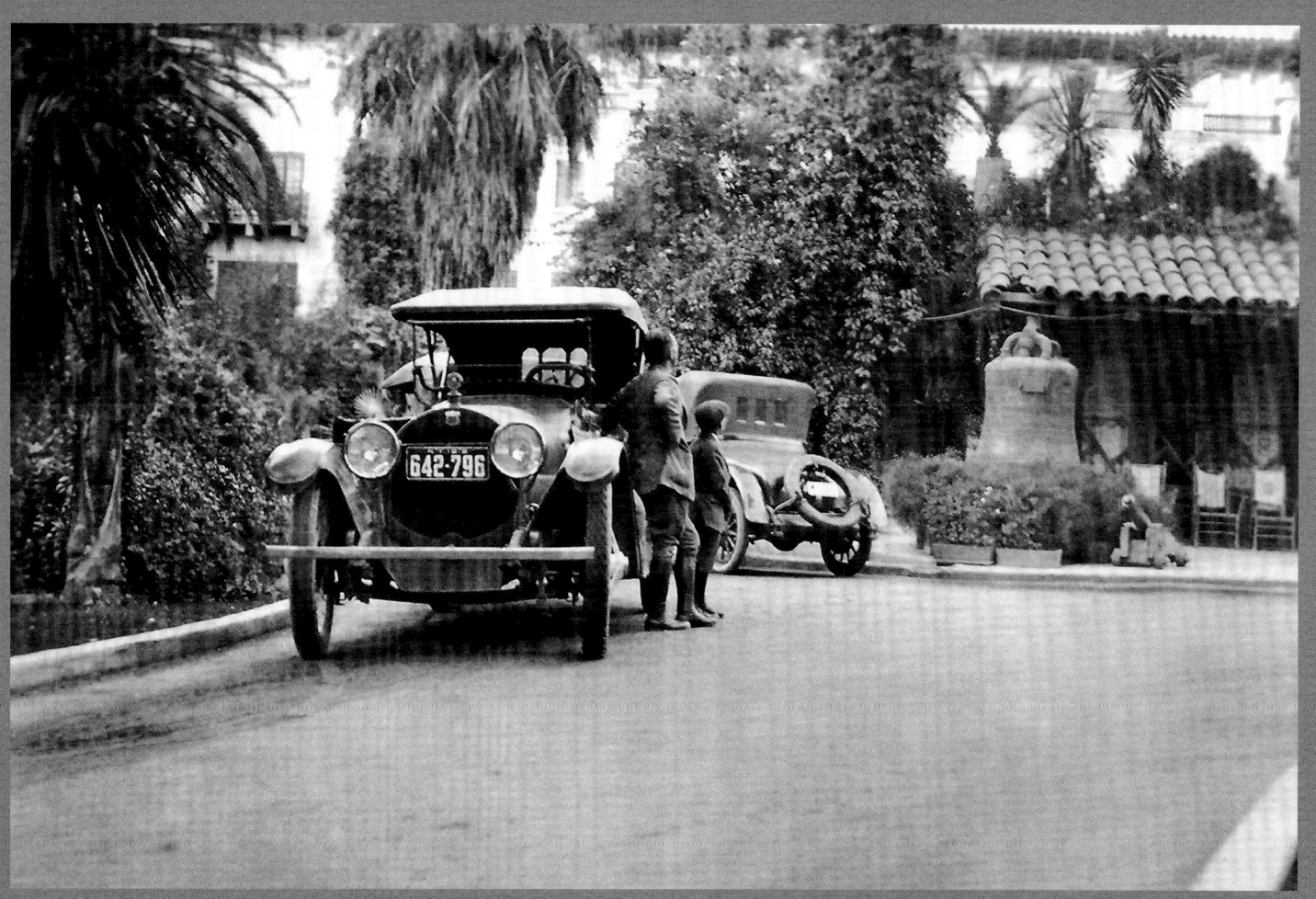

Henry and Ernest stand beside the Haynes looking at the Nanking Chinese Temple Bell at the Mission Inn in Riverside. The temple bell was brought to the Inn from China at the conclusion of the Boxer Rebellion in 1912. The bell is the focal point of the inn's courtyard.

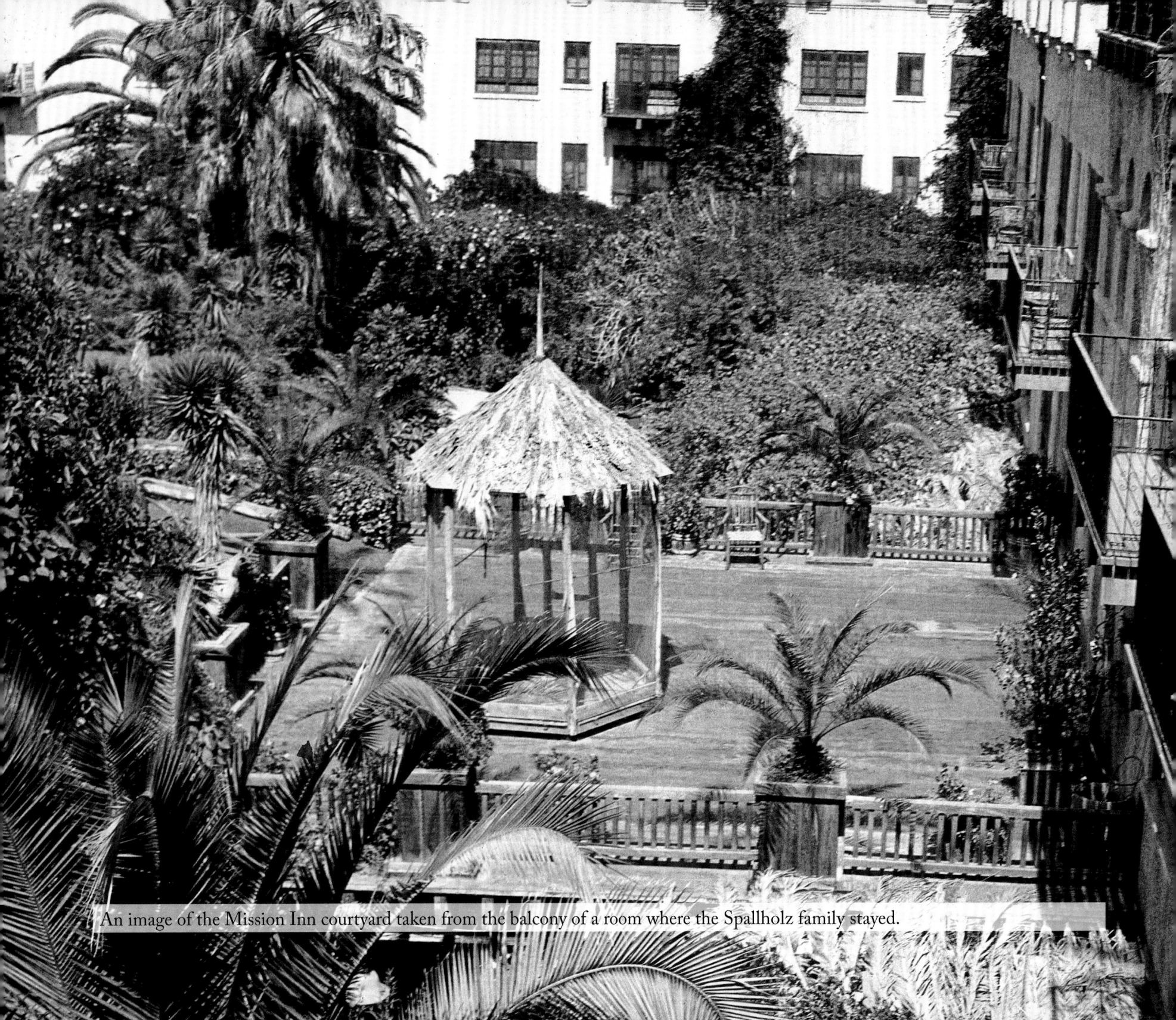
An image of the Mission Inn courtyard taken from the balcony of a room where the Spallholz family stayed.

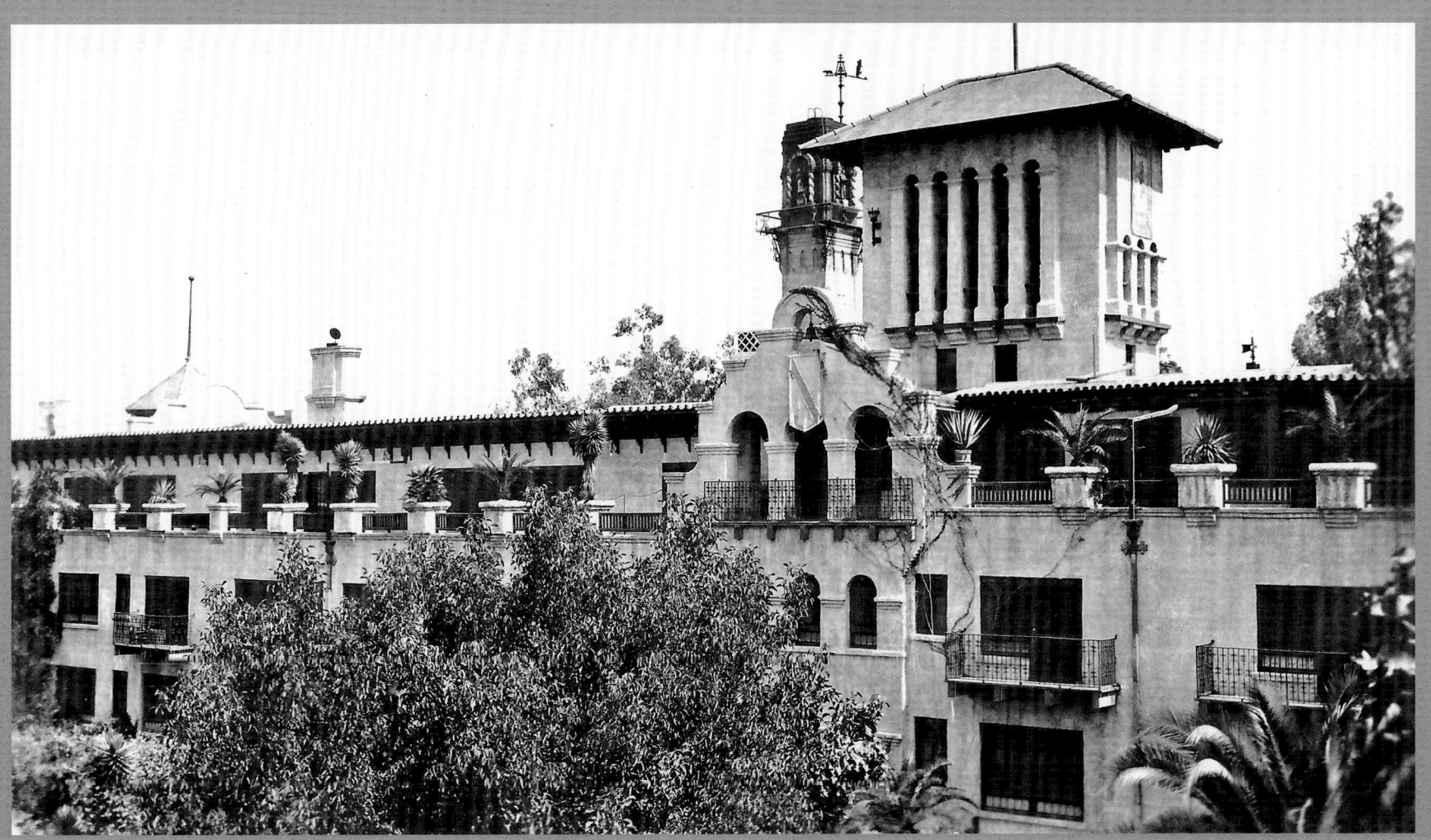

Front view of the wing emphasizing the inn's Spanish architecture. The screened gazebo is obscured by the trees in the center.

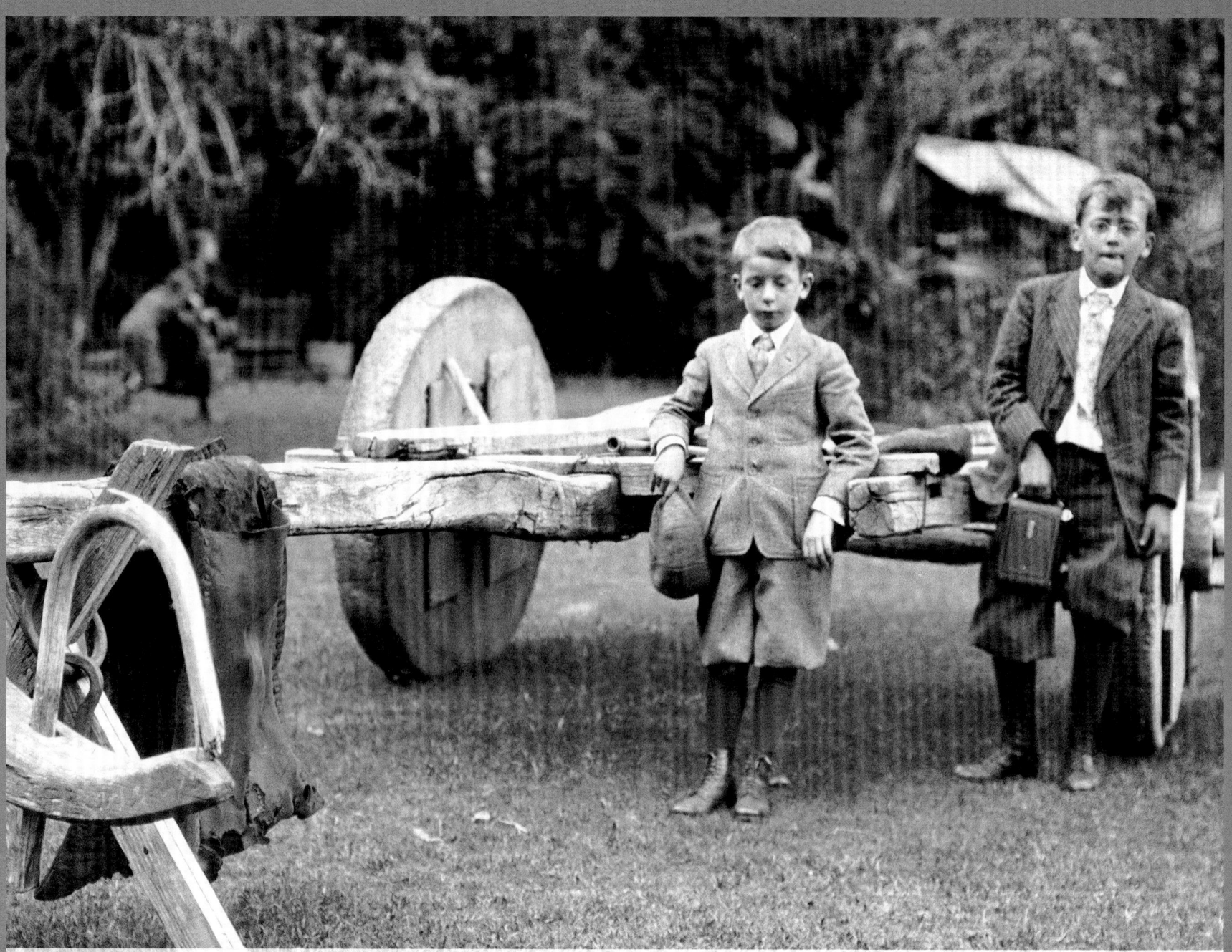

Ernest and Walter stand next to an old oxcart. Walter holds the Kodak camera, with the oxen yoke seen to the left. The boys are wearing attire appropriate for exploring the high-end neighborhood of the Mission Inn district.

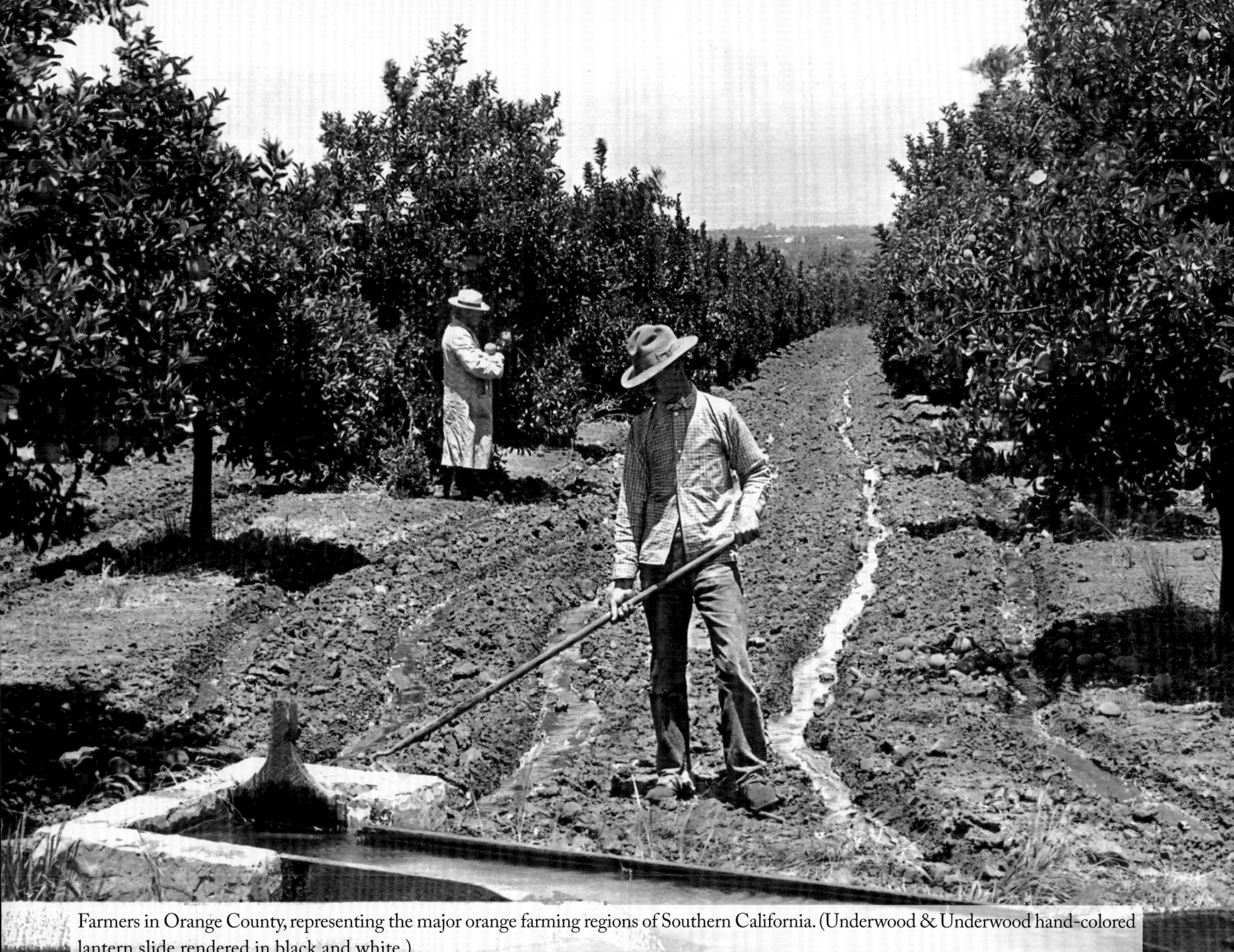

Farmers in Orange County, representing the major orange farming regions of Southern California. (Underwood & Underwood hand-colored lantern slide rendered in black and white.)

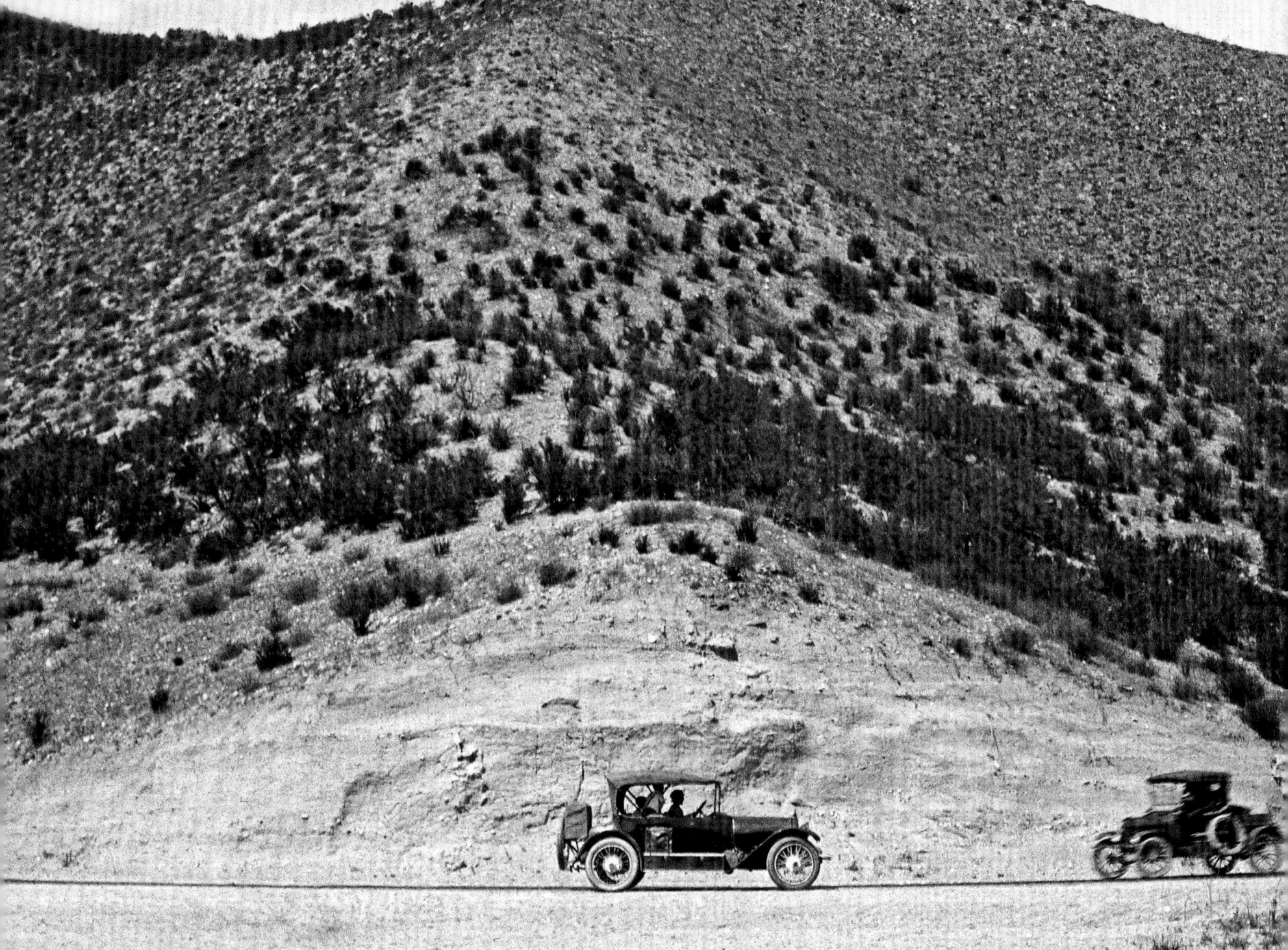

The sage-covered sand hills at Cajon Pass. This desolate climb out of the Los Angeles basin and coastal valley from Riverside to Barstow and the Mojave Desert is known today as Interstate 15, or the Mojave Freeway.

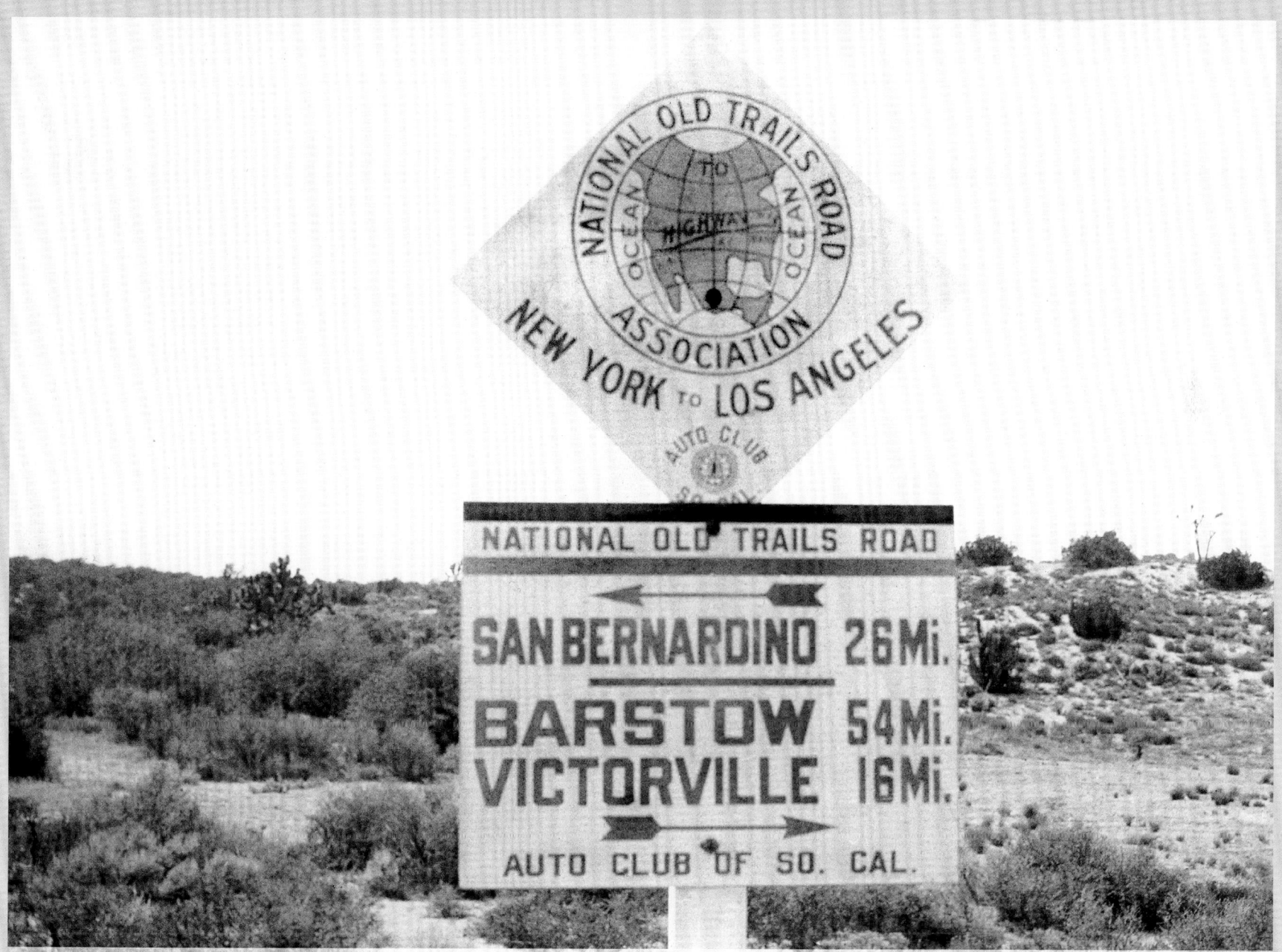

After crossing Cajon Pass, Henry stopped to take a picture of this sign marking the National Old Trails Highway, also known as the Ocean-to-Ocean Highway. Established in 1912, this route later became part of the western segment of the Santa Fe Trail.

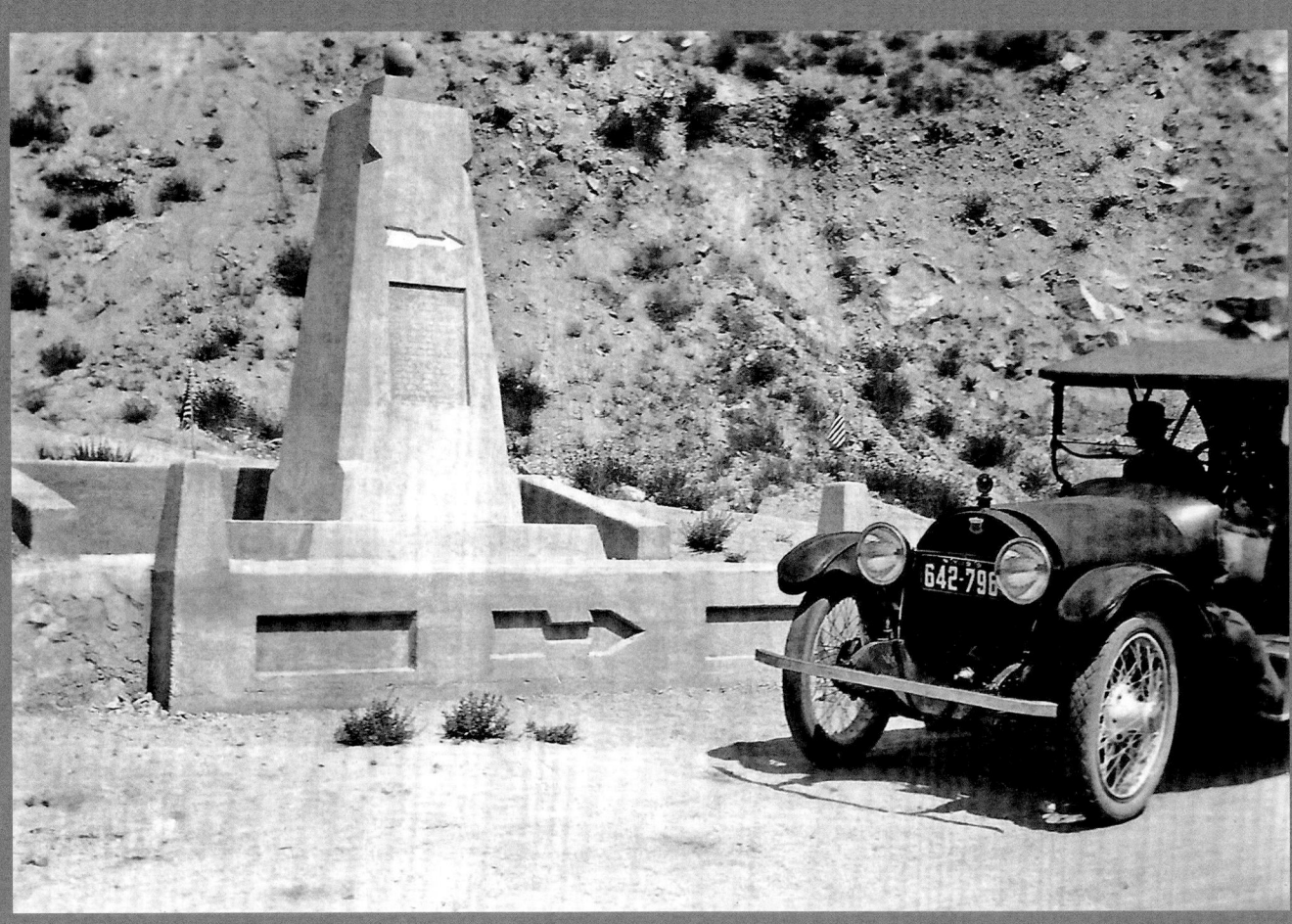

A monument dedicated in 1917 to honor the very early pioneers who entered California by crossing the Mojave Desert and traveled the Cajon Pass into San Bernardino County. The bronze plaque reads: *"Santa Fe and Salt Lake Trail, 1849. Erected in honor of the brave pioneers of California in 1917 by pioneers Sheldon Stoddard, Sydney F. Waite, John Brown, Jr., George Miller, George M. Cooley, Silas C. Cox, Richard Weir, Jasper N. Courbet."*

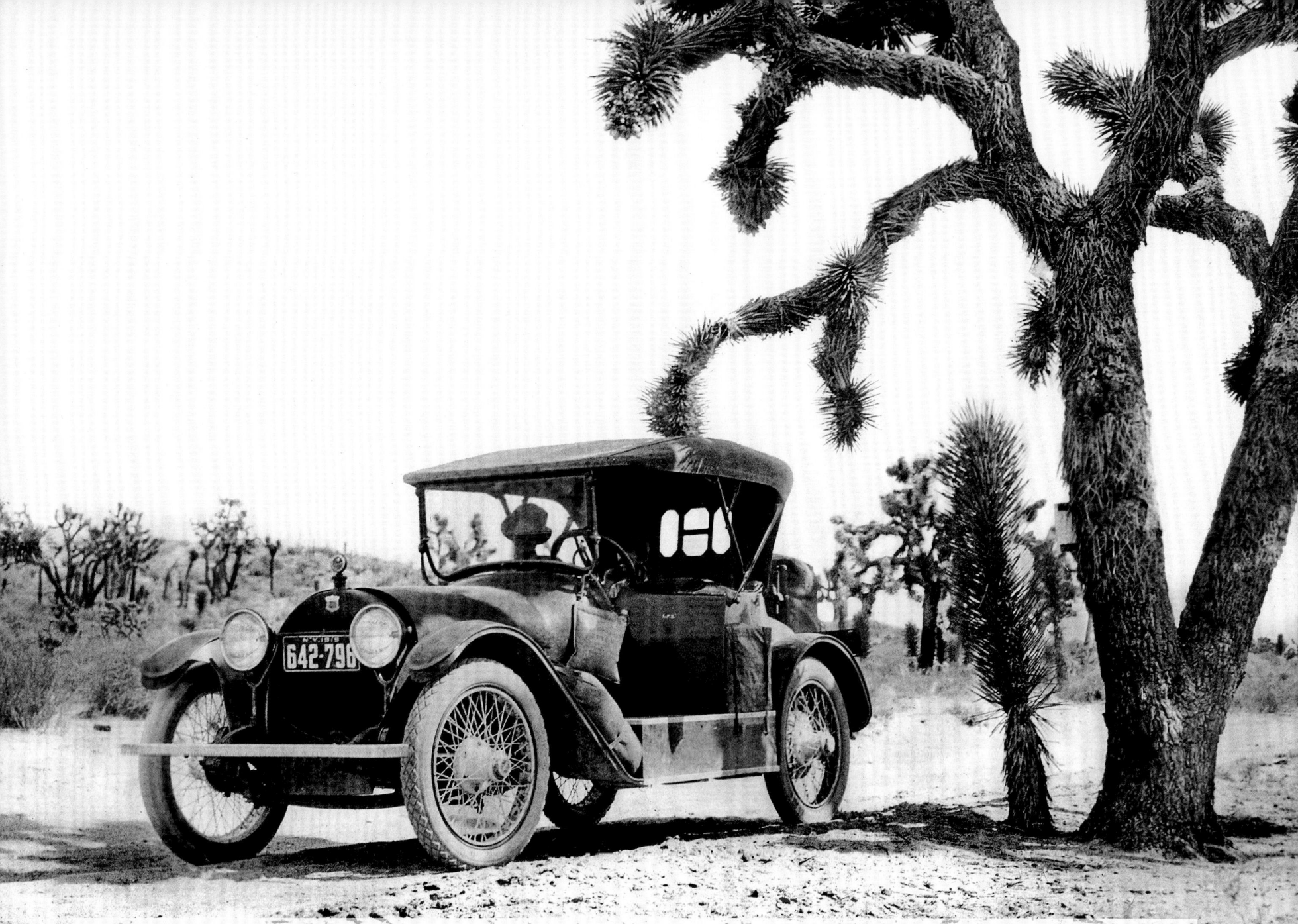

Henry photographed the Haynes parked next to a large and unusually symmetrical example of a Joshua tree, a species confined largely to the Mojave Desert. It is purported to have received this name in 1851 by the Mormons when they entered California. The trees' outstretched arms were a reminder of Joshua lifting his outstretched hands to the sky in prayer. Today the grove of Joshua trees comprises Joshua Tree National Park. Visible once more in this picture is the distinctive letter "H" in the rear window panels of the Haynes.

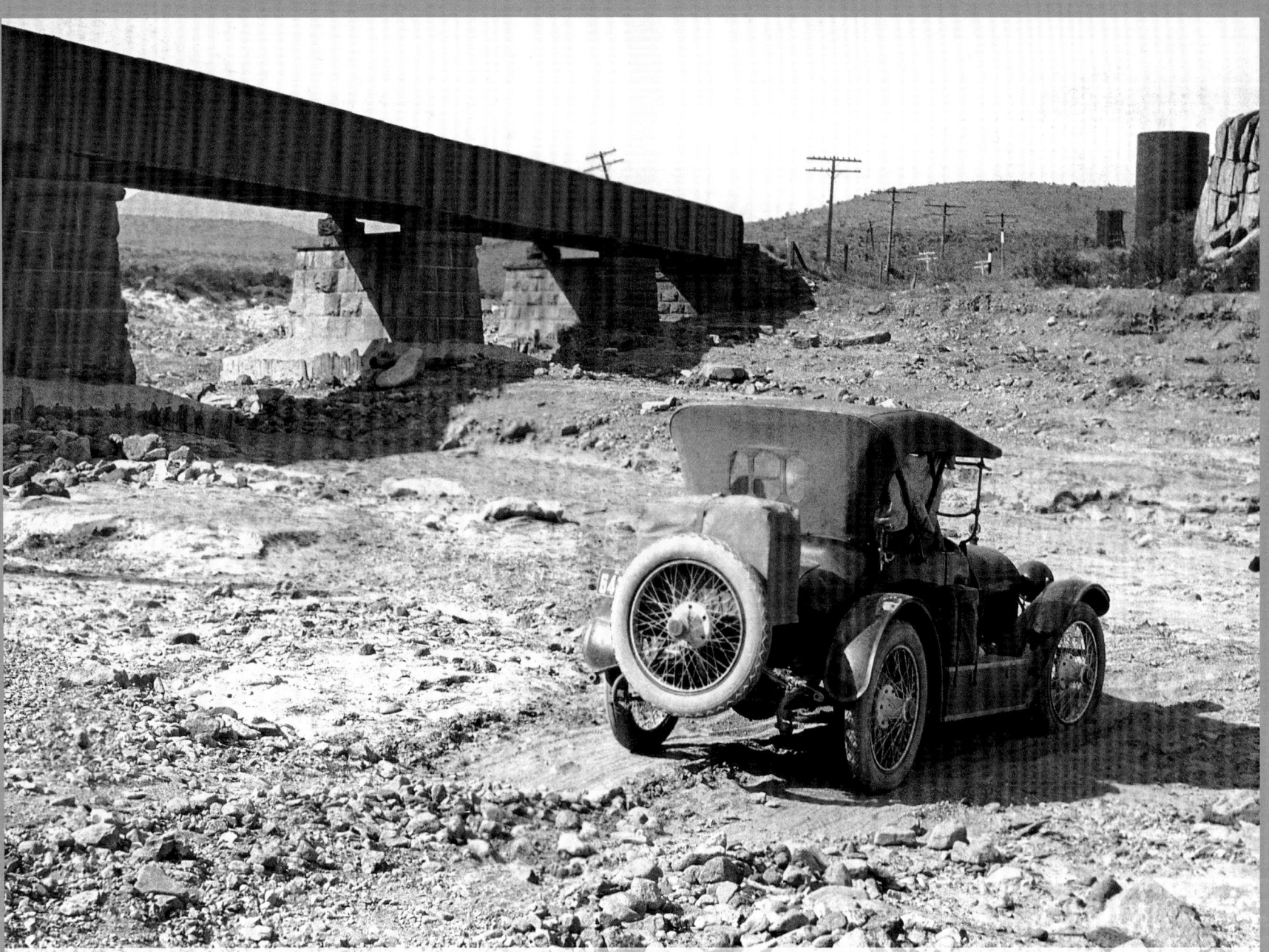

No wagon bridge existed for this dry riverbed crossing. After they reached the middle of the riverbed, the family passed under the first and the second pillars on their journey through the Mojave Desert. They were following the route of the AT&SF railroad across the desert for safety.

CHAPTER 12

ARIZONA: THE GRAND CANYON & PETRIFIED FOREST

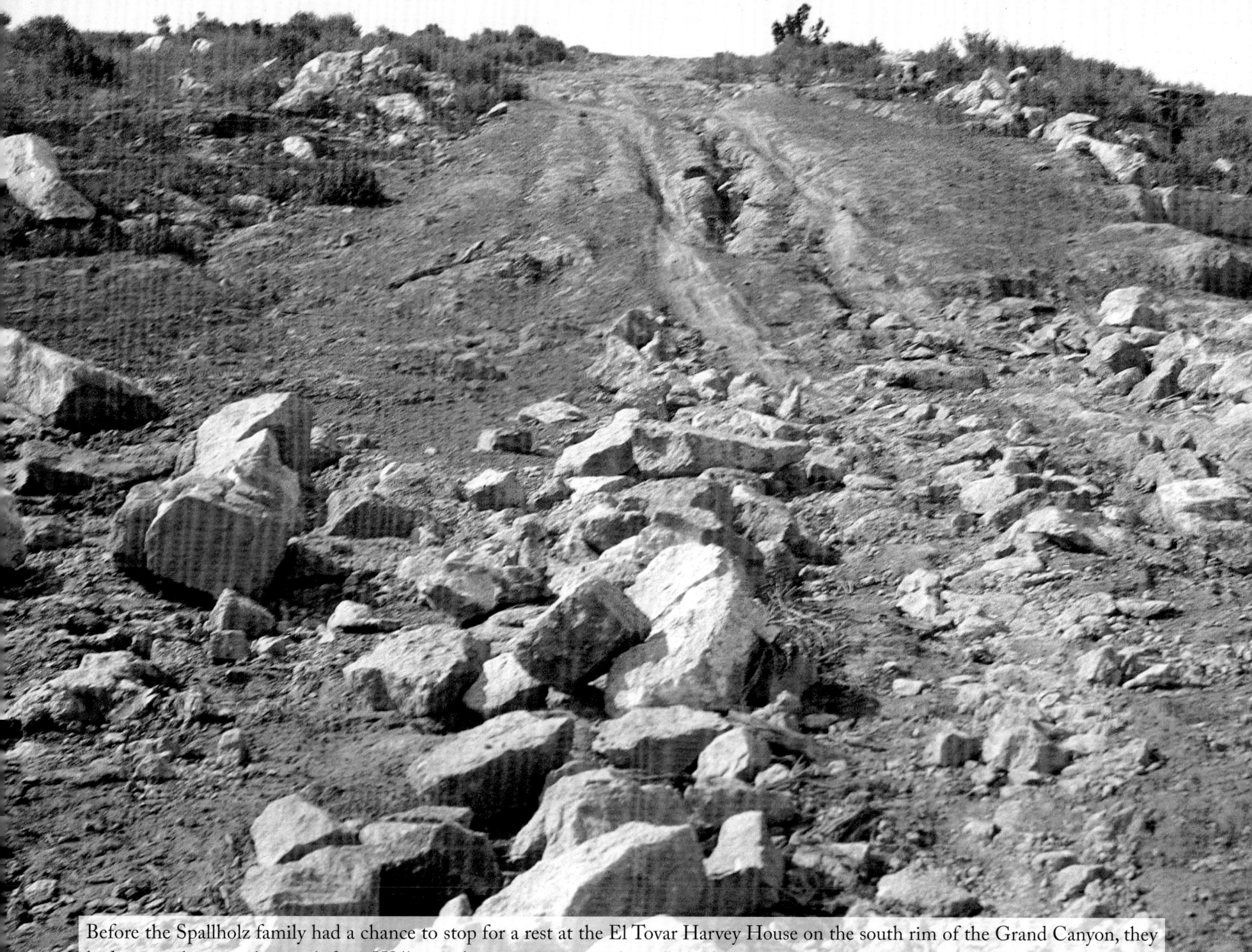

Before the Spallholz family had a chance to stop for a rest at the El Tovar Harvey House on the south rim of the Grand Canyon, they had to travel sixty miles north from Williams, Arizona, over a rough, rocky, and rutted macadam road.

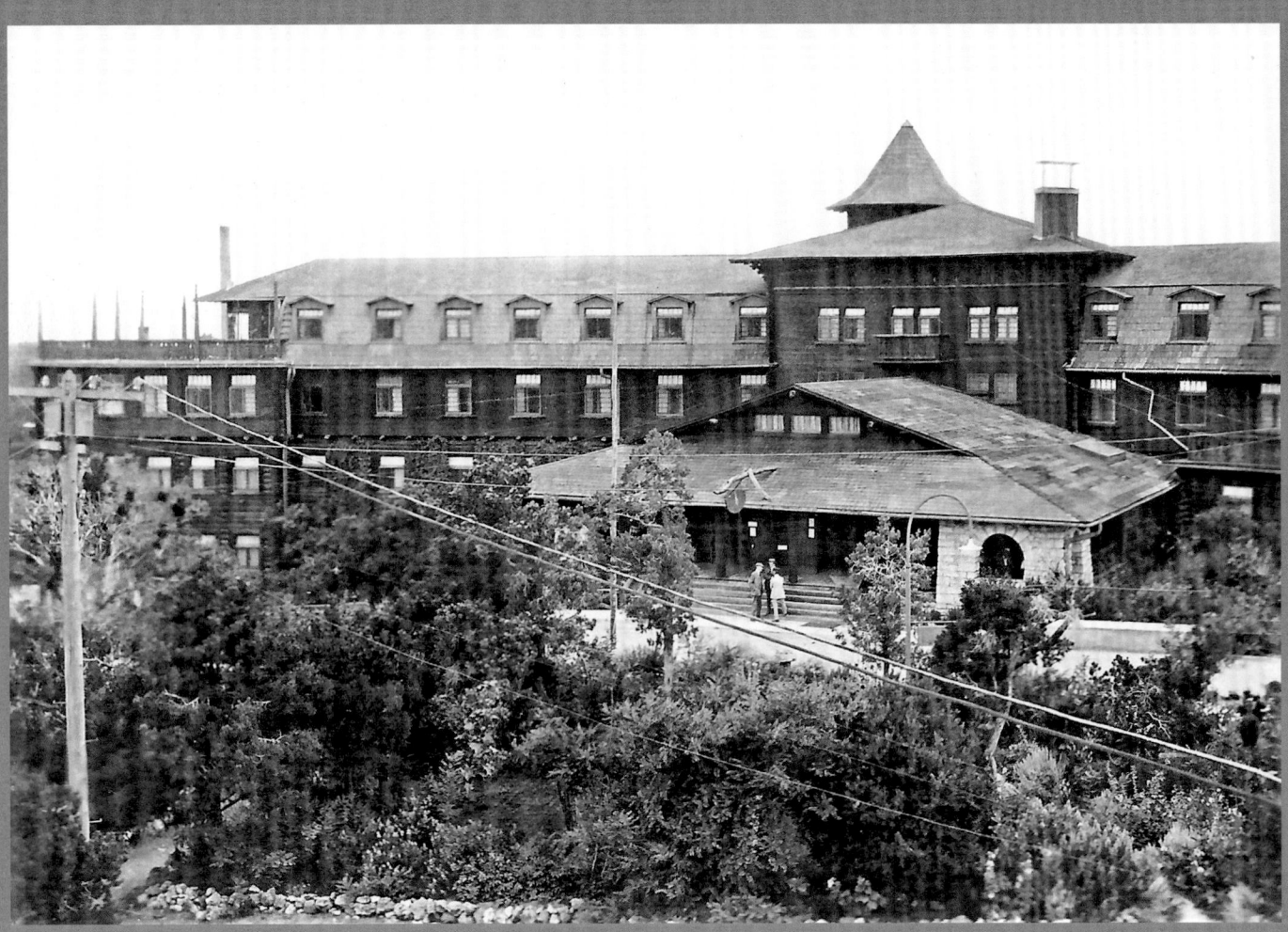

The El Tovar Hotel was designed by Charles Whittlesey, the chief architect of the Atchison, Topeka and Santa Fe Railway, in the National Park's rustic log style, opening in 1905. The Fred Harvey Company operated the hotel and restaurant for the Santa Fe Railroad. This Harvey House Hotel was named for the Spanish explorer Don Pedro de Tovar, the first European to report the canyon's existence circa 1540.

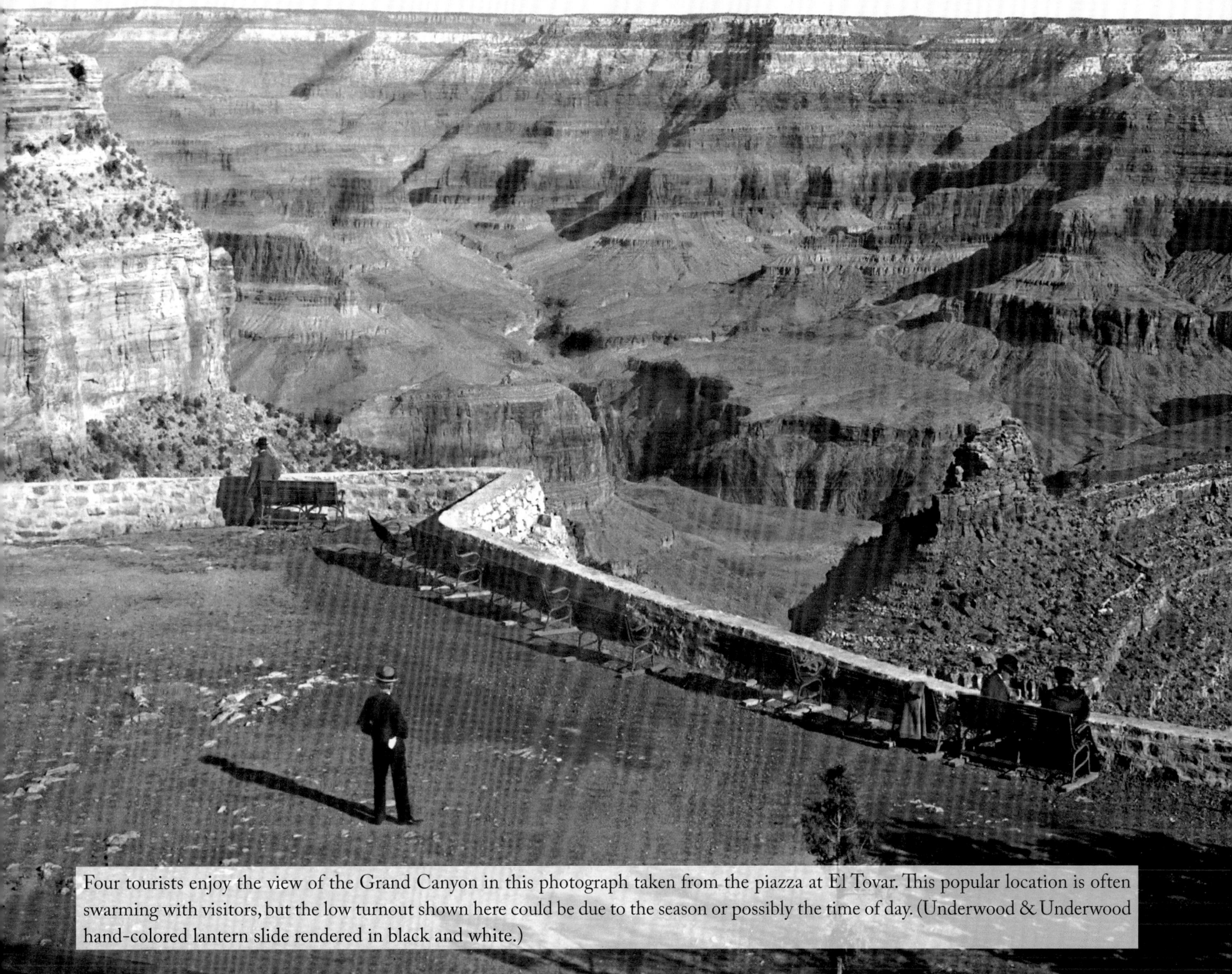

Four tourists enjoy the view of the Grand Canyon in this photograph taken from the piazza at El Tovar. This popular location is often swarming with visitors, but the low turnout shown here could be due to the season or possibly the time of day. (Underwood & Underwood hand-colored lantern slide rendered in black and white.)

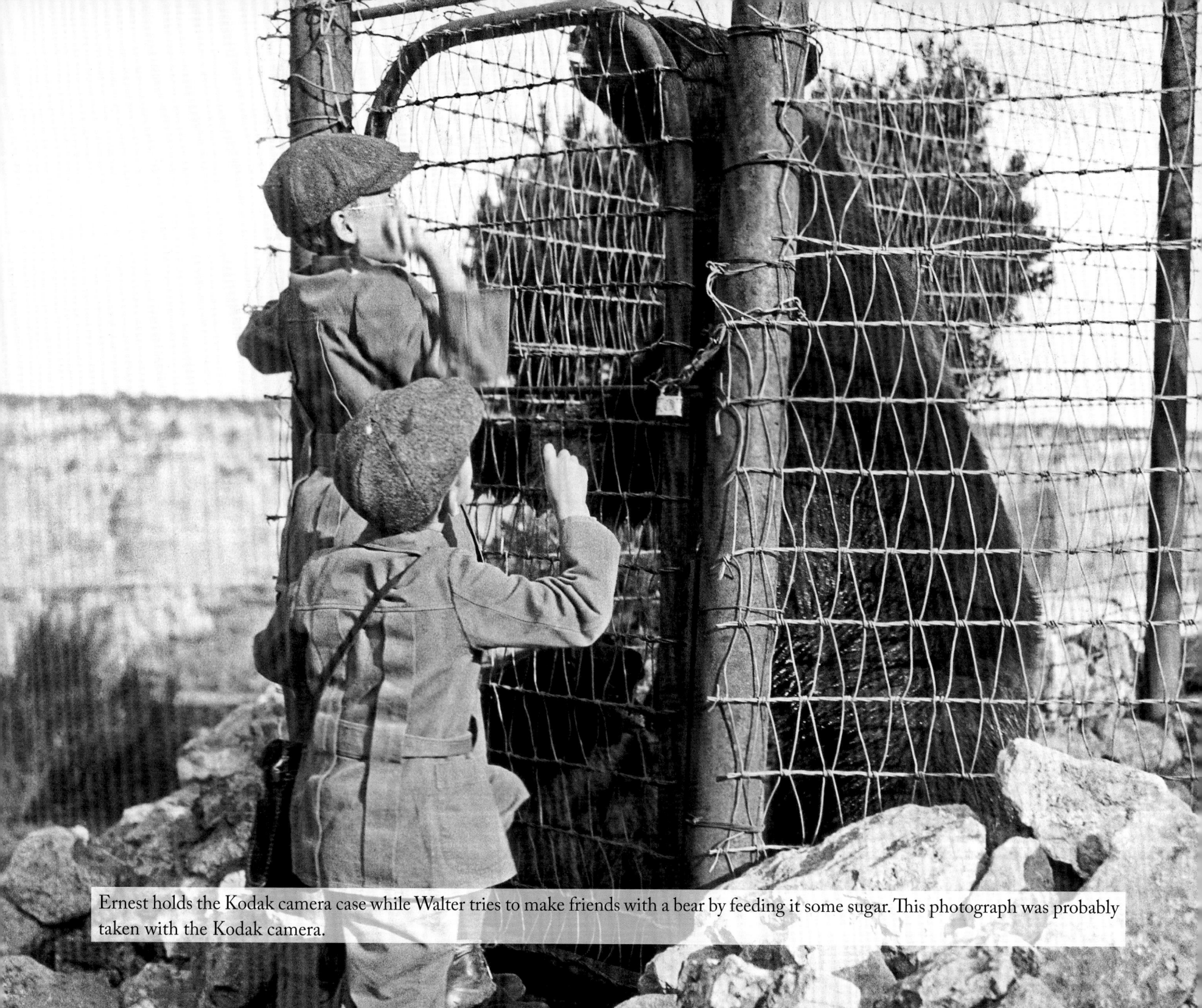

Ernest holds the Kodak camera case while Walter tries to make friends with a bear by feeding it some sugar. This photograph was probably taken with the Kodak camera.

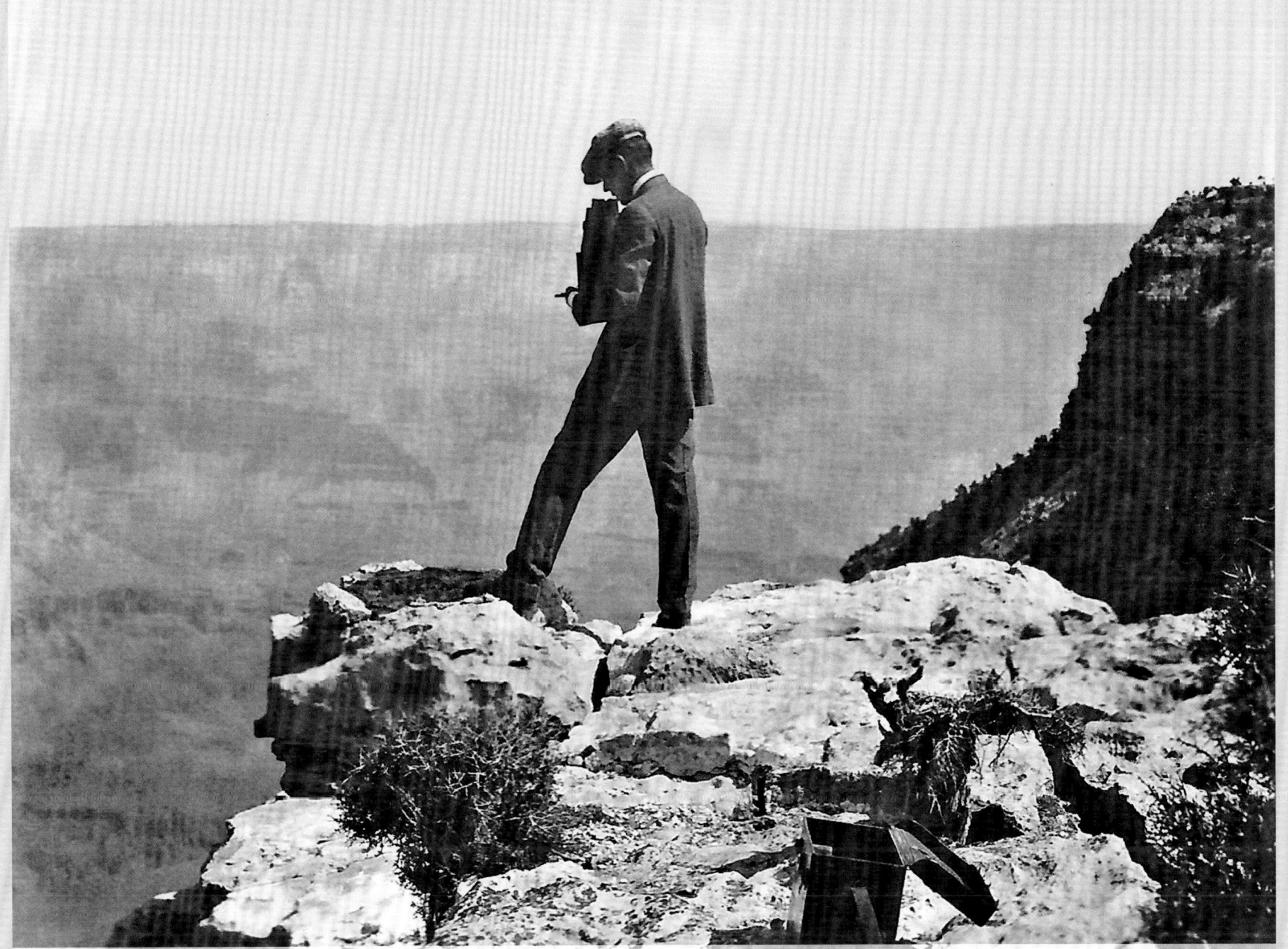

Taken with the Kodak camera, here's Henry standing on a rock ledge 5,000 feet above the Colorado River while using the Graflex camera.

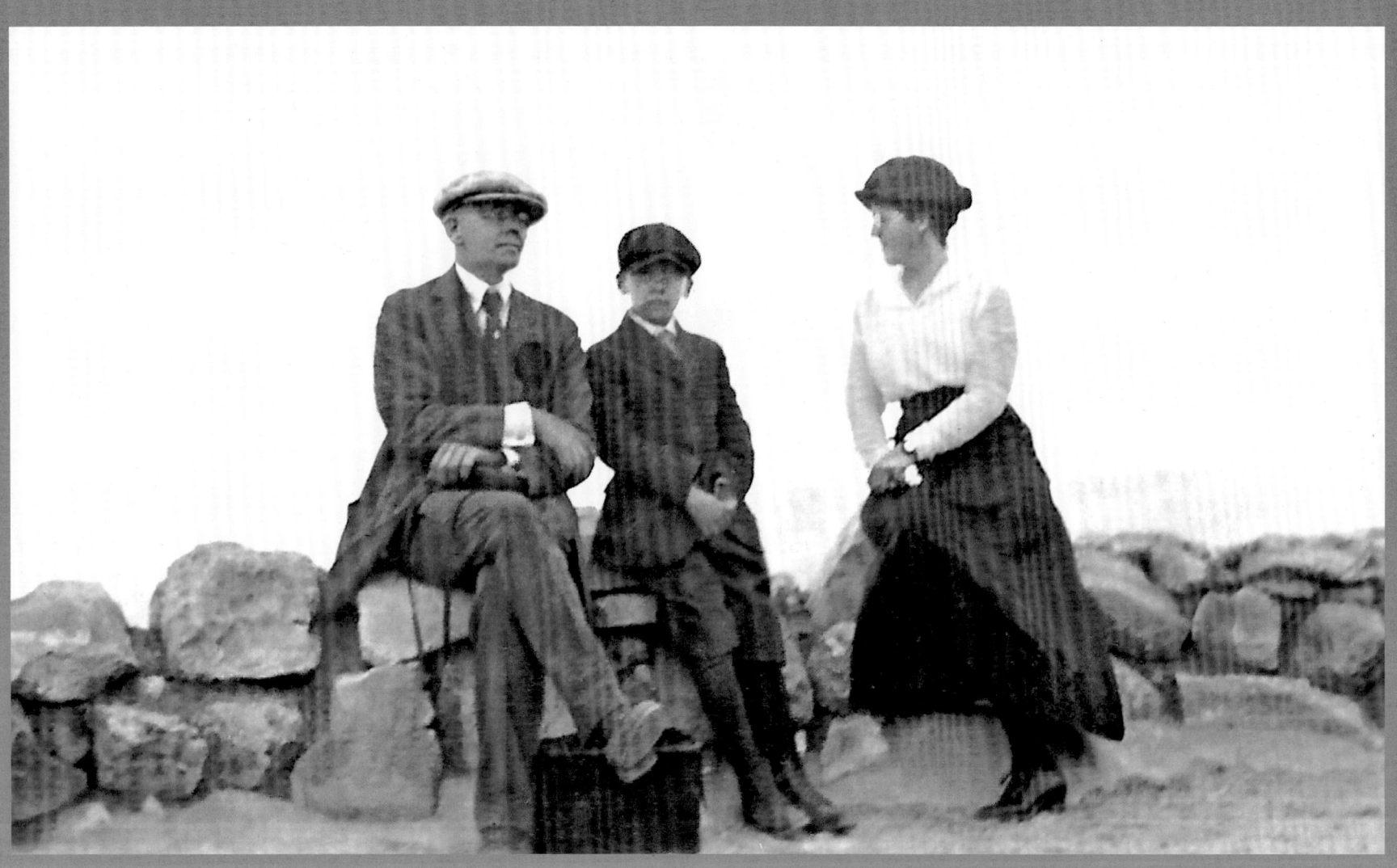

In a picture resembling a posed family portrait, Henry, Walter, and Lizzie Spallholz sit on the roof parapet of Hermits Rest, a structure designed by Fred Harvey Company chief architect Mary Colter. Henry is shown here with his lapel-mounted hearing aid, resting his foot on his camera case. Lizzie's lace shoes are visible in this photograph.

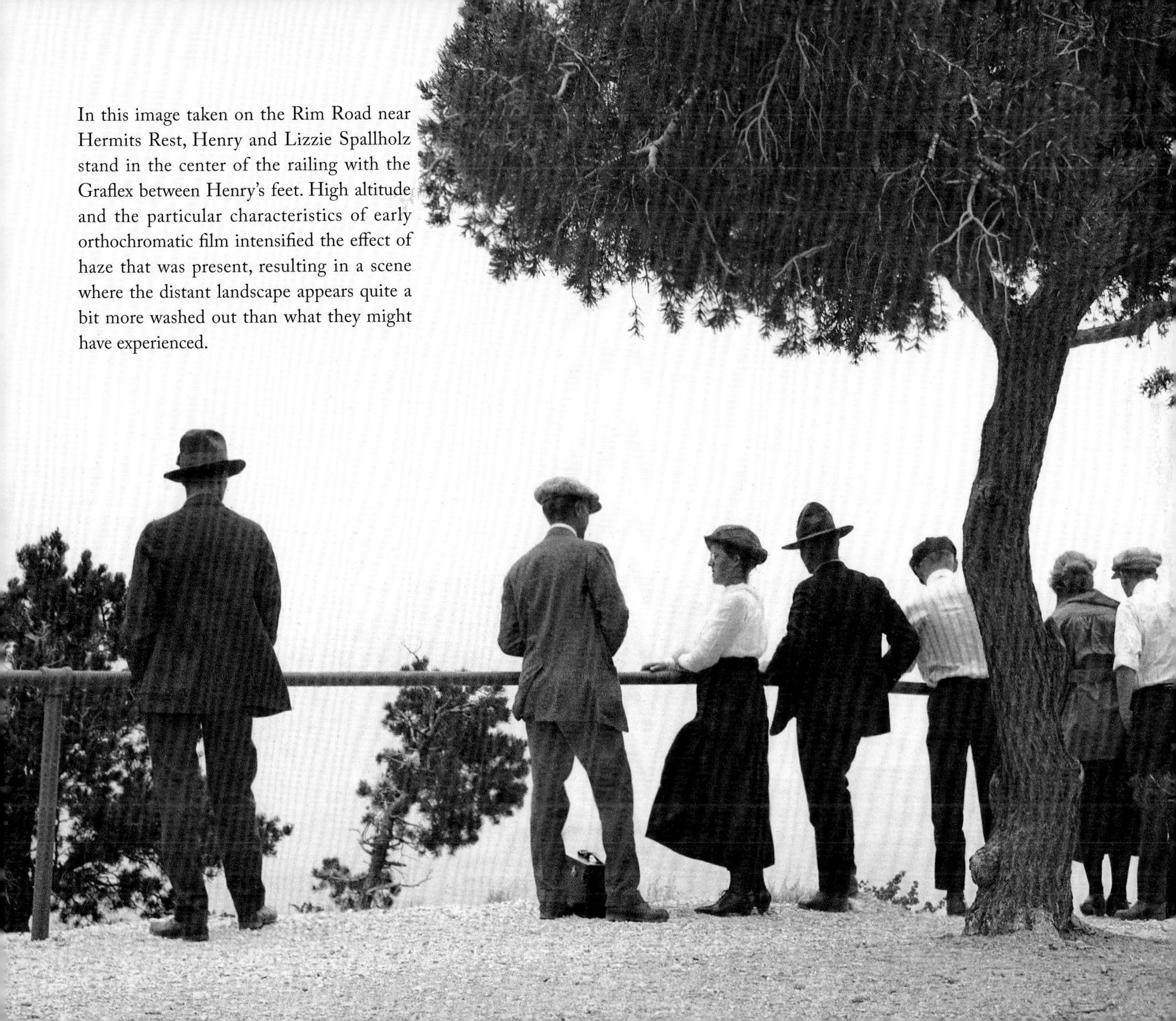

In this image taken on the Rim Road near Hermits Rest, Henry and Lizzie Spallholz stand in the center of the railing with the Graflex between Henry's feet. High altitude and the particular characteristics of early orthochromatic film intensified the effect of haze that was present, resulting in a scene where the distant landscape appears quite a bit more washed out than what they might have experienced.

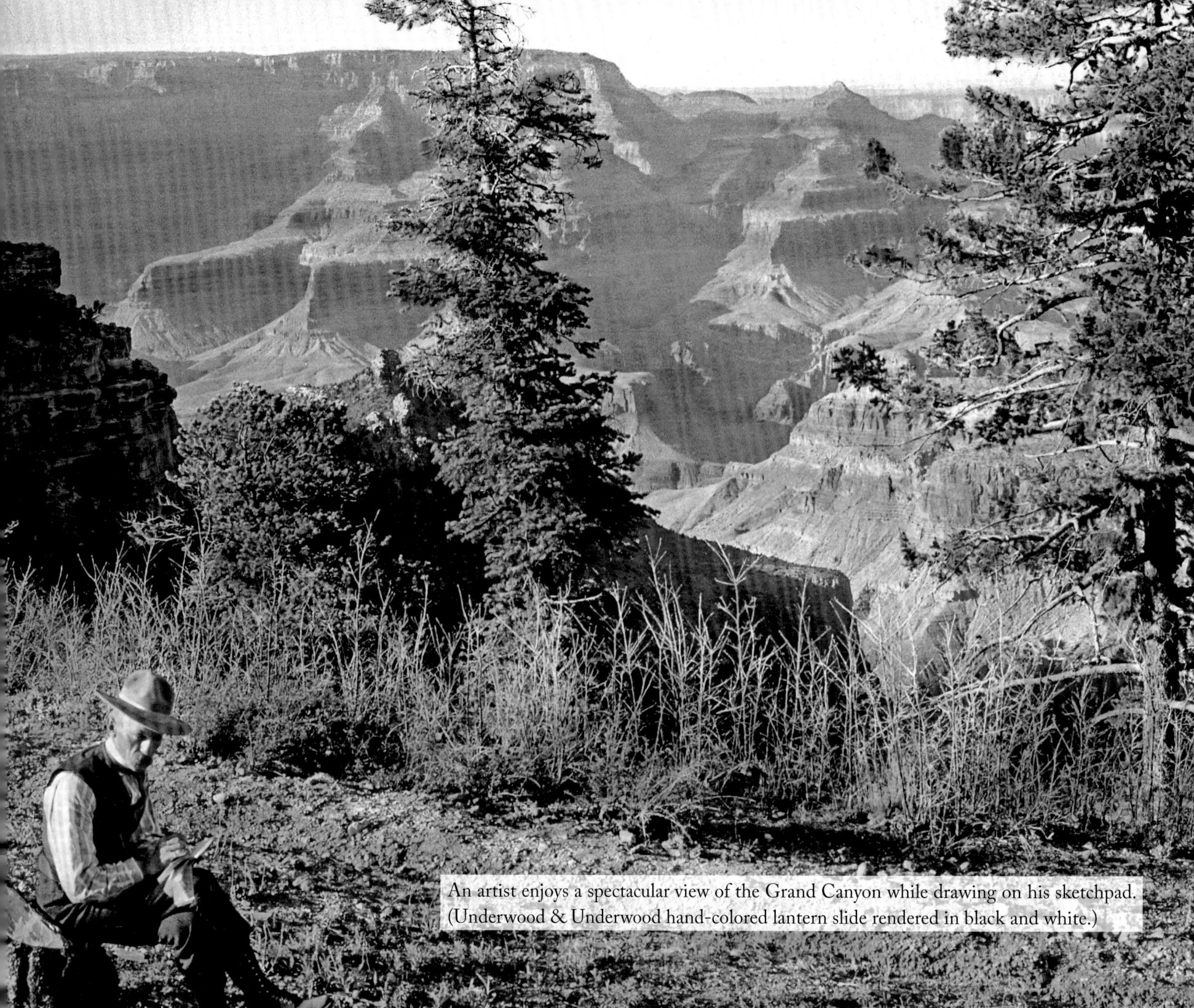

An artist enjoys a spectacular view of the Grand Canyon while drawing on his sketchpad. (Underwood & Underwood hand-colored lantern slide rendered in black and white.)

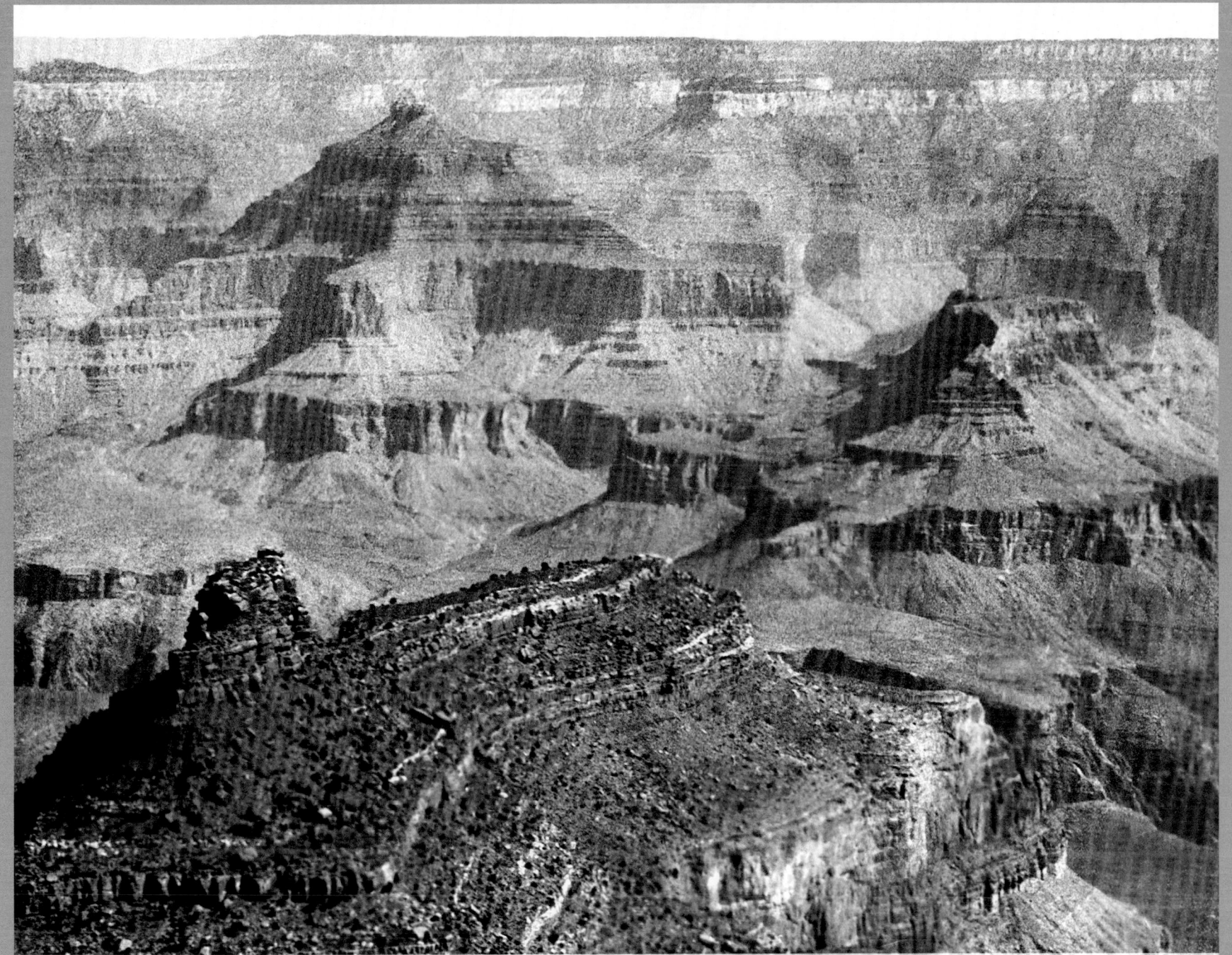

A view of the Grand Canyon from the El Tovar terrace shows the canyon's Battleship formation in the foreground.

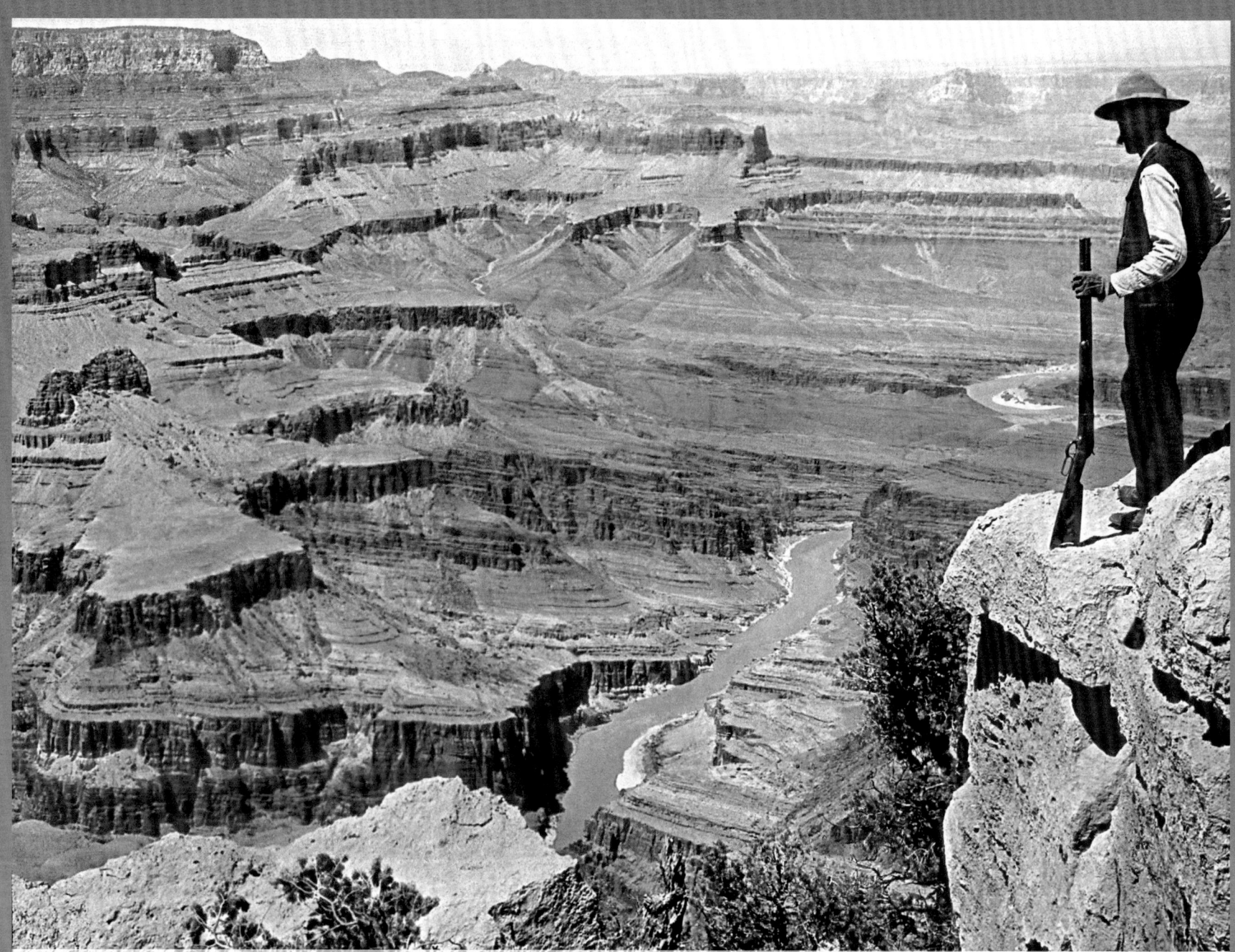

A man with a rifle looks over the Grand Canyon from Bissell's Point at an altitude of nearly 5,000 feet above the Colorado River. (Underwood & Underwood hand-colored lantern slide rendered in black and white.)

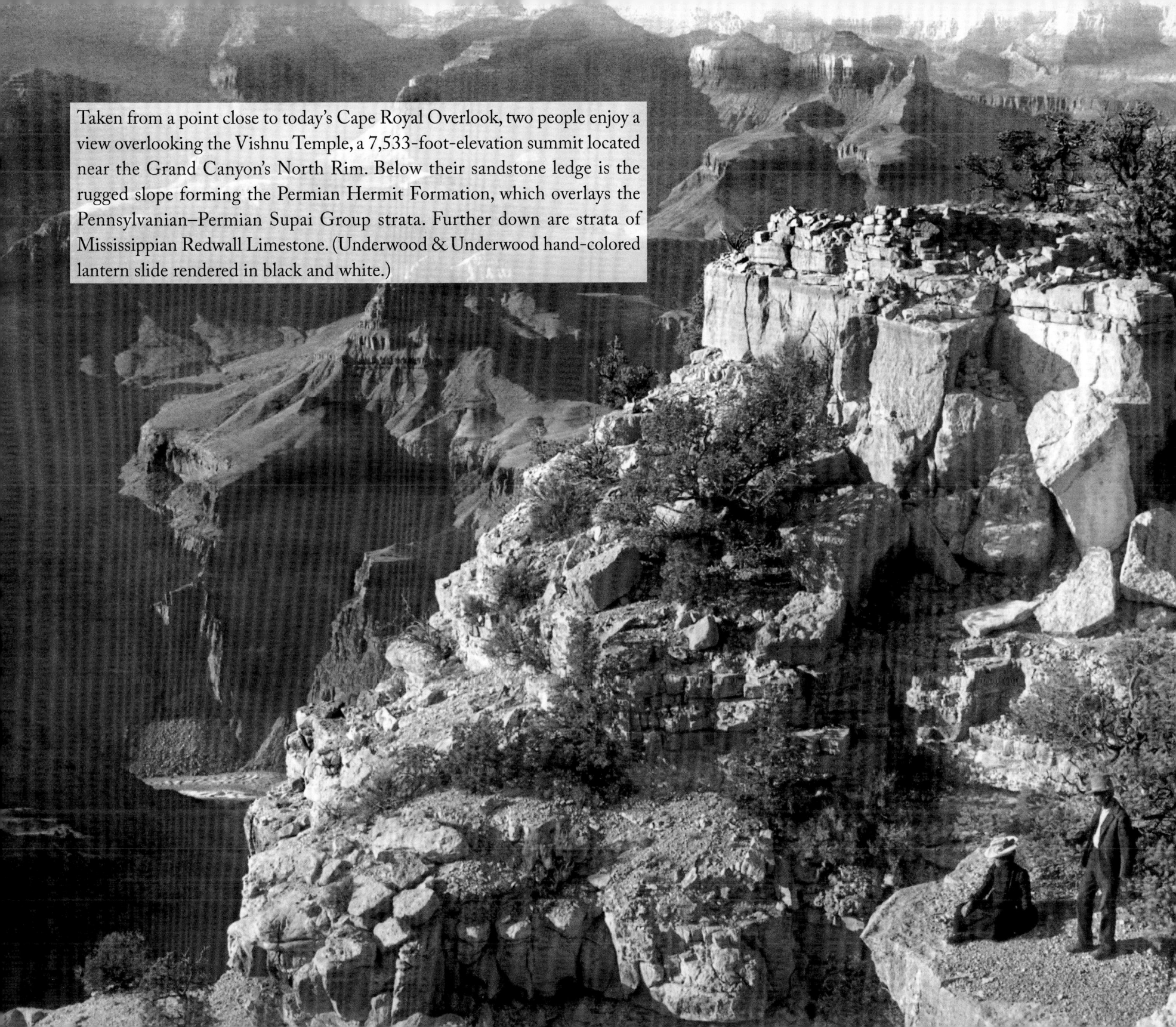

Taken from a point close to today's Cape Royal Overlook, two people enjoy a view overlooking the Vishnu Temple, a 7,533-foot-elevation summit located near the Grand Canyon's North Rim. Below their sandstone ledge is the rugged slope forming the Permian Hermit Formation, which overlays the Pennsylvanian–Permian Supai Group strata. Further down are strata of Mississippian Redwall Limestone. (Underwood & Underwood hand-colored lantern slide rendered in black and white.)

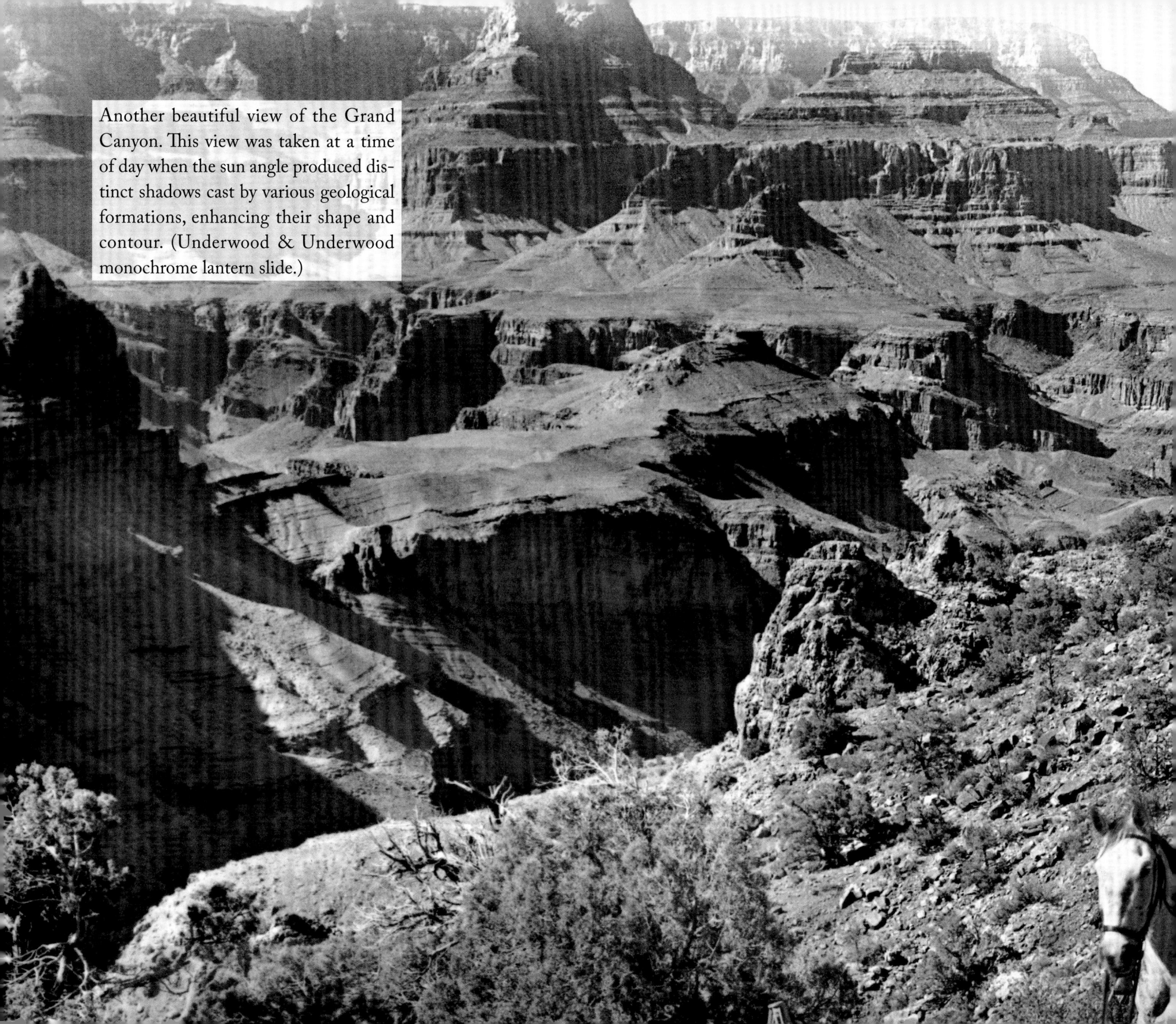

Another beautiful view of the Grand Canyon. This view was taken at a time of day when the sun angle produced distinct shadows cast by various geological formations, enhancing their shape and contour. (Underwood & Underwood monochrome lantern slide.)

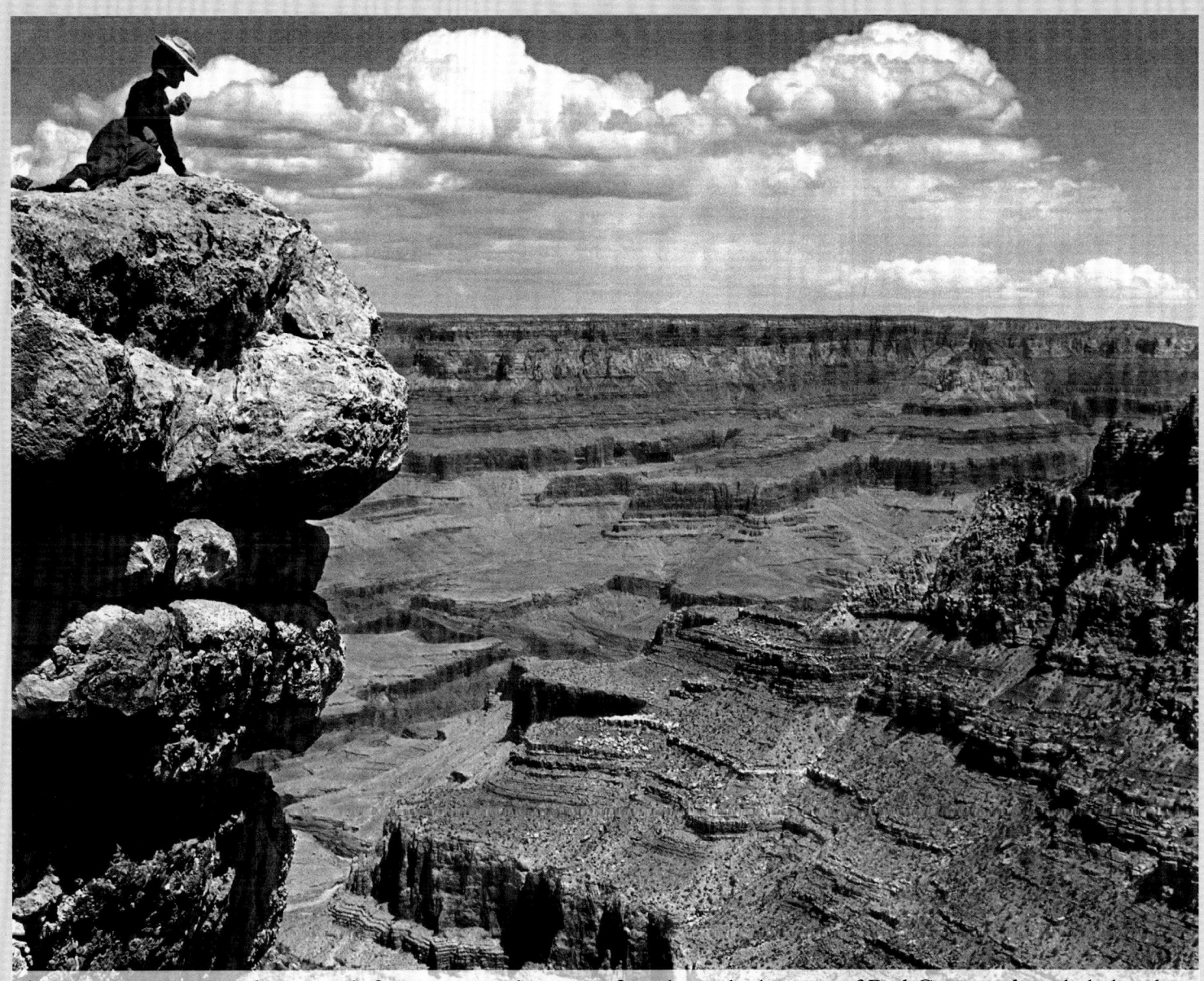

A woman prepares to drop a rock from a point about 600 feet above the bottom of Red Canyon, directly below her. Due to the possible presence of hikers below, engaging in this kind of activity is always dangerous. This view looks north from the height of land overlooking what is now a portion of the New Hance Trail. Red Canyon winds 2.5 miles north from this point, joining the Colorado River at Hance Rapids. (Underwood & Underwood hand-colored lantern slide rendered in black and white.)

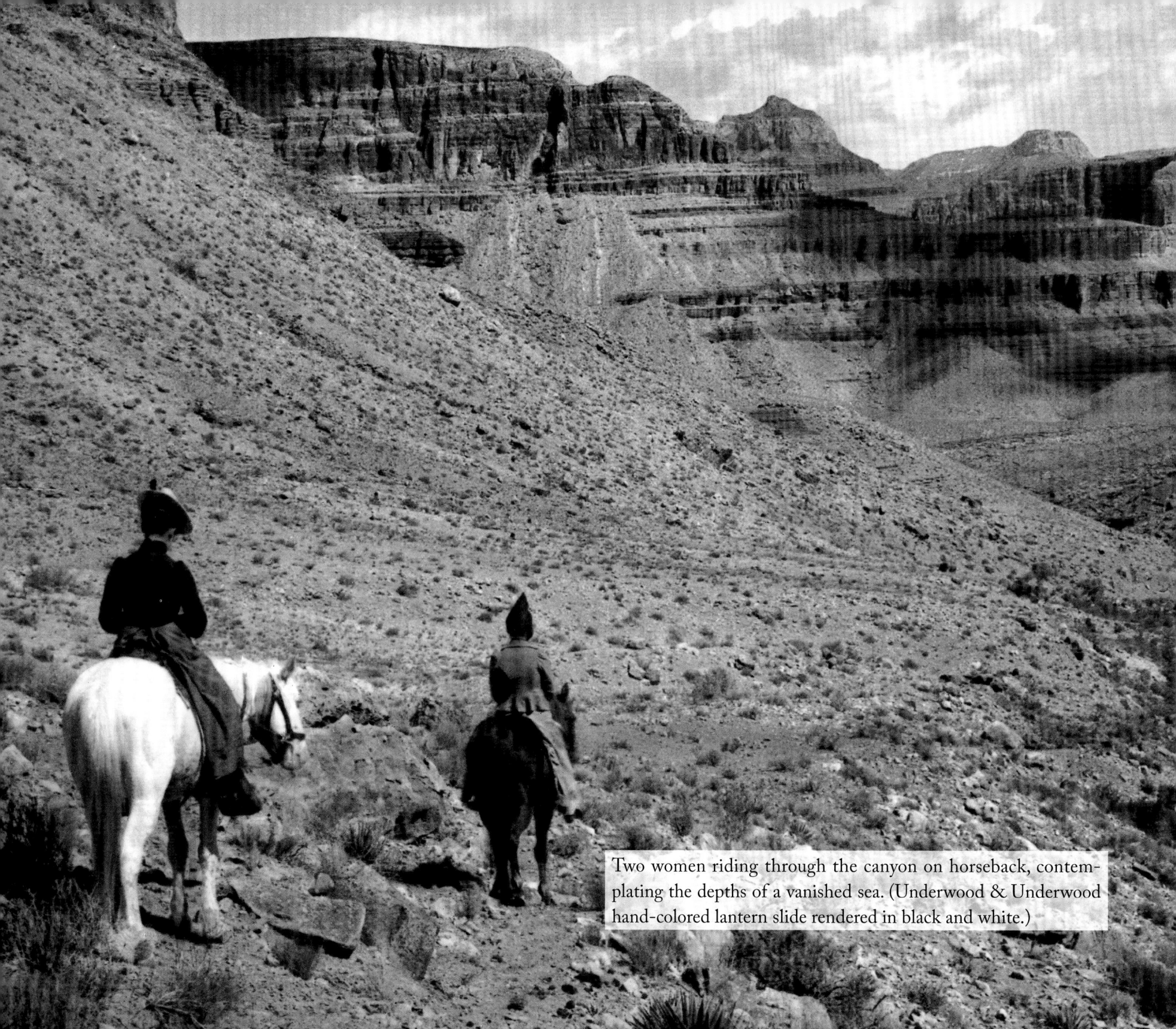

Two women riding through the canyon on horseback, contemplating the depths of a vanished sea. (Underwood & Underwood hand-colored lantern slide rendered in black and white.)

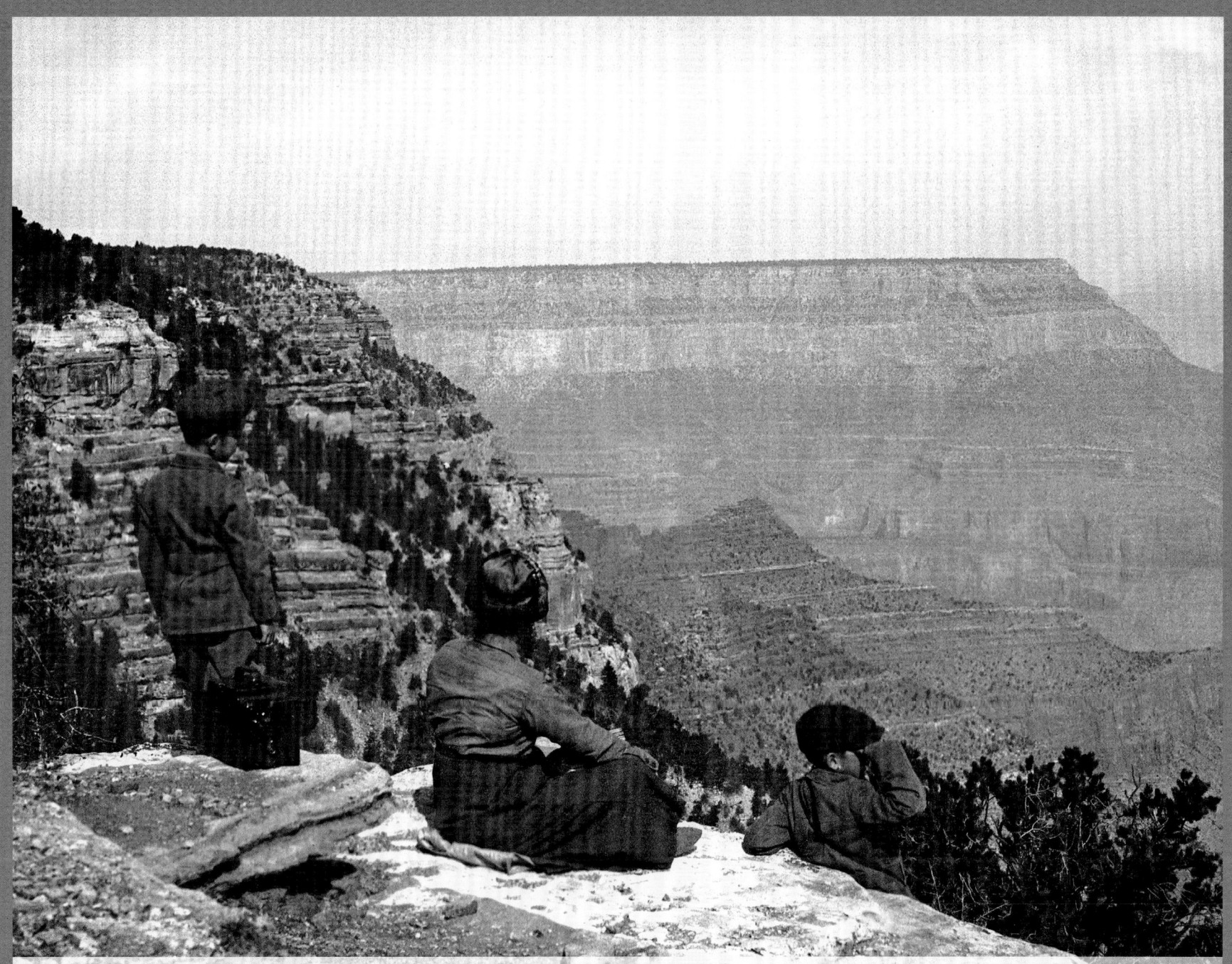

Walter, Lizzie, and Ernest perch on the edge of Grand View Point. The Graflex camera sits on the rock next to Walter, at Lizzie's left.

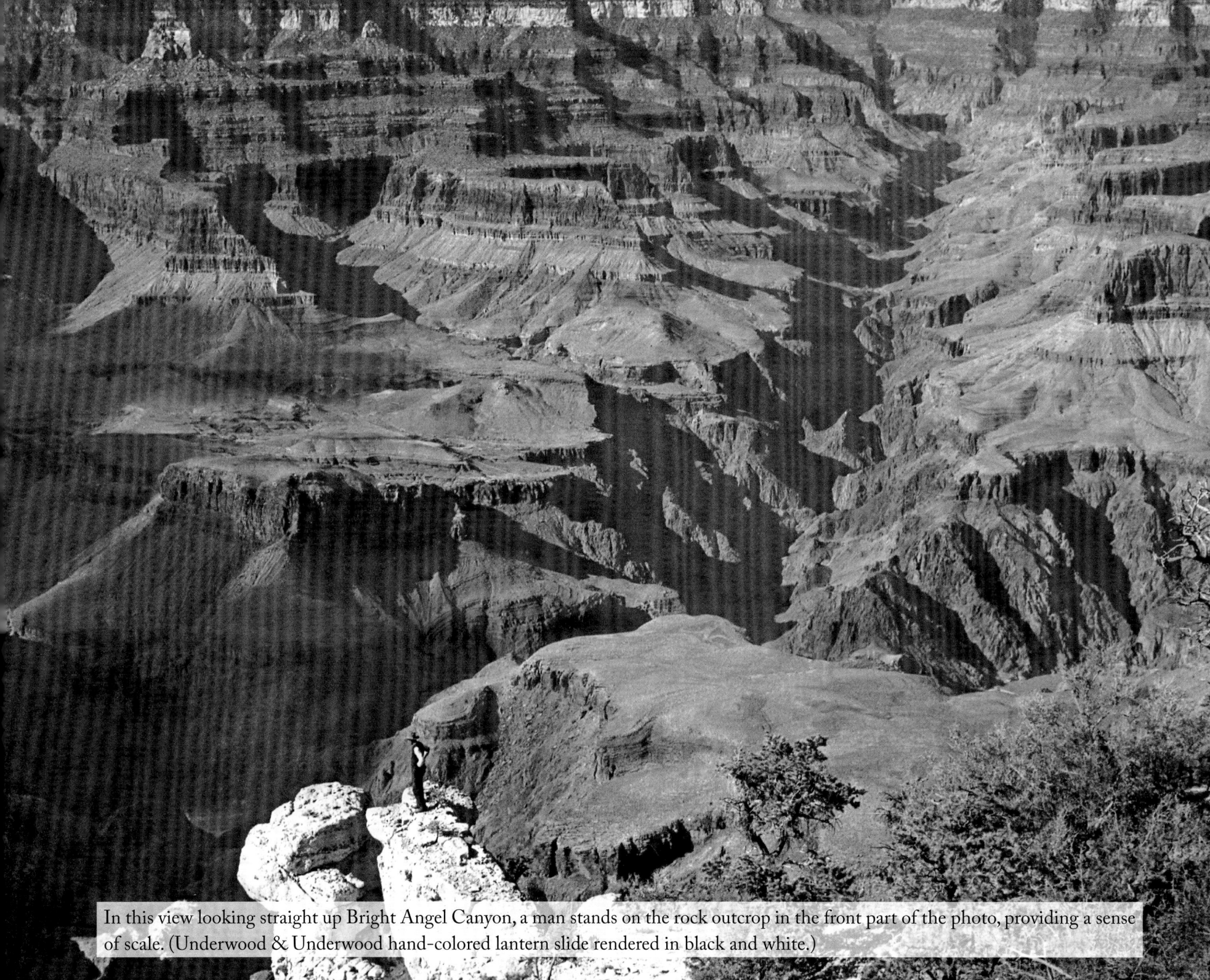

In this view looking straight up Bright Angel Canyon, a man stands on the rock outcrop in the front part of the photo, providing a sense of scale. (Underwood & Underwood hand-colored lantern slide rendered in black and white.)

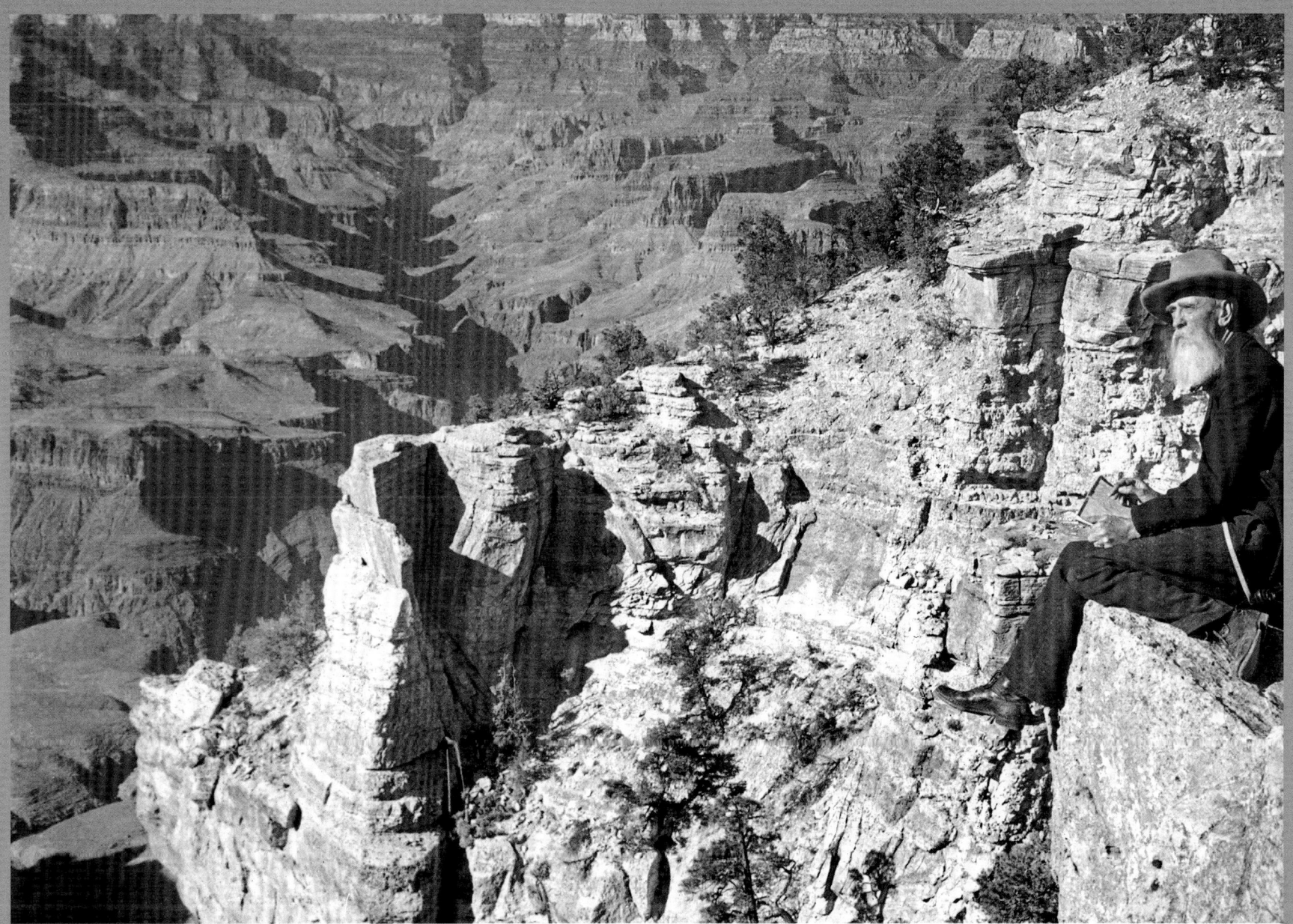

Thomas Moran, one of America's greatest scenic artists, sketching at Bright Angel Cove. Underwood & Underwood marketed their images in several formats. This lantern slide Henry purchased in 1919 is also the left-hand side of a pair of 3-D images found on a stereo view card that was part of a thirty-card set sold early in the twentieth century. (Underwood & Underwood monochrome lantern slide, copyright date 1903.)

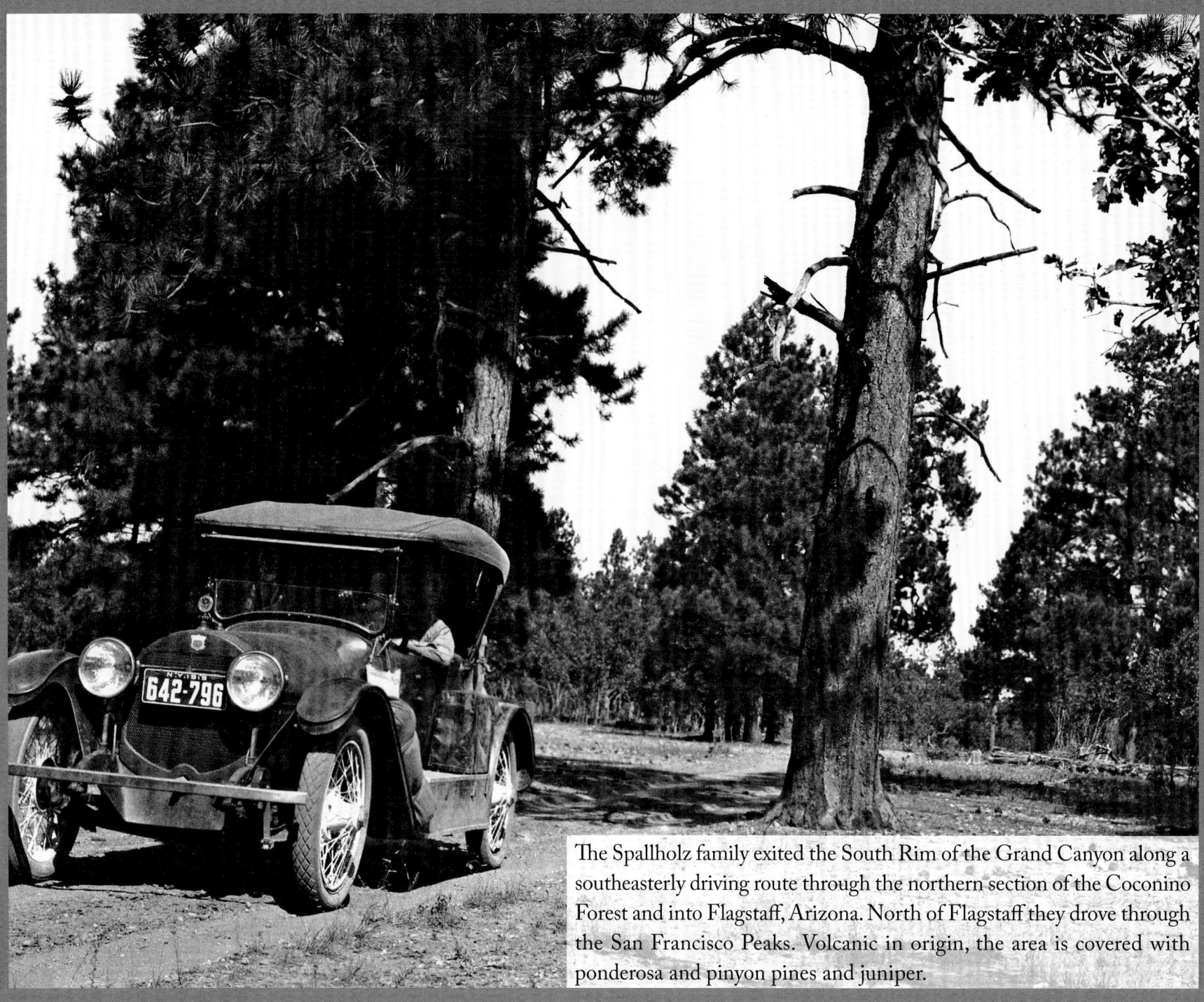

The Spallholz family exited the South Rim of the Grand Canyon along a southeasterly driving route through the northern section of the Coconino Forest and into Flagstaff, Arizona. North of Flagstaff they drove through the San Francisco Peaks. Volcanic in origin, the area is covered with ponderosa and pinyon pines and juniper.

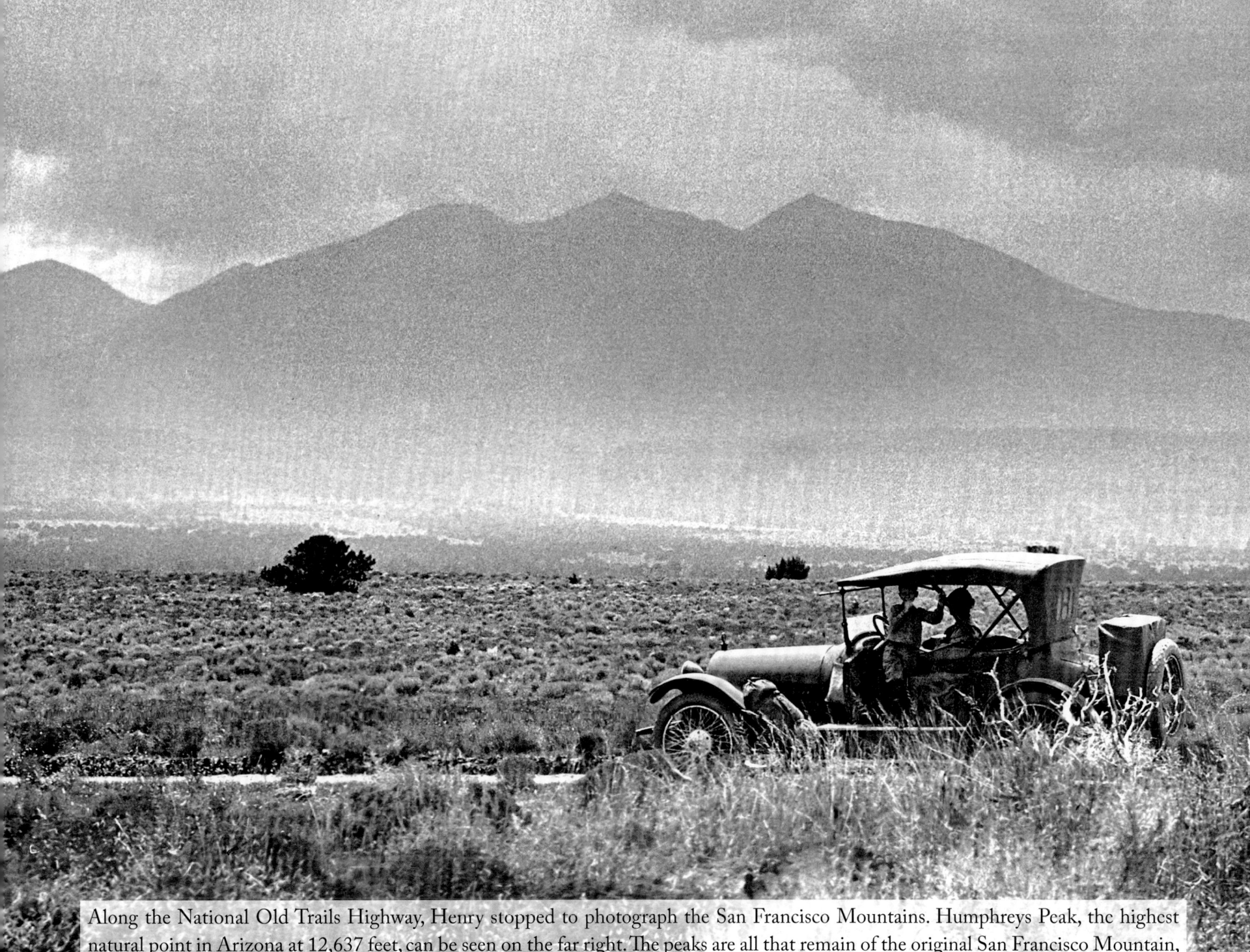

Along the National Old Trails Highway, Henry stopped to photograph the San Francisco Mountains. Humphreys Peak, the highest natural point in Arizona at 12,637 feet, can be seen on the far right. The peaks are all that remain of the original San Francisco Mountain, a volcano that was last active around 400,000 years ago.

Horseback riding in Arizona's San Francisco Peaks. Taken nearly fifteen years before the Spallholzes visited, this area of Northern Arizona continues to be a popular destination for tourists and hikers. (Underwood & Underwood hand-colored lantern slide rendered in black and white.)

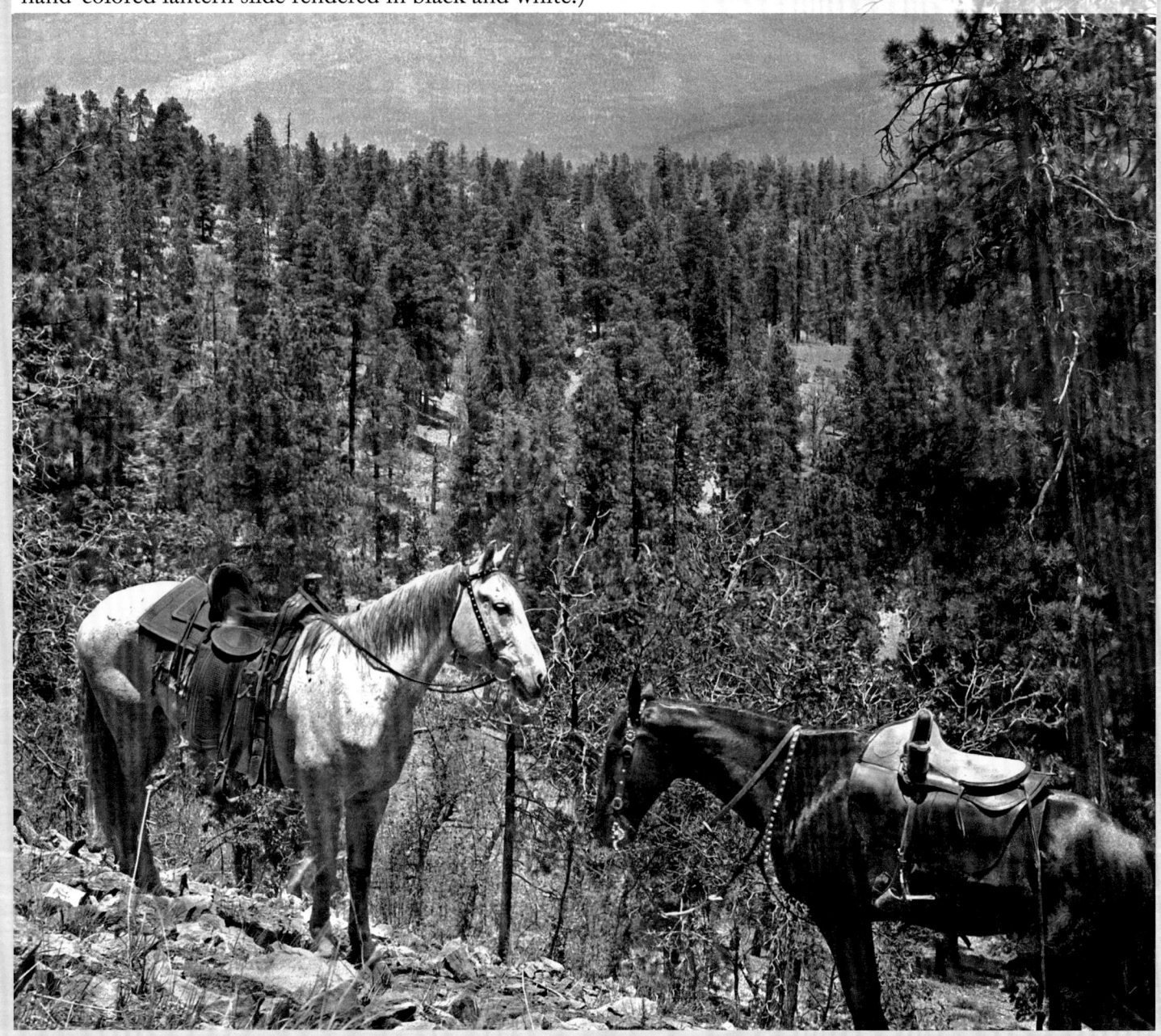

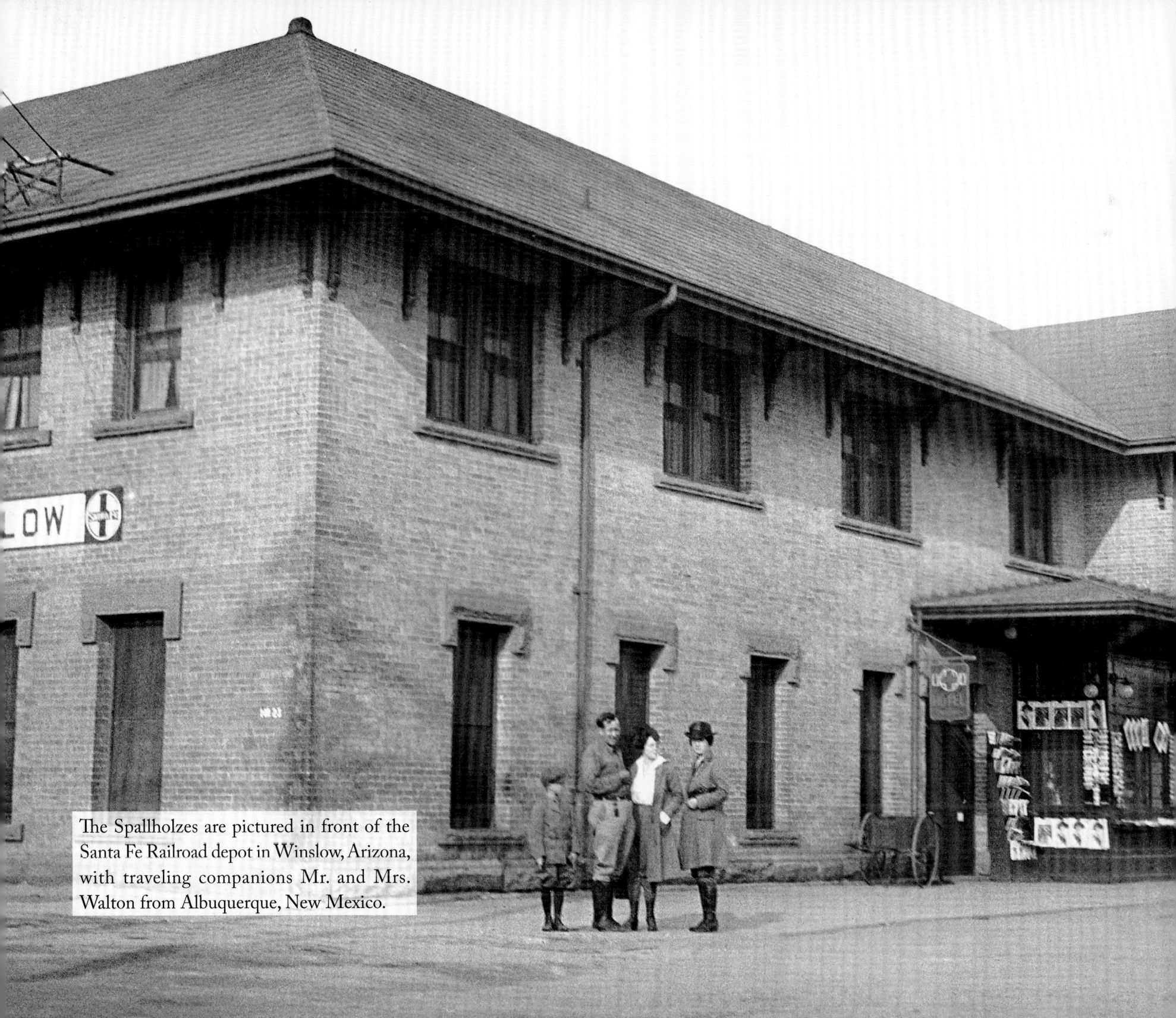

The Spallholzes are pictured in front of the Santa Fe Railroad depot in Winslow, Arizona, with traveling companions Mr. and Mrs. Walton from Albuquerque, New Mexico.

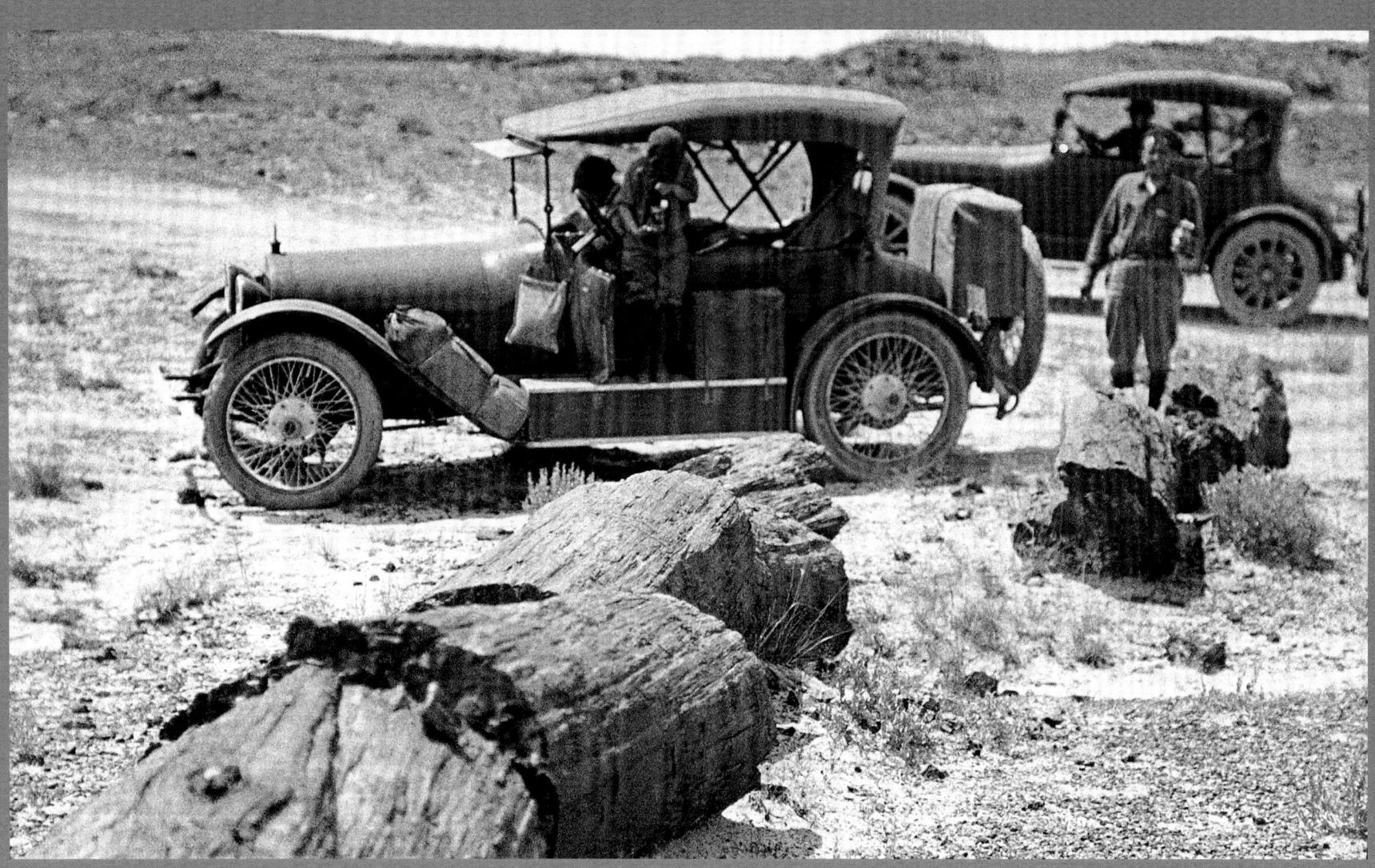

Taken in what is now the Petrified Forest National Park, Walter uses the Kodak camera to capture an image of an almost full-sized fossilized tree lying in sections in the foreground while traveling companion William Walton looks on in the background. Since Walter had the Kodak, Henry must have taken this photograph with the Graflex.

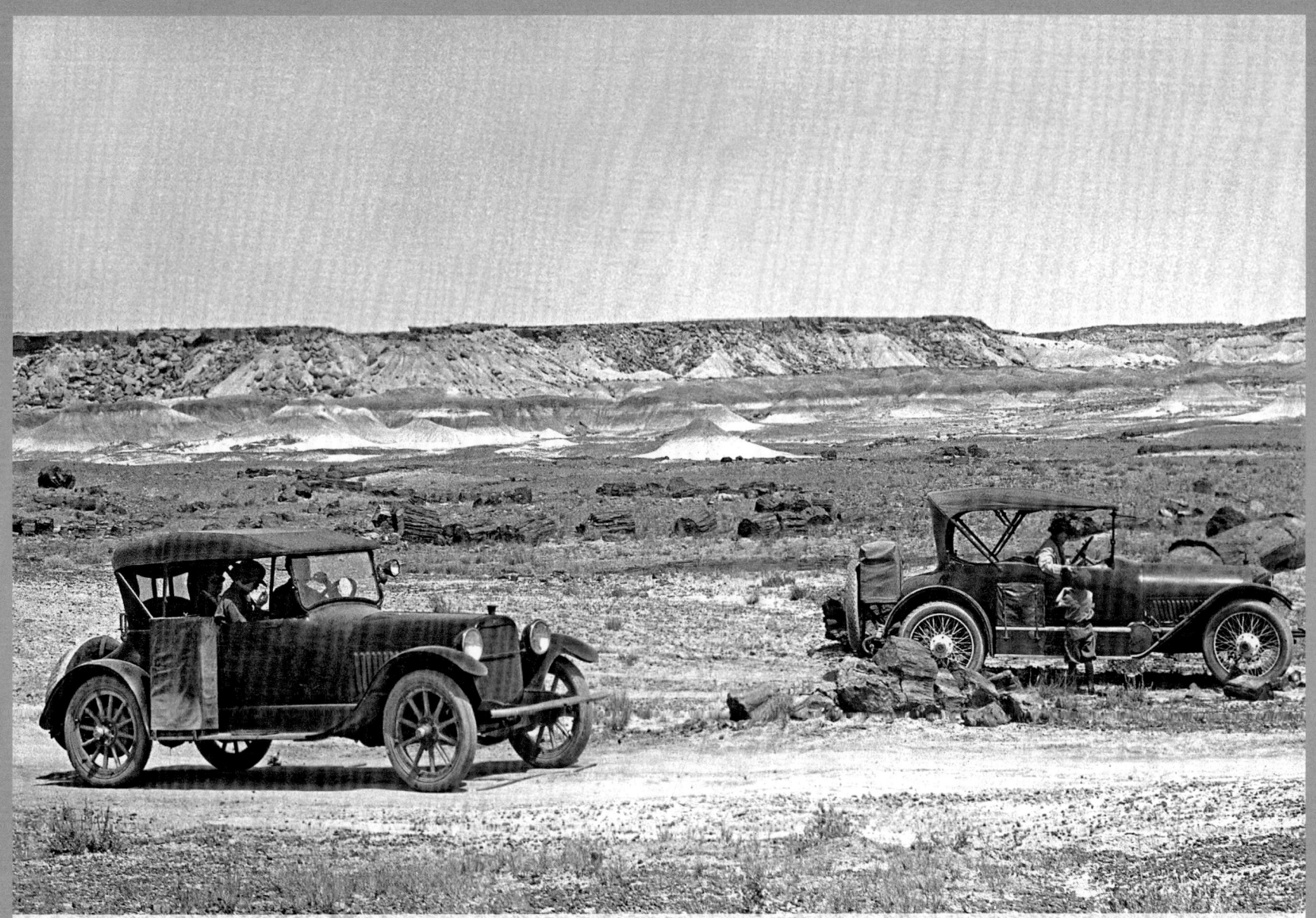

The Spallholzes and the Waltons stop to eat lunch in the shade inside their automobiles with the sun almost directly overhead. The Petrified Forest badlands are in the background.

Another view of the desolate Arizona badlands. The women prudently stay in the automobiles, shaded from the sun.

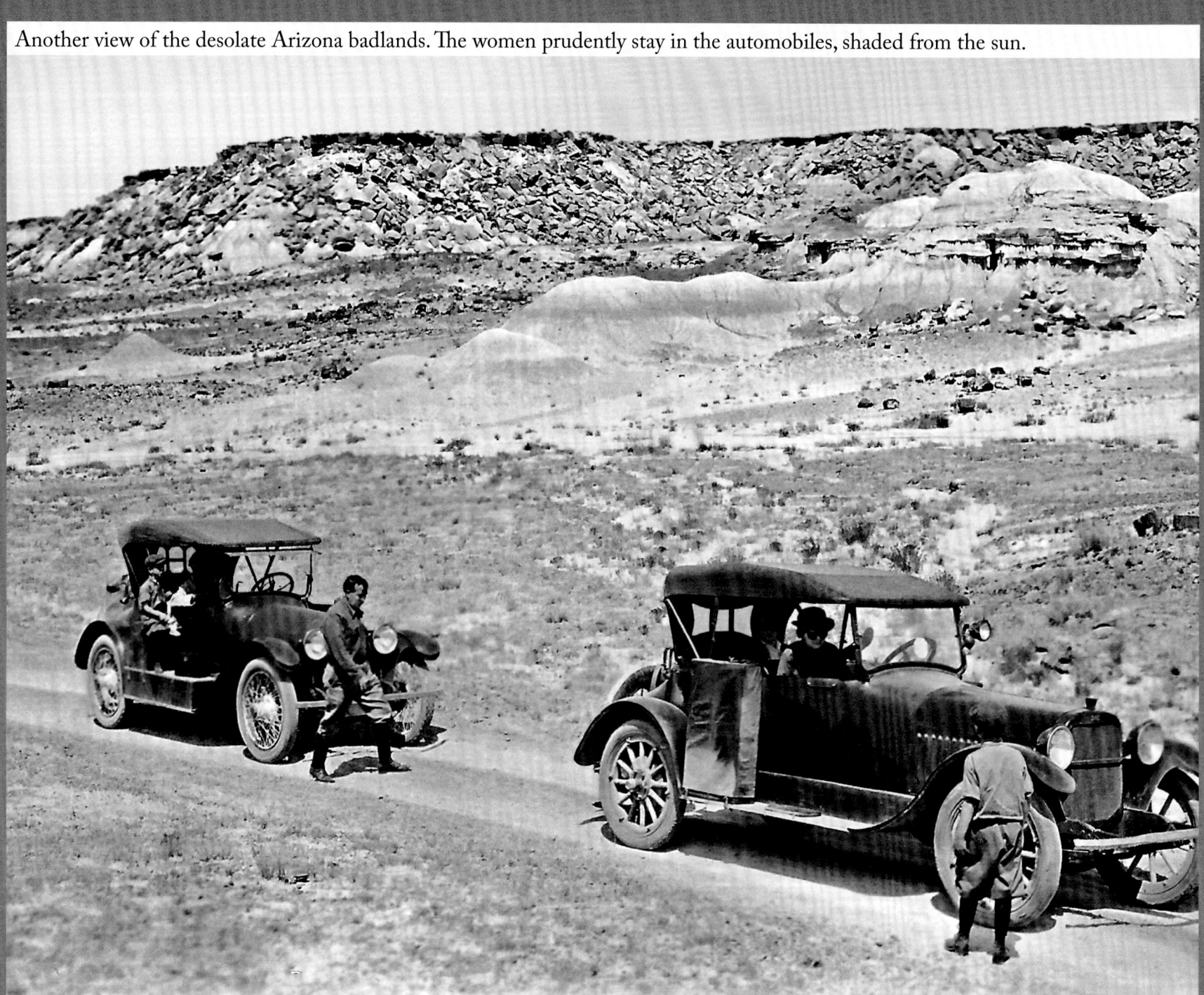

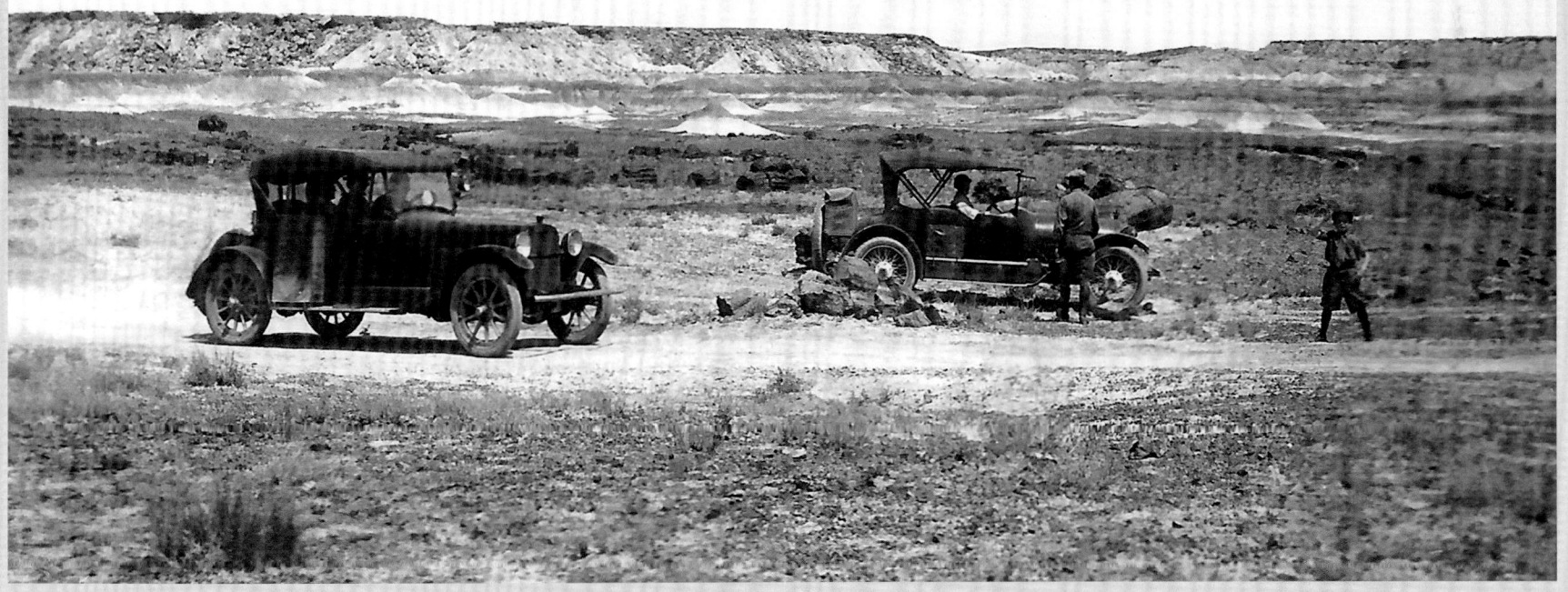

In another view showing their traveling companions, the Haynes is pulled off to one side of the road with the Petrified Forest in the background. Walter stands on the road in front of the two vehicles.

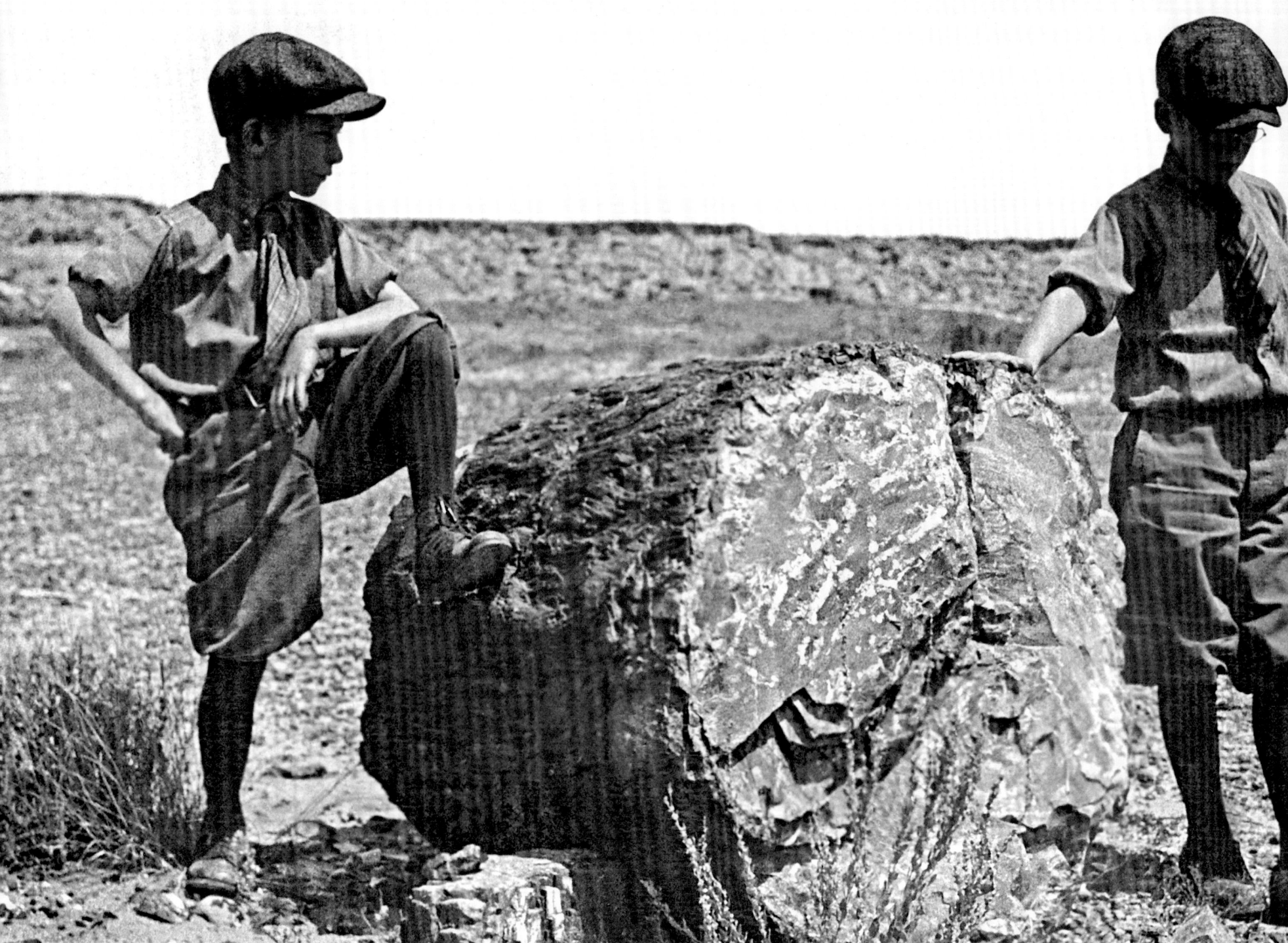

The boys stand under the hot Arizona sun next to a piece of petrified wood that is too large for them to carry off.

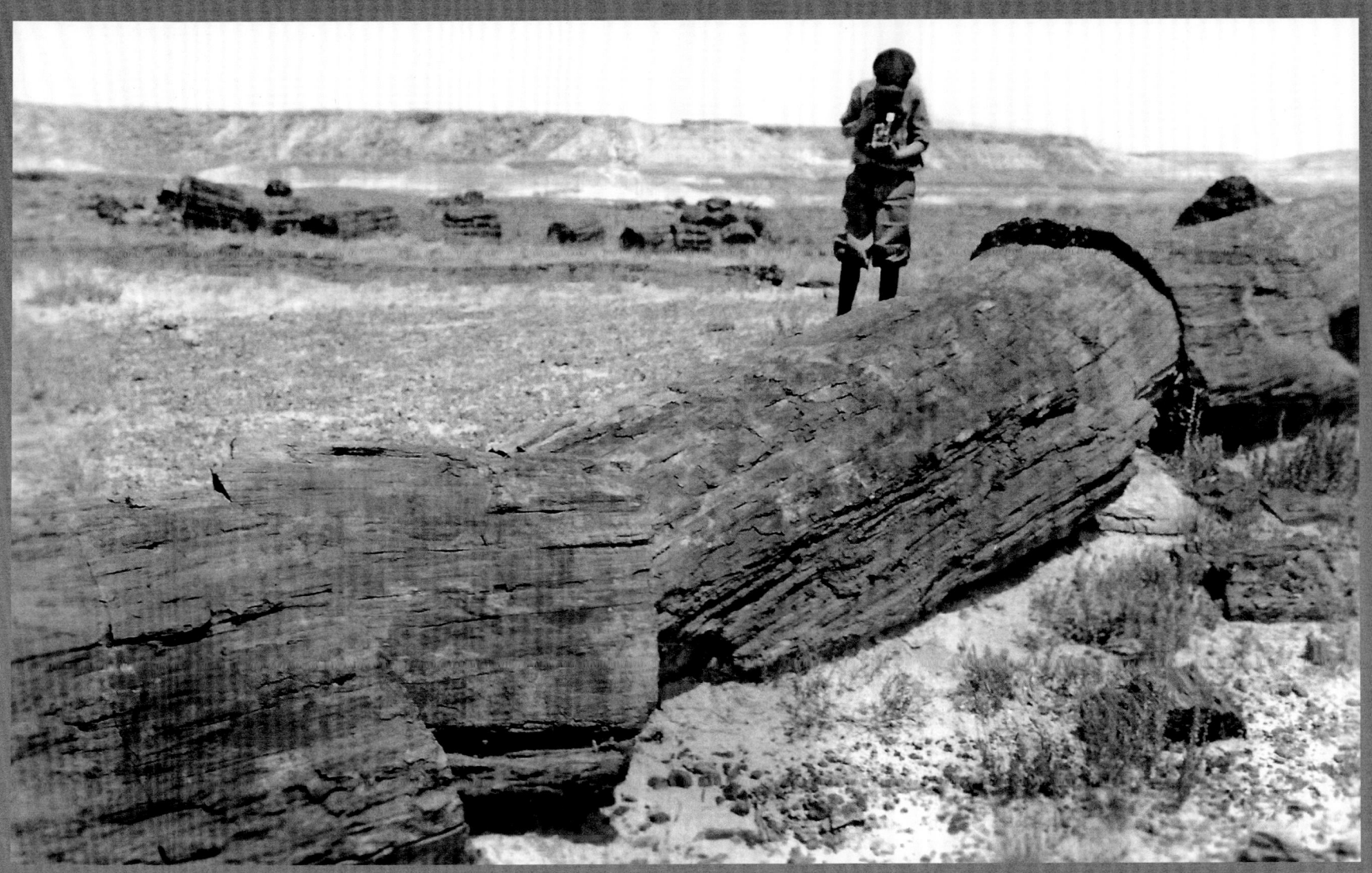

Walter snaps one more picture of a fossilized specimen of a conifer in the Petrified Forest, one he could not take as a souvenir.

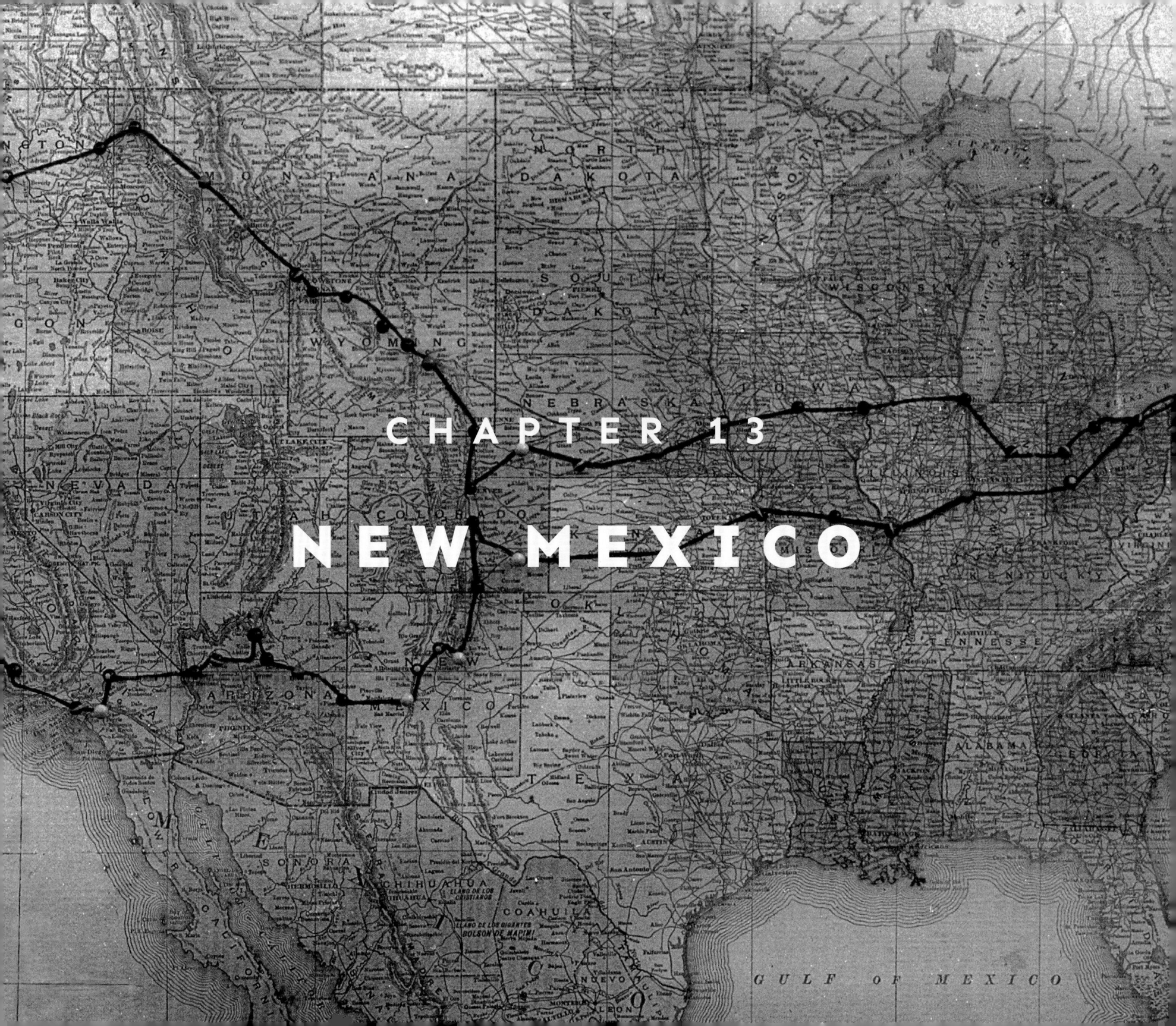

CHAPTER 13

NEW MEXICO

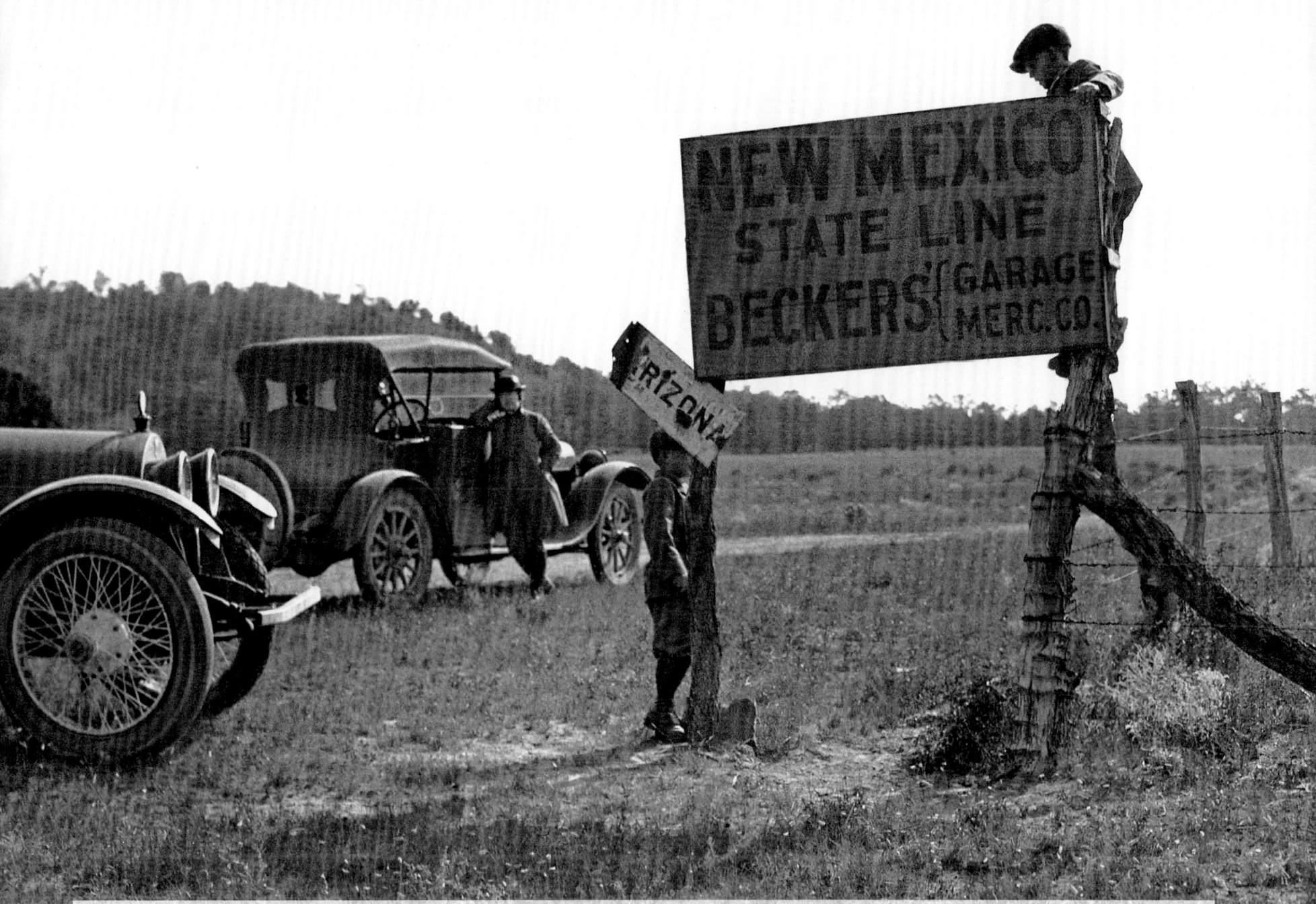

The travelers stop at the New Mexico state line. The state welcome sign shares space with that of a local business. Walter stands below the sign that points toward Arizona in the opposite direction, and Ernest balances on the fence post that also serves as a support for the state line signage. Mrs. Walton, wearing her duster, watches the boys as she leans against the couple's automobile.

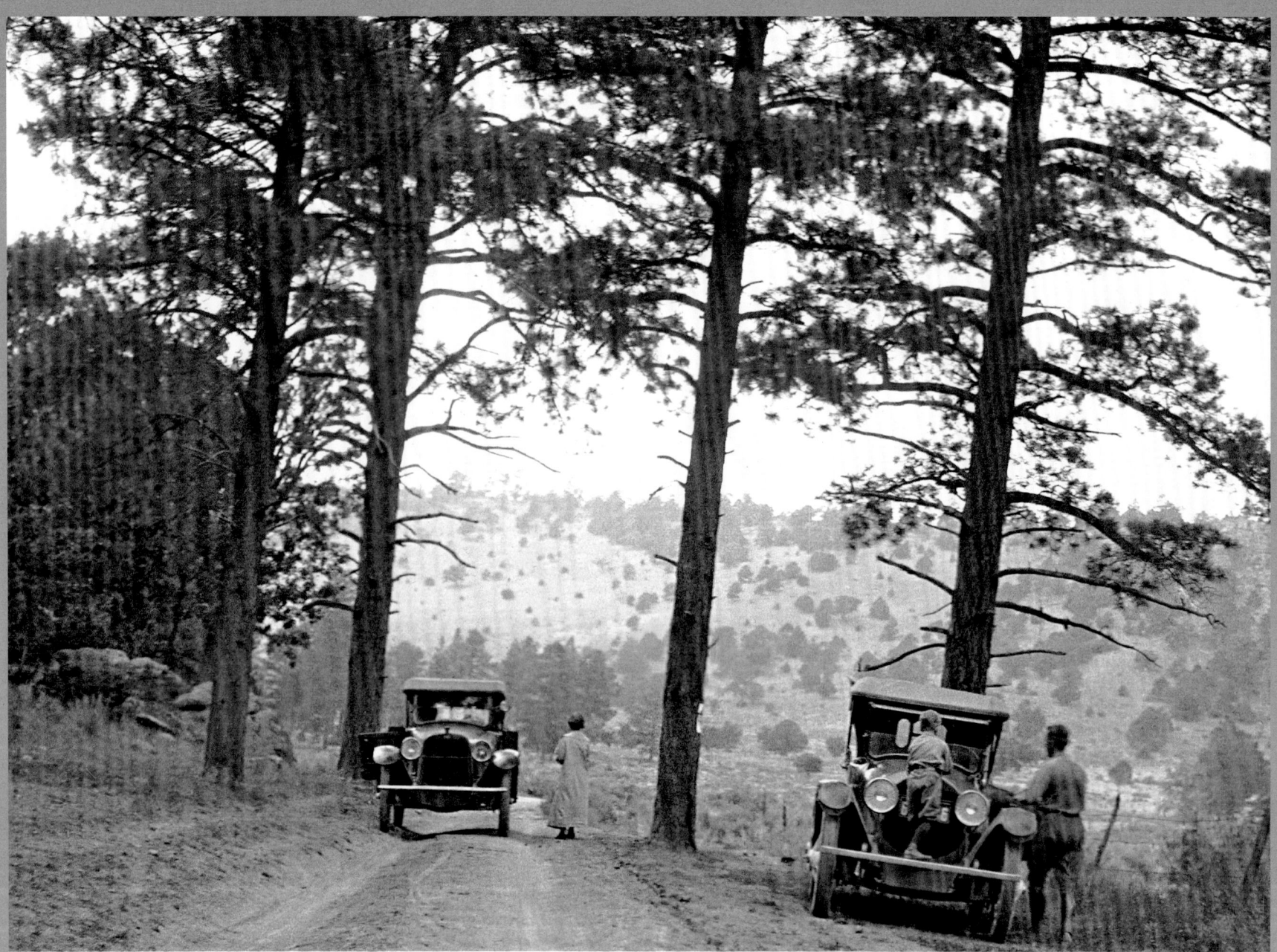

The Spallholzes and the Waltons stop beneath a group of ponderosa pines on a relatively well-maintained road in the Datil National Forest in Western New Mexico. Created in 1908, the Datil National Forest was merged with other forest lands, becoming part of the Cibola National Forest in 1931. Lizzie, wearing her daily duster, is standing in the road beside the Waltons' automobile.

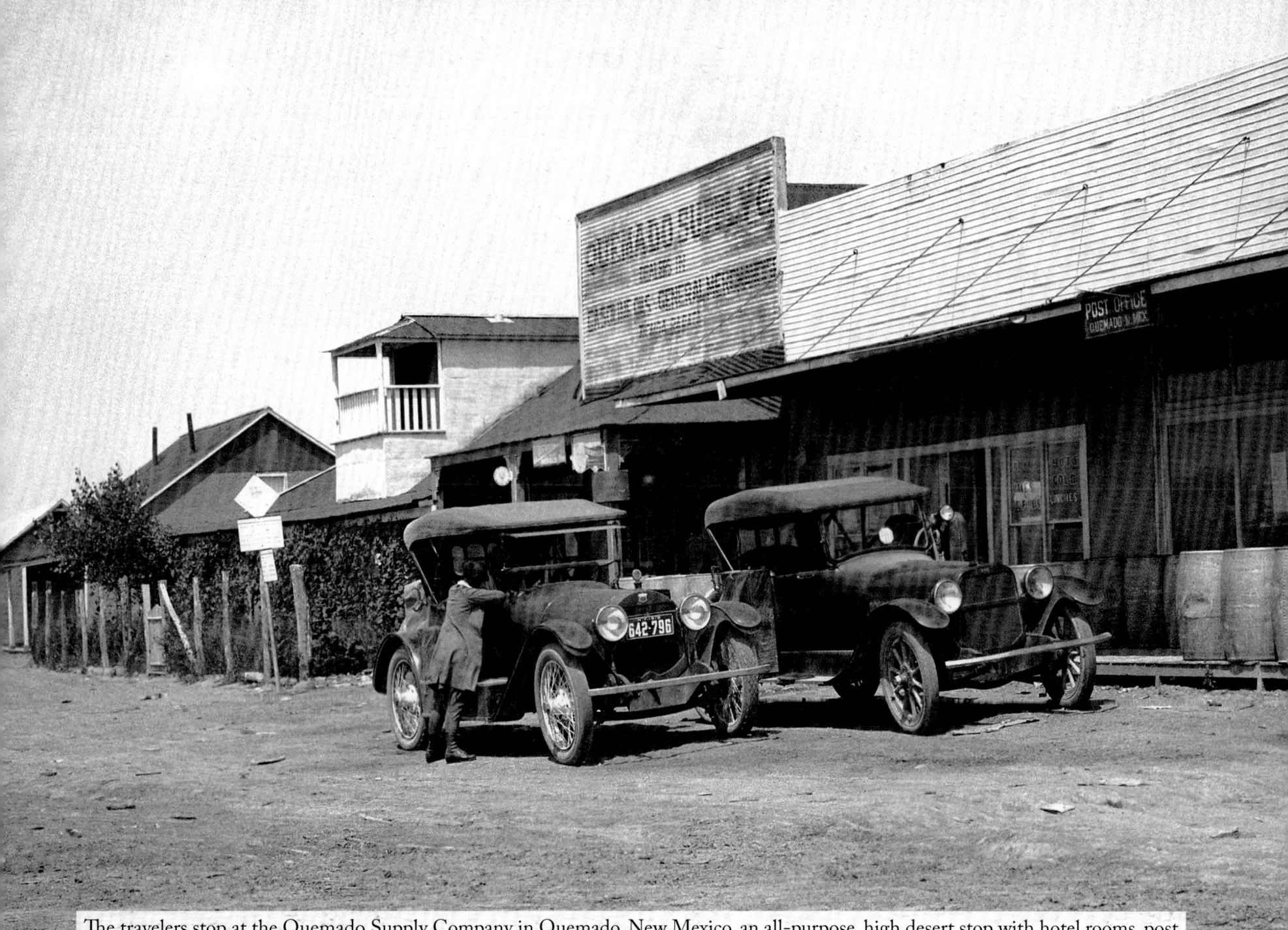

The travelers stop at the Quemado Supply Company in Quemado, New Mexico, an all-purpose, high desert stop with hotel rooms, post office, café, and gasoline at sixty cents per gallon.

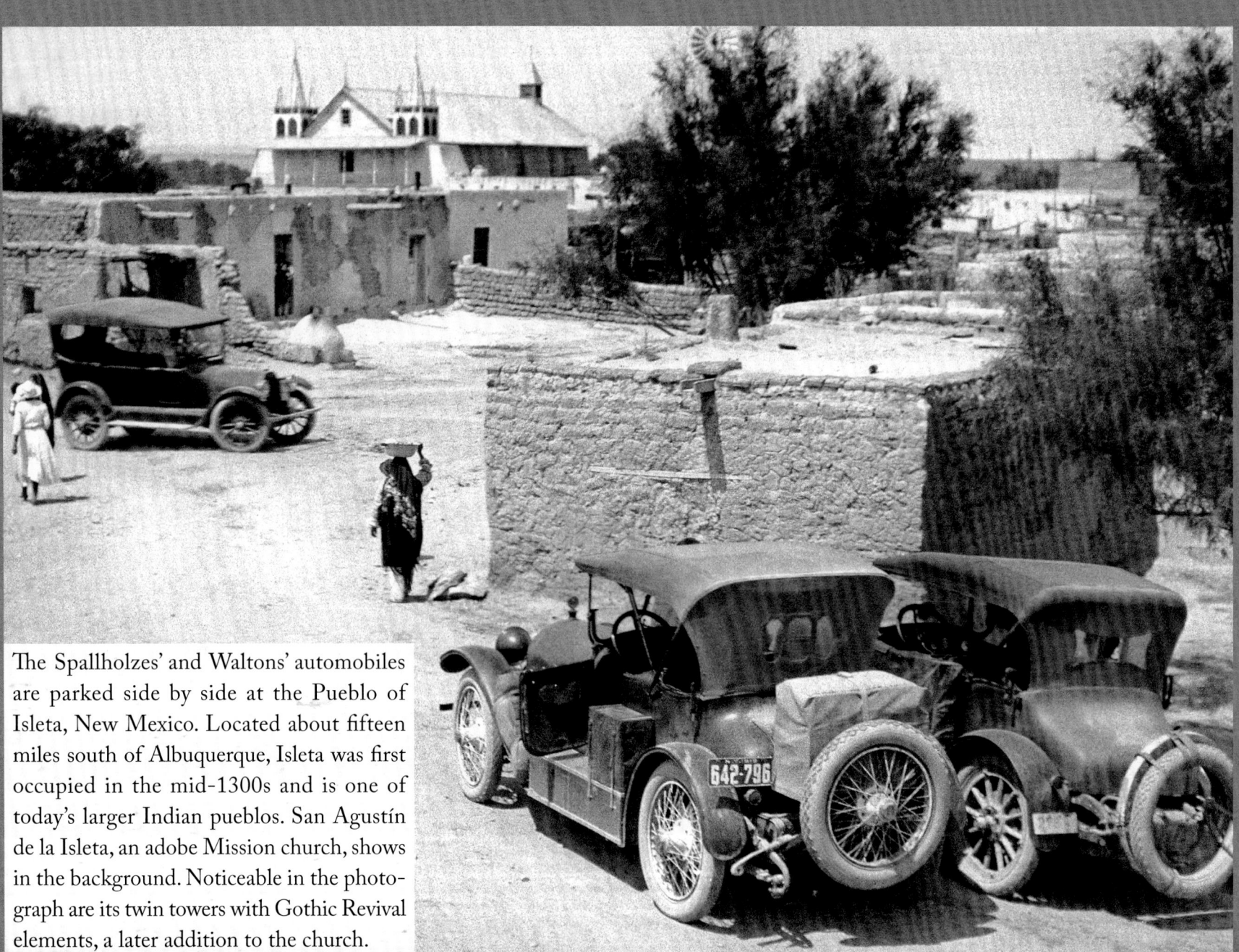

The Spallholzes' and Waltons' automobiles are parked side by side at the Pueblo of Isleta, New Mexico. Located about fifteen miles south of Albuquerque, Isleta was first occupied in the mid-1300s and is one of today's larger Indian pueblos. San Agustín de la Isleta, an adobe Mission church, shows in the background. Noticeable in the photograph are its twin towers with Gothic Revival elements, a later addition to the church.

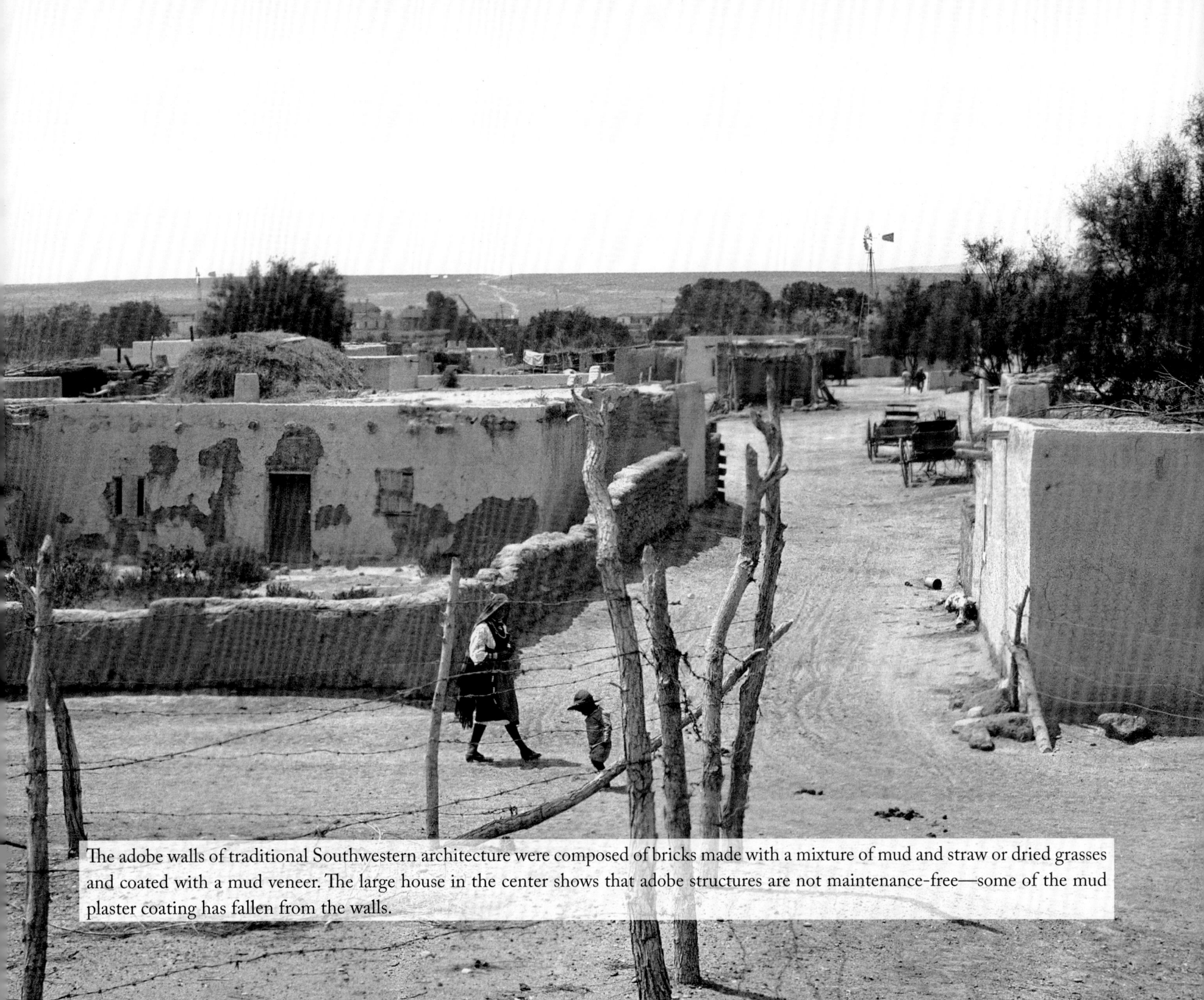

The adobe walls of traditional Southwestern architecture were composed of bricks made with a mixture of mud and straw or dried grasses and coated with a mud veneer. The large house in the center shows that adobe structures are not maintenance-free—some of the mud plaster coating has fallen from the walls.

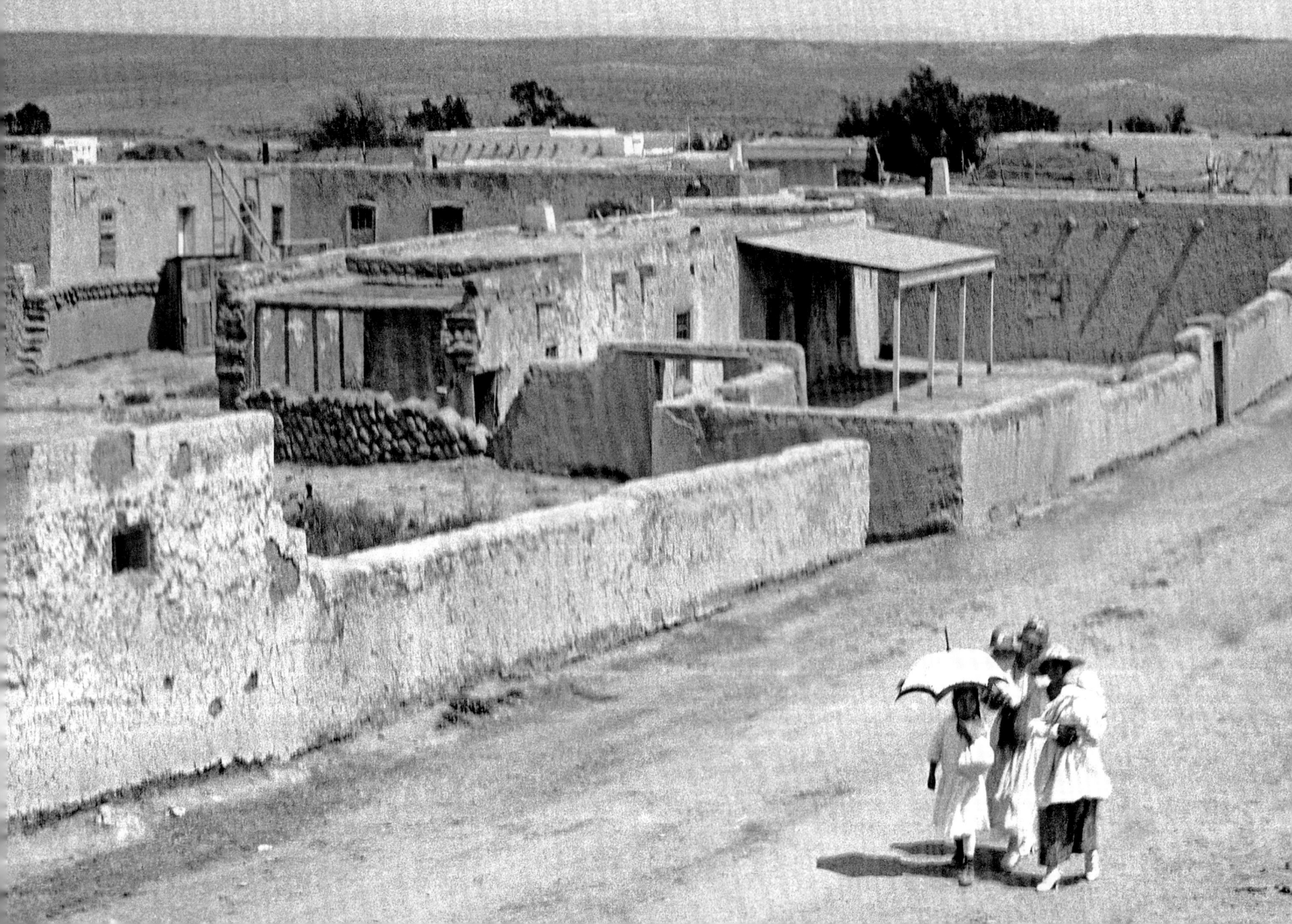

This interesting image taken from an elevated position shows people wearing what appears to be special-occasion clothing, possibly taken on a Sunday. The photograph features typical adobe-constructed homes and enclosing walls.

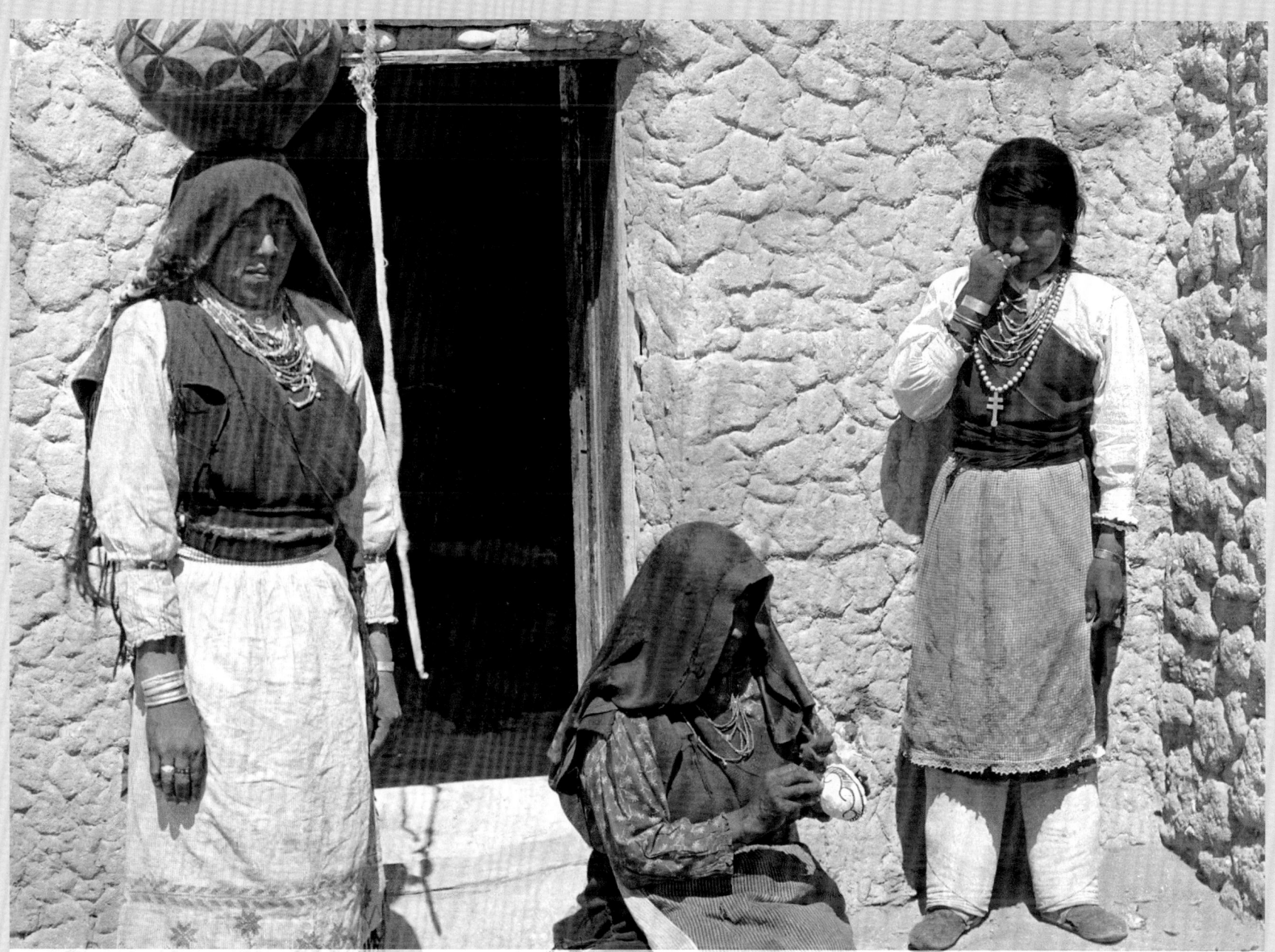

Posing in front of a doorway to an adobe house in Isleta, Pueblo women sell their wares, consisting of woven baskets, beaded necklaces, and pottery. The vessel on the woman's head could possibly have been used for carrying water from a common pueblo well. (Underwood & Underwood hand-colored lantern slide rendered in black and white.)

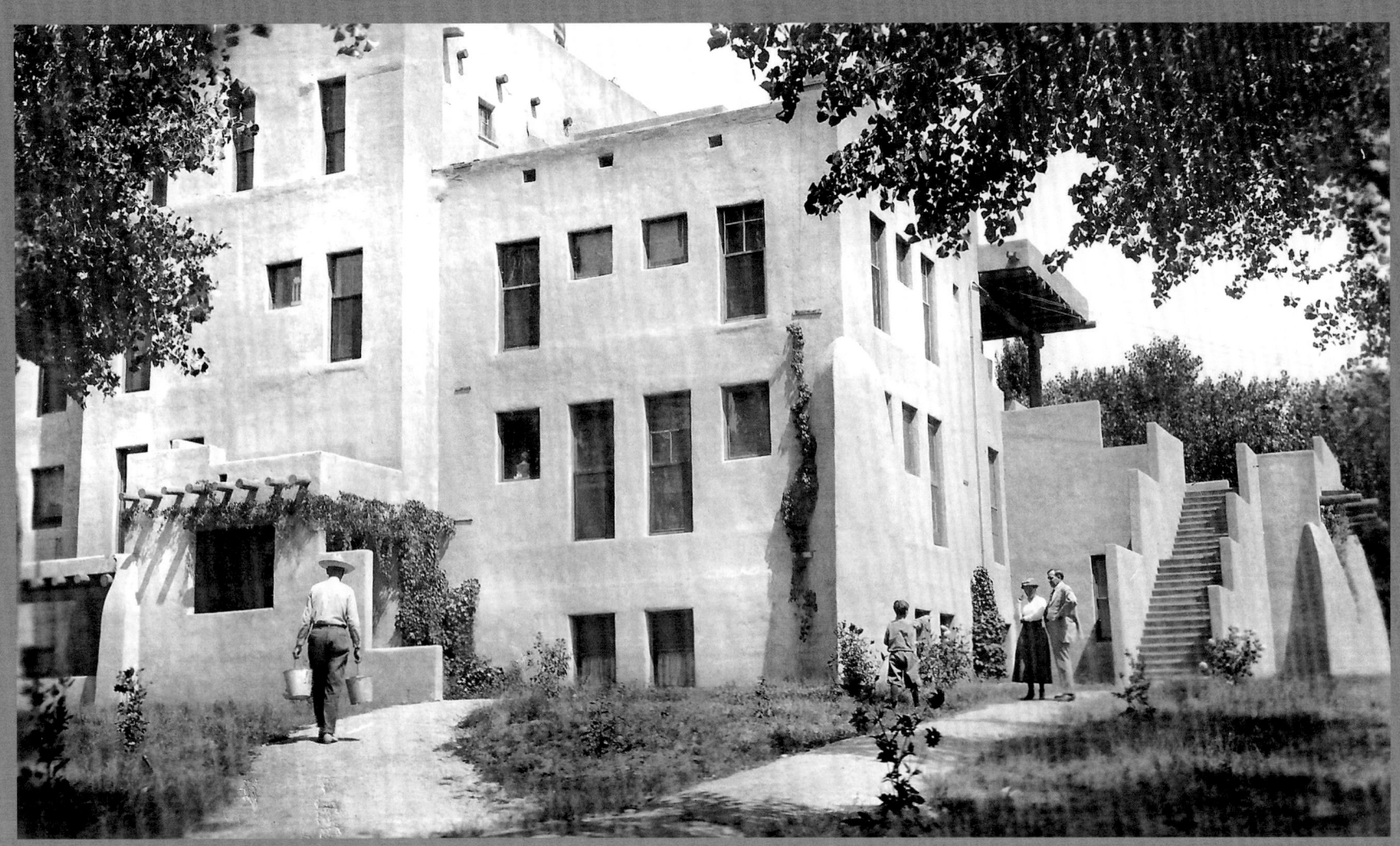

The Spallholzes stopped at the University of New Mexico in Albuquerque to observe a modern adaptation of the Pueblo architectural style. Lizzie converses with an unknown individual near the stairs at the right while a man carries buckets, probably filled with water, towards the entrance at the left. This design of Pueblo architecture dating back thousands of years was taken from Native people and adapted by settlers throughout the New Mexican territory.

With the Waltons remaining in Albuquerque, the Spallholz family headed towards Santa Fe, driving north on old New Mexico Route 1, later named New Mexico Route 85. Twenty-four miles north of Albuquerque, they came upon a large hand-excavated cut in the highway, known locally as the Big Cut. In this view from the south looking towards the north, Henry is seen standing beside the back of the Haynes. This cut would in time become part of the Albuquerque loop on Route 66.

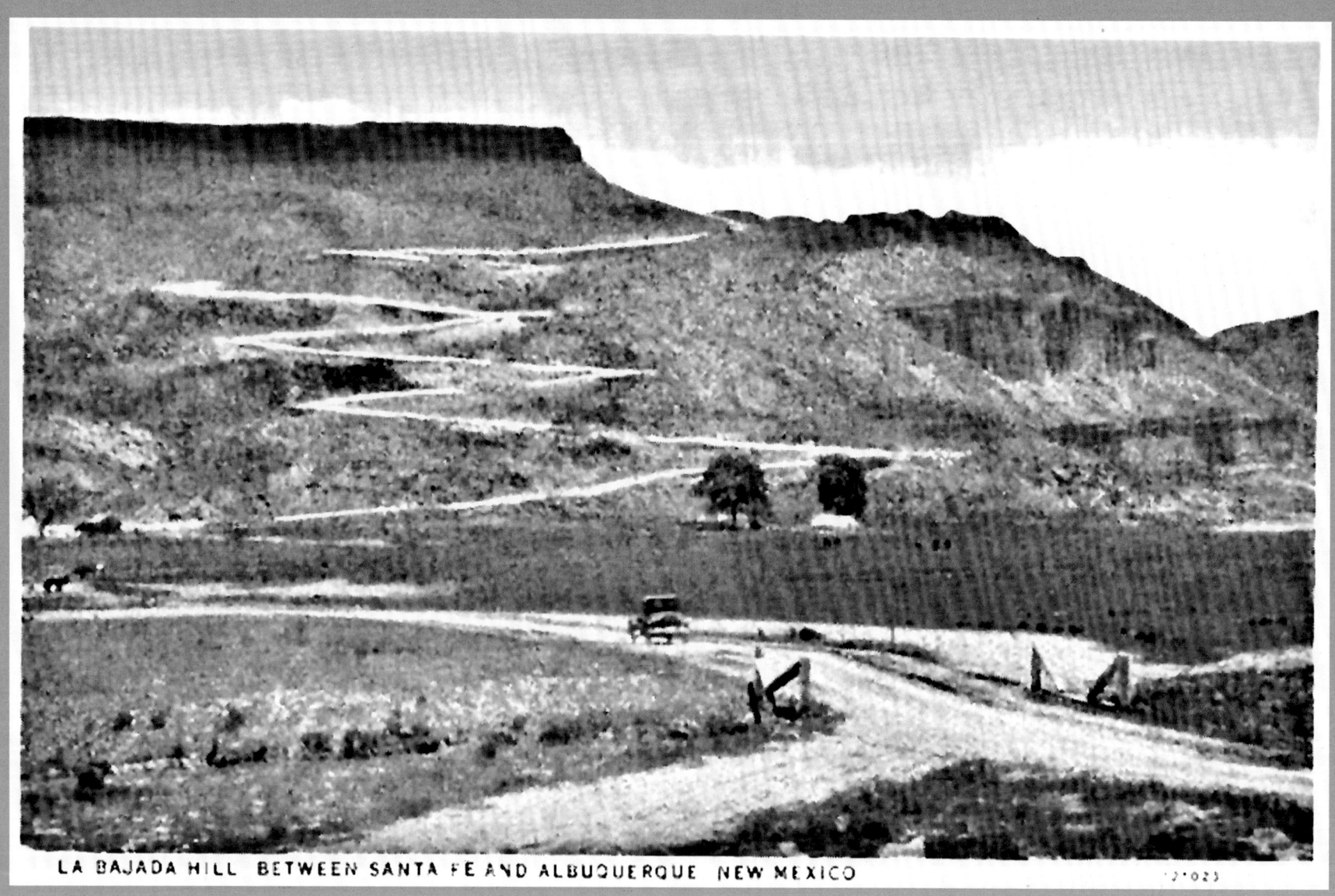

LA BAJADA HILL BETWEEN SANTA FE AND ALBUQUERQUE NEW MEXICO

La Bajada Hill between Santa Fe and Albuquerque, New Mexico. Further north on New Mexico Route 1, the Spallholzes encountered a very treacherous section of roadway with warnings and speed limit signs marked ten miles per hour. The ascending 1.5 miles of switchbacks from this perspective is known as La Bajada or, in English, The Descent. Henry noted that they had encountered eighteen switchbacks, some of which are seen in this postcard as the road zigzags its way up the basalt mountain.

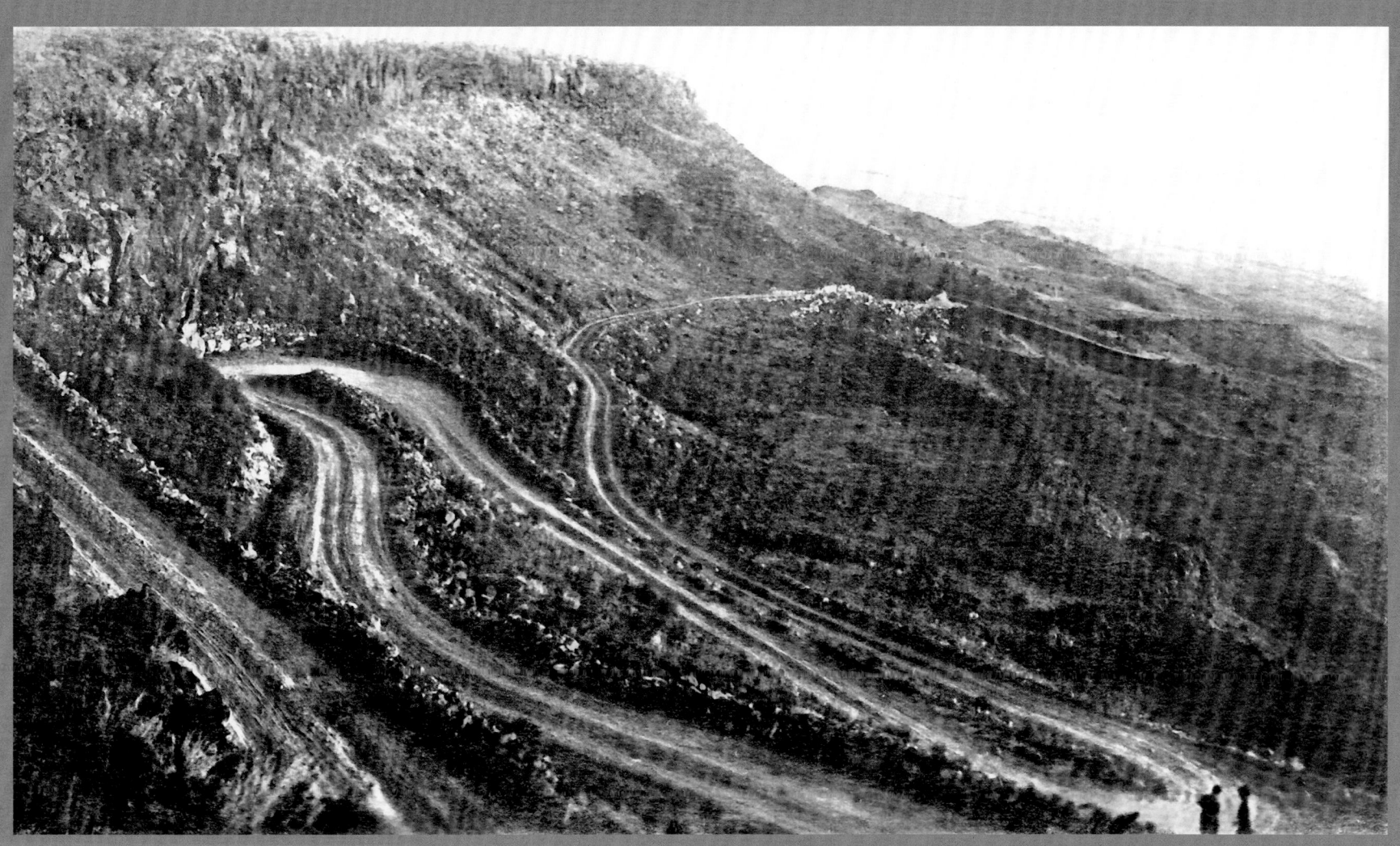

The hairpin turns on La Bajada were so sharp that long vehicles had to back up while ascending to get around them. Between 1926 and 1932, this road also became part of the southern section of the Route 66 loop between Albuquerque and Santa Fe. Today, the switchbacks have been bypassed and cars accelerate as they travel around a broad curve on I-25, passing through several ancient volcanic pyroclastic flows as it gains 600 feet of elevation climbing to the top of the escarpment. Nearby the Rio Grande River flows through a rift valley, showing evidence of considerable past volcanic activity.

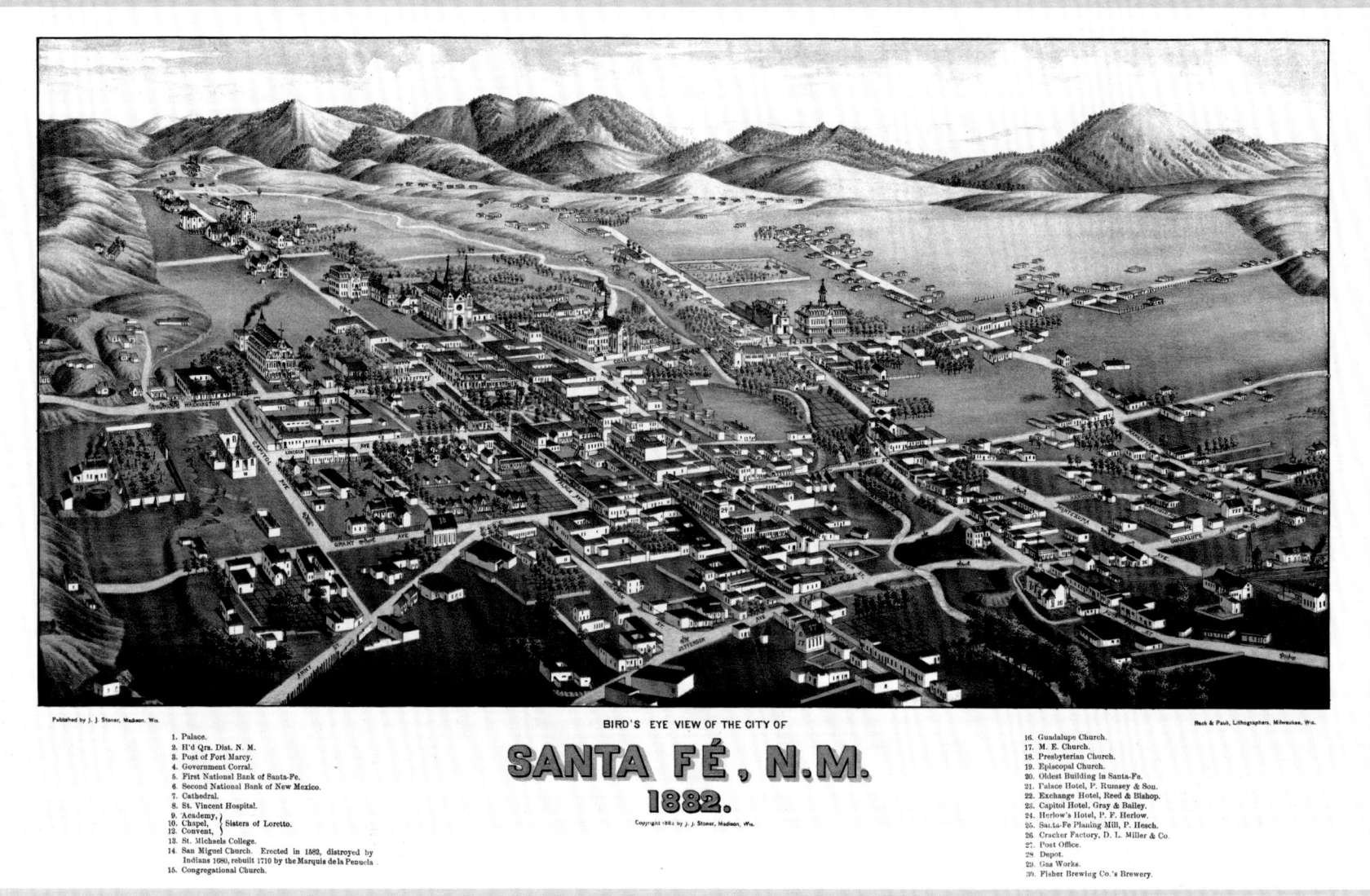

BIRD'S EYE VIEW OF THE CITY OF

SANTA FÉ, N.M.
1882.

Copyright 1882 by J. J. Stoner, Madison, Wis.

1. Palace.
2. H'd Qrs. Dist. N. M.
3. Post of Fort Marcy.
4. Government Corral.
5. First National Bank of Santa-Fe.
6. Second National Bank of New Mexico.
7. Cathedral.
8. St. Vincent Hospital.
9. Academy,
10. Chapel, } Sisters of Loretto.
12. Convent,
13. St. Michaels College.
14. San Miguel Church. Erected in 1582, distroyed by Indians 1680, rebuilt 1710 by the Marquis de la Penuela
15. Congregational Church.

16. Guadalupe Church.
17. M. E. Church.
18. Presbyterian Church.
19. Episcopal Church.
20. Oldest Building in Santa-Fe.
21. Palace Hotel, P. Rumsey & Son.
22. Exchange Hotel, Reed & Bishop.
23. Capitol Hotel, Gray & Bailey.
24. Herlow's Hotel, P. F. Herlow.
25. Santa-Fe Planing Mill, P. Hesch.
26. Cracker Factory, D. L. Miller & Co.
27. Post Office.
28. Depot.
29. Gas Works.
30. Fisher Brewing Co.'s Brewery.

Commercial lithograph of Santa Fe, New Mexico, from 1882. The local climate is high desert, with a city elevation of 7,198 feet. Sage brush, juniper, and piñon pine trees merge into forests of aspen and evergreen at higher elevations above the city.

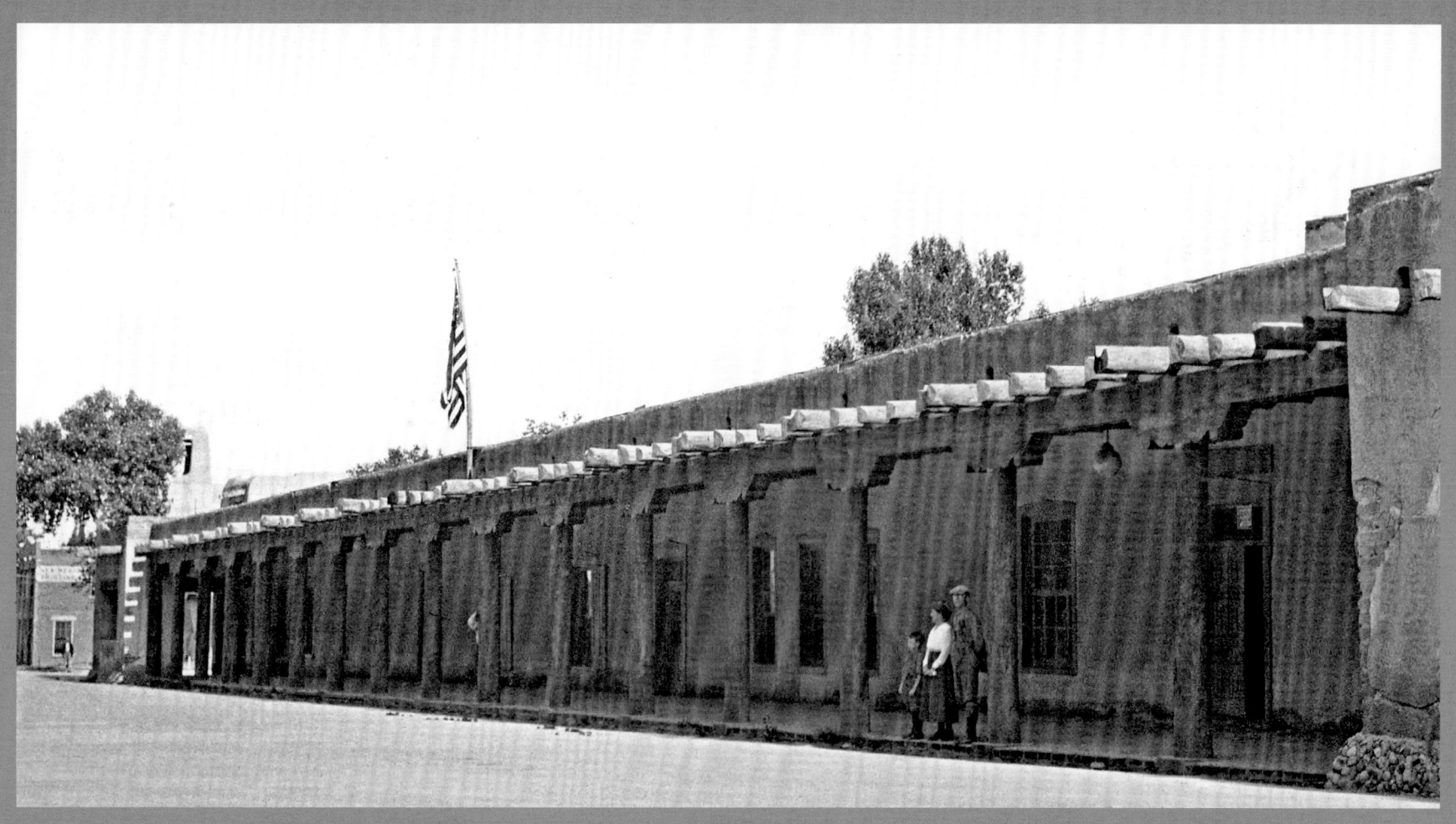

Ernest, Lizzie, and Henry stand in front of the historic Palace of the Governors in Santa Fe, which was occupied from 1620 to 1909 by Spanish, Pueblo, Mexican, and New Mexico governors. Seemingly deserted on the day of their visit, the site today is the location of a museum and a place where Native people hold their market for selling locally made goods.

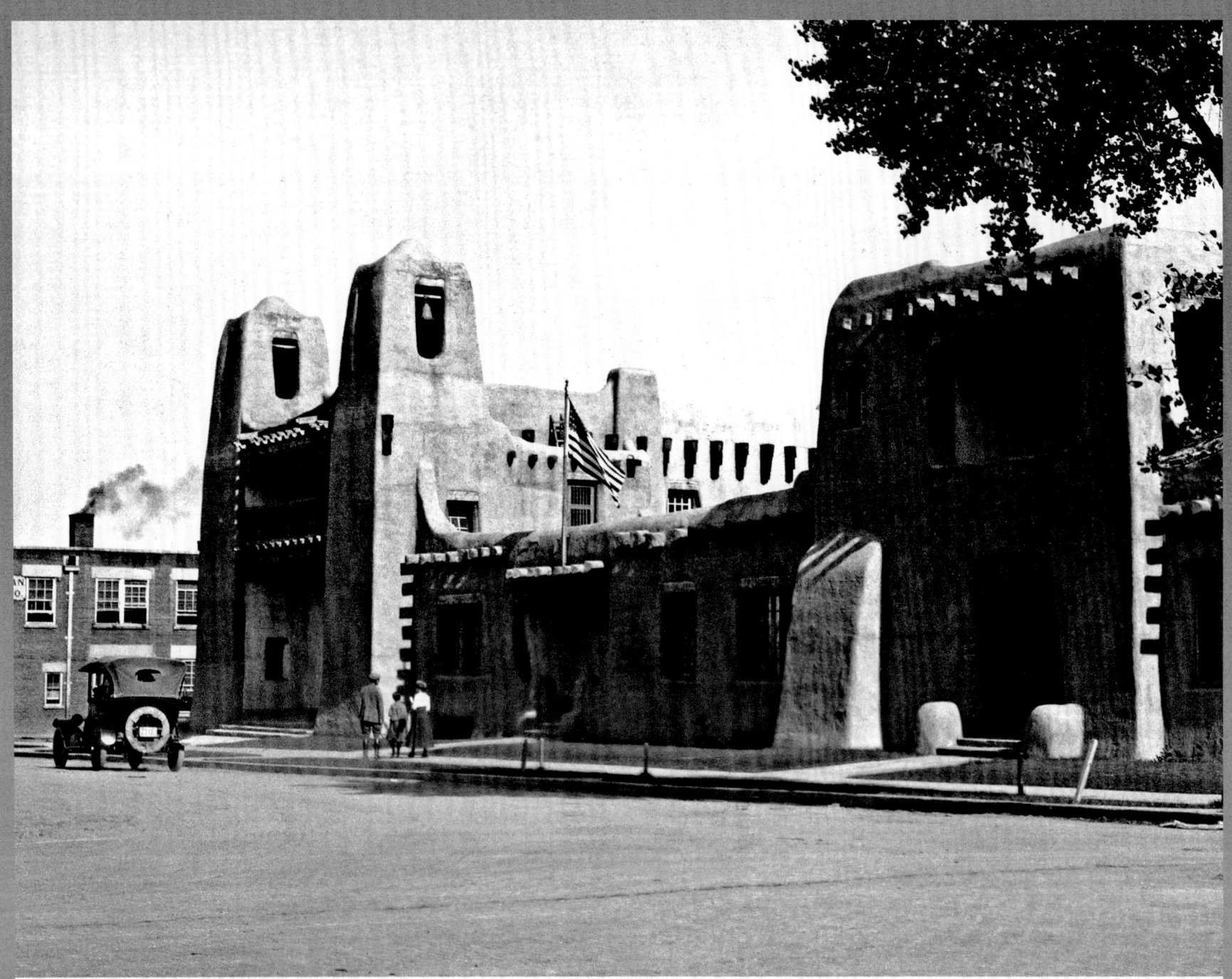

The Spallholzes stand in front of the Indian art museum, a splendid example of Mission architecture in Santa Fe.

Fifty yards southeast of the Museum of Indian Arts and Culture is the Roman Catholic Basilica of Saint Francis of Assisi. Although the basilica is one of the most photographed buildings in the Old Plaza area, no photo taken by Henry Spallholz is found in his collection. Given his propensity for photographing missions in California, it seems so unlikely that he would not have visited the church and photographed it that this "substitute photograph" has been included among his other Santa Fe photographs. Speculation suggests that something happened to either the camera or the development of the photograph at home to account for its being missing from the collection. (Saint Francis Cathedral, Santa Fe, New Mexico. Tyler Dingee, photographer. Courtesy of the Palace of the Governors Photo Archives (NMHM/DCA), negative number 051310.)

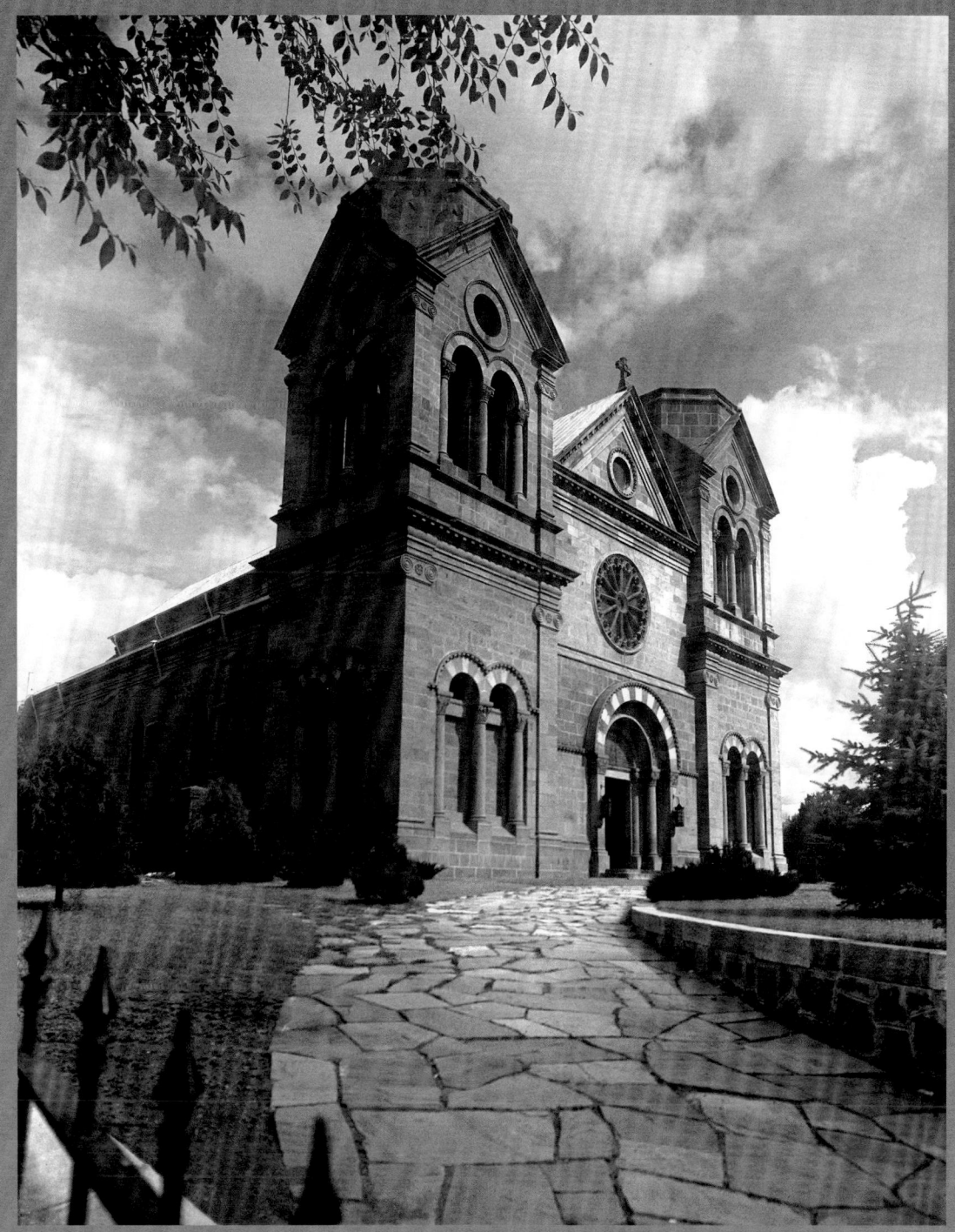

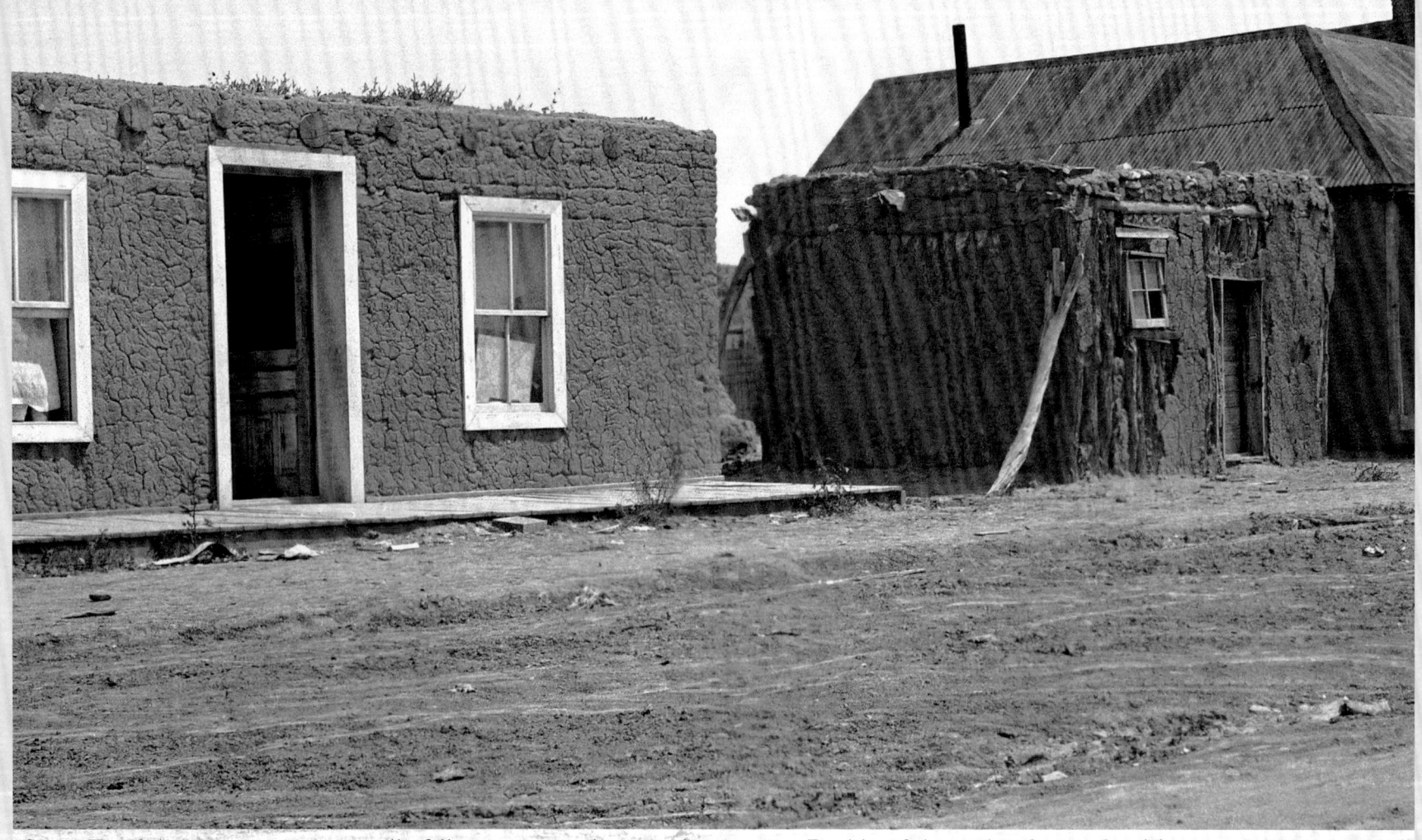

Santa Fe adobe construction generally falls into two architectural categories: Pueblo adobe with a flat roof, or Territorial with a pitched roof. Both styles of Santa Fe architecture were captured in this one photograph. The wooden ends protruding from the Pueblo style houses are structural beams (vigas) spanning the house's interior overlaid with a build-up of wooden tree branches called latias. A top layer of adobe forms the roof.

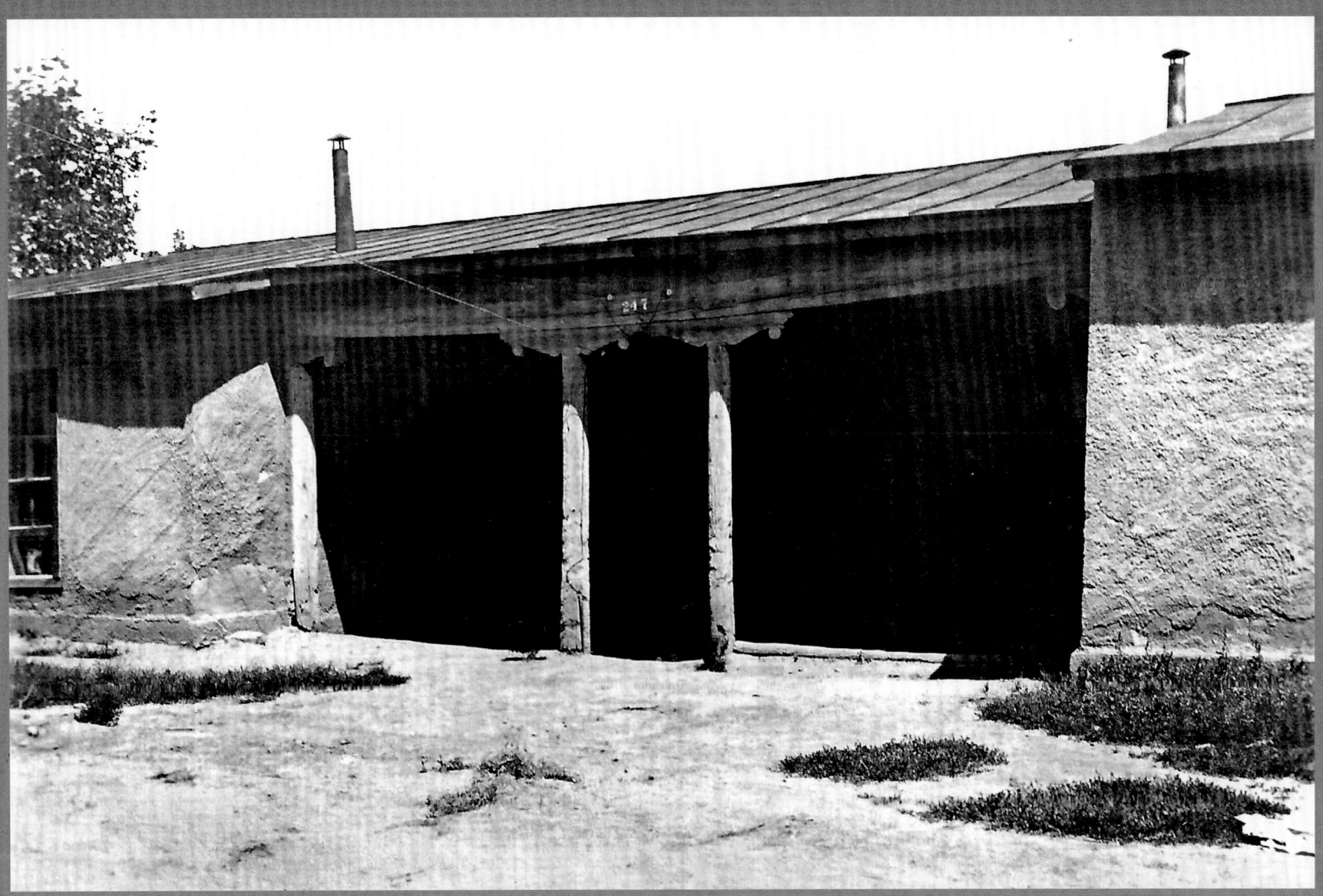

This house is constructed in a fancier Territorial style with a covered porch. The roof is supported by posts topped by corbels, which serve as support for the roof's viga beams forming the portal. Shown is one of the most common corbel styles with viga beams protruding from the front of the roof.

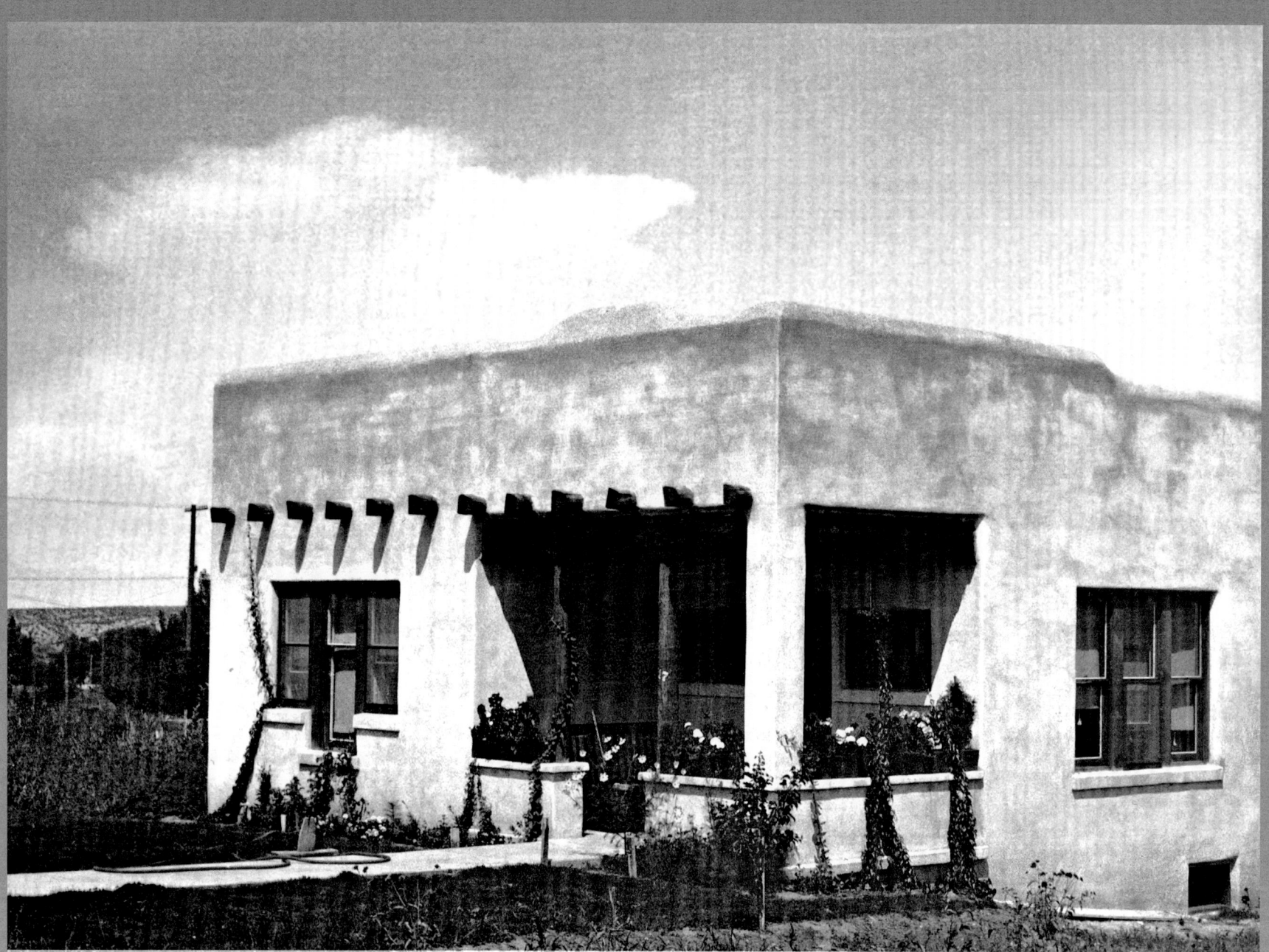

In the newer adobe Pueblo style of architecture, a house is constructed from some form of cement block or brick covered with a finish of adobe or stucco cement. The vigas protruding in the front of the house may be structural or simply ornamental. Vigas seen today in modern Pueblo style housing are usually decorative, not structural.

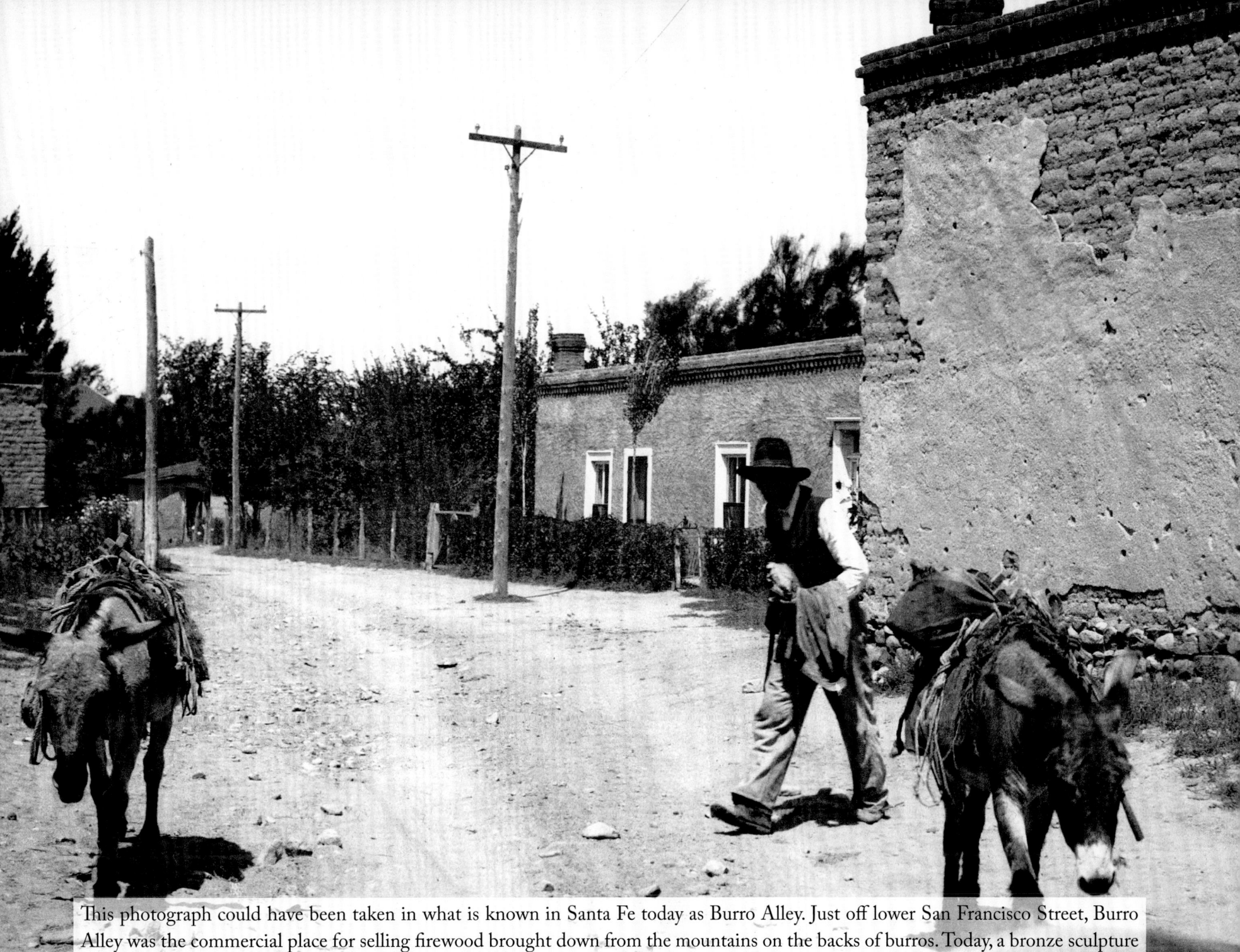

This photograph could have been taken in what is known in Santa Fe today as Burro Alley. Just off lower San Francisco Street, Burro Alley was the commercial place for selling firewood brought down from the mountains on the backs of burros. Today, a bronze sculpture of a burro loaded with wood stands at Burro Alley as a memorial to the past.

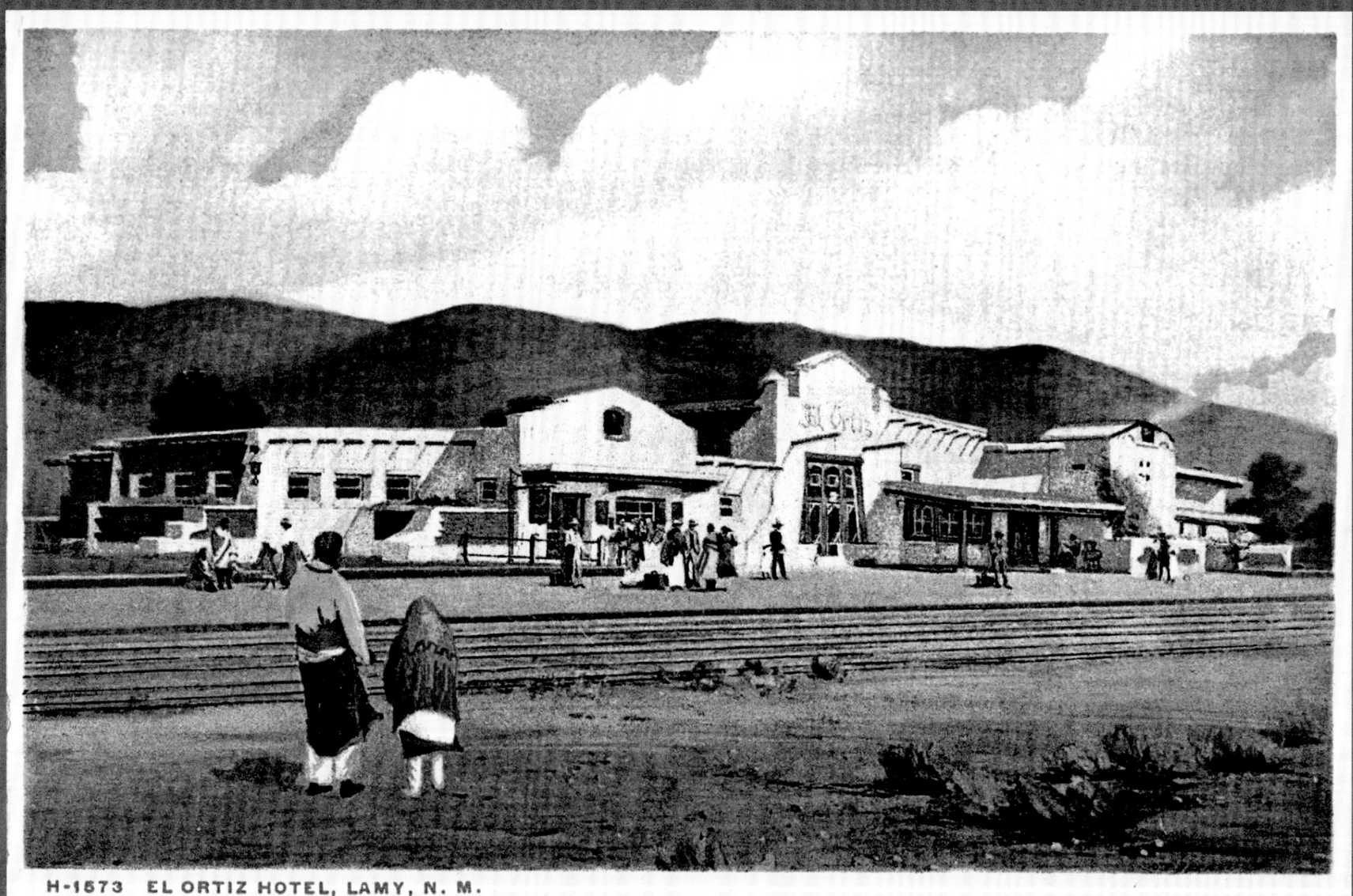

H-1573 EL ORTIZ HOTEL, LAMY, N. M.

As they left Santa Fe to resume crossing the Desert Southwest, the Spallholzes continued to follow the Santa Fe railroad for safety and to stay overnight at Harvey Houses along the way. There being no Harvey House Hotel in Santa Fe, they most likely stayed at the El Ortiz Hotel in Lamy, New Mexico, about fifteen miles south of Santa Fe. As seen in this vintage postcard image, the Atchison, Topeka and Santa Fe Railway tracks ran right in front of the hotel. From Lamy their driving route would continue to follow the Santa Fe Trail.

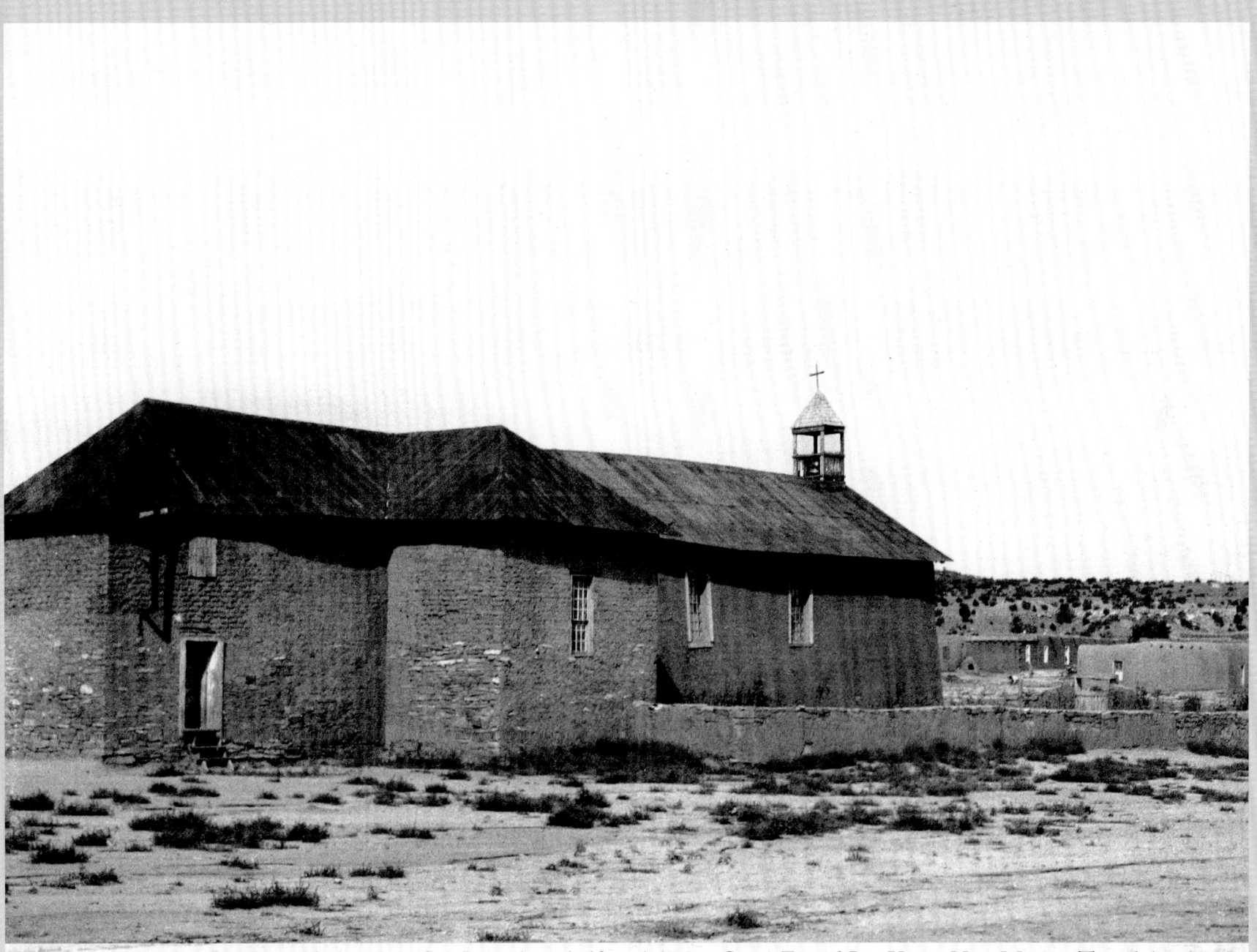

Henry took this picture of an old church in San Jose, about halfway between Santa Fe and Las Vegas, New Mexico. The adobe church was built in the Territorial New Mexico architectural style with a pitched roof rather than in the Pueblo adobe style with a flat roof. The church in this picture remains in San Jose today just as it appeared in 1919.

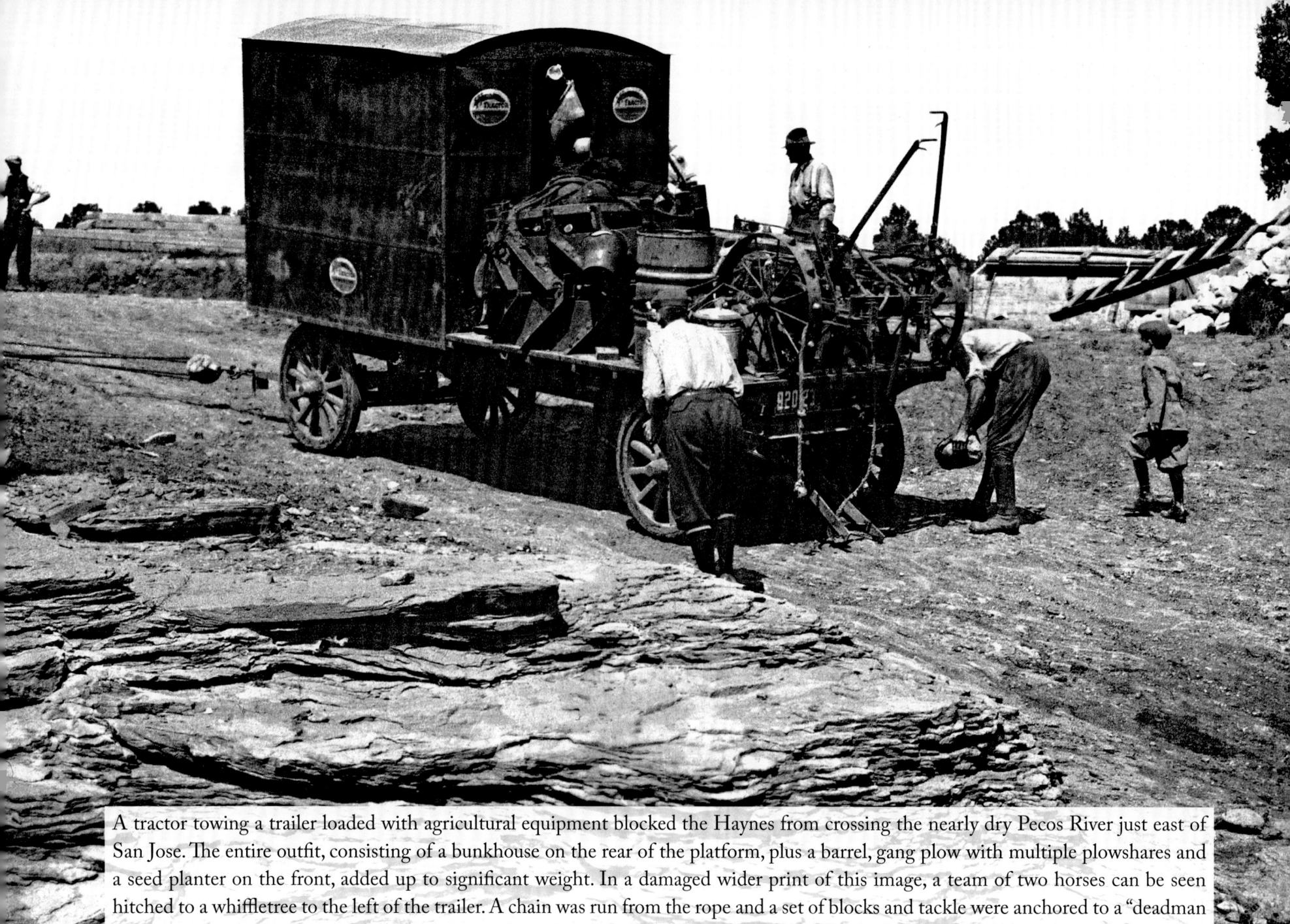

A tractor towing a trailer loaded with agricultural equipment blocked the Haynes from crossing the nearly dry Pecos River just east of San Jose. The entire outfit, consisting of a bunkhouse on the rear of the platform, plus a barrel, gang plow with multiple plowshares and a seed planter on the front, added up to significant weight. In a damaged wider print of this image, a team of two horses can be seen hitched to a whiffletree to the left of the trailer. A chain was run from the rope and a set of blocks and tackle were anchored to a "deadman anchor." The mechanical advantage provided by this apparatus allowed the team to slowly draw the load up the incline, a task they could not accomplish alone. The block and tackle can be seen suspended just above the ground. Two men are chocking the wheels with stones as Ernest walks behind the trailer.

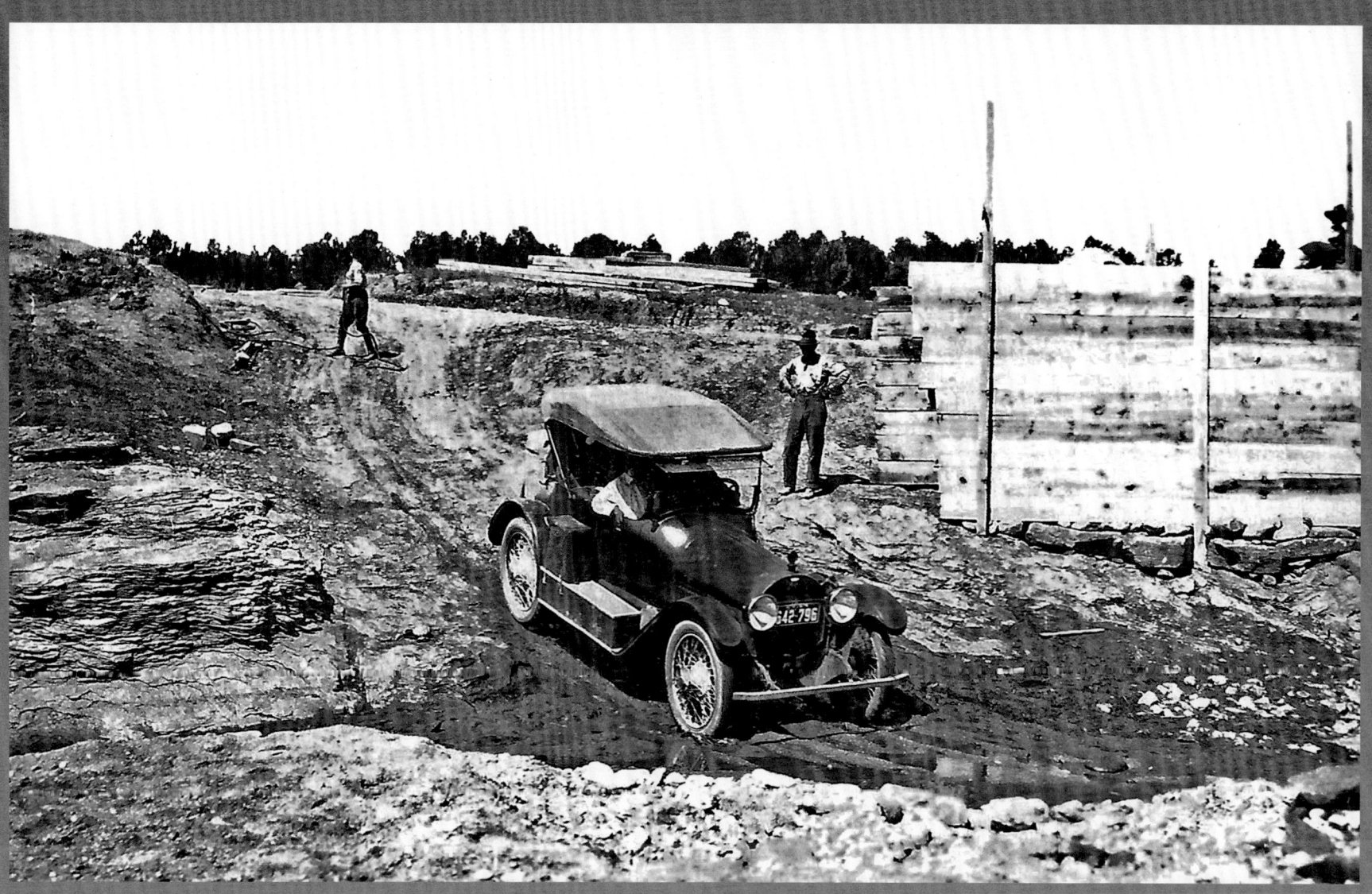

After the tractor outfit had moved on, the Spallholzes crossed the Pecos River along the Santa Fe Trail on their way north to Raton Pass, New Mexico. A steel truss bridge was built at this exact location in 1921, putting an end to the necessity for this kind of rough river crossing.

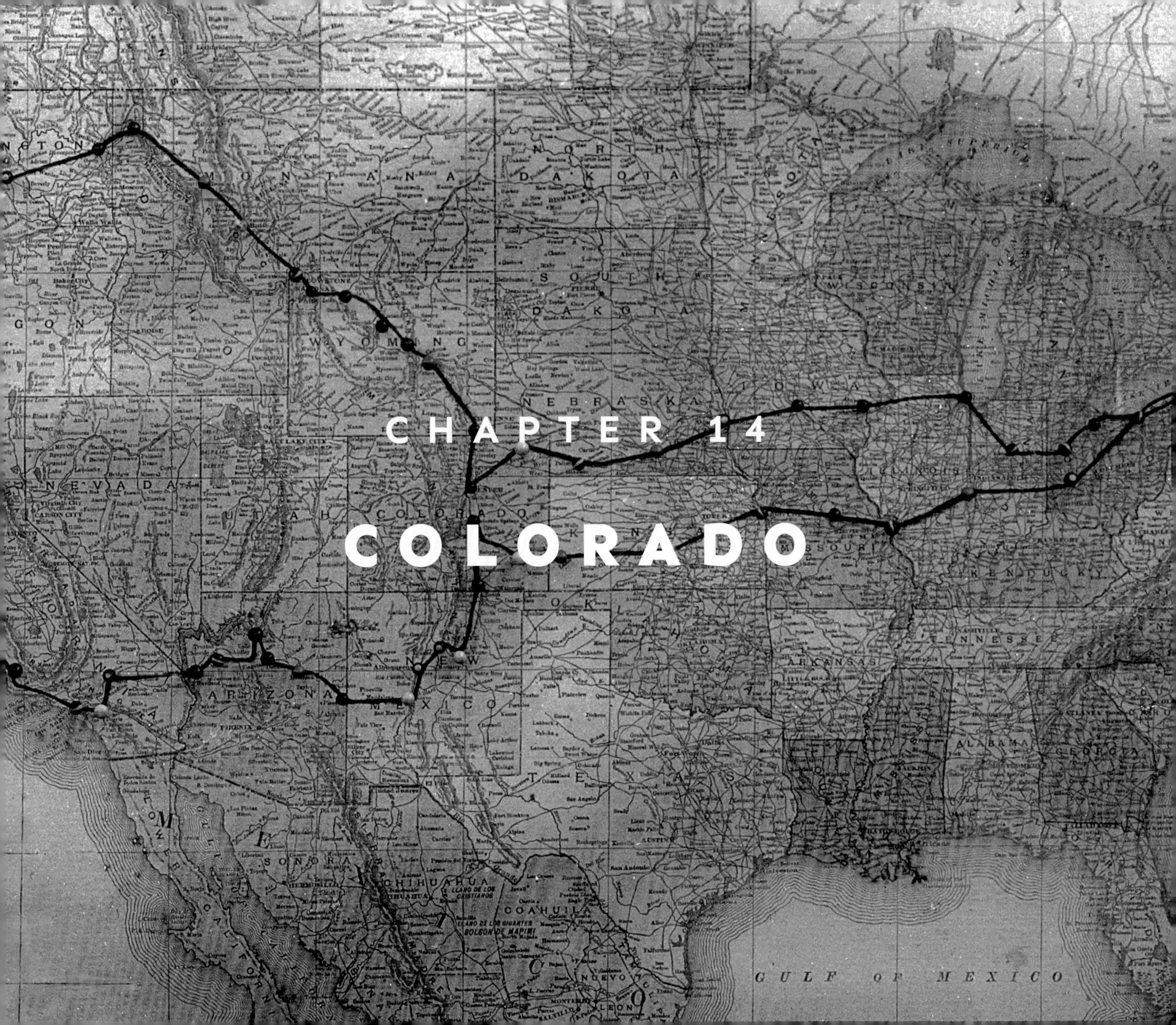

CHAPTER 14

COLORADO

The Santa Fe Trail traverses the Rocky Mountains through Raton Pass at an elevation of 7,934 feet between Raton, New Mexico, and Trinidad, Colorado. This Spallholz photo was taken from an elevation of about 7,000 feet, giving a view southward towards Raton. The mesas in this photo display Raton Pass's outcrop of volcanic rock, forming mesas extending from the Sangre de Cristo Mountains to the west and Santa Fe to the south.

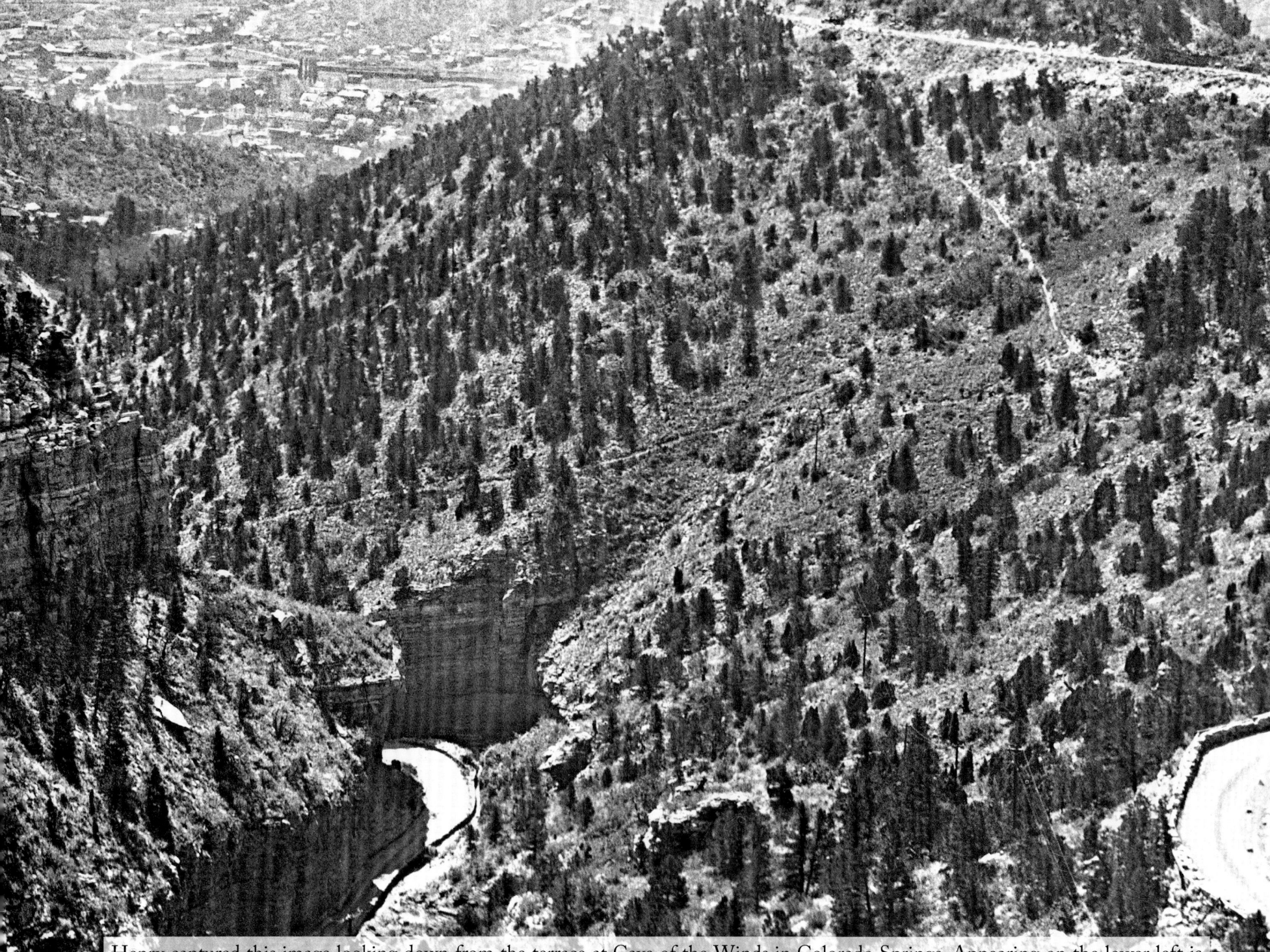

Henry captured this image looking down from the terrace at Cave of the Winds in Colorado Springs. Appearing on the lower left is Williams Canyon Road; the town of Manitou Springs is in the distance.

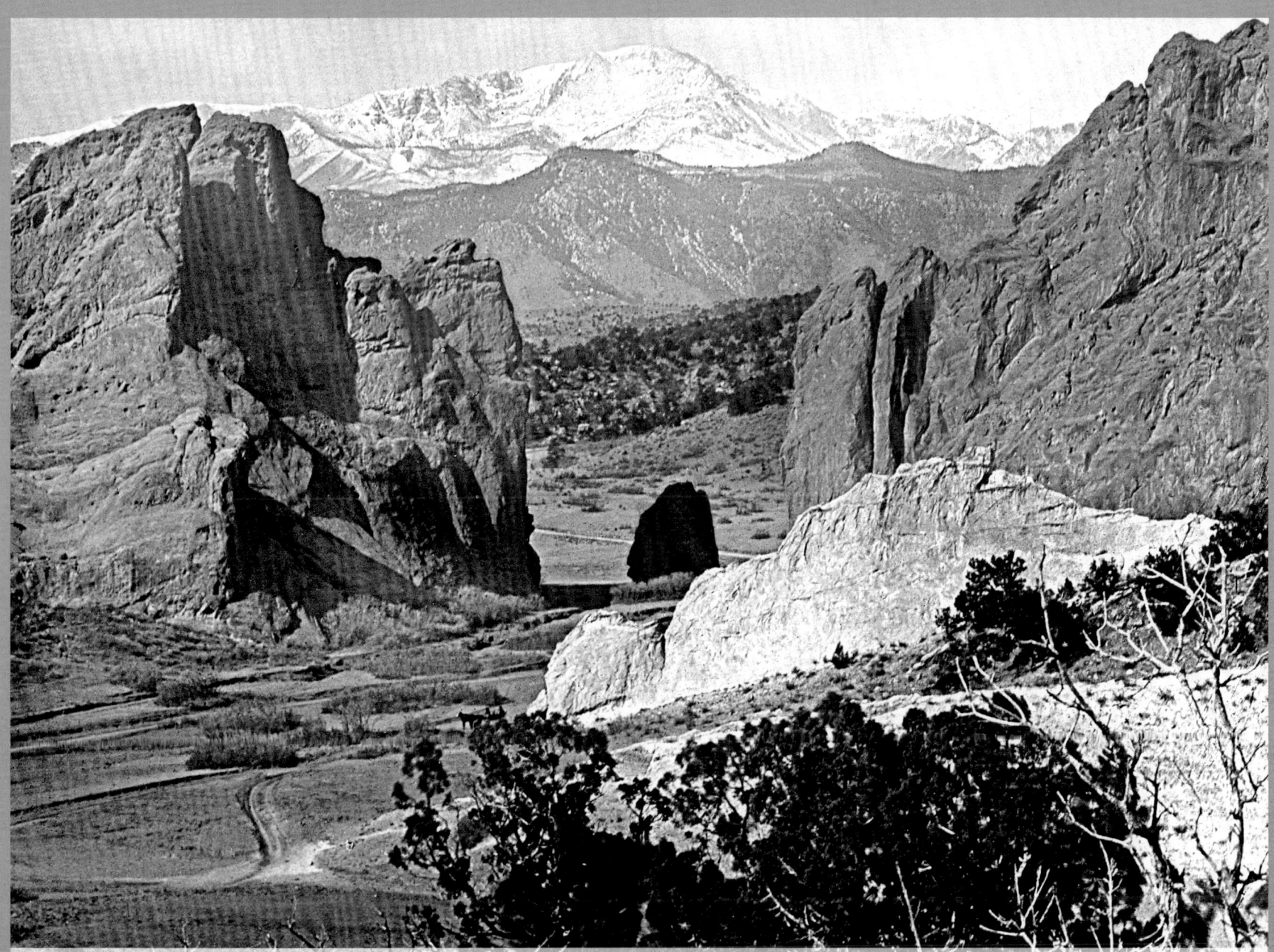

Gateway to the Garden of the Gods with Pikes Peak in the background. The hematitic dark red and pink sedimentary sandstone laid down horizontally has been turned up vertically by the Rocky Mountains uplift. Some of the larger sandstone formations reach up to 300 feet in height. (Underwood & Underwood monochrome lantern slide.)

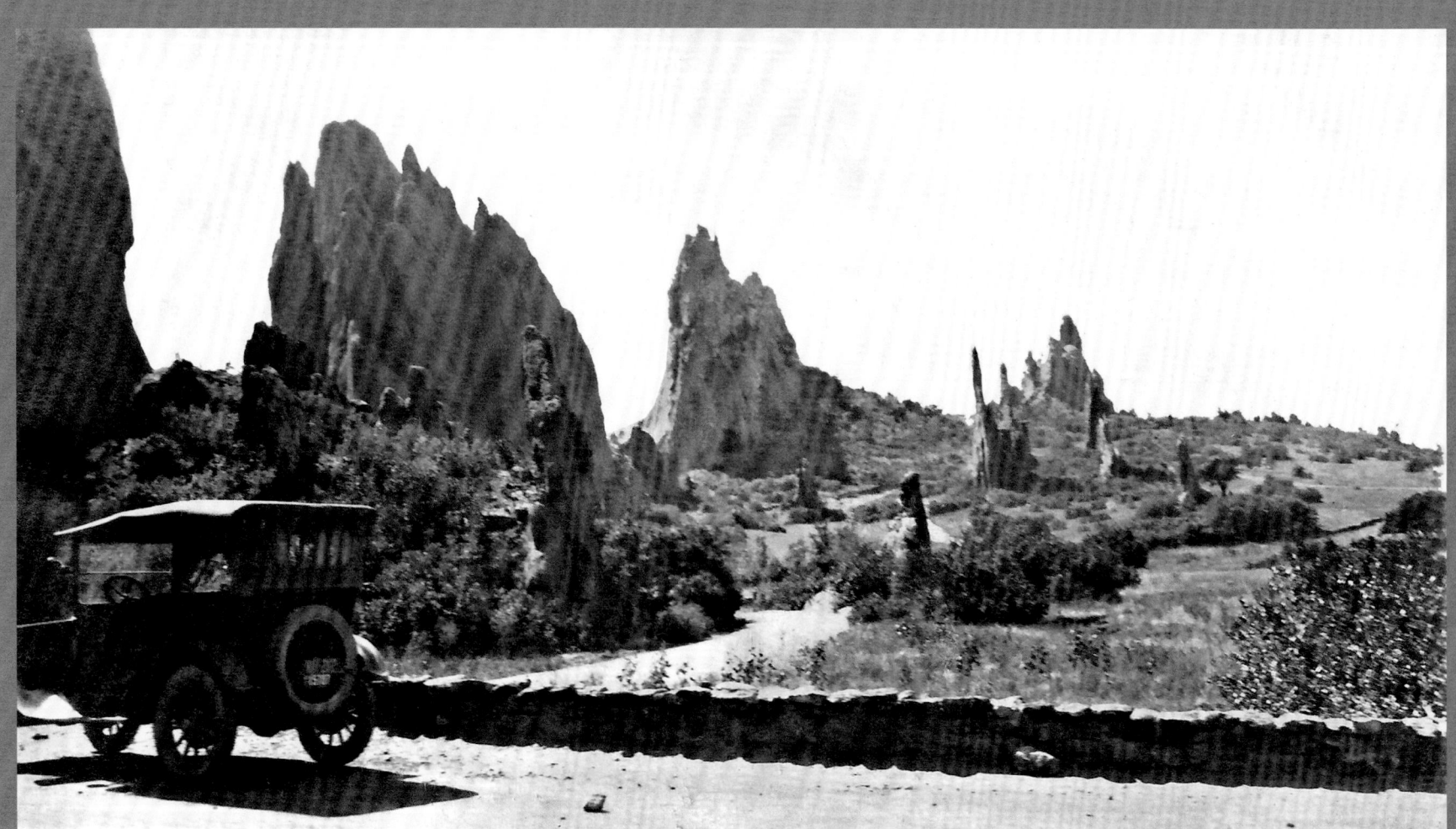

Henry captured a photo of another tourist's automobile in the foreground against a backdrop of the jagged red and pink uplifted sandstone rock formations that make up the Garden of the Gods in Colorado Springs.

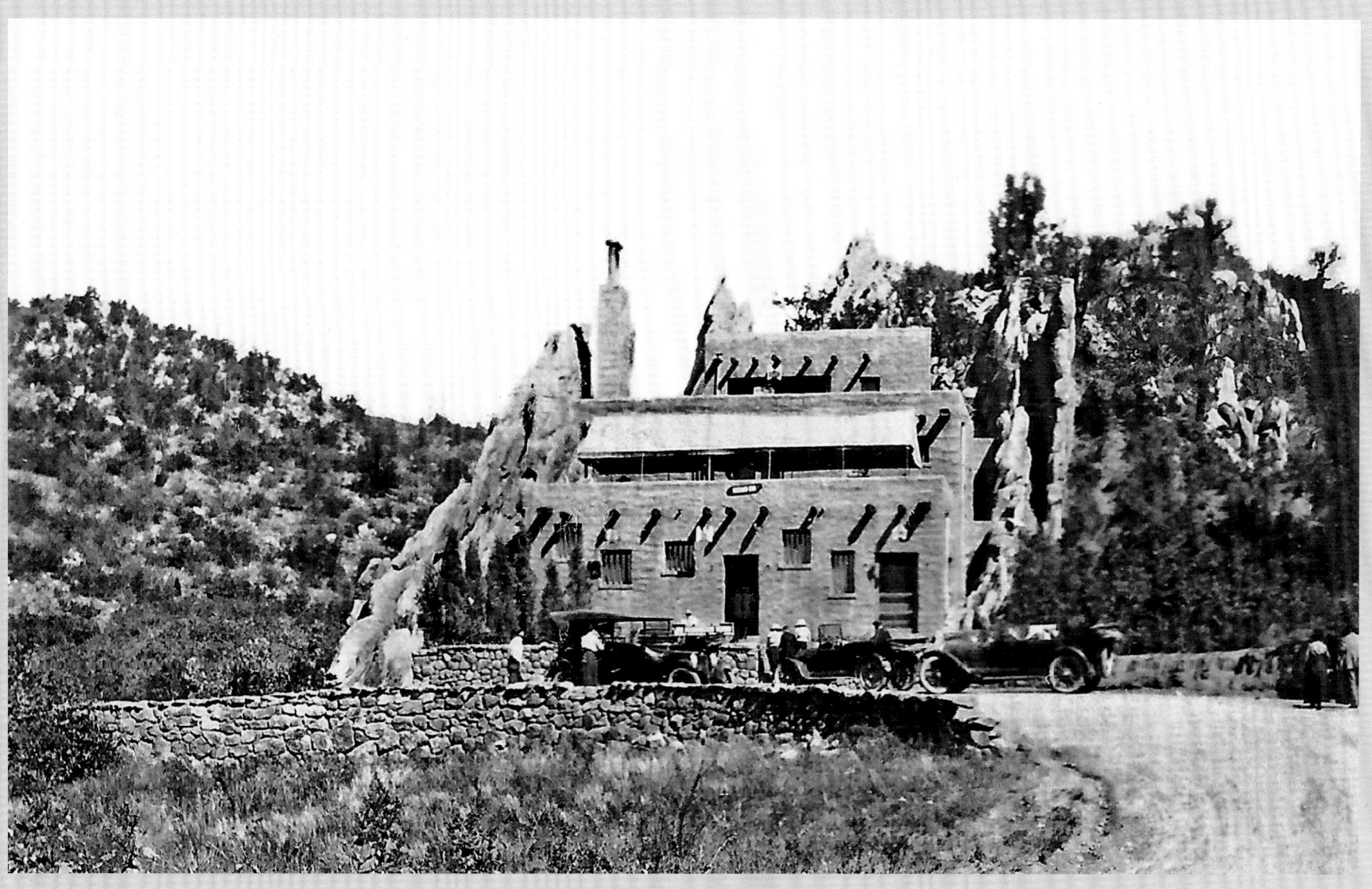

The Hidden House shown here was built within a large sandstone formation in 1915 as a visitors' center and restaurant. Originally constructed in the Pueblo Revival style with pink adobe, the building was demolished in 1999 and replaced by a larger, more modern visitors' center.

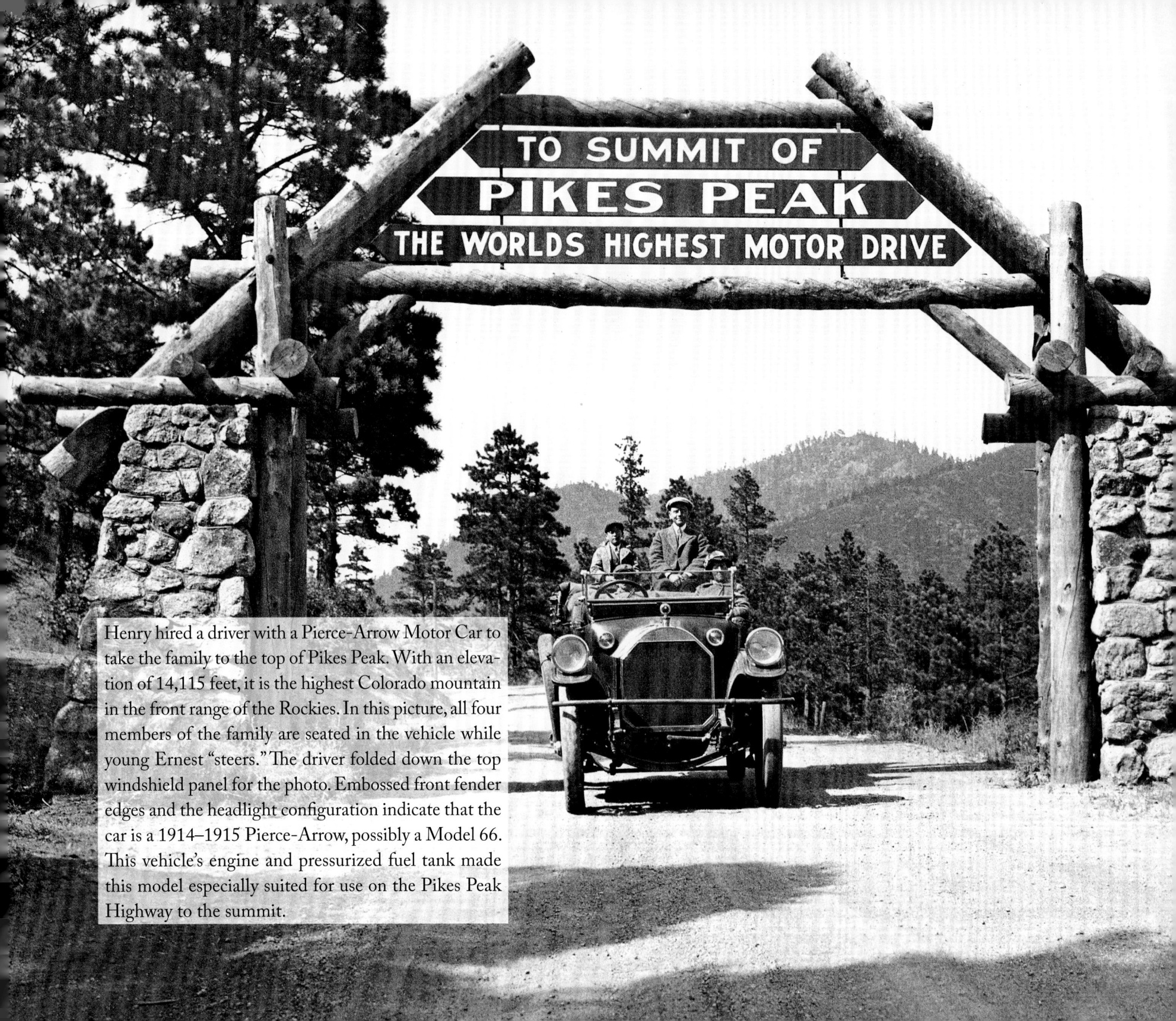

Henry hired a driver with a Pierce-Arrow Motor Car to take the family to the top of Pikes Peak. With an elevation of 14,115 feet, it is the highest Colorado mountain in the front range of the Rockies. In this picture, all four members of the family are seated in the vehicle while young Ernest "steers." The driver folded down the top windshield panel for the photo. Embossed front fender edges and the headlight configuration indicate that the car is a 1914–1915 Pierce-Arrow, possibly a Model 66. This vehicle's engine and pressurized fuel tank made this model especially suited for use on the Pikes Peak Highway to the summit.

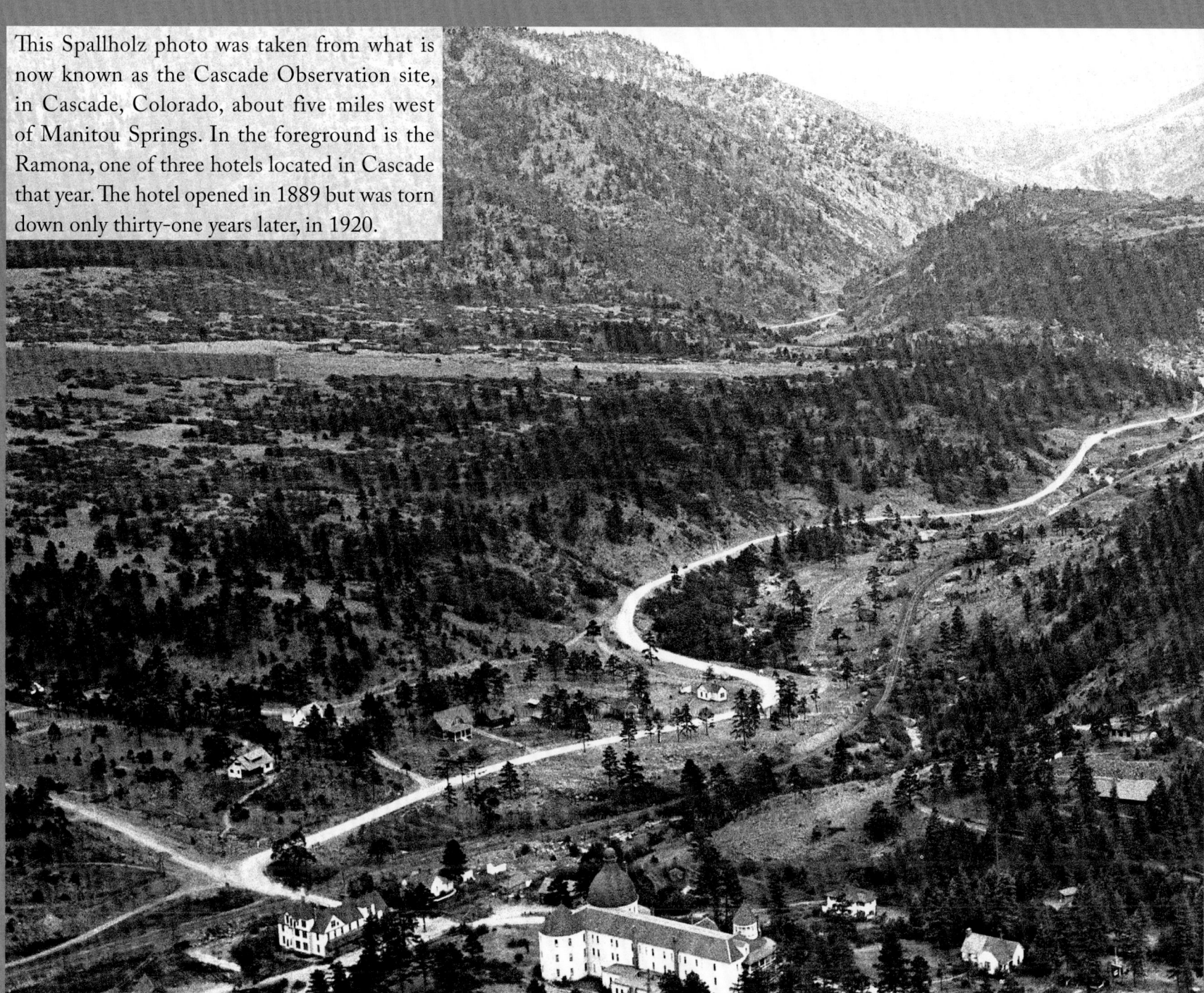

This Spallholz photo was taken from what is now known as the Cascade Observation site, in Cascade, Colorado, about five miles west of Manitou Springs. In the foreground is the Ramona, one of three hotels located in Cascade that year. The hotel opened in 1889 but was torn down only thirty-one years later, in 1920.

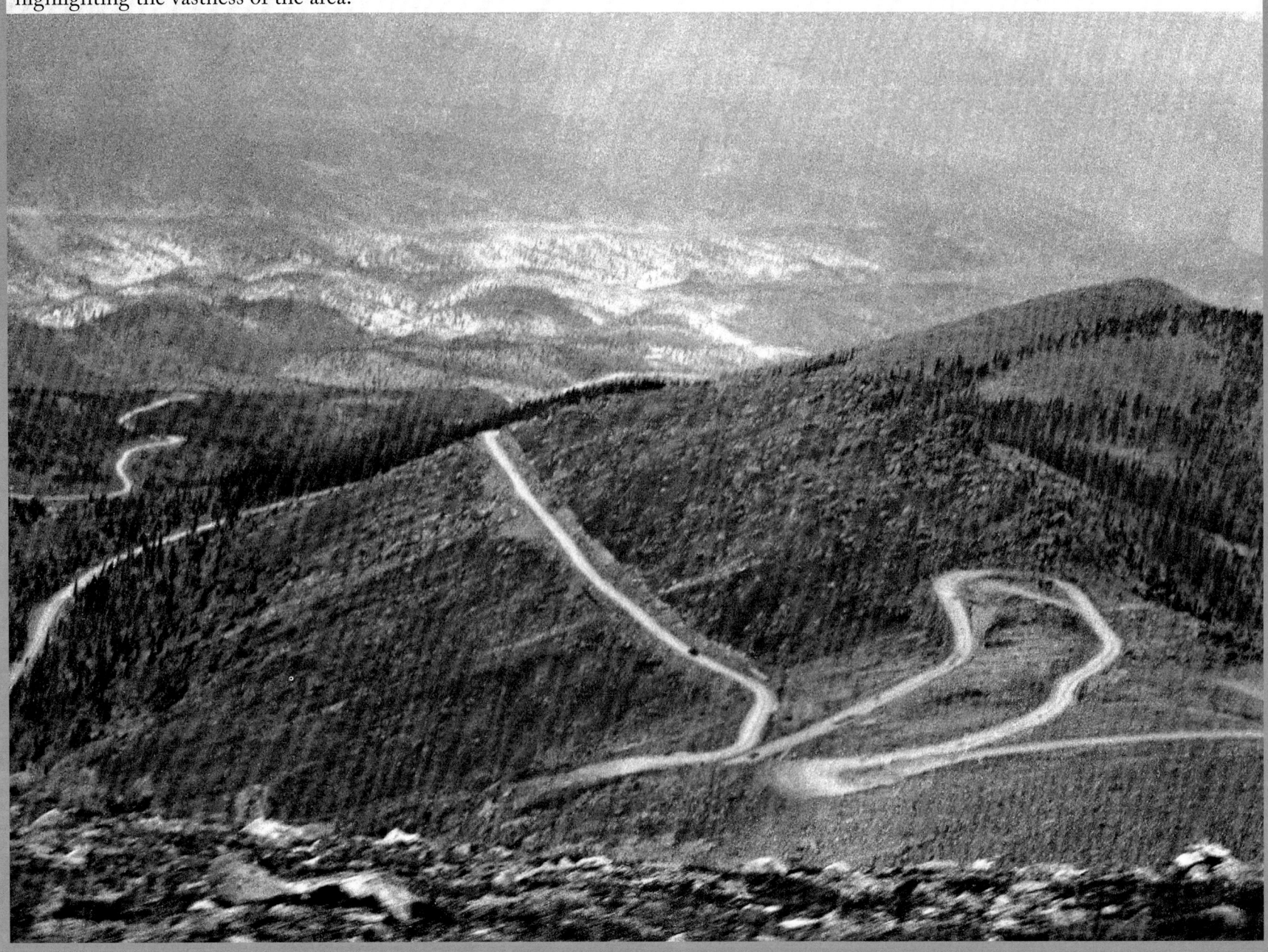

Looking somewhat like La Bajada in New Mexico, the multiple switchbacks along the Pikes Peak Road make the climb to the top by automobile possible. Much of the road has precipitous roadside drops with no guardrails. Note the automobile centered on the road below, highlighting the vastness of the area.

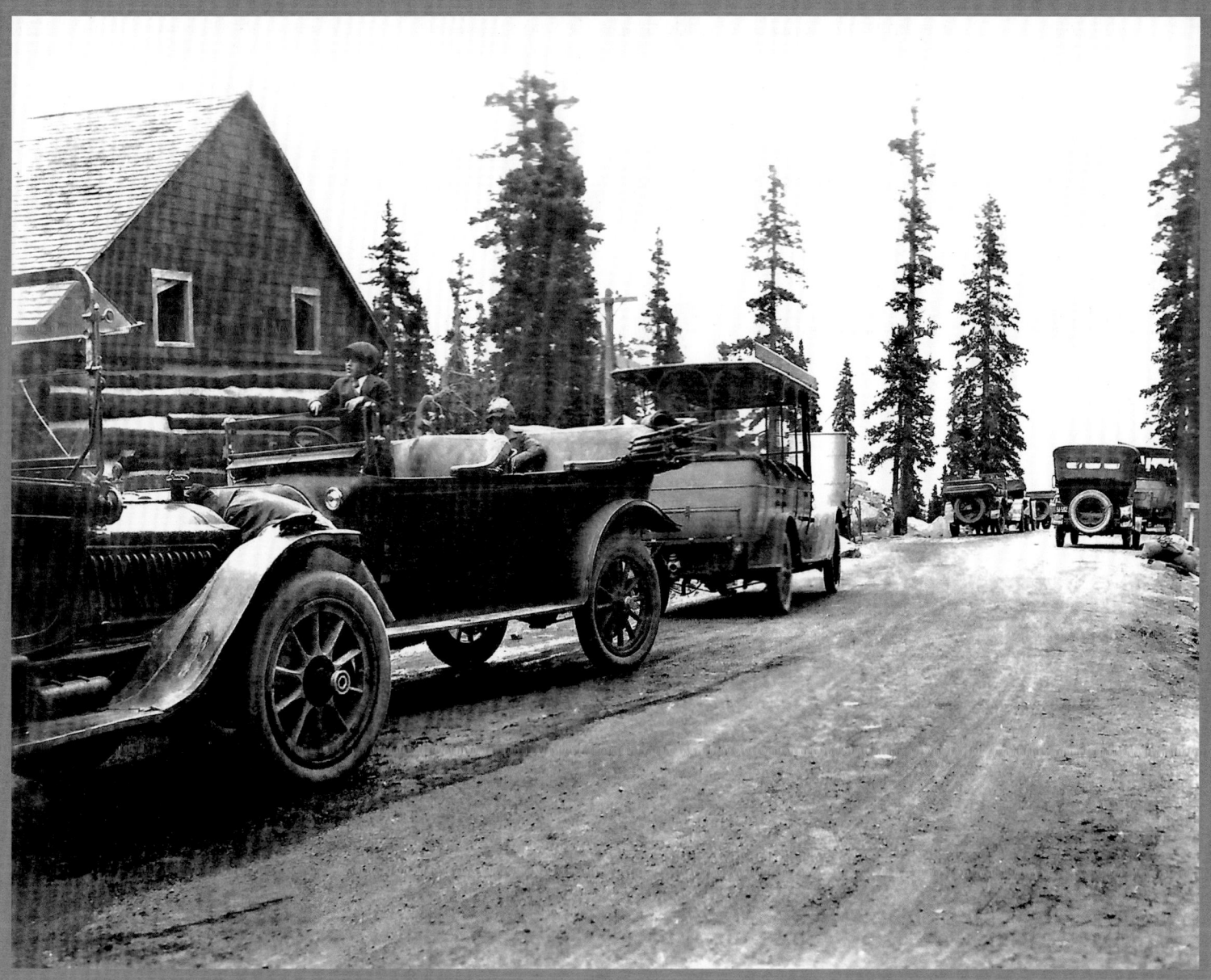

Along the Pikes Peak auto road, the Spallholzes and driver stop at a control station. From this point, the run to the top of Pikes Peak is nineteen miles. Ernest is standing behind the steering wheel of the Pierce-Arrow; Lizzie sits in the back seat.

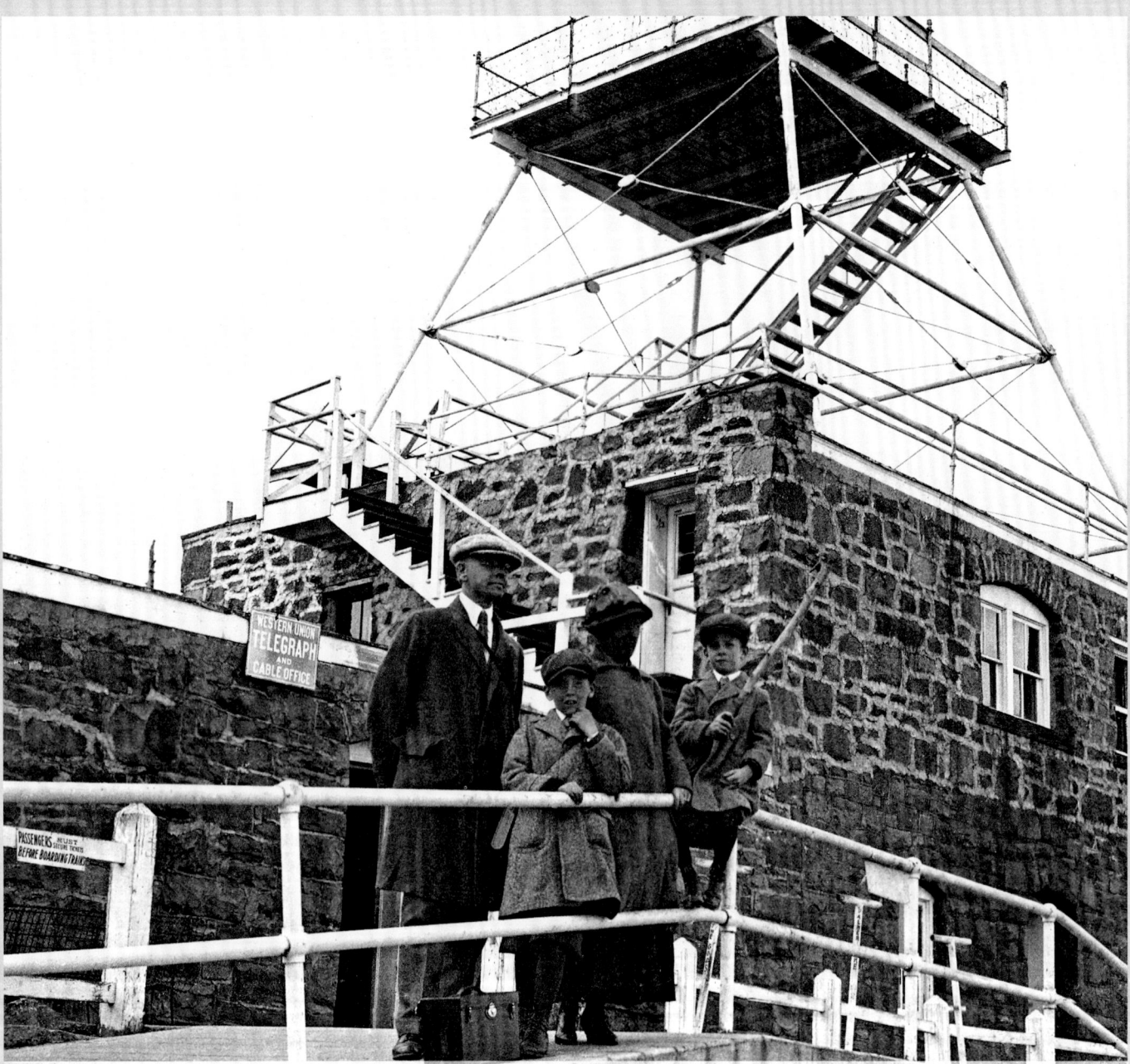

The Broadmoor Manitou and Pikes Peak Cog Railway is recognized as the world's highest cog railroad and is still in operation today. Henry and family are pictured standing on the train platform with the observation tower behind them and the Graflex camera at Henry's feet.

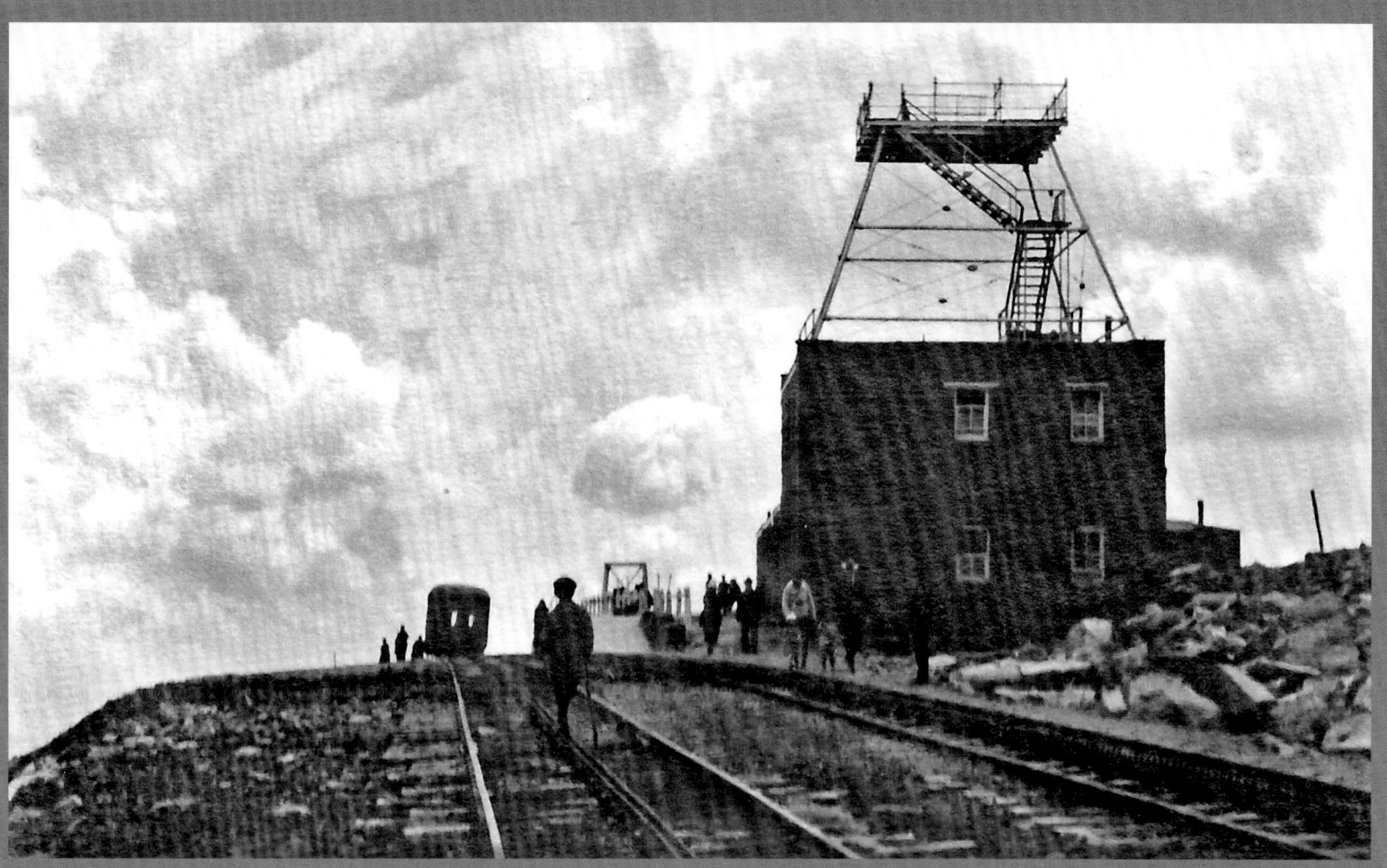

Shown here is the Broadmoor Manitou and Pikes Peak Cog Railway terminal and observation tower. Walter is standing on the central cog track that, when engaged by the cogwheel of the engine, makes train operation possible on the steep mountain grade.

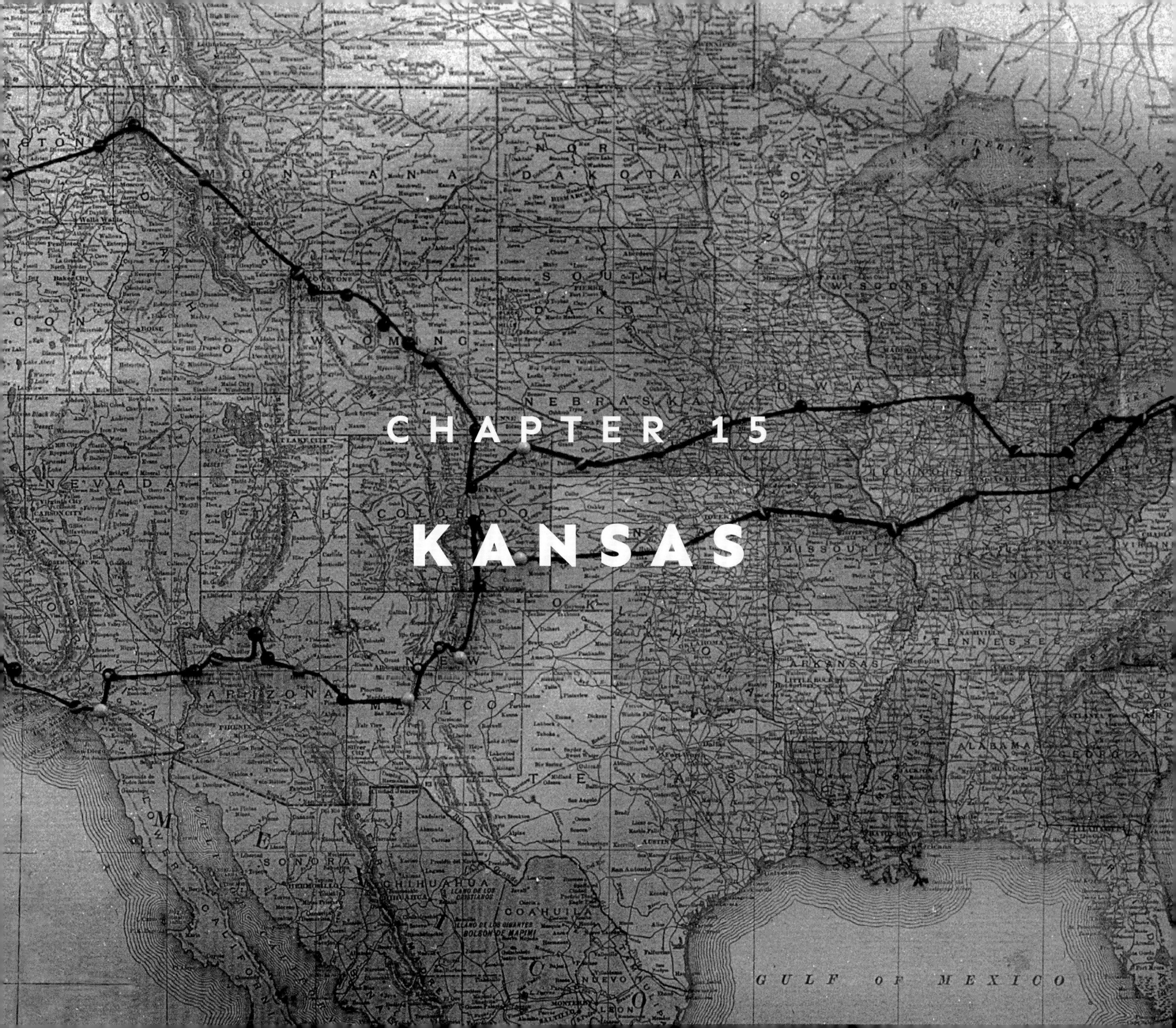

CHAPTER 15

KANSAS

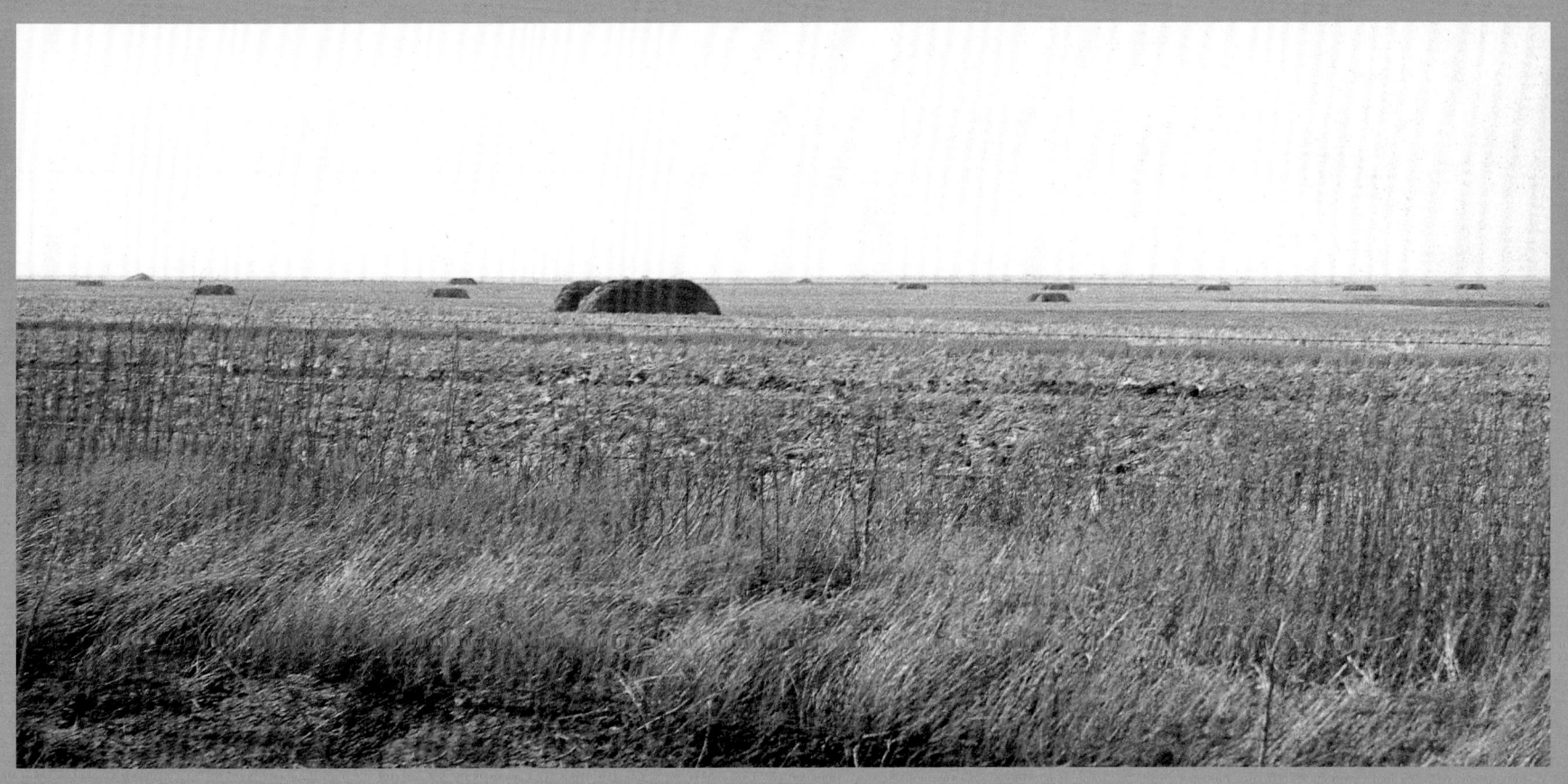

Leaving the Rocky Mountains behind, the family turned east from Colorado Springs and headed home. They encountered vast fields of wheat in Eastern Colorado and Kansas on the National Old Trails Road. Having seen broad wheat fields in Oregon, Lizzie had mentioned in her letters from Seattle that she hoped also to see the vast wheat fields of Kansas.

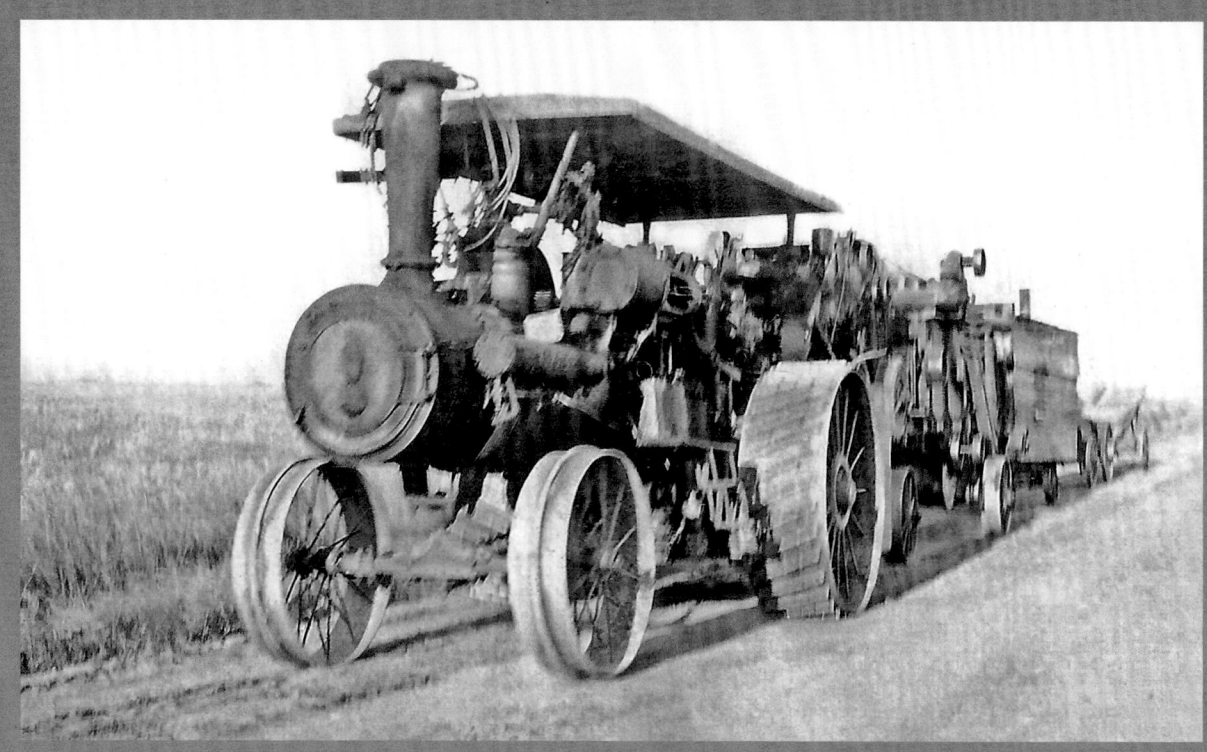

Traveling along the National Old Trails Road, Henry took a photograph of a modern steam-powered threshing machine and wagon, a Case Model 9-18, also known as the Black Lady. This steam-powered tractor threshing machine was manufactured by the J. I. Case Company. Complete threshing outfits of this type were seldom photographed while traveling on the road, making this a very rare image.

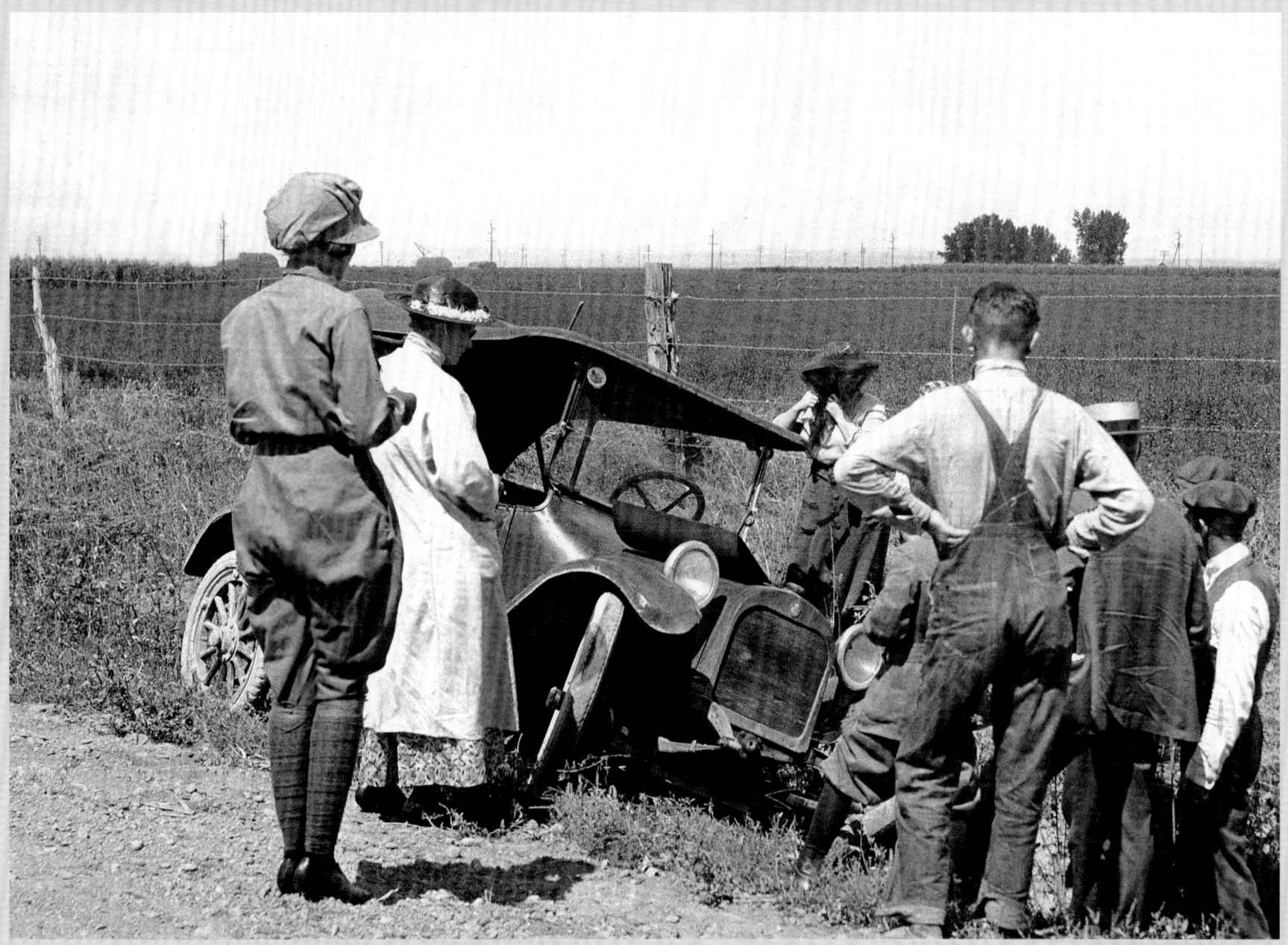

Vehicles created deep ruts in the muddy roads after almost any rain. These ruts would dry out to a cement-like consistency and could forcibly turn a car's front wheels, causing the driver to lose control and skid off the road. This accident took place right before the Spallholzes' eyes. The variety of clothing in this picture makes it possible to determine who were the occupants and who were the helpful locals.

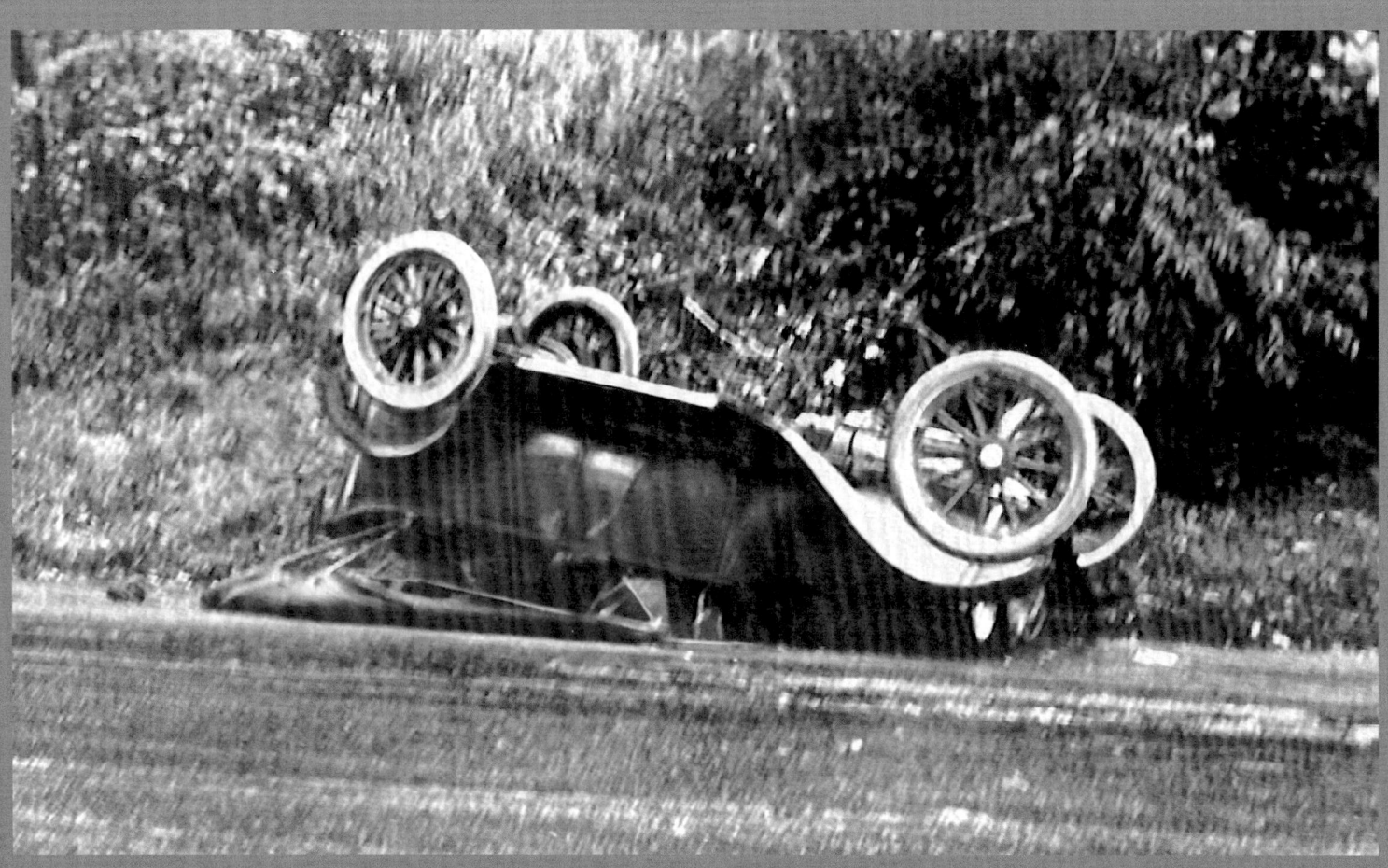

This accident undoubtedly resulted in severe injury or death to those involved. Automobiles sporting only a soft top supported by a collapsible metal frame provided absolutely no structural protection for the occupants in this rollover. The vehicle had sufficient weight to squash the top down to the level of the seat backs and base of the windshield. Fortunately, the car did not catch fire, which was always a possibility in this type of accident.

Walter and Ernest appear to play with a soccer ball while an unidentified friend of the Spallholz family living in Kansas City looks on.

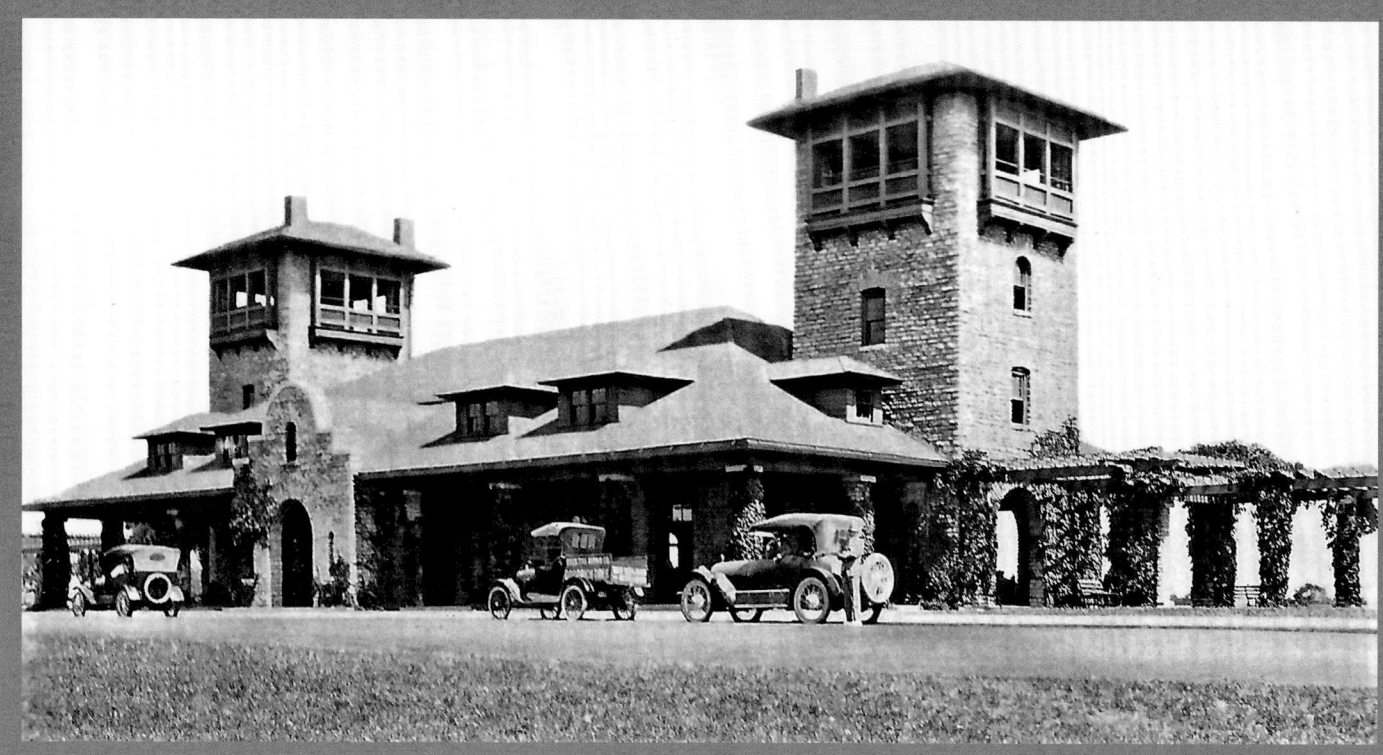

This structure is at the entrance to Swope Park in Kansas City. Built on land donated by Thomas H. Swope in 1895, the 1,805-acre Swope Park was at the time one of the largest municipal parks in the United States. Several vehicles, including the Haynes, are parked outside the ivy-covered visitors center. A family friend who traveled through the city with the Spallholz family is standing behind the Haynes.

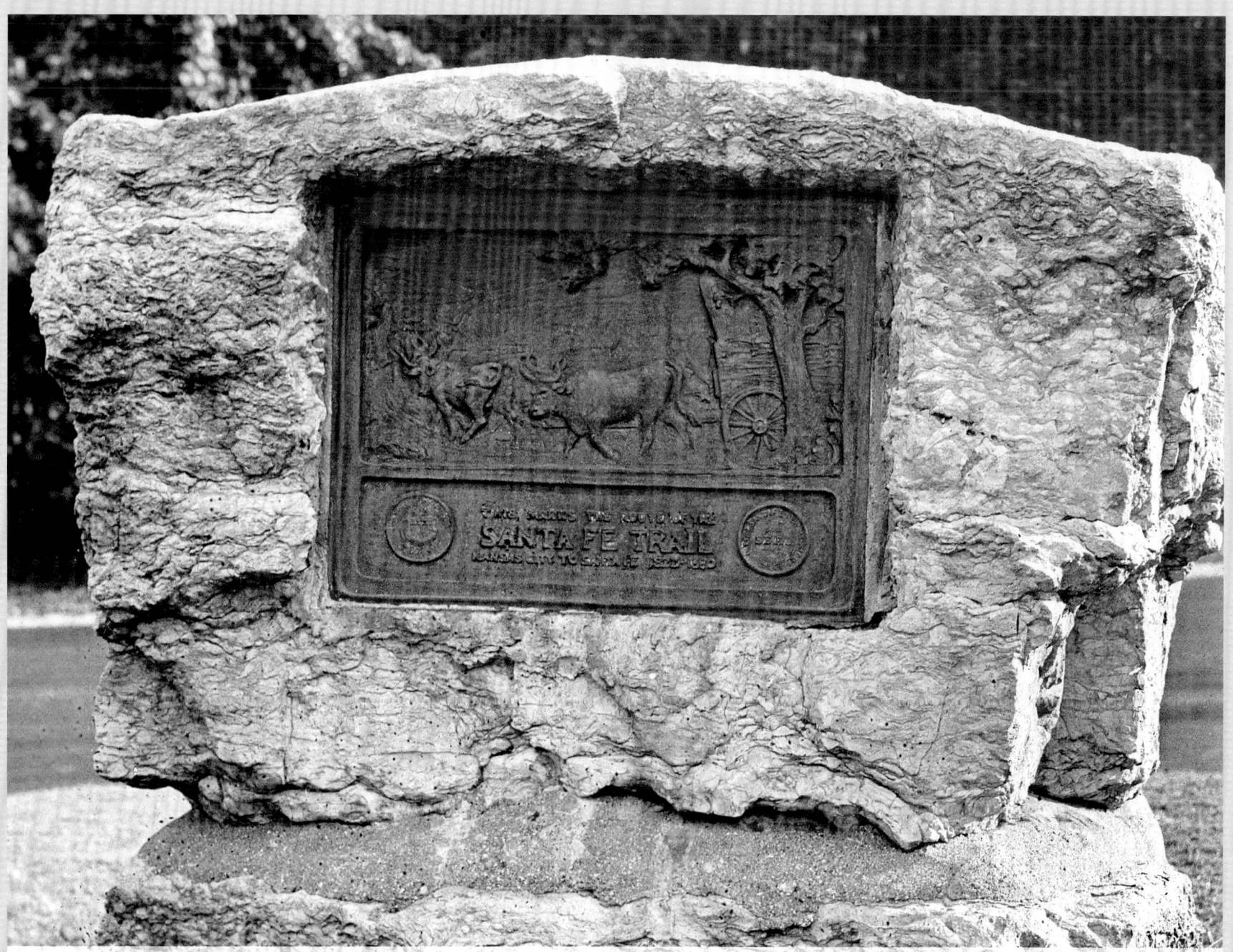

Stone marker in a Kansas City park along the Old Santa Fe Trail route. The inscription reads: "This marks the route of the Santa Fe Trail, 1820–1880; Kansas City to Santa Fe."

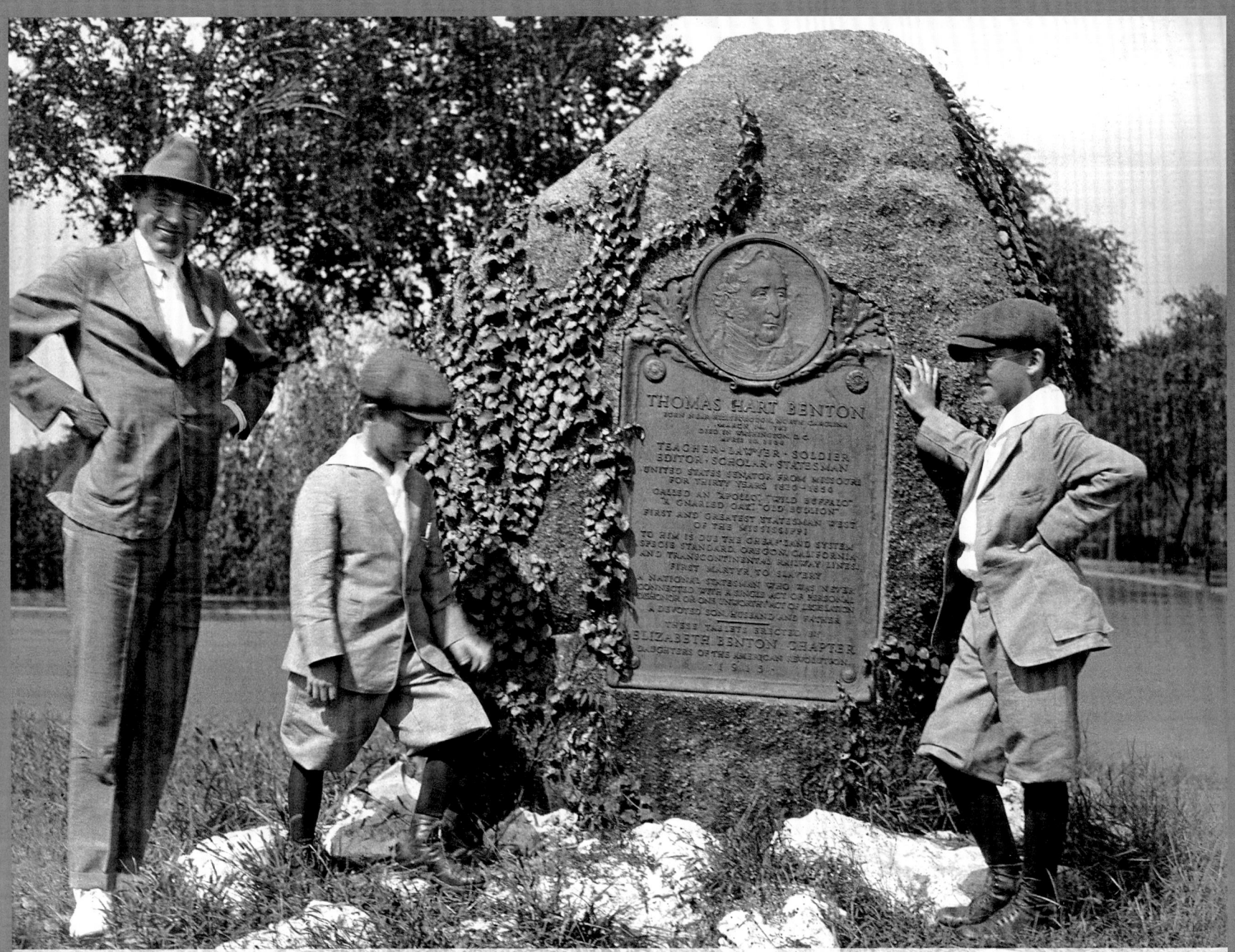

An unknown family acquaintance poses with Ernest and Walter for a photograph at the Senator Thomas Hart Benton Memorial, dedicated in 1915. Benton was a strong advocate for westward expansion of the United States, a philosophy known as Manifest Destiny.

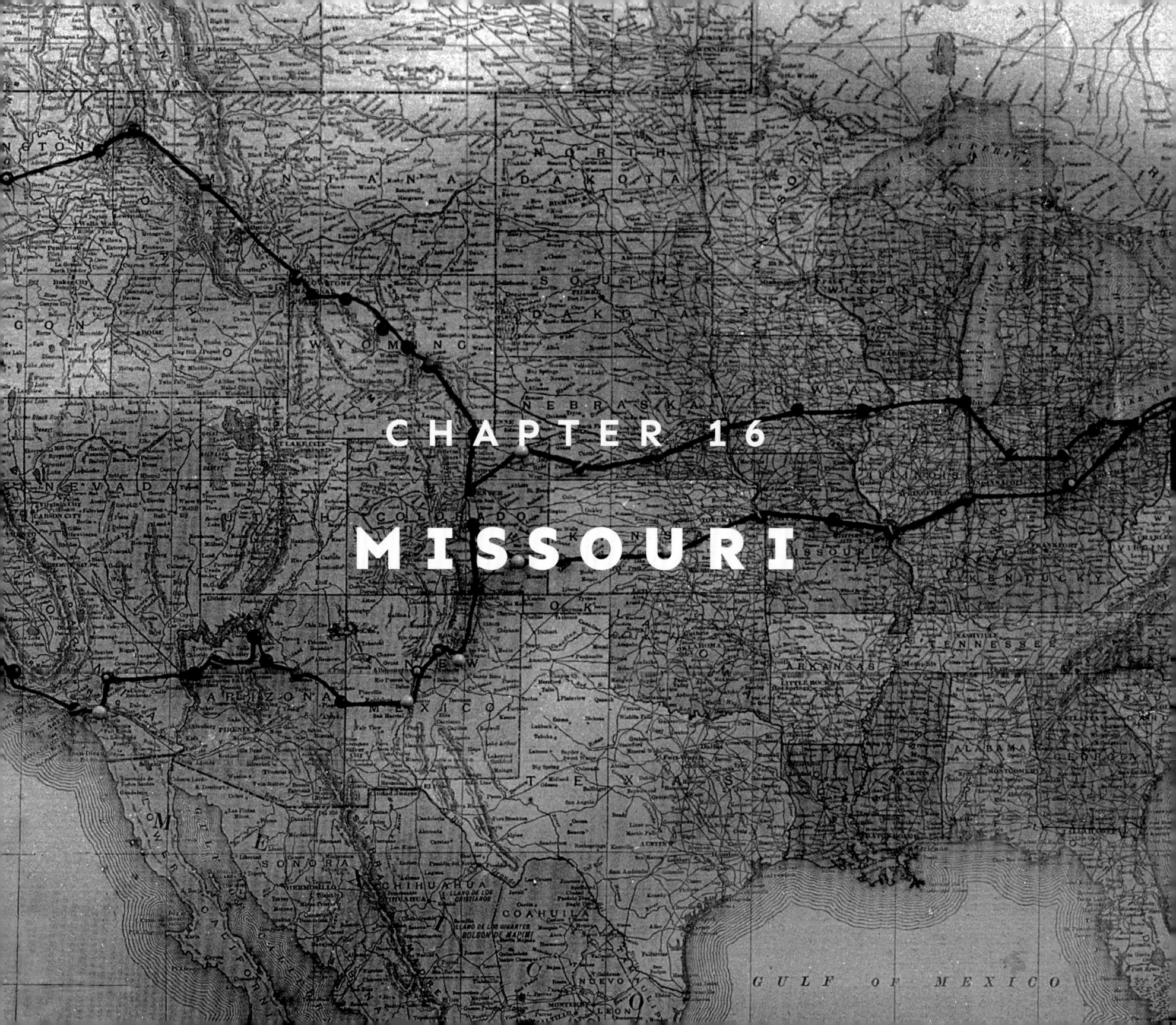

CHAPTER 16

MISSOURI

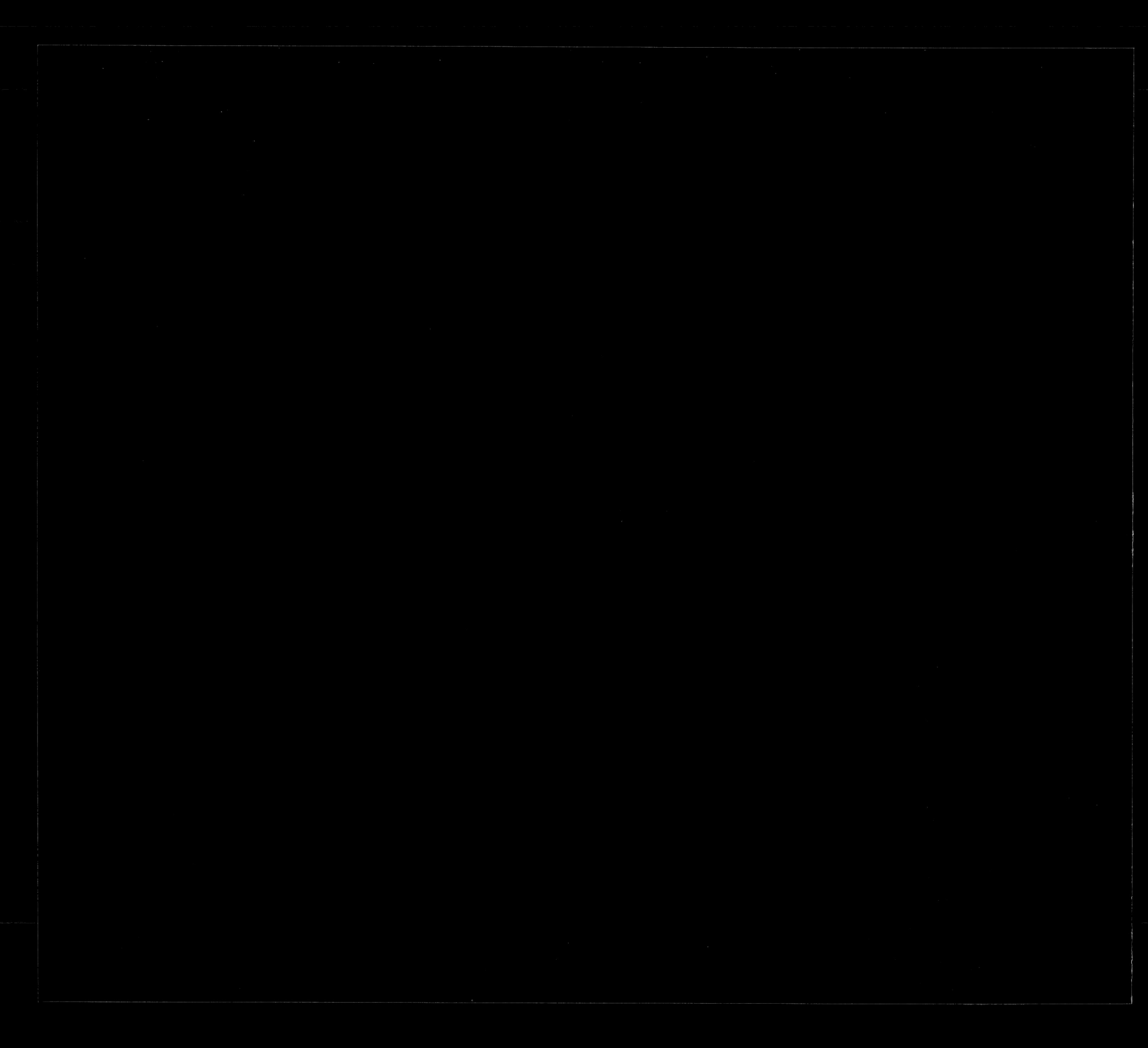

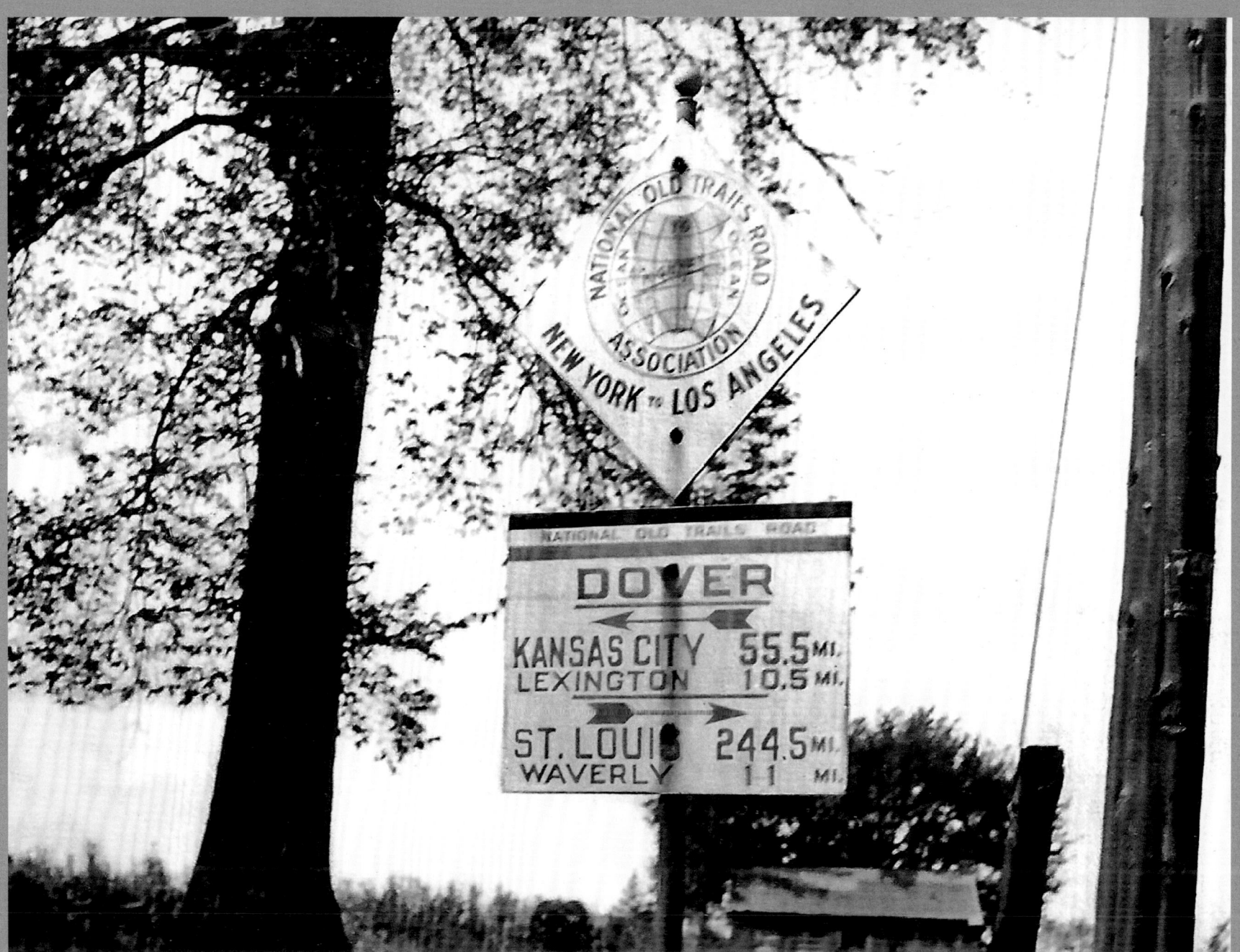

As the Spallholzes continued homeward bound on the National Old Trails Road, Henry snapped this picture of the sign marker that denoted a 244.5-mile drive between Dover and St. Louis, Missouri.

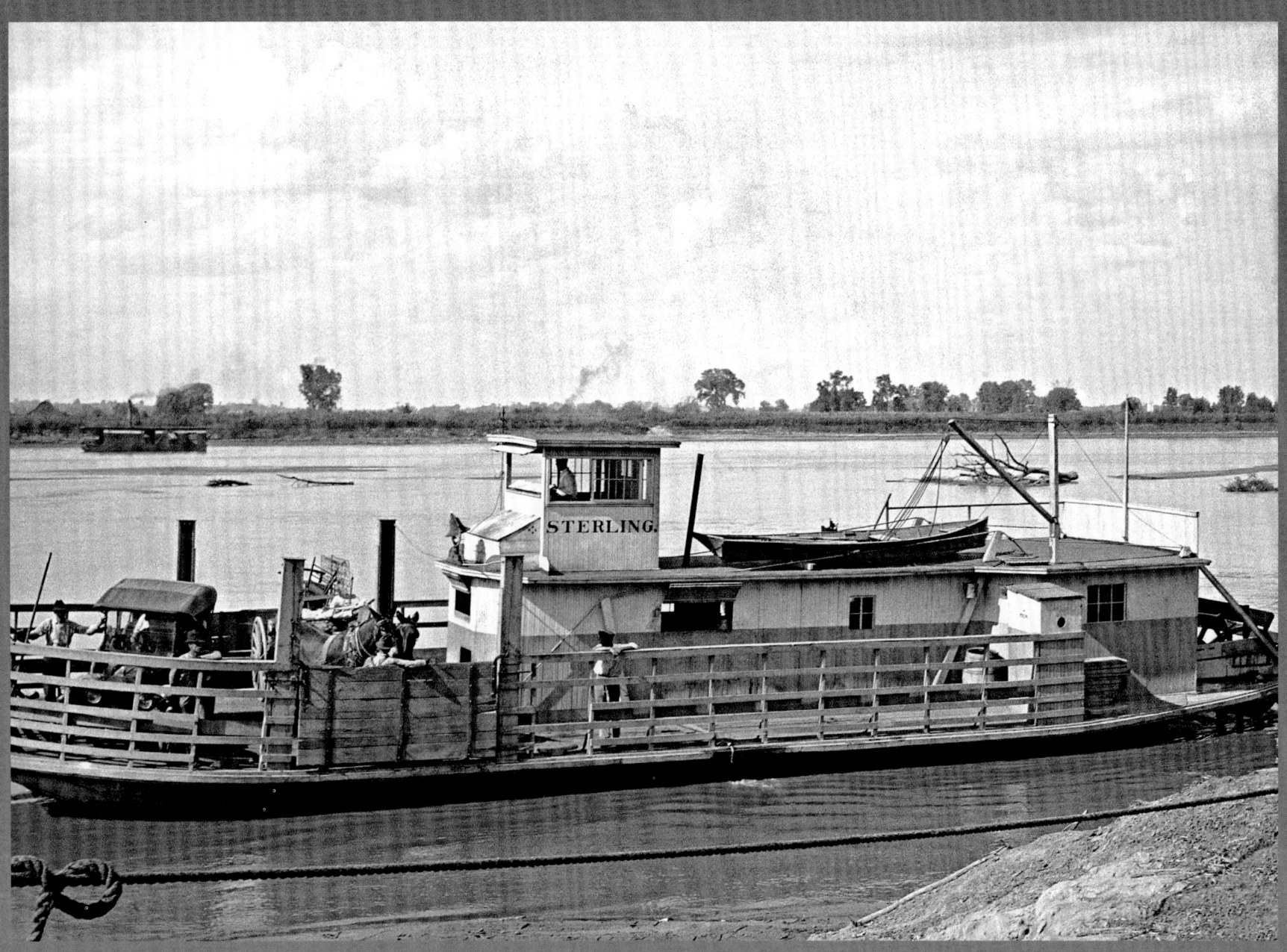

The Spallholzes crossed over the Missouri River at Booneville. Shown here is the paddlewheel steamboat *Sterling* as she slowly approaches the shore to unload. This view looks north towards New Franklin, Missouri.

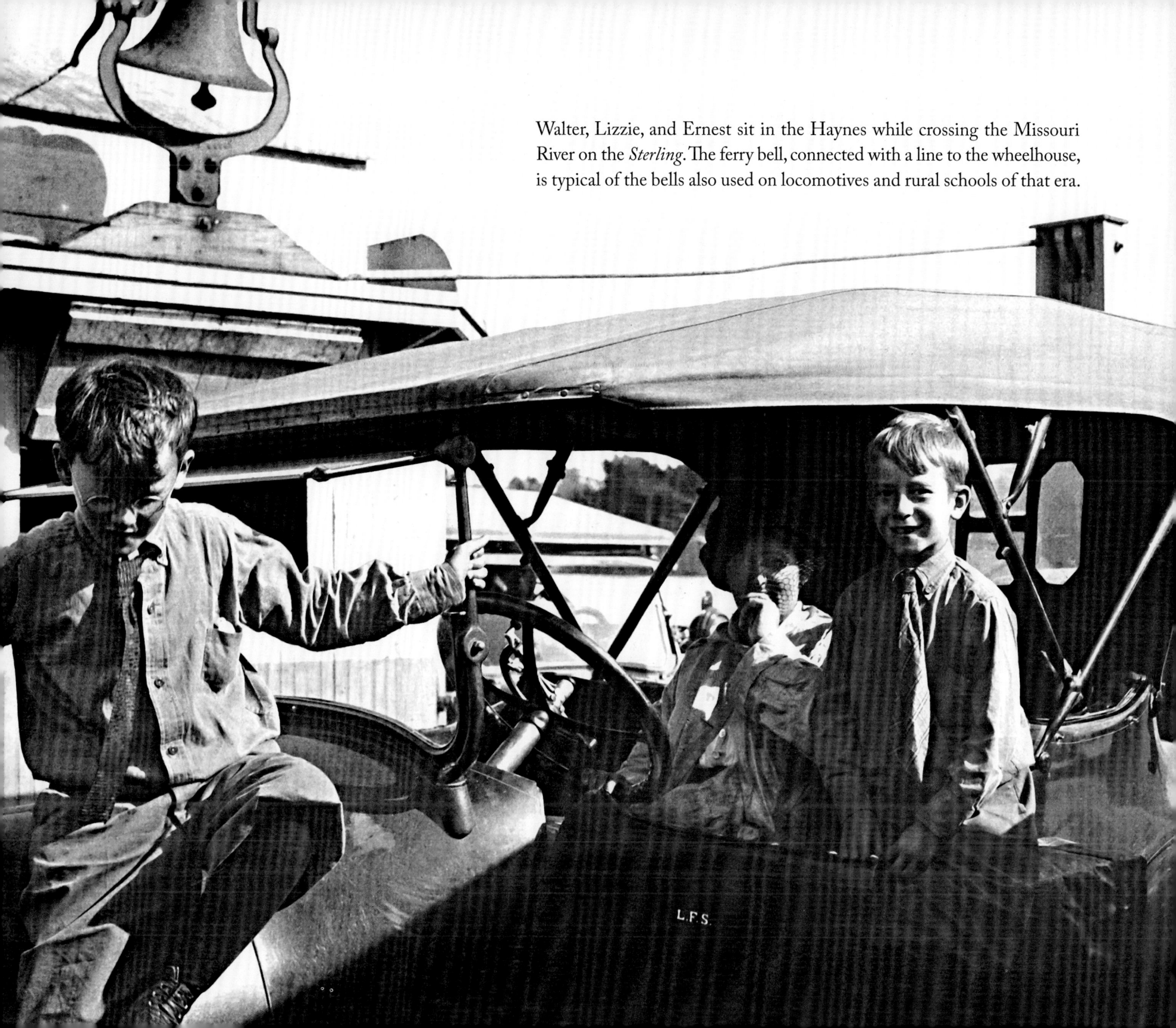

Walter, Lizzie, and Ernest sit in the Haynes while crossing the Missouri River on the *Sterling*. The ferry bell, connected with a line to the wheelhouse, is typical of the bells also used on locomotives and rural schools of that era.

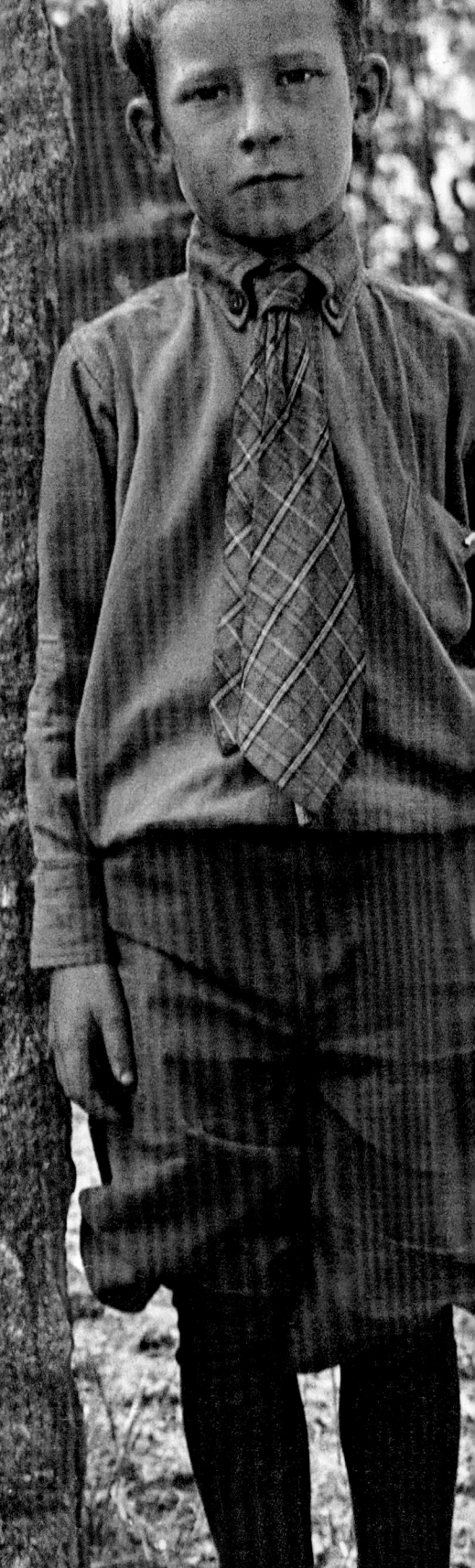

BOONE'S LICK ROAD
GRANT'S STAGE STAND 1821
MARKED BY THE
DAUGHTERS OF THE
AMERICAN REVOLUTION
AND THE
STATE OF MISSOURI
1913

Ernest stands next to a stone marker erected on Boone's Lick Road. The road was named for Daniel Boone's sons, who worked the salt trade on the Missouri River. Made of brown granite, the marker is one of a series of thirty-three placed by the Daughters of the American Revolution along the road that originally began in St. Charles and followed the Missouri River to Franklin, Missouri, and connected with the Santa Fe Trail.

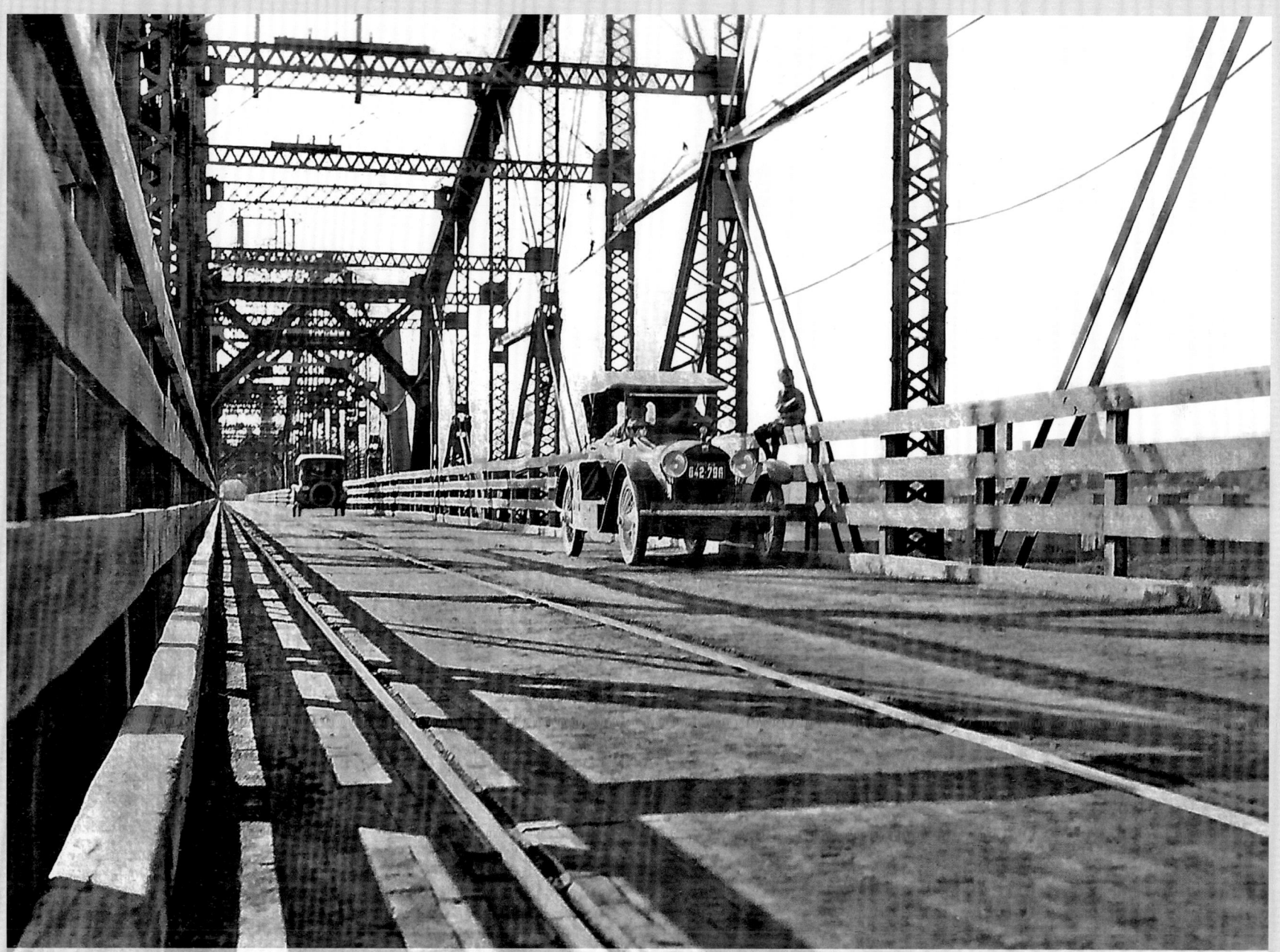

At St. Charles, the Haynes again crossed over the Missouri River to Bridgeton on the iron truss bridge, which opened in 1904 and was demolished in 1998. Henry parked the Haynes on the wrong side of the bridge, facing east in the westbound lane. Walter is sitting on the upper plank of the wooden guard rail.

The Spallholz family stopped in St. Louis to visit the Saint Louis Art Museum, shown in the background and to the left behind the parked automobiles. The statue in front of the museum is Saint Louis IX, king of France.

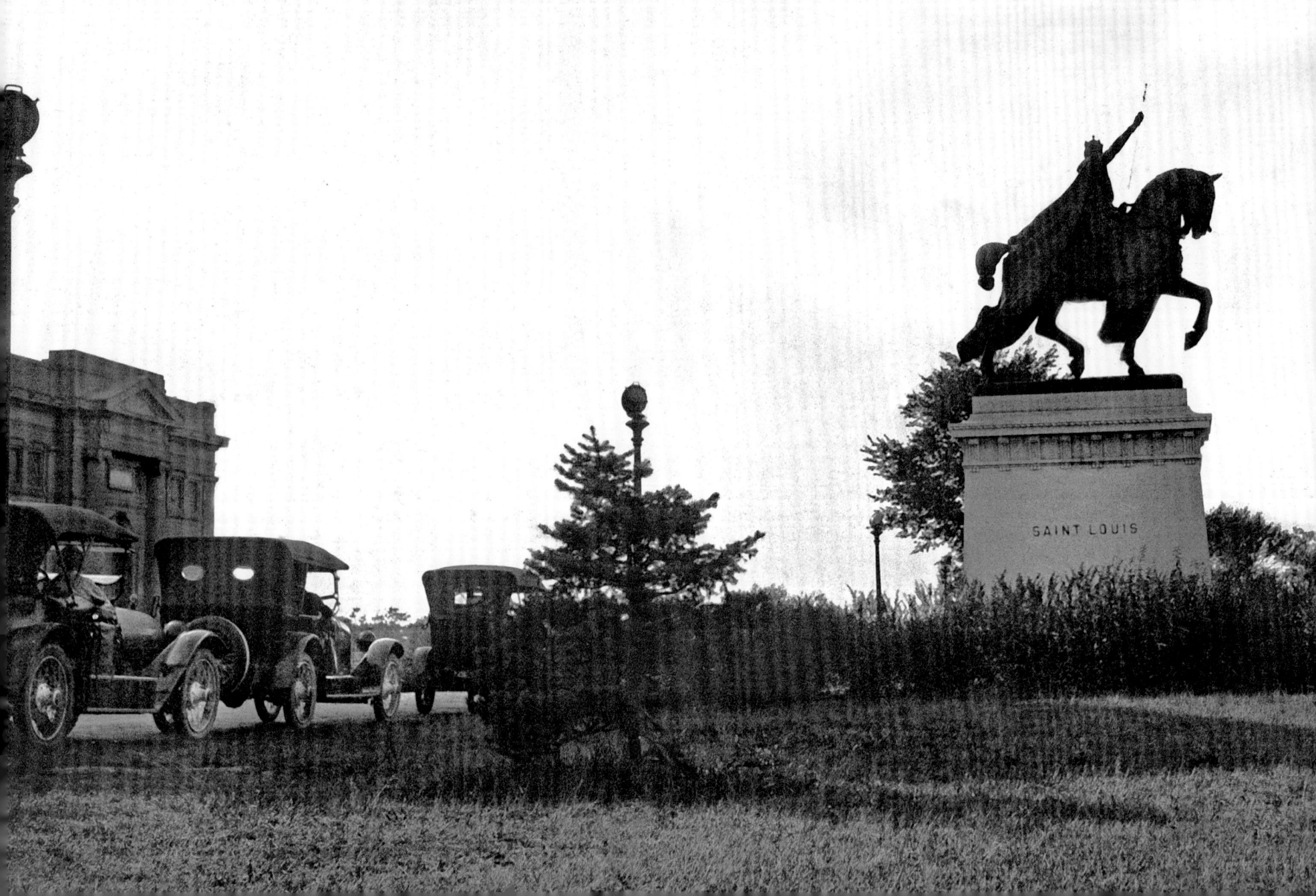

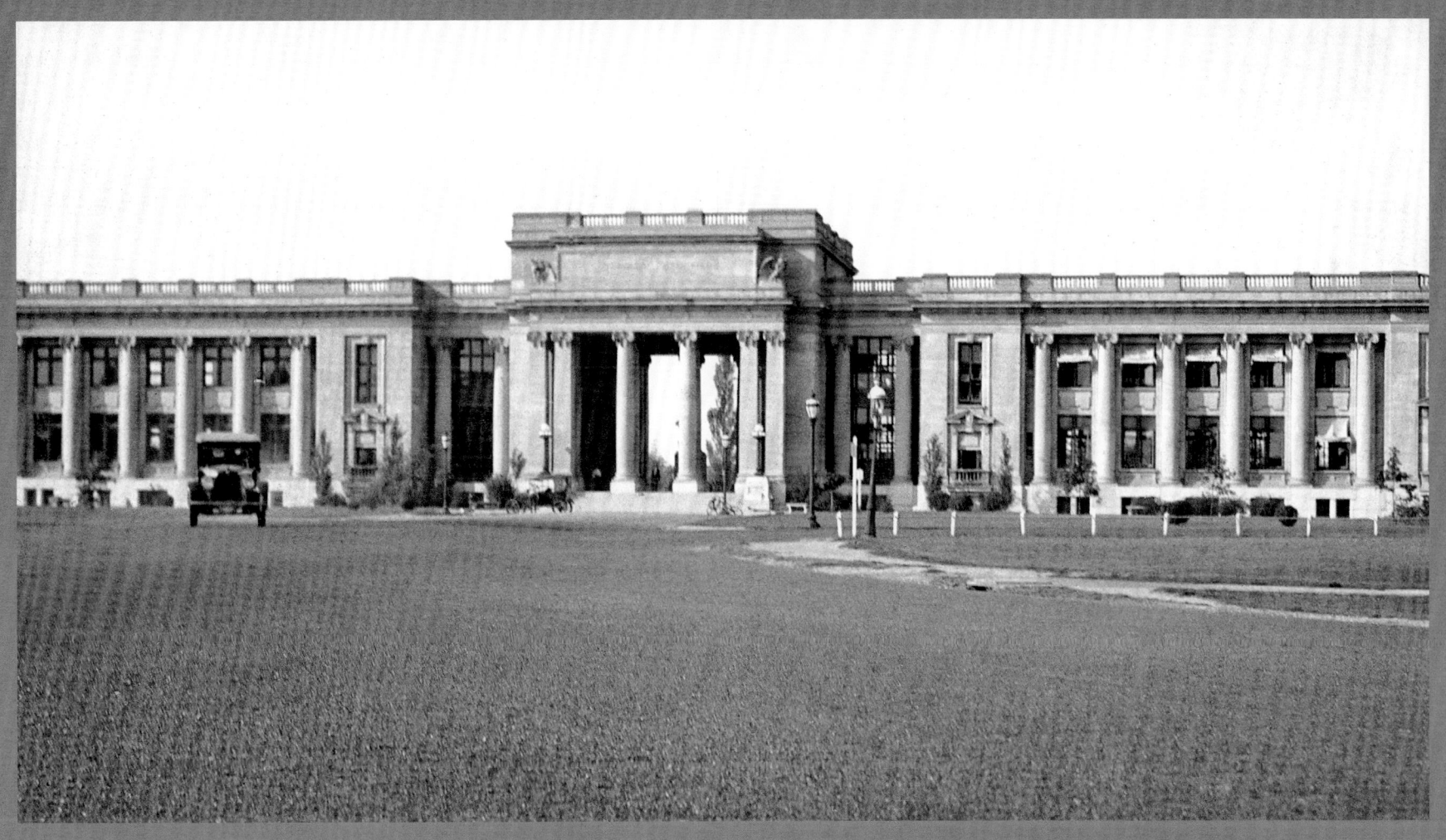

Henry captured a good view of the stone columns and expansive front of the Jefferson Memorial, which commemorates President Thomas Jefferson's role in the acquisition of French territory west of the Mississippi River by the Louisiana Purchase in 1803.

MADISON, OHIO, AND RETURN TO SALEM, NEW YORK

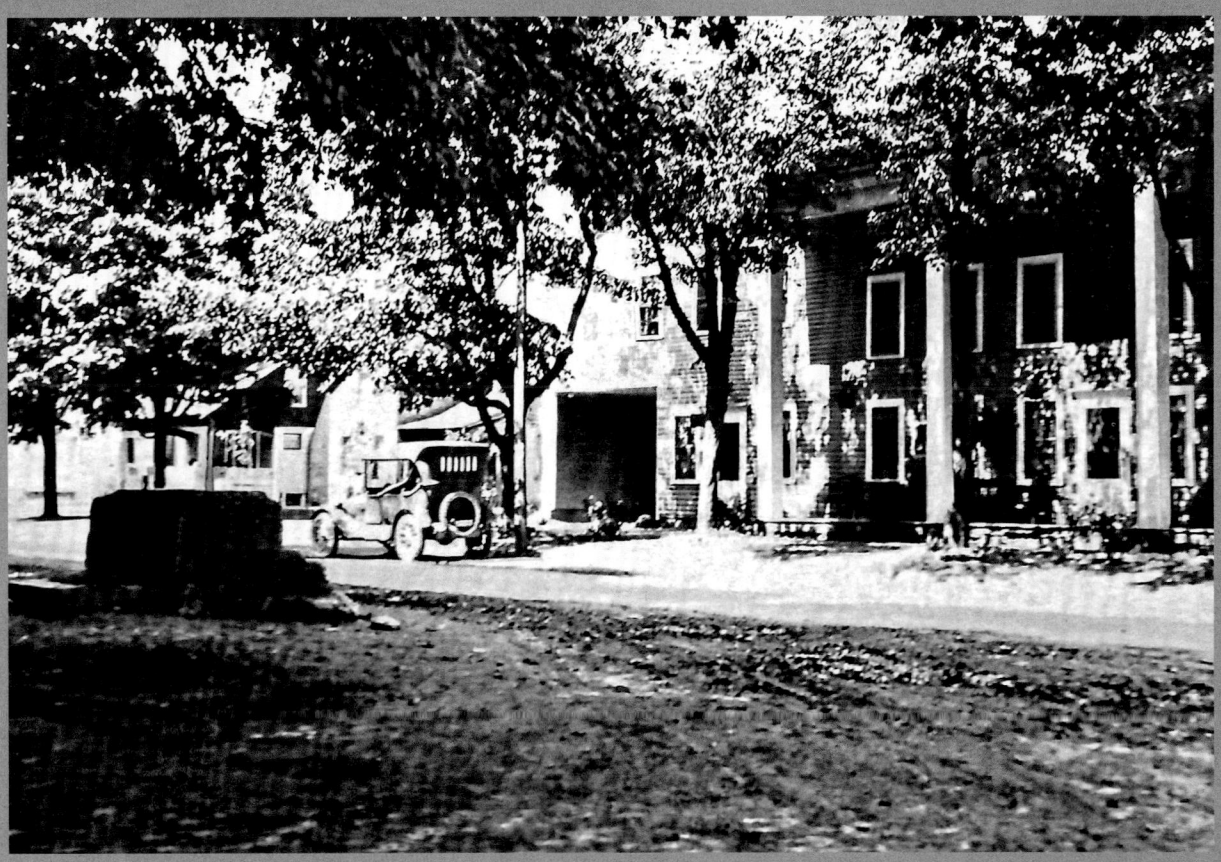

The final photograph Henry took on the road during the Spallholzes' return trip home was of the Unionville Tavern in Madison, Ohio. Built in 1798, the tavern was a convenient stopping place for travelers between Cleveland and Buffalo, New York. It also served as a way station along the Underground Railroad during the Civil War.

After 10,400 miles and ninety-six days, the Spallholzes returned home on September 15, 1919. They had camped out but also stayed at Harvey Houses along the Atchison, Topeka and Santa Fe Railway and historic hotels within national parks. This is their home on Park Place in Salem, New York, directly across the street from the Manhattan Shirt Shop and steam mill, the point where their journey began, nearly three months earlier on June 11. This photograph of their home was taken circa 1930. Theirs was the first house in the Village of Salem to have electricity and a telephone.

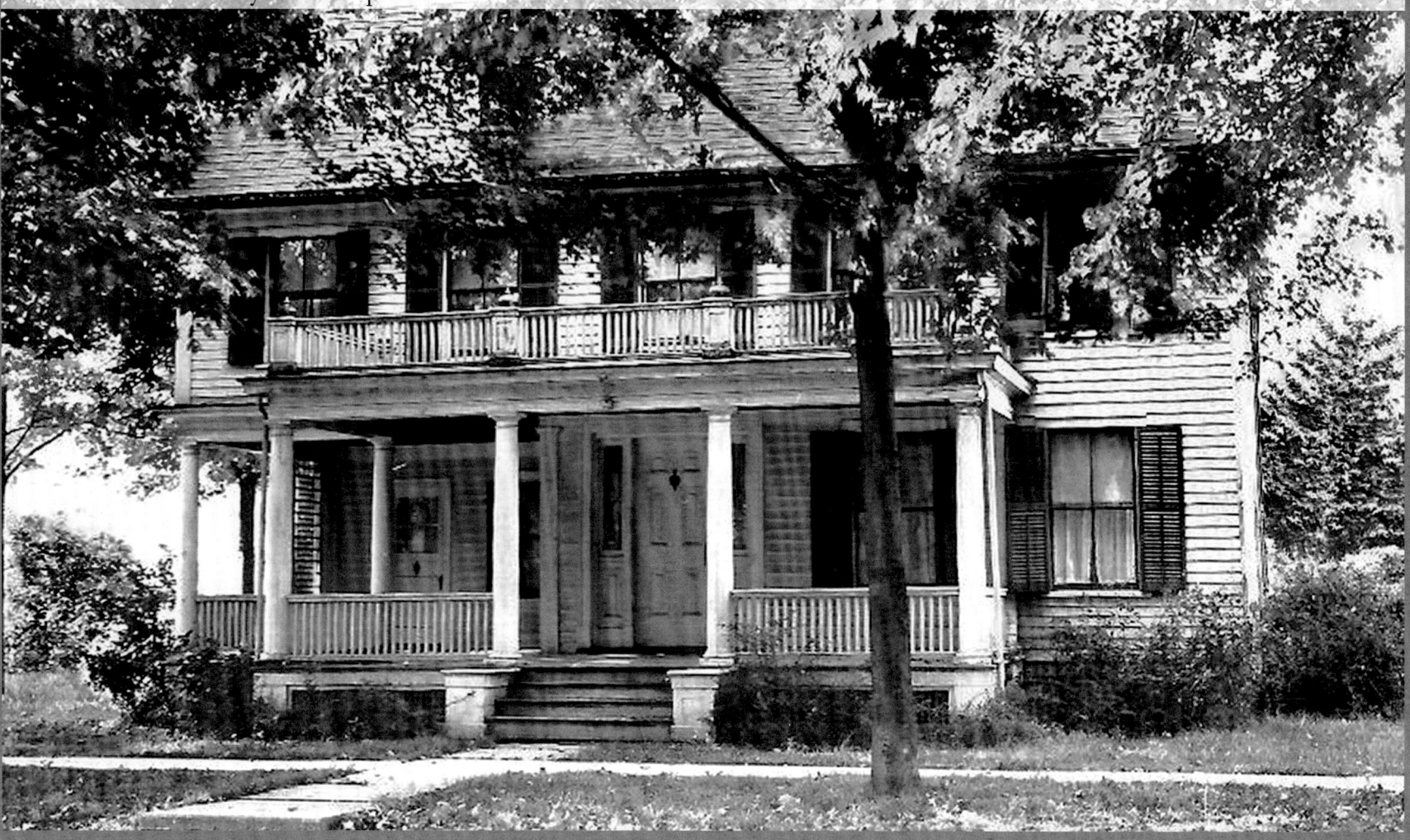

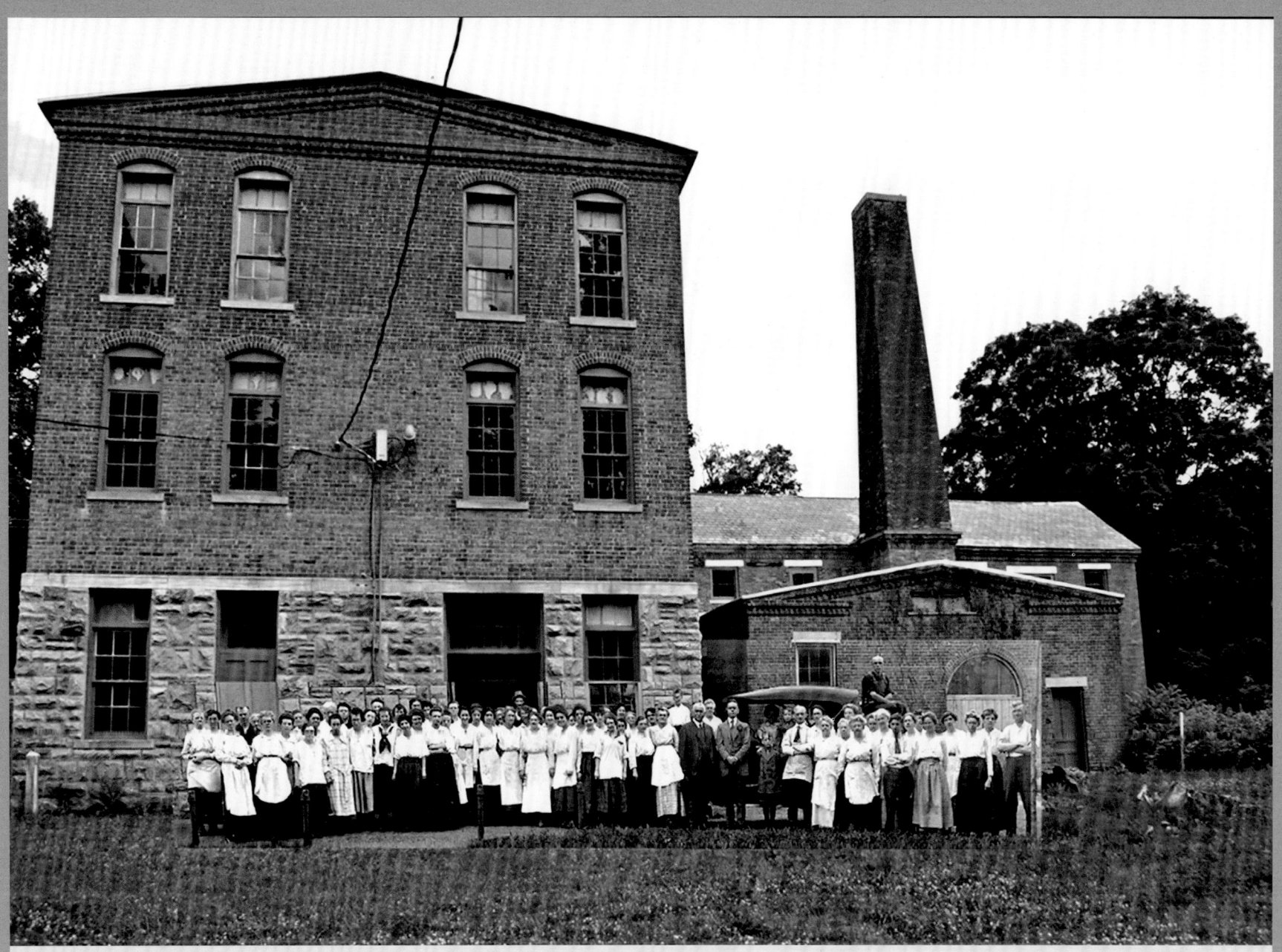

A modern-day photograph of the Manhattan Shirt Shop was overlaid and fused with a section from the 1919 photograph of the departing Spallholz family surrounded by company employees. It is scaled to appear as if it were taken from across Park Place by a photographer standing on the front porch of the Spallholzes' home.

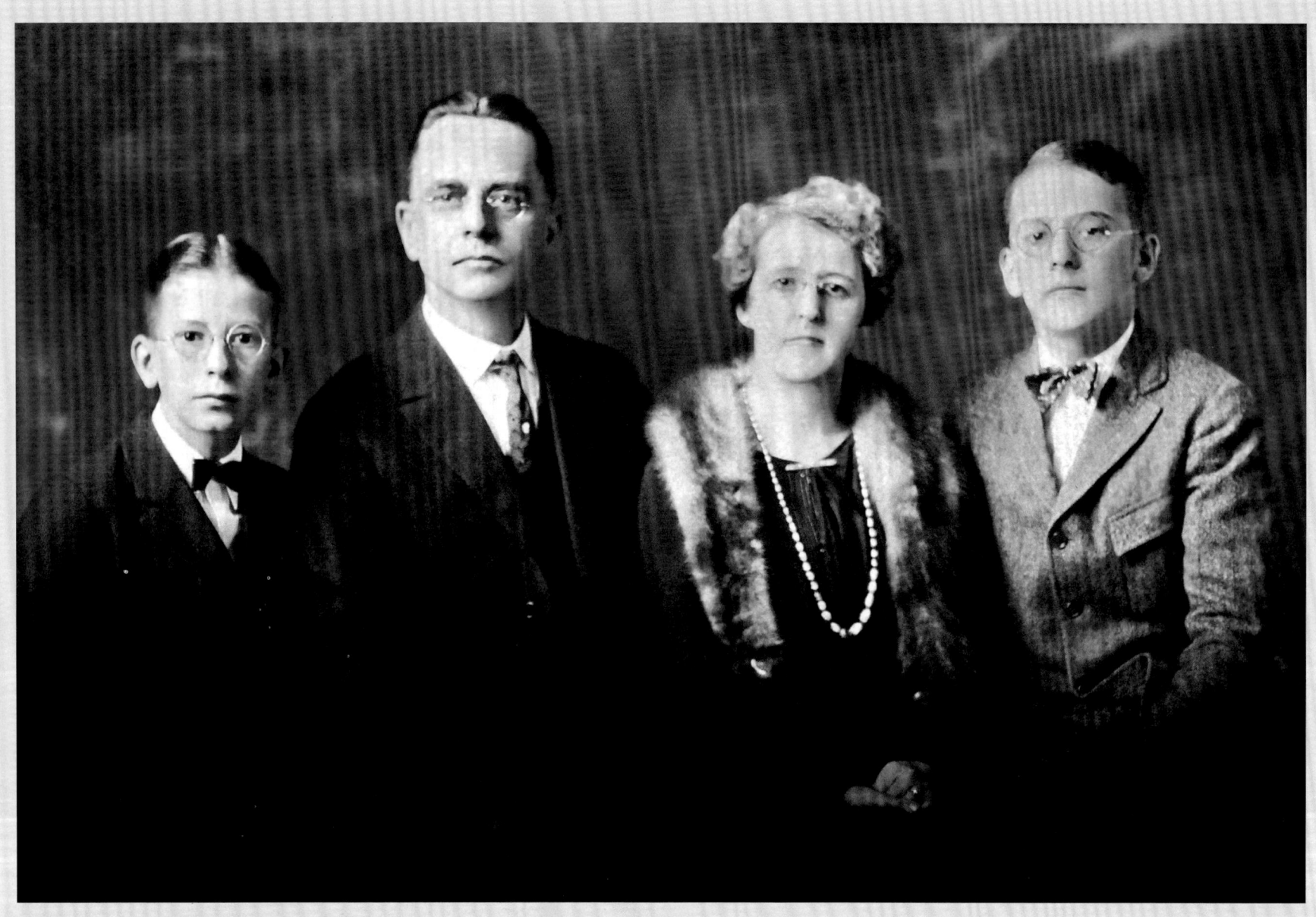

Spallholz family photo circa 1923. From left to right: Ernest H. Spallholz, Henry A. Spallholz, Lizzie M. Spallholz, and Walter L. Spallholz.

APPENDIX A

ASCENT OF MOUNT RAINIER

On July 28, 1919, Henry Spallholz set out from the Paradise Inn for his ascent of Mount Rainier, overnighting on the mountain at Camp Muir and making the descent on July 29. The following account was written by Mr. William F. Worner of Lancaster, Pennsylvania, his companion on the climb.

This is not the story of any great deed of valor, nor is it a minute record of the ascent of a peak hitherto unclimbed. Neither is it a glowing description of a peak that, as yet, is unexplored. This, then, is but an unembellished narrative of a climb made on foot by a novice in mountain climbing, up the highest volcanic peak in the United States, and the return to its base without any misadventure. Scores of hikers attempt the trip; many are taken sick while making the climb, and few reach the summit. I would not minimize its dangers. The climb is difficult and arduous, and fraught with many perils. Several climbers having lost their lives in the attempt, among them the gifted Prof. McClure. The Indians have never been known to reach the summit.

Our party was the sixteenth one to make the climb this summer. We made the ascent in ten hours and a half, breaking the former record for the season by thirty-one minutes. My only apology for this prosaic description lies in that fact.

Rainier National Park is situated in western central Washington and its area totals approximately 200 square miles. It has the largest active glacial area in the United States, 28 of its glaciers totaling 45 square miles of moving ice. A pleasing sight to behold are its many miles of beautiful, high-lying meadows, covered with wildflowers of many hues. Mt. Rainier, its perpetually snow-covered peaks, towers 14,408 ft. in the air.

From time immemorial, the Indians have called this noble peak by the musical and romantic name Tak-ho-ma, meaning the mountain (that to them) was God, as their legends inform us. An active volcano for many years, with frequent rumblings and eruptions, need we ask why the aboriginal Indian's deified it?

Captain George Vancouver, while cruising in the waters of the Pacific, and that of Puget Sound in 1792, saw the peak and named it Mt. Rainier after the distinguished British Admiral Rainier.

The Park is under the care of the Department of the Interior. There is but a small part of it visited by tourists most of whom spend their time in Paradise Valley.

Paradise Valley is aptly named. What memories it conjures up within us! Paradise Valley! The vale where the glaciers and wildflowers meet. What a picture it presents to the tourists. Myriads of avalanche lilies, bluebells and red Indian Paint Brushes pushing up through the snow and covering the hillsides far and wide evoke from the tourist the fitting exclamation, "Paradise Valley"! Paradise Inn—a magnificent hostelry of rustic architecture—is situated in Paradise Valley, 5,557 feet above the level of the sea. We approached it by automobile from Tacoma, sixty miles distant. The road winds thru avenues of pines, cedars and hemlocks, past giant waterfalls and over limpid mountain streams. From the entrance to the park proper (where all tourists must register), the road constructed by the government is so narrow that two vehicles cannot pass each other and the grade is quite steep. On one side towers the jagged peaks; on the other is a precipitation that would drop one thousands of feet below into the canyon of the Nisqually River, whose source is the melted snow and ice from the glacier bearing that name. We waited patiently for two hours and a-quarter at the ranger station while 245 automobiles, carrying 1,700 people motored down the narrow road bed before we were permitted to proceed up. The Inn had only been opened ten days before my arrival. Prior to my visit the tourists were compelled to travel the last ten miles on horseback thru the snow. When this hotel was opened for the season, entrance thereto was made by the caretaker at a garret window, which was approached on snowshoes. Tons of dynamite were used to blast away the snow surrounding the Inn and prepare space for parking automobiles. The snow and ice were piled seventy feet high before the hotel. The burning July sun rapidly diminished this towering mountain of dazzling white; from every direction, there flowed into the valley tiny rivulets of melted snow and ice.

We arrived at Paradise Inn on the afternoon of Monday, July 28, at 2 P.M. "Would you care to climb the summit" queried a park official? "That is what I came for," impulsively, I replied. I wasted no time, for at 2:40 P.M., in company with Henry A. Spallholz, the noted banker and globe trotter of Salem, N. Y., and Hans Fuhrer as guide, we began the ascent. We were accoutered for the climb in woolen shirt, tin-pan pants (of which more later) woolen cap, gloves and socks, hob-nailed boots, mackinaw and amber spectacles. We also carried Alpenstocks. Our faces were lathered with cold cream on top of which we applied a coat of actor's paint. Lunch, consisting of nuts, raisins, prunes, cheese and lemon drops, was tied to our belts. Before beginning the ascent, we were obliged to sign a release absolving the park officials from all responsibility should an accident occur. Our guide was a native of Switzerland and a mountain climber par excellence. As we left the Inn the many guests basking in the sunlight on the veranda wished us God-speed murmuring "Good luck to you." Our guide yodeled in true Alpine fashion; the crowd vociferated its appreciation. Hans impressed upon us the necessity of conserving every ounce of energy and forbade talking, much to the chagrin of Henry A. Spallholz. The pace set was uncomfortably slow.

The first part of the climb led us over immense fields of snow and ice. By 6 P.M., we had attained an elevation of

8,500 feet, where we ate supper, sitting on a narrow ledge of rock over which the water rushed madly. Continuing on our way up the snow field, we soon passed on our right, (elevation 9,500 feet), a projecting rock called Anvil Point, on which is located a diminutive Government ranger station. Here, high up among the clouds, resides for four months in each year a ranger whose duty it is to keep a close watch for forest fires. From this vantage point one can survey many miles of virgin forests. The little station is equipped with telephone and telescope. When a fire is sighted, the ranger residing nearest thereto is apprised of the approaching danger, and steps are taken to combat the fire.

At 8:20 PM Camp Muir was reached. The name sounded romantic but the glamor of it soon faded when I gazed upon that wretched hovel. It is built of mountain stone, ten by twenty feet in size and contains three windows and one door. The windows were minus sash and glass. Here we spent the night. The guide melted snow on an oil stove and brewed tea. Henry declared "it was the rottenest tea he had ever drunk" and further insisted that "it was made from weeds that grew in Paradise Valley." The guide protested that it was the best grade of Chinese tea. Thus we sat sipping tea and eating what little lunch remained, the wind meanwhile blowing in thru the windows and sending the black smoke from the oil stove into our faces and nearly blinding us.

The guide busied himself arranging our bed for the night. On the stone floor was placed a mattress, which he covered with eight army blankets. On this we quickly reclined, covering ourselves with twelve blankets. Hans was soon in the arms of Morpheus, and soon Henry was snoring sonorously. Outside the wind howled furiously. Presently what I took to be a kitten tripped across the blankets. Then another

scampered gleefully across our bed. By the dingy light of the lantern suspended from overhead I perceived that they were rats. I awoke the guide. He swore at them, shook the covers, and away they scampered. The guide soon fell into unconsciousness again and the rodents returned. Seizing my alpenstock I scattered them, and all thru the long night I chased rats while my comrades slept.

A 3:45 AM the guide got up and prepared coffee. Drawing on our caulked boots (we slept with all our clothing on), we sat up and drank coffee—a miserable trio we were, cold, dirty and hungry, our faces covered with grease and blanket lint. We were anything but comfortable at that time. At 4:30 AM we started for the summit. Dawn was just breaking in the east. As we proceeded the sun rose directly over the peak on our right called Little Tacoma. Presently the guide tied a rope securely to our waists, attaching one end to his own.

Up the Cowlitz Cleaver we scrambled, the ascent of which is quite taxing, being for the most part over rough, angular lava blocks. The wind was blowing at a terrific rate; at times it was difficult to keep our footing. At last the Bee Hive was reached, which is but a giant crevice in the rock. Down into this we had to slide on a rope to the footing thirty feet below. Continuing on the Cowlitz Cleaver, which is nothing more than a ledge of rock, on one side of which, thousands of feet below, moves the Nisqually Glacier, while on the other is the Cowlitz Glacier. The apex of the cleaver is but a foot or two in width at certain places. Our footing was most precarious at times, the shale and powdered rock giving way under our step.

Camp Misery was passed in due time, and presently the base of Gibraltar Rock—an immense overhanging cliff—was reached. The trail follows a narrow ledge along the face of the cliff, and was so precipitous that it was with difficulty we ascended. We pulled ourselves up the steep acclivity several hundred feet by the means of a rope. Overhanging rock masses and huge icicles made it difficult to assume an erect posture in climbing. Huge pieces of rock frequently rolled off the cliff and landed on the glacier, thousands of feet below. On we trudged, unmindful of the danger. The Saddle of Gibraltar was finally accomplished. This ledge led us to the base of a narrow chute between the ice of the upper Nisqually Glacier and the body of Gibraltar. The chute really offered the most serious difficulties in the ascent. Ordinarily the chute resembles the giant teeth of a hundred saws, paralleling each other about a foot apart. They are cones of ice, with spaces between wide enough for one's foot. Up this we clambered for about 800 feet until we reached another snow field (13,000 feet altitude). From here there remained only a long slope to climb, but this snow slope proved exceedingly fatiguing. Up its smooth side we zigzag our footing at times precarious, the grade precipitously steep. Immense crevasses in the ice made us detour not infrequently. Dull, gray clouds frowned upon us ominously. The wind blew at the rate of eighty miles an hour. It was difficult to maintain our equilibrium in the face of such a gale. At times, the guide ordered us to lie on our stomachs to escape the mighty blasts. We were cold, tired and hungry; my hands were frozen stiff. No other sound could be heard save the howling wind. It was almost impossible to breathe in the face of such an icy breeze.

At 14,000 feet altitude, we faced a bald rock. By its side we trudged on in this terrific windstorm until Registration Point (14,408 feet altitude) was reached. The summit was reached at last. We shouted for joy, but the sound died on our lips. There was nothing to fling back the echo. Registration Point is on the edge of the vast crater of Mount Rainier, the crater at this point being one and one-half miles wide. We descended into it to escape the stinging winds. Steam was issuing from the farther side of the rim. My hands were numb. It was only after a great effort that I could write my name in the book kept in the steel box on Registration Point for all who make the climb successfully. A glorious panorama was unfolded before us. To the right appeared the perfect snow-capped cone of Mount St. Helens, glistening in the sunlight. In front of us loomed Mount Adams and Mount Baker. In the distance could be seen the Tatoosh range of serrated mountains. Below at our feet lay Paradise Valley, the hotel obscured by clouds and vapor. All about us were mountain ranges and peaks innumerable, covered with snow—eternal ice and snow. At 9:40 A.M., we began the descent. The downward journey was accomplished more easily than the ascent. When Camp Muir was reached we were nearly famished, weak and exhausted. The guide prepared lunch, which we ate ravenously. We recuperated in due time. The balance of the descent was made in toboggan fashion. We sat down and held our alpenstocks before us and sped merrily over the snow hundreds of feet to the valley below. The "tin" pants served their purpose; for without them this part of the trip would have been impracticable. The Inn was reached amid the plaudits of the assembled guests, who welcomed us with open arms.

WILLIAM FREDERIC WORNER
SALEM PRESS 74, NO. 41, JUNE 11, 1920

HENRY'S TIME MACHINES

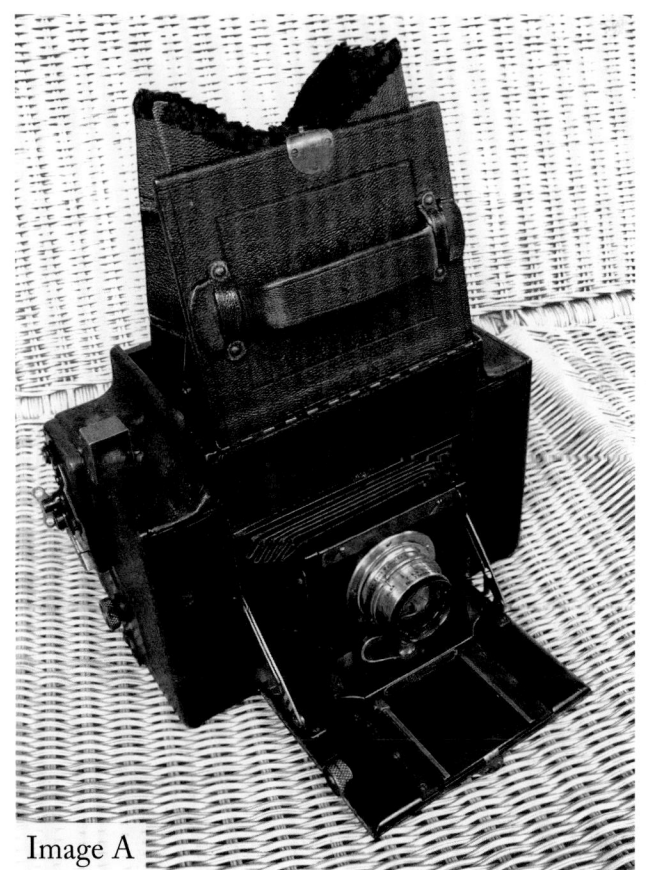

Image A

Cameras are visual time machines. They create images that transport us back to study and perhaps relive past experiences. They are especially valuable in providing visual eyewitness documentation of historical events. To document his family's 1919 road trip, Henry Albert Spallholz carried two cameras: a Bausch & Lomb-Zeiss 3A Graflex and a Kodak 3A. The Graflex (image A) weighed seven pounds and served as Henry's workhorse for precise framing and focusing of an image. The Kodak 3A rendered less precisely focused images than the Graflex; however, due to its lighter weight, it was more convenient for taking pictures at roadside stops.

The Graflex was a good choice for Henry to take scenic photos because it was a reflex camera with an internal first-surface mirror, angled to allow the photographer to view a subject through the lens up to the instant of exposure and immediately after the picture was taken. The only control on the lens itself was for aperture adjustment, with shutter speed controls located on the side plate. The photographer could achieve precise composing and focusing through the fur-lined view finder on the top. The large collapsible chimney-style hood on the Graflex shut out most of the ambient

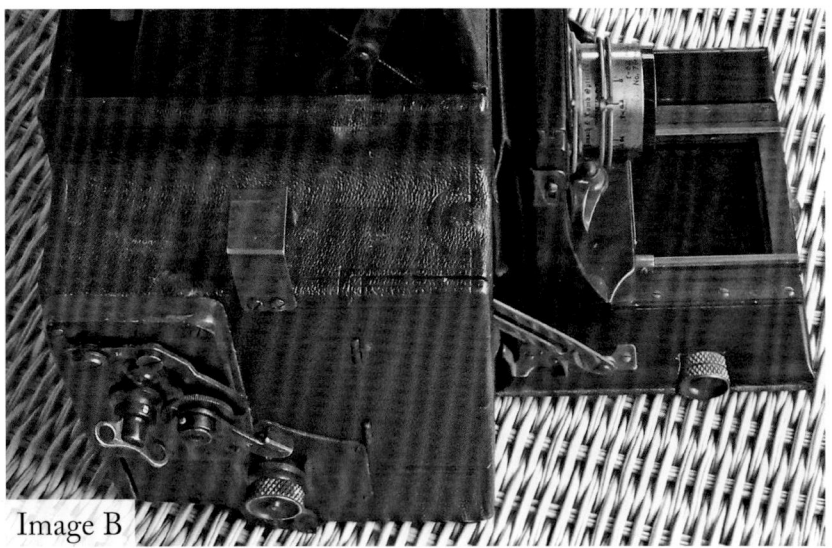

Image B

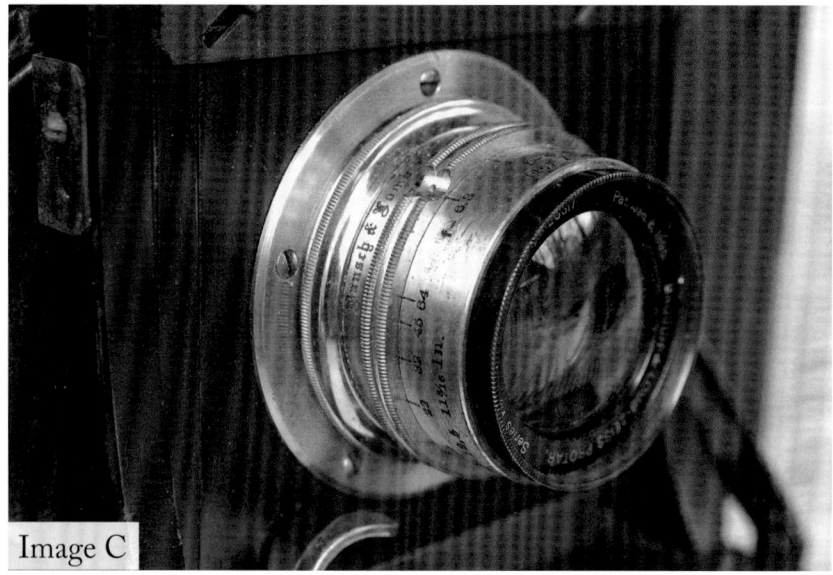

Image C

light and optimized photography work in sunny locations. The body of the camera (image B) provided a convenient place to carry extra rolls of film and a safe dark storage area for up to four rolls of film in its two side compartments.

Picture-taking using the Graflex required several steps. The photographer first had to set the curtain aperture and spring tension for the desired shutter speed, then press the reflex mirror lever to lock the mirror up into focusing position, compose the image, then make the exposure by tripping the shutter release lever on the forward left-hand side of the body. The mirror returned to its original position upon the lever's release. The Zeiss Protar 7a camera lens (image C) was convertible, meaning it was composed of two elements of different focal lengths, each of which could be used separately or in combination, producing three variations in focal length. This all-in-one feature eliminated the need for multiple lenses of different focal lengths.

By contrast, Henry's Kodak 3A autographic camera (images D-1/D-2 and E-1/E-2) was useful for quick photo opportunities. The small spring-loaded metal tab was lifted on the focusing scale and set into the notch corresponding with the subject's distance from the camera. To automatically be in focus for that distance, the photographer would slide the lens standard forward against the tab and lock it into place. All the exposure controls were on the shutter—none were on the body other than film advance, rewind, and a circular red window, which is typically found on older roll-film cameras. A small flip-down bed tab allowed for the camera to be placed on a surface for stability.

The Spallholz Collection is comprised of more than 330 Kodak prints and glass lantern slides (images F1/F2). Henry and Lizzie were meticulous in making notations on each photograph and on each slide. It is rare to find such a large collection of vintage photographic images where the photographer was so particular in logging the image location as well as additional bits of information relevant to what was happening in the photos. On the left side of the photograph album (image F3) is a specimen the Spallholzes brought back from the Petrified Forest.

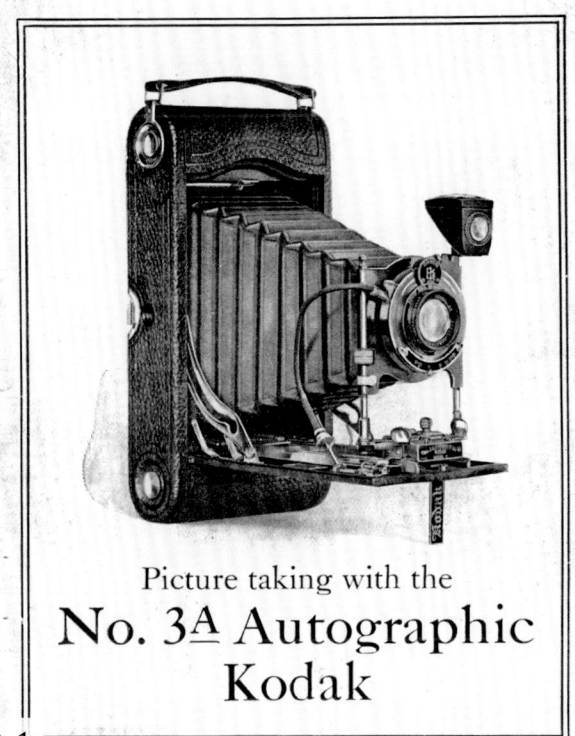

Picture taking with the
No. 3A Autographic Kodak

Image D-1

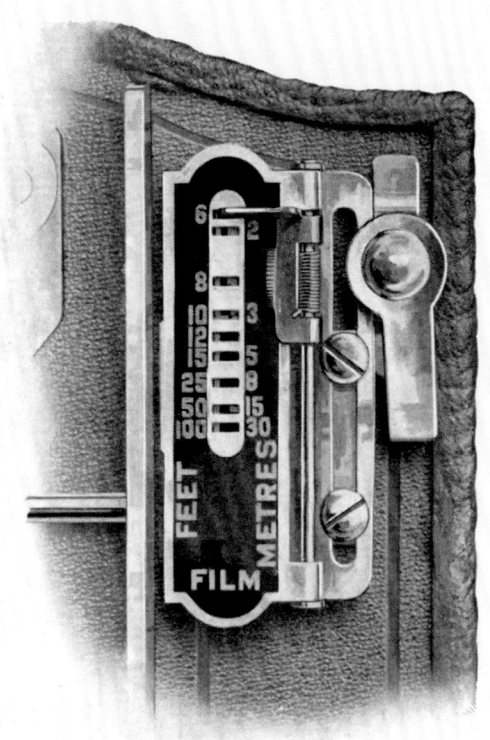

Image E-1

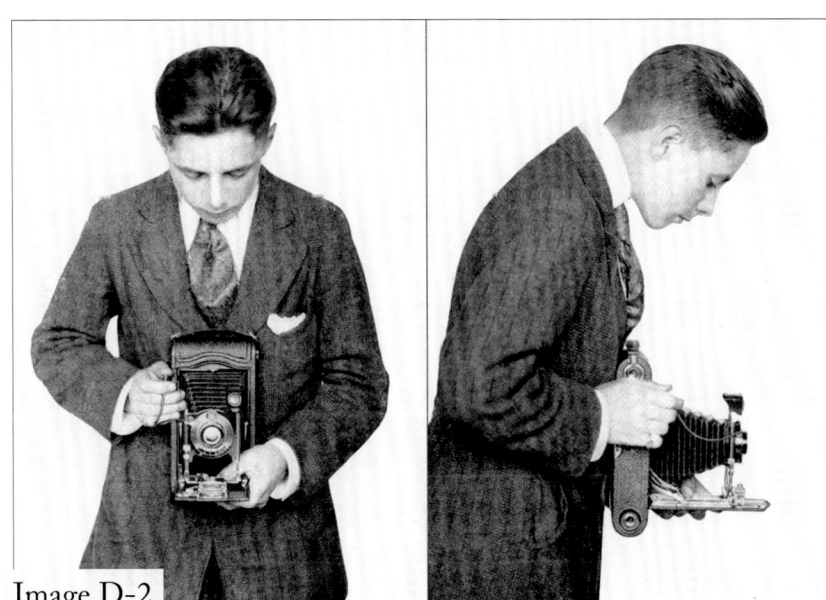

Image D-2

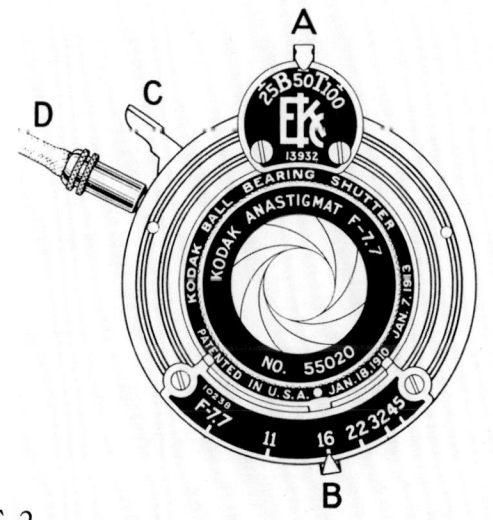

Image E-2

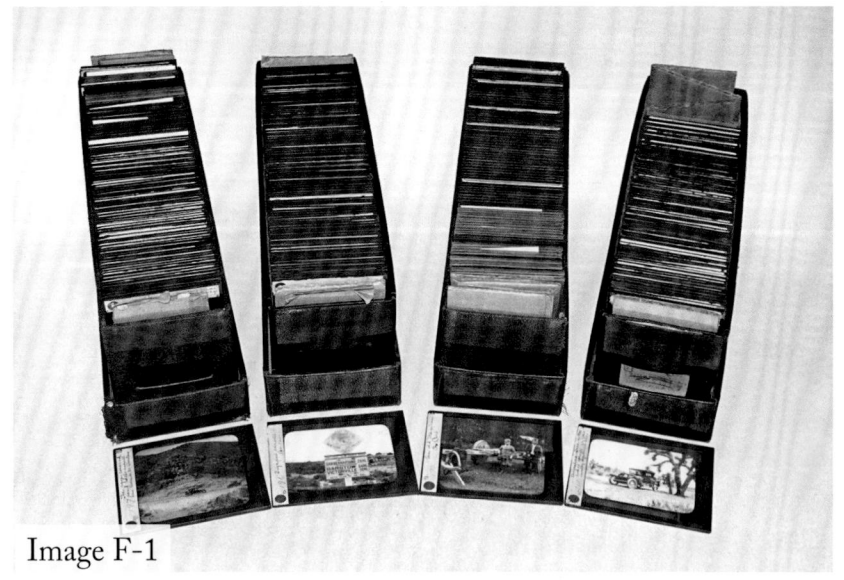

Image F-1

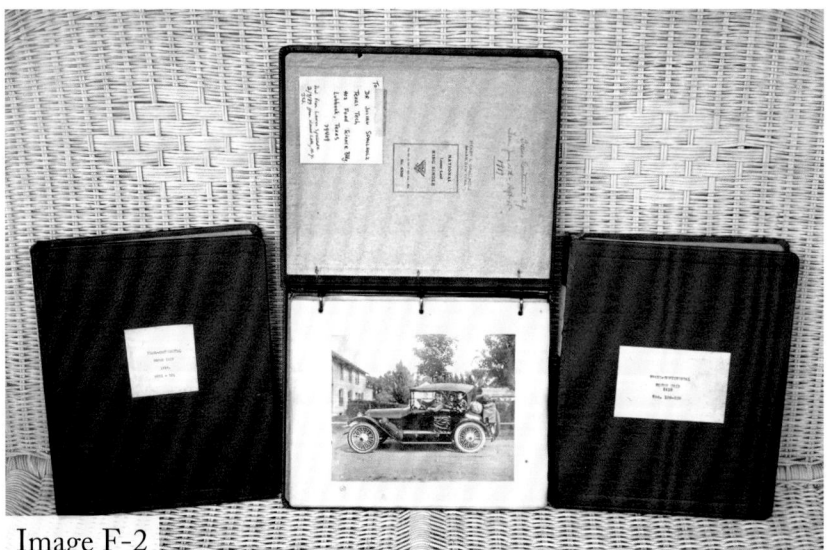

Image F-2

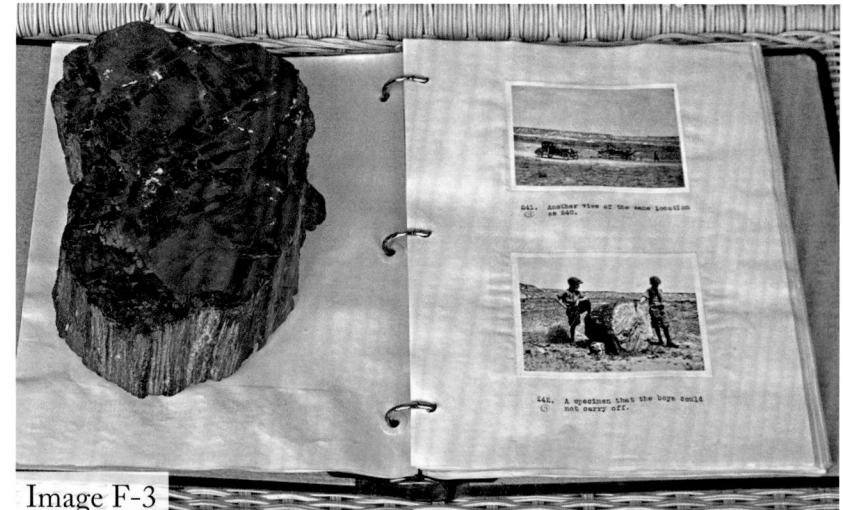

Image F-3

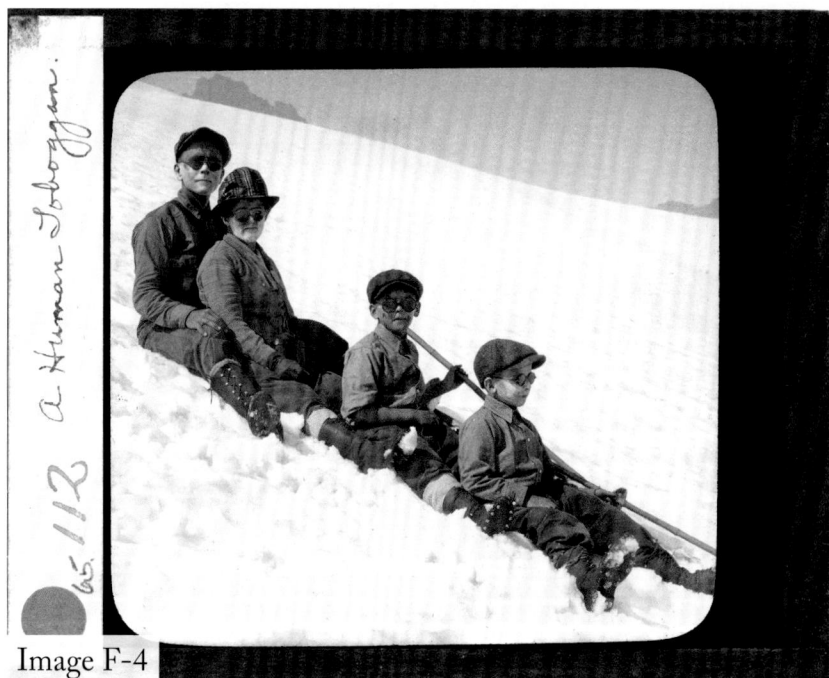

Image F-4

The image of the slide labeled "A human toboggan" (image F4) was prepared to illustrate the method Henry used to record information on his slides. A flatbed scanner was used to first scan the slide using top lighting, then perform a second scan with backlighting. Combining the two separate scans produced the slide-with-label image. Each label has a pre-printed thumb spot that establishes correct orientation for insertion into the projector's slide carrier.

Many slides and prints in the Spallholz Collection needed some level of restoration. Prints having some fading due to chemical instability in the paper could be corrected using an image-processing application's exposure and contrast correction tools. Damaged slides were a bit different. Henry likely paid to have the lantern slides produced by contact printing original negatives onto lantern slide plates. The plates were then developed in the method by which a sheet of film is processed. When dry, they were assembled by applying a slide mask to the emulsion (image) side of the glass plate, forming the border of the image. Then a clear protective "cover glass" was applied to the outer face of the mask, creating a "sandwich," with the image safely contained within the thin space between the plates. The thickness of the mask prevents the cover glass from contacting the image. This glass sandwich is then secured along the edges with paper binding tape, completing the slide.

In preparing images for this book, several slides were found to be damaged, likely by being dropped during projection and landing on a corner or edge, causing the glass cover and emulsion plate to shift position with respect to one another, creating one or more tears in the emulsion. Using modern digital technology, this damage was repaired by closing and blending in emulsion cracks, returning the image to its original undamaged state.

Henry Spallholz used a Bausch & Lomb Home Balopticon convection-cooled projector (image G) to present a number of slide programs of his family's trips. The unit could serve as both a conventional slide projector and as an opaque projector. When used as a slide projector, an internal mirror was positioned to direct light through the bellows slide projection lens assembly. Slides were loaded one at a time into the double-sided carrier. As a slide in the carrier was pushed into the light path, the other end of the slide carrier exited the projector and a small brass rod lifted the slide just slightly for easy removal. The unit also came with special holders

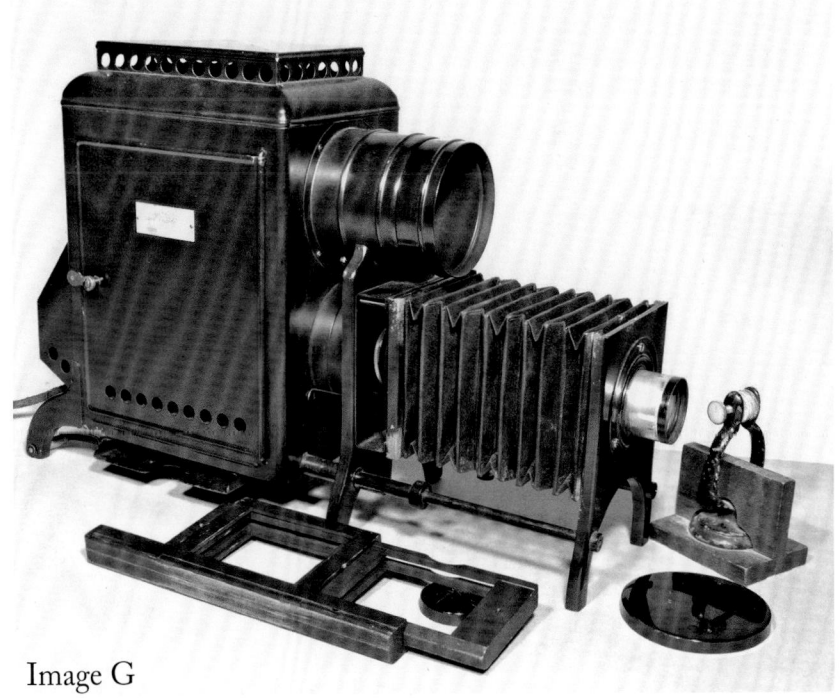

Image G

for projecting commercial postcards via the larger lens above the bellows. A postcard could be mounted on a flat holder and slipped into a slot in the floor of the lamp house. By flipping the internal front-surface mirror, the opaque projector portion of the unit could project any flat opaque material, such as the postcards Henry purchased to supplement his photographs.

By design, the unit did not contain any fan or cooling for the slide carrier. Instead, the lamp house was constructed with a series of vent holes that provided convection cooling. This means that the projector is totally silent, but the projector and slides can get quite heated.

APPENDIX C

"AMERICA'S FIRST CAR"

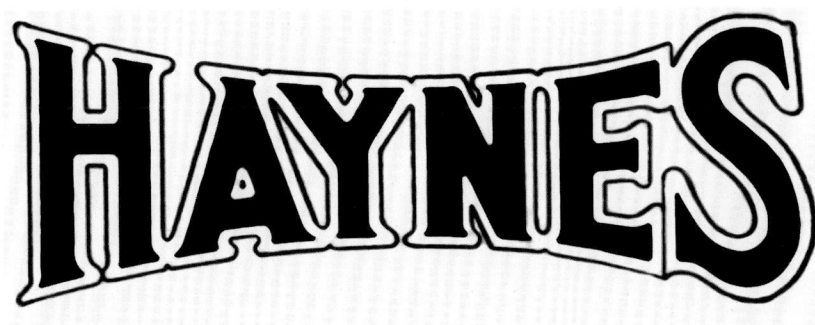

Elwood Haynes had a remarkable career, initially in business, in the exploration of natural gas in Indiana and later as one of the discoverers of stainless steel. His most remarkable engineering contribution, however, known but to few people, was his invention of the first motorized horseless carriage, the Pioneer, driven down Broadway in Kokomo, Indiana, on July 4, 1894, a full two years before Henry Ford would complete his motorized Quadricycle on June 4, 1896, in Detroit, Michigan.

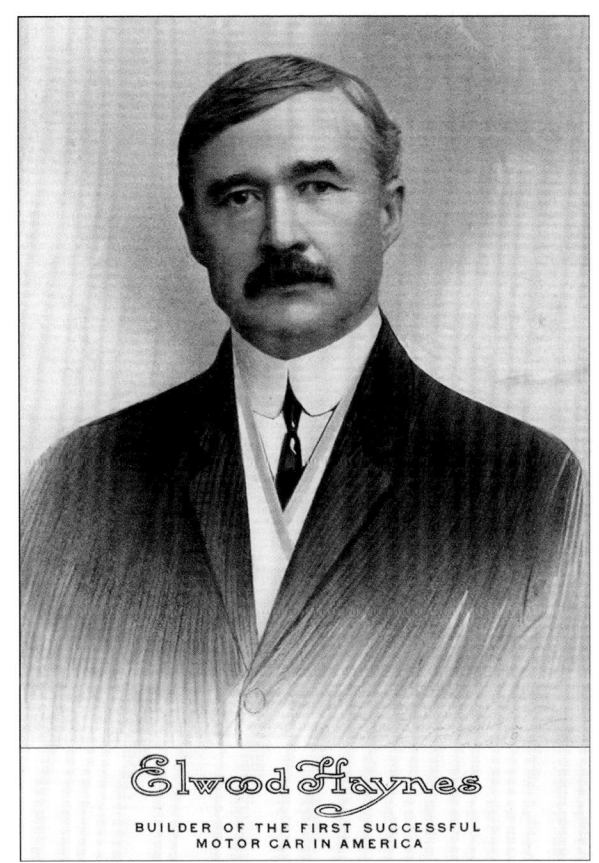

Elwood Haynes

BUILDER OF THE FIRST SUCCESSFUL
MOTOR CAR IN AMERICA

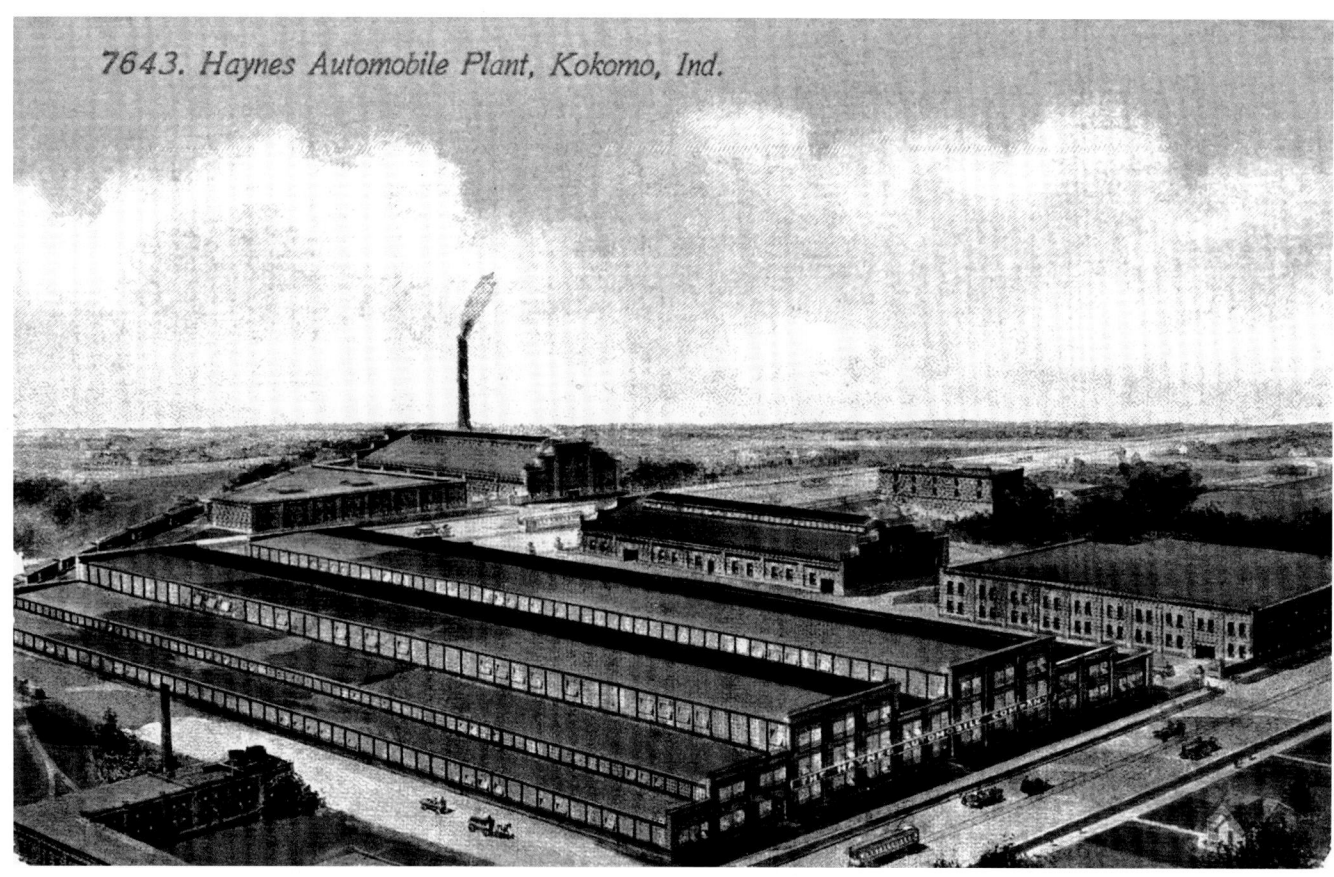

The Haynes Automobile Company, Kokomo, Indiana, as it appeared on a postcard in 1914. It was in this factory that the Spallholz Haynes Light Six was manufactured in 1917. Where the automobile was purchased by Henry Spallholz is unknown. Henry Spallholz visited the Haynes Factory on June 15, 1919.

Automobile manufacturing began in Kokomo under the joint venture of the Apperson brothers and Elwood Haynes circa 1898, leading to the very first commercial sales of automobiles under the Haynes-Apperson name. In 1905 with the dissolution of the Haynes-Apperson partnership, Elwood Haynes set up the Haynes Motor Car Company, commemorating production of the Light Six with a new logo and radiator badge bearing an embossed rendering of the Pioneer and the slogan "America's First Car." The company manufactured approximately 6,500 automobiles in Kokomo until 1924 when the company filed for bankruptcy and closed in 1925. A plant fire in 1911 and debt assumed in rebuilding followed by the downturn in the economy in the 1920s led to the factory's closure, the fate of many of the automobile manufactures in that decade.

Stock rendering of the 1917 Haynes Light Six Roadster (top) as compared with a photograph of the Spallholzes' car in "Loaded for the Trip" (bottom). The Haynes signature rear-window "H" is clearly visible in both the rendering and the photograph. While the Spallholz vehicle looked much like the stock rendering, with camping gear, running board boxes, and map case, Henry also extended the spare tire frame and added a front metal bumper.

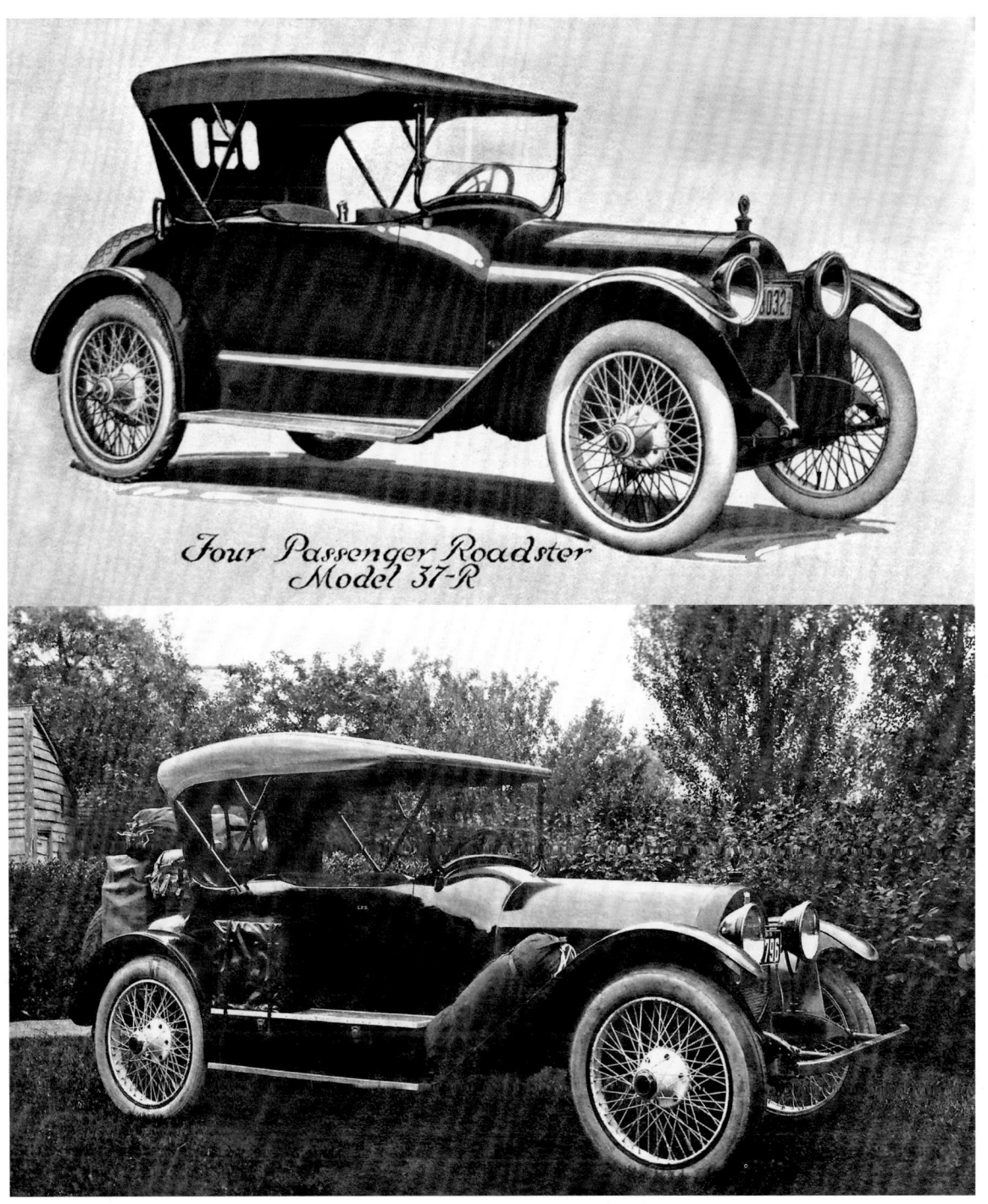

Four Passenger Roadster
Model 37-R

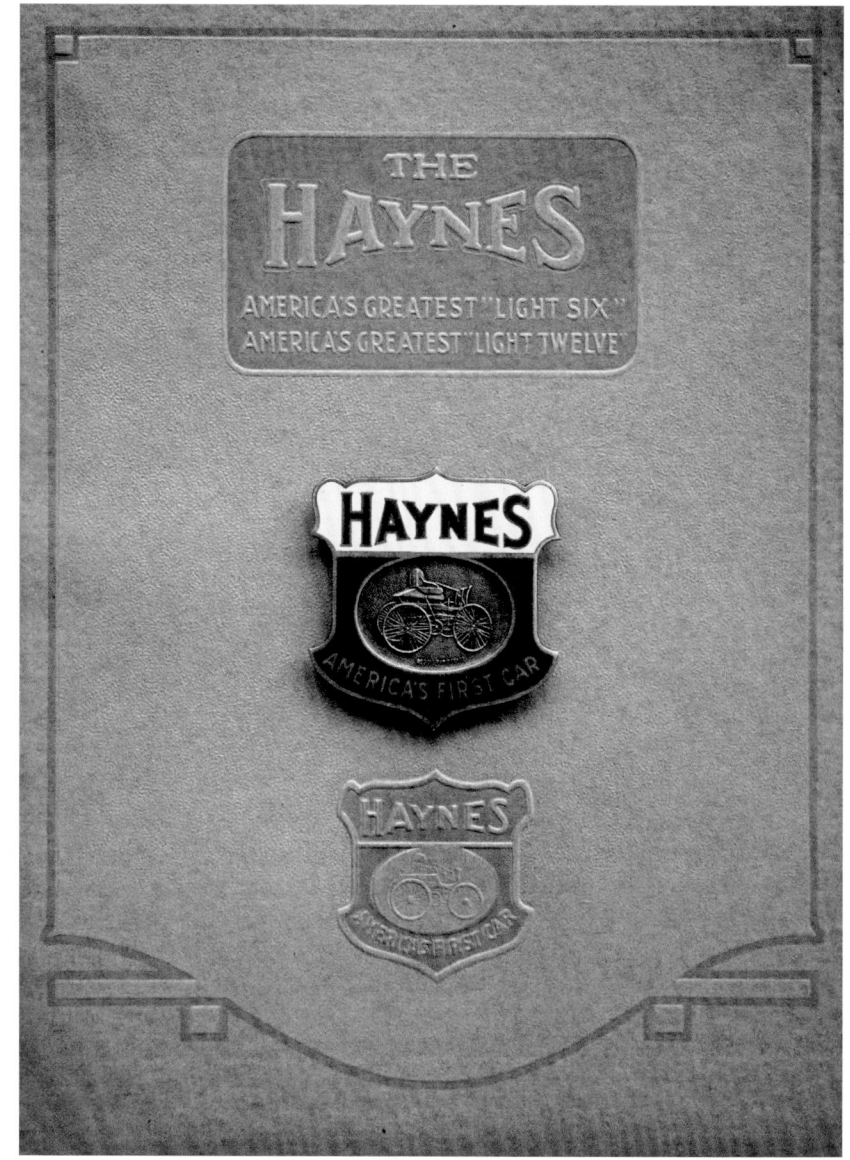

Reproduced photographically below by Art Vaughan is original Haynes Factory specification literature for the 1917 Light Six and Light Twelve automobiles. Henry Spallholz and family in 1919 drove a 1917 Light Six Roadster with wire wheels across the United States, June 11, 1919 to September 15, 1919; 96 days of travel and only one day of rain.

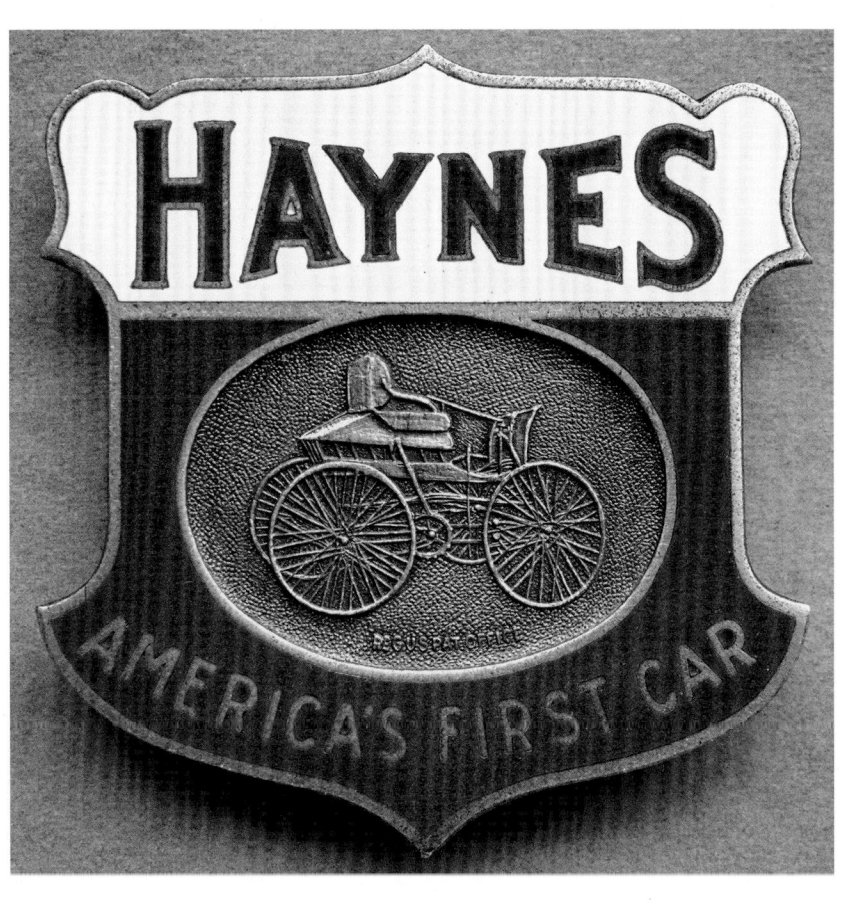

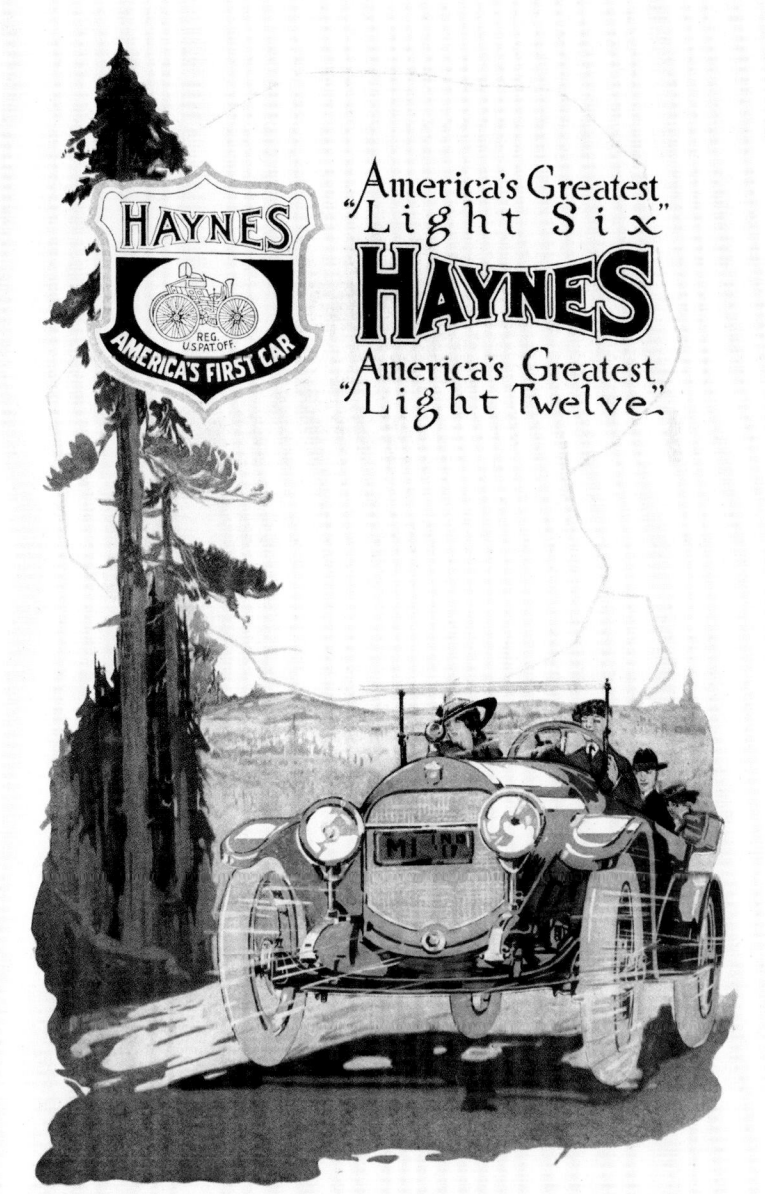

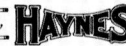

The Motor *of* the Haynes "Light Twelve"

THE constant trend of the automobile industry has been toward a motor car that would run without noticeable vibration, accelerate quickly and smoothly, and unite power with economy. The progress toward the achievement of this ideal brought out Elwood Haynes' first two-cylinder opposed motor in 1897. This came into being to displace the one-cylinder engine, and was in turn forced to give way to four and six-cylinder motors.

The fundamental problem of the automobile engineer has been the number of power impulses per revolution that he could apply to the crankshaft. In the four cylinder engine a noticeable gap occurred between each power impulse. The frequency of the power impulses was increased in the six cylinder engine and the gap eliminated. The eight cylinder V-type motor represented further achievement in the development of an even torque. Freedom from vibration demands that the power impulses completely overlap, and in this feature past motor car production culminates in twelve cylinder motors.

The "Light Twelve"

The Haynes Twelve is a "Light Twelve" because it is this type of car that has proved in every day use the best adapted for all travel conditions. Ample power with economy is the criterion it was built to meet. With this end in view its construction followed the general lines of the "Light Six." Wherever weight could be dispensed with, it was eliminated, and by the use of strong, light metals, the sturdiness of the car was not made to suffer.

After a year of constant experimenting, the Haynes "Light Twelve" is ready to make its bow to the multiple cylinder market. It is Haynes through and through — first devised and developed, and then perfected until it is a representative of Haynes quality in motor cars. Both motor car and body include the last improvements that the best minds of modern automobile engineering have contrived.

Motor

The motor is the high speed type, with light reciprocating parts. This construction gives a maximum speed, a fast pick-up, ability to make steep gradients, with a minimum cost of maintenance.

Cylinders

The cylinders are in two sets of six, each series cast en bloc. They are valve-in-head construction with a removable cylinder head, and the two series are set at an angle of 60 degrees on the motor base in the shape of a V. The bore and stroke are 2¾ by 5 inches, giving a piston displacement of 356 cubic inches. All the cylinders are separately ground after boring, insuring perfect compression.

Pistons

The pistons are made of an aluminum alloy, which gives durability and strength with little wear. The reciprocating weight of the engine also is materially reduced by the change from the old cast iron type with the advantage of a smoother running motor. The piston carries four high compression rings, with an oil groove to drain the oil to the reservoir, preventing its entrance to the combustion chamber and the formation of excessive carbon deposits.

Lubrication

The question of lubrication is the greatest barrier against which engineers have been fighting in designing twelve-cylinder motors. This has been solved in the Haynes "Light Twelve" by a gear pump. A hollow crankshaft with outlets into all the bearings keeps these friction surfaces well lubricated. All other bearing surfaces have small pipes, through which the oil is pumped to them. An indicator on the cowl keeps the driver posted on the exact condition of his lubrication system.

Cam Shaft

A single one-piece drop-forged open hearth steel cam shaft is used. If two cam shafts were used in the twelve-cylinder motor, the slightest inaccuracy in setting would prevent the motor from delivering the maximum power. In using one cam shaft this possibility is eliminated.

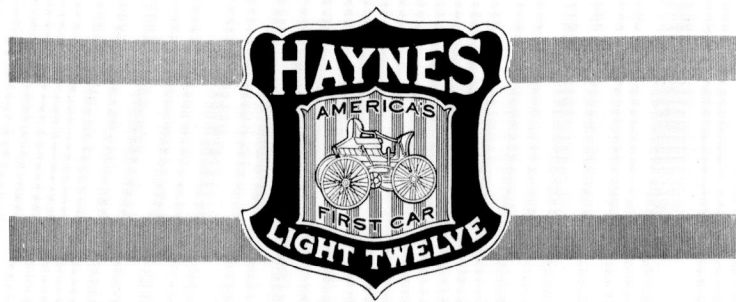

Rear View "Light Twelve" Motor

Ignition

A double Delco system of ignition is used on the "Light Twelve" motor to insure accurate firing at all times. Where perfect ignition is secured the maximum power from the minimum amount of fuel is obtained.

Carburetor

The carburetor is placed midway in the V between the cylinder blocks, where an equal distribution of fuel is assured each cylinder. The manifolds are surrounded by hot water jackets, to prevent any condensation of fuel before the gasoline reaches the combustion chambers. The position of the carburetor makes it readily accessible for any adjustments.

Cooling

An overheated motor can not give a maximum amount of power. This feature in a number of instances has not been given its due attention and has been considered a minor detail. In the Haynes "Light Twelve," the cooling system is driven by a centrifugal pump which keeps a constant flow of cool water around the valve seats and parts which might become overheated. Haynes motors never overheat and a thermostat control keeps the temperature up to the most efficient point at all times.

Valves

The twelve-cylinder motor is the logical place to use a valve-in-head cylinder. The valves are on top where adjustment can easily be made. The manifold is on the outside, and the exhaust pipe can come out of the center of the manifold. The exhaust can then go straight down and back under the car, and the heat is readily carried away.

The valve-in-head V-type motor permits an efficient arrangement of all accessories. The carburetor and the inlet valves it feeds are close together on the inside of the V. The water pump, generator, and air pump are in accessible places. The ignition is on the front end of the motor, and the vacuum tank on the rear. This arrangement keeps the carburetor and vacuum tank not only away from the ignition, but from the manifolds as well, thereby eliminating any chance of fire.

In an L-head V-type motor with the valves on the inside, the exhaust manifolds must be on the inside as well as the carburetor. This leaves the so-called valve alley very complicated, and it would be practically impossible to make an adjustment of the tappets without removing the carburetor at least. If the motor is L-head with the valves on the outside, the arrangement necessitates double cam shafts, a wide hood, and complicated methods of driving the water pump, ignition, lighting, and starting outfits. That is why the valve-in-head is the only logical arrangement for twelve-cylinder motors.

Accessibility

In the "Light Twelve" motor, every means has been taken to make every part requiring the least attention as easy of access as possible.

The valves which are located in a removable cylinder head, have been arranged on the alley side of the cylinder blocks so that push rod and valve adjustments are a simple matter.

The spark plugs have also been taken into consideration, being set on the valve side of the block. This brings all twelve spark plugs within arm's reach, affording less difficulty in removing.

Vacuum System

The same Stewart-Warner vacuum gasoline system is used on the "Light Twelve" as that used on the "Light Six." In place of being mounted on the dash a small bracket holds it in place in the "V" of the motor. The gasoline is warmed by the heat of the motor before coming to the carburetor, making vaporization more complete, which means a better and more powerful mixture in the combustion chamber.

Front View "Light Twelve" Motor

Crankshaft

The crankshaft in the twelve cylinder motor is of the hollow type to supply oil to crankshaft bearings. Two connecting rods are arranged side by side on the same crank pin. Each is readily adjusted without reference to the other—an arrangement not possible with the forked rod construction. In case the cylinders were placed exactly opposite, both connecting rods would come down to the crank pin for attachment at exactly the same place. To avoid this possibility, the right

series of cylinders is the width of a connecting rod bearing nearer the cowl. This arrangement is known as "staggering" the cylinders.

Circuit Breaker

An automatic circuit breaker protects the electrical equipment from damage by short circuits, by automatically breaking the flow of the current if trouble occurs. As soon as the short circuit is corrected the circuit breaker is closed by simply pressing down a button. It is impossible to keep the circuit breaker closed as long as there is a short circuit in the electrical system. This equipment takes the place of fuses, but it is far more reliable and convenient since it may be closed at will without having to insert new fuses.

The principle is the same as is employed in all large lighting and power plants for the protection of expensive electrical equipment.

Crank Case

A split type crankcase is used with all crankshaft bearings carried in the upper half. This section is aluminum, which accounts for its light weight combined with strength and durability.

The lower half is seamless pressed steel, and is used as the oil reservoir. The temperature of the oil is kept at a low point, as the pan is not covered by a mud shield. This item is cared for by steel webs running from the frame to the motor on a frame level.

Starting

The Leece-Neville starting and lighting system is used on the "Light Twelve." This system embraces a generator for charging the battery and a motor for cranking the engine.

The engine is assured of easy starting under all weather conditions. The Bendix drive flywheel starter is used. In this starter all cranking of the engine is performed through the flywheel. A small gear on the shaft of the starting motor is thrown into mesh with the large gear on the flywheel, the action being entirely automatic. This is an extremely simple mechanism, and one which cannot give trouble.

The New Series "Light Six" Motor

THE Haynes "Light Six" motor is of the light, high speed, high power type which has proved to be the most economical type of automobile motor. There are many high speed motors, but this motor is different. It possesses wonderful pulling power throughout the entire range of speeds. It may be throttled to forty revolutions per minute under load, or speeded up to the extreme of 3100 revolutions per minute. At forty revolutions per minute, the car is driven smoothly at the rate of one mile per hour on direct or high gear. Such wonderful flexibility of the Haynes "Light Six" motor gives unlimited possibilities.

The power plant is a single unit with three point suspension. Webs extend from the motor to the car frame so as to provide complete protection from mud and water. No mud pan is used.

The motor is perfectly balanced. An ordinary lead pencil may be stood on end on the cylinder block while the motor is running at 1500 revolutions per minute, equivalent to a speed of thirty-seven miles per hour.

Unusual Horse Power

On actual block test, the motor develops 55 horse power. Correct design, best materials and careful workmanship combine this abundance of power with light weight and economy. The "Light Six" motor will develop more power than any other motor of any make of equal bore and stroke.

Cylinders

The six cylinders are cast en bloc. Water is circulated between every cylinder and around every valve seat. The cylinder casting is unique in this respect. The cylinder dimensions are $3\frac{1}{2}$ by 5 inches. All cylinders are ground after being bored.

Push Rods

The valve lifters, or push rods, are of the "mushroom" type. There are no rollers in the lower ends to work loose and click. The push rods are made of nickel steel. They are heat treated and hardened to prevent wear. The adjusting screws in the upper ends of the rods are also hardened. The push rod adjustments are completely enclosed, yet they may be reached readily without having to disturb any other unit. All push rods may be taken out and replaced without having to remove the valve springs or valves.

Ignition

The modern generator-storage battery, dual ignition system is employed. During all ordinary running, the ignition current is supplied by the generator. The motor may be started on the storage battery, and as soon as it begins to fire, the generator automatically begins to supply the current without changing the ignition switch.

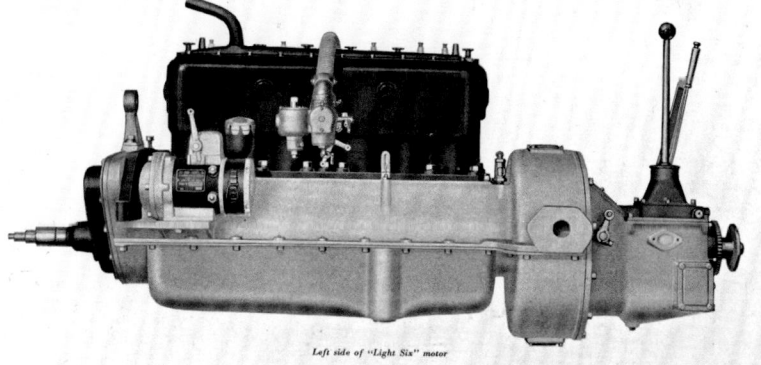

Left side of "Light Six" motor

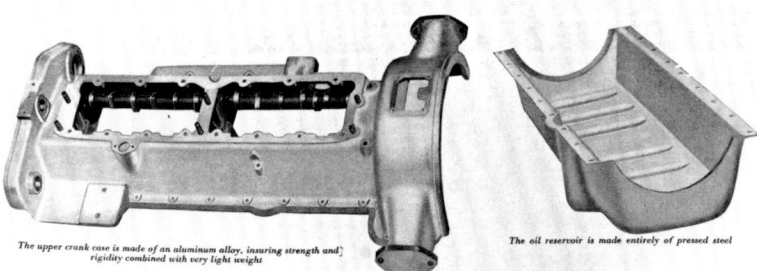

The upper crank case is made of an aluminum alloy, insuring strength and rigidity combined with very light weight

The oil reservoir is made entirely of pressed steel

The lower half of the crank case is made from pressed steel. There are no seams. A heavy leather gasket is used to insure an oil tight joint between the two sections of the crank case. The lower half contains the oil reservoir. No mud pan is used, in order that the air can strike the reservoir and cool the oil.

Three Bearing Crank Shaft

The three bearing crank shaft is recognized as the ideal construction for this type of motor. By its use the over-all length has been reduced to a minimum, resulting in greater strength, greater rigidity, and a higher ratio of horsepower to weight. This crank shaft is drop forged from .40% to .50% carbon steel and is subjected to a special heat treatment. Each crank shaft is carefully balanced to a perfect static and running balance after it is accurately finished.

All main bearings are two inches in diameter. The front bearing is $3\frac{1}{16}$ inches long; the center bearing is 3 inches long; and the rear bearing, $3\frac{3}{4}$ inches long. The bearing surface is unusually large for a $3\frac{1}{2}$ inch bore motor. Much of the success of this motor is due to the heavy crank shaft and the shape of the arms.

Lubrication

The proper lubrication of the automobile is as essential as is the design of the various parts. A combination of splash and force feed is employed. A plunger type oil pump with a capacity of $\frac{1}{2}$ gallon per minute at 1000 r. p. m., distributes oil to the main bearings, to the timing gears and to the connecting rod dip pans.

The connecting rod dip pins splash the oil so effectively that there is always a mist or vapor of oil throughout the crank case.

The oil reservoir has a capacity of 7 quarts. Oil is drawn from the bottom of this reservoir by the pump, which insures the motor receiving proper lubrication as long as there is any oil whatsoever in the reservoir. The oil is passed through a filtering screen each time it is circulated.

An improved oil level indicating gauge is used that will show at a glance the exact height of the oil in the crank case. No glass is used. An indicator raises and lowers with the oil level and shows on a scale the number of quarts of oil remaining. A glass sight feed is used in the pipe line coming from the pump.

Cooling System

Haynes cars never overheat. Water is circulated between every cylinder and up and around each individual valve seat. This is rarely the case even where cylinders are cast in pairs. A large centrifugal pump is used to force the water from the bottom of the radiator through the cylinder jacket. A wide cap extends the whole length of the cylinder block which may be removed easily so that the interior of the water jacket may be reached and kept clean of all sediment and scale.

The radiator is of the honeycomb type. It is made entirely of copper and is protected around the sides by a heavy steel shell. There is a half-inch air space between the radiator wall and the shell. This space prevents the heat from dulling the enamel on the outside of the radiator. A fifteen inch pressed steel fan is used and is provided with a quick adjusting belt tightener. The capacity of the cooling system is $5\frac{1}{2}$ gallons.

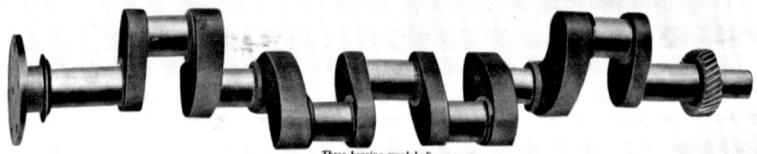

Three bearing crankshaft

No Intake Manifold

In the design of the Haynes "Light Six" motor, it has been borne in mind that gasoline is becoming heavier and its vaporizing point higher with consequent difficulty in making it evaporate easily. The carburetor has been mounted up high and attached directly to the cylinder block. There is no intake manifold. All gas passages are within the cylinder block where they are surrounded by the warm water.

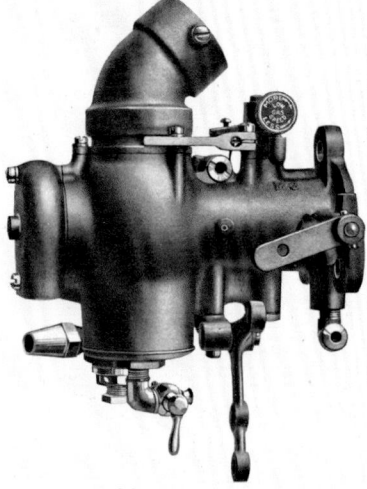

Carburetor used on "Light Six"

All carburetors will vaporize the gasoline in some sort of fashion but means must be taken to prevent the vapor or gas from condensing on its way to the cylinder. The exposed manifold is out where the draft from the fan can strike it and keep it cooler than the carburetor. When the warm gases strike the cold walls of the manifold, the gases condense exactly the same as one's breath when blown against a cold window pane.

When there is any appreciable condensation, more gasoline must be used, since the allowable time for the explosion in each cylinder is so short that the little drops cannot be broken up and burned. Only the gas that is mixed properly with the air is fully utilized.

The fact that the carburetor is attached directly to the cylinder block gives great fuel economy. There is no condensation in the gas passages of the motor. The gases are kept warm from the time they leave the

carburetor until they reach the various cylinders and are burned.

The Rayfield Carburetor is particularly well suited to the Haynes "Light Six." It has proved wonderfully economical and without change of adjustments shows power, speed and remarkable flexibility. The adjusting button on the cowl apron takes care of all adjustments necessary for temperature changes.

Starting and Lighting

The Leece-Neville electrical system is a separate unit system embracing a generator for charging the battery and a motor for cranking the engine. Higher

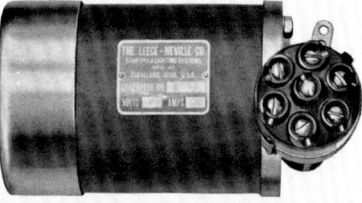

Generator and Distributor. Note accessibility and dust-proof construction

electrical efficiency is obtained from each of the units in building them separately, and a higher cranking speed of the engine is developed.

The entire electrical system operates on six volts. The Willard LBA, six-volt, 100 ampere hour storage battery has a large capacity and gives ample current at all times for the starting motor and electric lights. All wiring is enclosed in water and oil-proof conduits. An ammeter is provided to show the amount of current stored as well as the quantity used.

The starting motor is directly connected at all times to the crank shaft of the engine by a heavy chain. The large sprocket on the crankshaft contains an overrunning clutch. This clutch is essentially a Haynes design, and its construction is such that the chain and starting motor are in motion only when the engine is

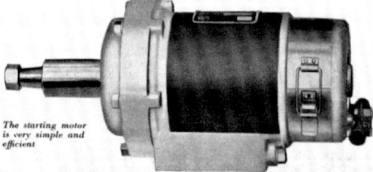

The starting motor is very simple and efficient

being cranked. When the engine is running, the chain is at rest. Back firing of the engine can do no harm. The starting of the engine is a wonderful example of what simplification may be had.

Haynes "Light Six" *and* "Light Twelve" Motors Are Mechanically Perfect

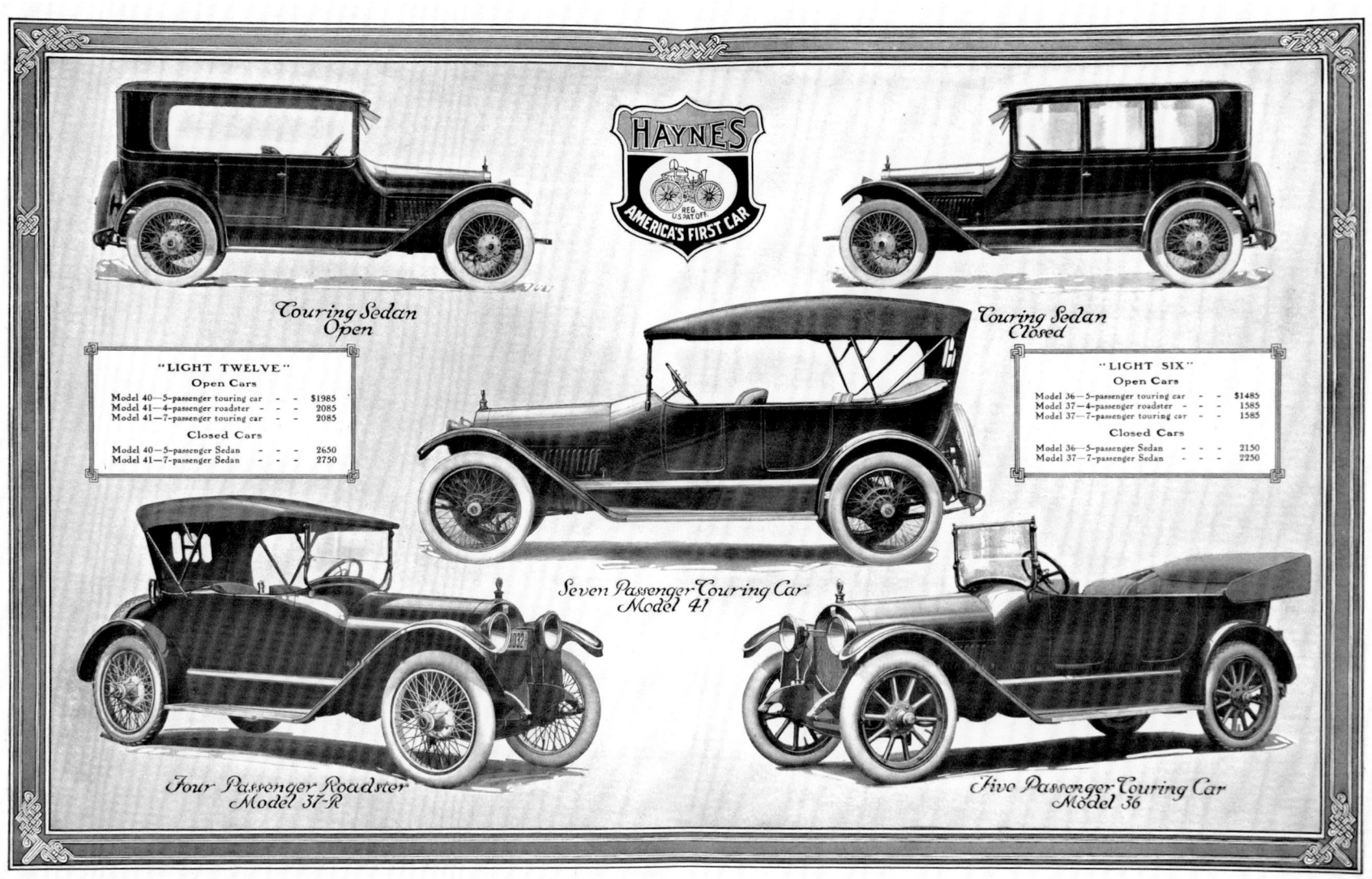

Touring Sedan
Open

Touring Sedan
Closed

"LIGHT TWELVE"

Open Cars

Model 40—5-passenger touring car	-	-	$1985
Model 41—4-passenger roadster	-	-	2085
Model 41—7-passenger touring car	-	-	2085

Closed Cars

| Model 40—5-passenger Sedan | - | - | 2650 |
| Model 41—7-passenger Sedan | - | - | 2750 |

"LIGHT SIX"

Open Cars

Model 36—5-passenger touring car	-	-	$1485
Model 37—4-passenger roadster	-	-	1585
Model 37—7-passenger touring car	-	-	1585

Closed Cars

| Model 36—5-passenger Sedan | - | - | 2150 |
| Model 37—7-passenger Sedan | - | - | 2250 |

Seven Passenger Touring Car
Model 41

Four Passenger Roadster
Model 37-R

Five Passenger Touring Car
Model 36

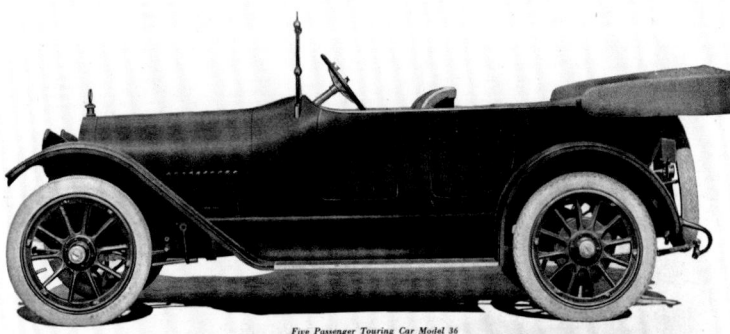

Five Passenger Touring Car Model 36

Refined Body Details for "Light Twelve" and "Light Six" Models

THE new 1917 models are designated as models 36, 37, 40 and 41. Models 36 and 40 are made in the five passenger touring style, model 36 being "Light Six," model 40, the "Light Twelve." Models 37 and 41 are seven passenger touring and four passenger roadster styles, model 37 being the "Light Six" and model 41 the "Light Twelve."

The cars are large and roomy, and the upholstering is deep and yielding. Real hand buffed leather is used throughout—the kind that feels soft to the touch. Big rolls over the backs of the seats add to appearance as well as to comfort. The rolls are permanently supported by thin flat springs.

The Models 36 and 40, five passenger touring cars are equipped with divided front seats. Direct entrance to the forward seats may be had through the front doors as usual, or through the rear doors and aisle-way. The individual seats give a greater sense of comfort and are a great convenience in many ways. The top can actually be handled by one man. A suitcase may be carried in the aisle-way. It is much more sociable with the car built in one big room.

The seven passenger Models 37 and 41 are likewise equipped with the individual front seats. The two auxiliary seats are of the stowaway type and are entirely out of sight when not in use. The seats drop down into the floor and all that remains visible are two rings. The floor is smooth and level at all times. There is ample room between all of the seats when seven passengers are carried. The unusually long wheelbase of 127 inches permits generous dimensions throughout the body.

The two auxiliary seats may be removed, if desired in taking long trips, by simply lifting them out. Two carrying spaces, measuring 18 by 22 by 7 inches are then available.

The four passenger roadsters, Models 37 and 41, are desirable cars for town driving and country touring. The well upholstered toy tonneau comfortably accommodates two passengers, while the driver's and the front passengers' seats are within easy speaking distance. The 127-inch chassis used for the seven passenger touring car is also used for the roadster so that there is an exceptional amount of leg room for the rear passengers.

The tonneau is upholstered on the sides with the best quality leather. Carrying space is provided under all seats, while the rear compartment is entirely devoted to storage space. The door of the rear compartment is large enough to admit suitcases.

The Sedan

The sedan body appeals to motorists who desire a car that offers complete comfort in any weather. The well appointed closed body formerly found a large following, that lately has increased with the advent of the closed car which could be quickly changed into a comfortable and well appearing automobile for summer touring. The Haynes sedan is in five and seven passenger models.

The interior of the sedan body is beautifully finished in a ribbed covert cloth upholstery of unusual weave. Grey silk window curtains carry out the scheme of the soft toned interior. The curtains are operated by a

---

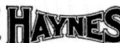
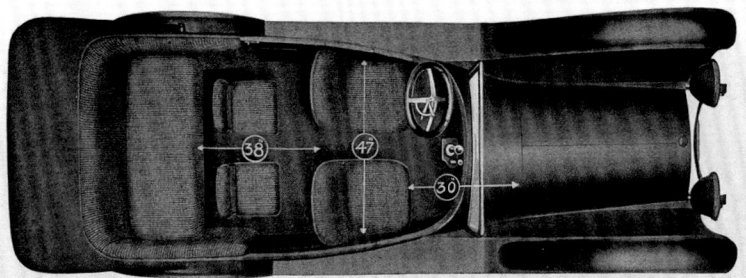

Showing seating arrangement and inside dimensions of models 37 and 41, seven passenger touring car

roller, and when the sedan is used as an open car, are completely contained and out of view.

The sedan body is designed for comfortable and luxurious travel. The wide, deep tonneau comfortably accommodates three passengers.

Entrance is made by a single door on each side of the car. Individual and adjustable front seats with a passageway between give convenient access to any part of the roomy enclosed body. A dome light of special pattern adds the final, pleasing touch for the enjoyment of evening driving.

The stuffiness of many closed bodies is avoided by double locking doors. The outer catch permits a gentle circulation of air in the car, while the inner lock closes doors tightly. The car is equipped with a double windshield, which prevents rain and snow from dimming the vision glass proper.

The sedan body can be converted into an open or closed body within a few minutes and without difficulty.

Perfection heaters are included as standard equipment, so that the closed car may always be kept warm.

Simplicity of Control

The Haynes control system gives an exhilaration that comes from complete mastery over the car. The few necessary levers and buttons are placed for the driver's greatest convenience.

It is an extremely simple matter to start the engine. There is but one thing to do at a time. Not even the clutch has to be thrown out. Lean back, comfortably in the seat and raise the hand to the ignition switch on the cowl apron less than an arm's length away. Then a slight pull on the starting motor switch sets the engine spinning and the car is ready to go. There is no noise, no fuss, no levers to shift. All is quiet obedience, ready for service at your will.

The 18-inch steering wheel is located on the left side and is so rigidly supported in passing through the cowl apron that no vibration can be transmitted from rough roads to the arms.

The gas and spark control levers are mounted on a stationary quadrant on top of the wheel, and in the center is the warning signal, all located at the finger tips.

The change speed and emergency brake levers are in the center of the car, so that the front seats are accessible from either side.

The gear shifting lever works in a ball and socket joint and engages directly with the shifter rods of the transmission gears, thus dispensing with the usual connecting rods.

The emergency brake lever is pivoted on the transmission case and engages with a rachet located below the floor. This construction leaves the floor clean and sightly, and there is nothing left around the levers to soil or catch skirts and overcoats.

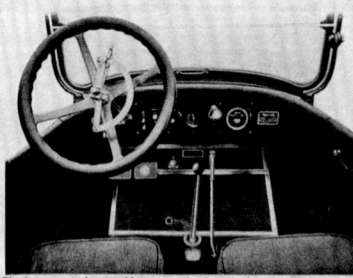

The few necessary levers and buttons are placed for the driver's greatest convenience

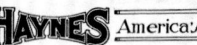

Showing seating arrangement and inside dimensions of Models 37 and 41, four passenger roadster

The foot accelerator is so located that there is a natural and comfortable position of the foot in operating it. It moves in a vertical direction and hence requires minimum muscular effort.

Both the clutch and brake pedals are adjustable to suit the individual driver. The foot pads may be pushed further away or brought closer according to his needs, and positively locked in each position.

The cowl equipment is complete in all respects. At the right of the steering column, flush with the cowl, is mounted the instrument board which contains the selective light switches, automatic circuit breaker, ignition switch, Waltham clock, ammeter and Stewart speedometer. These are all conveniently arranged and well lighted at night by the cowl light. At the left of the steering column is the starting motor switch and carburetor adjusting button—the entire equipment within easy reach of the driver.

The automatic circuit breaker takes the place of fuses and protects all of the electrical instruments against damage from short circuits and grounds. A Boyce Moto-Meter is mounted in the radiator cap where its red signal cannot escape the attention of the driver. It serves as a positive check on the memory, since the red column raises at once should water or oil be forgotten. An ammeter showing the charge and discharge of the battery is a part of the regular equipment.

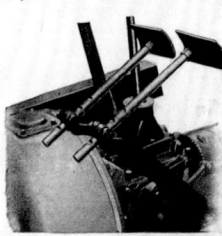

Adjustable Foot Pedals

One Man Top

The one man top is a reality on the 1917 Haynes cars. One man can loosen the top from the windshield and walk right back with it between the front seats. The tops are built in the Haynes factory. Five bows are used in the tops on all models and the front bow is reinforced with a strip of steel.

There are no bows to interfere with the elbows when lounging over the side. The top fastens directly to the top of the windshield by two ball and socket joints. The support is perfectly rigid and there are no unsightly and cumbersome rods or leather straps with which to bother.

Windshield

A rain vision and ventilating windshield is built integral with the cowl, making all brace rods and unsightly angle irons unnecessary. It is quickly adjusted for rain or ventilating purposes, and locks automatically in any position. Very substantial construction is used throughout, and sudden jolts or vibrations can have no effect upon it.

Economy

These cars are economical not only in the use of gasoline and oil, and the wear on the tires, but the up-keep cost is low on account of the fact that the greatest possible accessibility is to be had throughout the entire car. Adjustments must be made at some time on the best of cars. No machine outside of the human being is self-adjusting, and even it requires attention at times. Every adjustment may be made on the Haynes cars without having to remove any adjoining unit. The time is spent in making the actual adjustment in place of tearing down and replacing it in the car. This is a big item when adjustments are made by the garagemen whose charges are made according to the time spent.

Nickel Steel Reinforcement

Nickel steel is used generously throughout the entire chassis. Putting nickel in the steel allows the steel to withstand loads that would bend or break ordinary carbon steel. Nickel strengthens and hardens the steel. The nickel steel is used at all critical points, such as the steering knuckles, steering gear, transmission gears, and rear axle. Heat treated steels are used exclusively. Heat treatment rearranges the structure of the steel and makes it fine and silky. Heat treated steel will stand up under double the load taken by untreated steels. An ordinary piece of steel that will break under a pull of 60,000 pounds can be heat treated so that it will not break until the load is increased to 120,000 pounds. Heat treatment is essential in strain resisting chassis construction.

The Chassis

The chassis of the "Light Twelve" Model 40 is the same as that of the "Light Six" Model 36. The chassis of the "Light Twelve" Model 41 is the same as that of "Light Six" Model 37.

Every Haynes car is subjected to three exhaustive tests. Every motor is block tested and then torn down and inspected. The pistons are pulled out, bearings inspected and adjusted. The motor then goes into the chassis. The finished car receives a final road test before shipment. The Haynes car is built in the Haynes factory where one standard of quality prevails.

Vacuum Gasoline System

Both the "Light Six" and the "Light Twelve" are equipped with the Stewart Vacuum Gasoline System. This system is an automatic means of feeding the gasoline from the supply tank on the rear of the car to the carburetor.

It is absolutely automatic and requires no attention whatever. The gasoline feed is regular, as it depends in no way upon forced pressure or gravity.

Clutch

The single plate, dry disc clutch is completely enclosed in the fly wheel housing, yet it may be adjusted readily by removing a large cover plate. Neither water nor dirt can reach the clutch surfaces. A lining of Raybestos floats between the clutch surfaces and takes the wear exactly the same as the brake lining does in the brake drums on the rear wheels. No oil is used at any time on the friction surfaces.

The action of the clutch is extremely easy. A very slight pressure on the pedal controls the clutch at all times. The clutch has demonstrated its flexible action during the past year. It can not grab and it holds under the hardest pulls.

In making the clutch adjustment, the floor board of the front compartment is lifted and the large cover plate in front of the transmission removed. The engine is turned over so that the two adjusting bolts may be reached. Both are loosened. The clutch pedal is pressed down and one bolt is gently tapped to

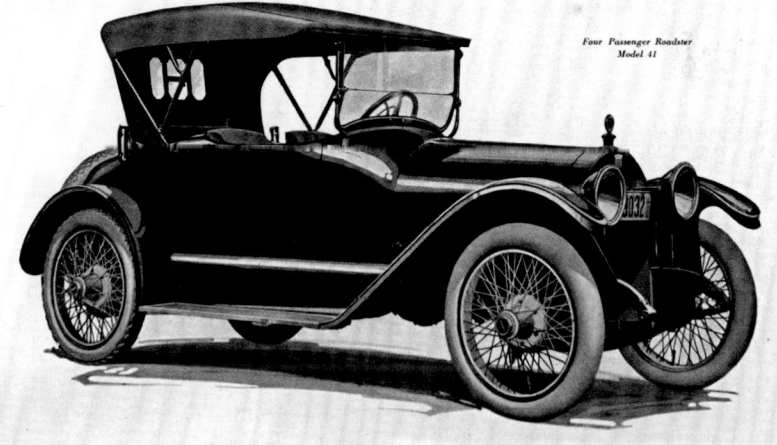

Four Passenger Roadster
Model 41

move it in a clockwise direction along the slot provided. The clutch is in perfect adjustment when the distance between the brake faces at the back of the clutch is about a half inch. The adjustment is completed by tightening up both bolts. The entire operation does not require more than five or ten minutes.

Transmission

The transmission unit is a Haynes design. It is of the selective sliding gear type with three speeds forward and one reverse. All gears heat treated after being cut from drop forged nickel steel. The shafts are likewise made of nickel steel and run in large Gurney ball bearings.

The shifting rods and interlocking pins are mounted in the upper cover plate so that they may be inspected as desired without having to go into the transmission. The walking stick type of gear shift lever is used to shift the gears. It is pivoted at the floor line by a ball and socket joint. Its action is very simple. It gives the entire front compartment a much neater appearance than the old style slot arrangement.

Front Axle

The front axle has an I-beam section and is inclined slightly to give the wheels the same caster action that may be observed in the casters on the ordinary bed It is the caster action combined with the proper weight distribution that makes the car hold the road at all speeds. The wheel spindles and steering knuckles are heat treated drop forgings of nickel steel.

The front wheels run on two sets of bearings containing ⅝ inch and ¾ inch balls. These balls have contact over a large area and are not supported merely at points. They take the side thrusts as well as the direct loads without the least wedging action.

Full Floating Rear Axle

The rear axle is designed and built in the Haynes factory.

It is a full floating axle, by which term is meant that the shafts turning the wheels float in the axle and do not carry any of the weight of the car. The wheels are mounted directly on the steel axle housing. The driving shafts may be removed at will without disturbing the wheels or wheel bearings. Although the shafts are relieved of carrying weight, they are 1½ inches in diameter and are made of nickel steel, heat treated.

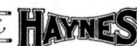
"Light Six" Chassis

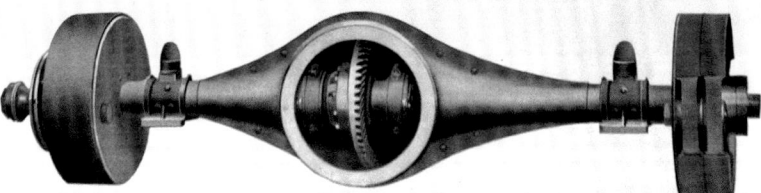
Haynes full floating rear axle

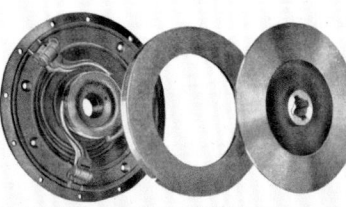
The clutch while free from complications is highly efficient and very easy to operate

Helical, or spiral bevel, drive gears are used in the axles of all models. The pinion gear and shaft are made of heat treated nickel steel. The entire differential may be removed from the axle by taking off four nuts that retain the bearings. There is no need of taking out the entire axle. The driving pinion gear shaft is supported by two bearings — one on each side of the gear. The adjustment is on the front side of the axle where it may be reached readily and operated in a simple manner.

Both the foot and hand brakes expand on the inside of a fourteen inch drum. They are completely enclosed and protected from mud. The linings last longer and the braking action is much more effective. There are no complicated toggle joints or spring releasing devices. The action is controlled entirely by cams that are positive. The brakes may be taken up from the outside.

Wheels

Wire wheels will be part of the regular equipment on the "Light Twelve" models. The regulation wooden wheels the same as last year will be used on the "Light Six," with wire wheels extra.

Tires

Goodyear Cord tires 34 x 4½ will be used exclusively on the "Light Twelve" models.

The "Light Six" models will be furnished with plain tread tires on the front and non-skid on the rear. An option is given of Goodyear or United States tires. Model 36 is equipped with size 34 by 4 inch and Model 37 with 35 by 4½ inch.

DEMOUNTABLE SEDAN TOPS

THE present year has seen as much progress in the construction of the demountable sedan tops as the past three years have witnessed in nearly any other branch of automobile building. This year's production is

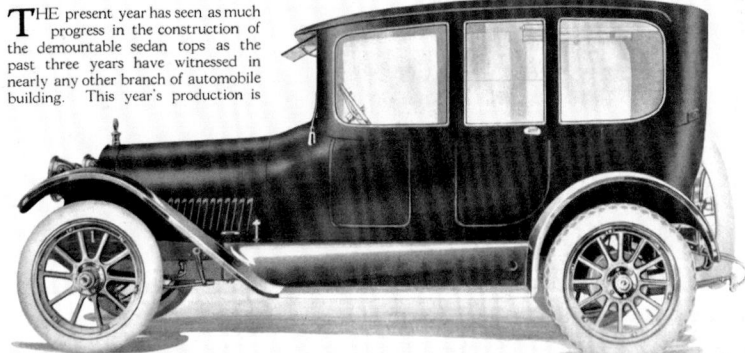

scarcely to be compared with the tops that were on the market last season, either in appearance and serviceability, or in refinement and finish.

All Haynes models, both in the "Light Six" and "Light Twelve" cars, can be equipped with De Luxe demountable tops. These can be firmly attached to the touring car and roadster bodies in a short time and removed with equal readiness without marring the car.

Both the interior and exterior of the De Luxe demountable tops are standard in essential and detail. The interior is neatly trimmed in a high grade and durable grey whipcord. The back and side tonneau

windows are fitted with roll silk curtains. An electric dome light illuminates the interior for night driving.

The frame is solidly built from hard wood, and the side panels and door frames are of rigid two inch stock. On touring car models, the forward side panel is curved with the body line.

The top doors are permanently attached to the automobile doors and hinged in such a manner to make the doors work as freely and silently as those of any limousine body.

The demountable tops for all models are priced at $275.

Detailed Specifications

"Light Twelve" Motor

Unit power plant, 3 point suspension, 12 cylinder, cylinders in 2 sets of six each, cast en bloc, light, high power, high speed type. It is of the valve-in-head construction. Develops over 70 horse-power.

Pistons. Aluminum alloy pistons are used, assuring maximum durability and strength with very little wear.

Leece-Neville separate unit starting and lighting system. Cranks through the flywheel.

Generator Storage Battery system of ignition. Gives greater flexibility at ordinary driving speeds. A double ignition system is used, assuring accurate firing, giving greater power and more economical fuel consumption.

Economical Rayfield Carburetor. By the use of one carburetor a like mixture of gas is given to all twelve cylinders.

Gear driven gear pump force feed lubrication, assuring perfect oiling of all parts.

Forced water circulation. Water space between all cylinders and around all valve seats. Large centrifugal pump. Haynes cars never overheat.

"Light Six" Motor

Unit power plant, 3 point suspension, 6 cylinder, 3¼x5-inch, cast en bloc. The high speed, high power construction is used, giving more power than any motor of a like bore and stroke. Actually develops 55 horse-power.

Pistons are made of aluminum alloy, four rings are used and an oil groove keeps the oil from working into the combustion chamber.

Ignition. Generator-storage battery system of ignition. Gives greater flexibility at ordinary driving speeds.

Leece-Neville unit starting and lighting system. No gears to shift. Assured starting in all weather conditions. Cranks through a chain, concealed in gear housing.

Economical Rayfield Carburetor with combination high and low speed adjustment assures proper mixture at all times. No intake manifold is used, the carburetor is connected directly on the motor.

Lubrication is of the force feed and splash type, a constant flow of oil at all times assured by the use of a plunger type oil pump with a capacity of ½ gallon per minute.

Cooling of all parts is assured by the large, centrifugal pump, which keeps cool water circulating around all valve seats and parts which have a tendency to overheat.

Body Specifications for both "Light Twelve" and "Light Six" Models

Body Styles. Model 36 "Light Six" and Model 40 "Light Twelve," five passenger touring car, Model 37 "Light Six," and Model 41 "Light Twelve," 7 passenger touring car and four passenger roadster.

Aisleway between front seats on both touring models. Roadster of "Cloverleaf" design, with the back seat reached by aisle between the two front seats.

Wheelbase. Models 36 and 40, 121 inches; Models 37 and 41, 127 inches, with turning radius of slightly over 21 feet. Left hand drive, center control with walking stick type gear shift lever. Enter front compartment from either side.

Stewart vacuum gasoline system with supply tank at rear of chassis. Indicating gauge in tank.

Clutch. Built in Haynes factory. Single plate dry disc type with facings of Raybestos. Requires very little pressure on pedal to operate. Cannot grab. Holds under hardest pulls.

Motor driven tire pump. Can not pump oil. Hose and tire gauge.

Stewart-Warner speedometer, driven from propeller shaft.

Five bow top. Can be operated by one man.

Improved Collins side curtains.

Windshield. Clear and rain vision ventilating.

Strapless, quick acting, single lock tire carrier at rear of chassis.

Running boards absolutely clear. Entire interior of body lined with real leather.

Headlights with Mazda bulbs and dimming device that saves two-thirds of the current. Outside focusing button. Duplex headlights on "Light Twelve."

Sparton electric horn under hood. Button in center of steering wheel.

Transmission. Selective sliding gear type, three speeds forward, one reverse. Heat treated, nickel steel gears.

Haynes full floating rear axle. Built in Haynes factory. Axle shaft, pinion gear and shaft of nickel steel.

Helical or Spiral bevel gear type drive gear used in rear axle. *Springs* 38 inches in front, 54 inches long in rear. Flat type insures easy riding. Chrome vanadium steel. Bronze bushings used in eyes. Spring bolts hardened and ground.

Crowned fenders. Low center of gravity with low running boards. Road clearance 10½ inches. Long sweeping stream lines.

Front and rear license brackets. Adjustable foot pedals. Foot and robe rails. Trouble lamp with cord.

Boyce Moto Meter. Waltham clock and Hydrometer.

Automatic circuit breaker. Protects electric system. Eliminates fuses.

Ammeter, showing charge and discharge of battery.

Wheels. Wire wheels are used on "Light Twelve." Regulation wooden wheels on the "Light Six" *Wire Wheels* for "Light Six" Models extra.

Auxiliary Seats. Two extra seats in Models 37 and 41. Drop down into floor when not in use. May be removed if desired, affording extra carrying space.

Complete kit of high grade tools, Tire Repair Kit.

Color. Body Brewster green, dark; black fenders and chassis.

Tires. Goodyear Cords on "Light Twelve." Goodyear or United States on "Light Six."

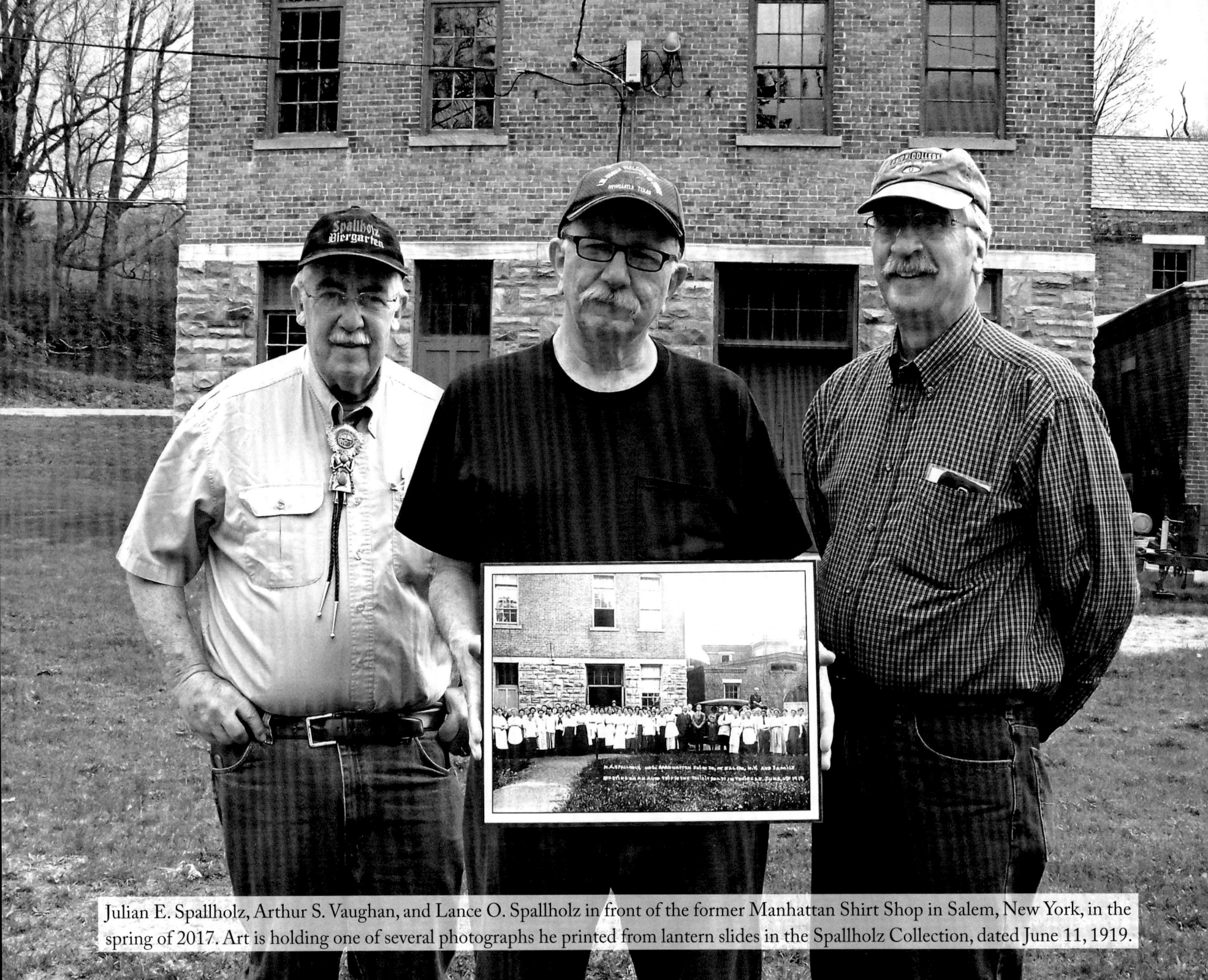

Julian E. Spallholz, Arthur S. Vaughan, and Lance O. Spallholz in front of the former Manhattan Shirt Shop in Salem, New York, in the spring of 2017. Art is holding one of several photographs he printed from lantern slides in the Spallholz Collection, dated June 11, 1919.

ABOUT THE AUTHORS

JULIAN E. SPALLHOLZ is a retired professor of nutrition/nutritional biochemistry from Texas Tech University. He attended high school at Salem Washington Academy, New York (1957–1961) and is a graduate of Colorado State University (BS 1965, MS 1968) and the University of Hawaii (PhD 1971). He has published over eighty peer-reviewed manuscripts, abstracts, textbooks, and international scientific proceedings. He is a member of the National Academy of Inventors with over fifteen US and foreign patents. He was selected as the Barnie E. Rushing Award recipient for research in 2010. Having given invited lectures throughout the United States and foreign countries, he has served as a consultant to industry, state, and federal governments. His primary research interest has centered around selenium toxicity. Dr. Spallholz retired from Texas Tech University in January 2019 after forty years of teaching and research. He now lives with his wife, Dr. Mallory Boylan, and two cats in Santa Fe, New Mexico.

LANCE O. SPALLHOLZ was born in Boston, Massachusetts. He graduated from Salem Washington Academy in 1965 and from Union College in 1969. He and his wife Norma started their careers as secondary school teachers. He returned to Union College to teach and retired after twenty-seven years. His children Julianna and Drue also graduated from Union. He and Norma live in Round Lake, New York, originally an 1867 Methodist Camp Meeting Association. They rehabbed one of the original cottages and later moved across the village to a larger home. He is involved in community activities as a member of the Village's Planning Board and a trustee for the Round Lake Library.

ARTHUR S. VAUGHAN is a retired laboratory technician (Western Electric, AT&T, Lucent Technologies, and Bell Laboratories), presently residing in North Andover, Massachusetts. He is a vice president of the New England Camera Club Council, where he served seventeen years as the NECCC Print Competition Director and live commentator for the Best of the NECCC Traveling Print Program. Art's photographic experience and interests include anamorphic (CinemaScope) photography, macro photography, stereo (3-D) imaging, photomicrography, color and black & white printmaking, and digital restoration of antique photographs, lithographs, engravings, and etchings.